The Black Abolitionist Papers

The Black Abolitionist Papers

VOLUME II
Canada, 1830–1865

C. Peter Ripley, *Editor*
Roy E. Finkenbine, *Associate Editor*
Paul A. Cimbala, *Assistant Editor*
Michael F. Hembree, *Research Associate*
Mary Alice Herrle, *Research Associate*
Debra Susie, *Research Associate*

The University of North Carolina Press
Chapel Hill and London

Manufactured in the United States of America

Library of Congress Cataloging-in-Publication Data
(Revised for vol. 2)
Main entry under title:

The Black abolitionist papers.

Includes bibliographical references and index.
Contents: v. 1—The British Isles, 1830–1865—v. 2—Canada, 1830–1865.
1. Slavery—United States—Anti-slavery movements—Sources. 2. Abolitionists—United States—History—19th century—Sources. 3. Abolitionists—History—19th century—Sources. 4. Afro-Americans—History—To 1863—Sources. I. Ripley, C. Peter, 1941– .
E449.B624 1985 973′.0496 84–13131
ISBN 0-8078-1625-6 (v. 1)
ISBN 0-8078-1698-1 (v. 2)

The preparation of this volume was made possible in part by a grant from the Program for Editions of the National Endowment for the Humanities, an independent federal agency, and by grants from the National Historical Publications and Records Commission, The Florida State University, the Ford Foundation, and the Rockefeller Foundation.

Contents

Illustrations

Maps

Acknowledgments

Thanking collaborators, colleagues, and supporters is one of the pleasures of an undertaking such as the Black Abolitionist Papers Project. Acknowledgments are a reminder that many hands shape each volume. They also signal that another volume is completed; that, too, pleases us.

The volumes are a collaborative effort, and volume II is no exception, particularly given the substantial contributions of Associate Editor Roy E. Finkenbine. Roy guided volume II through its daily regimen and helped us avoid the confusion that can arise during the long and complicated process of preparing a volume of documentary history. His scholarly contributions are evident in each phase of this volume, from selecting documents through writing notes, headnotes, and introductory material. His uncanny ability to suggest just the right document in which to locate specific information and his sophisticated knowledge of black abolitionists enriched the volume and speeded its completion.

Assistant Editor Paul Cimbala, who joined the teaching faculty at The University of South Carolina at Aiken after a year with the project, assisted in the selection of documents and the early note writing. His sense of historical subtleties and his hard work improved the volume; his good humor improved the process. Michael Hembree indexed many of the in-house research materials used in preparing volume II and then made good use of them as he wrote notes, headnotes, and introductory material. Although trained outside the field of antebellum American history, before the volume was completed Michael became our authoritative source on aspects of the Canadian experiment. Debra Susie transcribed documents with great accuracy, watched over the transcription guidelines, provided continuous demonstrations of the benefits of word processing technology, and kept us true to our style sheet. Her regular inquiries about "final copy"—that usually began, "do you mean to say here. . . ?"—reflect her writing skills and her good ear for the language. Mary Alice Herrle joined the project in the final phase of preparing the volume but arrived in time to catch writing slips, bad grammar, and inconsistent use of terms, names, and titles.

Jeffery S. Rossbach left the project after volume I was completed to pursue another career. His departure is a loss for the project and the profession. But he could not stay away and found the time and energy to contribute to this volume. We thank him for that. Professor Michael Wayne of the University of Toronto Department of History and Odette Langlais, a graduate student at that institution, took on the task of locating in Canada annotation materials that eluded us. They tracked down specific information from vague historical references, often about people and events that we had no reasonable expectations of ever finding. The Florida Resources and Environmental Analysis Center of the Florida State University prepared the maps that appear in this volume.

We wish to acknowledge the manuscript curators and repository directors who responded to our inquiries and allowed us to publish documents from their collections: Clifton H. Johnson of the Amistad Research Center, Thomas C. Battle of the Moorland-Spingarn Research Center, Edwin B. Bronner of the Haverford College Library, John D. Cushing of the Massachusetts Historical Society, Donald D. Eddy of the Cornell University Library, Patricia Kennedy of the Public Archives of Canada, Allan J. MacDonald of the Archives of Ontario, and Brian A. Young of the Provincial Archives of British Columbia. We offer continued and special thanks to Howard Dotson and the staff of the Schomburg Center for Research in Black Culture.

The project has several sponsors. The Florida State University, the National Endowment for the Humanities, the National Historical Publications and Records Commission, the Ford Foundation, and the Rockefeller Foundation have funded our work. At Florida State, Vice-President for Academic Affairs Augustus B. Turnbull, Dean of the College of Arts and Sciences Werner A. Baum, and Director of the Black Studies Program William R. Jones encouraged the project, dipped into their annual budgets on our behalf, and listened to my administrative complaints with great tolerance, usually. Frank G. Burke, Roger A. Bruns, Sarah Dunlop Jackson, Richard N. Sheldon, and Mary A. Giunta offered steady support and good cheer at NHPRC, even during a time when that agency faced dissolution by OMB. Through three directors, Kathy Fuller has monitored our NEH proposals with a cooperative spirit and high professional standards. Sheila Biddle of the Ford Foundation and Lynn Szwaja and Alberta Arthurs of the Rockefeller Foundation encouraged and supported the Afro-American Editing Consortium, and we have benefited from that in substantial ways.

The board of editorial advisors responded with wisdom to our queries. Lawrence J. Friedman of Bowling Green State University, John W. Blassingame of Yale University, Joe M. Richardson of Florida State University, and William H. Pease of the University of Maine were particularly helpful. Jerome Stern of the Florida State University English department once again refereed our editorial disputes and did his best to rid the volume introduction of fuzzy thinking and poor writing. We trust he will forgive us those instances where our stubbornness prevailed.

Martha, Hal, John P., Mary Ann, Joe, Jack, Jim, John Z., and Jerry listened attentively to my project stories with the patience we expect only from the best of friends.

Tallahassee, Florida
May, 1985

C. P. R.

Abbreviations

Newspapers, Journals, Directories, and Reference Works

AA	*Aliened American* (Cleveland, Ohio).
AAM	*Anglo-African Magazine* (New York, New York).
AAN	*Anglo-African* (New York, New York).
ACAB	James Grant Wilson and John Fiske, eds., *Appletons' Cyclopaedia of American Biography*, 6 vols. (New York, New York, 1888–89).
AHQ	*Arkansas Historical Quarterly.*
AM	*American Missionary* (New York, New York).
AMECR	*African Methodist Episcopal Church Review* (Philadelphia, Pennsylvania).
Amer	*Americas.*
Apal	*Apalachee.*
ASA	*Anti-Slavery Advocate* (London, England).
ASB	*Anti-Slavery Bugle* (Salem, Ohio; New Lisbon, Ohio).
ASR	*Anti-Slavery Record* (New York, New York).
ASRL	*Anti-Slavery Reporter* (London, England).
BC	*British Colonist* (Victoria, British Columbia, Canada).
BDAC	*Biographical Directory of the American Congress 1774–1971* (Washington, D.C., 1971).
BDGUS	Robert Sobel and John W. Raimo, eds., *Biographical Directory of the Governors of the United States* (Westport, Connecticut, 1978).
BE	*Brantford Expositor* (Brantford, Ontario, Canada).
BT	*Boston Evening Transcript* (Boston, Massachusetts).
CA	*Colored American* (New York, New York).
CBHMD	*Canadian Baptist Home Mission Digest.*
CF	*Christian Freeman* (New York, New York).
CG	*Christian Guardian* (Toronto, Ontario, Canada).
CHR	*Canadian Historical Review.*
CJ	*Chatham Journal* (Chatham, Ontario, Canada).
CJH	*Canadian Journal of History.*
CM	*Canadian Magazine.*
CN	*Christian News* (Glasgow, Scotland).
CP	*Chatham Planet* (Chatham, Ontario, Canada).
CR	*Christian Recorder* (Philadelphia, Pennsylvania).
CTWP	*Chatham Tri-Weekly Planet* (Chatham, Ontario, Canada).
CWD	Mark Mayo Boatner, ed., *Civil War Dictionary* (New York, New York, 1959).

CWH	*Civil War History.*
DAB	Allen Johnson and Dumas Malone, eds., *Dictionary of American Biography*, 20 vols. (New York, New York, 1928–36).
DANB	Rayford W. Logan and Michael R. Winston, eds., *Dictionary of American Negro Biography* (New York, New York, 1982).
DCB	George W. Brown, David M. Hayne, and Francess G. Halpenny, eds., *Dictionary of Canadian Biography*, vols. 1–4, 9–11 to date (Toronto, Ontario, Canada, 1966–).
DH	*Delaware History.*
DM	*Douglass' Monthly* (Rochester, New York).
DNB	Sir Leslie Stephen and Sir Sidney Lee, eds., *Dictionary of National Biography*, 22 vols. (London, England, 1885–1901; reprint, 1921–22).
DUB	*Imperial Dictionary of Universal Biography*, 3 vols. (London, England, n.d.).
E	*Emancipator* (Boston, Massachusetts; New York, New York).
ESF	*Elevator* (San Francisco, California).
FDP	*Frederick Douglass' Paper* (Rochester, New York).
FI	*Friends' Intelligencer* (Philadelphia, Pennsylvania).
FJ	*Freedom's Journal* (New York, New York).
FM	*Friend of Man* (Utica, New York).
FML	*Freed-Man* (London, England).
Found	*Foundations.*
G	*Gazette* (Cleveland, Ohio).
GSB	*Gerrit Smith Banner* (New York, New York).
GUE	*Genius of Universal Emancipation* (Mt. Pleasant, Ohio; Greenville, Tennessee; Baltimore, Maryland; Washington, D.C.; Hennepin, Illinois).
HF	*Herald of Freedom* (Concord, New Hampshire).
HP	*Harrisburg Patriot* (Harrisburg, Pennsylvania).
HT	*Harrisburg Telegraph* (Harrisburg, Pennsylvania).
I	*Inquirer* (London, England).
IC	*Impartial Citizen* (Syracuse, New York; Boston, Massachusetts).
JBS	*Journal of Black Studies.*
JIJ	*Journal of the Institute of Jamaica.*
JNE	*Journal of Negro Education.*
JNH	*Journal of Negro History.*
JPH	*Journal of Presbyterian History.*
JQ	*Journalism Quarterly.*
KA	*Kent Advertiser* (Chatham, Ontario, Canada).

LFP — *London Free Press* (London, Ontario, Canada).
LI — *Leeds Intelligencer* (Leeds, England).
Lib — *Liberator* (Boston, Massachusetts).
LM — *Leeds Mercury* (Leeds, England).
LP — *Liberty Press* (Utica, New York).
MDCB — W. Stewart Wallace, ed., *Macmillan Dictionary of Canadian Biography* (Toronto, Ontario, Canada, 1978).
MEB — Frederick Boase, ed., *Modern English Biography*, 6 vols. (New York, New York, 1892–1921; reprint, London, England, 1965).
MH — *Michigan History*.
MN — *Morning News* (St. John, New Brunswick).
MT — *Mirror of the Times* (San Francisco, California).
MVHR — *Mississippi Valley Historical Review*.
MWT — *Manchester Weekly Times* (Manchester, England).
NASS — *National Anti-Slavery Standard* (New York, New York).
NAW — Edward T. James, ed., *Notable American Women, 1607–1950: A Biographical Dictionary*, 3 vols. (Cambridge, Massachusetts, 1971).
NC — *Nonconformist* (London, England).
NCAB — *National Cyclopaedia of American Biography*, 61 vols. to date (New York, New York, 1898–).
NECAUL — *National Enquirer and Constitutional Advocate of Universal Liberty* (Philadelphia, Pennsylvania).
NEW — *National Era* (Washington, D.C.).
NHB — *Negro History Bulletin*.
NHS — *Niagara Historical Society*.
NNE — *New National Era* (Washington, D.C.).
NR — *National Reformer* (Philadelphia, Pennsylvania).
NS — *Novascotian* (Halifax, Nova Scotia).
NSFA — *Northern Star and Freeman's Advocate* (Albany, New York).
NSt — *North Star* (Rochester, New York).
NYH — *New York Herald* (New York, New York).
NYSu — *Sun* (New York, New York).
NYT — *New York Tribune* (New York, New York).
NYTi — *New York Times* (New York, New York).
OE — *Oberlin Evangelist* (Oberlin, Ohio).
OH — *Ohio History*.
OHA — *Onondaga Historical Association*.
OHSPR — *Ontario Historical Society Papers and Records*.
OntH — *Ontario History*.
OTNE — *Old-Time New England*.
P — *Philanthropist* (Mt. Pleasant, Ohio; New Richmond, Ohio; Cincinnati, Ohio).

PA *Pacific Appeal* (San Francisco, California).
PAC *People's Advocate* (Concord, New Hampshire).
PEB *Evening Bulletin* (Philadelphia, Pennsylvania).
PF *Pennsylvania Freeman* (Philadelphia, Pennsylvania).
PFW *Provincial Freeman* (Windsor, Ontario, Canada; Toronto, Ontario, Canada; Chatham, Ontario, Canada).
PH *Pennsylvania History.*
PHR *Pacific Historical Review.*
Phy *Phylon.*
PL *Palladium of Liberty* (Columbus, Ohio).
PMHB *Pennsylvania Magazine of History and Biography.*
PP *Pine and Palm* (Boston, Massachusetts; New York, New York).
PPr *Press* (Philadelphia, Pennsylvania).
PtL *Patriot* (London, England).
PtT *Patriot* (Toronto, Ontario, Canada).
RA *Rights of All* (New York, New York).
RAME *Anti-Masonic Enquirer* (Rochester, New York).
RDA *Rochester Daily Advertiser* (Rochester, New York).
RDD *Rochester Daily Democrat* (Rochester, New York).
RDT *Rochester Daily Telegraph* (Rochester, New York).
RMS *Renaissance and Modern Studies.*
RR *Rochester Republican* (Rochester, New York).
RUA *Rochester Union and Advertiser* (Rochester, New York).
SCJ *St. Catharines Journal* (St. Catharines, Ontario, Canada).
SL *Signal of Liberty* (Ann Arbor, Michigan).
SLO *St. Louis Observer* (St. Louis, Missouri).
TC *Constitution* (Toronto, Ontario, Canada).
TET *Evening Telegram* (Toronto, Ontario, Canada).
TG *Globe* (Toronto, Ontario, Canada).
TL *Leader* (Toronto, Ontario, Canada).
Trans London and Middlesex Historical Society, *Transactions.*
TRSC *Transactions of the Royal Society of Canada.*
US *Una Sancta.*
VF *Voice of the Fugitive* (Sandwich, Ontario, Canada; Windsor, Ontario, Canada).
WAA *Weekly Anglo-African* (New York, New York).
WC *Western Citizen* (Chicago, Illinois).
WH *Western Herald* (Sandwich, Ontario, Canada).

Manuscript Repositories

AMA-ARC American Missionary Association Archives, Amistad Research Center, New Orleans, Louisiana.
CaBViPA British Columbia Provincial Archives, Victoria, British Columbia, Canada.
CaOLU University of Western Ontario, London, Ontario, Canada.
CaOTAr Ontario Provincial Archives, Toronto, Ontario, Canada.
CaOTCi City of Toronto Archives, Toronto, Ontario, Canada.
CaOTP Metropolitan Toronto Central Library, Toronto, Ontario, Canada.
DHU Moorland-Spingarn Research Center, Howard University, Washington, D.C.
DLC Library of Congress, Washington, D.C.
DNA National Archives, Washington, D.C.
MB Boston Public Library and Eastern Massachusetts Regional Public Library System, Boston, Massachusetts.
MeU Raymond H. Fogler Library, University of Maine, Orono, Maine.
MH Houghton Library, Harvard University, Cambridge, Massachusetts.
MiD-B Burton Historical Collection, Detroit Public Library, Detroit, Michigan.
MWA American Antiquarian Society, Worcester, Massachusetts.
NIC Olin Library, Cornell University, Ithaca, New York.
NjP Princeton University Library, Princeton University, Princeton, New Jersey.
NN-Sc Schomburg Center for Research in Black Culture, New York Public Library, New York, New York.
NRU Rush-Rhees Library, University of Rochester, Rochester, New York.
NSyU George Arents Research Library, Syracuse University, Syracuse, New York.
OClWHi Western Reserve Historical Society, Cleveland, Ohio.
OO Seeley G. Mudd Center, Oberlin College, Oberlin, Ohio.
PHC Haverford College Library, Haverford College, Haverford, Pennsylvania.
PHi Historical Society of Pennsylvania, Philadelphia, Pennsylvania.
UkGM Mitchell Library, Glasgow, Scotland.
UkOxU-Rh Rhodes House Library, Oxford University, Oxford, England.

Editorial Statement

The Black Abolitionist Papers Project began in 1976 with the mission to collect and publish the documentary record of black Americans involved in the movement to end slavery in the United States from 1830 to 1865. The project was conceived from an understanding that broad spans of Afro-American history have eluded scholarly attention because the necessary research materials are not readily available. Many personal papers, business records, newspapers, and other documentary sources simply have not survived. Materials that have endured are often inaccessible to scholars and an interested public because they have not been systematically identified and collected. Except for several small manuscript collections of better-known black figures (usually those that continued to be public figures after emancipation),[1] the letters, speeches, essays, writings, and personal papers of black abolitionists have escaped professional attention. The same is true of antebellum black newspapers.

But the publications of individual historians demonstrated that black abolitionist documents could be unearthed.[2] The black documents that

1. See Mary Ann Shadd Cary Papers, Public Archives of Canada (Ottawa, Ontario), DHU, CaOTAr; Shadd Family Papers, CaOLU; Rapier Family Papers, DHU; Daniel A. Payne Papers, Wilberforce University (Wilberforce, Ohio); Anderson R. Abbott Papers, CaOTP; John M. Langston Papers, Fisk University (Nashville, Tennessee); Ruffin Family Papers, DHU; Amos G. Beman Papers, Yale University (New Haven, Connecticut); Charles Lenox Remond Papers, Essex Institute (Salem, Massachusetts), and MB; William Still Papers, Rutgers University (New Brunswick, New Jersey); Jacob C. White, Jr., Papers, PHi; Frederick Douglass Papers, DLC, NN-Sc, and DHU; Alexander Crummell Papers, NN-Sc; James T. Holly Papers, General Theological Seminary (New York, New York); J. W. Loguen File, NSyU; Paul Cuffe Papers, New Bedford Free Public Library (New Bedford, Massachusetts). Of these, only the Cary, Cuffe, Remond, Douglass, and Beman Collections have significant antebellum documents.

2. A number of black abolitionist documents were reprinted before this project began its work in 1976: Carter G. Woodson, ed., *Negro Orators and Their Orations* (Washington, D.C., 1925); Carter G. Woodson, ed., *The Mind of the Negro as Reflected in Letters Written during the Crisis, 1800–1860* (Washington, D.C., 1926); Dorothy B. Porter, ed., "Early Manuscript Letters Written by Negroes," *JNH* 24:199–210 (April 1939); Benjamin Quarles, ed., "Letters from Negro Leaders to Gerrit Smith," *JNH* 27:432–53 (October 1942); Philip S. Foner, ed., *The Life and Writings of Frederick Douglass*, 5 vols. (New York, N.Y., 1950–75); Howard H. Bell, ed., *Minutes of the Proceedings of the National Negro Conventions, 1830–1864* (New York, N.Y., 1969); Dorothy Sterling, ed., *Speak Out in Thunder Tones: Letters and Other Writings by Black Northerners, 1787–1865* (New York, N.Y., 1973). Pioneer scholarship on the subject that further suggested the availability of documents includes a number of articles on antebellum black Canadian fugitive communities by Fred Landon that appeared in the *Journal of Negro History* and *Ontario History* during the 1920s and 1930s; Dorothy B. Porter, "Sarah Parker Remond, Abolitionist and Physician," *JNH* 20:287–93 (July 1935), and "David M. Ruggles, an Apostle of Human Rights," *JNH* 28:23–50 (January 1943); Herbert Aptheker, *The Negro in the Abolitionist*

enriched those books and articles were not located in a single collection, repository, or newspaper in any quantity. They were found scattered in the manuscript collections of others (usually whites involved in nineteenth-century reform movements) and in newspapers of the day (usually reform papers but also in the traditional press). Clearly, a significant body of black abolitionist documents survived, but it seemed equally certain that locating the documents would require a thorough search of large numbers of newspapers and a systematic review of a wide range of historical materials, particularly the papers of white individuals and institutions involved in the antislavery movement.

An international search for documents was the first phase of the Black Abolitionist Papers Project. A four-year collection process took the project to thousands of manuscript collections and countless newspapers in England, Scotland, Ireland, and Canada as well as in the United States. This work netted nearly 14,000 letters, speeches, essays, pamphlets, and newspaper editorials from over 200 libraries and 110 newspapers. What resulted is the documentary record of some 300 black men and women and their efforts to end American slavery.[3]

The Black Abolitionist Papers were microfilmed during the second phase of the project. The microfilmed edition contains all the primary documents gathered during the collection phase. The seventeen reels of film are a pristine presentation of the black abolitionist record.[4] The microfilmed edition offers materials that previously were uncollected, unidentified, and frequently unavailable to scholars.

Now in its third phase, the project is publishing a five-volume series of

Movement (New York, N.Y., 1941); Benjamin Quarles, *Frederick Douglass* (Washington, D.C., 1948); Philip S. Foner, *Frederick Douglass* (New York, N.Y., 1950); Benjamin Quarles, "Ministers without Portfolio," *JNH* 39:27–43 (January 1954); Leon F. Litwack, *North of Slavery: The Negro in the Free States, 1790–1860* (Chicago, Ill., 1961); William H. Pease and Jane H. Pease, *Black Utopia: Negro Communal Experiments in America* (Madison, Wis., 1963); Benjamin Quarles, *Black Abolitionists* (London, 1969); William Edward Farrison, *William Wells Brown: Author and Reformer* (Chicago, Ill., 1969); Robin W. Winks, *The Blacks in Canada: A History* (New Haven, Conn., 1971); Jane H. Pease and William H. Pease, *They Who Would Be Free: Blacks' Search for Freedom, 1830–1861* (New York, N.Y., 1974); Floyd J. Miller, *The Search for a Black Nationality: Black Emigration and Colonization, 1787–1863* (Urbana, Ill., 1975); Richard Blackett, "In Search of International Support for African Colonization: Martin R. Delany's Visit to England, 1860," *CJH* 10:307–24 (December 1975). Several examples of early research on black abolitionists were reprinted in John H. Bracey, Jr., August Meier, and Elliott Rudwick, eds., *Blacks in the Abolitionist Movement* (Belmont, Calif., 1971).

3. This project has not collected or published documents by Frederick Douglass. Douglass's papers are being edited and published by John W. Blassingame and the staff of the Frederick Douglass Papers Project at Yale University.

4. The Black Abolitionist Papers are on seventeen reels of film with a published guide and index (New York, N.Y.: Microfilming Corporation of America, 1981–83; Ann Arbor, Mich.: University Microfilms International, 1984–). The guide contains a description of the collection procedures.

edited and annotated representative documents. Black abolitionist activities in the British Isles and in Canada are treated in separate volumes; three volumes will be devoted to black abolitionists in the United States. The volume organization was suggested by a systematic review of the documents. The documents made clear that black abolitionists had a set of broadly defined goals and objectives wherever they were. But the documents also demonstrated that black abolitionists had a set of specific goals and actions in Britain, another set in Canada, and a third in the United States.

The microfilmed and published editions are two discrete historical instruments. The 14,000 microfilmed documents are a rich Afro-American expression of black life in the nineteenth century. Those black voices stand free of intrusion by either editor or historian. The microfilmed edition presents the collected documents. The published volumes are documentary history. Substantial differences separate the two.

The five volumes will accommodate less than 10 percent of the total collection, yet the volumes must tell the ambitious history of a generation of black Americans and their involvement in an international reform movement that spanned thirty-five years in the United States, the British Isles, and Canada. We reconstructed that story by combining documents with written history. A thorough reading of the documents led us to the major themes and elements of black abolitionist activity—the events, ideas, individuals, concepts, and organizations that made up the movement. Then we sought documents that best represented those elements. But given their limited number, the documents alone could only hint at the full dimensions of this complex story. The written history—the volume introduction, the headnotes that precede each document, and the document footnotes—helps provide a more complete rendition by highlighting the documents' key elements and themes.

The documents led us to yet another principle that governs the volumes. Antislavery was a critical and persistent aspect of antebellum black life, but it cannot correctly be separated from the remainder of black life and culture. Antislavery was part of a broad matrix of black concerns that at times seemed indistinguishable from race relations in the free states, black churches and schools in northern cities, black family life, West Indian immigration, African missionary work, fugitive slave settlements in Canada, and a host of other personal, public, and national matters. Ending slavery was but the most urgent item on the crowded agenda of the black Americans represented in these volumes.

A number of considerations influenced the selection of specific documents published in the volumes. The most important was the responsibility to publish documents that fairly represent the antislavery goals, attitudes, and actions of black abolitionists and, to a lesser extent, that reveal their more personal concerns. There were other considerations as well.

We wanted to present documents by as many black abolitionists as possible. We avoided the temptation to rely on the eloquent statements of just a few polished professionals. We sought to document immediate antislavery objectives (often dictated by local needs and issues) as well as broad goals. A mix of document types—letters (both public and private), essays, scientific pieces, short autobiographical narratives, impromptu remarks, formal speeches, circulars, resolutions, and debates—were selected for publication.

We resisted selecting documents that had been published before our work began. But occasionally when a previously published document surfaced as a resonant black expression on an issue, topic, or incident, it was selected for publication. And, with the release of the Black Abolitionist Papers on microfilm, all the documents are more available than in the past. We often found different versions of the same document (usually a speech which appeared in several newspapers). When that happened, we selected the earliest published version of the most complete text. The cluster of documents around particular time periods and topics mirrors black abolitionist activities and concerns. The documents are arranged chronologically within each volume.

A headnote introduces each document. The headnote provides a historical context for the document and offers information designed to enhance the reader's understanding of the document and black abolitionist activities.

Footnotes identify a variety of items that appear within the documents, such as people, places, events, organizations, institutions, laws, and legal decisions. The notes enrich and clarify the documents. People and events that are covered in standard biographical directories, reference books, or textbooks are treated in brief notes. We have given more space to subjects on which there is little or no readily available information, particularly black individuals and significant events and institutions in the black community. A full note on each item is presented at the first appropriate point in the volume. Notes are not repeated within the volume. Information that appears in a headnote is not repeated in a footnote. The index includes references to all notes.

We have listed sources at the end of footnotes and headnotes. When appropriate, source citations contain references to materials in the microfilmed edition; they appear in brackets as reel and frame numbers (3:0070 reads reel 3, frame 70). The titles of some sources are abbreviated (particularly newspapers, journals, and manuscript repositories); a list of abbreviations appears at the front of the volume.

The axiom that "less is better" governed the project's transcription of documents. Our goal was to publish the documents in a form as close to the original as possible while presenting them in a fashion that enabled the reader to use them easily.

In the letters, the following items are uniformly and silently located regardless of where they appear in the original: place and date, recipient's name and address, salutation, closing, signature, marginal notes, and postscripts. In manuscript documents, idiosyncratic spelling, underlining, and quotation marks are retained. Words that were crossed through in the original are also retained.

The project adopted the following principles for documents found in published sources (newspapers, pamphlets, annual reports, and other nineteenth-century printed material): redundant punctuation is eliminated; quotation marks are converted to modern usage; obvious misspellings and printer's errors are corrected; printer's brackets are converted to parentheses; audience reaction within a speech is treated as a separate sentence with parentheses, for example, (Hear, hear.). We have let stand certain nineteenth-century printing conventions such as setting names or addresses in capital or italic letters in order to maintain the visual character of the document. A line of asterisks signals that material is deleted from a printed document. In no instance is black abolitionist material edited or deleted; but if, for example, a speech was interrupted with material extraneous to the document, the irrelevant material is not published.

The intrusive *sic* is rarely used. Brackets are used in their traditional fashion: to enclose information that we added and to indicate our inability to transcribe words or phrases with certainty. Some examples: we bracketed information added to the salutation and return address of letters; we bracketed material that we believe will aid the reader to comprehend the document, such as [illegible], [rest of page missing]; and we bracketed words and phrases that we believe appeared in the original but are uncertain about because of the quality of the surviving text. We have used brackets in the body of documents sparingly and only when necessary to avoid reader confusion. We have not completed words, added words, corrected spelling, or otherwise provided material in the text of manuscript documents except as noted above.

Our transcription guidelines for manuscript documents differ slightly from those we used for printed sources. We took greater editorial liberties with documents from printed sources because they seldom came to us directly from a black abolitionist's hand. Speeches in particular often had a long editorial trail. Usually reporters wrote them down as they listened from the audience; in some cases this appeared to be done with precision. For example, William Farmer, a British abolitionist and newspaper reporter, was an accomplished stenographer who traveled with William Wells Brown and took down his speeches verbatim, then made them available to the local press. More often, a local reporter recorded speeches in a less thorough fashion. Speeches and letters that black abolitionists sent to newspapers were apt to pass through the hands of an editor, a publisher, and a typesetter, all of whom might make errors in transcription. Because documents that were reprinted in newspapers often had sections changed or deleted, we have attempted to find the original publication of printed documents.

Our transcription guidelines were influenced by the availability of all the documents in the microfilmed edition. Microfilmed copies of the original documents give the reader ready access to unedited versions of the documents that appear in the published volumes.

A note on historical terminology: Throughout volume II, *Canada* is used to designate the area encompassed by the present-day Canadian nation. When discussing nineteenth-century Canada, we have used place names that were appropriate during the historical periods being considered. Prior to 1763, much of eastern Canada was part of the French colony of *New France*. Before 1841 present-day Ontario was called *Upper Canada* and present-day Quebec was called *Lower Canada*. Between 1841 and 1867, they were called *Canada West* and *Canada East* respectively. During both periods, they were collectively referred to as *the Canadas*, a term that excluded the *Maritime Provinces*—Nova Scotia, New Brunswick, and Prince Edward Island. Beginning in 1849, Vancouver Island was the *Crown Colony of Vancouver Island*. It did not unite with British Columbia until 1866. References to British Columbia before that date do not include the island. Until 1867 all of these British colonies were jointly known as the *British North American Provinces*.

The
Black Abolitionist
Papers

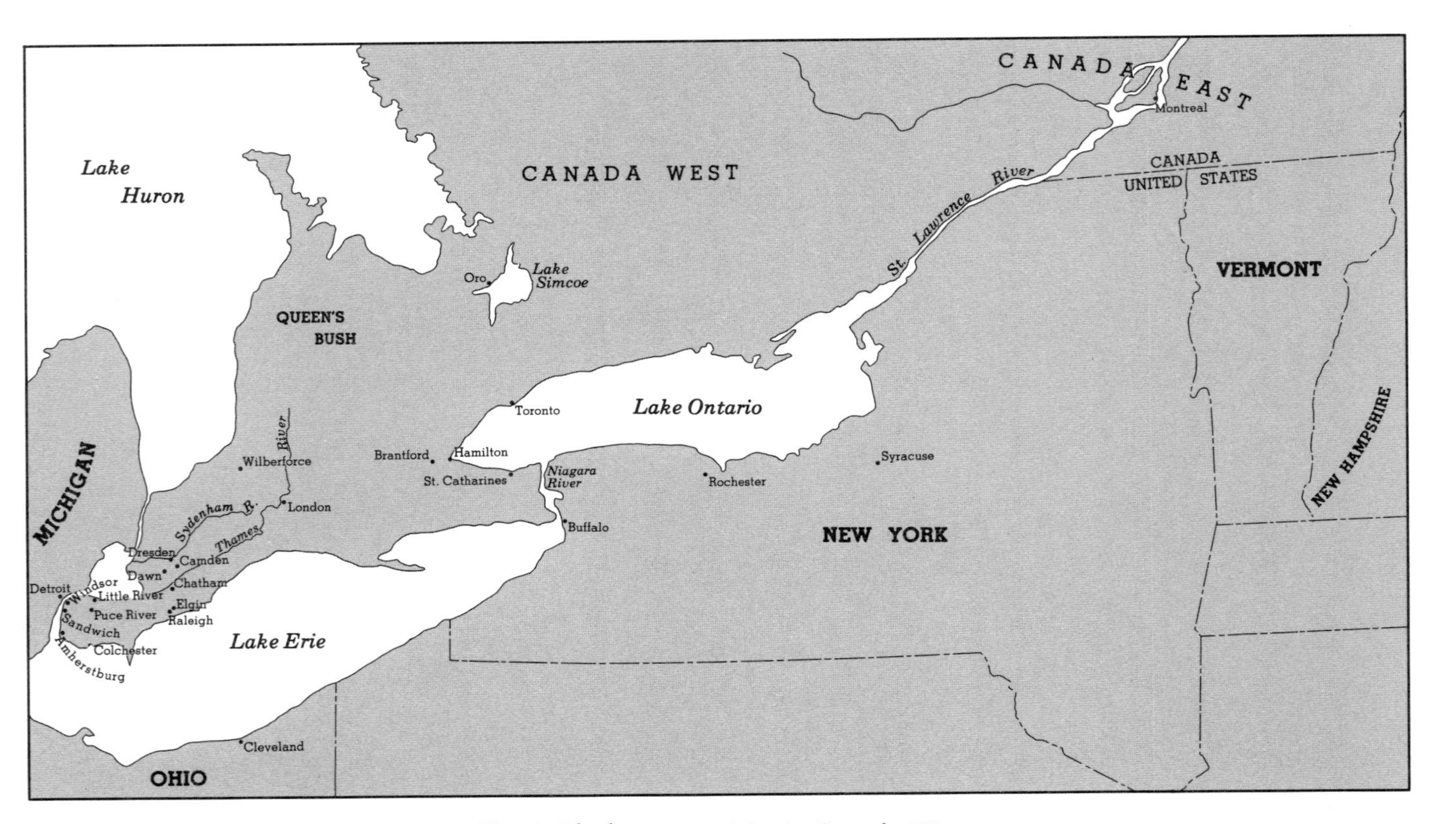

Fig. 1. Black communities in Canada West

Introduction

I'm on my way to Canada
That cold and distant land
The dire effects of slavery
I can no longer stand—
Farewell, old master,
Don't come after me.
I'm on my way to Canada
Where coloured men are free.
—George W. Clark, "The Free Slave"[1]

Canada seemed as remote as full freedom and equality to most eighteenth-century black Americans. Planters and proslavery advocates cautioned slaves that Canada was a distant, cold, barren, and hostile land inhabited by wild beasts and cannibals. But by the early nineteenth century, black Americans knew better. During the three decades preceding the American Civil War, some forty thousand blacks fled the United States into the British North American Provinces. They went to escape what black abolitionists often called the "twin evils" of slavery and racial prejudice. And Canada did not disappoint them. Fugitive slaves found there a sanctuary from southern bondage, and free blacks found relief from the social, economic, and political oppression that characterized black life in the northern states.

Once safely across the border, blacks discovered that Canada offered even more. As part of the British Empire, Canadians—regardless of color—enjoyed the right to participate in the economic, social, and political affairs of the nation. Freed from the constraints of American racial theory and practices, black emigrants went about the business of creating a prosperous and equitable life. Some did that in all-black settlements; others became part of thriving black communities in towns and cities; many worked the land as independent farmers. They entered trades and professions; bought land and businesses; established churches and schools; published newspapers and slave narratives; voted and held office; and organized self-help, literary, social, religious, and antislavery organizations.

Canada was mythologized in southern slave quarters and northern black communities as a haven that offered blacks an opportunity. But that opportunity also carried obligations. In time, as blacks settled in and

1. Various versions of this song by Clark, an American abolitionist, were well-known throughout the antislavery movement during the 1850s. See Daniel G. Hill, *The Freedom-Seekers: Blacks in Early Canada* (Agincourt, Ontario, 1981), 25, 220n.

grew successful, the Canadian experience became an antislavery symbol. Abolitionists in the United States, Canada, and the British Isles came to view black life in the provinces as a test of proslavery racial theories which held that blacks were inherently inferior, unfit for freedom, incapable of entering society, and therefore best left in bondage. Abolitionists reasoned that black success in Canada—where slavery was absent and prejudice was milder—would demonstrate black readiness for freedom, refute proslavery theories, and thereby achieve a critical victory in the struggle to free the slaves. What began as an exodus from oppression became both an experiment in opportunity and an obligation to do well.

Canada's reputation as a land of freedom and opportunity emerged from Canadian antislavery legislation, from the reluctance of Canadian courts to extradite American fugitive slaves, and from Canada's colorblind political and legal system. The Canadian slave population never exceeded a few thousand, and by the 1790s, antislavery sentiment was growing. John Graves Simcoe, Upper Canada's first lieutenant governor, persuaded the provincial legislative assembly to approve an antislavery bill in 1793 that prohibited the importation of slaves and provided for the gradual emancipation of blacks born into slavery. William Osgoode continued the process. As chief justice of Lower Canada, he issued a landmark decision that slavery was inconsistent with British law. Although this 1803 decision did not actually abolish the institution in Lower Canada, it left slaveholders without recourse to the courts, and it effectively freed the three hundred slaves in the province. This combination of administrative policy, legislation, and judicial rulings so discouraged slaveholding that few slaves remained in the Canadas by the time the Emancipation Act of 1833 formally abolished slavery.[2]

The demise of Canadian slavery and the abolitionist sentiment of key Canadian officials prompted American blacks—particularly fugitive slaves—to seek refuge north of the American border. By the 1820s, southern slaveholders began to view Canada as a threat to slavery and urged the U.S. government to conclude a treaty permitting recovery of runaway slaves, but Britain refused to depart from the principle recognized by the British courts that "every man is free who reaches British soil." When diplomacy failed, more persistent slaveholders sought other means to recover fugitive slaves. A few traveled to Upper Canada to bring back fugitives by force, but kidnapping violated Canadian law, often led to unpleasant confrontations with provincial authorities or hostile blacks, and, all in all, proved unsuccessful.[3]

2. Robin W. Winks, *The Blacks in Canada: A History* (New Haven, Conn., 1971), 96–113; Hill, *Freedom-Seekers*, 3–19.

3. Roman J. Zorn, "Criminal Extradition Menaces the Canadian Haven for Fugitive Slaves," *CHR* 38:284 (December 1957).

More litigious slaveholders turned to the extradition process. They hoped to return runaways to face criminal charges in southern courts. Periodic extradition requests tested the Canadian haven during the 1830s and 1840s. But as slaveholding pressure increased, so did British resolve. In February 1833, Upper Canada's legislative assembly enacted an extradition statute that allowed Lieutenant Governor John Colborne ample latitude to deny extradition requests. In the first test of the new law, Colborne refused to extradite Thornton and Rutha Blackburn, two Kentucky slaves who had fled arrest in Detroit, eluded a mob, and found refuge in Upper Canada. He argued that they had committed no crime punishable under Canadian law. The following year, Colborne refused to extradite a Virginia fugitive on similar grounds.[4]

In 1837–38 the Jesse Happy case solidified Anglo-Canadian extradition policy. During his escape, Happy, a Kentucky fugitive, stole a horse from his master. American authorities made a well-prepared request for his return based on the theft of the horse. An investigation by Canadian officials revealed that Happy had left the animal on the American side and had written to his former master to tell him where to find it. The Happy case prompted British officials to formalize a slave extradition policy; they concluded that a proper slave extradition request must include evidence of a criminal act that "would warrant the apprehension of the accused Party, if the alleged offense had been committed in Canada." Because slavery no longer existed in the Canadas, "self-theft" did not qualify as a crime. Happy was set free.[5]

The 1838 rule guided future slave-extradition cases. But it did not answer all the legal questions. What should be done with fugitive slaves who committed other crimes, particularly theft not essential to the escape? Britain and the United States agreed on the need for a treaty to cover extradition. American officials hoped that it would provide for the recovery of fugitive slaves. British officials determined that it would not and concluded that robbery or horse-stealing could become pretexts for recapturing runaways and, therefore, should not be extraditable offenses. But in 1842 Nelson Hackett, a fugitive from Arkansas, was extradited from Canada West because he stole goods that were not considered necessary to his flight. In ordering Hackett's return, the governor-general wrote that he was not willing to see Canada become "an asylum for the worst characters provided only that they had been slaves before arriving here." For the first time, criminal extradition proceedings returned a fugitive slave from Canada West.[6]

4. Winks, *Blacks in Canada*, 168; Norman McRae, "Crossing the Detroit River to Find Freedom," *MH* 67:39 (March–April 1983).

5. Winks, *Blacks in Canada*, 170–71.

6. Ibid., 171–72; Roman J. Zorn, "An Arkansas Fugitive Slave Incident and Its International Repercussions," *AHQ* 16:139–49 (Summer 1957).

Anglo-Canadian outrage at Hackett's return increased support for an extradition treaty. But the resulting Webster-Ashburton Treaty (1843) satisfied no one. Although Article X adopted provisions of the 1833 extradition statute, observers were not sure what that would mean in practice. The treaty may have been ambiguous, but Canadian officials were not. They had no intention of allowing it to endanger Canadian fugitives. And Anglo-Canadian abolitionists pressured government officials to insure that that was the case. No fugitive slave was extradited under terms of the Webster-Ashburton Treaty. The principles enunciated in the 1838 rule prevailed, even after passage of the Fugitive Slave Law of 1850.[7]

The last slave extradition case to come before the Canadian courts tested the antislavery convictions of Canadian officials. Fugitive slave John Anderson killed Seneca T. P. Diggs, a white neighbor of his master, who tried to stop Anderson during his escape from Missouri. In 1860, seven years after the incident, Anderson was arrested near Brantford, Canada West. Because Anderson had committed murder during his escape, there seemed a genuine chance that Canadian officials might surrender him to American authorities. Abolitionist reaction was intense. The Anderson extradition trial became a celebrated incident in the transatlantic antislavery movement. Abolitionists in both Britain and Canada petitioned key officials, instituted legal proceedings, and exerted all the pressure and influence they could muster. Anderson was acquitted in February 1861 on a technicality arising from a defective warrant. The Canadian haven remained exactly that, with the help of legal fine print. The outcome of the Anderson case and the coming of the Civil War closed the extradition issue.[8]

Canada's image as a haven developed from three conditions: the absence of slavery, protection from extradition, and the civil rights Canada offered to all its citizens regardless of color. Blacks found freedom and political and legal equality in the provinces. Precious rights denied in the United States—the right to vote, the right to serve on juries, equal protection under the law—were theirs in Canada. And black Canadians were able to guard those rights. During the 1850s, a growing black presence intimidated white Canadians and led to occasional attempts to keep blacks from exercising the franchise. But blacks used one right to defend another, took their case to the courts, and were supported by the Canadian judicial system.[9] Blacks in Victoria, Vancouver Island, struggled to fashion themselves into a substantial political force. In January 1860, less

7. Winks, *Blacks in Canada*, 172–74; Zorn, "Criminal Extradition Menaces Canadian Haven," 288–89.

8. Robert C. Reinders's articles provide the best overview of the John Anderson case. See "Anglo-Canadian Abolitionism: The John Anderson Case, 1860–1861," *RMS* 19:72–97 (1975); and "The John Anderson Case, 1860–61: A Study in Anglo-Canadian Imperial Relations," *CHR* 56:393–415 (December 1975).

9. Benjamin Drew, *A North-Side View of Slavery* (Boston, Mass., 1856; reprint, New York,

than two years after they first arrived in the city, a judicial decision disqualified nearly all of the black electorate, but black pressure and legal action brought about a provincial naturalization law that reinstated them. Thereafter, Victoria blacks voted as a matter of course, challenged irregularities in the balloting, occasionally ran for office, and elected black businessman Mifflin W. Gibbs to a seat on the city council in 1866.[10]

By the late antebellum period, integrated juries were common in most areas of Canada West, but only after the right of blacks to sit on juries was challenged and affirmed. With few exceptions, blacks received fair and impartial treatment in Canadian courts. Whites who committed acts of racial violence usually received appropriate punishment. After an antiblack riot in St. Catharines injured several blacks and damaged black property, many of the white rioters were arrested, and the property was repaired at their expense. When blacks were denied access to public facilities, the Canadian courts normally ordered those rights restored. Blacks gloried in the Canadian legal system; the *Provincial Freeman* urged blacks to leave "Yankeedom with disenfranchisement and oppression" and settle "in a land of impartial laws and a Constitution having no distinctions of color."[11]

Citizenship and legal equality reinforced black perceptions that Canada was a haven, albeit a less than perfect one. If black political and legal rights were rarely questioned, black social equality was. De facto discrimination and racism were not easily eliminated, even in the British North American Provinces. As more and more blacks reached Canada during the 1830s and 1840s, casual segregation patterns began to emerge. The situation grew worse after 1850. The increasing number of blacks (particularly fugitive slaves), the arrival of new immigrant groups, the decline of cheap land, and the consequent drift of blacks into towns accelerated the rise of Canadian racism. Blacks were victimized by verbal abuse, by public criticism, and by race-baiting politicians. They occasionally received shoddy treatment on public conveyances and in hotels, theaters, and churches, particularly those serving an American clientele.[12]

N.Y., 1968), 307; Alexander L. Murray, "Canada and the Anglo-American Anti-Slavery Movement: A Study in International Philanthropy" (Ph.D. diss., University of Pennsylvania, 1960), 324–25; Samuel Ringgold Ward, *Autobiography of a Fugitive Negro* (London, 1855; reprint, New York, N.Y., 1968), 148–49; *VF*, 21 October 1852; Winks, *Blacks in Canada*, 149, 214–15. See also Jason Howard Silverman, "Unwelcome Guests: American Fugitive Slaves in Canada, 1830–1860" (Ph.D. diss., University of Kentucky, 1981), which is the authoritative source on white racism and hostility toward blacks in Canada.

10. Crawford Kilian, *Go Do Some Great Thing: The Black Pioneers of British Columbia* (Vancouver, British Columbia, 1978), 64–74, 127–31, 140.

11. *FDP*, 16 July 1852; *PtT*, 13 May 1851; *Lib*, 8 August 1851; Murray, "Canada and the Anglo-American Anti-Slavery Movement," 325–27; *TG*, 31 July 1852 [7:0685]; Kilian, *Go Do Some Great Thing*, 126–27; *PFW*, 25 March 1854.

12. Winks, *Blacks in Canada*, 148, 211–15; *VF*, 26 February, 4 November 1852; *PFW*, 24

No matter how intense white racism became, attempts to abridge black rights generally proved unsuccessful, except in the case of education. Separate schools were commonplace in the Maritimes and, after 1840, increasingly so in Canada West. The Act of Union (1840) sanctioned the concept of separate schools in order to protect Roman Catholic and other denominational education. Whites in portions of Canada West interpreted the law to justify racially segregated schools. Before long, several communities established separate black schools, while others simply provided blacks no opportunity for public instruction. The Common School Act of 1850 guaranteed a public education to all Canadians, but it did not specify an integrated education. It required blacks to attend separate schools where they existed, although blacks could attend white schools when separate schools were not available. That stipulation legally entrenched the system of separate schools in the province.[13]

With the rise of racially separate education, blacks sought redress through the Canadian courts; but the critical case of *Hill* v. *School Trustees of Camden and Zone* upheld the separate school system allowed by the Common School Act. Justice John Beverly Robinson pronounced that "the separate schools for coloured people were authorized . . . out of deference to the prejudices of the white population" and explained that white Canadians feared that their children would be affected by the bad moral habits of black children. Such anxieties, he concluded, justified the system. During the following decade, blacks in communities throughout the province challenged separate schools in the courts and flooded government offices with letters of protest. For blacks, Canadian common schools represented the social egalitarianism that they sought in Canada; to accept racially segregated education would betray that objective.[14]

Despite these problems, the provinces retained their symbolic glow and practical appeal. Blacks remembered what they had left behind. They knew that American slavery and prejudice made the Canadian haven necessary. If the absence of slavery in Canada and the protection of Canadian courts made the provinces appealing to fugitive slaves, then Canada's reputation for political and legal equality made it appealing to free blacks. Thousands of black Americans fled to the British North American Provinces to escape slavery and racism. The migration followed a pattern tied to conditions and events in the United States.

June, 24 August 1854, 29 September 1855; *FDP*, 11 December 1851; *PtT*, 22 August 1852 [3:0125]; Kilian, *Go Do Some Great Thing*, 65–71, 82–83, 116–26; Murray, "Canada and the Anglo-American Anti-Slavery Movement," 298–303.

13. Kilian, *Go Do Some Great Thing*, 80; Jason H. Silverman and Donna J. Gillie, "'The Pursuit of Knowledge Under Difficulties': Education and the Fugitive Slaves in Canada," *OntH* 74:95–112 (June 1982); Winks, *Blacks in Canada*, 365–76.

14. Silverman and Gillie, "Pursuit of Knowledge Under Difficulties," 96–105; Hill, *Freedom-Seekers*, 100–103.

Although free blacks had settled in the Maritimes following the American Revolution and the War of 1812, the first substantial wave of immigrants, made up largely of blacks from the free states, moved north as a result of changing conditions in the United States. Beginning in the 1820s and continuing well into the 1840s, the social, economic, and political status of blacks in northern cities began to decline. Violence and segregation increased; voting rights and economic opportunity diminished. Northern urban centers became home for thousands of immigrants from Europe who competed for jobs, trades, and professions that had traditionally belonged to blacks. It was an economic competition that blacks lost. While group after group of new arrivals found a place in society, blacks remained economically dispossessed. The new conditions aggravated a persistent racism that kept blacks in poverty and on the periphery of American economic life. This sentiment was expressed by a revival of laws, regulations, proscriptions, and violence directed against free blacks, particularly in northern cities. Antiblack riots became common. Churches, schools, homes, and meeting houses were burned; blacks were abused, beaten, and sometimes murdered. Philadelphia alone witnessed seven riots between 1820 and 1849.[15]

Cincinnati provides the most dramatic example of the political and economic repression and mob violence that caused black Americans to emigrate during the 1830s and 1840s. In 1829 Cincinnati revised, amended, and codified a series of state and local laws and constitutional provisions designed to limit black rights and privileges. In July Cincinnati announced it would enforce the black codes. Blacks could not carry arms, sit on a jury, or serve in the militia. These statutes were demeaning, but more devastating was a provision that required them to complete a registration process and post a $500 bond or leave the county within thirty days. Without a certificate of registration, blacks could not legally obtain or hold a job. The black community requested a sixty-day extension of the registration deadline and then sent representatives to Upper Canada to investigate the possibility of settlement. The extension was granted, but white mobs periodically threatened the black community. An estimated 1,100–2,200 Cincinnati blacks eventually left the city in the months that followed.[16]

The Fugitive Slave Law of 1850 initiated the second and largest movement of blacks into Canada. The law addressed slave-owner dissatisfaction with the federal procedures for returning fugitive slaves. It created

15. Leon Litwack, *North of Slavery: The Negro in the Free States, 1790–1860* (Chicago, Ill., 1961), 66–75, 153–65; Philip S. Foner, *History of Black Americans: From the Emergence of the Cotton Kingdom to the Eve of the Compromise of 1850* (Westport, Conn., 1983), 203.

16. Winks, *Blacks in Canada*, 32–157; Richard Wade, "The Negro in Cincinnati, 1800–1830," *JNH* 39:48–57 (January 1954).

the position of federal hearing officer, who was given final authority over extradition proceedings; it stipulated heavy fines and possible prison terms for anyone aiding fugitive slaves; and it made the fugitive slave extradition process an administrative rather than a judicial matter, thereby robbing accused blacks of the right to testify on their own behalf, of the right to counsel, and of the right to a habeas corpus hearing. Free blacks and fugitives alike viewed the law as a threat to their freedom, with good cause. Slave catchers roamed northern cities seeking out fugitives with the assistance of local and federal authorities. Resistance to the law was fast and vigorous but so was the federal response. The act was enforced by the highest national authority: President Millard Fillmore, who had moved the bill through Congress, issued a stern proclamation on enforcement after an abolitionist mob interfered in an early fugitive extradition. In practical terms, the law had serious implications for black Americans. Obviously fugitive slaves could find no sanctuary from slave catchers in the United States. In addition, free blacks were threatened; the law so limited black rights, and so shaped the extradition process to the benefit of slave owners, that any black arrested as a fugitive seemed destined for slavery. No precise figures exist on the number of black Americans who left for Canada in response to the Fugitive Slave Law, but one reliable observer estimated that three thousand crossed the border during the fall of 1850.[17]

And cross they did. In the wake of the Fugitive Slave Law, when slave catchers traveled to northern cities, anxious fugitive slaves—many of them long removed from bondage and well situated in their communities—moved quietly into Canada. Runaways who had to make their way from a slave state had a more difficult time of it. It was a long and arduous journey to Canada under any circumstances. The drama and danger of escape cannot be exaggerated. Slave patrols, tracking dogs, a suspicious white population, the pass system, the rewards for capturing runaways, and the immense distance separating slavery from freedom made escaping a desperate act, particularly for plantation slaves, some of whom had never been more than a few miles from home. Methods of escape were varied and often creative and bold, but the hardships were common to all. Most fugitives walked, swam rivers, avoided whites, and nearly all suffered from a lack of food and adequate clothing.

An ironic twist of slave life made the dead of winter the best time to escape. During the Christmas holidays, it was common for slaves to receive passes to leave the plantation for a few days to visit family or friends on other plantations. Well-planned escapes often began with a holiday

17. Stanley W. Campbell, *The Slave Catchers: Enforcement of the Fugitive Slave Law of 1850* (Chapel Hill, N.C., 1968), 4–24, 110–45; Fred Landon, "The Negro Migration to Canada after Passage of the Fugitive Slave Act," *JNH* 5:22–25 (January 1920); *Lib*, 13 December 1850.

pass in hand. Winter also brought the advantage of frozen streams and rivers, which the escapees could cross on foot over the ice rather than risking the swim or finding a boat or ferry. But winter brought its own burdens. There were no standing crops or edible vegetation, and the cold defeated many runaways before they reached the free states. Frostbite and sickness were common. Romulus Hall traveled nine days and nights, went three days without food, and was so devastated by the cold that he died a week after reaching safety.[18]

In leaving master and plantation, slaves left home and family as well. Henry Atkinson recalled that "it went hard" to leave his wife, which he did only when he was certain they would be separated. "I expected to be taken away . . . so I concluded that it would be right to leave her. I never expect to see her again in this world—nor our child." For Canadian fugitives like Atkinson, the journey to freedom had a bittersweet quality. Anguish at the thought of abandoning family and friends kept them on the plantation until the threat of separation provided the incentive to begin the journey northward. The majority of runaways were males, yet some groups included women and children, and occasionally a mother and child made the journey alone.[19]

Arrival on Canadian soil, with its promise of freedom and equality, was often an exhilarating experience for black immigrants. But the circumstances of their arrival varied dramatically. Free blacks frequently crossed the border with personal belongings, money, a rudimentary education, and a trade. Fugitive slaves often came with little but their clothes. They all found that Canada offered freedom and perhaps the welcoming embrace of friends or family who had preceded them. Blacks and philanthropic whites organized relief efforts to feed, clothe, shelter, and find employment for the new arrivals. In time the fugitive slaves went about the business of arranging a life for themselves and their families.

The Canadian refuge began as a remedy, but it came to represent much more. The large numbers of American blacks fleeing slavery and racial prejudice for safety in Canada had an unavoidable symbolic value that permeated the entire black Canadian experience. By going to Canada, the fugitives made an implicit antislavery statement; each escape attempt gave lie to the "contented-slave thesis"—the proslavery fiction that blacks accepted, even preferred, a life in bondage. By thriving in Canada's free and open society, blacks effectively undercut proslavery claims of their inferiority and childlike dependence. The *Provincial Freeman* promised

18. Lewis Clarke et al., *The Agricultural, Mechanical and Educational Association of Canada West* (Sandwich, Canada West, 1859), 1; William Still, *The Under-Ground Railroad* (Philadelphia, Pa., 1872), 52–54, 121, 124, 125; *VF*, 22 April 1852.

19. *FDP*, 26 June 1851; *VF*, 1 January 1851, 4 November 1852; *PF*, 22 March 1856, 7 February 1857; Still, *The Under-Ground Railroad*, 27, 82–83, 129, 130, 190, 191; Drew, *North-Side View of Slavery*, 82–83.

that the progress of blacks in Canada would expose "the two great Yankee falsehoods": that blacks were unfit for freedom and that they could not live on terms of equality with whites.

Nowhere was the antislavery symbolism stronger and the hope of black progress more apparent than in the four major settlements of Wilberforce, Dawn, Elgin, and the Refugee Home Society. Wilberforce was founded by free blacks in response to the revived Ohio black laws in the late 1820s. Cincinnati blacks dispatched agents to Upper Canada to negotiate a land purchase in 1829. Concerned Quakers in Ohio and Indiana provided the funds to acquire eight hundred acres near Lucan, Upper Canada. Wilberforce attracted about two hundred free blacks and fugitive slaves, including Austin Steward, a former slave who left his grocery business in Rochester, New York, to direct the new settlement.[20]

Dawn and Elgin developed during the 1840s. The Dawn settlement grew around the British-American Institute, a black manual labor school founded near Dresden, Canada West, in 1842. The task of organizing and managing Dawn fell to fugitive slave Josiah Henson and white missionary Hiram Wilson. The prospect of educational opportunities, rare even for whites on the Canadian frontier, drew about five hundred blacks to the fifteen-hundred-acre settlement adjacent to the institute. Elgin was founded by William King, an Irish Presbyterian missionary, in 1849. King manumitted the slaves he had acquired through marriage and brought them to Buxton, Canada West, where they formed the nucleus of a black community. The Elgin Association, a joint-stock company incorporated in 1850, was responsible for the group's financial and legal affairs and arranged for the purchase and resale of fifty-acre parcels to the settlers. Under King's careful planning and supervision, Elgin became the most successful of the planned black settlements in Canada West. Buxton boasted three integrated schools, two hotels, a general store, and a post office. By 1861 three hundred families resided on Elgin's ten thousand acres.[21]

The last major black settlement, the Refugee Home Society (RHS), emerged from efforts to provide destitute fugitive slaves with land along the Detroit frontier in Canada West. The Detroit-based organization, founded in 1851 by Michigan abolitionists, merged one year later with the black Fugitive Union Society of Sandwich. The RHS remained under the broad control of white officers in the Detroit area. David Hotchkiss, an American Missionary Association (AMA) agent at Amherstburg, and Windsor fugitive slave Henry Bibb and his wife Mary directed the project.

20. Winks, *Blacks in Canada*, 156–62; William H. Pease and Jane H. Pease, *Black Utopia: Negro Communal Experiments in America* (Madison, Wis., 1963), 46–62.
21. Winks, *Blacks in Canada*, 178–81, 195–204, 208–16; Pease and Pease, *Black Utopia*, 63–108; Victor Ullman, *Look to the North Star: A Life of William King* (Boston, Mass., 1969), 91–177.

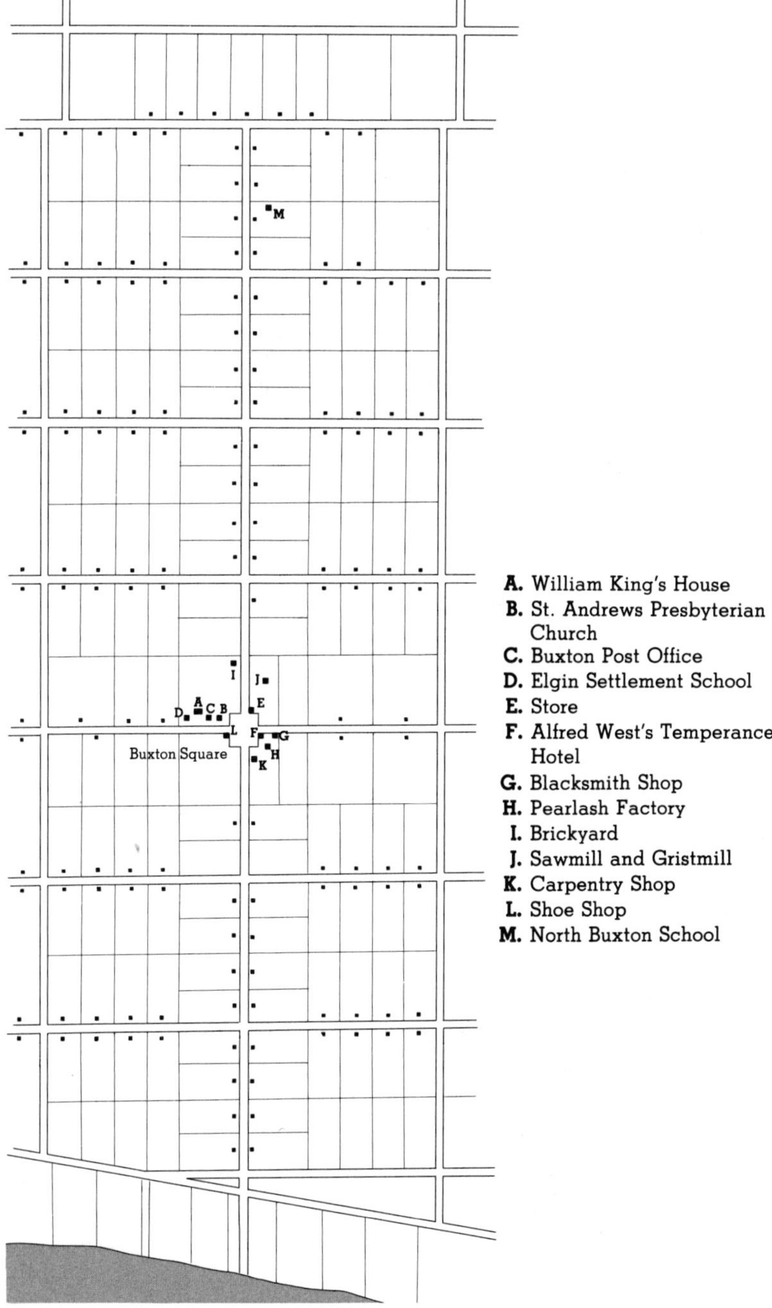

Fig. 2. Elgin settlement

Based on "Plan of the Elgin Settlement," a map held by Raleigh Township Centennial Museum, North Buxton, Ontario

Unlike the other three major planned black communities, the RHS did not establish a contiguous settlement but instead acquired several separate tracts of land south and east of Windsor. By 1855 the RHS had purchased two thousand acres and furnished land to one hundred and fifty black settlers.[22]

Religion and education guided the settlements, while ministers and missionaries provided much of the leadership. King conducted Presbyterian services at his Buxton Mission. The American Missionary Association's Canada Mission supported Hiram Wilson at Dawn and David Hotchkiss at the RHS. After the American Baptist Free Mission Society took control of Dawn in 1850, leadership fell to black ministers Samuel H. Davis and William P. Newman. The promise of education perhaps best symbolized the potential of the black settlements. The British-American Institute at Dawn received much publicity, but the Elgin schools left the most impressive legacy. King rejected vocational training for blacks in favor of classical studies. Knox College graduates taught the day classes while he conducted a night school for adults. The quality of education was such that whites in the surrounding Raleigh township closed their own school and sent their children to Elgin. "I left the States for Canada, for rights, freedom, liberty," black settler Henry Johnson recalled. "I came to [Elgin] to educate my children." And that he did. His son Richard Johnson later graduated from the Royal Surgeons' College in Edinburgh and served forty years as a Presbyterian medical missionary in Africa.[23] Many of the men and women educated at Elgin returned to the United States during and after the Civil War to assume prominent positions in southern black communities.

Abolitionists in the United States and Canada viewed the settlements as antislavery weapons that would provide indisputable evidence of black self-reliance and achievement. Ambitious things were expected of them. They offered freedom, security, and a sense of community unavailable to blacks—particularly fugitives—anywhere else on the North American continent. American and Canadian abolitionists reasoned that these favorable conditions would give blacks an opportunity to establish themselves as good citizens who prospered, voted, attended schools and churches, and by every measure became self-sufficient members of society. Black demonstrations of social, economic, and political achievement would indicate a readiness for freedom that would make a clear statement against slavery and prejudice in the United States.

The settlements were also viewed by many as experiments in social and moral reform. They provided a setting in which to infuse blacks with

22. Winks, *Blacks in Canada*, 204–8; Pease and Pease, *Black Utopia*, 109–22.

23. *VF*, 12 February 1851; Ullman, *Look to the North Star*, 164–77, 182–83, 240–322; Drew, *North-Side View of Slavery*, 306–7, 328; Pease and Pease, *Black Utopia*, 50–52, 67–69.

white, middle-class, Protestant values. Piety, education, moral uplift, and sobriety were the watchwords; thrift and industry were the economic imperatives. The work ethic filled the settlements. Community stability, social propriety, and conformity were prized. At Elgin, restrictions guided many aspects of the settlers' lives, even housing. Regulations specified the size and structural standards of the homes and their distance from the road; each home was required to have a front porch, a picket fence, and a flower garden. Imbued with utopian ideals of the day, the settlements were devoted as much to building citizens as to building communities.

But the black settlements never evolved into what their organizers and promoters envisioned. The presence of white leadership and the continued dependence on white philanthropy detracted from the settlements' image as self-sustaining, independent black enterprises. Wilberforce, Dawn, and the Refugee Home Society all suffered from periodic mismanagement, resulting in factionalism and a loss of public confidence in the settlements and their leaders. By 1836 Wilberforce was no longer an organized community. Dawn ceased functioning in the mid-1850s, although a legal battle for control of the British-American Institute property continued until 1868. The RHS disposed of its property during the Civil War and ended operations in 1876. The Elgin Association was dissolved in 1873.

Although the settlements never became what their organizers hoped for, to dismiss them as failures would be to lose sight of significant aspects of black life in Canada. Organizers and abolitionists in Canada and the United States wanted the settlements to become ideal communities of model black citizens. As supporters and leaders went about the business of raising funds and promoting the settlements, they promised all that and more; reformist optimism became antislavery propaganda. But converting the settlements into ambitious antislavery symbols ran counter to the realities of life on the Canadian frontier. The settlements could never keep pace with such myth-building, even with outside support. They could not fulfill the abolitionists' quest for an unequivocal demonstration of black self-reliance, and they could not conform to the reformers' model community, with its staid citizenry, flower gardens, and whitewashed picket fences. But stripped of antislavery symbolism and lofty expectations, the organized settlements were much like other communities in Canada West. Residents in the settlements endured the challenges and vicissitudes of pioneer life just as others did in the Canadian frontier towns and villages. On the frontier, some communities prospered; others languished and died. When the organized settlements declined, many inhabitants relocated while others remained on the land they had acquired. Pioneers more by circumstance than by choice, black settlers proved equal to the task of clearing the land, establishing homesteads, and tilling the soil. J. Dennis Harris, a Haitian immigration agent touring the Elgin settlement, expressed surprise when, instead of dense forest and marshes, he found "miles and miles" of cultivated farmland. Blacks helped transform Canada West and, in the process, were themselves changed by their newfound experience with freedom, new responsibilities, and participation in local political and economic life.[24]

The organized settlements provided opportunities for free blacks and helped facilitate the fugitive slave's transition from slavery to freedom. Black enclaves in predominantly white communities, in their own way, performed a similar function. By 1850 blacks had settled in six areas of Canada West: along the Detroit frontier, particularly at Windsor, Sandwich, Amherstburg, Colchester, and the surrounding region; in Chatham and its environs, including the all-black settlements at Dawn and Elgin; in the central section of the province, including London, Brantford, Queen's Bush, and the all-black Wilberforce settlement; on the Niagara frontier, particularly St. Catharines; in the urban centers of Hamilton and Toronto; and at the northern perimeter of Lake Simcoe. Although blacks never exceeded more than 1 percent of the Canadian population, their concentration in a few areas of Canada West gave them a local economic and political influence far greater than their total numbers would indicate. Blacks made up nearly 20 percent of the population of Chatham, 25 percent of Amherstburg, and 33 percent of Colchester in the decade preceding the Civil War.

A smaller black community developed along the Canadian Pacific coast after 1858. It was centered mainly in Victoria, Vancouver Island, although other settlements sprang up elsewhere on the island and on tiny Saltspring Island. A few adventurous types sought their fortune inland in the Cariboo gold-mining region. In all, perhaps eight hundred to one thousand blacks were settled on Vancouver Island and in British Columbia. By 1860 the black population of the British North American Provinces (including the Pacific Coast) was approximately sixty-two thousand with nearly two-thirds of this number in Canada West. More than two-thirds of the black migrants to the British North American Provinces left the United States in the decades after 1830, and a majority of them favored a destination in Upper Canada.[25]

Blacks gravitated to the urban areas of Canada West. Canadian communities such as Amherstburg, Windsor, and St. Catharines served as final stops on the underground railroad and offered arriving fugitive slaves temporary employment in these towns or on nearby road, rail, and canal projects. After earning enough to purchase land or establish themselves

24. *PP*, 3 August 1861 [13:0675].

25. Hill, *Freedom-Seekers*, 48–59; Kilian, *Go Do Some Great Thing*, 15–138, 147. More conservative population estimates appear in the Victoria *British Colonist*, 6 October 1868, and the *Victoria City Directory*, 1871.

in a trade, some moved elsewhere, while others remained in the towns, hoping to share in the opportunities and prosperity of the growing urban centers. If the organized settlements drew farmers, the towns attracted the shop-keepers, artisans, and laborers. One-half of Chatham's black workers were skilled or semi-skilled; many of those were shoemakers, carpenters, and blacksmiths. Blacks in gold-rush Victoria made exceptional gains from their business and property holdings. Driven from California by racial bigotry and legal discrimination, they brought their trades and considerable capital to Victoria and quickly became one of the most affluent, politically influential, black communities in the British North American Provinces.[26]

Unlike the settlements, the black communities were racial enclaves in predominantly white towns. Toronto was the focal point of black culture in Canada West until the 1850s. The *Provincial Freeman*, the most militant voice of black abolitionism in Canada, began regular publication in Toronto. The black community supported literary and benevolent societies, temperance groups, and a variety of church-related activities and organizations. Toronto blacks helped sustain the Upper Canada Anti-Slavery Society in the late 1830s. A decade later, they founded the short-lived British-American Anti-Slavery Society. The importance of the Toronto black community was underscored in 1851, when organizers of the North American Convention selected Toronto over larger American cities as the meeting site.[27]

Amherstburg and Windsor, both located near Detroit on the Canadian border, were convenient points of entry for fugitive slaves and, after 1850, became important centers of black Canadian life. Willis Nazrey founded Canada's first African Methodist Episcopal church in Amherstburg in 1828. Later the Amherstburg Baptist Missionary Association, organized by Anthony Binga and others, served as a provincial base for black Baptist activities. In the 1850s, Amherstburg was probably the most active center for the underground railroad in Canada. The first "true band" society, a black mutual-aid organization, was founded there in 1854 and served as a model for similar societies established in the province. The vitality of Amherstburg's black community was tacitly recognized when a black provincial convention met there in 1853. The black community in Windsor gained prominence due in large part to the work of Henry and Mary Bibb, James T. Holly, and Mary Ann Shadd Cary. There the Bibbs

26. Jonathan William Walton, "Blacks in Buxton and Chatham, Ontario, 1830–1890: Did the 49th Parallel Make a Difference?" (Ph.D. diss., Princeton University, 1979), 63, 321–23.

27. *VF*, 24 September 1851 [7:0109]; Winks, *Blacks in Canada*, 253–54; Daniel G. Hill, "Negroes in Toronto: A Sociological Study of a Minority Group" (Ph.D. diss., University of Toronto, 1960), 21–22; *TC*, 15 November 1837; *NSt*, 28 April, 1 December 1848 [5:0626, 0838]; *PP*, 7 September 1861 [13:0743].

and Holly published the first sustained black newspaper in Canada—the *Voice of the Fugitive*. Windsor also served as a Canadian base for the Refugee Home Society.[28]

By the mid-1850s, Chatham had given rise to a vibrant, prosperous black community. The transfer of the *Provincial Freeman* from Toronto highlighted the development of Chatham as a cultural mecca for black Canadians. For its size, it included an unusually large number of gifted black intellectuals, among whom were Martin R. Delany, Mary Ann Shadd Cary, Isaac D. Shadd, James Madison Bell, H. Ford Douglas, and William Howard Day. William H. Jones's British Methodist Episcopal congregation in Chatham rivaled the largest black churches in New York and Philadelphia. Chatham hosted several black conventions in the late 1850s. The British Methodist Episcopal church was organized at a religious convention in Chatham in 1856. The third National Emigration Convention, held there in 1858, intensified the debate in Canada over African and Caribbean immigration. John Brown's secret convention in 1858 added to Chatham's substantial legacy in black Canadian history.[29]

Black Canadians, by their daily lives, made a symbolic contribution to the antislavery cause, but many took more direct and formal action to free the American slaves. Abolitionism in Canada and the United States had common features—lecturing, raising funds, publishing newspapers, writing slave narratives, and convincing the uninitiated to do their part for the antislavery movement. But there were two substantial differences. First, blacks played a more influential role in the Canadian antislavery movement than they did in the United States. This was natural. Many black abolitionists arrived in Canada with substantial antislavery experience. They joined nearly every Canadian antislavery organization and formed societies of their own, and after the mid-1850s, the overall movement was largely in their hands. Second, black leaders, always mindful of the antislavery potential of the black experience in Canada, believed that assisting black refugees as they established a new life was critical to the antislavery struggle.

A sustained Canadian antislavery movement began in the 1850s, when the Fugitive Slave Law prompted the formation of the Anti-Slavery Society of Canada (ASC). On 26 February 1851, a public meeting at Toronto's city hall organized a society "to aid in the extinction of Slavery

28. Hill, *Freedom-Seekers*, 48–50, 155; *VF*, 21 October 1852 [7:0742, 0743, 0744]; *PP*, 7 December 1861 [13:0954].

29. *PFW*, 14 March 1857 [10:0580–81]; *PP*, 28 September 1861 [13:0774]; Floyd J. Miller, *The Search for a Black Nationality: Black Emigration and Colonization, 1787–1863* (Urbana, Ill., 1975), 166–67, 194–95, 179–82; Daniel A. Payne, *History of the African Methodist Episcopal Church* (Nashville, Tenn., 1891; reprint New York, N.Y., 1968), 361–92; Hill, *Freedom-Seekers*, 137; Walton, "Blacks in Buxton and Chatham," 62–76.

all over the world." Founded by local white clergymen and businessmen, three blacks—A. Beckford Jones of London, Henry Bibb of Windsor, and Wilson R. Abbott of Toronto—were among its fourteen vice-presidents. Fugitive slave and newspaper editor Samuel Ringgold Ward served on the executive committee and became the most visible, active, and successful advocate in both Canada and Britain. During its first year, the society focused its activities on aiding fugitive slaves, who arrived in staggering numbers during the winter of 1850–51. The ASC favored black Canadian settlements (such as Dawn and the Refugee Home Society) and opposed African colonization, West Indian immigration, and the extradition of fugitive slaves from the Canadas.[30]

The ASC promoted the cause by the time-honored method of sponsoring antislavery speakers, some of whom were brought in from the United States. Black lecturers—Ward, Frederick Douglass, Frances Ellen Watkins, and Jermain W. Loguen—persuaded white Canadians of the evils of American slavery. Ward, Douglass, and Loguen awed their listeners with first-person accounts of the horrors of slave life. Loguen recounted his experiences in bondage and spoke of his relatives and friends "still clanking their chains in the Southern prison-house."[31] During the early 1850s, white Canadians, angered and made curious by the passage of the Fugitive Slave Law, eagerly listened to former slave speakers, who confirmed their worst suspicions about the institution.

The society expanded its efforts by establishing local branches throughout Canada West. Ward was hired as a touring agent to speak and organize throughout the province during 1852 and into early 1853. He increased antislavery sentiment in Canada West and encouraged the formation of ASC auxiliaries in Hamilton, Windsor, Kingston, London, and Grey County. Ward's "natural, and . . . burning eloquence" and his imposing black presence had a powerful effect. He reported to the ASC that

> I had good audiences in the towns and villages which I visited throughout the country. Anti-Slavery feeling is spreading and increasing. The public mind literally thirsts for the truth, and honest listeners, and anxious inquirers will travel many miles, crowd our country chapels, and remain for hours, eagerly and patiently seeking the light. Surely this betokens a better, brighter day a-head.[32]

30. Winks, *Blacks in Canada*, 253–57; Hill, "Negroes in Toronto," 21–22; *TC*, 15 November 1837; *NSt*, 28 April, 1 December 1848 [5:0626, 0838]; I. C. Pemberton, "The Anti-Slavery Society of Canada" (M.A. thesis, University of Toronto, 1973), 17–40.

31. John W. Blassingame, ed., *Frederick Douglass Papers*, series one, 3 vols. to date (New Haven, Conn., 1979–), 2:327–30; *VF*, 5 November 1851; Pemberton, "Anti-Slavery Society of Canada," 52.

32. *TG*, 27 November 1851 [7:0199]; *First Annual Report, Presented to the Anti-Slavery Society of Canada, By Its Executive Committee, March 24th, 1852* (Toronto, Canada West, 1852), 15.

With these successes, the ASC grew ambitious and optimistic. After the first year, it broadened its activities from fugitive relief to more direct abolitionist labors. But that expansion required fresh funds as well as converts. So in April 1853, the society sent Ward to Britain to tap the purse of John Bull. Ward's British lecture tour lasted until 1855 and proved to be the ASC's outstanding contribution to the international antislavery movement. While Ward was abroad, the ASC was active at home. It established more local branches, and its women's auxiliary, the Toronto Ladies' Association for the Relief of Destitute Colored Fugitives, concentrated on relief work. In early 1855, the ASC opened a permanent office in Toronto under the direction of Rev. John B. Smith, a black American abolitionist who served on the society's executive committee, but the office soon closed because of financial problems and squabbling between Smith and ASC secretary Thomas Henning.[33] The closing of the Toronto office marked the decline of the society. By 1857 it had retreated to its initial role as a relief organization.

The ASC never approached the promise of its enthusiastic beginning. As early as 1854, black newspaper editor Mary Ann Shadd Cary rhetorically asked where the ASC could be found and sarcastically answered that it could only be located about the "middle of June"—a charge, fairly made, that the organization's annual meeting was its major antislavery activity. Continuing in that tone, Cary urged the society to apply for membership in the American and Foreign Anti-Slavery Society, itself a moribund association.[34]

Black abolitionists were more conspicuous in the mainstream Canadian antislavery movement than in the United States. They provided leadership, membership, and funds for the ASC, and they dominated many ASC branches; the London Anti-Slavery Society was directed by A. Beckford Jones during the early 1850s, and the Anti-Slavery Society of Windsor was a black-controlled ASC branch formed in October 1852 with Henry Bibb as its first president. The society held regular antislavery meetings, aided fugitive slaves, and provided a black antislavery presence in southwestern Canada West. In St. Catharines, Harriet Tubman was among the blacks who guided the activities of the interracial Refugee Slaves' Friends Society.[35]

33. Winks, *Blacks in Canada*, 257–59; Pemberton, "Anti-Slavery Society of Canada," 52–56, 76; Fred Landon, "Fugitive Slaves in London before 1860," *Trans* 10 (1919), 35; Murray, "Canada and the Anglo-American Anti-Slavery Movement," 398; C. Peter Ripley, Jeffery S. Rossbach, Roy E. Finkenbine, Fiona E. Spiers, eds., *The Black Abolitionist Papers: Volume I, The British Isles, 1830–1865* (Chapel Hill, N.C., 1985), 335–44, 362–66, 387–95, 412–23.

34. *PFW*, 3 June 1854 [8:0858].

35. *VF*, 11 March, 21 October, 18 November 1852 [7:0447, 0788, 0829]; Landon,

Blacks utilized independent means—black societies and lecture tours, black antislavery newspapers, and black national and provincial conventions—to promote their antislavery message. This was particularly true by the mid-1850s. When the ASC became lethargic and inactive, blacks pressed on. They had established several antislavery organizations during the 1830s and 1840s, but more groups formed in the trying times of the 1850s. Most were short-lived, but three were substantial. The militant Canadian Anti-Slavery Baptist Association emerged out of a schism among black Baptists in Canada West in late 1850. Congregations at Dawn, Chatham, Buxton, Colchester, London, Mount Pleasant, and Detroit joined the new association, which aided fugitive slaves, carried the antislavery message through sermons and lectures, and criticized moderate and proslavery churches. The Abolition Society of Halifax, Nova Scotia, the leading black antislavery group in the Maritimes, was formed by black American clergyman Richard Preston in 1846 and, after passage of the Fugitive Slave Law, became a full-fledged antislavery society. A self-consciously black organization, it remained independent of white-dominated groups in the United States and Canada but did maintain contact with like-minded black abolitionists in Boston. By 1860 blacks in Hamilton, Canada West, organized the Black Abolitionist Society, which sponsored black antislavery speakers and protested discrimination, although its effectiveness was limited by local white racism.[36]

Black Canadians took antislavery on the lecture tour. Although the Canadian lecturers generally were not as polished as the experienced black professionals from the northern United States, they attracted sizable audiences in the provinces, particularly in Canada West. Paola Brown, from Woolwich, indicted slaveholders and American churches for their actions and attitudes on slavery and the Fugitive Slave Law in a lengthy address that, in the best antislavery fashion, lasted over two hours. Henry Bibb, one of the talented professionals, toured the province during the summer of 1852 "to advocate the cause of the bleeding slave." Bibb's speeches were greeted by "continued cheers" and prompted Chatham blacks to

---

"Fugitive Slaves in London," 35; Pemberton, "Anti-Slavery Society of Canada," 52–53; Winks, *Blacks in Canada*, 258.

36. Richard Warren, *The Narrative of the Life and Sufferings of the Reverend Richard Warren (A Fugitive Slave) Written by Himself* (Hamilton, Canada West, 1856); Murray, "Canada and the Anglo-American Anti-Slavery Movement," 278–79; James K. Lewis, "Religious Nature of the Early Negro Migration to Canada and the Amherstburg Baptist Association," *OntH* 58:125–30 (1966); Winks, *Blacks in Canada*, 139, 259; James W. St. G. Walker, *The Black Loyalists: The Search for a Promised Land in Nova Scotia and Sierra Leone, 1783–1870* (New York, N.Y., 1976), 393; *NS*, 10, 24 August 1846; Michael B. Katz, *The People of Hamilton, Canada West: Family and Class in a Mid-Nineteenth Century City* (Cambridge, Mass., 1975), 3.

form an antislavery committee, to write an outline of their antislavery beliefs, and commit themselves to antislavery labors. Occasionally black antislavery speakers drew large audiences in Canada East and the Maritimes as well.[37]

Lecture tours often had several objectives. Antislavery headed a list that usually included more specific goals. Ward solicited money and members for the ASC. Mary Ann Shadd Cary, Isaac D. Shadd, and H. Ford Douglas enrolled subscribers for the *Provincial Freeman*. Henry Garrett raised money for a compensated emancipation plan. Martin R. Delany, J. Dennis Harris, Isaac N. Cary, William J. Watkins, William Wells Brown, William P. Newman, and Josiah B. Smith toured and lectured throughout Canada West and the Maritimes to recruit emigrants for West African or Caribbean settlement schemes.[38] Black abolitionists in the provinces adopted the style that characterized most antebellum reform lecturing in the United States and the British Isles. Lecturers usually based themselves in one location for several days and attempted to arrange speaking opportunities as they went along. Mary Ann Shadd Cary's July 1854 tour, devoted to obtaining subscribers for the *Provincial Freeman*, followed that approach. Arriving at Dawn, she contacted George Cary, a former Windsor acquaintance, and together they hastily arranged a meeting on behalf of the paper. At Chatham she spoke at a meeting of "the farmers in the neighborhood"; a day or two later, she attended a local political rally, where she was "kindly permitted to say a word of the paper." Upon reaching London, she again quickly organized several meetings, and at Toronto she offered to speak at the Emancipation Day celebration. H. Ford Douglas's 1857 tour demonstrated a growing sophistication and sense of organization. He allowed local abolitionists to arrange meetings in London, Woodstock, Stratford, Paris, Brantford, Dundas, and Hamilton before he arrived to deliver well-attended, well-advertised addresses. Yet planning ahead did not guarantee success, and once Douglas reached Toronto, his tour faltered. Isaac Shadd, acting as Douglas's advance agent, had obtained St. Lawrence Hall (Toronto's main meeting hall), placed a notice in the sympathetic *Globe*, and hung posters "in all the main thoroughfares." But when only sixteen people appeared, the meeting was canceled. After a second unsuccessful attempt, Douglas began lecturing in local black churches and found that word-of-mouth attracted large audiences in the Toronto black community.[39]

37. Winks, *Blacks in Canada*, 254; Paola Brown, *Address Intended to be Delivered in the City Hall, Hamilton, February 7, 1851, on the Subject of Slavery* (Hamilton, Canada West, 1851); *VF*, 17 June, 15 July 1852; *Lib*, 30 May 1851 [6:0949]; *FDP*, 27 April 1855 [9:0560].

38. *PFW*, 9 June 1855 [9:0692]; *CP*, 26 August 1858 [11:0334]; *CTWP*, 3 September 1858 [11:0342].

39. Jim Bearden and Linda Jean Butler, *Shadd: The Life and Times of Mary Shadd Cary* (Toronto, 1977), 148–50; *PFW*, 16 May, 20 June 1857 [10:0679, 0733].

The black press kept antislavery sentiment alive. Editors understood the importance of newspapers in forging public opinion, attracting converts, filling lecture halls, raising money, and uniting the black community. Several attempts were made to establish black antislavery papers in Canada West, and two—the *Voice of the Fugitive* and the *Provincial Freeman*—were successful. Henry Bibb, a former slave and an antislavery lecturer well known in Michigan and Canada West, began publishing the *Voice of the Fugitive* on 1 January 1851 in Sandwich. A comparison of his private correspondence and his editorial writings suggests that Mary Bibb, his wife, had a major role in the publication. Appearing bimonthly, the *Voice* conveyed the editor's concern with the issues of the early 1850s, particularly the arrival and condition of fugitive slaves and the proslavery American policies that drove blacks to Canada. The *Voice*, as the official organ of the Refugee Home Society, defended the organized black settlements. Henry Bibb's abiding interest in temperance, political antislavery, and black progress through agriculture received ample coverage. Subscription agents canvassed Canada West, Ohio, Michigan, New York, and New England and earned the *Voice* a wide readership. It was well respected and often quoted by the northern abolitionist press. In April 1852, the paper was moved to Windsor, and two months later, James Theodore Holly became coeditor and coproprietor. The office of the *Voice* burned in October 1853, and although Bibb announced that the paper was not finished, publication was suspended; with Bibb's death the following year, it never revived.[40]

In the spring of 1853, a second and equally vigorous black Canadian newspaper began publication. A sample issue of the *Provincial Freeman* appeared under Samuel Ringgold Ward's nominal editorship on 24 March 1853 in Windsor, and it began regular publication in Toronto a year later under the successive editorships of Mary Ann Shadd Cary, William P. Newman, H. Ford Douglas, and Isaac D. Shadd. Its editors, devoted Anglophiles, covered Canadian politics and other news from the British Empire. Ward and Cary's *Freeman* became a standard-bearer for Canadian immigration and for black assimilation into Canadian society. Cary's militancy and her caustic writings made the *Freeman* far more lively, provocative, and controversial than the *Voice*. At the same time, she brought a woman's perspective to a traditionally male domain. Early in her editorship, she cautioned readers to send no more letters to the editor that began "Dear Sir." The *Freeman*'s extensive commentary on women's rights and responsibilities carried her imprint, as did the selection of miscellaneous fillers such as "Modern Effeminacy" and "Why Modern Men Are Ugly." The *Freeman* moved to Chatham during the summer of 1855.

40. *CA*, 11 May, 22 June 1839 [3:0054, 0125]; Winks, *Blacks in Canada*, 394–97; *VF*, 1 January 1851, 22 April, 17 June, 16 December 1852; *Lib*, 28 October 1853 [8:0461].

But plagued by financial problems, publication of the paper became erratic in late 1857. The exact date of its demise is uncertain, but by September 1861, it was defunct.[41]

The two papers were an integral part and a valuable record of black Canadian life. In addition to reporting on antislavery, the *Voice* and the *Freeman* instructed their readers on proper social conduct and personal behavior, confirmed the credentials of agents soliciting funds for black concerns, and served as clearinghouses for information about the black Canadian community. They carried practical advice as well. Articles on planting wheat and potatoes, preserving foods, and identifying indigenous flora were of no small interest to former slaves who had little experience with agriculture in northern climates. The papers also provided space for black refugees to inquire about separated friends and families, an essential service later carried on by the black press in the United States during and after Reconstruction.

As black antislavery newspapers, the *Provincial Freeman* and the *Voice* had a great deal in common. Yet they had editorial differences that grew out of the expectations each had for black life in Canada. Bibb, the fugitive slave, began his work early in the decade, when Canada West was overwhelmed by newly arrived fugitive slaves in desperate need of assistance. Their needs were his primary concern. He wanted to relieve the urgency of their immediate situation and then see them well settled as landholding, yeoman farmers. Consequently he advocated sustained fund raising to support relief efforts, and he promoted land acquisition projects, most notably through separate black institutions such as the Refugee Home Society. The *Provincial Freeman* opposed both. The *Freeman* first appeared later in the decade, when the rush of fugitives had eased to a steady flow. The more sophisticated Ward and Cary took a longer and more philosophical view of life in Canada. Under the bannerline "self-reliance is the true road to independence," the *Freeman* editors urged blacks to avoid prolonged fund-raising efforts, to abandon separate institutions, and to integrate fully into Canadian society. For them, British citizenship offered blacks their best prospects. If the *Voice* spoke for the crisis of the moment, the *Freeman* addressed the hope of the future.

The antislavery mission of blacks in Canada looked both north and south of the forty-ninth parallel. Black abolitionists in the British North American Provinces struck at American slavery in a variety of ways: informing the public about slave life, raising funds, publishing newspapers, writing fugitive slave narratives, and organizing lecture tours. But the two

41. Winks, *Blacks in Canada*, 394–97; Alexander L. Murray, "*The Provincial Freeman*: A New Source for the History of the Negro in Canada and the United States," *JNH* 44: 123–35 (April 1959); William Howard Day to Gerrit Smith, 21 June 1858, Gerrit Smith Papers, NSyU [11:0253–254]; *GSB*, 28 October 1858 [11:0393]; *WAA*, 30 July 1859, 14 July 1860; *PP*, 28 September 1861 [13:0774].

aspects of antislavery in Canada that blacks considered particularly important were fighting the influence of American proslavery attitudes in Canadian society and aiding the fugitives as they struggled to become established citizens. Ward believed that keeping Canada free of American racial prejudice was critical to the antislavery movement. To allow American proslavery thought and racist practices to corrupt Canadian society would threaten the new homeland as a sanctuary for fugitives and as a showplace for black advancement.

Ward acknowledged that Canada protected runaways but warned that the U.S. government constantly pressured Britain and Canada to revise its policy on extraditing fugitive slaves; he insisted that combating those pressures was the responsibility of black abolitionists. Ward was alarmed by widespread proslavery attitudes—"friendliness to slavery is to be found in this Province in more forms than one." He saw people who "love slavery" and others who married into slaveholding families, or who had been slaveholders in the West Indies, or who came from America and "brought their pro-slaveryism with them." These white Canadians served as "the volunteer body-guard of slavery. . . ." Ridding Canada of proslavery thought and action and preserving Canada as a refuge, concluded Ward, was important antislavery business.[42]

When Ward ended a six-week, 565-mile tour on behalf of the Anti-Slavery Society of Canada, he provided a town-by-town report on black temperance meetings, churches, antislavery societies, Sabbath schools, landowners, farmers, and artisans. He concluded that progress in those Canadian towns and settlements was unmatched in American black communities. Ward implied that, given the opportunity to prosper and succeed, blacks would do exactly that, but that achievements would come slower in a society tainted by slavery and prejudice. The alliance between slavery and racism made combating "Canadian Negro-hate" an antislavery act—part of fighting the good fight.[43]

Assisting the thousands of fugitive slaves who flooded into Canada West was also important antislavery work. Blacks were conspicuous in relief organizations, on the underground railroad, and as members of vigilance committees. The Toronto Liberating Association was organized in the early 1850s "to assist the weary and wornout fugitive." The Society for the Protection of Refugees, the Ladies Coloured Fugitive Association, the Ladies Freedman's Aid Society, the Queen Victoria Benevolent Society, and various black church groups in Toronto had the same mission. Like-minded associations were established in black communities throughout the province. In St. Catharines, local blacks played a leading role in the work of the Refugee Slaves' Friends Society, a relief organization founded

42. *PFW*, 24 March 1853 [8:0175].
43. Ibid. [8:0172].

in 1852. Three of five members of the original executive committee were black. A second interracial society, the Fugitive Aid Society of St. Catharines, was organized in 1861. Harriet Tubman served on the executive committee and was a key figure in its success.[44]

The underground railroad and the vigilance committee were the most aggressive black efforts to assist fugitives. Canada was the northern terminus of the underground railroad—a historical phenomenon that abolitionists and southern propagandists alike mythologized into a highly complex, secret network that sent agents into the slave states to spirit thousands of bondsmen north to freedom. In reality the railroad consisted of haphazard, localized, and often semipublic groups that aided fugitives who came to them voluntarily. Blacks on both sides of the border joined with Quakers and other whites of conscience to make the system work. William Still in Philadelphia, Frederick Douglass in Rochester, Jermain W. Loguen and Samuel Ringgold Ward in Syracuse, and Lewis Hayden in Boston made their black communities centers of organized fugitive assistance.[45]

Black Canadians often helped to conduct slaves along the underground railroad. John Mason of Hamilton, a fugitive slave from Kentucky, claimed he returned numerous times to his home state to aid over thirteen hundred slaves in their escapes from bondage. He was captured, beaten, and returned to slavery, only to escape a second time. Harriet Tubman of St. Catharines—the "Black Moses"—is the best remembered underground railroad agent in Canada, making at least eleven trips into the slave states to bring out more than three hundred "charges." Other black Canadians consistently contributed to this effort in less daring but nonetheless important ways. Mary Ann Shadd Cary regularly corresponded with a free black aunt in the slave states and arranged to have individual fugitives directed to Chatham. John Henry Hill, a former slave from Virginia, maintained contact with William Still, who sent fugitives on to Toronto and placed them in Hill's care. Hill then obtained food, clothing, shelter, and employment for them. Mason, Tubman, Cary, Hill, and the many others like them enriched the symbolism of Canada as a haven.[46]

It is impossible to know how many fugitives traveled the underground railroad to Canada. There is a good deal of folklore as well as spotty and irregular information from contemporaries—some of it apocryphal and the best of it inconclusive. Loguen wrote that 1,500 fugitives passed

44. Winks, *Blacks in Canada*, 256, 258; Hill, *Freedom-Seekers*, 107, 179; *VF*, 6 May 1852; *Lib*, 25 October, 20 December 1861.

45. Larry Gara, *The Liberty Line: The Legend of the Underground Railroad* (Lexington, Ky., 1967), 1–18, 84–85, 90–106, 143–45; Winks, *Blacks in Canada*, 233–44.

46. Hill, *Freedom-Seekers*, 35–39; Elizabeth J. Williams to Mary Ann Shadd Cary, 18 January, 2 November 1858, Mary Ann Shadd Cary Papers, CaOTAr [11:0125, 0395]; Still, *The Under-Ground Railroad*, 189–200.

1. Harriet Tubman

From Sarah H. Bradford, *Scenes in the Life of Harriet Tubman* (Auburn, N.Y., 1869)

through Syracuse in a nine-year period but made no claim that they all went to Canada. George DeBaptiste reported that the Detroit Vigilance Committee sent 1,043 fugitives across to Canada between 6 May 1855 and January 1856, a figure that rings true for two reasons: Detroit was close to the border and had an aggressive vigilance committee, and DeBaptiste's position as president of the committee and the unusual preciseness of his report—"6 May 1855, 1,043 fugitives"—give him the authenticity of a record keeper, deserved or not. The most reliable modern study of the subject estimates, with great caution, that "by 1860 the black population of Canada West alone may have reached forty thousand, three-quarters of whom had been or were fugitive slaves or their children and, therefore, beneficiaries of the underground railroad."[47]

Once they safely reached Canada West, fugitive slaves found a militant community ready to protect their freedom. Although the Canadian courts seldom extradited fugitives, blacks were threatened by slave catchers, who tracked them across the border and attempted to return them to bondage through fraud and kidnapping. As the problem increased during the 1840s, blacks regularly rallied to prevent the reenslavement of fugitives, particularly along the Detroit and Niagara frontiers. Most interventions were impromptu actions brought on by the necessity of a situation. One incident, in an endless list of similar affairs, occurred when two slave catchers registered at Chatham's Royal Exchange Hotel and discussed their desire to locate the fugitive Joseph Alexander; the news spread through the community and drew "a large party of colored men," including Alexander. The white men, one of whom apparently was a New Orleans slave trader, were escorted to the train station by the crowd.[48]

After passage of the Fugitive Slave Law of 1850, when the threat from slave catchers became more acute, the organization of vigilance committees became a conspicuous part of life in many black communities, including Toronto, Chatham, and Amherstburg. The Toronto committee worked to prevent kidnappings and published notices warning newcomers of the presence of slave catchers in the city. The *Provincial Freeman* printed this warning in each issue:

> CAUTION
>
> From information received from reliable sources, we learn that parties are at present in Toronto endeavouring to induce coloured persons to go to the States in their employ as servants. From the

47. Gara, *Liberty Line*, 143–45; Jermain W. Loguen, *The Rev. J. W. Loguen, as Slave and as Freeman: A Narrative of Real Life* (Syracuse, N.Y., 1859), 444; *PFW*, 6 May 1856; Winks, *Blacks in Canada*, 240. Winks has the authoritative statement on this subject. He surveyed the literature and primary sources and considered all the possibilities and combinations to reach his conclusion about the underground railroad and the number of fugitives who were aided en route to Canada. See *Blacks in Canada*, 233–40, 485–96.

48. *PFW*, 8 August 1857.

> character of the propositions, there is reason to believe "foul play" is intended. . . . Individuals have proposed to women to go to Detroit to live in their service, and another party under circumstances of great suspicion to a boy, to go as far south as Philadelphia. We say to our people, listen to no flattering proposals of this sort. You are in Canada, and let no misplaced confidence in this or the other smooth-tongued Yankee, or British subject either, who may be mercenary enough to ensnare you into bondage by collusion with kidnappers in the States, deprive you of your liberty.

The Chatham Vigilance Committee—probably the most active and aggressive in the provinces—looked to black abolitionists Isaac D. Shadd, Mary Ann Shadd Cary, William Howard Day, and Martin R. Delany for leadership. It was involved in numerous dramatic rescues, the most impressive of which came in the fall of 1858 when it prevented the enslavement of a black youth, Sylvanus Demarest. The incident involved W. R. Merwin, who was taking Demarest into slavery. En route by train from Niagara Falls to Detroit, the two were observed in the London train station by Elijah Leonard, a former mayor of the city. Suspecting the correct circumstances, Leonard conspired with Anderson Diddrick, a local black, to send word down the line to Chatham. When Merwin and Demarest arrived there, they were greeted by an armed mob that numbered at least one hundred citizens. Demarest was removed from the train. The Great Western Railway insisted that charges be brought against the committee, and seven arrests were made (five blacks and two whites), including Isaac D. Shadd, an editor of the *Provincial Freeman*. New facts came out at the hearing. Merwin was not a southern slaveholder, did not own Demarest, and worked in New York City. The charges were dropped, and Demarest remained in Canada until his mother came to get him from Paterson, New Jersey; according to the New York *Tribune*, Merwin would "pocket the 'outrage' and will not hereafter claim the boy."[49]

Aiding fugitive slaves and supporting black interests in Canada required funds and material goods. Abolitionists undertook a long-standing and systematic fund-raising crusade in Britain and the northern United States on behalf of black Canadians. A host of agents traversed the American and British antislavery lecture circuits, appealing for donations to buy land for black settlements, to build schools and churches, to establish missions, and to feed and clothe destitute fugitive slaves.

Tours in Britain collected sizable contributions to aid the black settlements. Black fund-raising agents made it clear that the British could support fugitive slave activities in Canada with money and material goods and thus strike at American slavery from their own shores. The British

49. Hill, *Freedom-Seekers*, 39–43; *PFW*, 24 March 1855; *GSB*, 28 October 1858 [11:0393]; *NYT*, 4 October 1858; *NASS*, 30 October 1858.

found it appealing to have one of Her Majesty's dominions serve as an example of freedom next door to the republican, slaveholding United States—a flattering comparison that agents were quick to draw.[50] The promises made to British audiences by black abolitionists Nathaniel Paul, Josiah Henson, William Howard Day, Samuel Ringgold Ward, and others on behalf of black Canadians were timely, particularly among British reformers who put great stock in education, religion, honest labor, and good works. Black abolitionists stressed that money sent to Canada would start runaway slaves on a new life of freedom, prosperity, and progress. Land, clothes, farm tools, seed, and household goods were necessary for destitute fugitives aspiring to become middle-class farmers. Black churches and schools would provide the education and religious training necessary to make fugitives full and useful citizens.[51]

Fund raising did not go as well in the free states. A parade of both black and white abolitionists traveled through New England, New York, Pennsylvania, and the Midwest on behalf of the settlements, but the amount they raised was modest compared to that generated by their colleagues who went to Britain. American abolitionists were reluctant to finance missionary and relief efforts among black Canadians. They preferred to put their money where they thought the need was more immediate—the underground railroad, antislavery lecture tours, antislavery publications, local and state antislavery societies, and, occasionally, purchasing the freedom of slaves. Americans wanted to see their contributions doing good at home, where the slaves were.[52] American abolitionists made great promises on behalf of the settlements and built great expectations about successes there, but they were less willing to fund the hard work and steady demands those enterprises required.

They hesitated with good cause. Although most of these appeals were legitimate, the overall effort was troubled. Agents acted without authorization, used false or outdated credentials, solicited for nonexistent concerns, and refused to account for funds. Agents usually negotiated their fees with the organization authorizing their services. Twenty percent was common, 50 percent or more was not unusual, and the actual commission could be concealed by poor record keeping. Allocating money and material goods proved as controversial as the fund-raising process.

50. *CN*, 27 June 1850; Colonial Church and School Society, *Occasional Paper*, 1:8–10 (February 1854); *NC*, 18 May 1853; *PtL*, 9, 27 June 1853; Ripley et al., *The Black Abolitionist Papers*, 31–32, 37, 43n, 53, 57n, 362, 533–34, 535n.

51. *NSt*, 2 November 1849; *NC*, 26 January 1851; *CN*, 27 June 1850; *PtL*, 13 March 1851; *ASRL*, 1 November 1861; Pease and Pease, *Black Utopia*, 18–20; *LM*, 3 August 1861.

52. Murray, "Canada and the Anglo-American Anti-Slavery Movement," 22, 35–38, 45, 48–50; Pease and Pease, *Black Utopia*, 47–61, 67–68, 75, 115; *VF*, 29 January 1852 [7:0388]; Josiah Henson, *An Autobiography of the Rev. Josiah Henson*, ed. Robin W. Winks (London, 1881; reprint, Reading, Mass., 1969), 92.

Fugitive slaves complained about the patronizing, callous, and negligent behavior of agents entrusted with distributing the donations. Henry Bibb, himself a former slave, was charged with turning away ill-clad fugitives while his chickens "comfortably roosted" on donated clothes. Dennis Washington spoke for fugitive slaves forced to deal with patronizing white agents; when one snubbed his modest request for a few winter blankets, Washington responded bitterly: "I didn't come all the way from slavery to have a white man for my overseer." Such matters detracted from the Canadian appeal, particularly when some of the problems, frauds, and feuds were played out in the antislavery press.[53]

There were blacks and whites whose behavior, conduct, and attitudes did neither them nor the movement they represented credit. But it is risky to accept all the charges made against those who raised funds or distributed relief goods. Some of the accusations were fair; others masked personal and philosophical disputes. During the difficult years of the early 1850s, as blacks struggled to survive in Canada, they also struggled to define their place in Canadian society. Josiah Henson, James Theodore Holly, and Henry and Mary Bibb favored the black settlements, separate institutions, and white philanthropy to support them. Samuel R. Ward, Mary Ann Shadd Cary, and the *Provincial Freeman* group represented the opposition and urged blacks to be self-sufficient and to assimilate into Canadian society. This was a period of competing leaders, conflicting personalities, and clashing values.

In the context of these disputes, the fund-raising process (disparagingly called begging) aroused intense and acrimonious debate among Canadian blacks. Critics sought to demonstrate that the practice was not only corrupt but unnecessary. Why raise funds for large land acquisition schemes when inexpensive land was readily available to individual black settlers? Why send out "begging ministers" to collect funds for black churches and schools when adequate religious and educational institutions existed to meet the needs of the Canadian black community? Watchdog groups sprang up to oppose begging and assist fugitive slaves. Eight vigilance committees and fourteen true-band societies were formed in Canada West to coordinate and oversee the relief process.[54]

The intensity of the antibegging response cannot be explained solely by a moral aversion to the practice. Hostile opposition to begging arose

53. Winks, *Blacks in Canada*, 158–61, 195–206; Pease and Pease, *Black Utopia*, 52–58, 72–81; *PFW*, 3 November, 29 December 1855, 22 March, 5 April, 10 May 1856, 10 January, 14 March 1857; *FM*, 24 July 1839; Drew, *North-Side View of Slavery*, 339; Mary Ann Shadd Cary to George Whipple, 28 December 1852, AMA-ARC [7:1039].

54. *VF*, 12 February 1852; *PFW*, 17 May 1856; *Minutes and Proceedings of the General Convention for the Improvement of the Colored Inhabitants of Canada, Held by Adjournments in Amherstburgh*, C.W. (Windsor, Canada West, 1853), 8–9; Drew, *North-Side View of Slavery*, 236–38.

among those most conscious of the Canadian black community's role as an antislavery symbol. They argued that constant solicitations for money, clothes, and other resources for fugitives (whose destitution was described in the most agonizing terms) undermined the idea of Canada as a haven and suggested that blacks were incapable of taking care of themselves—all of which reinforced proslavery arguments of black inferiority. Many black Canadians stubbornly denied the need for assistance, even when the need was genuine. The myth of black dependence, so much a part of the proslavery argument, was the real target of the antibegging critique. Begging was anathema for those concerned with the antislavery message implicit in black self-reliance. A resolution by Windsor blacks, directed at the American public, denounced begging because it portrayed blacks as "a class of improvident, thriftless, and imbecile paupers."[55] Advocates of Canadian immigration believed that begging obscured the advantages and opportunities available to blacks in Canada. Incessant "appeals for the starving fugitive" damaged Canada's reputation as a positive alternative to African and Caribbean colonization. Osborne Anderson warned black Canadians that begging evoked the falsehood of black dependence—a falsehood that "lurks in the midnight hour . . . giving sanction to that doctrine of proslavery and colonization parties that claims we can't live on the continent of America, we must be expatriated to the shores of Africa."[56]

When Anderson raised the threat of colonization, he knew he invoked a powerful image. By the late 1830s, a majority of blacks had rejected white colonization schemes as an attempt to make the United States a white man's country. With few exceptions, black Americans considered the United States their home; they resolved to remain in the land they had helped build and struggled to eliminate slavery and racial prejudice. But that changed during the early 1850s when Canada became a centerpiece in the emigration debate, a debate that was influenced by American events and by the forceful personalities of several black leaders. Canada became an acceptable emigration site, in large part, because of despair over conditions in the United States. Black codes, economic difficulties, white violence, and vigorous enforcement of the Fugitive Slave Law convinced black Americans that the nation was drifting further from its democratic ideals. Even those blacks who insisted that staying in the United States and fighting against slavery and prejudice was the correct course of action came to praise Canada as a sanctuary from political and economic oppression. Canada was attractive because it met both prac-

55. *PFW*, 24 March 1853, 25 March, 22 July 1854, 30 June, 29 August 1855, 20 June 1857; *TG*, 24 December 1861; Winks, *Blacks in Canada*, 207; Drew, *North-Side View of Slavery*, 234–90, 321–40, 348–66; *Lib*, 29 October 1852.
56. *WAA*, 23 July 1859; *PFW*, 8 August 1857 [10:0781].

tical and tactical standards. On the practical side, it was accessible and it was safe. Tactically, it was close enough to the United States so that immigrants could continue in the antislavery struggle and could return home once conditions improved—a point that made resettlement in Canada more acceptable to antiemigrationists. This conditional endorsement represented the view of most black Americans throughout the decade. Permanent exile smacked of abandoning the homeland and the slave. That would not do.

Emigrationist sentiment in Canada increased in 1850–51 under the influence of Henry Bibb and James Theodore Holly. Holly, a thoughtful, early proponent of emigration, saw Canada as "a beacon of hope to the slave and a rock of terror to the oppressor." Proclaiming the "regenerative power" of emigration, he encouraged blacks in Canada "to facilitate the escape and comfortable settlement of more refugees in Canada. . . ." Holly and Bibb simultaneously conceived the idea of a convention that would discuss emigration and would create a Canadian organization dedicated to guiding the destiny of North American blacks.[57] By the summer of 1851, the debate was no longer limited to the idea of temporary refuge in Canada but was turning toward a formal organization that had as its objectives black unity and emigration from the United States.

The resulting North American Convention met in Toronto in September 1851. There was basic but not unanimous agreement on the emigration issue. The delegates generally favored Canada over Africa or the West Indies because, from Canada, blacks could better assist their "brethren who are daily fleeing from American slavery"; but there was some support for the British West Indies. The convention also gave organizational life to the North American League. This was Holly's "central authority" for unified action by American and Canadian blacks, which would help establish black Canadian settlers, would aid fugitive slaves as they arrived in Canada West, and would encourage free blacks to emigrate from the northern states. After the convention, Bibb and Holly (who left Vermont for Canada West in the spring of 1852) promoted the league as an instrument that would develop Canadian blacks into prosperous farmers.[58]

The convention and the league expanded the emigration debate. By mid-1852 a growing number of North American blacks no longer considered Canada as just a temporary sanctuary. Some promoted Canada and the West Indies as acceptable sites for permanent black resettlement and formally urged free blacks to leave the northern states. As the decade wore on, more and more Canadian black leaders demonstrated greater toler-

57. *VF*, 7 May, 2, 16, 30 July 1851 [6:0919, 0950–51, 0991, 7:004–5]; Miller, *Search for Black Nationality*, 110–11. Miller's book is the basis of our discussion on this subject.
58. "North American Convention Proceedings," in *VF*, 24 September 1851 [7:0110]; Miller, *Search for Black Nationality*, 111–12; *VF*, 19 November, 3 December 1851, 1 July 1852 [7:0181, 0205, 0211]; Ripley et al., *The Black Abolitionist Papers*, 150–51.

ance for emigration alternatives. The black convention held at Amherstburg, Canada West, in 1853 approved a resolution from the emigration committee that gave Canada "first consideration" but also viewed as acceptable the British West Indies (because of the British colonial government's position on slavery), Haiti (as a black republic), and certain locales in South America (as important points of "secondary interest"). Africa remained off limits. The *Provincial Freeman* group—Mary Ann Shadd Cary, S. R. Ward, and William P. Newman—supported permanent settlement in Canada West but tolerated the idea of immigration to other points in the Western Hemisphere. The *Freeman* editors staked out distinctive ground by urging Canadian blacks to become thoroughly British and to cast their lot as loyal British subjects. For them, Canada West was the place.[59]

It was largely through the influence of Martin R. Delany that regions other than Canada became respected rather than just begrudgingly accepted by black emigrationists, even by hesitant leaders in Canada West. Delany set forth his ideas about a black nationality in *The Condition, Elevation, Emigration and Destiny of the Colored People of the United States, Politically Considered* (1852) and then translated them into action by calling the first two National Emigration Conventions (1854 and 1856), both held in Cleveland. Delany rejected white colonization schemes, viewed black self-help and uplift as the proper means to end prejudice, and insisted that blacks should leave both the United States and Canada. He acknowledged Canada's importance as a refuge but considered it unfit for black resettlement because of its white-majority population and the threat of annexation by the United States. He argued that Central America, South America, and the British West Indies, with their majority nonwhite populations, were more suitable emigration sites.[60]

The response of black Canadian leaders Cary and Ward to the two Cleveland conventions marks a change in their ideas about emigration. The Cary-Ward group did not openly challenge the first convention, but they remained aloof because Delany had rejected Canada. And they were skeptical about his promotion of Central or South America. The *Provincial Freeman* ridiculed the idea of a separate black nation in the Americas and urged blacks to become part of the British nation in Canada. Bibb and Holly endorsed the 1854 convention. And although Henry Bibb died

59. *VF*, 17 June 1852 [7:0627]; *FDP*, 11 March 1852 [7:0455–56]; *Minutes of Convention in Amherstburg*, 11–16 [8:0302–5]; Mary A. Shadd, *A Plea for Emigration: or, Notes of Canada West* . . . (Detroit, Mich., 1852) [7:0244–65]; Miller, *Search for Black Nationality*, 143; *PFW*, 28 March 1857 [10:0598]; Robert L. Harris, Jr., "H. Ford Douglas: Afro-American Antislavery Emigrationist," *JNH* 62:223 (July 1977).

60. Martin Robinson Delany, *The Condition, Elevation, Emigration and Destiny of the Colored People of the United States* (Philadelphia, Pa., 1852; reprint, New York, N.Y., 1969); Miller, *Search for Black Nationality*, 126–27.

just weeks before it convened, Mary Bibb was an officer of the convention, and Holly was one of Delany's strongest advocates in the debate with antiemigrationists who opposed the gathering.[61]

In the time between the two Cleveland conventions, the *Provincial Freeman* faction joined the Delany forces. The shift probably occurred for several reasons, some of them unrelated to emigration. It is doubtful that Cary would have ever joined Delany as long as Bibb was Delany's ally and associate. But by late 1854, old antagonisms between the Bibb faction and the Shadd faction were gone. Bibb was dead, the *Voice of the Fugitive* was closed, Holly had left Canada West, and the Refugee Home Society was moribund. Antiemigrationist criticism brought Cary and Delany together. The antiemigrationists made no distinction between Cary's support for Canadian immigration and Delany's call for a black nation beyond the North American mainland; it was the idea, not the destination, that mattered. Stung by antiemigrationist attacks, the two groups represented by Cary and Delany defended the same principles. The union was completed when Delany acknowledged Canada as an alternative to American racial oppression and then moved to Chatham in early 1856. For her part, Cary supported the call for the 1856 Cleveland convention, used the *Freeman* to promote it, and then attended the meeting. The Cleveland delegates selected seven Chatham blacks to serve on the movement's National Board of Commissioners, appointed H. Ford Douglas as a lecturing agent, and named the *Provincial Freeman* the official emigrationist organ.[62]

This increasing openness toward the emigration movement found full expression two years later with the rise of black Canadian support for a series of specific emigration alternatives. Between early 1858 and early 1862, a growing awareness of white Canadian racial prejudice attracted several blacks in Canada West to programs advocating black emigration beyond the North American mainland. Many emigration choices confronted black Canadians, but West Africa and the Caribbean had the greatest appeal. From 1858 to 1861, Delany promoted a scheme to settle North American blacks in the Niger Valley region of West Africa. William P. Newman and J. Dennis Harris, a black plasterer from Cleveland, advocated Jamaican emigration. James Redpath's Haytian Emigration Bureau sent lecturers throughout Canada West and the Maritimes during the early 1860s to recruit black settlers for Haiti. There were other possibilities, but of these, the Niger Valley and Haiti proved to be by far the most attractive to black Canadians.[63]

61. Miller, *Search for Black Nationality*, 143.

62. *PFW*, 5 July 1851.

63. Miller, *Search for Black Nationality*, 134, 238; *WAA*, 12 May 1860, 30 November 1861 [12:0698, 13:0943]; Hollis T. Lynch, *Edward Wilmot Blyden: Pan-Negro Patriot*,

Delany announced in early 1858 that he intended to locate a black settlement in the Niger Valley. Beginning that spring, he spent the year gathering support and organizing a party to explore the region, then largely unknown to the western world. But he found it slow going. He was hampered by a lack of black enthusiasm, conflicts with sponsors, and the defection of members of the expedition. Delany and Robert Campbell explored the Niger Valley region in late 1859 and met with leading Egba chiefs, who signed a treaty that provided land for a settlement of North American blacks in the valley. Delany spent the following year in Britain, where he attempted to generate financial and moral backing for the proposed settlement and cotton-production scheme. He returned to Canada West in late December 1860. Based in Chatham, he spent early 1861 lecturing on "Africa and the African Race" and recruiting "mechanics," "cotton cultivators," and other settlers for his African venture. By April about thirty to forty Chatham blacks—including community leaders Osborne P. Anderson, Isaac D. Shadd, Amelia Shadd Williamson, J. H. Harris, and Amos Aray—planned to immigrate to the Niger Valley under the auspices of the African Aid Society, a British-based emigration organization.[64]

Yet many in the Chatham black community were ambivalent about Delany's African scheme. Some, like Mary Ann Shadd Cary, publicly lauded Delany's accomplishments in Africa and Britain but pointedly avoided endorsing his emigration program. And more problems lay ahead. Early in 1861, British Anglican missionaries in the Niger Valley convinced the Egba chiefs to repudiate their agreement with Delany. When news of this setback and of the coming of the Civil War reached Canada West, black support for the Niger Valley plan dissipated. Like many blacks in the British North American Provinces, Delany abandoned the emigration movement and turned his attention to the war, emancipation, and Reconstruction.

As support for Delany's Niger Valley venture waned, the idea of black resettlement in Haiti began to draw attention, particularly in the black communities of Canada West. Holly was attracted to Haiti as early as the mid-1850s and visited the island in 1855. Once there, he sought an agreement with the government of the island nation that would favor immigration, but his negotiations were unsuccessful. When a revolution installed Fabre Geffrard as the president of Haiti in 1859, the new leader

---

1822–1912 (London, 1967), 33; Winks, *Blacks in Canada*, 164. For a thorough overview of black support in Canada West for immigration to the Niger Valley or Haiti, see Miller, *Search for Black Nationality*, 170–263, and Winks, *Blacks in Canada*, 162–68. Except where otherwise noted, the following discussion of black emigrationism in the British North American Provinces is based on these two sources.

64. *PFW*, 29 January 1859 [11:0554].

sought out James Redpath, a young Scottish-American journalist, instead of Holly, to act as the black nation's general immigration agent in North America. Redpath responded to Geffrard's invitation with enthusiasm. He immediately visited Haiti and persuaded the legislature to pass a homestead bill providing land to immigrant families. Upon his return to the United States, he established the Boston-based Haytian Emigration Bureau (HEB), founded a proemigration newspaper (the *Pine and Palm*), and wrote and published *A Guide to Hayti*—all to inform, influence, and assist potential immigrants. Two black Canadians also boosted the Haitian movement. William P. Newman, the former colleague of Samuel R. Ward and Mary Ann Shadd Cary, visited the black nation in late 1859 and wrote letters to the *Chatham Planet*, in which he told blacks that "we may live here on one-half of the labor of the Northern States and Canada, and get rich." J. Dennis Harris's *Summer on the Borders of the Caribbean Sea* (1860) carried a similar message. Redpath's offer in early 1861 of free passage to Haiti further encouraged potential black emigrants.[65]

Redpath was eager to recruit emigrants from among the black communities in Canada West and the Maritimes. He enlisted an impressive group of traveling agents to labor in behalf of the HEB. John Brown, Jr. (the son of the antislavery martyr), Haitian Alexander Tate, and black abolitionists Isaac N. Cary, William Wells Brown, and William J. Watkins were among the handful of HEB agents who lectured and recruited potential black converts in every city and town with a black presence between Toronto and Windsor during 1861–62. Other groups were also active, and in all, several hundred blacks abandoned the British North American Provinces for the black island republic. But success was short-lived for the HEB. Haitian immigration attracted considerable black hostility. In October 1861, Chatham's large black community—including Isaac D. Shadd and Mary Ann Shadd Cary—gathered to approve several resolutions criticizing Redpath and his movement. That antagonism greeted HEB agents in subsequent visits to the village. One agent was nearly mobbed by hostile Chatham blacks and "escaped injury by the timely interference of some of the more considerate citizens."[66]

Mary Ann Shadd Cary, with her acid pen, flowery prose, and elegant hyperbole, led the opposition to Haitian immigration. She referred to Redpath as "Blackpath," described his agents as "maggots in the Haytian carcass," and charged them with sending "fugitives where they know that

65. *CTWP*, 18 January 1861 [13:0202]; *WAA*, 26 January 1861 [13:0224].

66. William Seraille, "Afro-American Emigration to Haiti During the American Civil War," *Amer* 35:194–96 (October 1978); William Edward Farrison, *William Wells Brown: Author and Reformer* (Chicago, Ill., 1969), 333–51; *WAA*, 19 October, 30 November 1861 [13:0837, 0943]; *PP*, 8 June, 6 July, 31 August, 14, 21 September, 9, 16, 23, 30 November, 21 December 1861, 2 January (supplement), 8 May 1862 [13:0617, 0754, 0761, 0987].

pestilential fevers, licentiousness, drunkness, heathenism and superstition abound," all for the sake of a few dollars. The "specious representations of paid agents of the Haytian government," she wrote, urged people to forsake a "healthy climate, British nationality, individual prosperity and the fullest exercise of freedom." Cary insisted that Haiti had nothing to recommend it over Canada. Only Redpath and his paid agents would profit from immigration there. She equated them to "the slave-trafficers" [sic] who preyed on "illiterate, foolish old people [and] ship them off [without] ceremony. . . ." Describing the Haitian alternative as "the nuisance of the hour," she informed her readers that Redpath's scheme was anathema to antislavery and akin to the earlier African colonization efforts of the American Colonization Society. She challenged Redpath's antislavery credentials and linked him to other attempts to make the North American mainland a white man's domain.[67]

The emigrationist debate became as much a philosophical and intellectual discussion and a critique of American society as it was a call for specific action. Canadian immigration was fundamentally a matter of necessity—a forced migration of refugees seeking safety and security from real threats in America. But sanctuary for the refugees was often viewed as a separate issue from the emigration debate, which engaged the attention and energy of many black leaders but never moved to action large numbers within the black communities. Throughout the time of the Canadian experiment, a majority of blacks were concerned with the demands of daily life, often under the difficult circumstances that came with being refugees. The debate over emigration from Canada touched few of them. Some were attracted to West Africa or the Caribbean because of growing racism in Canada, or because of their inability to become well situated there, or for other personal, political, or economic reasons. But with few exceptions, the debate was carried on by black leaders concerned with the destiny of North American blacks. Floyd Miller has argued that the emigration impulse was part of the search for a black nationality, a search by black leaders who believed that Afro-Americans, as a caste set apart by white society, needed to take united action. Martin R. Delany spoke for those who believed the search could never be concluded in a land where blacks were a despised and segregated minority, but even Delany was ambiguous about blacks surrendering all claims to their rights and privileges as Americans. Other leaders argued that self-help and elevation within white society was possible through black organizations and institutions—a view shared by many antiemigrationists, including Frederick Douglass. Antiemigrationists argued that blacks could gain those

67. *WAA*, 28 September, 19, 26 October, 9 November, 14 December 1861 [13:0777, 0836, 0851, 0886, 0976].

rights and privileges by changing American society. Emigrationists believed otherwise.

Canada proved to be a temporary refuge from southern slavery, slave catchers, legal inequality, and northern racial prejudice. But for all its symbolic value, it was not home. Blacks throughout Canada West spoke regularly of being driven from America and looked back to their homeland with the longing of exiles. They understood the lament of the elderly fugitive when she explained that she and her husband had been compelled to live in "a foreign country among strangers." Harriet Tubman, the celebrated former slave and underground railroad conductor, confided from St. Catharines: "We would rather stay in our native land, if we could be as free there as we are here." Parker T. Smith wrote that, after only five months, he was "home sick" and would likely return to Philadelphia soon. When white reformer Samuel Gridley Howe toured the black communities of Canada West in 1863, he found that blacks had "not taken firm root in Canada, and . . . desire to go to the southern region of the United States, partly from love of warmth, but more from love of *home*."[68]

This exile mentality is clearly evident in the immigrants' reaction to the Civil War. Throughout the British North American Provinces, blacks greeted the war as a crusade for emancipation and equality, and with that stake in the outcome of the conflict, they were eager to join in the struggle. Young, black Canadian males who attempted to enlist in the Union army during 1861–62 were rejected by the Lincoln administration, which feared that arming blacks would terrorize Southern whites into greater resolve and would alienate white Northerners from the war effort. But in 1863, Lincoln issued the Emancipation Proclamation and the Union army began to recruit black troops as a matter of policy. When news of those decisions reached the Elgin settlement, a town meeting brought forward forty black volunteers. In all, more than two-thirds of the settlement's young, adult male population enlisted in the Union army between 1863 and 1865. Hundreds of additional blacks throughout Canada West traveled to the recruiting station to join up.[69]

Black Canadian abolitionists who viewed the Civil War as a struggle

68. James W. St. G. Walker, "'On the Other Side of Jordan': The Record of Canada's Black Pioneers, 1783–1865," 39–40, an unpublished paper; Drew, *North-Side View of Slavery*, 30, 31, 273; Parker T. Smith to Jacob C. White, Jr., November 1861, White Papers, DHU [13:0860]; S. G. Howe, *The Refugees from Slavery in Canada West: Report to the Freedmen's Inquiry Commission* (Boston, Mass., 1864; reprint, New York, N.Y., 1969), 102.

69. Silverman, "Unwelcome Guests," 213–14; Walton, "Blacks in Buxton and Chatham," 143–44, 158; Donald George Simpson, "Negroes in Ontario from Early Times to 1870" (Ph.D. diss., University of Western Ontario, 1971), 895–97.

for freedom rallied fellow blacks to the conflict. They led by example. Osborne P. Anderson, Abraham W. Shadd, and Martin R. Delany of Chatham became Union field officers. When Delany was commissioned a major in the 104th United States Colored Troops in 1865, he became the first black field officer of high rank. Physicians Anderson R. Abbott and Alexander T. Augusta of Toronto served as medical officers and were later involved in the founding and operation of Freedmen's Hospital in Washington, D.C. Anderson spent several months raising black volunteers in Canada West before he enlisted. Delany did the same during much of 1863–65 for Massachusetts, Rhode Island, Connecticut, and Ohio units. After receiving a major's commission, he raised two regiments of former slaves in Charleston, South Carolina. Mary Ann Shadd Cary left Chatham and recruited for Connecticut and Indiana units. Solomon, a prominent Elgin resident and former slave of William King, sought volunteers throughout Canada West after serving as a recruiting sergeant for the First Michigan Colored Infantry. Josiah Henson advanced money to enlistees and personally escorted young black recruits to the Detroit recruiting station to make certain that they received the bounty to which they were entitled.[70]

Blacks promoted the Union at every turn. Clergymen of the black British Methodist Episcopal church instructed black males that they should be "shouldering arms and marching to the battle-field to put down the ungodly man-stealers. . . ." Toronto's black leaders issued an address "To the Colored Citizens of Canada" in 1863, which urged unqualified support for the war effort "because in that fratricidal war we recognize freedom and slavery marshalled against each other." Blacks used local, religious, and reform newspapers to rally black Canadians. Some writers, like "Violet" (probably Louisa E. Wilcox) of Victoria's black community, supported particular black regiments, viewing them as racial "instruments of [God's] retributive justice" and as symbols of racial pride. Black benevolent societies followed her advice by gathering supplies to aid black soldiers. They also sponsored bazaars, Sabbath-school exhibitions, and similar events to collect funds, bibles, and other goods for distribution to freedmen's schools and newly freed slaves in the South.[71]

70. *DANB*, 15, 19–20, 553; Hill, *Freedom-Seekers*, 87; Victor Ullman, *Martin R. Delany: The Beginnings of Black Nationalism* (Boston, Mass., 1971), 283–313; Simpson, "Negroes in Ontario to 1870," 897; Annie Straith Jamieson, *William King: Friend and Champion of Slaves* (Toronto, Ontario, 1925), 181; Winks, *Blacks in Canada*, 289; Martin R. Delany to Mary Ann Shadd Cary, 7 December 1863, Benjamin S. Pardee to Cary, 3 March 1864, Mary Ann Shadd Cary Papers, DHU [15 : 0108, 0266]; Walton, "Blacks in Buxton and Chatham," 158; Silverman, "Unwelcome Guests," 214–15.

71. Quoted in Silverman, "Unwelcome Guests," 215; *AA*, 9 May 1863, 9 April, 24 December 1864; *CR*, 13 June 1863 [14:0917]; *PA*, 12 September 1863, 6 February 1864

Rev. Thomas Kinnard, a black Toronto abolitionist, predicted in 1863 that "if freedom is established in the United States, there will be one great black streak, reaching from here to the uttermost parts of the South."[72] He was correct. The American Civil War rejuvenated black Canadian dreams of a return migration. Emancipation, Confederate defeat, and the potential of Radical Reconstruction seemed to pledge that the causes that had driven blacks from the United States would themselves be purged from the land. As reluctant exiles, black Canadians grew optimistic about the political, social, and economic opportunities in post-Civil War American life, and they sought an active role in reconstructing their war-torn homeland.

The residents at Elgin, the most successful black settlement in Canada West, developed a formal plan to relocate in the ruined Confederacy. They proposed to purchase twenty thousand acres on which to form an agricultural colony devoted to sugar and cotton in the hope that such an enterprise would provide guidance and inspiration to southern freedmen. In September 1865, Rev. William King visited Washington, D.C., to test the feasibility of such a project. There the dream died when federal officials outlined the difficulties facing a "New Buxton" and advised against it. King returned to Elgin and urged educated blacks to "go and give instruction to their brethren in ignorance" in the South. Many did. Elgin residents served black communities of the Reconstruction South as teachers, physicians, clergymen, lawyers, and political leaders. In all seven hundred blacks left Elgin for the United States.[73]

The postemancipation migration was less a mass movement and more a steady stream of individuals, families, and small groups. Some members of black communities joined the exodus; others remained behind. The issue split black families; the Shadds and the Hensons divided between those who chose permanent residence in Canada West and those who chose to return to the United States. A few individuals, like Abraham W. Shadd and Emaline Shadd, spent the early years of Reconstruction in the United States before resettling in Canada during the 1870s. But in the years immediately following the war, the black population of the British North American Provinces declined dramatically. A majority of blacks in Canada West, Canada East, and Vancouver Island returned to the United States (although relatively few left the Maritimes). Recent arrivals and blacks with family ties in the American South were the first to go. The

---

[14:1039]; Walton, "Blacks in Buxton and Chatham," 165; James W. Pilton, "Negro Settlement in British Columbia, 1858–1871" (M.A. thesis, University of British Columbia, 1951), 54; *NYT*, 2 June 1863.

72. Howe, *Refugees from Slavery*, 28.

73. Silverman, "Unwelcome Guests," 220–21; Walton, "Blacks in Buxton and Chatham," 167–68; Jamieson, *William King*, 179–84; Winks, *Blacks in Canada*, 289.

black population of Canada West dropped from a peak figure of approximately 40,000 in 1859 to fewer than 15,000 by 1871. A similar decline occurred in the British Pacific Northwest, where an estimated 800 to 1,000 blacks resided during the early 1860s; by 1871 the Victoria City Directory counted only 439 blacks in all of British Columbia.[74] No longer needing a refuge, blacks returned home.

The decline in the Canadian black population changed the life of those who remained behind. Black churches and schools closed, black cultural and benevolent societies disbanded, and some black communities and settlements virtually disappeared. The British-American Institute at Dawn was abandoned and sold in 1868, and the Elgin Association dissolved in 1873, believing its task completed. As most black Canadians returned southward, white benefactors in the United States and Canada turned their attention elsewhere, particularly to the emancipated slaves.[75]

The exodus drained away the leaders who gave purpose and energy to Canadian black communities. This was certainly the case at Elgin, and the Chatham black community lost its most able leaders with the departure of Mary Ann Shadd Cary, Isaac D. Shadd, Martin R. Delany, William H. Day, Amos Aray, James W. Purnell, Osborne P. Anderson, and William H. Jones. The leaving of Mifflin W. Gibbs, Jacob Francis, and Fielding Smithea had a similar effect on Victoria's blacks. In smaller, more isolated towns throughout the British North American Provinces, the absence of one key figure could be devastating. Only a few pre-Civil War black leaders remained in Canada. Frequently leaderless and reduced in numbers and influence, Canadian blacks fell prey to the increased discrimination, neglect, and stereotyping that characterized race relations in late nineteenth-century Canada.[76]

Many black leaders came to maturity during their Canadian years. They were tempered by assuming leadership roles in black communities and settlements, by creating political, antislavery, reform, and religious organizations, and by participating in a free society. Access to political or social institutions was not always easy or complete in Canada—there was prejudice, discrimination, and segregated education—but the rights were

74. Silverman, "Unwelcome Guests," 215–20; Winks, *Blacks in Canada*, 289; Hill, "Negroes in Toronto," 90–91; Walton, "Blacks in Buxton and Chatham," 164–74, 185–87, 221; Kilian, *Go Do Some Great Thing*, 147; Robert W. O'Brien, "Victoria's Negro Colonists—1858–1866," *Phy* 3:18 (First Quarter 1942).

75. Walker, "'Other Side of Jordan,'" 39–40; Silverman, "Unwelcome Guests," 220, 222–23; Winks, *Blacks in Canada*, 290–91; Pease and Pease, *Black Utopia*, 81, 107.

76. Walton, "Blacks in Buxton and Chatham," 165; *DANB*, 15, 38, 553; *NNE*, 2 March, 20 April 1871; Silverman, "Unwelcome Guests," 222; Miller, *Search for Black Nationality*, 182, 196–98; *FML*, 1 July 1866–1 August 1868; William H. Jones to J. J. Cary, 27 May 1870, AMA-ARC; Kilian, *Go Do Some Great Thing*, 144–47; *AA*, 8 July 1865; *San Francisco City Directory*, 1869; Winks, *Blacks in Canada*, 328–30.

theirs nonetheless, and blacks fought hard to protect them. They engaged in a life that only a limited number of northern blacks enjoyed and for which almost no southern blacks could have hoped. Slaves had skills, economic interchange, and, to varying degrees, rich social and personal lives within the confines of the slave community, but their limited rights and hard-won privileges were confined to the underside of southern society. Northern free blacks had social, religious, and educational institutions and organizations that provided the essentials of Afro-American life, and they held property and prospered in business, in the trades, or in one of the professions. But they also suffered economic and political oppression, they were denied access to courts and schools, relegated to menial jobs, and effectively excluded from full participation in American society. Canadian blacks exercised basic rights that antebellum American blacks fought to gain. When the war ended, Canadian blacks were experienced in the social, economic, and political matters that engaged black Americans during Reconstruction. The skills and experience they brought back to the United States helped shape postwar American life, particularly in the Reconstruction South.

Given their Canadian experiences, returning blacks naturally took the lead. They held prominent positions in nearly every Reconstruction state, as judges, legislators, Republican leaders, lawyers, teachers, ministers, Freedmen's Bureau agents, and organizers of civil, religious, and social organizations and institutions. Delany and Day worked with the Freedmen's Bureau. Delany in South Carolina, Gibbs in Arkansas, and James T. Rapier in Alabama became prominent Republican politicians during Reconstruction. Rapier was elected to the U.S. Congress, where he promoted a national civil rights bill. Abraham W. Shadd served as a judge in Arkansas. Charles Pearce sat in the state senate of Florida after organizing the African Methodist Episcopal church there. Jeremiah A. Brown was elected to the Ohio legislature. John J. Cary was an important figure in Nashville's black community and a cashier in the local Freedman's Savings Bank. George W. Brodie directed the North Carolina Insane Asylum in Raleigh. William Troy was the leading black Baptist clergyman in postbellum Richmond. James W. Purnell helped organize antidiscrimination efforts in Philadelphia. Mary Ann Shadd Cary studied law at Howard University and crusaded for women's rights in the District of Columbia. Eleven of the "eminent, progressive and rising" blacks singled out by Rev. William J. Simmons in his 1887 *Men of Mark* were former Canadian exiles.[77]

77. Ullman, *Martin R. Delany*, 314–506; Silverman, "Unwelcome Guests," 222–23; Tom W. Dillard, "Golden Prospects and Fraternal Amenities: Mifflin W. Gibbs's Arkansas Years," *AHQ* 35 : 307–33 (Winter 1976); Loren Schweninger, *James T. Rapier and Reconstruction* (Chicago, Ill., 1978), 36–179; William J. Simmons, *Men of Mark: Eminent, Progressive*

Mississippi offers the single best example of the ambitious role that black migrants from Canada played in post–Civil War American public life. Of the eight blacks admitted to the Mississippi bar during Reconstruction, three were from Canada West. Of the three blacks that exercised the greatest influence in the Mississippi state constitutional convention of 1868, two of them, Thomas W. Stringer and Henry P. Jacobs, had lived in Canada West until the Civil War. Stringer was the most powerful and influential black leader in the state from the end of the war until 1869. He served in the Mississippi Senate during the early 1870s. Jacobs, a Baptist preacher, organized black Baptist associations throughout western Mississippi after the war and was elected to the state legislature in 1870. Isaac D. Shadd, who left Chatham to settle on the Davis Bend plantation in 1871, later moved to Vicksburg, where he also gained a seat in the legislature. He was speaker of the Mississippi House of Representatives from 1874 to 1876.[78]

The ambitious undertakings that black leaders brought to Reconstruction echoed earlier efforts to establish a full and equitable life in Canada: organizing black churches and social organizations; supporting relief measures; establishing agricultural communities and family farms; providing access to public accommodations, to polling booths, to courts, and to schools. Blacks sought total participation in the life of both nations. In Canada they demonstrated that, given the chance, they could prosper in an open society; they found jobs, entered trades and professions, worked the land, educated their children, voted, held office, and generally demonstrated their readiness for freedom. Achieving the same in the United States became a measure of Reconstruction's success.

These aspirations, shared by blacks in both countries, had broad implications for the destiny of Afro-Americans. But in the United States, blacks had to contend with a pervasive body of racist thought and writings that shaped the racial attitudes of the day. Proslavery theorists insisted that blacks were inherently inferior and therefore unfit to partici-

---

and Rising (Cleveland, Ohio, 1887; reprint, New York, N.Y., 1968), 114–15, 145, 599–600, 621, 681, 862, 980–81, 1012–13; Carl R. Osthaus, *Freedmen, Philanthropy, and Fraud: A History of the Freedman's Savings Bank* (Urbana, Ill., 1976), 107, 232; Howard N. Rabinowitz, *Race Relations in the Urban South, 1865–1890* (Urbana, Ill., 1980), 145, 203; Miller, *Search for Black Nationality*, 182, 196–98; *DANB*, 553.

78. Irvin C. Mollison, "Negro Lawyers in Mississippi," *JNH* 15:40–42 (January 1930); Vernon Lane Wharton, *The Negro in Mississippi, 1865–1890* (1947; reprint, New York, N.Y., 1965), 148–51, 173–74, 176, 259, 262, 271–72; *NNE*, 20 April 1871; Janet Sharp Hermann, *The Pursuit of a Dream* (New York, N.Y., 1981), 183–84; Buford Satcher, *Blacks in Mississippi Politics, 1865–1900* (Washington, D.C., 1978), 25–26, 28–30, 37, 58, 76–78, 90, 148, 208.

pate in a free and democratic society. They argued that the United States was a land of opportunity for those able and willing to make their way in the world. They pointed to the greater achievements of various white immigrant groups to support that argument. The conclusion was inevitable: If blacks failed to achieve economic success, they must lack commercial ability; if they failed to train an educated elite, they must be intellectually unfit; if they lacked political rights, they must be incapable of exercising the franchise.

Black abolitionists struggled to educate the nation on these matters. They wrote and spoke about discriminatory laws, customs, and practices, and they insisted that white behavior—not black inferiority—best explained why blacks remained on the bottom rung. For them, the white argument was a self-fulfilling prophecy: a group legislated into second-class citizenship because it was considered inferior would, by virtue of those controls, become second-class citizens and thus give the appearance of being inferior.

Black success would refute oppressive racial theories. Black abolitionists understood the symbolic benefits derived from large numbers of blacks becoming skilled craftsmen, successful merchants, educated professionals, and prosperous farmers. Such a vision is precisely what motivated the reformers who organized the black settlements in Canada West as training grounds for black citizens and models of black achievement.

The published reports about black Canadian life emphasized black progress and praised Canada as a land of opportunity. The two ideas went hand in hand. The stories about black refugees who settled in Canada acknowledged the hardship of the journey and the difficult first year, but always—always—described black craftsmen, farmers, storekeepers, landowners, schools, and churches and praised the morality, sobriety, and religion found in various towns or settlements. "The road to elevation is open to the colored population," wrote Henry Bibb, to which Ezekiel Cooper added, if we "conduct ourselves in the capacity of respectable people[,] we can work wonders for our own redemption."[79]

Canada offered what antebellum America denied—the fair opportunity to succeed or fail. Radical Reconstruction promised that the United States too would become such a place. Constitutional and legal changes and the presence of federal troops in the South gave black Americans citizenship, with all that it implied. Blacks voted and held public office; helped write and pass state constitutions and legislation; organized, built, funded, and staffed schools and colleges; purchased farms and worked the land; and they became ministers, lawyers, doctors, merchants, and artisans. But the

79. *OE*, 30 August 1848 [5:0761]; *ASB*, 14 January 1854 [8:0601]; *VF*, 9 April 1851, 15 July 1852 [7:0658].

benefits of Radical Reconstruction were short-lived. By 1877 the troops were gone, white violence was on the rise, and the process of relegating blacks to second-class citizenship was well underway, as they lost land, schools, jobs, and the vote. The concern and the protection of the nation slipped away. American Reconstruction, like the Canadian haven, pledged a fair opportunity, but only Canada held firm to that promise.

1.
Austin Steward and Benjamin Paul to John G. Stewart
[August 1831]

American blacks looked to the British North American Provinces as a sanctuary from slavery and racial prejudice. Thousands flooded into the provinces between 1830 and the beginning of the Civil War. Many sought refuge in the organized black settlements that developed in Upper Canada. The settlements had philosophical as well as practical objectives. Contemporary reformers—black and white—viewed the settlements as potential showplaces for black achievement. Black uplift, they reasoned, would demonstrate black fitness for freedom and thus contradict proslavery theories of racial inferiority and childlike dependence. The Wilberforce colony, founded in 1830, was the first of four major, planned settlements. But in apparent contradiction to the objectives of black self-reliance and independence, Wilberforce was sustained by philanthropy. Always conscious of that dilemma, the Wilberforce managers attempted to solicit financial assistance without diminishing the credibility of their experiment. In an early progress report to the Albany *African Sentinel and Journal of Liberty*, a black newspaper, Austin Steward and Benjamin Paul carefully balanced images of a thriving, self-sufficient Wilberforce settlement with a plea for "pecuniary aid." They appealed to reformers by highlighting those characteristics—temperance, religion, education, self-reliance—that made Wilberforce both an experiment in social reform and an antislavery symbol. They also verified the credentials of two fund-raising agents, Israel Lewis and Nathaniel Paul. This progress report offered a subtle reminder to the friends of Wilberforce that their support for the settlement was a measure of their abolitionist commitment. William H. Pease and Jane H. Pease, *Black Utopia: Negro Communal Experiments in America* (Madison, Wis., 1963), 47–51; Robin W. Winks, *The Blacks in Canada: A History* (New Haven, Conn., 1971), 156–58.

WILBERFORCE SETTLEMENT,
U[pper] C[anada]

Mr. Editor:[1]

It will no doubt be gratifying to our friends who in different parts of the state of New York and elsewhere,[2] have taken an interest in our welfare, and have aided us in effecting this infant settlement,[3] to hear from us, to know how we are getting along; we therefore beg the favor of communicating to them, through the medium of your very useful paper, a short account of our affairs: Through the blessing of God, we have all enjoyed our usual degree of health. We have erected for our accommoda-

2. Austin Steward
From Austin Steward, *Twenty-Two Years a Slave, and Forty Years a Freeman* (Rochester, 1861)

tions comfortable log buildings, and have a portion of our land in a state of cultivation; our crops at present continue to smile upon the labor of our hands; we shall raise the present year nearly enough to supply the present number of settlers. The people are industrious, and well pleased with their present location; and it is believed that none of them could be hired to go back to the states. Two religious societies have been organized,[4] one of the Baptist, under the pastoral care of Elder Nathaniel Paul,[5] and the other of the Methodist, under the care of Elder Enos Adams; and we are happy to add, that the utmost degree of harmony exists between the two churches. A sabbath school,[6] under the superintendence of Mr. Austin Steward,[7] late of Rochester, is in successful operation; and a day school for the instruction of the children,[8] is taught by a daughter of Elder Benjamin Paul,[9] late of the city of New York; and in addition to which, a temperance society has been formed,[10] consisting of about thirty in number; and the voice of the people is decidedly against ardent spirits ever being introduced as an article of merchandise among us. There are, however, a number of families who have emigrated from the states, whose pecuniary circumstances will not admit of their coming at present to join us, but are compelled to take lands in the neighboring settlements upon shares, and hundreds more in the states are longing to join us, but on account of their limited means are not able to carry their designs into effect. We feel grateful for past favors, but will not the eye of the Philanthropist be turned toward their condition, and his hand opened to supply their wants, that they may thereby be enabled to join their brethren, to help forward one of the most noble enterprises that ever was started, to elevate the too long degraded African, this side the Atlantic?

The annual election of the Board of Managers, whose duty it is to appoint agents, and to take the oversight of the general concerns of the settlement, took place July 11th, when the following persons were duly elected: Austin Steward, Benjamin Paul, Enos Adams, William Bell,[11] Philip Harris,[12] Abraham Dangerfield, Simon Wyatt.[13] The newly elected board, considering the limited means of the colored people generally, and the absolute necessity of pecuniary aid, and in order to carry so desirable an object into effect, and to secure its permanent character, have reappointed Mr. Israel Lewis[14] their agent to obtain collections in the states, and the Rev. Nathaniel Paul, late of Albany, whose standing as a minister of the gospel, and whose devotedness to the cause of his colored brethren, are too well known to need any recommendation from us, to embark for England, for the same purpose. He will probably sail as soon as the necessary means shall be obtained to defray the expense of his voyage—and should a kind Providence smile upon the exertions of our agents, we have no doubt but in the course of a few years, that this settlement will present to the public such a state of things as will cheer the heart of every well wisher of the African race and put to silence the clamor of their violent enemies. By order and in behalf of the Board,

AUSTIN STEWARD, *Chairman*
BENJAMIN PAUL, *Secretary*

Liberator (Boston, Mass.), 17 September 1831.

1. Steward and Paul wrote to the editor of the Albany *African Sentinel and Journal of Liberty*, John G. Stewart (?–1849). Stewart, a barber and editor of several black newspapers, lived in Albany, New York, from 1824 until his death. Prompted by the failure of *Freedom's Journal* and the *Rights of All* and believing that blacks needed their own print voice, Stewart established the *African Sentinel and Journal of Liberty* in 1831. The monthly, which survived a little over a year, opposed slavery and racial prejudice and urged "Education, Temperance and Morality." In September 1838, Stewart announced plans to publish a weekly paper called the *Champion of Equal Rights* in New York City, but no evidence exists to suggest that any issues ever appeared. During 1842–43 he began his most successful publishing effort as coeditor with Stephen Myers and Charles Morton of the Albany *Northern Star and Freeman's Advocate*. In addition to his black newspaper ventures, Stewart was active in the antislavery and the black convention movements. As a delegate to the 1833 and 1834 black national conventions, he opposed the American Colonization Society plan for Liberian colonization and favored Upper Canada as an alternative black emigration site. During the mid-1830s, he was secretary of the Albany Colored Anti-Slavery Society. A temperance activist, he held office in the New York State Delevan Union Temperance Society during the early 1840s. Stewart's activism apparently gained him some respect in the Albany community, as he sought election to the state assembly from Albany in 1848. Joel Munsell, *The Annals of Albany*, 10 vols. (Albany, N.Y., 1850–59), 1:349, 373; *Albany City Directory*, 1824, 1831–48; *Lib*, 12 March [1:0043], 10 September 1831; Peter M. Bergman, *The Chronological History of the Negro in America* (New York, N.Y., 1969), 143; *CA*, 10 November, 15 December 1838 [2:0643, 0680]; *NSFA*, 1842–43; *Minutes and Proceedings of the Third Annual Convention for the Improvement of the People of Colour* . . . (New York, N.Y., 1833), 4, 22–23 [1:0304]; *Minutes of the Fourth Annual Convention for the Improvement of the Free People of Colour* . . . (New York, N.Y., 1834), 8; Charles H. Wesley, "The Negro in the Organization of Abolition," *Phy* 2:232 (Third Quarter, 1941); *CF*, 29 June 1843.

2. Wilberforce depended on the generosity of philanthropic friends. When Cincinnati blacks sent representatives to Upper Canada to arrange for the acquisition of land, they also sent out agents to solicit funds. Quakers of the Ohio and Indiana meetings purchased the acreage for the settlement; contributions also came from other benefactors in Ohio, Indiana, Pennsylvania, and New York. Austin Steward and the colony had close ties with several New York benefactors, including Lyman A. Spalding, a Lockport abolitionist; Everard Peck, a Rochester printer and newspaper publisher; Charles Davis of Ludlowville; John Budd, an Auburn minister; and Arthur Tappan, a New York City merchant-philanthropist—all of whom agreed to act as receivers for Wilberforce sometime in late 1832. In 1831 Spalding and Peck secured a loan for Israel Lewis, which he used to help

finance Nathaniel Paul's fund-raising trip to England. Austin Steward, *Twenty-Two Years a Slave and Forty Years a Freeman* (Rochester, N.Y., 1857; reprint, Reading, Mass., 1969), 114, 146, 176, 206–8, 210–11 [1:0225], 211–12; Pease and Pease, *Black Utopia*, 48; Richard C. Wade, "The Negro in Cincinnati, 1800–1830," *JNH* 39:158 (January 1954); Winks, *Blacks in Canada*, 158; *Lib*, 13 April 1833 [1:0274]; *CA*, 7 October 1837 [2:0213]; Peter Williams, *A Discourse Delivered in St. Philip's Church for the Benefit of the Coloured Community of Wilberforce, in Upper Canada, on the Fourth of July, 1830* (New York, N.Y., 1830), 10–11 [1:0006]; *CG*, 30 July, 22 August 1829.

3. The Wilberforce settlement, which was named after British antislavery leader William Wilberforce, was the first planned black community in Upper Canada. It was established in response to increasingly stringent enforcement of Ohio's black laws during the 1820s. In 1829 a group of Cincinnati blacks, led by James C. Brown, sent representatives to Upper Canada to investigate the possibility of black settlement there. Sir John Colborne, the lieutenant-governor of the province, encouraged them to relocate and the Canada Land Company offered land on which to settle. Israel Lewis and Thomas Cresap, agents for the Cincinnati blacks, negotiated for the purchase of four thousand acres in the western part of the province, but they lacked the capital to acquire the land. Instead, concerned Quakers in Ohio and Indiana, represented by Frederick Stover, purchased eight hundred acres near the village of Lucan, Upper Canada. About two hundred free blacks and former slaves soon settled there. They established farms and operated a small sawmill. Churches and a temperance society were organized to promote the moral elevation of the community; a common school, which also served whites students in the area, was opened. The leaders of Wilberforce also hoped to establish a manual labor college and seminary and sent Nathaniel Paul to Britain to raise funds for this purpose. Despite early progress and ambitious objectives, the Wilberforce settlement achieved only limited success. The experiment was hampered by incompetent, divided, and sometimes corrupt leadership. Paul's failure to secure funds in Britain doomed the manual labor college scheme. Austin Steward, a former slave and Rochester, New York, grocer, who had been appointed to direct the settlement's board of managers, became embroiled in a bitter dispute with Lewis over fund-raising practices. Steward and the Wilberforce board eventually dismissed Lewis and issued public disclaimers to that effect, but he organized his own colonization company and continued to solicit funds for the settlement. Lewis's misconduct, and the dissension and litigation it provoked, did much to discredit the settlement. By 1836 it was in decline and it soon ceased to be an organized black community. Winks, *Blacks in Canada*, 155–57; Pease and Pease, *Black Utopia*, 46–63.

4. Wilberforce residents founded both Baptist and Methodist churches by 1832. The settlement's First Baptist Church was the more prominent of the two; Nathaniel Paul, the congregation's first reported minister, was succeeded by his brother Benjamin Paul in 1831. Following Benjamin Paul's death in 1836, Daniel A. Turner assumed the position. By 1835 the church, with a congregation of twenty, was a member of the Western Baptist Association, and though it survived the settlement's decline through the next decade, by 1853 it claimed only ten members. In 1856 the Western Baptist Association dropped the church from its minutes. Little is known about the Methodist church. Donald George Simpson,

"Negroes in Ontario from Early Times to 1870" (Ph.D. diss., University of Western Ontario, 1971), 370–73; James K. Lewis, "Pioneer Coloured Baptist Life in Upper Canada," *CBHMD* 6:266 (1963–64); *Lib*, 23 February 1833 [1:0244].

5. Nathaniel Paul (1793–1839) was born in New Hampshire, one of six brothers of Thomas Paul, a Baptist minister and a leader of Boston's black community during the early nineteenth century. Paul probably attended the Free Will Academy in Hollis, New Hampshire (an integrated ministerial training school run by the Free Will Baptist church), before becoming pastor of the First African Baptist Church of Albany, New York, in 1820. From the beginning of his tenure, Paul boldly stated his antislavery convictions. He applauded the New York State emancipation law, called for a halt to the slave trade, and assured his congregation that slavery would be overthrown in the United States. For Paul, racial prejudice demonstrated white America's inability to judge man's moral worth, but he suggested that black sobriety, industry, and prudence could overcome racism. Paul's anticolonization views were moderate during the 1820s. He believed that black immigration to Africa was primarily justified as an antislavery tactic and as a missionary opportunity—a position that was consistent with his attachment to the Wilberforce settlement in Canada.

In 1830 Paul and his brother Benjamin were among the early settlers of the black agrarian community located twelve miles from the town of Lucan in Upper Canada. Nathaniel Paul was asked by Austin Steward, a leader of the community, to travel to Great Britain to raise money for a proposed black manual labor college. Paul arrived in England early in 1832. A year later, he married an Englishwoman and began a tour of Britain with William Lloyd Garrison, rebutting the claims of American Colonization Society agent Elliott Cresson, who was in England to raise money and support for the society. For the next three years, Paul continued his speaking, fund-raising, and organizing activities on behalf of American and British antislavery goals, particularly the Wilberforce settlement. Paul returned to Wilberforce (at Steward's request) in 1836; he reported that he had raised over $8,000 but had used nearly $7,000 for expenses, and that, combined with his monthly salary of $50 as a Wilberforce agent, left his mission $1,600 in debt. This severed Paul's relationship with Wilberforce. He moved back to New York State, and for the remaining three years of his life, he served as pastor of the Hamilton Street Baptist Church in Albany, where he continued to promote black antislavery activity, speak out against racial prejudice, and call for black moral and educational improvement. *Lib*, 17 September 1831, 14 January, 12 April, 25 August 1832, 22 June, 31 August 1833, 14 March, 19 December 1835, 15 September 1836, 26 July 1839 [1:0217, 0313, 0410, 0571]; *RA*, 14 August, 18 September 1829 [17:0624]; *FM*, 22 December 1836, 14 March 1838; *FJ*, 20 April, 10 August 1827 [17:0457, 0497]; *E*, 15 September, 1 December 1836 [1:0579]; *CA*, 15 April 1837, 27 July 1839 [2:0027, 3:0151]; Walter M. Merrill and Louis Ruchames, eds., *The Letters of William Lloyd Garrison*, 6 vols. (Cambridge, Mass., 1971–82), 2:53, 581; Winks, *Blacks in Canada*, 158–61, 263–64; Pease and Pease, *Black Utopia*, 50–53, 57–61; Steward, *Twenty-Two Years a Slave*, 216–17; Minutes of the Glasgow Emancipation Society, February 1835, March 1836, UkGM.

6. In January 1832, while visiting Wilberforce, Benjamin Lundy learned that Austin Steward taught the Sabbath school during the "warm season." Earlier,

during the summer of 1818, Steward had conducted a children's Sabbath school in Rochester, New York. Fred Landon, ed., "The Diary of Benjamin Lundy Written during his Journey through Upper Canada, January 1832," *OHSPR* 19:115 (1922); Steward, *Twenty-Two Years a Slave*, 81.

7. Austin Steward (1793–1865) was born in Prince William County, Virginia, to slave parents Robert and Susan Steward. When Steward was eight or nine years of age, his master, Captain William Helm, sold his Virginia plantation and moved his slaves to upper New York State. Steward was hired out to various employers, but sometime around 1813, he escaped to Canandaigua, where he labored summers for a local farmer and attended a Farmington academy during the winter. In 1815 Helm located Steward, who retained his freedom with the assistance of the New York Manumission Society through a legal technicality in the state's Gradual Emancipation Law of 1799. About 1817 Steward moved to Rochester and, despite violent opposition by local whites, developed a successful grocery business during the 1820s. He also taught a Sabbath school in the city. After being chosen by Rochester blacks to deliver an oration at their 5 July 1827 ceremonies celebrating slave emancipation in New York State, Steward became increasingly involved in the antislavery, temperance, and black convention movements. During the late 1820s, he served as Rochester subscription agent for *Freedom's Journal* and the *Rights of All* and hosted black reform meetings. He served as a vice-president at the first black national convention (1830).

In 1831 Steward joined the Wilberforce colony at the urging of a group of settlers. He organized and directed the settlement despite continual conflict with the Israel Lewis faction. Steward returned to Rochester in 1837, reentered business (this time with less success), and served on a committee appointed to oversee black schools in the city. After fire destroyed his business, he moved back to Canandaigua about 1842 and taught school. Despite these business failures, Steward regained his prominence among New York blacks during the early 1840s, presiding over New York State black conventions in 1840, 1841, and 1845 and simultaneously devoting new energy to the antislavery, black suffrage, and temperance causes. His evangelical approach to these struggles culminated in his attendance at the 1843 Christian convention at Syracuse, which attempted to harmonize reform ideals with New Testament principles. In later years, Steward's age forced him to localize his efforts; he chaired local black meetings, served as Canandaigua's subscription agent for the *National Anti-Slavery Standard*, and was a vocal opponent of the Fugitive Slave Law of 1850. He wrote and published his autobiography, *Twenty-Two Years a Slave, and Forty Years a Freeman*, in 1857; it sold well, and three other editions were printed during the following decade. The terminal illness of his talented daughter Barbara during 1860–61 placed Steward in a precarious financial situation and prompted his return to Rochester to sell copies of his narrative and to seek aid from former friends. Although he entertained the idea of going south to teach black contrabands during the Civil War, he remained in Rochester until his death. *NCAB*, 14:308–9; Steward, *Twenty-Two Years a Slave*; Philip S. Foner and George E. Walker, eds., *Proceedings of the Black State Conventions, 1840–1865*, 2 vols. (Philadelphia, Pa., 1979–80), 1:5, 10, 24, 37; *FJ*, 15 June, 27 July 1827 [17:0493]; *RDA*, 21 January 1831 [1:0017]; *RA*, 29 May 1829; *RDT*, 28 June 1828; *Lib*, 13 May 1833 [1:0274]; *RDD*, 19 April 1845; *RR*, 12 July 1841; *CA*, 11 September, 4 December 1841

[4:0191, 0318]; *ASR*, 30 June 1841 [4:0085]; *E*, 26 October 1843 [4:0688]; *NEW*, 21 November 1850 [6:0669]; *FDP*, 16 December 1853; *RUA*, 31 December 1861; Austin Steward to Gerrit Smith, 24 November 1861, Gerrit Smith Papers, NSyU [13:0931].

8. By 1832 Benjamin Paul's daughter turned over her teaching chores to her brother Thomas Paul, who conducted classes in a log schoolhouse built with funds donated by Oberlin, Ohio, Quakers. Education at Wilberforce, however, proved to be erratic, and by the end of 1836, the settlement was without a school. In 1839 residents reported a "flourishing school" under the direction of the Reverend Hiram Wilson, but the school closed sometime in 1842 when New York Quakers withdrew their support. A black public school was established in the area by the following year. *P*, 27 February 1838; *CA*, 24 August 1839; *NASS*, 3 June 1841 [4:0042]; Landon, "Diary of Benjamin Lundy," 115; Fred Landon, "The History of the Wilberforce Refugee Colony in Middlesex County," *Trans* 9:41 (1918); Simpson, "Negroes in Ontario to 1870," 365; Pease and Pease, *Black Utopia*, 52.

9. Benjamin Paul (?–1836) was born in Exeter, New Hampshire, the son of a black Revolutionary War veteran. Like three of his six brothers—Thomas, Nathaniel, and Shadrach—he became a Baptist clergyman. Paul served an Albany, New York, congregation until 1824, when he was appointed pastor of the black Abyssinian Baptist Church in New York City. There he actively involved himself in black community affairs, particularly black education; he served as attendance agent for the African Free Schools and supported Benjamin F. Hughes's School for Coloured Children during the late 1820s. In 1830, after resigning his New York City parish and moving to Rochester, he became enthused by prospects at the black Wilberforce settlement in Upper Canada. For nearly a year, he solicited funds throughout New York State for the enterprise before moving there with his family in the spring of 1831. Like four of his children and his brother Nathaniel, he played a prominent role in the young colony's affairs. When Nathaniel left Wilberforce in late 1831 on a fund-raising tour of Britain, Benjamin Paul replaced him as minister of the settlement's First Baptist Church, a position he retained until his death. Paul also was an early member of the Wilberforce board of managers, functioning as treasurer in 1832. When a protracted, bitter struggle for control of the colony emerged between Austin Steward and Israel Lewis after 1832, Paul joined the pro-Lewis faction. According to Steward, Paul was "inclined to pulmonary diseases," which likely contributed to his death at the Wilberforce settlement on 31 March 1836. *DANB*, 481–82; J. Marcus Mitchell, "The Paul Family," *OTNE* 63:75 (Winter 1973); George Walker, "The Afro-American in New York City, 1827–1860" (Ph.D. diss., Columbia University, 1975), 136, 142; *RA*, 12 June 1829; *FJ*, 23 March 1827, 1 February 1828 [17:0534]; *CA*, 7 October 1837 [2:0213]; Simpson, "Negroes in Ontario to 1870," 333, 362–74; *Lib*, 21 May 1831, 12 May 1832, 23 February 1833, 8, 29 March 1834 [1:0244, 0399, 0407]; Steward, *Twenty-Two Years a Slave*, 156.

10. Members of Wilberforce's temperance society pledged to discourage the sale and the use of alcoholic beverages, and in this they were successful. Nathaniel Paul testified before a House of Commons committee in 1832 that Wilberforce's residents "unanimously agreed to exclude the use of ardent spirits from the settlement." Landon, "Diary of Benjamin Lundy," 115; Great Britain, *House of Com-*

mons Sessional Papers, Reports from Committees (1831–32), 20:232.

11. William Bell, a local black farmer, remained a member of the Wilberforce board of managers through 1836. Bell later promoted local black education and served on the committee of the self-help oriented Provincial Union Association. Bell's moderate success antagonized local immigrant whites, who burned his barn and crops in 1848; despite this, he continued to reside in Canada West through the mid-1850s. Simpson, "Negroes in Ontario to 1870," 372; *CA*, 13 July 1839 [3:0133]; *Lib*, 13 April 1833 [1:0274]; A. Beckford Jones et al., Memorial of the Colored Inhabitants of London and Wilberforce, Canada West, 10 October 1842, Fred Landon Papers, CaOLU [4:0475]; *PFW*, 19 August 1854, 22 December 1855 [9:0018].

12. Philip Harris (1775–1857) and his wife, Vilana, were among the earliest Wilberforce settlers (1830) and remained at the colony until their deaths. As a member of the board of managers, Harris initially supported Israel Lewis in his struggle for control of Wilberforce but later opposed him. Landon, "History of Wilberforce Refugee Colony," 42; Pease and Pease, *Black Utopia*, 58.

13. Simon Wyatt was described in 1832 as "an old man, in his dotage," but he remained active in Wilberforce affairs throughout the 1830s. Initially a member of Wilberforce's small, pro–Israel Lewis faction, he later joined with the board of managers to condemn Lewis. Pease and Pease, *Black Utopia*, 58; Steward, *Twenty-Two Years a Slave*, 210; *CA*, 24 August 1839.

14. Israel Lewis (?–ca. 1841), a founder and early leader of the Wilberforce settlement, escaped with his wife from slavery, settled in Cincinnati, and became a prominent member of the city's black community by the late 1820s. In 1829, when a group of Cincinnati blacks decided to immigrate to Upper Canada, Lewis and Thomas Cresap met with Sir John Colborne, the lieutenant governor of the province, obtained his approval for the settlement, and negotiated the acquisition of a tract of land from the Canada Land Company. Arriving in Upper Canada during the summer of 1829, Lewis was one of the first settlers of the new colony and a prominent community leader. He marked out the settlement's land purchase into parcels, petitioned the Ohio legislature for assistance with the resettlement of the Cincinnati blacks, supervised the construction of a road at the settlement, and returned to the United States to solicit funds for the fledgling colony.

After Austin Steward arrived at Wilberforce in 1831, Lewis lost his position of prominence. He acted as an agent for the settlement until 1 April 1832 when he severed his connection with the board of managers. He formed a rival organization to challenge the leadership at Wilberforce and remained active in the settlement's affairs (thereby contributing to the factionalism) by establishing schools, distributing relief, and collecting funds. From the late 1830s until at least 1841, Lewis solicited contributions for Wilberforce in the Midwest, New York State, and Upper Canada despite condemnation in the press, in northern black communities, and at Wilberforce, where, by the summer of 1839, he had lost most of his support. Throughout the 1830s, Lewis's critics charged him with using the money he collected for his own benefit. The bickering and controversy his willfulness encouraged did much to damage the colony's chances for survival. His feud with Austin Steward brought the colony bad publicity; the shortcomings that it revealed persuaded the Baptist Missionary Society of Upper Canada to withdraw support from Wilberforce in 1837 and to encourage other philanthropists to follow their example, arguing that the colony was incapable of appointing competent agents. Nevertheless, Lewis pursued his plan to establish a manual labor institute; in 1840 he unsuccessfully petitioned the Upper Canada House of Assembly for a charter to form a black educational organization called the Wilberforce Benevolent School Company of Upper Canada. Lewis died in poverty in a Montreal hospital. *CG*, 30 July, 22 August 1829; *Lib*, 9 April 1831, 11, 23 February, 2, 9 March, 13 April 1833, 8 March 1834, 16 July 1836 [1:0245, 0271, 0273, 0399, 3:0133]; *P*, 17 June 1836 [1:0670]; *E*, 11 August 1836; *CA*, 15 July 1837, 16 February, 13 July, 24 August 1839, 18 September 1841 [3:0132, 4:0210]; *FM*, 14 March 1838; *NASS*, 3 June 1841 [4:0042]; Steward, *Twenty-Two Years a Slave*, 108, 171–73, 209, 214 [1:0288]; Pease and Pease, *Black Utopia*, 53–54, 57, 58; Winks, *Blacks in Canada*, 160; Landon, "History of Wilberforce Refugee Colony," 42; Marilyn Bailey, "From Cincinnati, Ohio, to Wilberforce, Canada: A Note on Antebellum Colonization," *JNH* 58:431–36 (October 1973); Journal of the Assembly of Upper Canada, 5th Session, 13th Parliament, 20–21 January 1840.

2.
The Israel Lewis Controversy

Israel Lewis to the Public
26 January 1833

The Wilberforce Board of Managers to William Lloyd Garrison
12 March 1833

The Canadian black settlements struggled to achieve stability. Their survival depended on hard work, skilled leadership, and the goodwill of outsiders. Soon after Wilberforce was established, factionalism disrupted the settlement's progress and diminished its public credibility. A personal and political rivalry developed between Austin Steward, the president of the board of managers, and Israel Lewis, the settlement's chief fund-raising agent. During 1831–32 Steward and other residents became concerned about Lewis's conduct, his long absence from Wilberforce, his infrequent progress reports on his fund-raising activities, and his reluctance to turn over funds collected for the settlement. In the spring of 1832, the Wilberforce board of managers dismissed Lewis, who then established the rival Wilberforce Colonization and High School Company of Upper Canada in an attempt to reassert his control over the settlement. Steward and his supporters prevailed in the ensuing struggle. Lewis's *Liberator* correspondence and the board of managers' subsequent reply are two of several letters that kept the internecine battles at Wilberforce before a concerned and increasingly skeptical abolitionist community. The latter document emerged from a 12 March 1833 "large and respectable meeting" of the residents of Wilberforce, which was called to condemn Lewis's actions and to express support for his replacement, Rev. James Sharp of London, Upper Canada. Pease and Pease, *Black Utopia*, 52–58; Winks, *Blacks in Canada*, 158–60; Steward, *Twenty-Two Years a Slave*, 209–12, 217; *Lib*, 13 April 1833 [1:0271].

Cazenovia, [New York]
Jan[uary] 26, 1833

TO THE PUBLIC:

I have just seen an article in the Rochester *Anti-Masonic Inquirer* of the 22d inst. signed by Austin Steward, and others,[1] of the Wilberforce Colony, declaring themselves to be the Board of Managers[2] of the legitimate affairs of that colony. This is not the first article that has been published by that undiscerning band of wicked men. I would have said something to confute the wickedness of that party before now; but knowing that a controversy among ourselves would go to retard our progress, I have heretofore refrained from saying anything in public print, in a party way. But in justice to the Wilberforce Colony, which I had the honor to plant, I will make a few remarks on the causes which have induced Austin Steward and his unprincipled band to pursue the course that he has. To be sure, it is painful for me to state acts of the kind about my own color; but necessity compels me to do so.

One year after I had planted the Wilberforce Colony, and commenced travelling for the purpose of getting aid for the Colony, I went to Rochester where this Austin Steward lived. He was recommended to me as a man of color supporting a fair character. I induced him to go to Wilberforce, and there got him in as one of the Board of Managers—took him into my house to live with me until he could get a home, knowing that he supported a good name where he came from. Some time in the course of the season, I lost a twenty dollar note of hand out of my house, which I found some time afterwards in the hands of a man, who said he got it of Austin Steward. I presented Steward to the grand jury, who have found a bill against him for felony, to be tried at the court of kings bench in August next.[3] This is one of the reasons that this man Steward is publishing his incendiary publications. In the article which appeared in the Rochester paper, it is stated that I have refused to submit monies collected by me, to him and others to distribute. This I do not deny, having the right to do so, guaranteed to me by the original Board of Managers. I feel myself quite responsible for all my acts, so far as they relate to that Colony. I will add by saying, there is no man of color living in the Wilberforce Colony by the name of *Sharpe*,[4] which the article seemed to say was an agent for the Colony. Nor neither do I recognize any board of managers but the one I belong to. I would say more; but knowing that all we say, not tending to unite, is so much wrong in most instances. There is one thing that gives me some satisfaction: that is, discerning men know that in all great undertakings like this, those engaged in them must be more or less persecuted; more especially when they stand in the midst of an ignorant people, coming from different sections of the country, under different views, and with different habits. A tight rein is the best to manage the affairs of such a people, under such circumstances.

ISRAEL LEWIS
President and Agent of Wilberforce
Colonization Company[5]

Liberator (Boston, Mass.), 23 February 1833.

WILBERFORCE, [Upper Canada]
March, 1833

FRIEND GARRISON:[6]

We saw in your paper a publication signed by the notorious Israel Lewis, in which he calls the lawfully constituted Board of Managers of this Colony, 'a few disaffected men of the Colony.' Sir, if you knew one half of the baseness of character of that Israel Lewis, you never would have admitted into your paper, which may emphatically be called the guardian of the black man, his libellous publication. In order that you may judge of the correctness of his statement, we shall send herewith the proceedings of a public meeting. It is at all times painful to us as a people, poor and despised as we are, and struggling for existence, to be called upon to record acts of unfaithfulness in those of our own color. But we have no other alternative left; we are compelled to go forward and publish Lewis' conduct to the world; and this we do out of no personal enmity, but as a duty we owe to this infant settlement, and also to our numerous friends every where, and, in so doing, we believe we have taken the only safe and sure path. The inhabitants of Wilberforce, are peaceable, industrious and happy, with a few exceptions; and they say by their votes that Israel Lewis should be removed from the Agency of this Colony, and that for good cause.

1. Israel Lewis never has rendered a satisfactory account for the money that he has received to relieve the wants of our poor, but has spent it in the most prodigal manner at the taverns and other public houses.

2. He has run into debt wherever he could, without, in our opinion, any reasonable probability of paying, and thereby brought a reproach upon us as a people.

3. Israel Lewis, who ought to be the guardian and protector of his colored brethren, is the first to cheat them in order that he may live in idleness; and to effect this, he will stop at nothing, no matter how base! how ungenerous! how unrighteous!

Israel Lewis would be glad to make the public believe that he is doing every thing in his power for the benefit of his colored brethren. Indeed, friend Garrison, to hear Lewis talk about exerting himself for an injured people, reminds us of the Devil chiding sin.

Let us review the ground, and see what this mighty man Lewis has done for his much oppressed colored brethren. Has he bought any land in Wilberforce? We answer, no—not one foot. Has Israel Lewis founded any schools at Wilberforce with the thousands of dollars he has drawn out of a generous public in the States? We answer, no. What then has he done of such great importance for the colored people? We answer, he has collected money and basely squandered it away; and shut the door where good might have been done for our colored friends.

Resolved, That the conduct of Israel Lewis is disgraceful in the extreme, in pretending that there is no Board of Managers at Wilberforce.

Resolved, That we know that all that Lewis has published is so completely void of truth, that it needs no refutation where he is known.

Resolved, That the foregoing, together with these resolutions, be sent on to Messrs. Garrison and Knapp,[7] to be inserted in the *Liberator.*

AUSTIN STEWARD, *Chairman*
JOSEPH TAYLOR, *Secretary*
PHILIP HARRIS
JNO. WHITEHEAD
WM. BELL
PETER BUTLER[8]
SAMUEL PETERSON

Liberator (Boston, Mass.), 13 April 1833.

1. Lewis refers to a circular issued by Austin Steward and the Wilberforce board of managers on 25 December 1832. It was widely republished in the abolitionist press and in the 22 January 1833 issue of the Rochester *Anti-Masonic Enquirer*, an Anti-Masonic party organ, published weekly from 1828 to 1834. The circular pleaded for aid from sympathetic northern philanthropists, criticized Lewis, and requested that several prominent, white New York friends act as receivers for donations to the settlements. Winks, *Blacks in Canada*, 159; *RAME*, 22 January 1833; Winifred Gregory, *American Newspapers, 1821–1936* (New York, N.Y., 1937), 488.

2. Wilberforce's board of managers evolved from an organization formed by Cincinnati blacks at the outset of their colonization effort into a permanent governing body empowered to oversee the settlement's public business. Consisting of seven men, including the president or chairman, the board's members were apparently elected each year at meetings open to all settlers. As of December 1832, the board consisted of Austin Steward (president), Joseph Taylor (secretary), Philip Harris, John Whitehead, Peter Butler, Samuel Peterson, and William Brown. Pease and Pease, *Black Utopia*, 48, 173; Winks, *Blacks in Canada*, 158; Steward, *Twenty-Two Years a Slave*, 114, 210–11 [1:0225].

3. In a 12 March 1833 letter to the *Liberator*, A. Talbot, a London justice of the peace, certified to northern abolitionists the accuracy of Austin Steward's "statement of facts" on the case. According to Steward, Israel Lewis charged him with taking a promissory note from Lewis's house, which led to Steward's indictment by a local grand jury in 1832. After considerable delay, the Court of King's Bench convened in 1833 under Chief Justice John Beverly Robinson and tried Steward. Lewis testified against Steward, but three prominent, local whites contradicted his testimony, and Steward was acquitted by a twelve-man jury. Steward, *Twenty-Two Years a Slave*, 144–46; *Lib*, 13 April 1833 [1:0274].

4. James Sharp (1799–1874) was born in Massachusetts but settled in Rochester, New York. A self-styled black minister with some education, Sharp frequently presided over local black citizens' meetings and celebrations. He moved to London, Upper Canada, in 1832 and replaced Israel Lewis as the authorized agent for the Wilberforce settlement. After returning to Rochester in 1838, he worked as a teamster and served as an agent for the *Palladium of Liberty*. He represented his city at the black state convention in Albany in 1840 and the black national convention in Buffalo in 1843. Sharp later appealed unsuccessfully to the American Missionary Association for a stipend for mission work with the Refugee Home Society in Canada. In the 1860s, he practiced folk medicine and advertised himself as a physician. Sharp joined a black Indiana regiment late in the Civil War; after the war, he returned to his Rochester medical practice. He died of Bright's disease in Fairport, New York. *FJ*, 25 July 1828; *CA*, 9 January 1841; *PL*, 27 December 1843; *NSt*, 27 July 1849; *FDP*, 27 August 1852, 28 October 1853; *Lib*, 11 July 1862; *RUA*, 16 May 1874; James Sharp to George Whipple, 19 September 1857, 19 November 1858, 19 October 1859 [10:0847, 11:0407, 12:0139], AMA-ARC; *Rochester City Directory*, 1841, 1853–71.

5. Israel Lewis and his supporters organized the Wilberforce Colonization Company on 11 July 1832. According to Lewis, the new company and a new board of managers was supposed to displace Austin Steward's board after a majority of settlers became dissatisfied with Steward and his board. In early 1834, Lewis stated that his company, now called the Wilberforce Colonization and High School Company of Upper Canada, would raise money to establish a manual labor school at Wilberforce that would educate black youths from throughout the United States. At that time, Thomas J. Paul was the company's corresponding secretary, Benjamin Paul, Jr., and Benjamin Bourn acted as agents, and J. T. Norton and the Reverend J. N. Campbell were trustees. Steward and his supporters, who never disbanded their own board, referred to the rival organization as "The African Canadian Colonization Company" and minimized the support that it received. Nevertheless, by early 1834, Lewis, his company, and its agents received notable white support at least in New York State, and by 1837 at least one-third of Wilberforce's residents backed the company. But by 1839, increasing condemnation of Lewis in the press began to turn his supporters against him and his project. *Lib*, 23 February, 13 April 1833, 8, 29 March 1834 [1:0245, 0271, 0399, 0407]; *CA*, 16 February 1839; Henry Shaw et al. to Joseph [Tallcot], with postscript from Benjamin Paul, [Jr.], 28 January 1837, Tallcot Family Papers, PHC [1:0919]; Pease and Pease, *Black Utopia*, 56.

6. William Lloyd Garrison (1805–1879) was born in Newburyport, Massachusetts, raised by a local minister, and apprenticed to a newspaper editor at age thirteen. After working at Benjamin Lundy's *Genius of Universal Emancipation*, Garrison, in January 1831, founded the *Liberator*, a Boston-based antislavery weekly. With intermittent assistance, he edited the paper for the next thirty-five years. It became the most controversial, best known and most widely read antislavery newspaper. In addition to advocating immediate abolition of slavery, the paper at various times supported anticolonization, free produce, disunionism, anti-Sabbatarianism, nonresistance (including opposition to political antislavery), and women's rights and generally gave a sympathetic hearing to most other mid-nineteenth-century reform causes. It informed readers about antislavery

meetings and activities, published letters from abolitionists and their critics, reviewed antislavery literature, and reported federal government actions concerning slavery.

From the 1830s on, Garrison was instrumental in organizing the antislavery movement and discrediting the American Colonization Society. He helped found the New England Anti-Slavery Society in 1832 and the American Anti-Slavery Society in 1833. During the 1840s, Garrison consolidated his control of the American society, rejected political antislavery, promoted international antislavery cooperation (touring England in 1846), and condemned the slave power conspiracy. Although he was disheartened by proslavery government actions in the 1850s, Garrison continued his antislavery efforts until the slaves were emancipated (January 1863) and the Thirteenth Amendment was passed. After the Civil War, Garrison ceased publishing the *Liberator* (December 1865) and left the American society but pursued various reform interests, including temperance, women's rights, and free trade. *DAB*, 7:168–72.

7. Isaac Knapp (1804–1843), a printer, was William Lloyd Garrison's boyhood friend and one of his earliest collaborators. They founded the *Liberator* in 1831 and copublished it through 1835, when Knapp assumed all publishing and financial responsibilities for the paper. He relinquished control of the *Liberator*'s business management in 1838 when his finances and health began to deteriorate. Knapp broke with Garrison in 1841 and published one issue of a rival newspaper, *Knapp's Liberator*. An active abolitionist, he helped organize the New England Anti-Slavery Society in 1832. Merrill and Ruchames, *Letters of William Lloyd Garrison*, 2:xxvi.

8. Peter Butler (1797–1872) was born in Baltimore to slave parents named Bowzer. As a young man, he escaped from slavery, changed his surname to Butler, then worked for seven years as a sailor on international voyages. Upon returning to the United States, he learned the caulking trade and married Salome Squawker, an American Indian woman. About 1829 Peter and Salome Butler moved their young family to Upper Canada, where he briefly worked as a caulker at Port Stanley, Port Dover, and St. Thomas on Lake Erie. Butler and his family were among the original settlers of the Wilberforce colony in 1830. There they farmed, raised seven children, and were active in the settlement. Elected treasurer of the settlement's board of trustees in 1836, Butler initially supported, then opposed, Israel Lewis's attempt to control the affairs of the colony. His knowledge of folk medicine, which he obtained on earlier voyages to Africa, earned him the sobriquet "Dr. Butler," and many settlers came to him for medical treatment. As settlers abandoned the Wilberforce colony during the 1840s and 1850s, Butler purchased much of their land. He continued to reside in the Wilberforce area until his death, accumulating a landed estate valued at $22,000. Landon, "History of Wilberforce Refugee Colony," 40–41; Winks, *Blacks in Canada*, 161; Pease and Pease, *Black Utopia*, 58; Daniel G. Hill, *The Freedom-Seekers: Blacks in Early Canada* (Agincourt, Ontario, 1981), 197, 227n.

3.
Austin Steward to Joseph Tallcot
2 December 1836

Factionalism, ineffective leadership, and a loss of public confidence contributed to the decline of the Wilberforce settlement. After six years, the black colony remained dependent on external support, even for the barest essentials necessary to survive the Canadian winter. Wilberforce's failure to achieve stability and self-sufficiency, particularly after an auspicious beginning, raised serious doubts about the feasibility of organized black settlements and threatened the relationship between white philanthropy and the black Canadian community. As Austin Steward prepared to leave Wilberforce to return to Rochester, New York, he wrote to Quaker philanthropist Joseph Tallcot of Skaneateles, New York, discussing the settlement's predicament. Pease and Pease, *Black Utopia*, 61–62; Winks, *Blacks in Canada*, 161–62.

Wilberforce, [Upper Canada]
December 2th, 1836

Joseph Tolkcot[1]
Dear Freind

I have jest seen aletter sent by you to Mr. Georg J. Goodhue informing him that you had sent on some clothes for our people and had raised about Eighty dollars for us.

I am constrained to returned you and other Freinds our humble thanks for your disinterrested benevelence in our behalf and hope you and others will not loose thair re[asons] in so good a couse—the Boxes containing the cloths have not arrived yet and I think it doubtfull weather they will come to hand this winter as the navagation must be closed for this Season. If those goods does not come to hand this winter I think that our people must suffer considable for the want of them. I think that Me[re]ssrs. Georg J. Goodhue & co.[2] is as good and safe house as could posibley have been surlected to forward whatever you may see fit to send for the Colony; my family[3] is now in the city of Rochester but I still remain in the Colony but I shall leave for Rochester in the course of four or five weeks. I may posibley mak you a visit this winter. We are making arangment for a school so that we can get your liberal donation. I am much obliged to you for those valuabl tracts that you sent me. The colonest is all well and joines me in love to you. I remain yours &c.,

Austin Steward

P.S. If you will send on the money to Mr. Goodhue without delay I will see it appied or distributed befor I leave the colony. We shall tak into considaration your hint about the sheep.[4]

A.S.

Quaker Collection, Haverford College Library, Haverford, Pennsylvania. Published by permission.

1. Joseph Tallcot (1768–1853), a Quaker reformer, lived in Skaneateles, New York. He wrote extensively on religious and educational matters, organized numerous Quaker meetings throughout the northeastern United States and Upper Canada, and served as the financial coordinator for various Quaker philanthropic causes. Joseph Tallcot, *Memoirs of Joseph Tallcot* (Auburn, N.Y., 1855); W. M. Beauchamp, "Notes of Other Days in Skaneateles," *OHA* 1:15, 21 (1914).

2. George J. Goodhue (1799–1870) was a Vermont-born resident of London, Upper Canada. From 1832 to 1840, Goodhue and his partner Lawrence Lawrason operated Lawrason and Company, a large general merchandise store in London. In this capacity, Goodhue also bought and sold land, loaned money, handled legal affairs, and served as a commission agent for various firms outside of the area. He served in the Canadian legislature from 1842 to 1867. *DCB*, 9:323–24; Clarence T. Campbell, *Pioneer Days in London* (London, Ontario, 1921), 29–31.

3. Austin Steward married a "Miss B——," described as the daughter of a Rochester friend and a "woman of talents and refined mind," on 11 May 1825. By 1836 the Steward family consisted of Austin, his wife, and seven children—two of whom had been born during the family's sojourn in Upper Canada. An additional child, a son, was born in 1840. The lives of the Steward children reflected the nineteenth-century pattern of premature mortality. The eldest child, a daughter, died in April 1837 at eleven years of age. A second daughter, eighteen-year-old Patience Jane, died in the mid-1840s. Two children are known to have survived to adulthood. Austin, Jr., continued his father's antislavery activities in Canandaigua, New York, during the 1850s. Barbara Ann (?–1861) became a teacher and abolitionist lecturer of some repute, touring throughout western New York and New England during the decade prior to her death in Wilkes-Barre, Pennsylvania. Steward, *Twenty-Two Years a Slave*, 92, 163–64, 177, 184–85, 218; Austin Steward to Asa Mahan, 25 February 1847, OO [5:0374]; *NEW*, 21 November 1850 [6:0669]; *WAA*, 1 October 1859, 21 April 1860, 14 December 1861; *FDP*, 24 June, 16 December 1853, 1 June, 14, 21 September, 19 October, 9 November 1855.

4. In 1832 blacks at Wilberforce owned one hundred head of cattle, in addition to horses and pigs. Tallcot apparently recommended four years later that the settlers also purchase and raise sheep. Pease and Pease, *Black Utopia*, 50.

4.
John Roberts to Richard C. Stockton
8 July 1837

In the decades preceding the Civil War, nearly forty thousand slaves escaped from southern bondage and made their way to the British North American Provinces. Many escapes were reported in the antislavery press, and these reports contributed to Canada's growing reputation as a haven from slavery and racism. John Roberts's flight to freedom was one such case. Roberts left his master, Baltimore slaveholder Richard C. Stockton, on 28 June 1837 while they were on a visit to western New York State. With the assistance of abolitionist Gerrit Smith, Roberts reached Upper Canada. Stockton wrote a letter to Roberts, which appeared as an advertisement in the 4 July 1837 issue of the *Rochester Daily Democrat.* In it Stockton proposed that the fugitive slave had been enticed away by "supposed friends" and promised that Roberts would be "kindly received" if he returned to Stockton's service. Roberts responded in an 8 July 1837 letter published in the Toronto *Christian Guardian.* He assured Stockton that he enjoyed freedom and would never again "assume the bonds of a Slave." Roberts's letter was widely reprinted in the antislavery press. *RDD*, 4 July 1837; *Lib*, 25 August 1837; *Baltimore City Directory*, 1831.

Toronto, Upper Canada
July 8, 1837

Sir:

I have seen in the Rochester *Democrat* of the Fourth of July, your publication inviting me again to assume the bonds of a Slave. And can you think, that I would voluntarily relinquish Freedom, fully secured to me by the British Government, to return to American Slavery, the vilest that now crushes man and defies God? Is this the appreciation you have of Liberty? If so, I value it more highly. No, Sir, dear to me as are the thoughts of my wife and child, I cannot again become a Slave, if this be the price at which I must purchase the enjoyment of their Society. For them would I freely expend my life—but to become a Slave again! no, never. To ask it, is an insult to the spirit of Liberty, to the Dignity of human nature, to that Heaven born religion you profess.

You say that with "an excellent character for integrity, stability, and sobriety," I have served you "upwards of twenty years." And does this expenditure of my primest manhood entitle me to no reward in my declining years? Send me, then, my wife, my child.[1] Disproportioned as would be the cost of doing this, to the value of the services I have rendered you, 'tis all I ask; it shall be your full acquittance. From one who feels anything of the power of the religion you profess—or who has any touch of humanity, or any regard for justice, I could not ask less, nor would he think of performing less.

You seem to doubt the *sincerity* of the friend, by whose aid I have been enabled to achieve my liberty.[2] How has the habit of oppression warped your judgment and dulled your sensibilities—that you should suspect the motives of those who strike from the helpless Slave his long worn chains. Take it to yourself: what would you think of the friendship of him who, at the hazard of all things, should deliver you or your child from Moorish or Algerine bondage?[3] Would you be so ungrateful as to suspect his motives, when you were a beggar in all things but in thanks? No: you would not. And you would feel a generous indignation, too, against the frozen-hearted traducer who would persuade you to suspect his sincerity. If you should ever be so unfortunate as to be in Slavery, may you find those who will deliver you as I have been delivered—who will make you, as I am made, a FREEMAN. *Then*; you will acknowledge their worth, and know how to honour their friendship. Farewell, Sir, may you enjoy the happiness of those who strive to make others happy,

JOHN ROBERTS[4]

Christian Guardian (Toronto, Upper Canada), 12 July 1837.

1. Roberts implies that his wife and child remained slaves, but newspaper reports indicated that they were free black residents of Baltimore. *NECAUL*, 17 August 1837 [2:0149].

2. Roberts refers to Gerrit Smith (1797–1874), a New York abolitionist who helped him obtain his freedom. Smith entertained Stockton during the latter's New York visit and attempted to convince him to emancipate Roberts. After Roberts escaped, undoubtedly with Smith's encouragement and assistance, the abolitionist drafted the necessary manumission papers and persuaded Stockton to sign them. Smith, the son of a wealthy New York landowner, used the family's vast property holdings and influence to support a variety of reform causes. By the mid-1830s, he headed a powerful circle of New York antislavery reformers. Smith left the American Anti-Slavery Society in 1840 in favor of political action against slavery; he served briefly in Congress but became disillusioned by federal support of slavery. He unsuccessfully attempted to establish a black agricultural settlement on a large tract of family land, assisted runaway slaves (participating in the famous Jerry rescue), subsidized free-state Kansas settlers, and conspired with John Brown to incite a slave insurrection at Harpers Ferry. After the Civil War, Smith worked for black suffrage. *Lib*, 25 August 1837; *NECAUL*, 17 August 1837; *DAB*, 9(1):270–71; Ralph V. Harlow, *Gerrit Smith, Philanthropist and Reformer* (New York, N.Y., 1939).

3. Roberts refers to the capture and enslavement of white Europeans by North Africans.

4. Roberts served his owner as coachman for about twenty years. While accompanying Stockton on a visit to New York state in 1837, he escaped. Roberts soon

settled in Toronto, Canada West. During the early 1840s, Roberts joined other Toronto blacks in vehemently protesting racist theatrical performances in the city. In 1852 Roberts frequently corresponded with *Frederick Douglass' Paper*, urging abolitionist unity and the election of antislavery candidates. He moved to Lockport, New York, late in that year. *RDD*, 4 July 1837; Wilson R. Abbott et al. to the Mayor of Toronto, 14 October 1841, CaOTCi [4:0256]; *FDP*, 17 September, 29 October, 12 November 1852.

5. Proceedings of a Meeting of Toronto Blacks

Convened at the Residence of William Osborne, 203 King Street, Toronto, Upper Canada, 13 January 1838

Comparing the United States to Canada was a standard strategy employed by black abolitionists. On 13 January 1838, Toronto blacks gathered at the home of white abolitionist William Osborne to consider a series of resolutions that challenged American proslavery practices, congratulated Britain for ending slavery in the British West Indies, and glorified Canada as a land of freedom and opportunity. Black abolitionists Stephen Dutton and William Augustus served as chairman and secretary of the meeting. The final order of business was to request that copies of the resolutions be sent to leading reform newspapers in Canada, the United States, and Britain. *CG*, 17 January 1838; *E*, 15 March 1838 [2:0432].

At a Meeting of the coloured inhabitants of the City of Toronto, convened by themselves, at the residence of Mr. Wm. Osborne,[1] on Saturday, Jan. 13th, 1838, Mr. Stephen Dutton[2] was called to the chair, and Mr. Wm. Augustus[3] was appointed Secretary.

The following Resolutions were unanimously adopted:

Moved by Mr. M. B. Truss,[4] seconded by Mr. H. Coles—

1. That we have learned with the most painful and indignant feelings, the continued determined opposition which is arrayed against the friends of our coloured brethren in the United States, in their efforts to secure the inalienable right of personal freedom to two millions and a half of human beings, who are held by tyrants in a state of abject slavery, and especially manifested in a resolution of the American Congress,[5] as published in a recent number of the *Emancipator*,[6] the effect of which is to stifle the voice of complaint and remonstrance, however respectfully presented in the petitions of the free in behalf of the oppressed.

Moved by Mr. John L. Randolph, seconded by Mr. Wm. Hickman[7]—

2. That the recent outbursting of the true spirit of slavery in a nominally free State, in the murder of that pious and talented advocate of human rights, the Rev. E. P. Lovejoy, has excited in our breasts feelings of the warmest condemnation of the perpetrators of that unparalleled outrage, mingled with the deepest and most affectionate commiseration for his bereaved widow and children;[8] and

has called forth our earnest prayers to Almighty God—prayers which we doubt not will be heard and answered—that this tragical affair may be overruled for the more speedy extinction of a system, the whole history of which presents an unbroken chain of deeds of cruelty, darkness, tyranny, and blood.

Moved by Mr. Samuel Thompson,[9] seconded by Mr. George Brown[10]—

3. That it is due, not only to ourselves and to the Government under which we have the happiness to live, but especially to our coloured brethren in the United States—as well the free as those who are yet groaning in slavery—and to that portion of the white population who are striving for universal emancipation, that they should be made acquainted with the true state of the coloured population of Canada, and with the happy situation in which we are placed as compared with our former condition.

Moved by Mr. Richard Burke,[11] seconded by Mr. George Williams[12]—

4. That we express the universal feeling of our coloured brethren throughout this Province when we state our perfect contentment with our political condition, living, as we do, under the influence of free and equal laws, which recognize no distinction of colour in the protection which they afford and the privileges which they confer;[13] and that we distinctly contradict all statements to the contrary which have been industriously circulated in the States, by slaveholders and others of a kindred spirit, for the purpose of creating a belief that coloured people are unprepared for freedom, and that our emigration to this country has effected no real improvement in our circumstances.[14]

Moved by Mr. Wm. Augustus, seconded by Mr. George Wilkinson[15]—

5. That we wish it to be known that the unfortunate occurrence which took place at Niagara in the month of September last, in the case of Moseby, the self-emancipated slave, and which has excited much painful feeling and some prejudice among our brethren in the neighboring States, is in reality mainly attributable to the unprincipled conduct of the slave master, who, in order to effect his design to re-enslave Moseby, alleged against him the commission of an offence—for which, whatever might be its character in the eye of Canadian law, he was not amenable to the laws of slave States;[16] and that we have every reason to believe that similar *pretences* in future will receive that degree of scrutiny from the authorities of this Province, which will afford ample protection to the injured.

Moved by Mr. William Hickman, seconded by Mr. J. C. Brown[17]—

6. That the philanthropy which induced the British Nation to strike the fetters from the limbs of our brethren in the West Indian colonies, at an expense of nearly a hundred millions of dollars, and which is now prompting the British public to demand the completion of their emancipation by the abolition of the apprenticeship system, has laid the whole family of coloured men under obligations of gratitude;[18] and that we earnestly hope and pray that the time is not far distant when America shall manifest similar magnanimity, and remove at once the stain which blots her banner, and the intolerable burden which oppresses two and a half millions of the natives of her soil.

It was then ordered that the proceedings of this meeting be sent to the *Christian Guardian*[19] and Toronto *Patriot*[20] for publication, and that other papers friendly to the cause of human rights, especially the Anti-Slavery Journals in the United States and in England,[21] be respectfully requested to copy them.

W. AUGUSTUS
Secretary

Christian Guardian (Toronto, Upper Canada), 17 January 1838.

1. William Osborne, a white land agent, resided at 203 King Street in Toronto. *Toronto City Directory*, 1837.

2. Stephen Dutton (?–ca. 1855), a Cincinnati resident during the late 1820s, was among the organizers of the Wilberforce colony and apparently served as an officer on the original colonization board; he recorded one of the first two deeds of the settlement in September 1830. Dutton left Wilberforce by the summer of 1831, presumably because of disputes among the colony's early leaders. He settled in Toronto, became a successful barber, and, by the early 1840s, was prominent in the local black community as the minister of the First Baptist Church—the city's oldest black institution and a center of antislavery activity. During the spring of 1841, Dutton visited New York to raise money for the congregation's new church building, which was completed before the end of the year. He became the first permanent pastor of the Zion Baptist Church of New York City in 1843 and remained there until 1848. In 1849 he was named pastor of a Baptist congregation in Patterson, New Jersey, where he remained until his death. Winks, *Blacks in Canada*, 155, 158; Landon, "History of the Wilberforce Colony," 41–42; Simpson, "Negroes in Ontario to 1870," 426; *GUE*, March 1831; *Lib*, 13 April 1833 [1:0271]; *CA*, 3 April 1841 [3:0973]; Walker, "Afro-American in New York City," 137; Michel Sobel, *Trabelin' On: The Slave Journey to an Afro-Baptist Faith* (Westport, Conn., 1979), 267, 269; *Report to the Fifteenth Anniversary of the American Baptist Missionary Convention* (Brooklyn, N.Y., 1877), 19.

3. William Augustus, a black Toronto dyer, resided in New York State before settling in Toronto, where, by 1837, he had an active role in the Upper Canada Anti-Slavery Society. *Toronto City Directory*, 1837; *Lib*, 17 September 1831 [1:0115]; *TC*, 15 November 1837.

4. Matthew B. Truss, a boot and shoemaker originally from Staunton, Virginia, was a prominent figure in the Toronto black community during the 1830s. An active lay leader in Toronto's Coloured Wesleyan Methodist Church, he served on its original board of trustees in 1838. *PFW*, 2 September 1854; *Toronto City Directory*, 1837; Daniel G. Hill, "Negroes in Toronto: A Sociological Study of a Minority Group" (Ph.D. diss., University of Toronto, 1960), 376.

5. Truss refers to the "gag rule" adopted by the U.S. House of Representatives in 1836 in response to the abolitionist petition campaign designed to pressure Congress to abolish slavery in the District of Columbia and the federal territories. Beginning in 1828, antislavery petitions arrived in such quantities during the next decade that they threatened to disrupt the congressional agenda. Antagonized southern congressmen reacted by passing the "gag rule," which automatically tabled such petitions. Passage of the rule broadened and strengthened the antislavery crusade by tying it to the constitutional issue of free speech and the right to petition. The rule was rescinded in 1844.

6. The *Emancipator* was founded by Arthur Tappan in New York City in 1833. Although it was initially a weekly antislavery journal, Arthur's brother Lewis Tappan began publishing it monthly two years later and informally linked it to three American Anti-Slavery Society papers. In 1840 Lewis Tappan converted the *Emancipator* into an American and Foreign Anti-Slavery Society organ. Elizur Wright took over direction of the paper shortly thereafter, and by 1842 he had moved it to Boston, where he continued to publish it as a political antislavery organ under various titles until 1850. Betram Wyatt-Brown, *Lewis Tappan and the Evangelical War Against Slavery* (Cleveland, Ohio, 1969), 102, 111, 143, 179, 195, 210, 218.

7. William Hickman (1758–1852), a black barber, was a veteran of the American Revolution and the War of 1812. As a resident of Toronto, Upper Canada, in the 1830s, he became active in black antislavery activities there. Hickman was living in Washington, D.C., at the time of his death. *VF*, 22 April 1852; *Toronto City Directory*, 1837; *CG*, 17 January 1838.

8. Elijah Parish Lovejoy (1802–1837), an antislavery preacher and editor, became an abolitionist martyr when he was murdered by an antiabolitionist mob in Alton, Illinois. Born in Maine, he studied at Waterville (now Colby) College and Princeton Seminary before being licensed to preach in 1833. That same year, he began publishing the *St. Louis Observer*, a Presbyterian journal, which he later moved to Illinois and published as the *Alton Observer*. Lovejoy reported extensively on the antislavery movement and organized an Illinois state auxiliary to the American Anti-Slavery Society. In 1835 he married Celia Ann French, the daughter of a Missouri planter. Lovejoy was shot and killed in November 1837 while defending his press against a mob. He was survived by his wife, who was then pregnant with a second child, and a one-year-old son, Edward Payson Lovejoy. *DAB*, 11:434–35; Merton L. Dillon, *Elijah P. Lovejoy: Abolitionist Editor* (Urbana, Ill., 1961), 40–43, 69, 76.

9. Samuel Thompson, a Toronto black, later served on the Committee of the Provincial Union Association, a black self-help organization, in 1854. *PFW*, 19 August 1854 [9:0019].

10. George Brown became a leader of the Toronto black community. During 1840–41, he joined protests against racist theatrical performances in the city.

Throughout the late 1840s, Brown served on the managing board of the British-American Anti-Slavery Society, an organization of Toronto blacks. Later, in 1852, he helped form the Canada Mill and Mercantile Association, a black-owned business in Buxton, Canada West, and he served as an officer and shareholder in the enterprise. Wilson R. Abbott et al., to the Mayor of Toronto, 20 July 1840, 14 October 1841, CaOTCi [3:0531, 4:0255]; *NSt*, 17 November 1848; *VF*, 22 April 1852.

11. Richard Burke, a baker, was a leader in the Toronto black community during the late 1830s and early 1840s. During 1840–41, he also protested racist theatrical performances in the city. *Toronto City Directory*, 1837; Wilson R. Abbott et al., to the Mayor of Toronto, 20 July 1840, 14 October 1841, CaOTCi [3:0531, 4:0255].

12. George Williams (ca. 1802–1862) was born a slave in Fairfax County, Virginia. He was separated from his family at age fourteen when his master took him to Maysville, Kentucky. Sometime around 1820, Williams began to actively pursue his freedom, and he and his master agreed upon a $250 purchase price. When his master then requested that Williams remain in slavery one additional year, the slave escaped. For six years, Williams lived in the free states, primarily on his Ohio farm. At the end of that time, racial discrimination and fear of the Ohio black laws prompted him to sell his land and resettle in Upper Canada. Williams soon established himself as a leader in the Toronto black community. In 1841 he moved to Sandwich, Canada West, where he worked as a whitewasher. By the early 1850s, he had achieved a position of prominence in the local black community. Williams contributed to the development of the settlement during 1851–52 as the leading trustee of the Colored Industrial Society. He also participated in the affairs of the Refugee Home Society, chaired numerous meetings of Windsor blacks, distributed goods to needy black fugitives in Windsor, and encouraged the convening of the black North American Convention (1851) in Toronto. He remained a prominent Sandwich resident throughout the 1850s. In 1861 Williams murdered his estranged wife during a marital dispute, and the following January was hanged for the crime before a crowd of three thousand people at Sandwich. Benjamin Drew, *A North-Side View of Slavery* (Boston, Mass., 1856; reprint, New York, N.Y., 1968), 343–44; Wilson R. Abbott et al., to the Mayor of Toronto, 20 July 1840, CaOTCi [3:0531]; *VF*, 1, 29 January, 26 February, 13 August 1851, 15 January 1852 [6:0717, 0834, 0840, 7:0055–56, 0349]; *Lib*, 4 March 1853 [8:0154]; *FDP*, 10 February 1854 [8:0645]; *WAA*, 18 January 1862.

13. Canadian law allowed blacks all rights of citizenship, including the franchise. But blacks did not find all of the personal freedom they hoped for in Canada, and they often faced open prejudice and hostility. They were considered inferior—not necessarily because they might have been slaves, but simply because they were blacks. Canadian racial attitudes often resembled those of northern whites, and some Canadians opposed the formation of black settlements. The situation worsened in the 1850s with fears that an influx of fugitives would mean more competition for jobs and would make things more difficult for Canadians in their own land. Although blacks were equal in the eyes of Canadian law, they faced social discrimination in schools, public accommodations, and housing.

Winks, *Blacks in Canada*, 20–21, 142–43, 248–51; Pease and Pease, *Black Utopia*, 8–12, 101–5, 165.

14. Antebellum slaveholders, and a few proslavery theorists, informed slaves that Canada was an extremely distant, barren, and inhospitable land. Hill, *Freedom-Seekers*, 25.

15. George Wilkinson, a baker, was active in the Toronto black community during the 1830s. A lay leader in Toronto's Coloured Wesleyan Methodist Church, he served on its original board of trustees in 1838. *Toronto City Directory*, 1837; Hill, "Negroes in Toronto," 376.

16. Solomon Moseby, a fugitive slave from Kentucky, settled near Niagara, Upper Canada, in 1837. In mid-September, Moseby's former owner attempted to extradite him. Although Canadian judicial procedure concerning fugitive slave extradition was not yet codified, in most cases Canadian officials refused to extradite fugitives unless they were charged with a crime for which they could be arrested in Canada. Because Moseby's owner charged him with stealing a horse during his escape, Moseby was jailed in Niagara by Canadian officials. A large number of area blacks, led by clergyman Herbert Holmes and community leader Sally Carter, surrounded the jail to prevent Moseby's return to his former master. They remained for three weeks and, in early October, attacked militiamen who attempted to remove Moseby to Kentucky. Moseby was finally freed, but Holmes and another black, Jacob Green, were killed. Twenty blacks were arrested but quickly released. Moseby fled to Montreal, then to England, but he eventually resettled in Niagara. Winks, *Blacks in Canada*, 169–70; Janet Carnochan, "A Slave Rescue in Canada Sixty Years Ago," *NHS*, no. 2 (1897), 8–17; Anna Brownell Jameson, *Winter Studies and Summer Rambles in Canada* (New York, N.Y., 1839), 246–50.

17. James Charles Brown (ca. 1796–?) was born in Frederick County, Maryland, to a white father and mulatto slave mother. While Brown was still quite young, his master separated him from his mother and took him to Kentucky. At age fifteen, Brown served as a fifer in a volunteer company at the battle of Tippecanoe (1811) and was promised freedom in return. But instead he was hired out for six years and required to pay his master a purchase price of $1,800. Freed about 1817, Brown worked as a mason in Bardstown, Shelbyville, and Louisville, where white mechanics became envious of his success and harassed him. In 1819, on the advice of Benjamin Lundy, Brown investigated Texas (then part of the Spanish Viceroyalty of New Spain) as a potential location for a black colony but rejected the site because of antiblack attitudes there. A short time later, he settled his family in Cincinnati, where he again gained employment as a mason, earning $600 annually. But racism intervened once more, and Brown's refusal to post the bond for good behavior required of Ohio's free blacks led to difficulties with authorities.

The rejuvenation of the Ohio black laws in 1829 prompted Brown to promote black immigration to Upper Canada. He served as nominal president of a black Cincinnati emigration society and engineered the migration of several hundred local blacks to what became the Wilberforce settlement. Conflicts with Israel Lewis prompted Brown to abandon the colony and settle in Toronto. His wife's dissatisfaction with Canada brought them back to Cincinnati in 1832, but

Brown's arrest in Louisville on the false charge of aiding fugitive slaves, his subsequent trial and acquittal, and Ohio racism led them to return northward. Brown apparently fought in the Coloured Corps during the Canadian Rebellion of 1837. After the war, he emerged as a leading figure in the Toronto black community by aiding fugitive slaves, exposing black begging imposters, and protesting Canadian racism.

Brown moved to Chatham in 1849 and immediately assumed a leadership role in the militant black community there. During the early 1850s, he chaired local antislavery meetings, continued his lifelong opposition to black begging, opposed segregated education, served as vice-president of the North American Convention (1851) in Toronto, held office in the Provincial Union Association (1854), and was an Elgin Association stockholder. From the mid-1850s on, Brown, an original Dawn trustee, invested most of his energies in an attempt to reform the management of the colony. He repeatedly attacked John Scoble and Josiah Henson for begging and mismanagement. He asked an August 1855 black convention to investigate Scoble and to remove Dawn from the Englishman's hands—a goal Brown pursued well into the early 1860s and one that caused some blacks to question Brown's integrity. But despite the loss of prestige and Brown's continuing legal difficulties engendered by the Dawn struggle, he remained a prominent figure in black Canadian affairs throughout the 1860s. Drew, *North-Side View of Slavery*, 239–48; Simpson, "Negroes in Ontario to 1870," 358–62, 670; Winks, *Blacks in Canada*, 155, 157–58, 161, 180, 202–3; Pease and Pease, *Black Utopia*, 53, 78; *E*, 15 March 1838 [2:0432]; *FM*, 24 July 1839 [3:0149]; *ASRL*, 8 March 1843; Wilson R. Abbott et al., to the Mayor of Toronto, 20 July 1840, 21 April 1843, CaOTCi [3:0531, 4:0562]; *VF*, 1 January [6:0694], 24 September 1851, 15 July 1852; *PFW*, 19 August 1854, 7 April 1855, 8 August 1857 [9:0017, 0525]; *KA*, 26 December 1850 [6:0694]; *Fifth Annual Report of the Directors of the Elgin Association* (Toronto, Canada West, 1854) [9:0062]; *Eighth Annual Report of the Directors of the Elgin Association* (Toronto, Canada West, 1857), 13 [10:0822]; *TG*, 11 August 1860, 24 December 1861 [12:0953, 13:1002]; Alexander L. Murray, "Canada and the Anglo-American Anti-Slavery Movement: A Study in International Philanthropy" (Ph.D. diss., University of Pennsylvania, 1960), 468–69, 474; *WAA*, 11 February 1860, 16 February 1861 [12:0486, 13:0326]; Legal Affidavits, *Canada West* v. *John Scoble and James C. Brown*, 1861–69, Regional History Collection, CaOLU.

18. Hickman refers to the Emancipation Act of 1833 (more commonly known as the British West Indian Emancipation Act), which took effect 1 August 1834 as a compromise measure between British antislavery forces and the West Indian colonial legislatures, which refused to undertake slave reform. Slave owners received 20 million pounds in compensation from the British government. Although slaves technically obtained all the rights and privileges of freedom, they actually became part of an apprentice system, as a first step toward complete emancipation. Only children under the age of six were totally and immediately emancipated. Even though the act did not fully satisfy most abolitionists, it was celebrated in both the United States and Britain every 1 August after 1834. As Hickman suggests, British antislavery forces then rallied against the apprenticeship system, causing Parliament to pass an 1838 law eliminating some of the system's harsher features; later that year, the Jamaica assembly ended the apprenticeship system in response

to persistent British pressure. William A. Green, *British Slave Emancipation: The Sugar Colonies and the Great Experiment* (Oxford, England, 1976), 99–161; William Law Mathieson, *British Slavery and Its Abolition, 1823–1838* (London, 1926), 183–242.

19. The Toronto *Christian Guardian* was founded in 1829 by Rev. Egerton Ryerson. Under Ryerson and later editors, the paper served a primarily Wesleyan Methodist readership. It initially supported the Liberal party but, by the mid-1830s, switched allegiance to the Conservatives. The paper ceased publication in 1926. Jesse Edgar Middleton and Fred Landon, *The Province of Ontario: A History, 1615–1927*, 4 vols. (Toronto, Ontario, 1927), 2:781–82; Edith Firth, ed., *Early Toronto Newspapers, 1793–1867* (Toronto, Ontario, 1961), 8.

20. The Toronto *Patriot* was founded by Thomas Dalton in Kingston, Upper Canada, during 1828, but it was moved to Toronto in 1832 for financial reasons. Dalton (1828–40) and his wife (1840–48) edited the paper, using it to oppose Liberal policies until its sale in 1848. Middleton and Landon, *Province of Ontario*, 2:783, 786.

21. In addition to the *Liberator* and the *Emancipator*, the leading American antislavery newspapers circulating at the time included the Cincinnati, Ohio, *Philanthropist* (1836–46?), edited after September 1837 by Gamaliel Bailey; the Utica, New York, *Friend of Man* (1836–42), edited by William Goodell; the Concord, New Hampshire, *Herald of Freedom* (1835–46), edited through 1837 by Joseph H. Kimball; La Roy Sunderland's Methodist *Zion's Watchman* (1836–42), published in New York City; and Orion S. Murray's Brandon *Vermont Telegraph* (1834–43). Benjamin Lundy's *Genius of Universal Emancipation* (1821–39) had been the major antislavery journal of the 1820s but was issued at this time from Philadelphia as a quarterly. The New York *Colored American* (1837–42), edited by Samuel E. Cornish, was the principal black paper. In Great Britain, the Central Negro Emancipation Committee had been publishing the *British Emancipator* (1837–40) since the previous November. Dwight L. Dumond, *Antislavery: The Crusade for Freedom in America* (New York, N.Y., 1966), 264–68; Gregory, *American Newspapers*, 274, 413, 463, 529; Howard Temperly, *British Antislavery, 1833–1870* (London, England, 1972), 272.

6.
Jehu Jones to Charles B. Ray
8 August 1839

Upon arriving in Canada, blacks were often exhilarated by the free and open society they encountered. Many became enthusiastic proponents of black Canadian settlement. Rev. Jehu Jones, a black Lutheran clergyman, reached Toronto on the eve of the annual 1 August celebration in 1839. He reported on the day's events to Charles B. Ray, the editor of the *Colored American*. Jones contrasted the interracial nature of the Canadian celebration with the exclusionary treatment he had faced in the free states. Like many other blacks, he was struck by the apparent lack of prejudice and the abundant opportunities that he found in Canada, and he marveled that information about life there was not more widespread among northern blacks. Jones encouraged young black Americans to consider emigration as the path to "being in reality free men." *CA*, 14 September 1839; Douglas C. Strange, "The Trials and Tribulations of One Jehu Jones, Jr., The First Ordained Negro Lutheran Clergyman in America," *US* 24:52–55 (Pentecost 1967).

Toronto, U[pper] C[anada]
Aug[ust] 8th, 1839

My dear sir:[1]

I am persuaded that you will be pleased to know, that, under the blessings of Divine Providence, I enjoy good health, and what are the impressions that was first made upon my feelings, which have been actively engaged for seven years in the States, carefully looking out for a home, but without success, to more favorable prospects under the crown of Great Britain. This letter will inform you that I arrived in this city on the evening of the 31st of July, in order to witness the celebration, of the 1st of August, being the 5th Anniversary of British West India Emancipation;[2] in this affair my expectations have been more than realized, in addition to my feelings—such as I never had before—that of feeling and knowing the importance and consequence of a man, and not to make me afraid. That I assure you, sir[,] my soul was absorbed in rejoicing, prayer and thanksgiving to the Author of all good gifts, that he has given me courage, through so many difficulties that I have experienced faithfully to pursue an object dear to my heart and to find a place where I am protected by law—besides that I can enjoy my peculiar Religious opinions, without giving offence to my neighbors.

On my arrival, I received a polite invitation from one of the Marshals of the day—Mr. Edwards,[3] in the name of the Association,[4] he represented, to dine with them and to participate, in all of the ceremonies on this grateful occasion; having cheerfully accepted the invitation, I accompanied, Rev. William Miller of Philadelphia,[5] who was appointed to deliver a sermon, in Westly Chapel, Hospital Street at 11 o'clock, A.M. I was highly gratified with his performance; his prayer was fervent and sublime, when he addressed the Throne of Grace, in behalf of Victoria, her Britannic Majesty, the Royal family and the British nation;[6] his subject was sublime, full of thrilling interest, not only to the loyal subjects of Toronto, but to Britons every where—he was equally happy in his discourse which, although brief, was lucid and distinct, such as the occasion called for. The exercise being over a respectable number of the party formed a procession, in front of the chapel and marched to the city hall, at 2 o'clock P.M., where Rev. Mr. Gassett,[7] after going through the usual and beautiful exercise of prayer, peculiar to the Episcopal church, he delivered an eloquent discourse on British West Indian Emancipation. On the service being ended in the city hall,[8] the procession was reformed, under the direction of the Marshals of the day, and marched to the Commercial hotel,[9] Front Street, where the rooms were handsomely decorated, with evergreens and the British flag, beautifully unfurled, in token of protection to the oppressed. At half past four o'clock, seventy-five of us sat down to a superb dinner, prepared by Mr. Carter, in his very best style. The Queen and Royal Family's health being drank and cheered, some appropriate, general and interesting remarks were made by various gentlemen, and at an early hour the company separated in peace, without the slightest accident or disorder to mar the joys of my first impressions under the British Crown.

Rev. Mr. Miller and myself were also invited to a tea party, at Mrs. Wilson's in Elizabeth Street, got up by the ladies of Toronto, in honor of the day. I scarcely need to add that the ladies sustained themselves, and the company in one of the neatest and social entertainment, that I ever had the pleasure to witness; at a late hour, worn down with the fatigue, incident to the occasion, I returned to my lodgings to contemplate on the magnanimity of the British nation, who under God, have given liberty to all her slaves. So, sir, you can readily perceive, that since first I inhaled the sweet zephyrs of British land, that it has made deep impressions upon my heart, not easily to be forgotten—having been introduced to his honor the Mayor,[10] who received and welcomed me in the most cordial, and friendly manner; I visited the city, public buildings, barracks, and the soldiers. There are several regiments stationed here, who parade every day; they have an excellent band of music attached to the regiment. The whole regiment is composed of young men, well calculated for the service in which they are engaged—the Scotch regiment is remarkable for their peculiarity of dress—their cap is splendid, has a number of rich, very costly feathers—in full dress they wear a red body jacket and in undress a white body jacket, either of which is very handsome with so many ornaments, besides that I cannot describe them accurately, a part of the leg however, is bare, with plaid garters, and old fashioned shoe and buckle to correspond such as was worn in by gone days. But to say the least of it, the regiment is very handsome—the officers in general are very fine, soldierly looking men.

There is a regiment composed entirely of colored men—the commissioned officers are white. I have seen several of the members in this city—the corps are stationed on the Frontier.[11] Great confidence is reposed in this regiment, and they have the most important post, in consequence of their acknowledged loyalty to the British Crown. When I reflect upon the known and acknowledged advantages to be derived by colored men, emigrating into the British provinces, where all distinction of caste is despised, and man known by his merits and loyalty to the Queen and country, I cannot but enquire how is it, that my brethren of the Northern States, who have the advantages of coming over, to examine the province for themselves, and to scrutinize the state of society, and report the result of their investigation in this matter have neglected to do so, it appears that our attention has never been properly directed or we have failed to accomplish any good end, can we always remain in a country, where prejudice against our complexion—which God and nature gave us—operates with violent and unholy hands upon us, to frown—wither and crush us for ever—even the prospects of comfortable living in security of the person and property of colored men are doubtful, and although there are no positive legislative enactments in the professedly free States, to deny us the privileges of advancing in knowledge and understanding of mechanical business and trades; still the blighting influence of prejudice, is so extraordinarily great, that it triumphs over every attempt as yet that has been made to give correct instructions to colored youths, in various & useful branches of mechanicism.[12] I must confess and acknowledge it is passing strange, that there should be so many intelligent and some learned men, residing in the Northern States, that are in possession of ample wealth for any good purpose—still as if infatuated, remain there deprived of every political and of many moral and religious liberties; whilst the kingdom of Great Britain is open to all men where life, liberty, and the pursuits of happiness, without dissimulation, is distributed with an equal hand, to all men, regardless of the country or condition of any. This province especially, seems to invite colored men to settle down among the people, and enjoy equal laws. Here you need not separate into disgusting sect of caste. But once your elastic feet presses the provincial soil of her Britannic Majesty, Queen Victoria, God bless her, you become a man, every American disability falls at your feet—society—the prospects of society, holds out many inducements to men of capital; here we can mingle in the mass of society, without feeling of inferiority; here every social and domestic comforts can be enjoyed irrespective of complexion. Tell my young countrymen this subject requires their most profound consideration—the subject of being in reality free men. I should like to continue this letter, but the bearer is about to depart, I have not time to correct inaccuracies. Yours, &c.,

JEHU JONES[13]

Colored American (New York, N.Y.), 14 September 1839.

1. Charles B. Ray (1807–1886) was born in Falmouth, Massachusetts, the eldest of seven children. Ray's father delivered mail to the islands off Cape Cod; his well-educated mother encouraged her children to attend the integrated public schools in nearby New Bedford. Ray worked as a farmer and a bootmaker before deciding upon a career in the ministry. After attending Wesleyan Academy in western Massachusetts, he enrolled in the Wesleyan Theological Seminary in 1832 but was forced to withdraw from the institution by white student protests and a faculty that viewed his departure as the "wisest course." Ray moved to New York City, opened a shoe store, and began a lifetime commitment to antislavery and to home missionary work among the poorest members of the city's black community. Ray believed in the importance of black self-discipline and economic security and was a proponent of temperance and dietary reform. He was an early abolitionist who believed that antislavery reform partially restrained racial prejudice against northern free blacks. During the mid-1830s, he helped found the New York Committee of Vigilance, participated in the black national convention movement, and belonged to the American Anti-Slavery Society. Because he believed in political action, he left the American society in 1840 and became a leader of the American and Foreign Anti-Slavery Society.

Ray was an eloquent spokesman for a national black press. In 1837 he was hired as a traveling agent for the New York *Colored American*, and by early 1840, he was its sole editor and proprietor. Ray used the paper to press his political antislavery convictions (he was a vigorous proponent of black suffrage throughout the 1840s and 1850s), to rebut arguments for African colonization and Canadian immigration, and to advocate the legal rights of fugitive slaves. Ray directed his attention to domestic missionary activity in the mid-1840s; he served as secretary of J. W. C. Pennington's Union Missionary Society and began an extended relationship with the New York City Missionary Society—an affiliate of the American Missionary Association. Ray became pastor of New York's Bethesda Congregational Church in 1845 and, at about the same time, helped select recipients for Gerrit Smith's black land grant plan. In 1848 he was appointed to the Committee of Twenty-Five, a group selected by that year's black national convention to devise a plan for establishing a black manual labor college.

Ray was infuriated by passage of the Fugitive Slave Law of 1850 and led a New York petition drive against it. At the 1853 Colored National Convention held in Rochester, he helped write the convention's "Report on Social Relations and Polity," a provocative analysis of black political economy. In 1859, as president of New York's Society for the Promotion of Education Among Colored Children, he focused on the need for quality black education and public school integration. In the 1860s, he was a leader of the African Society for Mutual Relief and dispensed private funds to black victims of New York's 1863 draft riot. In 1869 Ray renewed his call for black labor solidarity (a call he first made as a member of the American League of Colored Laborers in 1850) and helped organize the National Labor Convention of Colored People. In the mid-1870s, Ray aided black men and women immigrating to the Kansas frontier. M. N. Work, "The Life of Charles B. Ray," *JNH* 4:361–71 (October 1919); Florence T. Ray and H. Cordelia Ray, "Sketch of the Life of Rev. Charles B. Ray," in Florence T. Ray and H. Cordelia Ray to William H. Siebert, 12 April 1897, Siebert "Underground Railroad" Collection, MH; *NASS*, 6 June 1843, 24 October 1844, 26 August 1845, 16 July 1846, 3 May 1849, 17 July 1862, 5 September 1863, 24 March 1866, 5, 19 June, 23 October 1869, 1 October 1870 [4:0940, 0582, 5:0249, 1074]; *NSt*, 4, 11, 18 May, 23 November 1849, 13 June, 27 July, 5 September 1850; *FDP*, 16, 30 October, 13 November 1851, 27 May 1852, 15, 29 July, 28 October 1853, 3 February 1854, 25 April, 25 May, 3 August, 14 September, 16 November 1855; *OE*, 20 December 1843; *PL*, 27 December 1843; *LP*, 14 February 1846; *NEW*, 20 May 1847, 6 July 1848, 2 February, 14 March 1850 [5:0422, 0698, 6:0374, 0425]; Charles B. Ray to Thomas Lafon, 16 July 1845, AMA-ARC [5:0057]; Charles B. Ray to Gerrit Smith, 22 May, 2 December 1847, Gerrit Smith Papers, NSyU [5:0423, 0533]; *AAM*, July 1859 [11:0818]; *WAA*, 21 April 1860, 2 February 1861, 12 April 1862 [12:0646, 13:0254, 14:0237]; *DANB*, 515–16.

2. Celebrations on 1 August commemorated the end of slavery in the British West Indies. Blacks found Emancipation Day an appealing national holiday and contrasted it with slaveholding America's Fourth of July. First of August celebrations usually included street parades with brass bands and military companies, picnics, antislavery speakers (ranging from semiliterate recent fugitives to polished black and white professional abolitionists), dancing, and other amusements. These celebrations frequently included religious services. Benjamin Quarles, *Black Abolitionists* (London, 1969), 116, 123–28.

3. William H. Edwards emerged as a spokesman for the Toronto black community during the 1830s. In 1840 he attended the organizational meeting of the Canada Conference of the African Methodist Episcopal church; there he was ordained a deacon and assigned to the Toronto district. Edwards was ordained an AME elder in 1844. That same year, he visited England to raise funds to build a chapel for his Toronto congregation. He later served congregations in the St. Catharines district. Daniel A. Payne, *History of the African Methodist Episcopal Church* (Nashville, Tenn., 1891; reprint, New York, N.Y., 1968), 128, 145; *VF*, 12 August 1852; John Hooper to J. S. Hinton, 15 January 1844, British Empire MSS, UkOxU-Rh.

4. Jones evidently refers to the Abolition Society, an association of Toronto blacks organized in 1833. Among its other projects, it sponsored Emancipation Day celebrations in the city during the 1830s and 1840s. The society added a women's auxiliary in 1840. Hill, "Negroes in Toronto," 21–22.

5. William Miller (1775–1845), a free black, was born in Queen Annes County, Maryland. As a young man, he settled in New York City and practiced the cabinetmaking trade. Miller began preaching to black Methodists during the

1790s. Over the next three decades, he performed a major role in directing the withdrawal of these New York blacks from the larger Methodist body. He was ordained a deacon in 1808. But Miller's interests extended beyond religion. As early as 1810, his *Sermon on the Abolition of the Slave Trade* demonstrated a moderate antislavery view. He also helped found black masonry in New York City, started and directed the New York African Bible Society (an American Bible Society affiliate), and attended the 1831 black national convention in Philadelphia. In 1814 Miller led disgruntled members out of New York City's black Zion Church and formed the African Asbury Church. Despite his independent spirit, he was selected in 1820 to help draw up the discipline for an independent African Methodist Episcopal Zion denomination. Soon after, he began a flirtation with the rival African Methodist Episcopal church, which led to his ordination as an AME elder in 1823 and to his subsequent appointment to the pastorate of an AME congregation in Washington, D.C. Miller returned to the AMEZ church by the early 1830s and was given charge of the First Wesleyan African Church (Big Wesley) in Philadelphia, where he remained until his death in 1845. In 1840 he was elected bishop of the AMEZ's New York conference, but he functioned more in the role of assistant superintendent of that body. William J. Walls, *The African Methodist Episcopal Zion Church: Reality of the Black Church* (Charlotte, N.C., 1974), 44, 47–48, 63, 68–82, 90–91, 121–24, 129, 148, 172–73, 183, 567; William Miller, *A Sermon on the Abolition of the Slave Trade . . .* (New York, N.Y., 1810); *Minutes and Proceedings of the Convention of the People of Colour . . .* (Philadelphia, Pa., 1831), 3 [1:0077]; *Lib*, 7 July 1832; *CA*, 21 October 1837, 27 July 1839 [3:0151].

6. Queen Victoria (1819–1901) was the constitutional monarch of Britain and the British Empire from 1837 until her death. Together with her husband, Prince Albert, she symbolized domestic virtue to millions of Britons. Victoria and Albert produced nine children.

7. Henry James Grasett (1808–1882), the curate of St. James Anglican Church in Toronto, frequently addressed local Emancipation Day celebrations. Although reared in Quebec, Lower Canada, the controversial Cambridge-educated divine served the Toronto congregation from 1835 until his death. Grasett was considered the leading low-church cleric in the Toronto diocese, and he spearheaded opposition to high-church ritualism as leader of the Evangelical Association during the 1870s. He actively supported provincial tract and bible societies and pursued various educational reform causes. *DCB*, 11:367–69; *Toronto City Directory*, 1837; Hill, *Freedom-Seekers*, 182.

8. The original Toronto City Hall was built in 1831 at Front and Jarvis streets, a block north of the wharf on a site known as the Farmers' Market. The two-story, rectangular, brick structure functioned in its original capacity until 1899. *St. Lawrence Hall* (Toronto, Ontario, 1969), 18–24, 142; Bruce West, *Toronto* (Toronto, Ontario, 1967), 190–91.

9. The Commercial Hotel on Front Street, which was owned by John Raper, served visitors to Toronto during the 1830s and 1840s. *Toronto City Directory*, 1843–44.

10. Jones refers to John Powell (1809–1881), the Conservative mayor of Toronto from 1838 to 1840. Powell began the practice of law in Toronto in 1835 and was

first elected to the city council in 1837. After three undistinguished terms as mayor, he became a judge and later served as a registrar. *Mayors of Toronto*, 1 vol. to date (Erin, Ontario, 1982–), 28–30.

11. Jones refers to the several volunteer companies of black troops collectively named the Coloured Corps, which were formed during and shortly after the Canadian Rebellion of 1837 to defend the Niagara and Detroit frontiers. With one or two exceptions, these troops were commanded by white officers. In 1840 the companies were put to work clearing roads throughout Upper Canada. Three years later, following incidents between black troops and white civilians in several cities, they were transferred to the Welland Canal to maintain order between feuding factions of Irish laborers. The last of the Coloured Corps disbanded in June 1850. Winks, *Blacks in Canada*, 151–52.

12. Northern white prejudice effectively confined most free black workers to menial occupations and deprived their children of manual training even though no laws specifically kept blacks from practicing skilled trades. White customers refused to patronize black craftsmen, and white mechanics, fearing competition and the loss of status, refused to work with their black counterparts or to accept black apprentices. The 1831 black national convention proposed the establishment of a manual labor college at New Haven, Connecticut, but the town's residents roundly condemned the project and prevented its establishment. The only advanced school for blacks established on the manual labor principle in the United States during the 1830s was Gerrit Smith's short-lived Peterboro, New York, institution. In 1835, after one year of operation, the school had an enrollment of nine students. Leon F. Litwack, *North of Slavery: The Negro in the Free States, 1790–1860* (Chicago, Ill., 1961), 155–62, 172; Jane H. Pease and William H. Pease, *They Who Would Be Free: Blacks' Search for Freedom, 1830–1861* (New York, N.Y., 1974), 136, 138.

13. Jehu Jones, Jr., was the son of free black hotelkeepers Jehu and Abigail Jones of Charleston, South Carolina, and the brother of Edward Jones, a noted missionary to Sierra Leone. After spending most of his youth in Charleston, Jones moved with part of his family to New York City during the mid-1820s. He studied theology for a time and in October 1832 was ordained by the New York Ministerium of the Lutheran church, becoming the first black Lutheran pastor in the United States. Intending to do missionary work in Liberia, Jones returned to Charleston to join an expedition that was about to sail; when he arrived, authorities jailed him for violating a South Carolina law which forbade free blacks from reentering the state. He was later freed on the condition that he would not return. Heading back north, Jones met with officials of the American Colonization Society but was unable to persuade them to sponsor him for Liberian mission work. He then determined to obtain a Lutheran pastorate in the free states. Failing that, he eventually settled in Philadelphia, hoping to found a black Lutheran congregation in the city. Opposition from local white clergymen forced him in 1834 to settle for a four-month appointment from the Pennsylvania Synod to do itinerant preaching in the Philadelphia black community. Widening the scope of his labors, he eventually established small black congregations in Philadelphia, Gettysburg, and Chambersburg, Pennsylvania. Yet he directed most of his attention to St. Paul's Lutheran Church, his Philadelphia charge. Persistent financial problems and

northern racial prejudice prompted Jones to leave for Toronto, Upper Canada, in July 1839. He returned to Philadelphia by 1842 and supported himself for the remainder of the decade through the shoemaking trade. He attempted to reenter the ministry, and in 1849 he requested support from the New York Ministerium—a request that was hastily denied. Within two years, Jones returned to Philadelphia to do missionary work. *DANB*, 364; Strange, "The Trials of Jehu Jones," 52–55; *Philadelphia City Directory*, 1842, 1845–46, 1848–49, 1851.

7.
Nelson Hackett to Lord Sydenham
18 September 1841

During the 1830s and 1840s, American requests for the extradition of fugitive slaves continually tested Canada's status as a sanctuary for black Americans. Yet few incidents had the impact of the Nelson Hackett case. Hackett, the slave of Alfred Wallace, escaped from Washington County, Arkansas, in mid-July 1841. He eventually reached Chatham, Canada West. But on 7 September, Wallace located the fugitive in the Chatham black community and whipped and clubbed him until he submitted to arrest. Magistrates in Chatham remanded Hackett to the Sandwich jail, while Wallace began the process of extraditing him back to the United States. On 8 September, Hackett petitioned Lord Sydenham, the governor-general of the province, asking that the extradition request be refused. One hundred seventy-eight Hamilton blacks also petitioned Sir Allan McNab, a Conservative party leader, to oppose Hackett's extradition. Canadian officials seemed ready to comply. But Wallace returned South, initiated criminal charges against Hackett for theft, and persuaded the governor to formally request Hackett's extradition. In late December, the Provincial Executive Council reviewed the evidence and recommended that the application for extradition be approved based on the charge that Hackett had stolen property while escaping. Although black Canadians protested the decision, Hackett was surrendered to Arkansas authorities and returned to the United States in early 1842. The Hackett case outraged Anglo-American abolitionists, who worked hard to insure that the extradition process returned no additional fugitives to slavery. Further requests were made, but none were granted. Winks, *Blacks in Canada*, 168–74; Roman J. Zorn, "An Arkansas Fugitive Slave Incident and Its International Repercussions," *AHQ* 16:140–49 (Summer 1957); *PAC*, 7 October 1841 [4:0475].

Sandwich Gaol, [Canada West]
18 September 1841

To the Right Honourable Lord *Sydenham*, Governor-General of the Province of *British North America*,[1] &c. &c. &c.

The Petition of *Nelson Hackett*,[2] a Man of Colour, now confined in the Gaol of the Western District; Humbly showeth,

THAT your petitioner, who was a slave in Arkansas, in the United States of America, made his escape from that place to the province of Canada, where he had learned that the humanity of the British law made him a free man as soon as he touched the shores of the country; that after his arrival at Chatham, the person to whom he had belonged arrived at that place, and for the purpose of being enabled to take your petitioner back to Arkansas with him,[3] charged your petitioner with having stolen goods in your petitioner's possession, when, in fact and truth, the property belonged to your petitioner. When your petitioner was taken before the magistrates to be examined, from the blows that had the night before been inflicted on his head, he was in such a state as to be unconscious of what he said, he having been severely beaten over the head with the butt of a whip and a large stick. That to produce a feeling against your petitioner, his master charged him with having committed a rape, but did not attempt to make any proof thereof. Wherefore he prays your Excellency will be pleased to consider his case, and not authorize your petitioner to be given up, as should he be taken back to Arkansas, he will be tortured in a manner that to hang him at once would be mercy. Hoping that your Excellency will take pity on him, and not accede to the demands of his master without the most clear evidence of his guilt, which he is well assured can only be obtained by false swearing. And in duty bound will ever pray,

(signed)
his
Nelson X *Hackett*
mark

Canadian *Parliamentary Papers*, 2 (1842), Appendix S, n.p.

1. Charles Poulett Thomson, Lord Sydenham (1799–1841), the son of an English merchant, sat in Parliament from 1826 to 1839. He succeeded Lord Durham as governor-general of Canada in 1839 and was responsible for carrying out Durham's recommendations for Canadian union and responsible government. He received his peerage in 1840. *MDCB*, 812.

2. Nelson Hackett (ca. 1810–?) was purchased in June 1840 by Alfred Wallace, a Washington County, Arkansas, merchant and land speculator. Considered "a Negro dandy," Hackett, who performed the duties of valet and butler for Wallace, was handsome, well dressed, and of prepossessing manner. During Wallace's absence in July 1841, Hackett ran away, taking with him his master's beaver overcoat, gold watch, saddle, and best horse. Traveling only at night, he headed for Canada West, crossing over into the province at Detroit in September. Hackett settled in the black community at Chatham, but within a week of his arrival, Wallace had tracked him there. Wallace assaulted Hackett, recovered the stolen property, and had the fugitive arrested. The Chatham magistrates then remanded Hackett to Sandwich jail, and the Windsor authorities detained him there pending the next term of court. Meanwhile, Wallace and George Grigg, a Washington County lawman, returned to Arkansas, where on 26 November they persuaded the Washington County grand jury to indict Hackett for grand larceny. Four days later, Arkansas Governor Archibald Yell formally requested that Canadian authorities return the slave for trial in state court. In January 1842, upon the recommendation of the Provincial Executive Council, Canadian Governor-General Sir

Charles Bagot, amid vehement protests by Canadian blacks, ordered that Hackett be surrendered to Arkansas authorities. The authorities secretly ferried Hackett across to Detroit on 8 February, then transported him south. He escaped again in northern Illinois, only to be recaptured in late May and restored to Alfred Wallace a few weeks later. This case, which demonstrated that slave catchers could legally return slaves from Canada, outraged Anglo-American abolitionists. Zorn, "Arkansas Fugitive Slave Incident," 140–44.

3. From the time of the first formal American request for the extradition of a fugitive slave from Canada (1829), the official Canadian response was guided by a single legal premise: a fugitive could be returned only for an offense that would have made him liable to arrest in Canada. Because slavery was not legal in Canada, self-theft was not an offense for which a fugitive slave could be extradited. Over the next three decades, this guiding principle was formalized by Canadian legislation and legal decisions and by Article X of the Webster-Ashburton Treaty (1843) between Britain and the United States. Winks, *Blacks in Canada*, 168–74.

8.
Peter Gallego to Thomas Rolph
1 November 1841

Black abolitionists enjoyed full citizenship rights in Canada, but they came to understand that their new homeland was not free of racial prejudice. This was made clear to Peter Gallego, a Toronto black, during an 1841 tour of Canada West. Early in the year, delegates to a black convention asked him to visit Jamaica as their representative and to report on the possibility of black resettlement there. Gallego returned home an advocate of immigration to Jamaica. During July he promoted the scheme in the major towns of Canada West, although he repeatedly suffered mistreatment because of his race. Gallego reported on the tour, and on the discrimination he encountered, in a 1 November 1841 letter to Thomas Rolph, a white friend and a supporter of black settlement in the Caribbean. Gallego endured similar treatment on subsequent tours. Like other Canadian blacks, Gallego considered immigration to the Caribbean an appropriate alternative to North American racism. John K. A. Farrell, "Schemes for the Transplanting of Refugee American Negroes from Upper Canada in the 1840s," *OntH* 52:246 (1960); *CJ*, 1 June 1844.

Toronto, [Canada West]
1st November, 1841

TO DR. THOMAS ROLPH[1]
GOVERNMENT EMIGRATION AGENT FOR CANADA
DEAR SIR:

We owe it to your instrumentality, that, in this country, the imperial Government extends to us the protection of political refugees, and, in no small degree, that all the rights and privileges of naturalisation have recently been placed within the reach of not a few of us.[2] The first general petition ever drawn up on this subject in behalf of the coloured population was the fruit of your labours;[3] and, believing that you have not forsaken the cause of humanity, we would bring under consideration a series of facts, of daily occurrence, and at war with every feeling which our recognition as British subjects and as men has quickened in our breasts. Insult, outrage, and proscription, oppose themselves to us in all the channels of public circulation and entertainment. The steam-boat, the stage-coach, and the inn, deny to us the freedom of British subjects, and dedicate themselves as the sanctuaries of American prejudice. The power of the slave-driver is undisputed, and the appearance of a black man becomes the signal for the perpetration of atrocities, only equalled by those which are committed in the southern states of the neighbouring Republic.

But I will proceed to give the facts, by stating in the first place, the reason why they have of late come so repeatedly under my observation. You are aware that I hold the appointment from the Government of the island of Jamaica, as agent of emigration, to procure the coloured people of Canada to emigrate to that island, a circumstance which places me under the necessity of travelling about in almost every direction in the province. I had no sooner entered upon my tour, than, on leaving Toronto about the 13th of July last, in the steam-boat *Britannia*,[4] for Hamilton, on sitting down to dinner, one of the servants said, that he was ordered by the Captain to ask me to leave the table. I refused to comply with so polite a request, and informed him, that I would not move but upon violence being used against me; to which the servant good-naturedly replied, that no violence would be used, and left me without further interruption to finish my dinner.

From Hamilton I intended to have proceeded in the stage to Brantford; but it would seem that the Americans have entered into a compact to lose no opportunity of showing off that they are the "sovereign people" even in Canada, as may be seen by the toleration of their insults and outrages to the coloured people as often as we cross the lines, by placing ourselves in their stage-coaches, their inns, and their other territories—the steamboats under their influence. Not willing to believe but that I am under the jurisdiction of the British Government any where in Canada—having previously complied with the necessary rules, paying my fare to Davis, the stage proprietor at Hamilton, and being booked for Brantford, I was quietly awaiting the hour of departure. The hour arrived, when Davis, taking me aside into the passage, informed me that several of the passengers had clubbed together and refused to ride with me in the stage, and that in consequence of this, and some *ex post facto* regulation he had made on the occasion, I must either take the outside seat or not go at all. I chose the latter alternative, and came up to Ancaster on foot as you very well know, from whence, after enjoying the hospitality of Dr. Cragie,[5] I continued on to Brantford, walking the whole distance, with the exception of five or six miles, and at the time suffering severely from bodily weakness. I have understood since, that Davis treated me in this brutal manner at the instigation of Hewitt, the innkeeper at London, or some other Yankee as great a savage as himself.[6]

It was between seven and eight o'clock before we got into London. We were driven up to the Mansion-house;[7] I was the only one of the party that put up there on this occasion. After learning from the bar-keeper that I could be accommodated in the house, I walked out, and, during my absence, I met my friend Mr. Luis, a coloured man, who returned with me, and we supped together in the public dining-room. From the manner in which I was then treated, I felt no reason to anticipate any insult or annoyance as long as I might choose to remain. At the ring of the bell for breakfast, on the following morning, I went in and took my seat, and, having been helped by Mr. Andrew Caldwell, the person who sat at the head of the table, I was proceeding very comfortably with my meal, when the bar-keeper came in and observed to me, that my breakfast was not yet ready; but, telling him he need not trouble himself, as I was very well satisfied, he withdrew without further remark. In about ten minutes afterwards, a ruffianly, blustering-looking fellow entered the room, and abruptly said that he wished to speak to me. I remarked, that I would speak to him as soon as I had finished my breakfast. He insisted upon speaking to me immediately, and I returned him the same answer as before; whereupon he immediately seized hold of my chair, pulled it from under me, and prostrated me on the floor. I got up and demanded why he treated me in this manner? To which he replied, that he did not allow "niggers" any such privilege in his house, and thrusting his hand into my collar, he began to push me out backwards, when, coming upon some boxes that lay in the passage, he tumbled me over them and brought me down upon my back, endeavouring to hold me by the neck in this position. I contrived to loosen his grasp, and recovered my feet again; by this time, he had arisen also, and I gave him a couple of blows with my fist, which both he and his physician, upon oath, stated to have broken his jaw bone. I was then seized by the bar-keeper and some of the boarders, and dragged out into the street.

To obtain redress for this abusive treatment, I called upon Mr. Lawrason, a magistrate,[8] to get out a warrant against Hewitt, the innkeeper. His Worship refused to grant me one, and remarked, that I had been properly enough treated; at the same delivering himself of the most violent denunciations against amalgamation,[9] and evidently justifying any outrage which might have arisen from apprehension of the least approach thereto.

This bugbear of the Americans is causing, in a British community, no less a departure from their characteristic good sense than from their correctness of feeling. At the natural mixture of the races, the Americans are nothing horrified; but that this should take place according to religion, and with the sanction of just and equitable laws, is shocking to their moral sense. But shall an amalgamation mania imported into Canada from the United States, prohibit Her Majesty's coloured subjects from the enjoyment of rights and privileges which are extended to them everywhere else under the sceptre of British rule? Shall an integral portion of the British people be subject to every possible indignity and outrageous treatment to gratify the Americans? Shall the public tast[e] of this truly promising country be modelled upon that of the Yankees? They themselves are anxious that the public should speak out upon this subject; for, looking upon the boon of responsibility as an approach to their own "glorious free constitution," they only ask in addition, that the degradation of the blacks be conceded to form the corner stone of our rising political edifice. Grant this, and the highest object of American ambition would then be attained; and they would content themselves for the present with having [virtually] succeeded in making such an achievement in Canada as they have actually consummated in Texas.[10]

Proceedings were instituted against me by Hewitt for an assault, and I was convicted by the magistrates, Messrs. Lawrason, Douglas, and Smith, and sentenced to pay a fine of five pounds, or be imprisoned for a month. The case was heard at the General Quarter Sessions of the Peace, of the London district. The evidence went to prove, as clearly as evidence could do [one or two words illegible] several assaults were committed upon my person before I made any resistance; and there can be no question in any [unprejudiced] mind, that the verdict of the jury which sustained the [one word illegible] conviction would have been quite different, had the defendant been of white rather than of black complexion. A few more decisions like that of the magistrates, Messrs. Lawrason, Smith and Douglas, thus confirmed, will establish a precedent [of] legal proceedings with respect to the coloured people, which, [as far] as the interests of humanity are concerned, will make it a matter of indifference whether Canada may not fall under the political, as well as the moral subjugation of the United States.

Not having the money at the time to pay the fine imposed, I was cast into jail, and remained from Thursday night, the 14th, until about eight o'clock on the following Saturday night, confined in one of the cells with two other persons convicted of theft; when Judge Allen of the District Court,[11] true to the feelings of a Briton, upon hearing of my condition, came forward and caused me to be released. The Judge sat as a spectator amongst the magistrates before whom I was tried at the Quarter Sessions, and was a witness to the gross injustice done me in the verdict of a jury.

American prejudice has arrived at such a pitch in this country, that we cannot but avail ourselves of every possible means for its suppression. Public sentiment in Great Britain, so jealous of the rights of the coloured people in the West Indies, will not tolerate their oppression in this country by the Americans. Stanley, to whom belongs the honour of carrying the Bill of Emancipation, is Colonial Secretary,[12] and surely it were but to give the finishing stroke to that glorious measure, to see that the principles of equal justice to the coloured population are not thwarted in their operation, any where on British soil. The philanthropists of England, solacing themselves with the idea, that, in Canada, the coloured man has found an inviolable asylum from the persecution of his relentless and unnatural enemies, will be disturbed from their repose on being informed, that here we are exposed to outrages and atrocities which they would not hesitate to go even beyond the bounds of the British empire to put an end to. And what must be the general indignation, when it shall be known in Great Britain and Ireland, that very recently, in the village of St. Catharine, a number of Americans, or other persons instigated by Americans, fell upon an unoffending black man, and murdered him in a most cruel manner, in consequence of some vague rumour respecting a case of amalgamation that was said to be in contemplation; and that, not stopping at this atrocity, a white person, having, under a deep sense of duty to God and his fellow-creatures, given evidence against one of the principals concerned, was murdered in a still more savage and fiendish manner. The details are horrible in the extreme, and it is surprising that the public press has observed so dead a silence upon this matter. Will nothing but the daggers of the Americans drawn across their own throats quicken their sensibilities? Will nothing convince this infatuated country that when the liberties of the coloured population shall have fallen a victim to American barbarity, a similar fate will overtake them? They render themselves easy in that artificial security afforded by the regular forces, every day diminishing from desertion, and are slow to persuade themselves that a more natural defence is to be found in the protection of their coloured population.[13] In the event of an invasion, it will be disaffected British subjects that will oppose the greatest difficulties to us; what other policy, then, does the natural interest of this country dictate—that interest which in an individual we should call self-interest, but that our coloured population should receive every protection and encouragement? Will Canada do nothing for herself, but leave it altogether to a far-removed mother-country, to devise such means as may, at the distance she is placed from us, occur to her as calculated to promote our advancement. If so, the Americans are to be excused for the contempt they entertain for our disgraceful puerility—excused for the wish to make us manly as themselves, by giving us constitutions like their own, founded on bad faith and deceptive principles. But I will not despair. There is much of pure British feeling yet alive in this community, undazzled by the false glory of the Americans, and which will burn with all its natural lustre, undimmed by the moral humidity which is exhaled on every side. Many names might be enumerated which will be held in no less universal admiration than other distinguished philanthropists and benefactors of the human race. Feeling that the subject of my correspondence will receive your fullest attention, I have the honour to be, &c.,

PETER GALLEGO[14]

Patriot (Toronto, Canada West), 22 August 1842.

1. Thomas Rolph (1800–1858) left England in 1833 and established a medical practice in Ancaster, Upper Canada. From 1839 to 1842, he promoted ill-fated

Canadian immigration schemes in the British Isles. In 1843 the governor of Trinidad appointed him an agent of an unsuccessful venture to bring Canadian blacks to that island. He later retired to Portsmouth, England. *MDCB*, 721; Winks, *Blacks in Canada*, 166n, 171.

2. Although the administrative procedures of Canadian naturalization varied throughout the nineteenth century, the law merely required an individual to demonstrate three years' residence in the British North American Provinces in order to obtain British citizenship. W. P. M. Kennedy, *The Constitution of Canada, 1534–1937*, 2d ed. (London, 1938), 261–62, 302, 317, 699–701.

3. Rolph apparently acted as an adviser to Peter Gallego and two other Canadian blacks who drafted a memorial to Queen Victoria seeking protection (particularly jury trials) for Canadian blacks charged with crimes committed while in American slavery. They presented the petition to the secretary of Lord Durham, the governor-general of the Canadas in 1838, but it was misplaced and never reached the Queen. In 1839 Rolph visited England and inquired about its fate. Despite persistent appeals to the Colonial Office, he received no satisfactory response, even though he brought the matter before the World's Anti-Slavery Convention in London during June 1840. Evidence suggests, however, that Rolph falsely informed Canadian blacks that the mission had been successful. Murray, "Canada and Anglo-American Anti-Slavery Movement," 38–39, 133–43.

4. The *Britannia* was one of seven 350-ton steamboats built in 1833 to service Lake Ontario ports. Middleton and Landon, *Province of Ontario*, 2:679–82.

5. William Craigie (1799–1863), a Scottish-born physician and educational reformer, was licensed by the Edinburgh Royal College of Surgeons. He settled in Ancaster, Upper Canada, in 1834, then moved to Hamilton in 1845. He was a prominent public figure in both cities, particularly in educational and scientific matters. *DCB*, 9:165.

6. Joseph Hewitt was a wealthy, American-born hotel and real estate owner in Canada West. He constructed the American Hotel in the village of Newmarket, near York (Toronto), during 1826; it soon became famous in the province as the chief host for circuses and other mid-century traveling entertainments. Hewitt operated an inn in London during the 1840s. Edwin C. Guillet, *Pioneer Inns and Taverns*, 5 vols. (Toronto, Ontario, 1956–62), 1:222; *PtT*, 22 August 1842.

7. The Mansion House, built in 1828 on Dundas Street, was London's principal hotel. By 1857 a new Mansion House was built on the corner of Richmond and Bathhurst streets. Guillet, *Pioneer Inns and Taverns*, 3:208, 210.

8. Lawrence Lawrason (1803–1882) was a merchant in London, Canada West, where he owned a retail-wholesale business and was involved in land and railroad development. A steadfast Conservative, Lawrason participated in local political and civic affairs. He became a justice of the peace in 1835 and later sat briefly in the Legislative Assembly (1844). *DCB*, 11:500–501.

9. Amalgamation referred to the social and the sexual mixing of the races. Racial theorists argued, and most whites believed, that integration would encourage sexual relations between blacks and whites, thus causing the degeneration of the "superior" white race.

10. Gallego warns white Canadians that, by accepting American racial values, they run the risk of allowing Canada to fall victim to American influence. He cites Texas as an example. During the 1820s, Anglo-Americans settled on Texas cotton

lands, initially with the encouragement of the newly independent Mexican government. By 1836, despite Mexican attempts to curb what had become an alarming migration, Anglo-Americans were a majority in Texas. In 1835 they began a war for independence, which ended in victory in April 1836. Growing cultural, economic, and political ties with the United States led to the annexation of Texas in 1845.

11. W. Henry Allen, an English-born attorney who had practiced in the West Indies, was appointed judge of the London district in the 1830s, but his limited knowledge of Canadian law and culture led to his dismissal within a few years. Campbell, *Pioneer Days in London*, 74.

12. Gallego refers to Edward George Stanley (1799–1869), who joined Robert Peel's administration in 1841 as colonial secretary and was responsible for overseeing compliance with the Emancipation Act of 1833. Stanley, the earl of Derby, was educated at Eton and Oxford. He entered the House of Commons in 1822 and served as chief secretary for Ireland under Lord Grey (1830–33). He presided over short-lived Conservative governments in 1852, 1858, and 1866. *DNB*, 18:941–48.

13. Gallego refers to the tendency of Canadians to look to Britain for military protection against the United States. After the War of 1812, Canadian communities became dependent upon sizable garrisons of British regulars for their defense. By 1841 Canadian fears of an American invasion were heightened by American animosity toward the British, American support for Canadian rebels, rampant American expansionism, and the indefensibility of the U.S.-Canadian border. Gallego suggests that black Canadians would be particularly loyal to their adopted country in case of such an attack. J. M. S. Careless, *The Union of the Canadas: The Growth of Canadian Institutions, 1841–1857* (Toronto, Canada, 1957), 17–18.

14. Peter Gallego (1811–?), an early Toronto black abolitionist and emigrationist, is described as "carefully educated" and "thoroughly black." A protege of local Anglican bishop John Strachan, Gallego studied theology under Strachan and later enrolled at Upper Canada College and the University of Toronto. By 1837 Gallego had become involved in local antislavery activities as a prominent member of the Upper Canada Anti-Slavery Society. Gallego's concern for the local black community led him in 1839 to join Edward L. de St. Remy in planning publication of the *British American Journal of Liberty*, a Toronto paper aimed at Upper Canadian blacks and devoted to promoting black rights; it is not known if the paper was ever published. In 1840 he completed a census of the Toronto black community. One year later, as the agent of a black convention at Ancaster, Canada West, Gallego visited Jamaica to investigate and report on the advantages of emigration to the island. During the next three years, he made several additional voyages to Jamaica; he also crisscrossed Canada West, holding meetings to encourage black immigration to Jamaica. Simultaneously Gallego developed strong ties with Charles B. Ray and the New York City black community and often spoke at black anticolonization meetings there and in western New York State. When Gallego returned to Canada West in 1844, he published a promotional pamphlet encouraging black Canadians to settle in Jamaica. Although the pamphlet generated little interest, he remained a strong supporter of Jamaican immigration as late as the mid-1850s. Gallego's continuing involvement in emigration resulted

from Canadian racism. Perhaps more clearly than any other incident, his mistreatment by whites symbolized the worst of race relations in Canada West. On a well-publicized trip across the province in 1841, Gallego was refused a seat on a Hamilton-Brantford stage and denied service in a London stagehouse restaurant because he was black. In the latter instance, he was dragged out of the establishment, attacked for not knowing his place, refused legal aid, and then himself prosecuted for the disturbance. On another trip, despite purchasing a first-class ticket on a Toronto-Kingston steamer, he was physically assaulted by the captain for attempting to eat with white passengers. He complained to the Kingston courts, and the captain was fined £ 20. Gallego's opposition to separate schools and his continuing criticism of Hiram Wilson's Canada Mission also brought him verbal attacks even from those more sympathetic to the plight of his race. By 1856 he had apparently abandoned his promotion of emigration and settled in Chatham, Canada West. Simpson, "Negroes in Ontario to 1870," 294, 434–39, 883; *CJ*, 1 June 1844; Winks, *Blacks in Canada*, 166, 171; *TC*, 15 November 1837; *CA*, 22 June 1839, 20 March, 3 July 1841 [3:0125–26, 4:0087, 0090]; Massachusetts Anti-Slavery Society, *Tenth Annual Report* ([Boston], 1842), 21–22, Anti-slavery Pamphlets, MB [4:0352]; *PFW*, 22 September 1855 [9:0837]; *PtL*, 22 August 1842 [4:0465]; Samuel Ringgold Ward, *Autobiography of a Fugitive Negro* (London, 1855; reprint, New York, N.Y., 1968), 146; Pease and Pease, *Black Utopia*, 12, 63.

9.
Speech by Josiah Jones
Delivered at the Militia Parade Grounds, Chatham, Canada West 4 August 1842

Blacks in the Canadian provinces made 1 August a day of celebration to commemorate the Emancipation Act of 1833 that abolished slavery throughout most of the British Empire. By the early 1840s, it had become an annual event in most black settlements and in towns and cities with a sizable black population. Traditional Emancipation Day activities included parades, church services, dances, musical entertainment, banquets, teas, and speeches praising Britain for ending slavery and criticizing the United States for continuing the institution. The 1842 celebration in Chatham began at dawn, when twenty-one rounds were fired from the cannon at the militia parade grounds, and ran through the day. The evening's entertainment included a meal with "about sixty covers" and "many speeches." Josiah Jones, a local black farmer and militia member born in Tennessee in 1816, gave a well-publicized address. The celebration ended with a dance at the officer's building on the grounds. *CG*, 17 January 1838; *E*, 15 March 1838 [2:0432]; *CJ*, 6 August 1842; *WH*, 11 August 1842 [4:0461]; *Lib*, 23 August 1861 [5:0626]; Census of Canada, 1851.

Dear Beloved Brethren:

I am happy to inform the public, that I am very much gratified to see so many of our friends assembled together, to celebrate this great, and glorious day of liberty on which the shackles of slavery fell from so many of our Brethren. I am sorry that I am not better qualified to deliver a long speech, as we wish to show the public the respect we have towards our people, and also the great respect that we have for the British Constitution. Dear fellow Citizens and friends we find that when our foreign friends were oppressed and in a most deplorable situation, the British Government emptied their Coffers of Twenty millions of Pounds, of her precious gold and silver, to redeem them from their distressed condition.

Can we then forget such a friend? No! no! as long as we shall exist, our gratitude to her shall be manifested on every suitable occasion. Dear fellow men and Brethren, in the southern states, our friends are not asleep, they are known by all there to be true British subjects and all of the most loyal kind.

We also know what we are called by the southerners; they call us the tigers, and well might they so denominate us; but why dare that ferocious animal remain so harmless. I answer, because he is fettered and confined within a cage. Oh! that John Bull,[1] would roar in the East, and that the thunder of his voice might be heard by the tigers of the south, for then would they burst in sunder their prison house, and sweep with the besom of destruction, the enemies of liberty and of humanity.

Chatham Journal (Canada West), 6 August 1842.

1. John Bull was a standard term or symbol for Britain.

10. "The Coloured People of Hamilton" to Charles T. Metcalfe 15 October 1843

Segregated schools were common in Canada West and the Maritime Provinces. In Hamilton, Canada West, black children were excluded from public education during the early 1840s. Their fugitive slave parents sought redress from the city's board of police, which acted as the public school trustees. When that appeal brought no satisfaction, they petitioned Sir Charles T. Metcalfe, the governor-general of the Canadas, to rectify the matter. The 15 October 1843 petition, which was written by an anonymous local black, expressed deep disappointment at the treatment blacks received in the Canadian haven. When Rev. Robert Murray of the governor-general's office received the petition, he demanded an explanation from Hamilton's board of police. The board justified excluding blacks from the common schools on the basis of "strong prejudice" among local whites; but under pressure from Murray, the board reversed its decision and allowed black children into the schools. Winks, *Blacks in Canada*, 367; Robert Murray to George Tiffany, 19 October 1843, George Tiffany to Robert Murray, 9 November 1843, Egerton Ryerson Papers, CaOTAr.

Hamilton, [Canada West]
October 15th, 1843

Dear Sir/[1]

We the people of colour in the Town of Hamilton have a right to inform your Excellency of the treatment that we have to undergo. We have paid the taxes and we are denied of the public schools, and we have applied to the Board of the Police and there is no steps taken to change this manner of treatment, and this kind of treatment is not in the United States, for the children of colour go to the Public Schools together with the white children, more especially in Philadelphia,[2] and I thought that there was not a man to be known by his colour under the British flag, and we left the United States because we were in hopes that prejudice was not in this land, and I came to live under your Government if my God would be my helper and to be true to the Government. I am sorry to annoy you by allowing this thing, but we are grieved much, we are imposed on much, and if it please your Excellency to attend to this grievance, if you please Sir. I have left property in the United States and I have bought property in Canada, and all I want is Justice and I will be satisfied. We are called nigger when we go out in the street, and sometimes brick bats is sent after us as we pass in the street. We are not all absconders[.] Now we brought money into this Province and we hope never to leave it, for we hope to enjoy our rights in this Province, and may my God smile upon your public life and guide you into all truth, which is my prayer and God bless the Queen and Royal Family.

The Coloured People of Hamilton

Egerton Ryerson Papers, Ontario Provincial Archives, Toronto, Ontario, Canada. Published by permission.

1. Sir Charles T. Metcalfe (1785–1846) was born in Calcutta, India, and educated at Eton. He entered the Indian civil service in 1801 and served as provisional governor-general of India and as governor of Jamaica before succeeding Charles Bagot as governor-general of Canada in March 1843. He became a baron in 1845. *DNB*, 13:303–6.

2. Before the Civil War, most northern black children were excluded, either by custom or law, from attending school with their white peers. In 1834 Pennsylvania legislated a general system of public education that technically allowed black children to attend the schools of their choice, but segregation continued, particularly in the Philadelphia schools to which the author refers. An 1881 Pennsylvania law desegregated the common school system, but even after an 1882 court case upheld the intent of the legislation, local school boards continued to evade integration. Litwack, *North of Slavery*, 114–16; Harry C. Silcox, "Delay and Neglect: Negro Public Education in Antebellum Philadelphia, 1800–1860," *PMHB* 97:444–64 (October 1973); Edward J. Price, "School Segregation in Nineteenth Century Pennsylvania," *PH* 43:121–37 (April 1976).

11. Circular by Henry Gouins
22 December 1843

Slaveholders and their agents devised a variety of methods to capture fugitive slaves and return them to bondage. They attempted to lure fugitives back from the British North American Provinces with promises of money or employment, and they occasionally crossed the border to kidnap refugees. Black Canadians understood the need to remain alert to such practices. They formed vigilance committees to prevent kidnappings and published notices of suspicious individuals or schemes; the *Provincial Freeman* printed a general warning in each issue. At times, black Canadians even had to be wary of each other. In November 1843, a black man named George Wilson enticed Henry Gouins, a Chatham fugitive, to return to Ohio where Gouins was met and arrested by a slave catcher. Two local whites helped secure Gouins's freedom, and he immediately returned to Canada West and published a warning to other fugitives in the *Chatham Journal*. Hill, *Freedom-Seekers*, 39–43.

Dec[ember] 22, 1843

To the Colored People residing in the Province of Canada

MY FRIENDS AND COUNTRYMEN:

ALLOW me to avail myself of this opportunity of laying before you the situation, under the circumstances which I was placed. Some time las[t] month I was decoyed by one George Wilson, a man of color, to go into the State of Ohio, under pretence of his rendering me a service, but on my arrival in Perrysburg, Ohio, according to appointment, instead of meeting with the proffered services gratuitously promised by the deceiver, I was met by the Agent of a Slave Holder, and was arrested as a runaway slave; but through the kind interference of two professional gentlemen of that place, I was after a tedious investigation of the charge, once more set at liberty, on a promise on my part to see them fairly remunerated for their trouble.

In making this brief statement to my colored friends, I have two objects in view.

The first is to caution you against the impropriety of placing too much confidence in any person, particularly those of color, who can thus be guilty of such nefarious conduct to his own people, on a mere superficial acquaintance.

And secondly, as many of you whom I am now addressing, have by the permission of a kind Providence been allowed to make your escape from slavery and bondage, and through the wise and liberal policy of the British Government been allowed a place of refuge; I now with confidence appeal to your sympathy, and humbly solicit of you such assistance as you in your different circumstances can spare, in order to enable me honorably and honestly to redeem my promise to those, my benefactors, thereby showing to the world, that though we once were slaves, that now we are free we will be honest.

HENRY GOUINS[1]

Chatham Journal (Canada West), 23 December 1843.

1. Henry Gouins (1816–?) was a slave on plantations in Virginia, North Carolina, Tennessee, Alabama, and Mississippi. Gouins escaped from Alabama about 1839 using forged freedom papers. Although he was stopped twice and questioned about his papers, he reached Upper Canada, where he settled near Chatham and married Martha A. Bentley, also a fugitive slave; they produced three children. Gouins became a member of a local Baptist congregation. At the time of the 1851 census enumeration, he worked as a seaman, evidently in the Great Lakes maritime trade. In 1852 Gouins was a Chatham real estate agent, selling farmland near Buxton. By 1855 he was residing in Galt, Canada West, a settlement with about forty blacks. At that time, Gouins indicated he was writing a narrative of his life, which he intended to publish, but no evidence exists suggesting the project was ever completed. Census of Canada, 1851; Drew, *North-Side View of Slavery*, 138–43; *VF*, 16 December 1852.

12.
Speech by Lewis Richardson
Delivered at Union Chapel, Amherstburg, Canada West
13 March 1846

Famous fugitive slaves—Frederick Douglass, Samuel Ringgold Ward, Jermain W. Loguen, and others—thrilled antislavery audiences in Canada West. But less well-known fugitives, such as Lewis Richardson, the escaped slave of Senator Henry Clay, also attracted sizable crowds. On the evening of 13 March 1846, a large interracial audience pressed into Union Chapel in Amherstburg to hear Richardson speak about his slave experiences. Levi Foster presided over the gathering. After black abolitionist Henry Bibb explained the object of the meeting, Richardson rose and addressed his anxious listeners, detailing the conditions of slave life at Ashland, Clay's Kentucky plantation. When Richardson finished, Henry Bibb sang an antislavery song, "The Fugitive's Triumph," then made a brief speech welcoming Richardson to Canadian soil. I. C. Pemberton, "The Anti-Slavery Society of Canada" (M.A. thesis, University of Toronto, 1973), 39; *SL*, 30 March 1846; *ASB*, 24 April 1846 [5:0196].

Dear Brethren, I am truly happy to meet with you on British soil (cheers), where I am not known by the color of my skin, but where the Government knows me as a man. But I am free from American slavery, after wearing the galling chains on my limbs 53 years 9 of which it has been my unhappy lot to be the slave of Henry Clay.[1] It has been said by some, that Clay's slaves had rather live with him than be free,[2] but I had rather this day, have a millstone tied to my neck, and be sunk to the bottom of Detroit river, than to go back to Ashland and be his slave for life. As late as Dec. 1845, H. Clay had me stripped and tied up, and one hundred and fifty lashes given me on my naked back: the crime for which I was so abused was, I failed to return home on a visit to see my wife, on Monday morning, before 5 o'clock. My wife was living on another place, 3 miles from Ashland. During the 9 years living with Mr. Clay, he has not given me a hat nor cap to wear, nor a stitch of bed clothes, except one small coarse blanket. Yet he has said publicly his slaves were "fat and slick!" But I say if they are, it is not because they are so well used by him. They have nothing but coarse bread and meat to eat, and not enough of that. They are allowanced every week. For each field hand is allowed one peck of coarse corn meal and meat in proportion, and no vegetables of any kind. Such is the treatment that Henry Clay's slaves receive from him. I can truly say that I have only one thing to lament over, and that is my bereft wife who is yet in bondage.[3] If I only had her with me I should be happy. Yet think not that I am unhappy. Think not that I regret the choice that I have made. I counted the cost before I started. Before I took leave of my wife, she wept over me, and dressed the wounds on my back caused by the lash. I then gave her the parting hand, and started for Canada. I expected to be pursued as a felon, as I had been before, and to be hunted as a fox from mountain to cave. I well knew if I continued much longer with Clay, that I should be killed by such floggings and abuse by his cruel overseer in my old age. I wanted to be free before I died—and if I should be caught on the way to Canada and taken back, it could but be death, and I might as well die with the colic as the fever. With these considerations I started for Canada.

Such usage as this caused me to flee from under the American eagle, and take shelter under the British crown. (Cheers.) Thanks be to Heaven that I have got here at last: on yonder side of Detroit river, I was recognized as property; but on this side I am on free soil. Hail, Brittania! Shame, America! (Cheers.) A Republican despotism, holding three millions of our fellow men in slavery. Oh what a contrast between slavery and liberty! Here I stand erect, without a chain upon my limbs. (Cheers.) Redeemed, emancipated, by the generosity of Great Britain. (Cheers.) I now feel as independent as ever Henry Clay felt when he was running for the White House. In fact I feel better. He has been defeated four or five times, and I but once. But he was running for slavery, and I for liberty. I think I have beat him out of sight. Thanks be to God that I am elected to Canada, and if I don't live but one night, I am determined to die on free soil. Let my days be few or many, let me die sooner or later, my grave shall be made in free soil.

Signal of Liberty (Ann Arbor, Mich.), 30 March 1846.

1. Henry Clay (1777–1852) was born in Virginia but settled in Kentucky, where he became a wealthy, slaveholding landowner. Clay was in the forefront of American politics for thirty years. He served in the Kentucky legislature, the U.S. House of Representatives, and the U.S. Senate; he made two unsuccessful efforts for the presidency. His most enduring contribution to American political life was his negotiation of two Union-preserving compromises (1820, 1850) between proslavery politicians and their adversaries. *DAB*, 2(2):173–79.

2. Clay's white neighbors in Fayette County, Kentucky, insisted that he was an indulgent master, who manumitted some of his slaves, but blacks familiar with Ashland (Clay's plantation) provided contrary evidence. There were complaints of frequent floggings and inadequate food. One slave, whose wife belonged to Clay, asserted that Clay left the management of slaves to abusive overseers. The slave providing the above testimony, who was himself branded with the letters HC, indicated that Clay and an overseer flogged one slave so severely that he committed suicide. In 1840 a former Ashland overseer certified to a New York abolitionist that Clay regularly used the whip in administering discipline on the farm. Ash-

land also had a high number of runaways, admittedly an inexact gauge of Clay's harsh treatment. *NASS*, 7 May, 11 June 1846; Clement Eaton, *Henry Clay and the Art of American Politics* (Boston, Mass., 1957), 76.

3. When Lewis Richardson escaped from Henry Clay's plantation in December 1845, he left behind a slave wife in Lexington, Kentucky, and at least one child, a daughter, who was the property of Fayette County farmer E. A. Dudley. *SL*, 20 June 1846.

13.
Josiah Henson to George E. Ellis
16 March 1846

Fugitive slave Josiah Henson and white missionary Hiram Wilson organized and directed the British-American Institute, one of the more ambitious antebellum black educational ventures. Established in 1842 as an integrated manual labor school, the institute, located near Dresden, was so successful that the Dawn settlement developed around it. Henson was responsible for fund raising for Dawn. His letter to Boston Unitarian George E. Ellis describes his labors in Canada West. In typical fashion, Henson's appeal tactfully balanced talk of Dawn's promise with word of the settlement's urgent and immediate need for financial assistance. Pease and Pease, *Black Utopia*, 63–66; Winks, *Blacks in Canada*, 178–81.

Dawn, [Canada West]
March 16th [18]46

Dear Sir[1]

Having opportunity I readly embrace it to write you a few lines trusting that they may reach you finding you in good health and enjoying all the other necessary blessings of this life. Please pardon me for delaying to write so long; the only apology that I have to offer is simply this; I have en[d]ered your name with your kind Donation to the Committee of B.A. Institute;[2] consequently I supposed that they would have written before this late period.

Your kind treatment and benevolent act to me while at Boston can never be forgotten as long as my heart continues to beat & my pulse fails not to throb.

I spent most of the last summer, fall and winter visiting the schools and itinerating through out the whole Province;[3] for the purpose of hearing all the particulars relative the poor colored people who have been forced from their native home to hunt an Asylum in a strange land and among stra[n]g[ers] whose lots have been casted here with me: some of them are making as great proficiency as could be expected all things considered. Relative to the schools I will here remark that the scholars are doing very well.

P.S. Please accept of my most humble, earnest [&] sincere thanks for your kindness to me when at B. which your unmerited favor can never be forgotten.

P.S. I stated above that some of the people in Canada were doing very well[.] Permit me to say that others are entirely dependent upon the liberality of Gods people who truly feel for the oppressed.

Our Institution is in a prosperous condition and bids f[a]re to do well. The[y] have built the house which was in contemplation when I saw you last[.][4] It is not as large as we expected in consequence of our means being some what limited and the Committee thought that it would not be wisdom to go byond our ability.

We have about one hundred Students here this winter including the Juvenile Department[.] They are doing very well[.] Some have made rap[e]d progress.

We have a grist and Saw Mill intemplation which we believe will amply sustain the Institute if we can only get the means to carry it into effect.

I expect to visit Boston on or before the first of May next for the purpose of laying the project before my Unitarian friends;[5] whom the Lord has blessed with both means and hearts to give; & if I can only find forty good Christians there like yourselves who will give me one hundred dollars each I shall verily be able to carry out my scheme.

I will be better prepared to give you all the particulars relative to the sa[m]e when I see you face to face.

Please lay the project before some of your kind friends. Most Respectfully Yours,

Josiah Henson[6]

P.S. I have asked this favour from our Unitarian friends aside from anybody else and expect to be there at the time proposed to converse with you on the subject and if Blessed with Your concurrence I know it will be done.

J. H.

George E. Ellis Papers, Massachusetts Historical Society, Boston, Massachusetts. Published by permission.

1. George Edward Ellis (1814–1894), a Boston abolitionist, was pastor of the Harvard Unitarian Church in Charleston, Massachusetts. He edited the *Christian Record* (1842–45) and *Christian Examiner* (1849–55). Ellis lectured at the Harvard Divinity School from 1857 to 1863 and penned numerous biographical sketches and essays. Merrill and Ruchames, *Letters of William Lloyd Garrison*, 4:655–56n.

2. The Dawn settlement developed around the British-American Institute, a black manual labor school founded near Dresden, Canada West, in December 1842. Josiah Henson, together with Hiram Wilson of the American Missionary Association, organized the school; Quaker philanthropist James Canning Fuller raised the necessary funds in Britain. Located on three hundred acres, it provided academic and vocational training to black children and adults who otherwise had few educational opportunities in the northern states and Canadian provinces. During the 1840s, enrollment fluctuated between sixty and eighty students. Responsibility for the institute rested with a six-member board of trustees. An executive committee supervised the daily activities and coordinated community affairs.

The fifteen-hundred-acre Dawn settlement grew up adjacent to the school. It attracted nearly five hundred settlers, who supported themselves through agriculture and the sale of lumber products. Despite initial successes, the Dawn experiment was perpetually plagued by indebtedness, incompetent management, and unscrupulous agents. After Fuller died in 1847, Wilson disassociated himself from Dawn; thereafter, the settlement's leaders were continually charged with fraudulent conduct. In 1850 the American Baptist Free Mission Society assumed control of the institute and appointed Samuel H. Davis, a black Baptist clergyman, to manage affairs at Dawn. He revived the institute, but only briefly. John Scoble, secretary of the British and Foreign Anti-Slavery Society, came to Dawn in 1851 to investigate the settlement. Within a year, he took complete charge of the institute. Scoble's patronizing attitude toward blacks alienated many Dawn settlers and his authority was eventually challenged. Led by James C. Brown, one of the original Dawn trustees, blacks in the Dresden-Chatham area organized in the summer of 1855 and initiated a protracted court battle for the control of Dawn. During the course of this struggle, which continued into the 1860s, the institute became moribund. Dawn ceased to be an organized black community long before it was officially disbanded in 1868. Pease and Pease, *Black Utopia*, 63–83; Winks, *Blacks in Canada*, 143, 178–81, 195–204.

3. Henson had spent most of the summer and fall of 1845 "itinerating at his own charges" throughout Canada West. In October Henson and Rev. Hiram Wilson left Dawn on a fund-raising mission, the success of which was essential to keeping the school open. *CF*, 27 November 1845 [5:0114]; William P. Newman to Hamilton Hill, 21 October 1845, Autograph File, OO [5:0083].

4. Henson probably refers to the schoolhouse at Dawn, which was completed by the end of November 1845. *CF*, 27 November 1845 [5:0114].

5. In the spring of 1845, during a trip to Boston as an agent for Dawn, Henson met the Reverend Ephraim Peabody (1807–1856), a Unitarian minister. Peabody introduced him to Samuel A. Eliot (1798–1862), a politician and moderate antislavery advocate and eventually the amanuensis and sponsor of Henson's autobiography. Eliot arranged the initial funding for Dawn's sawmill by introducing Henson to Amos Lawrence (1786–1852), a Unitarian merchant-philanthropist, and other Bostonians who contributed $1,400 to the institute. Henson consistently returned to his Boston sources for additional financial assistance. Henson, *Autobiography*, xiii, 93–94; *CF*, 27 November 1845 [5:0114]; *NCAB*, 12:200; *DAB*, 6:80–81, 11:46–47; Pease and Pease, *Black Utopia*, 75; *NASS*, 11 November 1847 [5:0513].

6. Josiah Henson (1789–1883) was born a slave in Maryland, where he became a plantation manager and respected local preacher. In 1825, on the orders of his owner, Isaac Riley, Henson transported eighteen slaves to Kentucky—an act he regretted, as reported in his autobiography. In the late 1820s, Henson decided to purchase his freedom. He struggled to collect the necessary money, but after his owner deceived him about the purchase price, then threatened to sell him, Henson fled to Upper Canada with his wife and four children in the fall of 1830. He became an influential black preacher in Dresden, Canada West, and led two successful forays into Kentucky to free slaves.

Henson devoted the next twenty-five years to improving the educational and economic situation of Canadian blacks. In 1842 he helped found the British-

American Institute at Dawn and was recognized as the school's de facto leader. Although Henson was responsible for the school's initial success, his work at Dawn was hampered by unproved accusations of financial mismanagement. Despite this he remained at the settlement until the school closed in 1868. In 1849 and again in 1851, Henson visited England to lecture and raise funds for the institute. During the latter trip, he displayed examples of the institute's products at the Great Exhibition of 1851 in London. Today Henson is remembered less for his antislavery activity and his work at Dawn than for the myth that he was the model for Uncle Tom in Harriet Beecher Stowe's *Uncle Tom's Cabin*. Despite early hesitation by Henson and Stowe to acknowledge his identification with Uncle Tom, that identification became generally accepted in the public mind. It enlarged Henson's reputation and made him one of the best known Canadian black leaders. It also enhanced Canada's image as a prejudice-free haven for blacks. Henson made a final trip to England in 1876 and was received by Queen Victoria and large crowds wishing to hear "Uncle Tom" speak. *DAB* 7:564–65; Winks, *Blacks in Canada*, 181–95; W. B. Hartgrove, "The Story of Josiah Henson," *JNH* 3:1–21 (January 1918); Josiah Henson, *Father Henson's Story of His Own Life . . .* (Boston, Mass., 1858); *DANB*, 307–8.

14.
Mary E. Bibb to [Gerrit Smith]
8 November 1850

The rapid growth of the Canadian black community after 1850 prompted the development of a black antislavery press there. The *Voice of the Fugitive*, the first black Canadian newspaper, spoke for fugitive slaves in Canada West. Dedicated to social reform, the *Voice* covered a broad range of issues—antislavery, temperance, education, religion, and moral elevation. It became the official organ of the Refugee Home Society in 1852 and was thereafter linked to the controversies that arose from RHS activities. Fugitive slave Henry Bibb founded and edited the *Voice*, but the contrast between his private correspondence and the paper's polished style suggests that his well-educated wife, Mary E. Bibb, had a good deal to do with the paper's style and content. Recognizing that black Canadians alone could not sustain the publication, the Bibbs directed the prospectus for the *Voice* to American abolitionists and appealed to their interest in the condition of fugitive slaves in Canada West. *VF*, 1 January 1851; Pease and Pease, *Black Utopia*, 111, 116–19.

Sandwich, C[anada] West
Nov[ember] 8th, 1850

My Dear Friend

Will you aid us by sending as many subscribers as convenience will permit, There are hundredrs of Slaves coming here daily. My husband[1] & self consider this the field for us at present. He is about to engage in this. ~~While~~ I expect to take a school next week[2]—any aid from the friend will be very acceptable. Please let me know what you think of the movement. In haste,

M. E. Bibb[3]

PROSPECTUS
VOICE OF THE FUGITIVES[4]
(IN CANADA)
Is to be the title of a Newspaper to be published by
MR. HENRY BIBB
AT SANDWICH, CANADA WEST
(NEAR DETROIT, MICHIGAN)

It is designed to be an organ through which the refugees from Southern Slavery may be heard both in America and Europe. The first copy will be issued in January, 1851, on a medium sized sheet, and will be published but twice a month, until we shall obtain a sufficient number of subscribers to support a weekly.

To do this, and spread out our cause widely before the world, we would most respectfully solicit all to whom this may come—and especially such as are interested in the elevation of those of us who, after many long years of unrequited toil, have succeeded, by the help of God, in making our way to where we may glorify Him with our bodies and spirits, which are His—to subscribe for the paper! And if any should wish to know whether Fugitives can take care of themselves, after becoming free from bondage, subscribe for the paper! If any wish to know how we enjoy liberty, and what we think of those who have robbed us of our wives, children, and all that is sacred and dear, let them subscribe for the paper! If you would like to give utterance to the dumb by aiding us in proclaiming liberty to the captives, and the opening of the prison to those that are bound, contribute and subscribe for the paper!

—THE TERMS WILL BE—

DOLLAR A YEAR

TO BE PAID ALWAYS IN ADVANCE,

Will those who are interested in the success of our enterprise, give us a lift in the start? Will you act as Agents, and forward to us before the first of January next? Only make us to feel that we shall be backed up by anti-slavery sympathy, and we shall go forward with strength and courage.

All letters from the United States must be directed to Detroit, Michigan, and those from Canada and England, to Sandwich,

NAMES.	RESIDENCE.	No. COPIES.

Gerrit Smith Papers, George Arents Research Library, Syracuse University, Syracuse, New York. Published by permission.

1. Henry Bibb (1815–1854) was the eldest of seven children born to Kentucky slave Mildred Jackson. Bibb's father was a slaveholder named James Bibb. When he was "young and small," Bibb was separated from his mother and hired out for several years to a succession of cruel masters. During this service, Bibb acquired the rudiments of education. Bibb met and married a slave named Malinda in 1834; they had one child, Mary Frances. In December 1837, Bibb fled slavery and briefly settled in Perrysburg, Ohio. Determined to rescue his family, he returned to Kentucky in June 1838. He was captured but managed to escape and make two

more unsuccessful rescue attempts before being recaptured and shipped with his family to New Orleans. After another escape attempt, Bibb was separated from his family. He endured a journey that took him into Texas and Indian Territory (where he was sold to a part-Indian owner) and culminated in 1841 with his final, successful flight to freedom. Bibb settled in Detroit in January 1842. He briefly attended a school for blacks run by Rev. William C. Monroe. He again attempted to locate his family, but when he discovered in 1845 that his wife had been sold and was the mistress of her new owner, he made no further rescue attempts.

Bibb returned to Detroit and increasingly involved himself in antislavery and Liberty party ventures. He became employed as an antislavery lecturer, joined Joshua Leavitt's bibles-for-slaves crusade, and gained notoriety, along with Frederick Douglass, William Wells Brown, and J. W. C. Pennington, as one of the most dynamic former slave abolitionist speakers. Bibb married Boston abolitionist Mary Miles in January 1848. In October 1849, Bibb published the highly regarded *Narrative of the Life and Adventures of Henry Bibb, An American Slave.* In the fall of 1850, passage of the Fugitive Slave Law forced Bibb to flee to Canada. He and his wife soon (January 1851) established the *Voice of the Fugitive*—an antislavery weekly with an emigrationist message—which was meant to serve the burgeoning black community of Canada West.

Working with black abolitionists James Theodore Holly and J. T. Fisher, Bibb organized a convention of North American blacks in Toronto during September 1851 that led to the founding of the North American League—an organization meant to serve as a central authority for blacks in the Americas as well as an agency for promoting immigration to Canada and aiding blacks once they arrived. The league was short-lived, but Bibb, in January 1852, again tried to institutionalize his emigrationist efforts by joining with Michigan philanthropists to form the joint-stock Refugee Home Society—an association whose purpose was to acquire thousands of acres of Canadian land for sale to black immigrants. Friction between Bibb and other black Canadian leaders doomed the society. Bibb died on Emancipation Day in 1854. Henry Bibb, *Narrative of the Life and Adventures of Henry Bibb, An American Slave* (New York, N.Y., 1850; reprint, Miami, Fla., 1969); *DANB*, 44; *NSt*, 29 March 1848; *E*, 19 April 1848.

2. Mary Bibb had opened a school in Sandwich, Canada West, in November or December 1850. By January 1851, she was instructing twenty-five day and evening students in her home; one month later, the day-school enrollment had grown from twelve to forty-six students, who met in a makeshift classroom lacking desks and other equipment. The school, never financially secure, closed by the spring of 1852, if not earlier. *VF*, 1 January, 12, 26 February 1851 [6:0721, 0815, 0836]; *ASB*, 12 April 1851 [6:0899]; H[enry] Bibb to American Missionary Association, 14 December 1850 [6:0686], Samuel J. May to Lewis Tappan, 3 August 1852, AMA-ARC.

3. Mary Elizabeth Miles Bibb (ca. 1820–1877), a free black native of Rhode Island, was the only child of Quaker parents. She was educated at a Lexington, Massachusetts, normal school and taught at several schools, including an Albany, New York, school for blacks and Hiram S. Gilmore's Cincinnati high school. She later taught in Boston, where she met and married abolitionist Henry Bibb in June 1848. After passage of the Fugitive Slave Law of 1850, they settled in Sandwich, Canada West, where Mary opened a school. It foundered in 1852, and she

worked as a dressmaker until the spring of 1853, when she took charge of a flourishing government-sponsored black school of sixty-nine students. Bibb's interest in advancing the status of blacks reached beyond education. She influenced the editorial direction of the *Voice of the Fugitive*, and during part of 1851, when her husband Henry was traveling in Wisconsin and Illinois, she oversaw the paper's production. In the early 1850s, she sponsored the establishment of a mutual improvement society, was a founding member of the Anti-Slavery Society of Windsor, served as an officer of the National Emigration Convention (1854) in Cleveland, and, like Henry, was involved with the operation of the Refugee Home Society, which selected her as its corresponding secretary in January 1852. An ardent supporter of the RHS, she defended it against opponents and argued that its land policy provided the best opportunity for black self-help. She became a rival of Mary Ann Shadd Cary; the two clashed over RHS policies and over the principle of establishing segregated schools. Cary believed Bibb responsible for her school's loss of American Missionary Association support and accused her of being "a profane swearer and a drug taking woman." Whether those charges were true or not, Bibb's assistant teacher described her as an erratic personality. After Henry's death, an AMA missionary accused Mary of depriving her mother-in-law, Mildred Jackson, of a living despite the $10,000 property she was said to have controlled. Mary Bibb later married Isaac N. Cary and ran a private school in Windsor. During the early 1870s, she moved to Brooklyn, New York, where she spent the remainder of her life. In her will, she bequeathed $3,000 to charitable organizations, including the Howard Colored Orphan Asylum in Brooklyn. *ASB*, 12 April, 4 October 1851 [6:0898]; *VF*, 13 August, 19 November 1851, 29 January, 17 June, 15 July, 21 October 1852 [7:0051, 0184, 0788]; *Lib*, 12 November 1852 [7:0825], 29 September 1854; *PP*, 19 October 1861 [13:0835]; Mary E. Bibb to Rev. George Whipple, 22 May 1853, AMA-ARC [8:0267]; *NYT*, 9 August 1877; Jim Bearden and Linda Jean Butler, *Shadd: The Life and Times of Mary Shadd Cary* (Toronto, 1977), 34–36, 121–23, 152; Carleton Mabee, *Black Education in New York State: From Colonial to Modern Times* (Syracuse, N.Y., 1979), 312; *New York City Directory*, 1876–77; *DANB*, 44.

4. Henry Bibb began publishing the *Voice of the Fugitive* on 1 January 1851 in Sandwich, Canada West. Mary Bibb, his wife, also appears to have played a major part in editing the paper. As the title implied, the *Voice* was intended to appeal to fugitive slaves in both Canada West and the United States. Subscription agents soon recruited readers in Canada West, Ohio, Michigan, Pennsylvania, New York, and New England. As a result, the *Voice* obtained the widest readership of the two black newspapers published in the province during the 1850s. Within the first year, the *Voice* boasted one thousand subscribers. It was widely quoted in the northern abolitionist press. The *Voice* promoted immediate abolition of slavery, temperance, black education, black agriculture, Canadian immigration, and moral reform. Every other week, it published antislavery and temperance news, black abolitionist correspondence, black meeting reports, word of the fugitive slaves arriving in Canada West, and numerous editorials by Bibb. It functioned as the official organ of the Refugee Home Society and informed readers of the progress of the society's settlements. The year 1852 brought several changes. In April Bibb moved the paper to Windsor. Two months later, James Theodore Holly became coeditor and coproprietor. In December Bibb announced that the paper

would be renamed the *Voice of the Fugitive and Canadian Independent.* But in October 1853, the office of the *Voice* burned to the ground. Although Bibb informed readers that the paper "is not dead," publication was suspended. Bibb's death the following year prevented it from being revived. *VF,* 1 January 1851, 22 April, 17 June, 16 December 1852; Winks, *Blacks in Canada,* 395–97; Simpson, "Negroes in Ontario to 1870," 168, 171–74; *Lib,* 28 October 1853 [8:0461].

15.
Henry Bibb to the Executive Committee of the American Missionary Association
14 December 1850
14 April 1851

The survival and success of the black refugees who fled to Canada West in the wake of the Fugitive Slave Law often depended upon the resourcefulness of black leaders. Henry Bibb, a former slave and prominent black abolitionist, was a persistent and energetic leader of the movement to assist Canadian fugitives. He published the *Voice of the Fugitive*, helped organize fugitive-slave settlements, and coordinated relief efforts in the Windsor area. During the difficult winter months of late 1850 and early 1851, he contacted the Executive Committee of the American Missionary Association with word of those activities. The AMA—an antislavery organization dedicated to Christianizing and educating nonwhites in the United States and abroad—seemed a natural ally. Bibb reported on conditions among the refugees, discussed efforts on their behalf, hinted at future plans, and requested AMA advice on several matters, all in the hope that the AMA would provide much-needed assistance. The AMA responded by endorsing the Refugee Home Society and increasing the number of missionaries it supported in the Windsor area. *AM*, June 1851; Murray, "Canada and Anglo-American Anti-Slavery Movement," 436.

Sandwich, [Canada West]
Dec[ember] 14th, 185[0]

To the American Missionary Association[1]
Messrs. L. Tappan &c.
Gentlemen

After a long silance to you on my part, respecting the Bible for the slave,[2] I would now respectfully call your attention to it, in relation to the refugees from southern slavery who are so rapidly settling in Canada. This class of persons are almost entirly destitue of th[is m]ost important of all books. I think if your society would forwared a lot of Bibles and Testimants to this place, they would be very acceptable—and would be profitablly distributed among the fugitives. My wife has just commenced teaching a school in Sandwich, for them—she has quite a large school, but has not a suppy of school books for the children.

I have not corasponded with lately with you concerning the Bible cause, not having any thing of importance to report.

Since & for a long time befor the passage of the fugitive slave law[3] my time & energies were taken up in doing what I could through this state in

3. Henry Bibb

From Henry Bibb, *Narrative of the Life and Adventures of Henry Bibb, An American Slave* (New York, 1849)

exposing it. Soon after the law was passed fugitives were fleing to Canadan in such vast nombers that I was induced by the friends of humanity to come here & commence an organ through which their wants & conditions might be made known to our friends in the States, & which should be devoted to the elevation of the condition of our people genrally. I here inclose the prospectus,[4] & I hope that you will inform me what you think of it (the object).

I have had the pleasure of forming an acquaintance with Br. ~~Hogkiss~~ Hotchkiss, your Agent or Missionary.[5] Judgeing from what I have seen of Him I think he is well quallified for the station in which you have placed him.

Sevral persons have been to this section of Canada just befor the close of navigation with boxes of things for the suffering fugitives & so far as clotheing is concerned I think those who are now here will be able to stand the winter. However others are still coming every week more or less, but the most they nede is shelter & something to eat. For the last 6 or 8 weeks our house has been filled with strangers almost every day & night but we have never turned one from our door without food or lodging if they could put up with such ~~a~~ as we had. Ever true to the cause of suffering humanity,

H. Bibb

American Missionary Association Archives, Amistad Research Center, New Orleans, Louisiana. Published by permission.

Sandwich, C[anada] W[est]
April 14th, 185[1]

To the Ex Com of the American Missionary As[6]

Your communication of March 20,th was thankfully received. I showed it to Br. Hotchkiss, who was much pleased with the idea of making a united applycation to the American Bible Society[7] for a donation of Bibles for the fugitives in Canada. I have been waiting for him to write until I think it is not best to wait longer. I therefor write myself. Enclosed you will find my applycation to them for Bibles, which you will please present. If the~~y~~ request should be granted—let the Bibles be forwared to Detroit Mich. to my care. If they refuse you will of course ~~forwared~~ forwared me their answer.

There is another subject to which I would respectfully call your attention and solicit your advice thereon. It is with regard to procuring land for the fugitives in Canada as a perminant means of self support and of Educating their children &c. My views are briefly setforth in an article which I here enclose.[8] Without confering with Br. Harned[9] on the subject I have taken the liberty of anouncing that He would receive contributions for that object. Such an enterprise commenced I think here just at this time would be one of the greatest temeral blessings that could be confered on this people. It would save many form being lofers and idellers—it would make the way possible for all to get homes by their own industey and to follow agracultural pursuits if they wish to do so—it would furnish the means for Educating hundreds who would perhaps otherwise grow up in ignorance, and last but not least it would put a check the American Colonceation Society or scheme.[10] And I have faith to belive that if your society would only take hold of the work, it could be easely accompished. Shall I not hear from you soon on the subject? Let it be born in mind that this is the most southern part of Canada; the most conveninant crossing place for the fugitives and that the land is now very cheap but cannot be so long. Yours for God & humanity,

H. Bibb

American Missionary Association Archives, Amistad Research Center, New Orleans, Louisiana. Published by permission.

1. The American Missionary Association was founded at Albany, New York, in 1846. The society's affairs were initially directed by treasurer Lewis Tappan and secretaries Simeon S. Jocelyn and George Whipple. Whipple also edited the *American Missionary*, an AMA organ, until the Civil War. AMA membership was open to all nonslaveholding Christians. The association promoted mission work and Christian education among nonwhite peoples in the Americas and abroad. By 1855, it had missions in Egypt, Siam, Haiti, Jamaica, and West Africa, in addition to the more than one hundred "home" missions in North America. After the Civil War, the AMA became the largest supporter of freedmen's education in the South, founding and funding over five hundred black schools and colleges. Today blacks remain the AMA's primary focus. Clifton H. Johnson, "The American Missionary Association: A Study in Christian Abolitionism, 1846–61" (Ph.D. diss., University of North Carolina, 1958); Joe M. Richardson, *Christian Reconstruction: The American Missionary Association and Southern Blacks, 1861–1890* (Athens, Ga., 1986); W. Augustus Low and Virgil A. Clift, eds., *Encyclopedia of Black America* (New York, N.Y., 1981), 101–2.

2. Bibb believed that the Bible was a potent antislavery document that would hasten the demise of slavery if read by slaves. In February 1849, he joined the American Missionary Association campaign to distribute bibles to slaves, and throughout the spring of 1850, he conducted fund-raising lectures in the Northeast. Despite Garrisonian opposition, Bibb had supported earlier, unsuccessful efforts to convince the American Bible Society to assume that task. Bibb believed that the bible campaign opened the antislavery debate to people that otherwise would oppose or ignore "naked" abolitionism. *E*, 2 June 1847, 17 May 1849 [5:0434, 1091]; *Lib*, 25 June 1847 [5:0437]; Henry Bibb to Executive Committee of the American Missionary Association, 14 February 1849, Henry Bibb to Lewis Tappan, 16 March 1849, H[enry] Bibb to L[ewis] Tappan and W[illia]m Harned, 6 May 1850, AMA-ARC [5:0972, 1007, 6:0502]; John R. McKivigan, "Abolitionism and the American Churches, 1830–1865: A Study of Attitudes and Tactics" (Ph.D. diss., Ohio State University, 1977), 292–96.

3. The Fugitive Slave Law of 1850 was one of the five congressional enactments passed in September and collectively designated as the Compromise of 1850. The law was meant to address slave-owner dissatisfaction with the federal procedures for returning fugitive slaves; it created the position of United States commissioner, a federal hearing officer loosely affiliated with northern state courts, who had final authority over extradition proceedings. The law also ordered state and federal authorities to cooperate in capturing fugitives, and it imposed a $1,000 fine or six-month jail sentence on anyone that aided a runaway. Most important, the law

made the slave certification hearing an administrative, and not a judicial, procedure. Blacks could not testify on their own behalves and had no right to counsel or to a habeas corpus hearing; free blacks regarded the law as a severe threat to their freedom. Abolitionists used the law to rouse northern antislavery sentiment and to reinvigorate fugitive slave rescue committees. Ultimately the law and the confrontations it precipitated moved the North and South closer to war. Stanley W. Campbell, *The Slave Catchers: Enforcement of the Fugitive Slave Law, 1850–1860* (Chapel Hill, N.C., 1968), 15–25.

4. Bibb refers to the prospectus of the *Voice of the Fugitive*, which appears as Document 14 in this volume.

5. David Hotchkiss, a Wesleyan Methodist minister from Pennsylvania, did missionary work among the Choctaws and French along the frontier from 1835 to 1839. In 1850 the American Missionary Association appointed him to replace Isaac Rice at the Amherstburg, Canada West, mission. While there, Hotchkiss helped found the Refugee Home Society, briefly served as the society's corresponding secretary, and acted as subscription agent for the *Voice of the Fugitive*. He left the Amherstburg mission in 1853 but returned in 1855 to establish a mission on RHS property at Puce River, where his condescending treatment of blacks and his close ties to the RHS provoked opposition from some black settlers. Arsonists destroyed two buildings at his mission in 1857; the following year, he moved to Rochester, Canada West. After the Canada mission closed in 1862, Hotchkiss settled in Michigan. Johnson, "American Missionary Association," 329–52; *AM*, December 1850, January 1860; Fred Landon, "Work of the American Missionary Association Among the Negro Refugees in Canada West, 1848–64," *OHSPR* 21:198–205 (1924); *SLO*, 7 September 1835; *VF*, 1 January 1851; Murray, "Canada and Anglo-American Anti-Slavery Movement," 456–57.

6. In April 1851, the Executive Committee of the American Missionary Association consisted of Arthur Tappan, Simeon S. Jocelyn, Charles B. Ray, William Harned, Anthony Lane, Thomas Ritter, Samuel E. Cornish, William E. Whiting, J. W. C. Pennington, J. O. Bennett, Josiah Brewer, and M. S. Scudder. *AM*, November 1850.

7. The American Bible Society was founded in 1816 by representatives of New York, Philadelphia, and Boston associations that had originated the free distribution of bibles early in the century. Wealthy New Yorkers concerned with the moral reform of American urban society led this effort to distribute the Bible to the lower classes and newly arrived immigrants. The ABS printed and distributed over six million bibles by 1840. Now an international organization, the ABS distributes more than 200 million bibles annually. Paul Boyer, *Urban Masses and Moral Order in America, 1820–1920* (Cambridge, Mass., 1978), 23–24, 35, 80, 83, 308; *The Directory of Religious Organizations in the United States*, 2d ed. (Falls Church, Va., 1982), 16.

8. Bibb evidently refers to an editorial entitled "What do the fugitives in Canada stand mostly in need of," which appeared in the 26 March 1851 issue of the *Voice of the Fugitive*. It outlined a land-purchase plan advocated by a black convention held at Sandwich, Canada West, during November 1850. The editorial announced the creation of a stock fund to finance the purchase of twenty thousand acres of Canadian government land for subdivision into small farms and resale to fugitives from American slavery. One-third of all monies paid by fugitives

would then be appropriated for the education of their children. Subscribers to this effort were asked to forward their names to William Harned at the American and Foreign Anti-Slavery Society office in New York City or to Bibb. *VF*, 26 March 1851.

9. William Harned (?–1854) spent his early life in Philadelphia, where his Quaker predilections led him to active involvement in antislavery, pacifist, and temperance circles by the mid-1830s. In 1836 he joined in a call to organize Pennsylvania's immediatist abolitionists and then served on the executive committee of the resulting Pennsylvania Anti-Slavery Society's Eastern District. Convinced of the efficacy of political antislavery, Harned actively supported the Liberty party during the early 1840s. By mid-decade he had moved to New York City to become office agent of the American and Foreign Anti-Slavery Society. After 1848 he worked closely with the local black community as corresponding secretary and treasurer of the New York State Vigilance Committee and local subscription agent for Frederick Douglass's *North Star*. During his decade in New York, he abandoned his Quaker roots and became a Congregationalist. Harned was assistant treasurer of the American Missionary Association during the early 1850s. *AM*, October 1854; *NECAUL*, 29 October 1836, 14 January, 11, 18 February, 29 April 1837, 22 February, 1 March 1838, 30 May 1839; *PF*, 14 June 1838, 18 January 1844; *Lib*, 20 April 1838, 24 April 1846, 29 June 1849, 15 February 1850; *E*, 4 January, 20 May, 29 July 1841; Lewis Tappan to J[oshua] P. Blanchard, 15 May 1848, "Circular of the New York State Vigilance Committee," [August 1848], W[illiam] Harned to J[oshua] P. Blanchard, 11 April 1849, Drayton, Sayres, and English Papers, DLC; *NSt*, 18 May 1849, 27 June 1850, 10 April 1851, 18 March 1852; *FDP*, 11 March 1853.

10. The American Colonization Society was founded in 1817 with a primary goal of removing free blacks from the United States, particularly to its colony in Liberia; secondarily, the ACS sought to aid the manumission of slaves and to suppress the slave trade. The society lobbied without success for congressional endorsement of African colonization as national policy. Ralph R. Gurley, longtime ACS secretary and editor of the society's organ, the *African Repository*, forged the ACS into a prominent national association with hundreds of state and local auxiliaries. But during the 1830s and 1840s, the society was weakened by strong opposition from northern free blacks and the growing abolitionist movement, by the conversion of some leading members to abolitionism, by competition from independent and local societies, and by internal division. When Liberians won their independence in 1847, the ACS became merely an advocate of black emigration. Although it was inactive after the Civil War, a skeletal organization remained into the 1960s. During its initial fifty years, the ACS claimed to have collected $2,500,000 for Liberian colonization and transported twelve thousand blacks to Africa. P. J. Staudenraus, *The African Colonization Movement, 1816–1865* (New York, N.Y., 1961).

16. Editorial by Henry Bibb
15 January 1851

To antebellum black Americans, education symbolized racial achievement, in part, because it was denied in slavery and difficult to obtain in the free states. Southern whites outlawed slave education, fearing that literacy might lead to revolt, and free blacks in the northern states were often denied access to public schools or were compelled to attend separate and inferior ones. Henry Bibb's 15 January 1851 editorial in the *Voice of the Fugitive* defined black attitudes about education. Bibb informed readers that schooling would clothe blacks with a "power which will enable us to rise from degradation and command respect from the whole civilized world." Like Bibb, many black abolitionists believed that education was an important component of the struggle to overcome slavery and racial prejudice. The fugitive slaves and free blacks who fled to Canada West found educational opportunities there that were unavailable to them elsewhere on the continent. And they took full advantage, establishing schools at Wilberforce, Dawn, Elgin, the Refugee Home Society, and other black settlements and successfully fighting for admission to public schools—albeit segregated ones—in the towns and cities of the province. Jason H. Silverman and Donna J. Gillie, "'The Pursuit of Knowledge Under Difficulties': Education and the Fugitive Slaves in Canada," *OntH* 74:95–112 (June 1982).

EDUCATION

We regard the education of colored people in North America as being one of the most important measures connected with the destiny of our race. By it we can be strengthened and elevated—without it we shall be ignorant, weak, and degraded. By it we shall be clothed with a power which will enable us to arise from degradation and command respect from the whole civilized world: without it, we shall ever be imposed upon, oppressed and enslaved; not that we are more stupid than others would be under the same circumstances, indeed very few races of men have the corporal ability to survive, under the same physical and mental depression that the colored race have to endure, and still retain their manhood.

In most of the slave States where the colored people are compelled to work under the slave-driver's lash, without wages, they are often sold apart from their families, handcuffed and branded with hot irons, and forbid by statute law to read the name of God.[1] Under such treatment, almost any other race would have sunk in despair.

Show us a community of white people, even in a free country, where they may possess all the natural advantages of climate and soil that the world was ever blessed with, and let there be no schools, no post-offices, no newspapers circulated or read, no mental instruction given, orally or otherwise, and we could write out the character of that people. They would have a grog-shop at almost every public place; they would be ignorant, vicious and licentious; the county jails would seldom be unoccupied by prisoners, the courts would be continually annoyed by petty lawsuits, and the county heavily taxed for the support of paupers.

With this mass of degradation before us, we say that the most effectual remedy for the above evils is education. It is the best fortune that a father can give his son; it is a treasure that can never be squandered, and one that will always command respect and secure a good livelihood for an industrious person.

But we speak now especially to our fugitive brethren. We frequently hear persons say that they are too far advanced in life to learn to read and write. To all such we say, be not discouraged. We think there are but very few who could not be taught to read the Bible, if they would only commence and persevere. If we learn to read that, we can then learn to read other books and papers, and we should understand the laws of the Government under which we live. To do this we should read, in order to become wise, intelligent, and useful in society. We should at least know how to read and write; and when we have learned this, we have the best means with which to educate ourselves.

Voice of the Fugitive (Windsor, Canada West), 15 January 1851.

1. Southerners were generally opposed to the education of blacks, be they free or slave. South Carolina, Missouri, Virginia, Louisiana, North Carolina, Mississippi, and Alabama had statutes prohibiting the teaching of reading to slaves. Carter G. Woodson, *The Education of the Negro Prior to 1861* (Washington, D.C., 1919), 159–64.

17. Henry Bibb "To Our Old Masters"
January–February 1851

Black abolitionists used many weapons to attack slavery. They took particular care to inform the transatlantic community about the institution in all its dimensions, from the conditions of slave life to the fallacies of proslavery arguments. In a series of three essays prepared for the *Voice of the Fugitive* in early 1851, Henry Bibb presented an historical and philosophical critique of proslavery charges that blacks were slaves because they were innately inferior and contented with their lot in life. Like many black leaders, Bibb added a touch of irony to his writings. He apologized—as an uneducated former slave—for basing his arguments on historical research; he addressed the essays "to our old masters," a poignant reminder that he spoke for fugitive slaves who had outwitted their masters; and he explained to the slaveholders that their Anglo-Saxon ancestors had themselves been slaves of the Romans.

TO OUR OLD MASTERS
[No. 1]

GENTLEMEN:

Though we cannot be supposed to be profoundly versed in historical lore—our education not commencing until we become fugitives—yet we have made certain discoveries in the history of bygone times, which we wish to bring under your notice; not that we imagine you to be ignorant of the facts we are about to introduce, but simply for the purpose of refreshing your memory, and informing you that *we* have acquired the knowledge that you are the descendants of men who were placed much in the same position as ourselves, namely, fugitive slaves.

In passing, we may observe, that in the course of our researches we have discovered, that ever since mankind formed themselves into communities, slavery, in various modifications, has had an existency. We also learn, from the same source, that the individuals held in bondage never submitted to the yoke with cheerfulness, nor acknowledged the Divine right of their masters to the property which they claimed in them. We furthermore learn that this unjust appropriation has invariably been productive of hate, discord and bloodshed between the parties, and that frequently the degraded portion have, by their perpetual struggles with their oppressors, compelled the acknowledgement of their claims to equality.

Now, throughout the whole course of slavery exhibited in past ages, we cannot conceive a solitary argument, in a moral point of view, which could be adduced in its favor; it has invariably been the strong against the weak. Men possessed of the same intellectual power, and the same general attainments, have been enslaved by their fellow-men, simply because they were their superiors in numbers, or greater favorites of fortune, or, perhaps, better skilled in the use of the sword.

It is contended by many of you that our enslavement is just,[1] inasmuch as we are an inferior race, and not susceptible of the same degree of cultivation as the white men. We will take another opportunity of answering you on this point, as our business is with yourselves at present, merely observing, that every negro in the South is aware that he is placed in a false position, and that it is only "might" which constitutes the "right" of his master to rob him of his liberty; and the thinking portion of them (there are negroes that *think*) are fully persuaded of the fact that

> Freedom's battle, once begun,
> Though baffled oft, is ever won.

We, who have escaped from your toils, can perceive that the traffic in the flesh and blood of our brethren must have a speedy termination—that you must adopt one of the many proposed schemes which the benevolent have put forth for our emancipation—or take the consequences of your blind obstinacy, which can only result in confusion and ruin to yourselves.

But we have not taken up the pen to write on our own position at present. We mean to show that you are the most inconsistent race of slaveholders that the world has yet produced; that your practice is entirely at variance with your preaching; that in prosperity you have repudiated the doctrines which in adversity you promulgated; in fact, that you are now inflicting upon us a tyranny similar to that under which your forefathers groaned, and against which they rebelled.

We understand, that about 2,000 years ago, your ancestors were roaming about in the forests of Britain—a horde of painted savages, similar in character to the Indians of the present day—that their customs were of the most barbarous description, and that they even indulged in human sacrifices. While in this state, their country was invaded by a warlike people, who, although in a semi-barbarous state themselves, had progressed infinitely beyond the Britons in the arts and in general civilization. Your forefathers, though savages, had the spirit of liberty strongly implanted in their breasts, and they fought like demons to secure that liberty; yet, notwithstanding their almost super-human exertions, the determination and genius of their Roman invaders proved too powerful for them; they were obliged to bend their necks to the yoke—they became the slaves of their conquerors.

Notwithstanding this prostration, they experienced many changes of fortune. Their burning thirst for liberty appeared to be unquenchable—it was perpetually showing itself in a variety of ways, and it was not until a deluge of blood had been spilt on both sides, that your predecessors were reduced to anything like perfect subjection.

For many centuries they remained in a state of servitude; and it may be said that they derived an advantage from their enslavement, for the Roman yoke was very light, and that great people, unlike you tyrants of the present day, endeavored to enlighten those whom they subdued. But circumstances compelled the Romans to leave your forefathers to themselves; nations whom they (the Romans) had enslaved in other parts of the world were bursting their bonds, their own frontier was threatened, the magnitude of their conquests had enfeebled them, and they were in danger of losing all by having grasped too much.

After the Romans had abandoned Britain, the country became the prey of a variety of conquerers, until the nation was consolidated under the peaceful rule of the Saxons, who intermingled with the aboriginal race. The arts of peace were cultivated, and civilization was rapidly progressing, when a band of determined warriors, who had spread desolation in various parts of Europe, rushed in upon your forefathers, killed their king and took possession of their country. William the Conqueror divided the lands of Britain among his followers, and those who had hitherto been the proprietors of the soil were compelled to toil on it as slaves for their imperious masters. The condition of your ancestors, at this period of their history, was as degraded, under the iron rule of their masters, as ours is at present under the domination of yourselves—the descendants of those reluctant slaves. William the Conqueror and his followers were not more enlightened than the people whom they enslaved—in military tactics only did they excel—and the sword had become the umpire in all cases of dispute; the strong arm constituted the law—"might was right."[2]

The oppressed were both mentally and physically degraded; but the undying spirit of liberty still existed among them: there were not wanting, in the prostrate herd, men of powerful minds, who stood forth boldly to advocate the cause of their fallen race, and, by their eloquence, succeeded in enlisting the sympathies of the more intelligent and humane of their oppressors in their favor. Struggle succeeded struggle, and concession followed concession; but it was by tardy steps that liberty advanced. The discovery of this continent afforded a shelter from oppression, and thousands of fugitives from slavery found their way across the Atlantic. The principles of liberty, which they had so long cherished, continued to animate the greater portion of them in their new home; and, by their perseverance, they have rendered themselves independent of all who would enslave their kind. But you—the degenerate offspring of a noble race—you are infinitely behind the tyrants from whom your parents fled. While those have advanced, you have retrograded, and, if you can understand anything that is going on around you, you will be aware that you elicit the contempt of the whole civilized world—hated at home for the discord you produce among a free people, and despised abroad for your vain pretensions to that which you do not possess.

In closing, we will recapitulate: We have shown that your predecessors were once naked savages, possessed of less intelligence than the negroes of the present day; that in the course of a thousand years they had advanced very slowly in civilization, and were then completely enslaved by a foreign power; that they remained in this state for centuries, acquiring their freedom by small instalments, though full liberty as citizens was never conceded to them;[3] that on this continent you are now following the same line of conduct which the conquerors of your mother country pursued, and that while you are thus engaged, the lordly descendants of the conquerors of England have gone considerably ahead of you in the recognition of human rights and liberties; and the descendants of the Anglo-Saxons in England are ashamed of their monstrous offspring.[4]

No. 2

In our last number we endeavored to show that human slavery had not invariably depended upon the inferiority (or the supposed inferiority) of the persons enslaved—that all classes and colors had alike been subjected to its influence, and that its existence, in the majority of instances, hinged upon the physical powers at the command of the enslavers. It is now our intention to show that the present humiliating position of our race forms no exception to the general rule—that we are slaves because you are stronger physically, not because of any natural or intellectual inferiority in us. This fact, by your own conduct, you admit; or why do you so carefully block up every channel which has been opened for our instruction? Are we not justified in concluding that you are impregnated with the idea, that could we receive the same amount of care and attention which has been bestowed upon yourselves, that we could, in all probability, exhibit an equal degree of mental power, by which means you would entirely lose your control over us? This conclusion appears to us inevitable; and we will give you what we conceive to be a very strong reason for our conviction: Many of you have taken considerable pains to instruct domestic animals in various branches of knowledge. Horses and dogs—those two most invaluable servants of man—have received the greatest amount of attention in this respect, and, the more apt the scholar appeared to be, the more assiduous has his master become in affording him instruction. Now, we have never known an instance where the master of any domestic animal thus in course of training, has abandoned the educational process in the apprehension that the dog or the horse could possibly become as learned as himself; and yet, in our own case, it is evident, that, while the majority of you endeavor to persuade the world that our intellectual capacity is very little above the level of the brute creation, you are so afraid that we should arrive at your own standard, that you dare not allow any one to instruct us.

We find that this assumption of our mental inferiority is not generally entertained among the highly enlightened; they are disposed to admit us into the ranks of progressive beings; it is among the badly educated, arrogant, and half finished portion of your race—men, diminutive in intellect, but giants in self-esteem—who are compensated for their lack of wisdom by their measureless stock of impudence, imagining, forsooth, because they belong to an elevated class of beings, that all who differ from them in color are little better than a superior order of monkeys; while, in reality, if these inflated intellectual abortions were placed in the position best adapted for them in creation, they would form the *tails* of the colored races, thereby rendering the assumed resemblance to the brute creation more striking.

Many men of great attainments, and who are entitled to rank as philosophers, have fallen into the vulgar prejudice on this subject. De Vastey,[5] one of our brethren, an African of St. Domingo, thus alludes to this class of writers:

> Posterity will find it difficult to believe that, in an enlightened age like ours, there are men, who call themselves philosophers, willing to reduce human beings to an equality with brutes, merely for the sake of sanctioning the abominable privilege of oppressing a large portion of mankind. While I am now writing, I can scarcely refrain from laughter, at the absurdities which have been published on this subject. Learned authors, and skilful anatomists, have passed their lives in discussing facts as clear as daylight, and in dissecting the bodies of men and animals, in order to prove that I, who am now writing, belong to the race of Ourang-Outangs! Edward Long gravely advances, as a proof of the moral inferiority of the black man, that our vermin are black, and that we eat wild-cats. Hanneman maintains that our color originates in the curse pronounced by Noah against Canaan; others affirm that it was a mark fixed upon Cain, for the murder of his brother Abel. For myself, I see strong reasons to believe that the white men are the real descendants of Cain; for I still find in them that primitive hatred, that spirit of envy and pride, and that passion for riches, which the Scriptures inform us led him to sacrifice his brother.[6]

Here it will be observed, that one of our calumniated race shows himself capable of entering the arena and vindicating his claim to an equality with the whites, in a diction as polished, and with ideas as forcible as have been elicited on the opposite side of the question.

Want of space necessarily compels us to be brief; but we will continue this subject in our next and following numbers.

No. 3

In accordance with the promise, given in our last, we resume our remarks; and, notwithstanding the probability of being accused by you of presumption, in endeavoring to establish for ourselves a common origin with your own race, we will fearlessly pursue the subject, feeling confident, that as long as we promulgate nothing but what will bear the test of strict investigation, and make no deductions but what are strictly warranted by the premises, we can defy calumny, and at the same time promptly grapple with fair argument.

Before proceeding we may remark that Professor Lawrence, of London, in his Lectures on Zoology, Physiology, and the Natural History of Man,[7] though he endeavors to prove a distinct origin for the various races, makes this admission in our favor: "Of the dark colored people, none have distinguished themselves by stronger proofs of capacity for literary and scientific investigation, and, consequently, that none approach more nearly than the negro to the polished nations of the globe."

The great error committed by nearly all writers who have endeavored to form estimates of the character and capabilities of the different branches of the human family has been, that they have taken a survey of the various kinds as they were placed before them, without reference to what they had been, or what they were likely to become, as circumstances operated upon them. This is an unphilosophical mode of procedure; but it is from such superficial observations as these that the opinions of mankind have been formed with regard to us. They lose sight of the fact that circumstances are all powerful in the formation of character; that by the operation of favorable causes, men and nations may be elevated to the highest possible standard of excellence—that, in combination with the most perfect development of the bodily powers an intellect may be generated among them capable of fathoming the most profound mysteries in nature, by which means, elements which were once an object of dread, may be converted into peaceful auxiliaries for assisting them in the pursuit of happiness—that, like Ajax of old, they may not only defy the lightning, but control it and command its services.[8]

Reverse the circumstances which lead to these results; cut off from a society its most highly cultivated minds; let education cease; enslave the mass; let toiling, eating, and sleeping, constitute their only employment; let their whole time be devoted to ministering to the wants of the animal portion of their nature; while the moral and intellectual are lost sight of—what a marked change will be observable in a few generations! If the labor should not be carried to excess, no particular deterioration will be seen in the general formation of the individuals; but the forehead will become low and retiring while the back part of the head, the seat of the animal passions, will be increased in proportion to the decrease in the anterior region; they will become grovelling in their ideas; of morals they will have a very imperfect conception, and anything of an intellectual character they will be unable to appreciate. Any one attempting to enlighten them would, in all probability, become an object of derision—it would be "casting pearls before swine." Instruction could only be received in the same simple form as it is administered to children—their degraded intellect being unable to comprehend anything of a high character; and several generations would have to pass before they could again take their place among civilized beings.

Facts can be adduced to show that these results have been produced in various societies of men. Examples are now in existence, among civilized nations, of this mental inferiority—the agricultural laborers in England and the lower class in the South of Ireland, have been degraded below the level of their original standard; and, though possessed of the use of a language, their acquirements are exceedingly limited—exhibiting only the common instincts which animate the brute creation. If it were not known that these men belong to a race which has developed extraordinary intellectual powers, that same class of physiologists who have adjudicated on our claims to equality with the whites, would likewise consign their English and Irish brethren to the level of the lower animals.

The following evidence, in support of this view, is extracted from one of the most philosophical works which this age has produced, namely, *The Vestiges of the Natural History of Creation:*[9]

> About two hundred years ago, a number of people were driven by a barbarous policy from the counties of Antrim and Down, in Ireland, towards the sea-coast, where they have ever since been settled, but in unusually miserable circumstances even for Ireland;[10] and the consequence is, that they exhibit peculiar features of the most repulsive kind, projecting jaws with large open mouths, depressed noses, high cheek bones, and bow legs, together with an extremely diminutive stature. These, with an abnormal slenderness of the limbs, are the outward marks of a low and barbarous condition all over the world; it is particularly seen in the Australian aborigines. On the other hand, the beauty of the higher ranks in England is very remarkable, being, in the main, as clearly a result of good external conditions.

On this subject the celebrated naturalist, M. Buffon,[11] remarks: "Coarse, unwholesome and ill-prepared food makes the human race degenerate. All those people who live miserably are ugly and ill-made. Even in France, the country people are not so beautiful as those who live in towns; and I have often remarked that in those villages where the people are richer and better fed than in others, the men are likewise more handsome and have better countenances."

Voice of the Fugitive (Windsor, Canada West), 29 January, 12, 26 February 1851.

1. In reaction to the rise of militant abolitionism during the early 1830s, southerners defended slavery as a "positive good." They argued that it produced bene-

fits for the white master race and for the permanently inferior black slaves, who were considered incapable of assuming the responsibilities of freedom. By the 1850s, proslavery writers turned the defense of slavery into a critique of northern society, damning it for, among other things, its materialism and individualism. George M. Fredrickson, *The Black Image in the White Mind: The Debate on Afro-American Character and Destiny, 1817–1914* (New York, N.Y., 1971), 43–70.

2. Bibb's description of the indigenous peoples of pre-Roman England—Celts, Britons, Picts, and Scots—probably comes from Tacitus' *Life of Cnaeus Julius Agricola.* Roman legions invaded England in 55 B.C. and extended their control over the island until the late fourth century, when the legions were withdrawn to defend Rome against barbarian attacks. Without the Roman military presence, England was open to invasion by Angles, Saxons, and Jutes. The Saxons, who were converted to Christianity in the sixth century, slowly reunified the island. The Anglo-Saxons were subjugated by the French Norman forces of William the Conqueror in 1066.

3. Bibb's statement is incorrect. The inhabitants of Roman England, except slaves, were granted full Roman citizenship by Emperor Caracalla in 212 A.D.

4. Bibb refers to the fact that most European nations had abolished slavery by 1851, while the United States still allowed the institution to exist, despite widespread criticism from the British.

5. Pompee Valentin, Baron de Vastey (?–ca. 1820) was a French-educated mulatto, who served as private secretary to King Henri Christophe (1806–20) of Haiti. De Vastey defended the monarchy and African civilization in several published works on Haitian politics, European colonialism, and Franco-Haitian relations. Roland I. Perusse, *Historical Dictionary of Haiti* (Metuchen, N.J., 1977), 102.

6. De Vastey's quote surveys the explanations of racial differences used by antebellum philosophers, ethnologists, and other scientists. In the decades preceding the Civil War, many racial theorists attempted to use scientific, historical, and scriptural arguments to demonstrate black inferiority. During the 1840s and 1850s, the theory of polygenesis, which posited that the races were separate creations, became popular among many intellectuals, particularly the "American school" of ethnology. Most adherents to this theory believed that racial characteristics were irreversible, thereby lending credence to the notion of permanent black inferiority. Some saw blacks as a lesser species, closer to animals than to the white race, and linked them to various species of apes. At that time, the term *orang-outang*, to which De Vastey refers, usually meant the African chimpanzee, not the Asian orangutan. A few racial theorists depended upon historical observations, including those of Edward Long (1734–1813), a Jamaican planter, who wrote extensively on the history, society, and economy of the island. The antiblack statements in his *History of Jamaica* (1774) became part of a corpus of information they used to demonstrate black inferiority. Many theorists used Old Testament references in an attempt to explain the skin color of blacks and to justify Afro-American slavery. According to Genesis 9:20–27, Noah's son Ham observed his father lying drunk and naked in his tent. When Noah awoke, he was angered and cursed Ham's son Canaan and all of Canaan's descendants to be the "servant of servants." Nineteenth-century proslavery apologists, who believed that the black

race descended from Canaan, used this story as a rationale for black bondage. Others preferred the biblical tale of Cain and Abel. According to Genesis 4:1–15, Cain murdered his brother Abel out of jealousy and was marked by God as punishment. Many proslavery preachers argued that Cain was marked with a black skin, which was passed on to his descendants. Frederickson, *Black Image in White Mind*, 71–96; William Stanton, *The Leopard's Spots: Scientific Attitudes toward Race in America, 1815–59* (Chicago, Ill., 1960); Winthrop D. Jordan, *White over Black: American Attitudes toward the Negro, 1550–1812* (Chapel Hill, N.C., 1968), 17–20, 32, 216–39, 242, 285, 416, 491–511.

7. Sir William Lawrence (1783–1867), an English physician, became a member of the College of Surgeons in 1813 and later served as sergeant-surgeon to Queen Victoria. He published a number of essays and lectures, including "On the Physiology, Zoology, and Natural History of Man" (1819). *DNB*, 11:727–28.

8. Ajax is a giant, slow-witted Greek warrior in Homer's *Iliad.* Bibb refers to the fierce engagement in the Trojan War, during which Ajax successfully appealed to Zeus to end a violent thunderstorm that had enveloped the field of battle.

9. Robert Chambers (1802–1871), brother of the eminent British encyclopedist, William Chambers, wrote *The Vestiges of the Natural History of Creation* in 1845. The work was widely read and received favorable comment in Darwin's introduction to *On the Origin of the Species. DNB*, 4:23–25.

10. Chambers refers to Oliver Cromwell's reorganization of Ireland in 1653. After a brutal pacification program, Cromwell ordered the forced resettlement of the Irish in the Connaught province. The vacated land in Down, Antrim, and other Ulster counties was divided among English soldiers and investors. D. M. R. Esson, *The Curse of Cromwell* (London, 1971), 156–87.

11. Georges-Louis LeClerc, compte de Buffon (1707–1788), a French naturalist, was the premier scientist of the Enlightenment. He promoted Newtonian scientific principles and investigated a variety of subjects in his multivolumed *Histoire naturelle, generale, et particulière* (1749). Buffon's pioneering work in anthropology and zoology anticipated much nineteenth-century scientific thought on race and evolution. Otis E. Fellows and Stephen F. Milliken, *Buffon* (New York, N.Y., 1972).

18.
Editorial by Henry Bibb
26 February 1851

On 15 February 1851, authorities in Boston arrested fugitive slave Frederick "Shadrach" Wilkins and took him to the city courthouse for an extradition hearing. As the court adjourned, a crowd of black Bostonians entered the room, surrounded the defendant, and ushered him to safety; eventually, he was conveyed to Montreal, Canada East. The Shadrach rescue was the first organized challenge to the Fugitive Slave Law. The American federal government responded swiftly. Three days after the rescue, President Millard Fillmore issued a special proclamation ordering that federal charges be brought against those involved. The proclamation, also signed by Secretary of State Daniel Webster, brought the arrest of several members of the Boston Vigilance Committee, including blacks Robert Morris and Lewis Hayden. In the 26 February 1851 issue of the *Voice of the Fugitive*, Henry Bibb criticized the government's response to the Shadrach rescue and defended the right of civil disobedience, especially by those on the periphery of American society. Bibb anticipated the political polarization that eventually resulted from strict federal enforcement of the Fugitive Slave Law. Austin Bearse, *Reminiscences of Fugitive-Slave Law Days in Boston* (Boston, 1880; reprint, New York, N.Y. 1969), 117–22; Merrill and Ruchames, *Letters of William Lloyd Garrison*, 4:49–50n.

THE PROCLAMATION

We have inserted, in another portion of our paper, a proclamation issued by President Fillmore,[1] in consequence of disturbances which have taken place in Boston on an attempt having been made to recover a fugitive slave. It will be seen, by the proclamation, that it is the intention of the President fully to carry out, by force of arms, the fugitive law, as he therein gives instructions to the various military bodies in the vicinity to assist in the recapture of the said slave, who had been set at liberty by the populace; and that all persons who lent their assistance in effecting the escape, are to be "immediately arrested and prosecuted according to law."

This may be considered the commencement of hostilities between the friends of liberty and the supporters of slavery; and it remains to be seen how far despotism can be carried out in a country like the United States, which has so long boasted of the liberality of its institutions.

We can imagine the Emperors of Russia and Austria issuing a mandate of the same character as this proclamation of President Fillmore—their governments being absolute,[2] and backed by powerful standing armies; while their subjects, who are enveloped in the most profound ignorance, tacitly admit the Divine right inherited by their masters to use them as they list, but in the United States the case is different: despotic laws can never have permanent existence among free people.

The people against whom this proclamation is issued are denominated as "lawless persons." These are the usual cant terms employed by all tyrants, and men of sense attach no importance to them. Laws, from time immemorial, have so seldom been founded in justice, that it is not singular that honest men should invariably be found opposing them. The men of Boston who threw the tea overboard were lawless men;[3] but their want of veneration for law established the Republic of the United States.

In the proclamation the persons of color are alluded to as chiefly composing the "lawless" mob. We admit the lawlessness of our people—they are outlaws—the only way in which the law recognizes them is in punishment; they are beyond the pale of its protection,[4] consequently they cannot be censured for opposing its execution.

On the whole, we are rather rejoiced than sad at the issue of this proclamation, for it will have the effect of bringing matters to a crisis more speedily. We are likewise glad to know that a library is being established at the Presidential mansion[5] for the purpose of affording instruction to future Presidents, as nothing but a total lack of knowledge of the effects which follow such a course of policy as that which is now pursued, could have induced President Fillmore and his besotted gang to send forth such an edict.

Voice of the Fugitive (Windsor, Canada West), 26 February 1851.

1. Millard Fillmore (1800–1874) was the thirteenth president of the United States. Born at Locke, Cayuga County, New York, he served in the New York state legislature and in the United States Congress between 1828 and 1847. With the death of President Zachary Taylor on 9 July 1850, Vice-President Fillmore became president and served through the end of Taylor's term. *DAB*, 3(2):380–82.

2. The autocratic regimes of Nicholas I (1796–1855) of Russia and Ferdinand I (1793–1875) of Austria were widely regarded as models of despotism and bulwarks against unfulfilled nationalist and democratic aspirations in nineteenth-century Europe.

3. On 16 December 1773, a group of Massachusetts colonists, poorly disguised as Mohawk Indians, boarded three British merchant ships in Boston harbor and threw 342 chests of tea (valued at $90,000) overboard. Samuel Adams organized the "tea party," which highlighted colonial protests against British taxation policies. The British responded by closing the port of Boston.

4. Law, custom, and prejudice frequently combined, as Bibb suggests, to place blacks "beyond the pale of protection." No northern state expressly prohibited all black rights to legal protection and redress of injuries during the antebellum period. But blacks were vulnerable, particularly in the courtroom. Although practices varied from state to state, blacks often could not give testimony in cases in-

volving a white person, were not allowed to sit on juries, and held no judgeships. Rampant racial prejudice on the part of white judges and juries further undermined black opportunity for a fair trial. Penal statistics reveal that a disproportionate number of antebellum northern blacks were arrested and imprisoned for minor offenses. Litwack, *North of Slavery*, 93–112.

5. Upon the recommendation of first lady Abigail Powers Fillmore, Congress appropriated funds for a White House library during the early 1850s. Charles Hurd, *The White House Story* (New York, N.Y., 1966), 80, 90, 142, 196.

19.
Thomas H. Jones to Daniel Foster
5 May 1851

Arrival on Canadian soil often had a powerful impact on fugitive slaves reaching the end of a dangerous journey to freedom. One observer reported that "they seemed to be transformed; a new light shone in their eyes. . . ." Letters written by black refugees back to American friends reflect Canada's transforming effect. Fugitive Thomas H. Jones offered his reaction in a letter to Daniel Foster, his Massachusetts benefactor. Jones, who had escaped from slavery two years earlier, was forced by slave catchers to flee to the Maritime Provinces, leaving his wife and children with friends in Salem, Massachusetts. Even so, Jones confided to Foster that, upon arriving in Canada, he felt, for the first time, "that my bones are a property bequeathed to me for my own use." Hill, *Freedom-Seekers*, 59; *Lib*, 30 May 1851.

ST. JOHN, N[ew] B[runswick]
May 5, 1851

DEAR BROTHER:[1]

From my knowledge of your generous nature and kind Christian hospitality, I know it will be a source of pleasure to you to be informed of my safe arrival here on British ground. Quite free from terror, I now feel that my bones are a property bequeathed to me for my own use, and not for the servitude or gratification of the white man, in that gloomy and sultry region, where the hue of the skin has left my race in thraldom and misery for ages.

O, my dear friend! how good it is to live on the poorest fare, where the mind may apply its immortal powers to the contemplation of heaven and heavenly things, unawed by the monsters who would tie us to a tree and scourge us in our nakedness for attempting to worship the Creator in spirit and in truth!

The atrocity of the hideous system under which I groaned for more than forty years was never so strikingly demonstrated to my mind as it has been by breathing under the auspices and protection of a Government that allows all its children to go abroad in the true liberty of nature, every person free to frequent the altar or the sanctuary to which Conscience would lead him; no cause for degradation but vice, and no lever of promotion but virtue and intelligence.

I begin to see clearly, and to hope with reason, that the Refugee Law has or will awaken the world to a sense of our deep wrongs; and I feel warranted in saying, that the nations of the earth will soon give an expression of opinion upon our cause which will shame the Southern white man out of his cruelty, and cause him to unchain his sable victims. The Ethiopian will ere long be redeemed from his bondage,[2] for Jehovah will be his Emancipator, as he is his King, Creator and Judge.

As to this Province, I have found a home of refuge, full of true, warm, generous Christians, whose hearts, abounding with the love of God, are full of sympathy for the slave, whom they will help to free in due time, as far as human means can extend. The citizens of St. John have received me in the spirit of brotherhood, and only that my mission calls me beyond the seas, I might remain here, and be an instrument of good for many years to come.

In a few days, I proceed to Halifax, and thence to England, as soon as circumstances will permit.[3] Hoping that you will remember me to every kind friend taking an interest in my destinies, I am, Your brother in Christ,

THOMAS H. JONES[4]

P.S. Wherever I preach or lecture, I am followed by enthusiastic houses.

T.H.J.

Liberator (Boston, Mass.), 30 May 1851.

1. Daniel Foster (?–1864), a Massachusetts minister, studied at Dartmouth and Andover. He embraced Garrisonian abolitionism in 1848 and served as an agent for the Massachusetts Anti-Slavery Society in the early 1850s but broke with the Garrisonians in 1853. He taught at a black school in Boston for a time, served briefly as chaplain of the state house of representatives (1857), and joined the free settlers' struggle in Kansas. Foster enlisted in the Union army in 1862 as a chaplain and received a captain's commission before he was killed in action at Chapin's Bluff, Virginia. *Lib*, 21 June 1861, 25 March, 17 August 1862, 29 November 1863, 21 October 1864; *WAA*, 29 October 1864; *NASS*, 6 June 1863.

2. Jones refers to members of the black race, particularly New World slaves.

3. Jones intended to leave for London during the month in order to be an antislavery representative at the Great Exhibition of 1851. In July 1852, he was still planning to visit England, this time to solicit funds to purchase his wife's son out of slavery in North Carolina. No evidence exists to suggest that Jones ever crossed the Atlantic to Britain. *Lib*, 30 May 1851, 13 August 1852 [7:0697].

4. Thomas H. Jones (1806-?) was born to slave parents near Wilmington, North Carolina. He lived on the plantation of John Hawes until about 1815, when he was sold to a Wilmington storekeeper from whom the slave obtained his surname. While working as a house servant, then as a store clerk, Jones obtained a rudimentary education. Upon reaching adulthood, he married a slave named Lucilla Smith, and they produced three children before being separated several years later when her mistress moved to Alabama. Following his master's death in 1829, Jones was sold to Owen Holmes of Wilmington, who hired him out as a stevedore. By the mid-1830s, convinced that he would never see his family again, Jones remarried, this time to a slave named Mary R. Moore. She bore several children before Jones purchased her out of slavery. They lived in the free black com-

munity of Wilmington until 1849, when a white lawyer friend warned Jones about plans to reenslave his children, who were technically still slaves. The lawyer attempted to maneuver a special act for their emancipation through the North Carolina legislature. When this effort failed, Jones sent his wife and children—except a son, Edward, who remained in slavery—to safety in the free states. In August 1849, Jones stowed away on the brig *Bell* until it reached New York City, where he rejoined his family. He was quickly drawn into the antislavery movement and lectured for several months in Connecticut and western Massachusetts before settling in Salem, where he preached regularly at the local Wesleyan church. At the 1850 meeting of the Massachusetts Anti-Slavery Society, he defended William Lloyd Garrison against clerical critics, which gained him the attention of Garrisonians and earned him the friendship and support of Massachusetts clergyman-abolitionist Daniel Foster. In May 1851, the threat of slave catchers forced Jones to flee to the Maritime Provinces, leaving his family behind in Salem. Basing himself in St. John, he gave antislavery lectures throughout New Brunswick and Nova Scotia, frequently attracting sizable audiences. He also enlisted subscribers for the *Liberator*. Word reached Jones in 1852 that he could purchase his eldest son Edward for $850. His wife raised $324 in the Boston area, but the remainder came in slowly, so Jones turned his full attention toward redeeming his son from slavery. He solicited contributions throughout the Maritimes and considered a fund-raising tour of England that never materialized. Jones returned to Massachusetts in August 1853. His treatment on the steamer *Eastern City* during the trip back briefly made him an antislavery cause célèbre; a clerk who had assaulted Jones during the voyage to Boston and forced him to pass the night on deck was eventually arrested for his actions. After arriving in Boston, Jones toured New England and penned his narrative, *The Experience of Thomas Jones* (1854), to raise funds to free his son. Although Jones's narrative sold well, it remains unclear when (or if) he completed his son's purchase. But by 1859 he had settled in Worcester, Massachusetts, and reemerged as a minor figure in the antislavery movement. He attracted considerable attention with a speech given before the August 1859 New England Colored Citizens' Convention in Boston, in which he urged black Americans to militantly "strike for liberty." He also became a vocal critic of black emigration projects, particularly those advocated by the African Civilization Society. Jones continued to reside in Worcester through 1862. Thomas H. Jones, *The Experience of Thomas Jones, Who was a Slave for Forty-Three Years* (Springfield, Mass., 1854); Massachusetts Anti-Slavery Society, *Eighteenth Annual Report* (1850), 98 [6:0364]; *Lib*, 30 May 1851, 13 August 1852, 19 August, 2 September 1853, 18 August 1854 [6:0949, 7:0697, 8:0430]; Thomas H. Jones to William Lloyd Garrison, 10 February 1854, Anti-Slavery Collection, MB [8:0650–51]; Foner and Walker, *Proceedings of Black State Conventions*, 2: 216, 223; *Worcester City Directory*, 1860–62.

20.
Editorial by Henry Bibb
21 May 1851

Black abolitionists in Canada were concerned about American influences on the Canadian haven. They believed that Canada offered blacks freedom and opportunity, and they regularly praised "Her Majesty's government" for ending slavery in the empire, for protecting fugitive slaves, and for supporting the transatlantic antislavery movement. But they also knew that the haven required their constant vigilance. Black abolitionists feared that the United States would annex Canada, thus destroying their sanctuary. They were also concerned that American racial prejudice would corrupt white Canadians. Black leaders were particularly worried by the rise in racist behavior that followed the rapid growth of the Canadian black population during the 1850s. Henry Bibb's 21 May 1851 editorial in the *Voice of the Fugitive* addressed the problem and his attendant anxieties.

COLOR-PHOBIA IN CANADA

This most obnoxious and fatal disease has made its way into this province where it is destined to make havoc among the ignorant and vicious if a speedy remedy is not applied. Its allies are mostly among the lowest class of white people, who are used as mere stepping stones or political hobbies for the more refined and enlightened to ride into office upon. Its origin sprang from old Capt. *Slavery*, who has enlisted thousands in his services to carry on the work of prejudice, malice, and hatred, death and devastation among the human family. He has ever been opposed to the spread of knowledge among the common people. The rum shop is substituted for the school house and his soldiers are mostly men [of] intemperate habits; always ready to go at the bidding of their leader to break up an anti-slavery meeting, to engage in the work of kidnapping, man stealing, breaking up the bands of human affections by selling children from parents and husbands from their wives.

In thousands of instances he has enlisted the press and the pulpit in his services, and especially in the U.S. He has secured the Executive and Legislature power of that Government in passing and enforcing the fugitive slave law which is regarded as a disgrace to the christian world.

But the old deceiver is not satisfied with what has been accomplished in the states; but is now striving to get a foot-hold in Canada where many of the objects of his prey have settled under the protection of Her Majesty's law.

Color-phobia is a contagious disease. It is more destructive to the mind than to the body. It goes hard with a person who is a little nervous. It makes them froth and foam as if the Bengal Tiger was in them. Its symptoms are various. It makes them sing out "darkey," "darkey," "nigger," "nigger"—sometimes "long-heel"—"long-heel."[1] It sometimes makes them quack like crows. It frightens them up from the dining table at public houses, not because of a black man's cooking the dinner or waiting on the table, but because of his sitting down to eat. It excites them awfully when colored passengers enter the rail cars or stage coaches, but not when they come in the capacity of waiters or servants.

It sometimes gets into children through the wicked and unnatural teaching of parents. Whenever you hear a parent saying to a child "hush and go to sleep, or the nigger will catch you"—the black man will kill you, &c. It is pretty good evidence that they have got the color-phobia. When they have it bad they will turn up their noses when they get near a colored person, as if they smelt something disagreeable and often say there is a cloud rising. It sometimes gets holds of professors of religion, and shows itself at the communion table, especially if a colored sister offers to partake of the emblems of the dying Saviour with her white brethren—she is modestly asked by one of the Deacons or class leaders to wait until the white folks are done and she is seated up in the back corner of the gallery or in the back part of the house (perhaps under the steps).[2]

In Canada, it gets hold of the very dregs of society. It makes them shudder at the idea of "negro settlement" "they will ruin the country" &c. The objection most generally brought up is that we shall have negro lawyers, doctors, judges &c. It seems to excite their imagination so much that they become alarmed about amalgamation—the white girls are all going to make choice of black men, and the white gents will be left without wives, and what then? Don't be alarmed friends, you shall not be hurt. All this is the workings of a diseased imagination, of which you must be cured, or it will destroy your souls and bodies both. Anti-Slavery is the very best remedy for it. It will cure you of prejudice and hatred, and prepare you for a happier state of existence.

Voice of the Fugitive (Windsor, Canada West), 21 May 1851.

1. Long-heel is a disparaging, archaic term used by southern whites to refer to a black person. Harold Wentworth and Stuart Berg Flexner, eds., *Dictionary of American Slang*, 2d suppl. ed. (New York, N.Y., 1975), 324.

2. Most antebellum Protestant churches that celebrated the Eucharist compelled black communicants to wait until after all whites had partaken of the bread and wine at the Communion table. While waiting, blacks were required to remain in racially separate "Negro pews" or balconies. Catholic churches rarely observed this practice. Litwack, *North of Slavery*, 196, 204.

21.
James Theodore Holly to Henry Bibb
May 1851

Deteriorating race relations in the United States and the passage of the Fugitive Slave Law of 1850 convinced a growing number of black leaders of the efficacy of emigration. The emigrationist debate began cautiously with talk of temporary Canadian resettlement and peaked in the late 1850s and early 1860s with specific West African and Haitian immigration projects. James Theodore Holly helped shape the discussion through a series of letters written to Henry Bibb during the spring and summer of 1851, which Bibb published in his *Voice of the Fugitive*. Holly supported Canada as an immigration site because it was accessible to fugitives and because immigrants could strike at slavery from there. He believed that black resettlement in Canada would have "regenerative" powers and that black achievement there would be "a beacon of hope to the slave and a rock of terror to the oppressor." Holly proposed that Canadian blacks organize additional settlements to aid fleeing refugees, that a "central authority" be created to unite and direct black action, and that a convention be called to consider the destiny of blacks on the North American continent. In his May 1851 letter, Holly explained the advantages of black immigration to Canada over white-sponsored African colonization. *VF*, 7 May, 1 June, 2, 16, 30 July 1851 [6:0919, 0950, 0991, 7:0004, 0021].

VOICE FROM THE "GREEN MOUNTAINS"

Dear Sir:

I was agreeably surprised, on the receipt of the late copies of your valuable journal, to learn that you had already projected, and was agitating a plan for the systematic colonization of refugees in Canada West; and that you had thereby anticipated the suggestion contained in my former communication.[1] Your plan meets my hearty approbation, and I give in my adhesion to it, as an humble supporter of the same. And I design hereafter to give testimony in *deed* as well as in *profession*. I think it has now become the duty of the whole free colored population of the United States, to support your project as the most practicable one ever presented for their consideration, and the most available for the speedy emancipation of our enslaved brethren. We should regard you and those that immediately surround you in the noble project, as the head and centre of all our future efforts. We should organize state and local associations, throout all of the free states, for auxiliary cooperation with your chief central authority in Canada West.

When another National Convention of our people shall assemble from all the free states, I trust it will be in obedience to a call emanating through the *Voice of the Fugitive*, and that we will convene with you, on your territory, to concert and consolidate a general effort for Canadian colonization.[2]

Let it be an understood matter from now and henceforth, that the central authority of the colored people of the United States, is in your asylum of the refugee, and that hereafter it is to be the grand rallying point of all our efforts. I have long been impressed with the necessity of some project to withdraw our people from the drudging employment of menials, about the towns and cities of the free states, and to locate them in a primitive community, where they might lay the foundation of their own future greatness, and at the same time afford a hospitable home to the escaping bondmen.

Three great schemes have been hitherto pressed upon our attention, viz.: African, Haytian, and British West India colonization. But the distance of these locations from our enslaved brethren still clanking their chains, and their tropical latitudes, are insurmountable objections to the free colored people of the United States. And the persons with whom, and the circumstances in which, the African scheme originated, makes that project the most intolerable of all others, and it is not likely that any considerable number of our people will ever look upon Liberia with any degree of favor, no matter what advantages it may present for *individual enterprise*, until American Slavery is abolished.[3]

But happily the question of Canadian colonization presents itself to us, divested of all these objections. It is on the North American continent, in close proximity to the United States, and convenient to the North-western slave states.[4] There is but a slight variation of climate from that we have all been used to. The project is an alternative we can spontaneously adopt ourselves, without having it marked out for us by doubtful philanthropists. Therefore we should vigorously pursue this project, and swarm in a ceaseless tide to Canada West, and hang like an ominous *black cloud* over this guilty nation, until the precipitated occurrence of providential circumstances—the terrible thunderbolts of Omnipotent judgment hurled from the hand of Jehovah, shall scale the Alleghany summits, and reverberate through the valley of the Mississippi, breaking every chain and letting the oppressed go free. To be an humble instrument in producing so glorious a result, is worthy of a lifetime of self-sacrificing toil, and heroic effort. I freely consecrate myself and my all to do the humblest share of the work.

I submit myself to the leadership you have so worthily assumed, and I doubt not but that in proportion, as the knowledge of your project becomes disseminated, it will enlist firm supporters for you, from amongst the earnest portion of our people throughout the country in word and deed. I think I am justified in assuring you of a full quota of noble spirits in Vermont, who will rally around your standard, after the project has assumed a more tangible shape. But we must move patiently, what though it should require years of labor, and succeeding generations to perfect the design? It is the eternal truth of God, the destiny of a vast portion of the human race, and the fate of nations that engages our attention, and we cannot move too securely. Let us not forget that by time, patience and perseverance, all things are accomplished.

J. T. H.[5]

Voice of the Fugitive (Windsor, Canada West), 1 June 1851.

1. Holly apparently refers to the constitution of the Fugitive Union Society, which Bibb published in the 1 January 1851 issue of the *Voice of the Fugitive*. The society was created to aid the settlement of fugitive slaves in Canada West in the wake of the Fugitive Slave Law of 1850. In his "former communication," written to Bibb on 7 May 1851, Holly had proposed a similar Canadian agency to deal with the economic, social, political, religious, and educational needs of blacks fleeing into the province. *VF*, 15 January, 7 May 1851 [6:0919].

2. During the 1850s, the black convention movement shifted its emphasis from ridding American society of slavery and racism to debating the merits of emigration. Free blacks held nine national conventions between 1830 and 1848. The various convention agenda shared the goals of ending slavery, elevating the status of all blacks, and providing a national focus for black reform. During the 1830s, influenced by William Lloyd Garrison and other white reformers, delegates pursued a wide range of reforms while diluting their uniquely black perspective. Consequently, from 1836 to 1843, the national movement was inactive while local conventions maintained interest in cooperative action and eventually revitalized the broader movement. During the 1840s, black national conventions became more militant and independent, emphasizing black priorities. Beginning with the North American Convention (1851) in Toronto, the movement focused on black nationalism and emigration. Holly called for the Toronto convention in order to encourage black immigration to Canada. A spirited debate over emigration dominated the convention movement through the last antebellum national convention in 1855 and engaged the attention of some black leaders until the start of the Civil War. The convention movement encouraged reform activity, nurtured black leadership, and generally aided the cause of abolitionism. Howard H. Bell, ed., *Minutes of the Proceedings of the National Negro Conventions, 1830–1864* (New York, N.Y., 1969); Jane H. Pease and William H. Pease, "Negro Conventions and the Problem of Black Leadership," *JBS* 2:29–44 (September 1971); Pease and Pease, *They Who Would Be Free*, 119–23.

3. Antebellum efforts to resettle American free blacks outside of the United States attracted support from many white Americans. Some philanthropists, including many Quakers, believed that colonization was a way to assist free blacks while promoting Christian missionary work on the African continent. Others viewed it as the solution to a troublesome social problem—the presence of free blacks in a white-dominated, slaveholding society. In order to promote colonization and encourage governmental assistance, a group of white politicians and phi-

lanthropists founded the American Colonization Society in 1816. In the decades that followed, many other colonization societies, some affiliated with the ACS, were organized on the state and local levels. Haitian independence (1804) and the emancipation of slaves in the British West Indies (1834) stimulated some interest in Caribbean colonization alternatives. These efforts proved relatively unsuccessful. Subsidized by the Haitian government and endorsed by colonizationists, an estimated eight thousand American free blacks did settle in Haiti during the 1820s. But black immigration to Haiti soon slowed, as settlers became disenchanted with political and economic conditions in the island nation. The most ambitious and controversial colonization project was the effort of the ACS and allied colonization societies to settle American free blacks in Liberia. A group of American free blacks, working under ACS sponsorship, founded the colony of Liberia on the West African coast in 1822. Although settled on land rich in timber, rubber, and iron ore, the colony, which was run by ACS agents for its first seventeen years, managed a rather tenuous existence. The hostility of the indigenous population and the opposition of an overwhelming majority of American free blacks hindered its development. In 1839 the dotting of essentially coastal settlements was reorganized by the society into a commonwealth. In 1847 Liberia gained its independence. Floyd J. Miller, *The Search for Black Nationality* (Urbana, Ill., 1975), 43–51, 54–90; C. Abayomi Cassell, *Liberia* (New York, N.Y., 1970), 1–205.

4. Holly probably refers to the slave states of Missouri, Kentucky, Tennessee, and Arkansas.

5. James Theodore Holly (1829–1911) was the son of a free black Washington, D.C., shoemaker. The younger Holly spent his early years in the district and attended a segregated school there until the Holly family moved to Brooklyn, New York, in 1844. A baptized Roman Catholic, he was persuaded by a priest to continue his education in mathematics and the classics. Through the late 1840s, he also worked as a clerk at Lewis Tappan's American Missionary Association offices. In 1850 Holly moved to Burlington, Vermont, where he operated a bootmaking shop with his brother Joseph. More important, he began to give serious thought to the direction of the Afro-American destiny. Holly temporarily embraced colonization, but he soon abandoned it in favor of Canadian immigration and black unity. He initiated a correspondence with Henry Bibb, a leading black Canadian abolitionist and the editor of the *Voice of the Fugitive*. During the summer of 1851, with Bibb's encouragement, Holly called for the formation of the North American League; he envisioned it as a centralized organization whose objectives would include forging continental black unity, assisting fugitive slaves in Canada West, encouraging Canadian immigration, and aiding black agricultural development. During 1852 and 1853, Holly labored for Bibb's *Voice*, first as a corresponding editor and subscription agent and then as coeditor and coproprietor. He also supported the Refugee Home Society, an experiment directed by Bibb that attempted to create agriculturally-based fugitive slave communities in southwestern Canada West.

The black emigration cause remained Holly's primary focus through the early 1860s. He helped organize the General Convention for the Improvement of the Colored Inhabitants of Canada, which met at Amherstburg during June 1853, and he convinced delegates to adopt a proemigration stance. He attended the

1854 Cleveland meeting of the National Emigration Convention. When delegates to that gathering selected Holly as their representative to visit Haiti and negotiate an immigration treaty with the government there, he abandoned support for Canadian settlement in favor of a lengthy commitment to Haitian immigration. He soon seized the leadership of the nascent Haitian movement by linking it with black Episcopalian missionary ventures. During the next two years, he sought church assistance for Haitian settlement projects. In 1856 Holly, who had converted to Episcopalianism during his Vermont days, was ordained an Episcopal priest and appointed rector of St. Luke's Episcopal Church in New Haven, Connecticut. After the second National Emigration Convention (August 1856), he organized the West Indian Trading Association and the Protestant Episcopal Society for Promoting the Extension of the Church Among Colored People to serve as advocates for the Haitian cause. In 1857 he published *Vindication of the Capacity of the Negro Race*, a brief for Haitian immigration. Holly broke with the National Emigration Convention in 1858, but he continued to serve the broader movement by encouraging church support, lecturing, and writing a series of promotional essays for the *Anglo-African Magazine*. When enthusiasm for Haitian immigration peaked between late 1859 and early 1861, Holly shared leadership of the movement with white journalist James Redpath. Early in 1861, Holly organized the New Haven Pioneer Company of Haytian Emigration and led 111 blacks from New Haven, Boston, and Canada West to a settlement in Haiti. Within nine months of their arrival, four members of the Holly family had died along with thirty-eight other settlers.

But Holly refused to abandon Haiti. In the fall of 1862, he obtained missionary sponsorship for his venture, and two years later, he secured a regular missionary appointment to Haiti from the Episcopal church. He was consecrated bishop of Haiti in 1874. Holly remained a resident of the West Indies until his death in 1911; during these years, he founded medical clinics, schools, and a theological college for blacks. Holly's appointment in 1900 as regional representative of the Pan-African Association provided a significant link between the antebellum black emigration movement and twentieth-century black nationalism. Miller, *Search for Black Nationality*, 94, 105, 107–15, 135–37, 142–49, 157, 161–71, 181, 186, 230–49, 266–67, 272; David M. Dean, *Defender of the Race: James Theodore Holly, Black Nationalist and Bishop* (Boston, Mass., 1979); *VF*, 7 May, 1 June, 2, 16, 30 July, 24 September 1851, 15 July, 2 December 1852 [6:0919, 0950, 0991, 7:0004, 0021, 0112, 0657, 0845]; *AAM*, June, July, August, September, October, November 1859 [11:0763, 0820, 0896, 0991, 12:0079, 0173]; *WAA*, 15, 24 January, 9, 16 February 1861 [13:0217, 0300, 0325, 0362]; *PP*, 5 June 1861 [13:0677]; J. Carleton Hayden, "James Theodore Holly (1829–1911) First Afro-American Episcopal Bishop: His Legacy to Us Today," in *Black Apostles: Afro-American Clergy Confront the Twentieth Century*, ed. Randall K. Burkett and Richard Newman (Boston, Mass., 1978), 129–40; *DANB*, 319–20.

22.
Editorial by Henry Bibb
18 June 1851

Henry Bibb was a vigorous advocate of the Canadian sanctuary and used his *Voice of the Fugitive* to keep Americans and Canadians informed about the conditions and needs of the thousands of fugitive slaves who crossed into Canada West after 1850. Bibb's 18 June 1851 editorial emerged from a May meeting of the Refugee Home Society that he attended in Detroit. That gathering had endorsed a plan to purchase fifty thousand acres of land in Canada West and resell them to fugitive slaves. In the editorial, Bibb exaggerated the number of fugitives in Canada West and described their pitiful state but insisted that with temporary philanthropy and assistance the fugitives could develop into prosperous farmers. Like many black leaders, Bibb believed that Canada West could become a black showplace that would demonstrate their readiness for freedom. Bibb's editorial reflected the philosophical base and practical program of the Refugee Home Society. *VF*, 1, 18 June 1851 [6:0972].

THE AMERICAN REFUGEES HOME

To the friends of civil liberty and education, we would most respectfully represent that the number of human beings held in chattel slavery in the U. States is over and above 3,000,000; and that they are not only prohibited in several of the slave States[1] by statute law from reading, the scriptures of Divine Truth as a means of grace—but the most sacred ties of the human family are frequently and wickedly broken up by selling husbands from wives and children from parents.[2] From such oppression as this, people are constantly running away to the North, and thousands of whom have been compelled to take refuge in Canada under the British flag, which protects them in the enjoyment of that liberty which the American Government has so earnestly sought to take from unoffending people.

It is not now our purpose, however, to enlarge upon the evils of that system "one hour of which is fraught with far greater misery than ages of that which" the fathers of the American Republic, "rose in rebellion to oppose," for we presume there are none who will read this circular but what will admit its intrinsic sinfulness. But our object is simply to lay facts before the public, relative to the rapid influx and actual condition of our refugee brethren in Canada since the enactment of the notorious Fugitive Slave Law in the U.S., and to arrive at, if possible, what kind of assistance would result in the most permanent good to the greatest number of this people who are now in Canada and who may hereafter come.

It was generally supposed before the passage of the fugitive slave law that there were from 25 to 35 thousand who had taken refuge here, and since that enactment the number has greatly augmented[3]—from the fact that it is now well understood that there is no protection to the liberty of a refugee slave in America, until the Canadian line is drawn between him and his pursuer.

The sad story of the fugitives *Long, Syms, Wordman* and a host of others who have been dragged back into perpetual slavery by the strong arm of the American government, furnishes sufficient proof of the truthfulness of this assertion.[4]

The condition of this people in Canada, as a general thing, is that they are here in a strange land from necessity, uneducated, poverty stricken, without homes or any permanent means of self support; however willing they may be to work they have no means to work with or land to work upon. The natural inference is that they must either beg, starve or steal. To prevent this much has been sent to Canada during the last 7 months by the friends of humanity, in the way of food and clothing for the fugitives.[5] But such help is only temporary and must be repeated again and again, while it is degrading to some extent to all who are recipients thereof—for no people can be respected who live beneath the dignity of manhood. Ignorance, dissipation and pauperism are the landmarks of slavery, and the great aim and object, therefore, should be to enable this people to arise above it by their own industry. The remedy for the physical wants of this people, those especially specified, lies slumbering in the virgin soil of C. W. To improve the moral, mental and political condition of a poverty stricken and degraded people, they must become owners and tillers of the soil—and PRODUCE WHAT THEY CONSUME.

It is no exaggeration for us to say that more than two-thirds of the refugees in Canada understand agricultural labor and would follow it for a livelihood, had they land or the means to purchase it. They would also gladly open schools for their children that they might be educated for usefulness in life, had they the means with which to do it.

Without homes or employment they are poorly qualified to produce the necessaries of life, to educate the youth or extend the hospitable hand to the gradual emigration of other fugitives who are constantly arriving here, who go up and down these shores hunting shelter and employment but finding none. In order that there may be a permanent asylum to conduct such persons to on the Queen's soil, where the cause of education, industry and morality may be promoted, the friends of humanity in Michigan have organized a state society for the purpose of making an "effort at home and abroad" to purchase 50,000 acres of Canada land for this object, and they propose to deed to the family of every actual settler 5 acres of said land and to leave adjoining it 20 acres which may be purchased by said settler at cost and that one-third of all money paid in for said land by settlers should be appropriated for the support of schools for their children, and that the balance should be kept at interest in the bank for the purchase of more land for the same object from time to time while slavery exists in the United States.[6]

The undersigned being a resident of Canada, has been solicited to write a circular embracing such facts as might be necessary to throw light upon the subject; but for want of time we have not been able to give the subject that consideration which its overwhelming importance demands.

In conclusion we would remark that the Canada Company[7] offer 700,000 acres of land in blocks containing from 2000 to 9000 acres each, situated in the Western District, and scattered lots containing from 100 to 200 acres each, situated in almost every township in Canada West.

The above land is located in the most *southern and western* part of Canada, and is selling from $2 to $4 per acre.

The land is rich and generally well stocked with valuable timber. It is surrounded on either side with lasting and navigable waters. The climate is as mild and congenial to the physical and intellectual development of the African race as a part of Missouri, Ohio, Michigan, Wisconsin or New York; and the argument which is frequently brought up by pro-slavery men that it is so cold that colored people cannot live here is a falsehood and the facts in the case will prove it to be so, from the fact that there are at the present time some thirty-five thousand living here who generally arrive at as old an age as they do in the south, and from the fact that when negro slavery was tolerated and practised here under the colonial government[8] that there was no complaint about the climate's being too cold for the colored people then, affords the most striking proof to our mind that wherever a white man can live and prosper that a colored man can also, if he is given an equal chance. There will always be objections enough brought up against any scheme to settle the colored people this side of Liberia, by prejudiced pro-slavery men. But we say to the true friends of the refugees in Canada, that there never was a time when they could have conferred a more permanent blessing upon this people than to enable them now to purchase some of this land to settle upon.

H. BIBB

Voice of the Fugitive (Windsor, Canada West), 18 June 1851.

1. Slave states is a term used to describe those states that allowed slavery within their borders. The slave states in 1851 were Delaware, Georgia, Maryland, South Carolina, Virginia, North Carolina, Kentucky, Tennessee, Louisiana, Mississippi, Alabama, Missouri, Arkansas, Florida, and Texas.

2. Southern state laws defined slaves as the property of their masters, who had a virtually unrestricted right to dispose of their chattels as they saw fit. Slave marriages were not recognized by law, and consequently, slave families were separated

by sale, forced migrations, estate settlements, and gift transfers. In some areas of the South, as many as one in six or seven slave marriages ended on the auction block, and the separation of husband and wife or parent and child had an impact on the black community beyond the immediate family. Kenneth M. Stampp, *The Peculiar Institution: Slavery in the Ante-Bellum South* (New York, N.Y., 1956), 197–200, 252, 257–58, 348–49; Herbert G. Gutman, *The Black Family in Slavery and Freedom, 1750–1925* (New York, N.Y., 1976), 318–19.

3. Few reliable statistics exist on the number of fugitive slaves that reached the British North American Provinces prior to the Civil War. Biased underenumeration troubled the 1851 and 1861 Canadian census data. Both the abolitionist and proslavery presses frequently distorted their estimates of the size of the fugitive slave population. But certainly the trickle of fugitive slaves that regularly reached Canada after the War of 1812 turned into a torrent after the passage of the Fugitive Slave Law of 1850. The vast majority of these fugitive slaves settled in Canada West. By 1860 thirty thousand fugitives had apparently settled in the province; they represented three-fourths of the black population there. Although the number of blacks in the total Canadian population probably never exceeded sixty-two thousand (about 2.5 percent) before the Civil War, black numbers may have appeared larger as a result of heavy concentrations in certain Canada West communities, particularly Chatham (20 percent), Amherstburg (25 percent), and Colchester (33 percent). Winks, *Blacks in Canada*, 233–40, 484–96.

4. Bibb refers to three early 1851 incidents involving fugitive slaves Henry Long, Thomas Sims, and Woodson. Long was arrested in New York City on 8 January 1851. The American Anti-Slavery Society supplied funds for his defense, but failed to free him through the courts. They were opposed by the Union Safety Committee, a local businessmen's group. A federal commissioner ordered Long returned to slavery and, despite threats by black and white abolitionists to resist the Fugitive Slave Law, he was led through the streets to a waiting ship by an escort of two hundred policemen. No attempt was made to free him, and he was returned to slavery at government expense. Long was sold in Richmond for $750. Woodson, a Kentucky slave who had lived in Pennsylvania for seven years, was arrested in Beaver, Pennsylvania, on 12 March 1851. He was tried before a federal tribunal in Pittsburgh, which ordered him returned to his master at government expense. Woodson was returned to Louisville, but by early April, abolitionists and family friends in Pittsburgh and Beaver raised the funds necessary to purchase his freedom. Sims, who had escaped only two months earlier from a Georgia rice plantation, was arrested in Boston on 13 April 1851. Members of the Boston Vigilance Committee made several unsuccessful attempts to free him by physical force, but he was remanded to slavery and escorted by three hundred soldiers to the *Acorn*, a waiting vessel. Federal marshals delivered him to his owner in Savannah and he was later sold in Vicksburg, Mississippi. These three cases, among others, helped turn the tide of public opinion against the Fugitive Slave Law. Campbell, *Slave Catchers*, 116–21, 200; Carleton Mabee, *Black Freedom: The Nonviolent Abolitionists from 1830 Through the Civil War* (London, 1970), 307; *NSt*, 16 January 1851; *Lib*, 4 April 1851; *ASB*, 22, 29 March, 5 April 1851; Leonard Levy, "Sims' Case: The Fugitive Slave Law in Boston in 1851," *JNH* 25:39–74 (January 1950).

5. During late 1850 and early 1851, supporters contributed food, clothing, and

funds to assist fugitive slaves in Canada West. Bibb reported that antislavery friends in Michigan, Ohio, and New York assisted about one hundred families at Sandwich. American Missionary Association agent Rev. David Hotchkiss and Rev. Elias E. Kirkland aided nearly two hundred families in the Amherstburg area. Fugitives at Chatham received "considerable" assistance. Several committees in Canada West solicited contributions, and in January 1851, William P. Newman had made a successful fund-raising foray into Michigan on behalf of the Dawn settlement. Bibb publicized contributions received from the states in his *Voice of the Fugitive* and apparently coordinated relief distribution in the Sandwich area. *VF*, 1, 15 January, 12, 26 February, 12 March, 21 May 1851 [6:0721, 0839, 0846, 0938].

6. Bibb refers to the Refugee Home Society, an organization that grew out of efforts to create a settlement for fugitive slaves along the Detroit frontier in Canada West. The Detroit-based society was founded in 1851 by Michigan abolitionists concerned with the condition of fugitive slaves. By 1852 it had merged with the Fugitive Union Society, a black Windsor-based moral improvement association. Ultimate control of the new RHS rested with the white officers in Michigan—Horace Hallock, Elias P. Benham, Abraham L. Power, and J. Nathan Stone. They authorized white clergyman Charles C. Foote and others to raise funds for the project in the United States. Local RHS leadership fell to David Hotchkiss, an American Missionary Association agent in Amherstburg, and to Windsor blacks Henry and Mary Bibb. Over the next three years, the RHS acquired two thousand acres and settled 150 blacks on its lands. Unlike other planned black communities in the Canadas, the RHS did not establish a contiguous settlement but instead bought several separate tracts of land south and east of Windsor near the Puce and Little Rivers. These tracts were then divided into twenty-five-acre parcels and sold to fugitive slaves. As stated in its constitution, the RHS was committed to moral elevation through temperance, industry, religion, and education. The American Missionary Association supported several missions for RHS settlers. Laura Haviland opened a school at Little River and Mrs. David Hotchkiss conducted classes at Puce River, but more ambitious educational plans never materialized. The RHS received considerable criticism from the black community in Canada West. The Bibbs defended the project through the *Voice of the Fugitive*, the RHS's official organ. But opponents, led by *Provincial Freeman* editors Samuel Ringgold Ward and Mary Ann Shadd Cary, derided the land acquisition scheme as an unnecessary embarassment to black Canadians. They objected to RHS fund-raising methods—the "begging" tours of Foote and others. They reported settlers' objections to RHS ownership restrictions and the patronizing attitude of many RHS officers. After Henry Bibb's death in 1854, Foote and George De Baptiste, a black caterer and community leader from Detroit, assumed local leadership of the RHS. But weakened by factionalism and black criticism, the society failed to construct a lasting, viable fugitive slave community. With the coming of the Civil War, the RHS began to dispose of its assets—a process that continued through 1876. Winks, *Blacks in Canada*, 204–8; Pease and Pease, *Black Utopia*, 109–22; Peter Carlesimo, "The Refugee Home Society: Its Origins, Operation and Results, 1851–1876" (M.A. thesis, University of Windsor, 1973), 121, 123–24.

7. The Canada Land Company, a colonizing company, was organized by John

Galt in 1824 and received a British government charter in 1826. The government of Upper Canada sold the company over 1.3 million acres of Crown Reserves and 1.1 million acres of the Huron Tract. The company then sold lots, built roads, and promoted settlement on these lands. Contractual obligations with the government ended in 1843, although the company operated well into the twentieth century. *Encyclopedia Canadiana* (Toronto, 1957), 2:182–83; Winks, *Blacks in Canada*, 156–58.

8. Slaves were first introduced into New France (later called Quebec) in 1628. King Louis XIV of France officially permitted residents of the colony to import and own slaves during the late seventeenth and early eighteenth centuries, and shortly thereafter, the institution reached as far west as the Detroit frontier. Slavery continued under British rule in the latter part of the eighteenth century. American Loyalists brought their slaves when they resettled in the Maritimes and Quebec after the American Revolution. Some Canadian Indians also owned and traded slaves. But the brief growing season and the high cost of maintaining slaves limited the growth of slavery in Canada; and increasing British antislavery sentiment soon precipitated its decline. John Graves Simcoe, the lieutenant-governor of Upper Canada in the 1790s, considerably hastened the end of the institution in the Canadas by urging the legislative assembly of Upper Canada in 1793 to outlaw the importation of slaves and to grant Canadian-born slaves their freedom at twenty-five years of age. In 1803 a legal decision of Justice William Osgoode freed the three hundred slaves in Lower Canada. The few slaves remaining in Upper Canada were freed by the Emancipation Act of 1833, which outlawed slavery throughout much of the British Empire. Hill, *Freedom-Seekers*, 3–20; William R. Riddell, "The Slave in Canada," *JNH* 5:261–377 (July 1920).

23.
Proceedings of the North American Convention
Convened at St. Lawrence Hall, Toronto, Canada West
11–13 September 1851

The North American Convention was an organizational expression of the burgeoning emigrationist sentiment among black leaders on the North American continent. Called by Henry Bibb and encouraged by James Theodore Holly, the session convened at St. Lawrence Hall in Toronto from 11–13 September 1851. Fifty-three delegates from Canada West and the United States considered a series of resolutions on several issues, particularly emigration and Holly's call for the creation of the North American League. Although there was some dissent over specific issues, the meeting condemned slavery, endorsed Canadian immigration (while generally rejecting more distant sites), praised the British government, and outlined a plan for black uplift based on temperance, agriculture, skilled trades, and accumulated wealth. Holly and James L. Taylor, a Vermont colleague—neither of whom were able to attend the meeting—sent a prepared document outlining their plan for the league. They envisioned a permanent organization, which would be based in Canada West and designed to aid fugitives, to encourage immigration from the free states to Canada, and to help establish blacks in farming. The meeting expanded Holly's program by authorizing the league to raise funds to purchase and distribute land and agricultural implements to fugitives. The proceedings of the session, which were based on secretary James D. Tinsley's minutes, were printed in the *Voice of the Fugitive*. *VF*, 24 September 1851; Miller, *Search for Black Nationality*, 111–12.

SEPT[EMBER] 11

THURSDAY [MORNING]

Pursuant to a Call, the convention assembled in the St. Lawrence Hall,[1] at the hour of 10 o'clock.

The House was called to order by Mr. J. T. Fisher,[2] who moved the appointment of Mr. Henry Bibb as chairman, pro tem, and, on motion of Mr. J. J. Cary,[3] seconded by Mr. Thomas Smallwood,[4] Mr. James D. Tinsley[5] was appointed secretary, pro tem.

On motion of J. T. Fisher, seconded by D. Hollins,[6] the chair appointed a committee to nominate permanent officers, and the same committee to examine the credentials of delegates.

Moved by Jabez P. Campbell,[7] seconded by J. T. Fisher, that this committee consist of three persons, and that they report at two o'clock.

Committee—James Thomas Fisher, Hiram Wilson,[8] and Josiah Henson. On motion of W. H. Harris,[9] credentials were received from the following delegates:[10]

TORONTO—Thomas Smallwood, James D. Tinsley, John J. Cary, William H. Harris, David Hollins, J. T. Fisher.

NIAGARA—Rev. F. Lacy, B. Hoyt, William Scott, Isaac Washington, D. Goodler, G. Morgan, G. Brackston.

DAWN—Josiah Henson, G. Cary, W. P. Newman, J. Willson.

ST. CATHARINES—L. P. Barton, J. Anderson, E. B. Dunlop, H. Gray, H. Wilson, Dr. Lawson.

BUFFALO, U.S.—H. K. Thomas, P. Harris, B. F. Young, Rev. Jabez P. Campbell, J. Simpson, G. Weir, jun., J. McLean.

BURLINGTON, VERMONT, U.S.—J. T. Fisher.

UTICA—Free Will Baptist Mission—R. Cheney.

MONTROSE, PA.—A. L. Post.

SANDWICH, C.W.—H. Bibb, A. Smith, H. Brant.

WINDSOR—Israel Campbell.

CHIPPEWA—A. Anderson.

TOLEDO, OHIO—H. F. Stanton.

HAMILTON—F. Russel, J. Burns.

NORWICH—J. Wainer, E. De Groat.

CHATHAM—J. C. Brown.

SYRACUSE—J. Lisle, James Baker.

ALBANY—William H. Topp.

ENGLAND—John Scoble, Esq.

PORT HOPE—Henry Gray.

JAMAICA, W.I.—Mr. Anderson.

PITTSBURGH, PA.—Dr. M. R. Delany.

DOVER, C.W.—Isaiah Clifford.

Moved by J. T. Fisher, that the convention now hear the report of delegates, which was carried.

Moved by the Rev. J. P. Campbell, that the chair address the convention, and also state the object of the call.

On motion of Rev. H. Wilson, a business committee of five persons was appointed: the following persons were nominated by the chair to act in that capacity, and report at two o'clock: J. T. Fisher, Hiram Wilson, J. P. Campbell, George Cary[11] and B. F. Young.

On motion, the convention adjourned to meet at two o'clock.

AFTERNOON SESSION

Minutes of the forenoon session were read and approved.

The president announced the first business in order would be to hear reports from committees.

The committee on officers reported the following persons:

President—Henry Bibb.

Vice-Presidents—J. C. Brown, Chatham, C.W.; T. Smallwood, Toronto; H. F. Stanton, Toledo, Ohio.[12]

Secretary—James D. Tinsley, Toronto.

Assistant Secretary—J. J. Cary.

On motion of Rev. H. Wilson, that the report be adopted: while this motion was pending, an amendment was offered by Mr. Scoble,[13] seconded by Mr. Campbell, that Mr. J. C. Brown's name be stricken from the list as vice-president, and some respectable person be appointed in his stead; the subject of which was referred to a committee of seven, which made the following report:

> The committee, to whom was referred the investigation of the case of J. C. Brown, beg, leave to state, that they have duly considered the case, and from the nature of the circumstances, are not justified in declaring him guilty of the charge, neither can they entirely exonerate him from acting wrong: and as the case is undergoing a legal investigation, they therefore recommend that Mr. J. C. Brown's name be withdrawn as a candidate for any office in this convention.[14] The committee on "Rules" reported the following:
>
> 1. Resolved, that each session of the Convention be opened by addressing the Throne of Grace.
>
> 2. At the time appointed for the assembling of each session of the convention, the president shall take the chair, and call the convention to order.
>
> 3. The minutes of the preceding session shall be read at the opening of each session, at which time all mistakes, if there be any, shall be corrected.
>
> 4. The president shall decide all questions of order subject to an appeal of the Convention.
>
> 5. All motions and addresses shall be made to the President; the member rising from his seat.
>
> 6. All motions, except those of reference, shall be submitted in writing.
>
> 7. All committees shall be appointed by the chair unless otherwise ordered by the convention.
>
> 8. The previous question shall always be in order and, until decided, shall preclude all amendment and debate of the main question, and shall be put in this form, "shall the main question be now put?"
>
> 9. No member shall be interrupted while speaking except when out of order, when he shall be called to order through the chair.

10. A motion to adjourn shall always be in order, and shall be decided without debate.

11. No member shall speak more than twice on the same question, without the consent of the convention, nor more than fifteen minutes at each time.

12. No resolution except of reference shall be offered to the convention, except it come through the business committee: but all resolutions rejected by the committee, may be presented directly to the convention, if the maker of such wishes to do so.

13. Rule as amended. Sessions of the convention shall commence at half-past nine o'clock, a.m., and shall close at one o'clock, p.m.; to commence at half-past two o'clock, p.m., and close at six, p.m.; evening session shall commence at half-past seven o'clock, and close at the discretion of the convention.

The business committee then reported the following resolutions, which, after a spirited debate, were received and adopted.

1. Resolved, that the infamous fugitive slave enactment of the American Government—whether constitutional or unconstitutional, is an insult to God, and an outrage upon humanity, not to be endured by any people; we therefore earnestly entreat our brethren of the northern and southern states to come out from under the jurisdiction of those wicked laws—from the power of a Government whose tender mercies, towards the colored people, are cruel.

2. Resolved, that we feel truly grateful, as a people, to her Britannic Majesty's just and powerful Government, for the protection afforded us; and are fully persuaded from the known fertility of the soil, and salubrity of climate of the milder regions of Canada West, that this is, by far, the most desirable place of resort for colored people, to be found on the American continent.

3. Resolved, that we warmly recommend to colored settlers in Canada, to use all diligence in obtaining possession of uncultivated lands, for the laudable purpose of making themselves and their offspring independent tillers of a *free soil.*

The following protest against the first resolution was entered by the undersigned delegates:

Whereas, the convention, in adopting the first resolution, inviting the colored people to leave the northern part of the United States, has done so contrary to the desires and wishes of those of us, from the states, who believe it to be impolitic and contrary to our professed policy in opposing the infamous fugitive slave laws, and schemes of American colonization; therefore we do hereby enter our solemn disapprobation and protest against this part of the said resolution.

M. R. Delany, Penn.
Wm. H. Topp, New York[15]
Henry F. Stanton, Ohio
Payton Harris, New York[16]

On the motion of Rev. J. P. Campbell, Resolved, that all persons present, who come from places from which no delegates have been appointed, and who concur in the spirit of the call, and are desirous of participating in the deliberations, shall by having their names enrolled, be considered delegates of this convention.

On motion, the convention adjourned until seven o'clock this evening.

EVENING SESSION

The minutes of the afternoon session were read and approved.

Several eloquent and effective addresses were delivered by Messrs. Bibb, Lisle,[17] Hiram Wilson and J. P. Campbell.

Moved by J. T. Fisher, that the business committee be enlarged by an addition of four—W. H. Topp, J. Lisle, F. Russel, and H. K. Thomas,[18] were added.

Moved by Mr. Baker,[19] that a committee of three be appointed, to wait on the Trustees of the First Baptist Chapel, of this city, to ascertain whether they will grant the use of it for the holding of this convention.

D. Hollins, J. Lisle, and J. D. Tinsley were appointed. On motion, the meeting adjourned to meet to-morrow, the 12th instant, at nine o'clock, a.m.

SEPTEMBER 12
FRIDAY MORNING

The convention met according to adjournment.

Prayer by Mr. Lisle, after which the roll was called, and minutes of previous day were read and adopted.

On motion of Mr. Harris,[20] reports from the several delegates, setting forth the moral, civil, and pecuniary condition of our people, in their respective localities, were listened to with much attention, and, in some instances, with great satisfaction.

On motion, the following resolution reported by the business committee was called up for consideration, when Mr. Scoble of England arose, and in an able and eloquent manner, recommended its adoption.

Resolved, that chattel slavery, as now existing in the United States, is repugnant to Divine Revelation—to reason, conscience, and common sense—that it is a most flagrant violation of the letter and spirit of Christianity, and ought, at once, and for ever, to be abolished.

On motion, the convention adjourned to meet at two o'clock, p.m.

AFTERNOON SESSION

The convention met as per adjournment.

Prayer by Rev. J. P. Campbell, minutes of the morning session were read and adopted.

The following additional resolutions were reported by the business committee:

1. Resolved, that this convention impress upon the minds of our people the great necessity of acquiring education and wealth.

2. Resolved, that we recommend to the people, abstinence from all intoxicating liquors, that they may, by so doing, save dollars for themselves and their children.

Whereas, the independence and stability of the farmers' life throw around them the elements of character essential to happiness and progress, therefore,

Resolved, that this convention recommend to the people to cultivate the soil as one of the surest means by which to attain to respectability, influence, and independence.

Resolved, that this convention impress upon the minds of parents the necessity and advantage of their children learning trades: and that parents do not discharge their duty to their children, who do not make sacrifices to promote that end.

Resolved, that the convention recommend to the colored people of the U.S. of America, to emigrate to the Canadas instead of going to Africa or the West India Islands, that they, by so doing, may be better able to assist their brethren who are daily flying from American slavery.

On motion, the report was received, and the resolutions were adopted excepting the fourth which was laid over for the time, but adopted at a subsequent period.

On motion, a committee on statistics, consisting of the following gentlemen, was appointed by the president: J. P. Campbell, Wm. H. Topp, and H. K. Thomas.

On motion, the convention adjourned to meet again at seven o'clock this evening.

EVENING SESSION

President in the chair.

Messrs. W. W. Anderson,[21] of Jamaica, and John Scoble, Esq., of England, being solicited, came forward, and occupied the attention of the convention, with able and eloquent addresses in favor of emigration to Jamaica.

Mr. Scoble spoke, at great length, on the duty of looking upon all available locations on this continent whether Canada, West Indies, or South America, as offering especial inducements, to the colored man to promote enterprise, intelligence and industry, and as furthering the great designs of the Deity in his final success.

On motion, a vote of thanks was tendered to those gentlemen for their information and able addresses.

SEPTEMBER 13
SATURDAY MORNING

President in the chair.

Divine blessing was invoked by the Rev. Israel Campbell, of Windsor.

The minutes of the previous session were read and approved.

The business committee then presented the following resolutions:

> Resolved, that slavery being a sin against God, and an outrage upon man, we feel sacredly bound, as a convention and as individuals, to make common cause with the enslaved, and never to cease our efforts against slavery until it is swept from the face of the earth, or our vital breath and pulsation cease.
>
> Resolved, that in the opinion of this convention, the establishment of exclusive churches and schools for colored people, contributes greatly towards the promotion of prejudice, heretofore unknown in the Canadas, and we do hereby recommend that all such organizations be abandoned as speedily as may be practicable.
>
> Resolved, that the British Government is the most favorable in the civilized world to the people of color, and is thereby entitled to our entire confidence.
>
> Resolved, that we recommend to the friends of humanity, to support such presses only as will faithfully vindicate our cause; and that we use our best endeavors to extend the circulation of the *Voice of the Fugitive*.

On motion, the convention adjourned to meet at two o'clock, p.m.

AFTERNOON SESSION

President in the chair.

Prayer was offered by the Rev. J. Lisle, after which, the minutes were read and approved.

Moved by John Scoble, Esq., seconded by William H. Harris, that a committee be formed to draw up an address as emanating from this convention,[22] and embodying in its spirit the sentiments embraced in the various resolutions which have been adopted, and that the same committee be a committee of revision and publication.

Moved by Mr. Scoble, and seconded by Rev. J. Henson, that Mr. Bibb be one of that committee; J. T. Fisher and J. D. Tinsley were also appointed to complete that committee.

The following amendment, offered by Mr. Scoble to a resolution offered by Mr. Fisher, was unanimously adopted.

> Resolved, that the formation of a great league of the colored people of the North and South American continents,[23] and of the West Indies, for the general abolition of slavery, for the protection of the common rights of their brethren throughout the world, and for their social, political and moral elevation, be recommended to the consideration of a committee of five persons, to be appointed by this convention; and that they take the necessary steps to acquire information, and to report at such time, and in such manner, as they may think proper, the result of their inquiries and deliberations.
>
> Resolved, that this convention recommend, as worthy of our support, the Government of Great Britain and her West Indian colonies and Canadian provinces, in preference to Central America, or any other country tainted with slavery; and we do recommend to all our friends in the free states, to settle under its protection.

On motion, the convention adjourned to meet at seven o'clock, p.m.

EVENING SESSION

The convention was called to order by the president.

Prayer was offered by Rev. Israel Campbell:[24] minutes of afternoon session were read and approved.

On motion, resolved that we tender our thanks to the anti-slavery societies of the city of Toronto and the Elgin Association, for their kindness toward our friends since the passage of the fugitive slave enactments.[25]

On motion, resolved that a committee of seven persons be appointed to correspond on the subject of calling another convention.

The following gentlemen were appointed a committee of correspondence.

Henry Bibb, Sandwich, Canada West
Samuel R. Ward, Boston, Massachusetts
Wm. H. Topp, Albany, New York
A. D. Shadd, West Chester, Pennsylvania[26]
David Jenkins, Columbus, Ohio[27]
A. G. Beman, New Haven, Connecticut[28]
William Lambert, Michigan[29]

On motion, Mr. Hiram Wilson was added to the business committee.

The convention was then addressed by Dr. M. R. Delany, in an eloquent manner.

On motion, a vote of thanks was tendered by the convention to the chairman and officers for the very able and impartial manner in which they have discharged their several duties.

On motion, the convention adjourned *sine die.*

Voice of the Fugitive (Windsor, Canada West), 24 September 1851.

1. St. Lawrence Hall, a three-story sandstone building, was the first major building erected following the Toronto fire of 1849. The hall served as the social and cultural center of the city during the 1850s and was frequently the site of Anti-Slavery Society of Canada meetings. *St. Lawrence Hall.*

2. John T. Fisher, a black Toronto saloonkeeper, advocated unified black action against slavery, black prosperity and independence based on agriculture, and enforcement of civil rights for black Canadians. At one time, Fisher advocated the use of violence against southern slaveholders, arguing that they had declared war on black people. He was associated with the *Voice of the Fugitive.* During 1851 and 1852, he worked to establish an agricultural league that would hasten the demise of slavery by placing the free labor products from Canada and the West Indies in direct competition with U.S. goods on the British market. After the North American Convention endorsed his views, he became a vocal supporter and organizer of the unsuccessful North American League. In March 1852, Fisher became an organizer and officer of the Canadian Mill and Mercantile Association—another attempt to encourage black business independence through the establishment of a sawmill, a gristmill, and a country store near Buxton. By 1855, having received a significant response to its request for pledges, the company was able at least to construct the sawmill. *Toronto City Directory,* 1850; *VF,* 29 January , 23 April, 21 May, 16 July, 3 December 1851, 26 February, 22 April 1852 [6:769, 0908, 0932, 0933, 7:0004, 0203, 0430, 0532]; Simpson, "Negroes in Ontario to 1870," 483–86; Jonathan William Walton, "Blacks in Buxton and Chatham, Ontario, 1830–1890: Did the 49th Parallel Make a Difference?" (Ph.D. diss., Princeton University, 1979), 100; Annie Straith Jamieson, *William King: Friend and Champion of Slaves* (Toronto, 1925), 110.

3. John J. Cary, the brother of George, Isaac N., and Thomas F. Cary, was probably born in southern Virginia. During the 1830s, he lived in Cincinnati, where he received his early education from John W. Alvord, the Lane rebel and future Freedmen's Bureau school superintendent. By 1850 Cary had moved to Toronto, where he plied the barbering trade. He was later employed by his brother Thomas and successful black businessman Richard B. Richards as an agent for their three ice houses. Cary was active in local and provincial black meetings and conventions during the 1850s and early 1860s; he signed the call for and attended the North American Convention (1851) and was appointed by the Amherstburg Convention (1853) to a Toronto vigilance committee charged with curbing begging practices in the city. Late in the decade, he urged local blacks to abandon the Conservative party and support Reform candidates. He

chaired a June 1861 meeting of Toronto's black citizens that expressed concern with the Canadian government's handling of the John Anderson extradition case. Cary settled in Nashville, Tennessee, after the Civil War and became a prominent figure in the freedmen's community there. In 1870 he chaired the local celebration of the ratification of the Fifteenth Amendment. He was the principal cashier of the Nashville branch of the Freedman's Savings Bank from 1870 until its failure in 1874. After the bank's demise, he sold real estate and worked at various other occupations in the city through the early 1880s. Carl R. Osthaus, *Freedmen, Philanthropy, and Fraud: A History of Freedman's Savings Bank* (Urbana, Ill., 1976), 107, 172, 179, 232; Bearden and Butler, *Shadd*, 186; Thomas F. Cary to [Mary Ann Shadd Cary], 21 January 1858, John J. Cary to [Thomas F. Cary], 19 May 1858, Mary Ann Shadd Cary Papers, CaOTAr [11:0127, 0223]; *VF*, 27 August 1851 [7:0068]; *PFW*, 24 March 1853 [8:0175]; *Nashville City Directory*, 1867–81.

4. Thomas W. F. Smallwood, the proprietor of a Toronto saw factory, was born free in Maryland, the son of former slave and underground railroad activist Thomas Smallwood. The younger Smallwood arrived in Toronto with his family in October 1843, after suspicion concerning his father's antislavery activities forced the family to flee from Washington, D.C. Smallwood's involvement with racial concerns made him a prominent member of the city's black community in the 1850s. He signed the 1851 call for the North American Convention and served as a vice-president of the gathering. In 1854 he helped arrange the city's Emancipation Day celebration, was elected a vice-president of the self-help-oriented Provincial Union Association, and opposed the Colonial Church and School Society's efforts to establish a separate school in the city. He also worked to repair the growing division between free blacks and fugitive slaves in the Toronto community. Although initially a supporter of the *Provincial Freeman*, Smallwood began to organize subscribers dissatisfied with the paper's editorial direction in 1855, and he broke with Mary Ann Shadd Cary, the *Freeman's* editor, one year later. He remained a leading member of the city's black elite well into the 1860s. *VF*, 27 August 1851, 11 March 1852 [7:0068, 0447]; *PFW*, 24 March 1853, 3, 17 June, 5, 19, 26 August, 14 October 1854, 17, 24 March 1855, 25 November 1856, 18 June 1859 [8:0175, 0858, 9:0017, 0044, 0139, 0503, 0994, 10:0385, 11:0792]; *TG*, 11 August 1860 [12:0953]; Thomas Smallwood, *A Narrative of Thomas Smallwood (Colored Man)* (Toronto, Canada West, 1851), 33, 34, 36; *AA*, 9 May 1863.

5. James D. Tinsley (?–1854), a Virginia-born fugitive slave (and a friend of Samuel Ringgold Ward), became prominent in the Toronto black community before leaving for the Australian goldfields. Arriving there in November 1852, he became active in Melbourne's Young Men's Christian Association and taught at the all-white Melbourne Baptist Sabbath School. He apparently enjoyed some success and planned to return to his Canadian home after a stop in England, but he lost his life when his ship sank in the Atlantic. *PFW*, 5 August 1854 [8:0991]; E. Daniel Potts and Annette Potts, "The Negro and the Australian Gold Rushes, 1852–1857," *PHR* 37:387 (November 1968).

6. David Hollins, a black Toronto currier, was an early member and a stockholder of the Elgin Association and served as one of the vice-presidents of Toronto's 1854 Emancipation Day celebration. *Toronto City Directory*, 1850;

Winks, *Blacks in Canada*, 212; *Fifth Annual Report of the Directors of the Elgin Association* (Toronto, 1854), 12 [9:0062]; *Eighth Annual Report of the Directors of the Elgin Association* (Toronto, 1857), 14 [10:0822]; *PFW*, 29 July 1854.

7. Jabez Pitt Campbell (1815–1891) was born to free black parents, Anthony and Catherine Campbell, at Slaughter Neck in Sussex County, Delaware. When he was ten, a Christmas day conversion experience began his lifelong involvement with religion and the African Methodist Episcopal church. After Campbell's father mortgaged him to a local white man and then abandoned him, an attempt was made to sell the boy into slavery. When rumors of the plan reached Campbell, he escaped to Philadelphia, where he resided with his mother for several years. Licensed to preach in 1837, he served for four years in eastern Pennsylvania and then as an AME missionary in New England. Following his ordination as a deacon, he concurrently served congregations in Providence, New Bedford, and Boston. In Providence Campbell met Stella Medley, whom he married in 1844. When she died a decade later, he married Mary Ann Shire of Philadelphia (1855). Campbell was reassigned to the New York Annual Conference in 1843, ordained an elder, and then successively served numerous congregations in New York State. In 1854 Campbell moved to the Philadelphia area and served churches there for the next decade. For several years, he was also book agent of the AME Book Concern. From 1854 to 1858, Campbell edited the *Christian Recorder*, an AME organ.

While in Philadelphia, Campbell developed an active interest in temperance and antislavery. During the early years of the Civil War, he became a vocal critic of the Lincoln administration's inertia in emancipating the slaves. He left Philadelphia's Bethel Church in 1863 and transferred to the Baltimore Annual Conference. The following year he was elected an AME bishop and spent the remainder of his life supervising the administrative affairs of regional episcopal districts, primarily in the South. Campbell sailed to California in 1865 and established the first AME conference there. During Reconstruction, he supervised AME mission work among former slaves in the Mississippi Valley. That experience apparently disillusioned him with southern race relations, and he briefly flirted with emigrationist schemes. In 1876 this led to his election as a vice-president of the American Colonization Society. During the 1880s, Campbell established AME conferences in Santo Domingo, Haiti, and Bermuda. He simultaneously labored to improve the educational facilities of the church and, from 1883 until his death, chaired the board of trustees of Wilberforce University. An elder statesman of the AME, Campbell was sent as a delegate to the Wesleyan General Conference in England in 1876 and 1879. He also was recognized late in his life with honorary doctorates from Wilberforce and the University of Pennsylvania. B. W. Arnett, "Biographical Sketch of Jabez Pitt Campbell," *CR*, 20 August 1891; Alexander Wayman, *Cyclopaedia of African Methodism* (Baltimore, Md., 1882), 6–7; Charles Spencer Smith, *A History of the African Methodist Episcopal Church* (Philadelphia, Pa., 1922; reprint, New York, N.Y., 1968), 39, 71–72; *Lib*, 23 December 1859; Clarence E. Walker, *A Rock in a Weary Land: The African Methodist Episcopal Church during the Civil War and Reconstruction* (Baton Rouge, La., 1982), 34–35; August Meier, *Negro Thought in America, 1880–1915: Racial Ideologies in the Age of Booker T. Washington* (Ann Arbor, Mich., 1963), 66.

8. Hiram Wilson (1803–1864) was born in Acworth, New Hampshire, and re-

ceived his early training at the Kimball Union Academy and Oneida Institute. He entered Lane Theological Seminary in Cincinnati in 1833, but he soon joined the abolitionist Lane Rebels and left to complete his studies for the ministry at Oberlin College. Wilson settled in Toronto in 1836 and became an agent for the American Anti-Slavery Society—one of the select group of antislavery missionaries known as the Seventy. He traveled throughout Upper Canada and established at least ten schools in the province. In 1842 he joined Josiah Henson and James Canning Fuller in establishing the British-American Institute, a manual labor school around which the Dawn fugitive slave settlement developed. One year later, he toured Britain to raise funds for the settlement, and in time he acquired financial support from the American Missionary Association. Discouraged by managerial controversies at the settlement and by the death of his wife, Hannah, Wilson left Dawn in 1850. He considered leaving Canada West, but passage of the Fugitive Slave Law and the subsequent influx of black refugees into the province prompted him to settle in St. Catharines. He remarried, and with a small stipend from the AMA, he preached, established an evening school, and operated a fugitive relief station. Wilson abandoned his missionary and relief efforts in 1861. William H. Pease and Jane H. Pease, *Bound with them in Chains* (Westport, Conn., 1972), 115–39.

9. William H. Harris, a black billsticker and provisions dealer, was a trustee of the Coloured Regular Baptist Church of Toronto—a life-time office that became a point of controversy in 1855 when parishioners accused him of abusing his position by interfering with the church's finances and denying members access to the building. A supporter of the *Provincial Freeman* and a vice-president of the Provincial Union Association, he was active in the Toronto black community throughout the decade, helping to organize the 1854 Emancipation Day celebration and attending political caucuses and other meetings. In 1860 he chaired a meeting that resolved to secure the release of the fugitive John Anderson by legal means. *Toronto City Directory*, 1850; *PFW*, 3, 17 June, 29 July, 5, 19 August, 24 November 1854 [8:0858, 0994, 9:0017, 0959]; *TG*, 15 September 1858; *WAA*, 7 April, 15 December 1860 [12:0622, 13:0039].

10. The fifty delegates who attended the North American Convention represented a mix of demographic characteristics and a wide range of previous antislavery experience. They were overwhelmingly black; only four whites—John Scoble of Britain, William Wemyss Anderson of Jamaica, and Hiram Wilson and physician Daniel Lawson of St. Catharines—were delegates. In contrast to other black national conventions, no delegates attended from the eastern, urban black communities of Boston, Providence, New Haven, New York City, and Philadelphia; but thirty-one delegates represented black communities in Canada West. The fifteen American delegates came from western New York, the Pittsburgh area, and Ohio. The men who gathered at Toronto followed a variety of occupations. Francis Lacy (Norwich), George Weir, Jr. (Buffalo), R. Cheney (Utica), Albert L. Post (Montrose, Pa.), and seven others were clergymen. Four, including John Simpson (Buffalo), were barbers. The delegate list also included blacksmith Andrew Smith (Sandwich), farmer John Willson (Dawn), teamster David Goodler (Niagara), cooper Elijah De Groat (Norwich), laborer Benjamin Hoyt (Niagara), two tailors, a factory owner, a billsticker and provisions dealer, a currier, a saloonkeeper, a teacher, and a mason. A few, like Henry Bibb and Martin R.

Delany, were professional black abolitionists, and nearly half had significant experience in the antislavery or black convention movements. Yet only five delegates—John Willson, Josiah Henson, George Cary, Henry Bibb, and Israel Campbell—would attend the Amherstburg Convention, which was called two years later to address similar issues. Simpson, "Negroes in Ontario to 1870," 843; Census of Canada, 1851; *FDP*, 10 June 1853, 3 February 1854; *Buffalo City Directory*, 1868; Foner and Walker, *Proceedings of Black State Conventions*, 1:64; United States Census, 1850; *NSt*, 24 November 1848, 23 March, 20 April 1849; *P*, 31 May 1843; *PL*, 27 March, 9 October 1844; *AA*, 9 April 1853; *Report of the Convention of the Colored Population held at Drummondville, Aug., 1847* (Toronto, Canada West, 1847), 5–6; *Minutes and Proceedings of the General Convention for the Improvement of the Colored Inhabitants of Canada, Held by Adjournments in Amherstburg, C.W.* (Windsor, Canada West, 1853), 2–3 [8:0297–98].

11. George Cary (1807–1862) lived in southern Virginia until he was twenty-one years old. For the next fourteen years, he resided in Cincinnati, Ohio, where he was active in the black community as a reformer and the president of the Cincinnati Iron Chest Company. An opponent of begging and of African colonization, he believed that the proper course for black Americans was one that would allow them to improve their own condition through education and hard work. As early as May 1832, he advocated establishing a black college in Canada, where, he believed, American prejudice would not hinder its development. By November 1838, he was involved with a Cincinnati organization that planned to purchase land and establish a sawmill and a gristmill as means for exhibiting black industry. The plan was never executed, but Cary became involved in a similar project when he moved to Canada West about 1842 to assume a role in establishing the British-American Institute. Dresden remained Cary's home throughout his Canadian career. He was active in community and reform affairs, serving, at various times, on the executive committee of the institute, as principal instructor at the institute, as a trustee of the Fugitive Union Society (1851), as one of the founders of the Refugee Home Society (1852), as a vice-president of the Anti-Slavery Society of Canada, and as an officer of the Amherstburg Convention (1853). He eventually broke with the RHS, charging its white officers with being more interested in speculation than antislavery, and became a supporter of the anti-RHS faction. Beginning in May 1854, he acted for a time as an agent for the *Provincial Freeman*. The prejudice he encountered in Canada led him to advocate Haitian immigration despite Mary Ann Shadd Cary's reservations about the movement. During the summer of 1861, he formed a cotton-growing association with the intention of establishing a permanent settlement in Haiti and demonstrating to blacks what could be accomplished there. He left Canada for Haiti the following December, found work cutting sugar cane, and died within three weeks after his arrival. George Cary to [William Lloyd Garrison], 5 May 1832, Antislavery Collection, MB [1:0162]; *P*, 20 February 1838, 4 November 1840, [2:0386, 3:0690]; *CA*, 23 February 1839, 20 November 1841 [3:0008, 4:0307]; *NASS*, 5 November 1847; *VF*, 1 January, 11 March, 1 July, 21 October 1852 [7:0320, 0450, 0647, 0784]; Mary A[nn] Shadd [Cary] to G[eorge] Whipple, 28 December 1852, 15 January 1853 [7:1039, 8:0093], AMA-ARC; *PFW*, 22 July 1854 [8:0935]; *WAA*, 23 July 1859, 26 April 1862 [11:0865, 14:0271]; *PP*, 14

September 1861 [13:0754], 13 February 1862; Simpson, "Negroes in Ontario to 1870," 208.

12. Henry F. Stanton (1824–?), a Pennsylvania-born black Ohioan, was selected by Toledo blacks as a delegate to the North American Convention (1851) in Toronto. Employed as a barber in Toledo during the early 1850s, he moved to Cleveland late in the decade and there supported himself by his musical talent. James deT. Abajian, *Blacks in Selected Newspapers, Censuses and Other Sources: An Index to Names and Subjects*, 3 vols. (Boston, Mass., 1976), 3:395; *Cleveland City Directory*, 1859; United States Census, 1850.

13. John Scoble (1799–ca. 1867) was born in Kingsbridge, Devonshire, England, and was ordained a Congregational minister. Scoble joined the British antislavery movement in the 1820s and in 1831 was appointed a lecturer for the Agency Committee, an organization founded by the Anti-Slavery Society and meant to arouse British popular opinion against colonial slavery. Scoble toured the West Indies in 1836, published his findings in the book *British Guiana* (1837), and aided Joseph Sturge's investigation of the oppressive apprenticeship system that had replaced slavery in the islands. Scoble helped Sturge found the British and Foreign Anti-Slavery Society (1839) and organize London's World Anti-Slavery Convention (1840). In 1842 Scoble was appointed secretary to the society and, for the next ten years, promoted the antislavery cause in Great Britain and Europe while engaging in an ongoing confrontation with British and American Garrisonians over antislavery tactics. He assumed managerial control of the British-American Institute at Dawn, Canada West, in 1852. Scoble's patronizing attitude and ineffective leadership provoked controversy and litigation over control of the settlement. He severed his relationship with Dawn in 1861, but remained active in the antislavery movement, most notably in his efforts to protect fugitive slave John Anderson from extradition. Scoble entered Reform party politics in the late 1850s and held a seat in the Canadian parliament from 1863 to 1867. *DCB*, 9:704–6.

14. No evidence exists to suggest that James C. Brown was involved in any legal proceedings at this time. The committee probably refers to an investigation being conducted by John Scoble, the representative of a British antislavery committee concerned with allegations of improprieties in the administration of the black Dawn settlement. Shortly before the North American Convention convened, Scoble held a meeting at Dawn to clear Josiah Henson of these charges, which were made by Brown and others. Questioning Brown's credibility before the convention delegates may have been a means used by Scoble to discredit Henson's detractors. *VF*, 10 September 1851; *PFW*, 26 August 1854.

15. William H. Topp (1812–1857) of Albany, New York, was a successful, self-educated free black tailor of mixed African, Indian, and German ancestry. A respected community leader with a lifelong commitment to united black action and to reform, he regularly participated—often as an officer or committee member—in local, state, and national black conventions. He was president of the New York State Council (1854) and a member of the National Council of the Colored People (1855), short-lived coordinating bodies established to advance the status of blacks. Topp's name also frequently appeared on remonstrances emanating from the Albany black community. A pragmatist in his approach to abolitionism,

Topp energetically pursued equal political rights for blacks. Although an active member of the American Anti-Slavery Society and a friend and admirer of William Lloyd Garrison, he vigorously advocated political antislavery action. In 1852 he supported Free Soil presidential candidate John P. Hale and attempted to rally delegates to the Liberty party convention behind him. Topp's other reform interests included women's rights and integrated education; his support for the latter led him to oppose Frederick Douglass's 1853 proposal to establish a black industrial college; this conflict cooled the friendship between the two reformers. Topp urged free blacks to remain in the United States, as he considered colonization and emigration schemes to be tantamount to abandoning the slave. His health failed in 1857, and he died of consumption on 11 December. *E*, 10 December 1840 [3:0740]; *ASRL*, 30 June 1841 [4:0085]; *NSt*, 3 December 1847, 14, 21 January, 11, 18 February 1848, 19 January, 7 September 1849 [5:0054, 0957, 6:0135]; *FDP*, 15 January, 12 February, 10 September, 15 October 1852, 25 November 1853, 3 February, 25 August 1854, 25 May 1855 [7:0356, 0419, 0780, 8:0501, 0640]; *ASB*, 13 November 1852, 25 February 1854, 19, 26 May 1855 [9:0664]; *Lib*, 19 March 1852, 8 January 1858; *NASS*, 29 January 1846, 28 February, 19 December 1857 [5:0152]; William H. Topp, J. W. Randolph, and William P. McIntyre to W[illia]m H. Seward, 22 April 1850, William H. Seward Papers, NRU [6:0451]; Martin Robinson Delany, *The Condition, Elevation, and Destiny of the Colored People of the United States* (New York, N.Y., 1969), 102; Merrill and Ruchames, *Letters of William Lloyd Garrison*, 4:379–81; Foner and Walker, *Proceedings of Black State Conventions*, 73–75 [7:0018]; Quarles, *Black Abolitionists*, 219.

16. Payton Harris (1794–?), a Virginia-born tailor and clothes cleaner, was prominent in the Buffalo black community. Although illiterate, Harris played an active role in directing local black antislavery affairs. In 1841 he presided over an effort by Buffalo blacks to confront the problem of racially motivated mob violence. He was a delegate to the Colored National Convention (1848) in Cleveland, the North American Convention (1851) in Toronto, the Colored National Convention (1853) in Rochester, and several state and local conventions. Harris vehemently opposed black emigration and colonization activities. *CA*, 13 November 1841; *NSt*, 10 March 1848; United States Census, 1850; *VF*, 24 September 1851, 29 January, 9 September, 1 October 1852; *FDP*, 10 June 1853, 24 March 1854, 12 January 1855, 17 September 1858; *E*, 25 October 1873; *Buffalo City Directory*, 1868.

17. John Lisle (1828–?), a black Syracuse clergyman, was born in New York. Local blacks selected him as a delegate to several antebellum black conventions, including the Drummondville Convention (1847) and the Colored National Convention (1848) in Cleveland, where he urged blacks to agitate continually against slavery. Because of his efforts to subvert the Fugitive Slave Law of 1850, and particularly because of his involvement in the Jerry rescue, Lisle was forced to flee to Dawn, Canada West, in 1851. He was an agent for the Sandwich Mission during the early 1850s. He supported the call for the North American Convention (1851) in Toronto, attended the convention as a delegate, and there encouraged blacks to develop an agrarian culture and immigrate to Canada West. Lisle later served churches in Detroit. *Convention of the Colored Population*, 6; *NSt*, 14

January, 29 September 1848; United States Census, 1850; *VF*, 15 January, 13, 27 August, 24 September, 19 November 1851, 12 February, 3 June 1852; Abajian, *Blacks in Selected Newspapers*, 2:501.

18. Henry K. Thomas (1817–ca. 1888), the uncle of noted black, Reconstruction-era politician James T. Rapier, was born to a slave mother and white father in Virginia. After spending his early years in Nashville, Tennessee, he escaped from slavery in 1834, then sojourned briefly in several midwestern states before settling in Buffalo, New York. Thomas opened a barbershop in the fashionable Hotel Niagara in 1842 and developed a thriving trade. About this time, he began to purchase real estate in the city and near the Seneca Indian Reservation in western New York State. He also married a black woman named Maria; they produced eleven children. During his Buffalo years, Thomas became active in the local antislavery and black convention movements and was a particularly vocal advocate of political antislavery. Buffalo blacks selected him as a delegate to the North American Convention (1851) in Toronto. One year later, fear of slave catchers led Thomas to resettle his family at the Elgin settlement near Buxton, Canada West. He purchased one hundred acres, which he promptly cleared and planted in wheat, corn, and barley. Although he proved to be a poor farmer, he took an active part in the life of the community. He joined St. Andrew's Presbyterian Church and devoted much time to church affairs. Together with Wilson R. Abbott, he raised $3,000 among friends in Toronto and Buffalo to form the Canada Mill and Mercantile Company, the first major black-owned commercial venture in the province. They soon established a sawmill, gristmill, and general store at Buxton. Thomas remained a moving force behind the enterprise. During the Civil War, he joined a local militia unit. After the war, he continued to exercise a leadership role in the affairs of the local black community. Loren Schweninger, *James T. Rapier and Reconstruction* (Chicago, Ill., 1978), 1, 3–4, 14–15, 17, 34; *NASS*, 20 October 1845; *SL*, 16 January 1843 [4:0525]; *VF*, 24 September 1851 [7:0109]; Simpson, "Negroes in Ontario to 1870," 535–36; Walton, "Blacks in Buxton and Chatham," 105.

19. James Baker (1810–?), a Georgia-born black, was a leader of the Syracuse black community during the 1850s. Local blacks selected him as a delegate to the Cazenovia (New York) Fugitive Slave Law Convention (1850) and the North American Convention (1851) in Toronto. United States Census, 1850; *VF*, 24 September 1851; Foner and Walker, *Proceedings of Black State Conventions*, 1:43.

20. Payton Harris.

21. William Wemyss Anderson (1802–1877), a Scottish lawyer, immigrated to Jamaica in 1833. He wrote numerous essays on the local economy and society, was elected to the legislature in 1837 and appointed commissioner of immigration in 1851. He promoted black immigration to Jamaica on his tours of North America but had little success. "Jamaica Worthies. XIII. William Wemyss Anderson," *JIJ* 2:218–21 (1896).

22. The address is published as the following document in this volume.

23. Fisher refers to the North American League.

24. Israel Campbell (1815–?) was born a slave in Greenville County, Kentucky. Separated from his mother, he served several masters in Tennessee and Mississippi. In 1837 he became a Baptist preacher and ministered to fellow slaves in

Winchester and Franklin counties, Tennessee. Campbell learned a number of trades, including bootmaking; an industrious entrepreneur, he exchanged his wares for other goods that he then resold. Campbell planned to buy his freedom until he discovered that his master intended to sell him southward. After one unsuccessful attempt, he escaped to Canada West in the late 1840s. As late as 1855, he corresponded with his former master to arrange for the purchase of his freedom papers. After arriving in Canada, Campbell farmed near Chatham with an older brother. He soon became a popular speaker, exhibiting his antislavery principles as well as his concern for black civil rights and white prejudice. Beginning in 1851, he traveled through the midwestern United States as an agent for the Fugitive Union Society. Campbell was a vice-president of the Amherstburg Convention (1853) and in 1854 attended Martin Delany's National Emigration Convention in Cleveland. That same year, he spent six months as a student at Oberlin College. After returning to Canada West, he continued to preach to Baptist congregations, was ordained, acted as a missionary and pastor to a number of black congregations, and became a naturalized Canadian citizen. In 1856 he left Canada West to organize a Baptist church in Toledo and to serve as minister at the Sandusky (Ohio) Regular Baptist Anti-Slavery Church. Campbell preached in Ohio until 1862, when he decided to write and sell his autobiography in hopes of raising sufficient funds to purchase the freedom of his children. Near the end of the Civil War, he began missionary work among the freedmen in Louisiana. In 1866 he moved to Texas, where he organized churches and became known as the "father of the Baptists of Texas." He served as the minister of the Missionary Baptist Church in Galveston through the early 1890s. Israel Campbell, *Bond and Free: or, Yearnings for Freedom from My Green Brier House* (Philadelphia, Pa., 1861); A. W. Pegues, *Our Baptist Ministers and Schools* (Springfield, Mass., 1892; reprint, New York, N.Y., 1970), 100–102; Simpson, "Negroes in Ontario to 1870," 680, 701; Carlesimo, "Refugee Home Society," 130, 134; *VF*, 29 January 1852 [7:0388]; *PFW*, 8 December 1855 [9:0976].

25. The Toronto antislavery societies referred to were the Anti-Slavery Society of Canada (headquartered in Toronto), which was founded in February 1851 in response to the passage of the Fugitive Slave Law of 1850, and its auxiliary, the Toronto Ladies' Association for the Relief of Destitute Colored Fugitives, which was organized in April 1851. Before the end of their first year of operation, the two organizations collected $1,108 for Canadian fugitive slaves, and the ladies' association assisted more than one hundred black families. The convention also recognized the Elgin Association for its work in establishing a fugitive slave settlement near Buxton, Canada West. The Elgin Association, a joint-stock company incorporated in the summer of 1850, was legally responsible for overseeing the black Elgin settlement. The association raised the funds necessary to acquire land for the settlement; nearly nine thousand acres were purchased by 1854. Winks, *Blacks in Canada*, 210–11, 252–59, 265; Murray, "Canada and Anglo-American Anti-Slavery Movement," 213, 214, 271–78, 339, 388–95, 399–400, 548.

26. Abraham D. Shadd (1801–1882), a Pennsylvania-born free black, operated a shoemaking business in Wilmington, Delaware, before moving to nearby West Chester, Pennsylvania, in the early 1830s. He used both his Wilmington home and his West Chester farm to hide fugitive slaves escaping along the underground railroad. A vigorous opponent of slavery, Shadd was one of five blacks who served

on the Board of Managers of the American Anti-Slavery Society at its founding meeting in 1833. He acted as a local subscription agent for several antislavery papers—particularly the *Liberator*, *Emancipator*, *National Reformer*, and *Colored American*—during the following decade. Shadd was also a prominent figure in the early black convention movement. He attended the first four black national conventions and presided over the third, which was held in Philadelphia in 1833. He was a leading delegate to Pennsylvania's 1841 and 1848 black state conventions. Shadd, a militant advocate of black civil rights, helped lead an extensive protest against Pennsylvania's disenfranchisement of black voters in the late 1830s. Although he was an early critic of colonizationist efforts, he later endorsed Canadian immigration, resettled his family in Canada West in 1851, and served on the General Board of Commissioners of the National Emigration Convention, which gave tepid support to Martin R. Delany's Niger Valley Exploring Party in 1858. But Shadd refused to abandon Canada West. An active participant in local politics, in 1859 he gained a seat on the Raleigh Town Council, becoming the first black to hold elected office in the British North American Provinces. Shadd remained in Ontario after the Civil War. He and his wife Harriet Shadd produced thirteen children, including five—Mary Ann Shadd Cary, Isaac D. Shadd, Alfred S. Shadd, Emaline Shadd, and Abraham W. Shadd—who had distinguished careers in Canada and the United States. Winks, *Blacks in Canada*, 215; Harold B. Hancock, "Not Quite Men: The Free Negroes of Delaware in the 1830s," *CWH* 17:329 (December 1971); Hill, *Freedom-Seekers*, 202–5; William Lloyd Garrison, *Thoughts on African Colonization* (1832; reprint, New York, N.Y., 1969), 36–40 [1:0098]; Foner and Walker, *Proceedings of Black State Conventions*, 1:110, 118–19; *Minutes of Third Annual Convention*, 5 [1:0294]; *CA*, 25 July, 15, 22 August 1840 [3:0534, 0563, 0578]; *WAA*, 14 December 1861 [13:0976]; Martin R. Delany, *Official Report of The Niger Valley Exploring Party* (Leeds, England, 1861), 12–13 [11:0336]; *NR*, February 1839; *IC*, 5 December 1849 [6:0234].

27. David Jenkins (1811–1877) was born in Lynchburg, Virginia. Although it is unclear whether his father, William Jenkins, was a white slaveholder or a free black, the younger Jenkins was reared in circumstances well beyond the reach of most of his race, including a thorough education at the hands of a private tutor hired by his father. In 1837 Jenkins settled in Columbus, Ohio, where he managed a boardinghouse and worked as a painter, plasterer, and paper hanger. Through thrift and industry, he amassed a considerable sum of money, which he invested in real estate. Jenkins agitated against slavery from the time of his arrival in Columbus until the end of the Civil War. On 27 December 1843, he began publishing the *Palladium of Liberty*, a Columbus weekly devoted to the abolition of slavery and the advancement of the black race. Although the paper obtained a sizable readership in Ohio and the eastern United States, it ceased publication in late 1844. After the *Palladium*'s demise, Jenkins frequently wrote on antislavery matters for Frederick Douglass's *North Star*. He remained a leading figure in Ohio abolitionist circles, as he participated in the underground railroad, lectured against slavery, organized Emancipation Day celebrations, coordinated mass rallies to protest the Fugitive Slave Law of 1850, and helped to found the Ohio State Anti-Slavery Society. Jenkins also played a key role in the black convention movement. He attended the 1843 National Convention of Colored Citizens in Buffalo, the

1848 National Convention of Colored Freemen in Cleveland, and the 1853 Colored National Convention in Rochester, and he coauthored the "Address to the Colored People of the United States" that emerged from the 1848 meeting. A prominent delegate at every state black convention held in Ohio between the late 1840s and the early 1870s, he frequently served on statewide black coordinating committees. Jenkins advocated mass black emigration as late as 1849, but he became a critic during the decade that followed, urging blacks to remain in the United States "under the tree [they had] planted." During the Civil War, he vocally supported the Union cause and enlisted troops for the Fifth U.S. Colored Infantry. Jenkins was intensely interested in state and local politics and regularly attended sessions of the Ohio legislature, offering petitions on behalf of black civil rights and earning the sobriquet "member at large." After the war, he became a ward committeeman in the local Republican party, but his attempts to obtain political office and to become sergeant-at-arms of the Ohio legislature were thwarted because of his race. Disgusted by the racism he encountered in Ohio and encouraged by the promise of Reconstruction, Jenkins moved to Canton, Mississippi, in 1873 to teach at a Freedmen's Bureau school. During the final two years of his life, he served in the Mississippi legislature. Dennis Charles Hollins, "A Black Voice of Antebellum Ohio: A Rhetorical Analysis of the *Palladium of Liberty*, 1843–1844" (Ph.D. diss., Ohio State University, 1978), 14–41; Frank R. Levstik, "David Jenkins: Eagle That is Forgotten," *NHB* 38:464 (October-November 1975); *NSt*, 20 October, 3 November 1848 [5:0807, 0819]; *Lib*, 27 October 1848 [5:0812]; *Report of the Proceedings of the Colored National Convention, Held at Cleveland, Ohio*. . . . (Rochester, N.Y., 1848), 3 [5:0769]; *Proceedings of the Colored National Convention, Held in Rochester July 6th, 7th, 8th, 1853* (Rochester, N.Y., 1853), 5 [8:0327]; Miller, *Search for Black Nationality*, 140; *FDP*, 4 January 1855 [9:0362]; Foner and Walker, *Proceedings of Black State Conventions*, 1:219, 242, 257, 274, 305, 319, 338, 342.

28. Amos G. Beman (1812–1874) was the son of Jehiel C. Beman. The elder Beman, pastor of a black church in Middletown, Connecticut, was a prominent abolitionist and early supporter of William Lloyd Garrison. Amos Beman was privately tutored before attending several schools, including Oneida Institute (1835–36). He taught in Hartford while a candidate for the ministry. In June 1838 he moved to New Haven, Connecticut, to serve the Temple Street Colored Congregational Church. Throughout his reform career, Beman focused his attention on temperance, antislavery, and moral improvement. He sponsored educational lectures, library clubs, protective associations, and "elevation meetings"; he cofounded the Connecticut State Temperance Society for Colored People (1836), wrote a series of newspaper articles on the subject for the *Colored American* (1839), and organized the New Haven Literary and Debating Society (1841).

Beman was a vigorous abolitionist, who, with his father and J. W. C. Pennington, became one of the most important antislavery spokesmen for Connecticut's black community during the 1840s and 1850s. When the American Anti-Slavery Society became factionalized in 1840, Beman helped found the American and Foreign Anti-Slavery Society and served on its executive committee. Beman also understood the necessity of a vital black press and edited the short-lived *Zion's Wesleyan* in 1842. As president of the 1843 National Convention of Colored Citizens held in Buffalo, New York, his speech helped defeat a resolution by

Henry Highland Garnet that sanctioned slave violence. During the 1840s, Beman devoted increasing amounts of time to abolition and the struggle for black civil rights. He led the black suffrage movement in Connecticut, made his church a station on the underground railroad, and counseled disobedience to the Fugitive Slave Law of 1850. At the Rochester Colored National Convention (1853), Beman was elected to the National Council of the Colored People—an executive committee meant to serve as the convention's administrative arm—and he was appointed to the Manual Labor School Committee.

In 1856 and 1857, Beman faced personal tragedy when his wife and two of his four children died of typhoid fever. He remarried in 1858. That same year Beman was appointed pastor of the Fourth Colored Congregational Church of Portland, Maine. Beginning in mid-July 1859, Beman served a year as an agent of the American Missionary Association. He traveled throughout the Northeast, lecturing, raising funds, and assessing the state of the black church. Throughout the 1860s, Beman supported himself and his family by serving a number of short-term ministerial appointments, by working for the freedmen in Tennessee, and by advising the African Civilization Society's freedmen's school project in Washington, D.C. Beman's contributions to black civil rights were honored in 1872 when he was appointed chaplain to the Connecticut legislature. Robert A. Warner, "Amos Gerry Beman—1812–1874: A Memoir on A Forgotten Leader," *JNH* 22:200–221 (April 1937); *Lib*, 7 January, 7 July, 11, 25 August 1832, 11 May, 11 August, 7 September, 2 November 1833, 2 March, 3 December 1836, 8 September 1843, 26 September 1856, 9 September 1864 [1:0092, 0218, 0283, 0341, 0651, 0751, 4:0660, 15:0517]; *FDP*, 22 July 1853, 8, 29 September, 13, 27 October 1854, 12 January, 4 May, 14 September 1855 [8:0373, 9:0072, 0116, 0133, 0168, 0374, 0578, 0832]; Amos G. Beman to Lewis Tappan, 11 October 1841, 27 September 1843, AMA-ARC [4:0251, 0673].

29. William Lambert (ca. 1818–1890) was born to free black parents in Trenton, New Jersey, and received an excellent education "at the hands of Quakers." He settled in Detroit by 1840 and entered the garment trade, working first in the clothing shop of West Indian black Robert Banks, then establishing a thriving tailoring business of his own. Between the early 1840s and the Civil War, the controversial and militant Lambert devoted much of his time to the flood of fugitive slaves that poured through Detroit on their way to Canada West. He cofounded the city's Colored Vigilant Committee in the early 1840s and, as secretary of that organization, coordinated efforts to aid and protect black refugees, kept records of the hundreds he helped, and participated in several fugitive slave rescues. With the assistance of George De Baptiste, another local black, he founded a second effort in the late 1850s that combined elements of a vigilance committee and a fraternal order. About that same time, Lambert was attracted to the revolutionary ideas of abolitionist John Brown. He attended Brown's Chatham Convention (1858) and was selected to serve as treasurer of the government that Brown intended to establish in the Appalachian mountains after the Harpers Ferry raid. Lambert also contributed to abolitionism in more public ways. He frequently spoke out against slavery and was an active member of several state antislavery societies. During the early 1840s, he endorsed political antislavery and joined the Liberty party. He also labored for a variety of other reform causes, including civil rights, black education, and temperance; he helped lead a movement that at-

tempted to obtain the franchise for Michigan blacks, combated racism in the Detroit press, worked for black admission to the city's public schools, and organized a black day school (1842). Lambert participated in the black convention movement, attending two antebellum national meetings and calling and organizing Michigan's 1843 black state convention. Although an early opponent of black emigration, after 1854 he advised blacks to resettle beyond the North American continent. Lambert represented Detroit blacks at the 1854 and 1856 National Emigration Conventions in Cleveland, where he rallied behind James T. Holly's plan for Haitian immigration. At the 1856 meeting, he was elected treasurer of the National Board of Commissioners, the emigration movement's administrative arm. He also worked for Holly's Protestant Episcopal Society for Promoting the Extension of the Church among Colored People, which advocated Episcopalian missionary work among Haitian blacks. Lambert continued in the movement through the early 1860s. He remained a leader of Detroit's black community after the Civil War, when he helped to found black Masonic and Oddfellows lodges, held prominent positions in local Episcopal lay affairs, and represented the community at several black state conventions. A force in local Republican circles, he made unsuccessful bids for election to Detroit's board of estimates in 1875 and 1877. After a period of deteriorating mental health, Lambert hanged himself in 1890. He left an estate valued at more than $70,000. Undated newspaper clippings, William Lambert Folder, MiD-B; David M. Katzman, *Before the Ghetto: Black Detroit in the Nineteenth Century* (Urbana, Ill., 1973), 3, 5, 13–14, 21, 23, 27, 32–33, 38–43, 95, 138–39, 148–49, 161, 176–77, 180; Katherine DuPre Lumpkin, "'The General Plan Was Freedom': A Negro Secret Order on the Underground Railroad," *Phy* 28:63–77 (Spring 1977); *SL*, 23 January, 25 December 1843, 23 March 1846 [4:0527, 0711]; *Lib*, 18 November 1853 [8:0495]; Foner and Walker, *Proceedings of State Black Conventions*, 1:181–87, 190, 194; Miller, *Search for Black Nationality*, 161, 166–67, 233; Undated newspaper clipping, Stanley Smith Collection, CaOLU; *WAA*, 31 March 1860 [12:0598].

24.
Address by Henry Bibb, John T. Fisher, and James D. Tinsley
[September 1851]

Delegates to the North American Convention asked black abolitionists Henry Bibb, John T. Fisher, and James D. Tinsley to "draw up an address as emanating from this convention, and embodying the spirit and sentiment embraced in the various resolutions . . . and . . . be a committee of revision and publication." The committee consisted of a former-slave-turned-newspaper-editor (Bibb), a Toronto saloonkeeper and militant black activist (Fisher), and a fugitive slave who would leave Canada West for the Australian goldfields within the year (Tinsley). They issued an aggressive assault upon American slavery, an eloquent brief for emigration, and an ambitious call to action for blacks on the North American continent. Their "Address to the Colored Inhabitants of North America" conveyed the energy and passion of the North American Convention. *VF*, 22 October 1851.

AN ADDRESS
TO THE
Colored Inhabitants of North America

DEAR BRETHREN:

The Committee appointed to prepare this Address, would most respectfully, earnestly, but very briefly call your attention to several topics, which to them appear of the most vital importance to the general well being of our people.

In the first place let it be borne in mind that we are an oppressed and much degraded people; not in Canada, thank Heaven! nor by the laws of Great Britain, for under this government we have no reason to complain, as here, and here only, we participate in all the rights and privileges which other men enjoy. But, on the other hand, was ever any class or portion of the human family so persecuted and oppressed as the colored inhabitants of the United States of America? Nearly the entire population of our people in that country are held and treated as slaves by Church and State, notwithstanding that they proclaim theoretically to the world—and even keep the proclamation standing at the head of their national text book—that "*all men* are created *equal*, and endowed by their Creator with certain inalienable rights, and that among these are life, *liberty*, and the pursuit of happiness."[1]

This political or practical falsehood looks well on paper, and strikes harmoniously on the American ear, especially on the 4th day of July; but it sounds like base hypocrisy to every colored American[2] who knows that under the same government three millions and a half of his race are tyrannically robbed of their manhood. While this is the case, those who are nominally free will be little better off, in point of fact, than those who are actually slaves; for let it be remembered, that there can be no real freedom in the land while the great body of our people are held in slavery. We have, therefore, all one common interest at stake, which is the abolition of slavery and the mutual improvement of our people. Let us then be united in sentiment and in action upon this work until it is accomplished. It is emphatically a moral duty which God requires at our hand—He requires that we should "remember those in bonds as bound with them," and we shall have yet to come to that point. Too long, brethren, have we been conniving at our own oppression, by leaving the work which we should have done in the hands of others; by not giving our testimony at all proper times, and under all favorable circumstances, against slaveholding; by not doing our part in sustaining either the pulpit or the press which have faithfully vindicated our cause before the public; by not giving countenance to anti-slavery meetings, and by throwing off responsibilities which rightfully belonged to us; by imitating our oppressors in vanity and extravagance in dress, &c., which is unbecoming and impracticable; and finally, by neglecting to educate ourselves and children, which is the most essential step to our moral and intellectual advancement. Only let this effectually be done, and our great object is more than half accomplished.

With the map and the history of human bondage before us, we are led to believe that the abolition of American slavery is now in the hands of the people of color in North America. Not that we would have the true-hearted abolitionists, who have stood by us in the darkest hours of adversity, to cease their efforts until the work is done; but we should be found standing in the front ranks of the battle, until our kinsmen, according to the flesh are disenthralled. Men who have had to contend against "fearful odds," and who have received succour in the hour of peril, should certainly be the first to fly to the rescue when the oppressed and the afflicted are crying out for deliverance.

The history of the oppressed in all ages of the world, plainly shows that they have emerged from degradation to social and political equality with their oppressors, only in proportion to their own exertions in their own cause. In the emphatic language of the poet—

> Know ye not, hereditary bondsmen?
> He that would be free, himself must strike the blow[3]

We have dwelt much on the subject of American slavery because we consider it a matter of the greatest importance. It is the great stumbling-block in the way of our social and political advancement, and it is also the main key which locks the door against our general improvement. But notwithstanding, we believe as long as American slavery exists, an impetus will be given to the exertions of the liberated few which will cause them to rise in general intelligence, and enable them to realize a like elevation for the whole race.

We have already said that the destiny of slavery is in the hands of our people in North America, and the time has now fully come when we should apply the remedy: but let us first look and calculate what is our relative strength in the United States; and secondly, see how we can most effectually bring it to bear on the great objects which we have in view.

In the northern and southern states there are about 700,000 free people of color. In the southern states there are about 3,500,000 slaves, while the slaveholders number about 250,000. Should the slaves rise to a man, and demand their freedom at the hands of their oppressors, and say that they would no longer work without wages—that they would no longer suffer their wives and children to be lacerated by cruel slave-drivers, or allow them to be sold apart as cattle in the market, how long would slavery last? It would be abolished in even less than a single day, were it not that the strong arm of the whole American Government is under a pledge to keep the slave in his chains. Three millions and a half of men, armed with the righteous cause of freedom, and the God of Justice on their side, against two hundred and fifty thousand tyrants, could sweep them like chaff before the wind. It is the knowledge of this fact that causes the slaveholders and their supporters to dread the increase of the free people of color—that induces state after state to pass laws prohibiting their settlement—that causes them to interfere with the private right of individuals to emancipate their slaves—and that systematically organizes plans for transporting men from the land of their nativity to Liberia.[4] But we have great reason to thank God that notwithstanding the gross ignorance of our people, very few of them can be gulled into that scheme of prejudice and deception. We know that the great battle between freedom and slavery is to be fought on this continent and not in Africa. Our oppressors seek to divide our forces by inducing the most energetic of our brethren, by deceptive premises, to embark for a distant shore. We wish our friends to understand this trick of the slaveholders, as we disapprove of the scheme in toto.

If we are asked, then, where shall we go, or what is to be the remedy—whether it is to be moral or physical force? We say to our brethren, Be patient, enter into no conspiracies for the shedding of human blood, not only because of the improbability of your success against the government of the United States in such a contest, but because it is contrary to the will of God; because we believe that there is a better way; because we know that we have truth and justice on our side, and "the weapons of our warfare should not be carnal, but mighty, through God, to the pulling down of the strong holds" of human bondage; and we shall pursue a course that will secure the approbation of Him who is greater than all that can be against us. We give our unqualified verdict in favor of self-emancipation, for we have authority from the Inspired Volume, which says, "If ye are persecuted in one city, flee away to another." We believe it to be an indispensable duty that every "hereditary bondsman" owes to himself, first to run away from slavery, and to carry off with him whatever may be necessary to effect his escape.

2nd. That he should go with a determination never to be re-captured and carried back into bondage alive. If the man of blood is on his trail, let the fugitive exert himself to the utmost in baffling the skill of the hunter—if his efforts prove fruitless, then, we say, let him stand at bay and boldly face his pursuers, for it would be more glorious for such an one to die in defence of his own liberty, than to be carried back into perpetual slavery. Self-preservation is the first impulse of nature, and if there is any cause in which a person can be justified in shedding blood it must be when it is shed in the defence of Liberty.

3rd. It is inexpedient in the extreme for such persons to stop short of Canada or the West Indies, where the soil is untainted with human slavery, and where the fugitive is protected in the enjoyment of liberty by one of the most powerful governments on the globe.

4th. We recommend a thorough reorganization of the free people of color, and their friends in the States, in Canada, in the West Indies, and in England, to facilitate the escape of refugees from American slavery, and also to advance their social, moral, political, and intellectual improvement.

As we regard education as being one of the most important items connected with our destiny, and as it is more dreaded by the slaveholders than bowie-knives or pistols, we therefore recommend, that there should be no time nor opportunity lost in educating the people of color. Let there be put into the hands of the refugee, as soon as he crosses Mason and Dixon's Line,[5] the Spelling Book. Teach him to read and write intelligibly, and the slaveholder won't have him on his plantation among his slaves. It is emphatically the most effectual *protection to personal or political liberty* with which the human family can be armed.

For the carrying out of the above, and other kindred objects connected with our destiny, your Committee would strongly recommend the formation of a great Agricultural League of our people of the United States, the British American Provinces and the West Indies.[6] We suggest that such an organization should be linked together with capital, which would not only give it a power and influence which would be felt by the community at large, but enable it to accomplish something for the elevation of our race. One prominent object should be to purchase large tracts of land in Canada and Jamaica, with agricultural implements, and to establish farms throughout those colonies, as far as it may be practicable for the purpose of encouraging industry among refugees from American slavery, and other persons of color who may be disposed to become owners and tillers of the soil.

In order to become members of such an association, and to raise the necessary means to carry on such an enterprize, let the initiation fee be $5, and the stock be divided into shares of $50 each, to be paid in ten annual instalments, and the money to be deposited in the Bank of Upper Canada,[7] subject to the order of an Executive Committee of the Association. Such an organization would give a new impulse to the Under-ground Railroad,[8] and give profitable employment to thousands of colored persons who never aspire higher than to be hewers of wood and drawers of water for the white man.

Let one thousand out of the thirty thousand refugees in Canada, unite with such an Association, within one year from this day, and it will give us a fund of $5,000 capital to commence with.

Let the state of New York, with her 60,000 free colored inhabitants, unite with us by adding 2000 members within one year, and we should have $10,000 to work with, and so could other states do likewise. How much this would gladden the fugitive's heart even to hear of such an organization located in Canada; and what man of color will say that this is not a desirable object? Who among us will pretend to say that it is impractible? Who will say that we have not the ability to carry it out? "Where there is a will there is a way."

We cannot close without referring to the Refugee's Home Society in Michigan, which is now making an effort in connection with the Fugitives' Union Society,[9] of Sandwich, Canada West, for the purpose of settling fugitives in Canada on land. They are aiming to purchase 50,000 acres of land to be divided into 25 acre lots, to be sold to actual settlers at cost, &c. Their object is a noble one, and they are succeeding well. Too much praise cannot be awarded to them for what they are doing for the fugitive.

In conclusion, brethren, let us remember the great responsibility that rests upon the free people of color. Every refugee in Canada is a representative of the millions of our brethren who are still held in bondage; and the eye of the civilized world is looking down upon us to see whether we can take care of ourselves or not. If our conduct is moral and upright, in spite of all the bad training we have had, it will reflect credit on ourselves, and encourage our friends in what they are doing for our elevation. But if, on the other hand, it should be seen, that under a free Government, where we have all our political and social rights, without regard to our color, and where we are permitted to sit under the sanctuary of God, "where there is none daring to molest us or make us afraid," and where we are supported by the prayers and sympathies of all good men, we should prove ourselves to be incapable of self-government, it would bring down reproach and disgrace upon the whole race with which we are connected, and would be used as an argument against emancipation. The slaveholders' predictions would be pronounced true, and society would consider the whole of us unfit for the enjoyment of liberty. How important it is, then, that we should each and all feel our responsibility and conduct ourselves accordingly.

Voice of the Fugitive (Windsor, Canada West), 22 October 1851.

1. The committee quotes from the Declaration of Independence.

2. For many antebellum free blacks, Fourth of July celebrations symbolized the hypocrisy of slaveholding America's professions of liberty and equality. A large number of northern blacks instead observed the First of August—the anniversary of West Indian emancipation. Black leaders registered their objection to black Fourth of July celebrations in 1834 when a national black convention went on record opposing the practice. Quarles, *Black Abolitionists*, 119–23.

3. Bibb, Fisher, and Tinsley paraphrase a line from Lord Byron's *Childe Harold's Pilgrimage*, canto 2, stanza 76:

> Hereditary bondsmen! Know ye not
> Who would be free themselves must strike the blow?
> By their right arms the conquest must be wrought?

George Gordon Noel Byron, *Childe Harold's Pilgrimage and Other Romantic Poems*, ed. Samuel C. Chew (New York, N.Y., 1936), 76.

4. Bibb refers to the movement in the southern states to tighten manumission regulations and to restrict the freedom of free blacks. The southern states permitted relatively unrestricted slave manumission practices during the decades immediately following the Revolution; by the mid-1830s, however, most required slave owners to obtain judicial or legislative permission to free slaves and required those freed to leave the state. Even those states that did not restrict an owner's right of manumission stipulated that freed blacks either migrate or risk deportation or reenslavement. Ira Berlin, *Slaves Without Masters: The Free Negro in the Antebellum South* (New York, N.Y., 1974), 138–39.

5. The Mason and Dixon Line, the symbolic border between the North and South, originated as a line surveyed in 1763 and 1767 by Charles Mason and Jeremiah Dixon to settle boundary differences between Pennsylvania and Maryland. In the antebellum era it was understood to be the dividing line between slave and free territory and was the actual boundary separating Pennsylvania from Delaware, Maryland, and Virginia. *CWD*, 516.

6. Bibb, Fisher, and Tinsley refer to the North American League, the creation of black abolitionist James Theodore Holly, which was envisioned as a "central authority" to coordinate black political and social actions in North America. Holly hoped it would "mold the destiny of the whole Afro-American race." He called for a convention to implement his plan in a series of letters published by Henry Bibb in the *Voice of the Fugitive* during June and July 1851. With Bibb's assistance, the resulting North American Convention convened in Toronto from 11–13 September. Although Holly was unable to attend the gathering, he coauthored a letter to the convention (with James L. Taylor) that outlined the primary objectives of the proposed league: to provide aid to fugitive slaves upon their arrival in

Canada West, to promote free black immigration into the province, and to establish a black agricultural presence in Canada West with an eye toward future commercial endeavors. The convention adopted Holly's proposal and wrote a constitution for the new league that included support for West Indian immigration and called for the sale of shares in the league in order to finance black land purchases. Despite Holly and Bibb's support, the new North American League never really functioned. Miller, *Search for Black Nationality*, 110–12.

7. The Bank of Upper Canada received its charter in 1821. The government owned one-fourth of the bank's stock, and the remainder was controlled by a group of York Conservatives led by John Strachan. Initially, the bank thrived, but it was severely weakened by the depression of 1857 and finally closed its doors in 1866. G. P. de T. Glazebrook, *The Story of Toronto* (Toronto, 1971), 56–57, 109.

8. The underground railroad describes antebellum networks of sympathetic free blacks, Quakers, and other abolitionists that assisted fugitive slaves as they escaped to northern cities and Canada. Abolitionist and southern propaganda frequently mythologized these networks as highly complex secret organizations, but they were often haphazard, localized, and semipublic in nature. Few conductors went south to entice slaves away from their masters, as southerners charged, but rather, most gave assistance (shelter, transportation, and money) to fugitives that came to them voluntarily. Major routes went through Cincinnati and Philadelphia, which were primary centers of organized fugitive assistance, in no small measure because of the active free black communities there. Following the passage of the Fugitive Slave Law in 1850, fear of slave catchers led to the development of "vigilance committees" to protect and assist escaped slaves in many northern cities. Larry Gara, *The Liberty Line: The Legend of the Underground Railroad* (Lexington, Ky., 1967).

9. The Fugitive Union Society was a forerunner of the Refugee Home Society.

25.
Samuel Ringgold Ward to Henry Bibb
16 October 1851

When Samuel Ringgold Ward arrived in the Canadian provinces in October 1851, he brought with him the credentials of a professional black abolitionist. The New York Congregationalist minister and newspaper editor was well known in the American antislavery community. He had edited the *Impartial Citizen* in Syracuse, New York, and had assisted the local vigilance committee in the rescue of fugitive slave William "Jerry" McHenry from federal officers. Fearing prosecution for his role in the Jerry rescue, Ward resettled with his family in Canada West. In his 16 October 1851 letter to Henry Bibb's *Voice of the Fugitive*, Ward announced his arrival and offered an insightful commentary on Canadian racial prejudice. Drawing on personal experience, he demonstrated that legal equality in the Canadas did not mean that racial discrimination was absent, and he explained how American economic and social influences helped shape Canadian race relations. C. Peter Ripley, Jeffery Rossbach, Roy E. Finkenbine, and Fiona Spiers, eds., *The Black Abolitionist Papers*, two vols. to date (Chapel Hill, N.C., 1985), 1:300–301.

Beauharnois, Canada
Oct[ober] 16, [1851]

Dear Bibb:

The *Impartial Citizen* breathed its last,[1] after a lingering illness of the spine, and obstructions, impurities and irregularities of the circulation. *Requiescat in pace!*

I am, like yourself, a refugee. President Fillmore has issued orders for the "arrest of all, without distinction of persons, who were engaged in, or directly or indirectly aided in, or encouraged" the rescue of poor Jerry. I am so much afraid that his Excellency's order would include me, and that trial would be conviction, and as the President has been kind enough to designate treason as the crime committed,[2] I so much suspect that conviction would be suspension, that I have determined to let 'catching' precede any other step. To insure this, I have come to Canada, and I am now on my way from Montreal to your part of the province, making, or intending to make, Toronto my head-quarters for the winter. In the spring I may be a candidate for a job of hoeing in your garden.

I do not, of course, find Canada free from negrophobia. I am not disappointed in this, as it is not my first entrance into your beautiful and progressive province. As an instance of Canadian Negro hate, I took passage to-day, at Lachine, for Kingston. I could get a cabin passage, on the steamer *St. Lawrence*, which carries Her Majesty's Mail, upon no terms whatever! Mr. Kelly, the Purser, declared that there was no room for me.

4. Samuel Ringgold Ward
From I. Garland Penn, *Afro-American Press and Its Editors* (Springfield, Mass., 1891)

There were half-a-dozen state-room keys, uncalled for, in the office at the time. And the cabin saloon was much less crowded than was the deck. I concluded to sail but a short distance upon the infernal craft, but I could not have a cabin passage for even three hours! I therefore staid at this point, running the risk of finding a better chance in some other boat this evening. On Lake Champlain, the *Francis Saultus* gave me a cabin passage without hesitancy. So the *America*, *Fashion*, and *Buckeye State*, on Lake Erie, and the *Arctic* on Lake Michigan. The same is true on the Hudson River. All of these are Yankee vessels, plying in Yankee waters, and run by Yankee captains. But the *St. Lawrence*, under the patronage of the British Government, and sailing upon British waters, with a British subject for a captain, compels a black man to take a deck passage—or none. I shall see how far British law sustains all this. My opinion is, that Englishmen, like Yankees, love the gold of northern and southern slaveocrats; and to get such gold, the Englishman, like the Yankee, will trample upon a black man's rights. There are exceptions to this rule, on both sides of the line, but there are precious few of either who will stand by us when interest bids in an opposite direction. The boast of Englishmen, of their freedom from social negrophobia, is about as empty as the Yankee boast of democracy. In all this, I repeat, I am not at all disappointed; and I believe that a universal agitation, by the press and the tongue, in church and at the polls, will rid our beloved adopted country of this infernal curse. God forgive me when I shall refuse or neglect to do my humble part in this agitation!

Your paper is not known in Montreal. This I very much regret. You would do well to send exchanges to the *Montreal Witness*,[3] and the Montreal *Pilot*.[4] Specimen numbers would speak for themselves, if sent to Rev. Dr. Wilkes, D. P. Jones, Esq.,[5] Shadrack Minkins,[6] and Francis Fransisco. Most happy would I have been to show it to those gentlemen, if I had had a copy with me. Please send to me at Toronto, and I will pay you in cash or labor in a few weeks. If you choose to make me one of your agents, so be it; if not, I shall act as such, quite as free and as faithfully.

I did not come to Canada to relinquish labor, nor to be a burden to my fellow-subjects. Rum and Negro hate, the two great public evils of our adopted land, shall receive unyielding fight from me during my life. And, that the result of my next decade's labor may not, like that of the last, be bankruptcy, I purpose to base the support of my family upon the tilling of the soil, or some other handicraft by which a poor man with a family can live.

But I must close. If you choose to have me do so, I will scrawl a little for your columns, now and then; if not, please say so, and I shall not be displeased. Yours in exile and in hope,

S. R. Ward

Voice of the Fugitive (Windsor, Canada West), 5 November 1851.

1. The *Impartial Citizen*, a semimonthly antislavery and reform newspaper, began publication in Syracuse on 14 February 1849, the product of a merger between Samuel Ringgold Ward's Cortland, New York, *True American* and black activist Stephen Myer's Albany *Northern Star and Freeman's Advocate*. Myer's affiliation with the *Citizen* ended in June 1849, and at that time, Ward converted the paper into a weekly Liberty party organ. By the end of its first year, the *Citizen* had seventeen hundred subscribers (out of the two thousand Ward thought necessary to ensure its success), but delinquent subscribers created financial difficulties, which were only partially alleviated by donations from abolitionist Gerrit Smith and women's antislavery fairs. Despite these problems, Ward and his assistant Seymour King published the paper in Syracuse through 19 June 1850, suspended publication briefly, but resumed on 10 July 1850 in Boston. Ward considered merging the *Citizen* with the *North Star* but instead discontinued publication by October 1851, declared bankruptcy, and soon went to Canada. Although Jermain W. Loguen, a former subscription agent for the *Citizen*, accused Ward of defrauding paid subscribers, Ward noted that the paper failed because less than one-tenth of the subscribers had paid, and many stopped subscriptions "without paying up arrearages." *IC*, 28 February, 14 March, 17 June, 25 July, 5 December 1849, 13 February, 19 June, 14 September, 7 December 1850; Ronald K. Burke, "The *Impartial Citizen* of Samuel Ringgold Ward," *JQ* 49:759–60 (Winter 1972); *NSt*, 5 June, 30 October 1851; *PF*, 19 June 1851; *FDP*, 26 June, 30 October 1851; *VF*, 29 July 1852 [7:0677]; Quarles, *Black Abolitionists*, 88.

2. The rescue of William "Jerry" McHenry (?–1853) was one of the best known slave rescue incidents of the 1850s. McHenry, who had escaped from his owner, John McReynolds of Madison County, Missouri, was residing in Syracuse, New York, and working as a cooper when McReynolds sent an agent to retrieve him under the terms of the Fugitive Slave Law of 1850. The authorities arrested McHenry on 1 October 1851, but an interracial crowd freed him and helped him escape to Kingston, Canada West. According to an 18 February 1851 special proclamation by President Millard Fillmore, those who aided fugitive slave rescues were to be prosecuted for obstructing the Fugitive Slave Law. Ward was implicated in the rescue because he had visited McHenry on the day of his arrest and had delivered a speech to the waiting crowd. Twenty-six men, including twelve blacks, were indicted by the grand jury investigating the case. Nine of the accused blacks, including Ward and Rev. Jermain W. Loguen, vice chairman of the local vigilance committee that had participated in the rescue, escaped to Canada West. Three whites were brought to trial, but only Enoch Reed, the one black to stand trial, was convicted. Campbell, *Slave Catchers*, 154–57; Ward, *Autobiography of Fugitive Negro*, 117–18.

3. The *Montreal Witness* was founded in 1846 by John Dougall, in partnership with his father-in-law John Redpath. The paper grew steadily, achieving a sufficiently large circulation in English-speaking areas around Montreal to ensure moderate financial success. Dougall edited the paper until 1871; under his control, it championed evangelical Christianity, temperance, Sabbatarianism, economic progress, and free trade. Although politically independent, it frequently favored Reform politicians. The *Witness* was intolerant of Catholics and, although not particularly sympathetic to blacks, vigorously opposed Southern slavery. The *Montreal Witness* ceased publication in 1938. *DCB*, 11:270, 975; Winks, *Blacks in Canada*, 261–62, 473.

4. The Montreal *Pilot* was founded by Francis Hincks in 1844. He sold the pro-Reform paper in 1848; one year later, the *Pilot*'s interim proprietors, "entirely ruined" by a £ 500 libel verdict, resold the paper to Rollo Campbell. Under Campbell's ownership, the *Pilot* published two editions—a tri-weekly, and a weekly for rural Canada East. Endorsed by Montreal's Reform party, the *Pilot* became an object of Conservative attack, and its offices were wrecked during riots over the Rebellion Losses Bill (1849). William Bristow, who used the *Pilot* to rally Reform opinion in Canada East and to oppose annexationism, and Rev. John Mockett Cramp edited the paper during the 1850s. Campbell's financial difficulties forced the *Pilot* to cease publication in 1862. *DCB*, 9:83, 10:129–30, 757, 11:409–10.

5. D. S. Janes of Montreal was a vice-president of the Anti-Slavery Society of Canada during the early 1850s. Pemberton, "Anti-Slavery Society of Canada," 49.

6. Frederick "Shadrach" Wilkins (also called Minkins), a Virginia slave, escaped from the service of John Debree of Norfolk, a purser in the U.S. Navy, in May 1850. He made his way to Boston, obtained work as a waiter at the Cornhill Coffee House, and joined the Twelfth Baptist Church. In time, Debree learned of Wilkins's whereabouts, had an affidavit made out in the Virginia courts, and sent slave catcher John Caphart to Boston to recapture and return his slave. Caphart obtained a warrant in Boston, located Wilkins, and secured his arrest by a federal marshal on 15 February 1851. The fugitive slave was taken directly before a federal commissioner, but a large crowd of local blacks forcibly freed him and spirited him away from the courtroom. Through the covert assistance of the Boston Vigilance Committee, Wilkins reached Montreal, Canada East, within ten days. Although initially dependent upon the aid of Boston antislavery friends, he soon established himself in Montreal. Within the year, he opened a saloon and restaurant, joined a local Methodist congregation, married an Irishwoman, and fathered a child.

Word of the Shadrach rescue soon reached Washington. On 18 February, President Millard Fillmore issued a proclamation calling for strict enforcement of the Fugitive Slave Law of 1850 and ordering the arrest and prosecution of all who had "aided, abetted, or assisted" in Wilkins's escape. Four blacks and four white abolitionists were eventually arrested, but none were ever convicted. As a result, the Shadrach rescue proved to be the federal government's greatest defeat in its effort to enforce the Fugitive Slave Law. Campbell, *Slave Catchers*, 148–51; Sobel, *Trabelin' On*, 258; *NSt*, 10 April 1851; *PF*, 21 August, 11 September 1851.

26.
Samuel Ringgold Ward to Henry Bibb
6 November 1851

Black leaders in Canada West insisted that there was great antislavery value in their efforts to create a new life north of the forty-ninth parallel. They believed that black progress in Canada's open and free society would refute widely held assumptions about black inferiority that were the intellectual and emotional underpinnings of American slavery and racial prejudice. In his 6 November 1851 letter to Henry Bibb, Samuel R. Ward explained why he believed that Canada would become the "great moral lighthouse for the black people" and why he planned to make Canada West his "field of labor." *VF*, 19 November 1851 [7:0180].

Toronto, [Canada West]
Nov[ember] 6, 1851

H. Bibb, Esq.
Dear Sir:

Yours of the 27th ult. should have been answered before, but for my absence from town. Please accept my thanks for the very cordial welcome you are pleased to extend to me. I agree with you perfectly as to the importance of this field of labor. What we do here must exert a most powerful influence upon our cause in the United States. Indeed I believe that should our improvement, here, go on regularly, steadily, progressively, two results would follow which our friends in the States are very backward in seeing and acknowledging. In the first place, all the boasted influence for good flowing from Liberia, would be realizing more at home, and with it must go down for ever the old, oft refuted lie, of our incapacity for social equality with the Anglo-Saxons.[1] In the second place, persecution must cease in the North, and the more rigorous features of slavery in the South, for our enemies will feel unwilling to do anything that will even indirectly tend to driving us where we can be freemen to the fullest extent. Well, ameliorate the condition of the free black, and you injure slavery. Diminish the rigors of slavery, in respect to the slave himself, and you both feed the flame of liberty in his bosom, and increase his facilities for running away.

Our friends in the United States are not so clear sighted as our enemies. They would not really like to abandon the fugitives here, but they very greatly undervalue this field.[2] If it be not the great moral lighthouse for the black people, free and enslaved, on this continent, I am altogether mistaken. This seemed so to me, long before I came here; every day confirms me in the opinion. Our enemies see it, know it, deplore it, hate it.

Still, every letter I get, remonstrates against my remaining here, and demands my return!

S. R. Ward

Voice of the Fugitive (Windsor, Canada West), 19 November 1851.

1. Before 1830 most white Americans believed that blacks were inferior, but few assumed that the condition was permanent. This belief changed by the mid-1830s with the emergence of a systematic proslavery argument. Proslavery apologists believed blacks to be constitutionally indolent, vice-ridden, sensual, and lacking the intellectual capacity necessary for freedom and equal participation in a civilized, democratic society. During the 1840s and 1850s, the "American school" of ethnologists buttressed these assertions with "scientific opinion." They examined the nature of racial diversity and concluded that the black and white races were two distinct, separately created, and unequal species. *Crania Americana* (1839) by Samuel George Morton, leader of the "American school," posited the thesis that blacks were permanently inferior to whites. Morton's thesis gained wide acceptance among the defenders of slavery. By the outbreak of the Civil War, the notion of permanent black inferiority was the prevailing popular and scientific view. Frederickson, *Black Image in White Mind*, 43–97.

2. Many American abolitionists were reluctant to offer financial support to the various missionary and relief efforts among black Canadians. Instead, they preferred to contribute where they thought the need was more obvious—the underground railroad, antislavery lecture tours, antislavery publications, local and state antislavery societies, and, occasionally, purchasing the freedom of slaves. Before the passage of the Fugitive Slave Law of 1850, American abolitionists received limited information about the fugitive slave population in the British North American Provinces. After 1850 the large number of fraudulent fund-raising agents and widespread black Canadian opposition to the "begging" system limited contributions to the Canadian field. Murray, "Canada and Anglo-American Anti-Slavery Movement," 22, 35–38, 45, 48–50.

27.
Mary Ann Shadd Cary to George Whipple
27 November 1851

The black Canadian community acquired dynamic new leadership with the arrival of the Shadd family in 1851. Mary Ann Shadd Cary, her brother Isaac, and sister Amelia attained prominence for their antislavery and civil rights activities in Canada West. As an editor of the *Provincial Freeman*, Mary Ann Shadd Cary became a tenacious, outspoken advocate of black self-reliance, racial assimilation, British institutions, and Canadian immigration. Concern for the growing number of fugitive slaves in the province prompted her to open a day school for children and adults in Windsor, Canada West, during the fall of 1851. She turned to the American Missionary Association for financial assistance to sustain the project. Her 27 November 1851 letter to AMA secretary George Whipple corrected his impression that her efforts promoted segregated education. She justified her school by arguing that legal and social circumstances excluded many blacks, especially fugitive slaves, from the public schools. Although critical of public and persistent fund raising to support black efforts in the province, Cary conceded the propriety of soliciting money for educational and religious objectives. As this letter demonstrates, she occasionally turned to white philanthropy to further her causes. *NAW*, 1:300–301; *DANB*, 552–53; Mary A[nn] Shadd [Cary] to George Whipple, 27 October 1851, AMA-ARC [7:0160].

Windsor, C[anada] W[est]
Nov[ember] 27, 1851

Professor G. Whipple[1]
Sir:

In reply to yours of Nov., 4th, which has been recd., I beg you will not consider my effort here, an attempt to encourage the spirit of caste. I am utterly opposed to such a thing, under any circumstances, and would consider an attempt to enlist the sympathy of your society in favor of a project of the kind, decidedly reprehensible.

Whatever excuse may be offered in the states for exclusive institutions, I am convinced that in this country, and in this particular region, (the most opposed to emigration of colored people I have seen), none could be offered with a shadow of reason, and with this conviction, I opened school here with the condition of admission to children of all complexions.[2]

In answer to your first question, there is no doubt, that colored children would be admitted into the Governmt. schools of this village, if a process of law were resorted to; the Trustees of those schools, base their refusal, at present, on a provision (not at all mandatory) for colored people, in the "School Act.["][3] The parents are indifferent to the necessary measures, hence their exclusion. 2. There are, at least, forty children of suitable age, and many grown persons, who would frequent the day school, and who plead inability to pay, as an excuse for not sending or attending now; the frequent arrivals, make an exact estimate a difficult matter, but in a sch. among fugitives, grown persons contribute largely to the numbers.

If I should receive foreign aid, my dependence on parents would be at an end, I am convinced, as the sum realized from a day school, at one shilling per week, and an evening school, for adults, at sixpence, is insufficient to support any one comfortably, and is accompanied with protestations of poverty. One might get on, for a time, with the very poor accommodations the Barracks afford for a school on a small sum, but if an estimate of expenses (as room fuel ect.,) is included, as would have to be, $250. per annum would be the smallest sum reasonable. At present, parents furnish fuel, and take room rent out of it, the consequence is, a very cold, open apartment, unfurnished & objectionable in every way, and a scanty supply of fire-wood.

In the states, I was connected by membership, with the African Methodists[4] but have not renewed my membership with that body of Christians in this country, because of its distinctive character and do not purpose to do so.

By way of testimonial as to personal reputation, or qualifications for this employment, I take liberty to refer you to Rev. C. B. Ray or Professor Charles Reason[5] of your City, to whom I am personally known, or to Dr. J. McCune Smith[6]—Rev. S. E. Cornish[7] or Mr. Wm. P. Powell,[8] members of the "Society for the Promotion of Education Among Cold. Children," in whose employ I was, as a teacher in the Centre St., School in July last.[9] I am unmarried. Respectfully Sir,

Mary A. Shadd[10]

American Missionary Association Archives, Amistad Research Center, New Orleans, Louisiana. Published by permission.

1. George Whipple (1805–1876) was born in Albany, New York. He studied at Oneida Institute and Lane Seminary. As one of the Lane rebels, he transferred to Oberlin College and was appointed professor of mathematics there in 1838. He was a founder and chairman of the Western Evangelical Missionary Society. In 1846 Whipple became the corresponding secretary for the newly organized American Missionary Association, a position he held for thirty years and one that made him responsible for publishing the monthly *American Missionary*. *AM*, November 1876.

2. During the fall of 1851, Mary Ann Shadd Cary established a private school in deteriorating Windsor army barracks built during the War of 1812. Cary shared the barracks with an African Methodist Episcopal church congregation and fugitives in need of shelter. By October 1851, she was teaching twenty-four

children and adults in day and evening classes—an attendance figure that varied little during the life of the school. When Cary failed to secure a living from school fees, she turned to the American Missionary Association for assistance and obtained a stipend of $125 a year. The AMA withdrew its support in January 1853, ostensibly because of Cary's religious beliefs, but she believed that the action resulted from her vocal disagreement with the Bibbs over the Refugee Home Society. Unable to maintain the school without aid, she closed it in March and apparently never reopened it. Mary A[nn] Shadd [Cary] to George Whipple, 27 October 1851, 14 February, 21 June, 21 July, 28 December 1852, 7 February, 28 March, 2 April 1853 [7:0160, 0421, 0636, 0667, 1039, 8:0122, 0184, 0192], Mary A[nn] Shadd [Cary] to the Executive Committee of the American Missionary Association, 3 April, 24 October 1852 [7:0497, 0800], AMA-ARC; *VF*, 13 August 1851 [7:0052].

3. The Common School Act of 1850 allowed separate schools for racial or religious reasons while providing for black education. Blacks could attend white schools when separate schools were not provided, but blacks were required to attend separate schools if they were available. But in practice Canadian racism and local decree frequently kept blacks unschooled or relegated them to inferior separate schools, particularly in the southwestern portion of Canada West, where the majority of fugitives lived. As a result, blacks often had to establish their own schools, frequently with the assistance of white missionary organizations; the best examples were schools in the black settlements at Windsor, Wilberforce, and Dawn, and the Colonial Church and School Society's institution at London. In 1853 the case of *Hill* v. *School Trustees of Camden and Zone* upheld, clarified, and further rigidified this practice. The separate school system remained intact well into the 1860s. Winks, *Blacks in Canada*, 368–76.

4. Cary refers to the African Methodist Episcopal church (often called Bethel Methodists), a leading black denomination during the antebellum period. The AME came to life when discriminatory seating practices prompted black parishioners to withdraw from individual Methodist congregations in Baltimore (1787) and Philadelphia (1792) in favor of establishing their own semi-independent black Methodist churches. In 1816, seeking greater black control over congregational affairs, these congregations joined three other black churches in the middle-Atlantic states to found the AME church. The denomination grew rapidly, soon establishing foreign missions and a thriving publishing program for its religious materials. The AME flourished in the black communities in Canada West, although after 1856 most Canadian members joined the newly formed British Methodist Episcopal denomination. After emancipation, the AME actively competed for converts among black Methodists in the South and dramatically increased its numbers and influence. By the 1970s, the AME claimed one million members. Low and Clift, *Encyclopedia of Black America*, 32–36; Carol George, *Segregated Sabbaths: Richard Allen and the Rise of Independent Black Churches, 1760–1840* (New York, N.Y., 1973), 51–119; Walker, *Rock in a Weary Land*, 4–5, 8–15, 19, 46–81, 99–103.

5. Charles Lewis Reason (1818–1893) was born in New York City, the son of Haitian immigrants to the United States. Along with his brothers, Patrick and Elmer, Reason was educated at the New York Manumission Society's African Free School. He received additional instruction from private tutors. In 1832, when the

society decided to employ only black staff members at the school, Charles's academic accomplishments and his special aptitude for mathematics led to his appointment as an instructor. In 1837 Reason began his active participation in the reform life of New York's black community, first as a member of the Colored Young Men of New York City, a group pressing for black suffrage, and then as a founder and executive committee member of the New York Political Improvement Association, an organization that helped win the right of jury trial for blacks accused of being fugitive slaves (1840). He also successfully lobbied (1841) the state legislature to revoke the sojourner law, which guaranteed slaveholders the right of unimpeded movement through the state with their slaves. Throughout the 1840s, Reason spoke against colonization and for black equality in northern society. He helped organize a number of black citizens' conventions (often serving as the meeting's secretary), repeatedly protested black exclusion from public institutions, and urged blacks to support a black national press.

Throughout his life, Reason advocated black self-help through education. In 1847 he cofounded the Society for the Promotion of Education Among Colored Children; the society organized two schools, and he became principal of one in 1848. That same year, he served on the education committee at the National Convention of Colored Citizens meeting in Troy, New York, and he attended the founding of the Free Soil party in Buffalo. During the 1840s, Reason continued his own educational activities as well. He was a leader of New York's Phoenix Literary Society; he contributed poetry to the *Colored American*; and he wrote the verse "Freedom" as an introduction to Alexander Crummell's *The Man, the Hero, the Christian: A Eulogy of the Life and Character of Thomas Clarkson* (1849). In September 1849, Reason was appointed a professor of literature and language at Central College, located in McGrawville, New York, but he maintained his affiliation with New York City's black community and served on the executive committee of the city-based American League of Colored Laborers. In the fall of 1851, feeling that abolitionists had not tried to keep the "avenues of industrial labor" open to free blacks and that blacks were thereby denied the opportunity to become "self-providing artisans," Reason left Central College to direct Philadelphia's Institute of Colored Youth, a Quaker-sponsored coeducational school that taught vocational and academic subjects. At the Rochester Convention of Colored Citizens in 1853, Reason served on the committee that investigated the possibility of founding a black manual labor college. A year later, he wrote "The Colored People's 'Industrial College'" and an introduction to Julia Griffiths's *Autographs for Freedom* (1854). In 1855 Reason was appointed principal of a black public school in New York City, a position he held for the next thirty-seven years. During the Civil War, Reason served on the city's Citizens' Civil Rights Committee. Throughout the 1870s and 1880s, he continued his struggle against race prejudice as an active member of black educational and protective organizations. Anthony R. Mayo, "Charles Lewis Reason," *NHB* 5:212–15 (June 1942); *CA*, 19 August, 2, 23 September 1837, 15 March, 16 June, 1, 8 September, 6, 22 October, 16 December 1838, 14 September, 28 November 1840, 16, 30 January, 5, 19 June, 3, 10 July 1841 [2:0152, 0167, 0196, 0198, 0436, 0494, 0572, 0580, 0608, 0622, 0680, 3:0615, 0722, 0834, 0857, 4:0047, 0068, 0091, 0099]; *NSt*, 21 January 1848, 11 May 1849, 13 June, 24 October 1850; *PF*, 2 October, 9 December 1852, 7 April, 28 July 1853, 30 April 1854 [8:0199, 0706]; *IC*, 14

February 1849; *WAA*, 21 April, 26 May 1860, 2 November 1861 [12:0646, 0650, 0685, 0728]; *NASS*, 28 May 1864 [15:0362]; Bergman, *History of Negro in America*, 174, 188; *DANB*, 516–17.

6. James McCune Smith (1813–1865) was born in New York City, the son of former slaves that fled from Charleston, South Carolina, and settled in New York State. Smith excelled at the city's African Free School but was denied admission to American colleges. Rev. Peter Williams, the black minister of New York's St. Philips Episcopal Church, helped him enroll in Glasgow University during 1832. Smith received a bachelor's (1835), a master's (1836), and a doctor of medicine degree (1837), while playing an active role in the Scottish antislavery movement as an officer of the Glasgow Emancipation Society. After a brief internship in Paris, Smith returned to New York City in 1837. He established a successful and integrated medical practice and opened the first black-owned pharmacy.

In 1839 Smith began his lifelong dedication to black equality within the antislavery movement when he chaired a committee of New York City's Young Men's Anti-Slavery Association, which debated the best way for free blacks to aid the abolitionist cause and discussed what white abolitionists must do to secure both black trust and participation in the movement. Throughout the 1840s, Smith pondered the validity of political antislavery. Although he rejected affiliation with the Liberty party, he consistently championed unrestricted black suffrage. During these years, Smith continued his support for black-run organizations and for black economic and educational opportunity. He sold subscriptions for Samuel Ringgold Ward's *Impartial Citizen* and Frederick Douglass's *North Star*, acted as an agent for Gerrit Smith's land scheme (1845–46), and collected funds for the integrated, abolitionist-sponsored Central College of McGrawville, New York (1850). During the 1850s, Smith became concerned about racial prejudice among white abolitionists, and he engaged in a protracted debate with Robert Purvis over the issue. Smith and his wife, Malvina, faced personal tragedy when, over a six-week period in the summer of 1854, three of their four children died of illnesses. Smith returned to his antislavery work in April 1855 with a newfound willingness to support political antislavery. In the late spring, he cochaired a Syracuse convention of the Radical Political Abolitionists party, called for federal intervention to end slavery, and defended the constitution as an antislavery document.

Although Smith briefly edited the *Colored American* in the late 1830s, he did his most important writing during the mid-1850s as New York correspondent (sometimes under the pseudonym "Communipaw") for the *Frederick Douglass' Paper*. He used his column to discuss a variety of issues: defects in the antislavery movement, integration, and scientific theories of race. A partial list of Smith's other writings shows the eclectic nature of his interests. They include an essay entitled "On the Influence of Opium on Calamenial Functions" (1844), two pamphlets entitled *A Lecture on the Haytian Revolution* (1841) and *The Destiny of the People of Color* (1843), the eloquent introduction to Frederick Douglass's second autobiography, *My Bondage and My Freedom* (1855), and an introductory biographical sketch of Henry Highland Garnet in Garnet's *Memorial Discourse* (1865). Smith also published a number of important articles in the *Anglo-African Magazine* and, in the early 1860s, reaffirmed his lifelong anticolonizationist stance by attacking the positions of leading black emigrationist-nationalist theorists in the columns of the *Weekly Anglo-African*. He died of a heart ailment in 1865. George Forbes, Biographical Sketch of James McCune Smith, Antislavery Collection, MB; *CA*, 9 September, 28 October 1837, 9 February 1839, 15 August 1840 [2:0175, 0245, 0998, 3:0561]; *NASS*, 8 March 1841, 1, 8 February, 17 October 1844, 28 June 1848, 3 May 1849, 31 October 1850, 27 March, 23 August, 11 September 1851, 12 December 1854, 25 November 1865 [4:0749, 0750, 0935, 5:1085, 6:0655, 0863, 7:0077, 0092]; *NSt*, 4 May 1849 [5:1082]; *FDP*, 16, 30 July, 13 August 1852, 15 April 1853, 6 October, 3, 17, 24 November 1854, 26 January, 2, 9 February, 27 April, 18 May, 6 July, 21 September, 12, 26 October, 9 November 1855, 13 November 1856 [9:0562, 0644, 0645, 0647, 0650]; *IC*, 27 June 1849, 7 September 1850; *Lib*, 6 October 1854; *E*, 1 February, 20 December 1838, 17 January, 28 November 1839 [2:0369]; *PF*, 24 January, 10 October 1839 [2:0982]; *P*, 17 October 1837, 16 January, 22 May 1838, 19 January 1842 [2:0351]; *AAM*, May, August, September 1859 [11:0708, 0888, 12:0029]; *DM*, June 1859, October 1860, March 1863 [12:1022]; *WAA*, 5, 12, 26 January, 23 March 1861 [13:0174, 0190, 0226, 0362].

7. Samuel Cornish (ca. 1796–1858) was born free in Sussex County, Delaware, moved to Philadelphia in 1816, was educated by black minister John Gloucester, and eventually taught at Gloucester's African School. Cornish was licensed to preach in 1819 and ministered two years in Maryland before moving to New York City as pastor of the First Colored Presbyterian Church (later Shiloh Presbyterian Church). He remained there until 1828, when he relinquished the post to his protege, Theodore S. Wright. Cornish's first years in New York reveal many of the ideas that framed his future reform activity. He opposed colonization, and though he flirted with emigration, he rejected it as a solution to black problems. He believed that education, moral reform, and self-help were the means to improve the condition of free black Americans but never hesitated to censure white prejudice. Cornish's first public forum was as senior editor of *Freedom's Journal*, the first black American newspaper, which was established by Cornish and John Russwurm in 1827. Cornish remained with the paper until its demise in March 1829 and, two months later, established the short-lived *Rights of All*.

Cornish also devoted his energies to black organizations that sponsored practical programs for black improvement. He supported the black citizens' movement during the early 1830s and worked as an agent for the Phoenix Society of New York (a black protective association that sponsored the Phoenix High School for Colored Youth in New York); he was an organizer of the American Moral Reform Society; and he helped Lewis and Arthur Tappan establish the New York Anti-Slavery Society. In 1835 Cornish became a member of the executive committee of Garrison's American Anti-Slavery Society, a position he held until 1840. In March 1837, he founded the *Colored American*, the most successful of the early black newspapers.

During the late 1830s and early 1840s, Cornish's positions on antislavery and black self-help led him into a series of conflicts and controversies. In June 1839, he was attacked for his opposition to the idea of an antislavery political party, and as a member of the executive committee of the New York Committee of Vigilance, Cornish forced the resignation of David Ruggles as the committee's secretary because of Ruggles's belief in extralegal activities to free fugitive slaves. Cornish was also involved in the schism within the American Anti-Slavery Society, because he objected to William Lloyd Garrison's anticlerical tone and his stance on the role of women in the movement. Although he did not support an antislavery political party, he believed in political action as an antislavery instrument and supported the black suffrage movement. For those reasons, as well as his longtime friendship with Lewis Tappan and his anger with the American Anti-Slavery Society for its 1838 decision to drop agents assigned to educate free blacks, Cornish helped organize the American and Foreign Anti-Slavery Society in May 1840 and became a member of its executive committee.

By the mid-1840s, Cornish was estranged from many of his associates in the American and Foreign Anti-Slavery Society over the issue of an antislavery political party. But Cornish did not allow antislavery controversies to interfere with his role in the black church. He helped J. W. C. Pennington organize the Union Missionary Society (1841), assisted Lewis Tappan when he reorganized the society into the American Missionary Association (1845), and served as pastor to Presbyterian churches in New Jersey and the Emmanuel Church of New York City. Cornish continued as an active antislavery reformer well into the 1850s. Pease and Pease, *Bound with Them in Chains*, 140–61; David E. Swift, "Black Presbyterian Attacks on Racism: Samuel E. Cornish, Theodore S. Wright and Their Contemporaries," *JPH* 51:433–70 (Winter 1973); Quarles, *Black Abolitionists*, 6, 33, 68, 79–80, 109; Howard Bell, "The American Moral Reform Society, 1836–1841," *JNE* 27:34–40 (Winter 1958); Bella Gross, "*Freedom's Journal* and the *Rights of All*," *JNH* 27:241–86 (July 1932); Howard H. Bell, "Free Negroes of the North, 1830–1835: A Study in National Cooperation," *JNE* 26:447–55 (Fall 1957); Pease and Pease, *They Who Would be Free*, 12, 24–26, 31, 71, 79–84, 113, 122, 133–34, 136, 175, 194–95, 209–11, 257–58, 291–92; Miller, *Search for Black Nationality*, 82–84; *DANB*, 134–35.

8. William P. Powell (1807–ca. 1879) was born free in New York State. Powell's grandmother was Elizabeth Barjova, a cook for the Continental Congress, and his father was a slave named Edward Powell, who was freed when New York abolished slavery in 1827; William was described on his passport application as "of a mulatto colour but of Indian extraction." Powell was educated before serving as an apprentice sailor. He settled in New Bedford, Massachusetts, married Mercy O. Haskins from nearby Plymouth (who was probably part Indian), and established a boardinghouse for sailors.

Powell was an early Garrisonian abolitionist. He signed the constitution of the American Anti-Slavery Society in December 1833, helped found a local antislavery society in the New Bedford area, and was one of the first members of the New England Anti-Slavery Society. An anticolonizationist, he believed that blacks should participate fully and equally in American society. In 1837 Powell and other free blacks appeared before the Massachusetts legislature to protest racial discrimination in the state. Their efforts began a long struggle that culminated during the mid-1840s, when blacks won the statewide right to send their children to integrated public schools and saw an end to the Massachusetts ban on interracial marriage.

Powell promoted women's rights and black self-help. He was chairman of New Bedford's Young Men's Wilberforce Debating Society and supported the temperance crusade. In 1839 Powell moved to New York City and opened an employment agency and home for sailors under the auspices of the American Seamen's

Friends Society. Powell continued his antislavery activity by founding the Manhattan Anti-Slavery Society (1840) and by using the sailors' home to host abolitionist gatherings. Throughout his antislavery career, Powell maintained his allegiance to the American Anti-Slavery Society and Garrisonian principles. He served on the society's executive committee, opposed political abolitionism, and criticized the slaveholding American church. When the Fugitive Slave Law of 1850 was passed, Powell led black efforts to prevent state and local police involvement in extraditions.

Powell's concern about the law and his desire to ensure an adequate education for his seven children prompted a ten-year residence in Liverpool, England. While living there, Powell worked for a trading company and continued his antislavery efforts by hosting black abolitionists during their British tours; he served as a conduit between reform allies in America and Britain and coordinated shipment of British goods to the Boston Anti-Slavery Bazaar.

Powell returned home during the secession crisis. His son William, Jr., was commissioned as a surgeon for the Union army. In 1862 Powell reopened his seamen's home in New York City; a year later, the home was ransacked and his family threatened by antidraft rioters. Powell helped found the American Seamen's Protective Union Association (1863); he served as a delegate to the National Colored Labor Convention held in Washington, D.C. (1869); and he was chairman of the New York Civil Rights Committee (1873). He was a participant at a William Lloyd Garrison Memorial meeting held in San Francisco in June 1879. Philip S. Foner, "William P. Powell: Militant Champion of Black Seamen," in *Essays in Afro-American History* (Philadelphia, Pa., 1978), 88–111; George W. Forbes, Biographical Sketch of William P. Powell, William Powell to Maria Weston Chapman, 30 October 1857, 12 January 1859, William Powell to Samuel J. May, 21 October 1859, Antislavery Collection, MB [10:0880, 11:0545, 12:0142]; Constitution of the American Anti-Slavery Society, American Anti-Slavery Society Papers, DLC [1:0352]; *Lib*, 24 May 1834, 13 June 1835, 19 July, 27 September 1839, 21 July 1843, 7 February 1845, 13 March, 24 July 1863, 29 September 1865 [1:0456, 0609, 3:0141, 0207, 4:0613, 0987, 14:0762, 0974, 16:0236]; *NASS*, 6 May 1841, 24 February 1842, 28 March 1844, 3 May 1845, 10 August, 10 September, 29 October 1846, 9 January, 6 February 1851, 12 February 1859, 23, 30 July 1863 [3:1022, 4:0369, 0774, 5:0267, 1071, 6:0726, 11:0585]; *NSt*, 7 April 1849, 24 October 1850 [5:1051]; *ASA*, August 1853; *WAA*, 10 August 1861 [13:0685]; *PP*, 17 August 1861 [13:0693, 0694].

9. John Peterson and Charles L. Reason joined New York City blacks to form the Society for the Promotion of Education Among Colored Children in July 1846. Society leaders included President William P. Powell, Treasurer James McCune Smith, and trustees Samuel E. Cornish and Charles B. Ray. The nominally interracial organization was established to increase black access to city schools, to encourage black school attendance, and to operate black charity schools. During the spring of 1847, the society founded a high school for black youths; the school had an enrollment of 112 students within two years, but the lack of public support forced it to close. Public funds did help the society operate two elementary schools: Primary School No. 1 (at which Cary taught in 1851), located in the basement of the black St. Philip's Church on Center Street, and Primary School No. 2, located on Thomas Street. The three schools were primarily staffed by

black teachers. Combined enrollment rose to 975 before the city board of education absorbed the two elementary schools into the public system in 1853. The society continued to monitor black school attendance and facilities in the city throughout the decade. In 1857 it lobbied state officials for the physical renovation of New York City's black schools. Walker, "Afro-American in New York City," 77–80; Mabee, *Black Education in New York*, 63–67, 155, 188.

10. Mary Ann Shadd Cary (1823–1893) was the oldest of thirteen children born to free blacks Abraham and Harriet Shadd of Wilmington, Delaware. Abraham Shadd, a prosperous shoemaker and respected political activist, was a leader of the black convention movement, an anticolonizationist, and an early member of the American Anti-Slavery Society. The Shadds were devoted to educating their children, and Mary Ann began her studies by attending a school for free blacks sponsored by the African School Society of Wilmington. After moving to West Chester, Pennsylvania, in the mid-1830s, the Shadds enrolled Mary Ann in a Quaker-owned, private school for free blacks, where she was tutored by Quaker antislavery activist Phoebe Darlington. For the next twelve years, Mary Ann Shadd Cary taught at black schools in the mid-Atlantic region and in New York City. Her experiences led her to publish *Hints for the Colored People of the North* (1849), an analysis of the manner by which the northern political economy repressed blacks. The pamphlet began Cary's lifelong examination of the interrelationship between economics and racism.

In 1851 Cary immigrated to Canada West with her brother Isaac and her father, hoping to assist blacks fleeing there after passage of the Fugitive Slave Law of 1850. Settling in Windsor, she opened a school for blacks and wrote *Notes on Canada West* (1852), an immigration guide for fugitives. In March 1853, she joined with Samuel Ringgold Ward to publish the first edition of the *Provincial Freeman*, a newspaper addressed to Canadian blacks. A year later, she helped transform the paper into a regularly published, Toronto-based weekly. Between 1854 and 1857, Cary, the first black woman newspaper editor in North America, dominated the journal despite staff and location changes. She used the paper to express her commitment to integration, her criticism of self-segregated black Canadian communities, and her vision of Canada as a permanent place of settlement. She also attacked corruption and mismanagement among the black and white leaders of the Canadian fugitive slave community.

In January 1856, Mary Ann married Thomas J. Cary, a Toronto businessman and antislavery activist who died in 1860. The Carys had two children. From 1860 to 1863, Mary Ann Shadd Cary operated a black school at Chatham. She also penned numerous letters to the *Weekly Anglo-African* and *Liberator* and edited Osborne P. Anderson's memoir, *A Voice from Harpers Ferry* (1861). During the last years of the Civil War, she recruited black soldiers for the Union army. Cary moved to Detroit in 1864 and continued to teach. After settling in Washington, D.C., in 1869, she served as principal of a black grammar school (1872–84) and continued her reform activities as a suffragist and as an advocate of black economic self-sufficiency. In 1883 Cary received a law degree from Howard University. *NAW*, 1:300–301; *DANB*, 552–53; Harold Hancock, "Mary Ann Shadd Cary: Negro Editor, Educator, and Lawyer," *DH* 15:187–94 (April 1973); Bearden and Butler, *Shadd*.

28.
Jermain Wesley Loguen to Washington Hunt
2 December 1851

Passage of the Fugitive Slave Law of 1850 turned the trickle of black refugees reaching the Canadas into a torrent. Some arrivals were fugitives fresh from slavery. Others had resided in the North for a period of years. A few fugitives, like Samuel Ringgold Ward or Jermain W. Loguen, feared arrest because of their militant resistance to the Fugitive Slave Law. When the law was passed, Loguen's wife and friends urged him to flee to Canada West. But he publicly announced his intention to stay and fight, telling audiences, "I don't respect the law—I don't fear it—I won't obey it." He called on other Syracuse residents to resist the law. One year after the law was passed, Loguen participated in the 1 October 1851 rescue of William "Jerry" McHenry, a fugitive slave jailed in Syracuse by federal authorities. With his arrest a virtual certainty, Loguen fled to St. Catharines, Canada West. Shortly thereafter he was indicted by a Buffalo grand jury. On 2 December, he wrote to Governor Washington Hunt of New York State, seeking a promise of protection should he return to stand trial. Although no such promise was made, Loguen returned to Syracuse but was never tried. He spent the remainder of the decade aiding fugitive slaves escaping through the city on their way to Canada West. Philip S. Foner, *History of Black Americans: From the Compromise of 1850 to the End of the Civil War* (Westport, Conn., 1983), 21; Quarles, *Black Abolitionists*, 209–10; Hiram Wilson to William Harned, 3 December 1851, AMA-ARC; *VF*, 1 July 1852 [7:0642].

St. Catharines, C[anada] W[est]
Dec[ember] 2, 1851

To his Excellency WASHINGTON HUNT[1]
Governor of the State of New York
DEAR SIR:

As a citizen of the State of New York, now in exile for the sake of liberty, which is dearer to me than life, I take it upon me to address to you a few lines upon the subject, to which a prompt reply is most respectfully solicited.

Your Excellency may perhaps have been made acquainted with the fact, that the Grand Jury, recently empanelled by the United States District Court, at Buffalo, have found a bill of indictment against me, as one of the actors on the 1st of October last, in the rescue of a certain supposed fugitive slave, in Syracuse, called *Jerry*.

I am not disposed, sir, to deny my presence in Syracuse at the time of that notable event, or that, in common with thousands of my fellow-citizens I felt sincerely desirous that the conflict should result as it did, in favor of freedom. I am aware, sir, that you have long acted in good faith as a minister of justice, and that your exalted seat, as the Governor of a great and enlightened people, is filled with dignity and honor; I can, therefore, with the greater confidence, approach your Excellency upon a matter of vital importance, to me especially, and also to the cause of universal freedom.

I have long cherished the truly democratic motto of 'exact and equal justice to all men,' and trust that you possess sounder judgment and better sense than to conclude that my absence from Syracuse, and from 'the Empire State,' when hotly pursued and ardently sought for, is *prima facie* evidence of guilt. To draw so rash and uncharitable a conclusion would, in effect, be to take part with Austria and the proud autocrat of Russia, against the renowned and noble Kossuth.[2] It would go to justify an all-pervading suspicion towards that great champion of human freedom, upon his advent to our American shores, instead of the sunshine of confidence from the happy countenances of the millions of his admirers. As is his position with Austria, so is mine at present with the United States. On this point, your Excellency will allow me to define my position more clearly. It was my misfortune, not my fault, that I was born in the South, contrary to the Declaration of American Independence, which solemnly avers that 'all men are created equal, and are endowed by their Maker with certain inalienable rights, among which are life, liberty and the pursuit of happiness.' In short, according to a fundamental law of American despotism, more direful and damning than ever darkened or cursed an Austrian Hungary, I was born unconstitutionally.

I served out my time at the South, at least as long as God required me to remain there, and with Divine approbation, I burst my galling chains, and came out of slavery twenty years ago. I have resided long enough in her Britannic Majesty's dominions to have become a British subject; but having lived for many years in the State of New York, at Syracuse, as a minister of the Gospel and 'citizen of no mean city,' I have never been able to produce any other certificate of freedom[3] than the one which was indelibly written upon my constitutional nature, by the finger of the Almighty. With this God-given guarantee of my right to freedom, which no human power could obliterate, I felt in some degree secure among the sons of noble sires who gallantly fought and bled for liberty, until my confidence in the protection afforded me was shaken by the passage of the horrible Fugitive Slave enactment, and for a long time after the passage of that notoriously wicked and cruel enactment, I felt disposed to maintain my ground, and sooner pour out my heart's blood, as a libation upon the holy altar of liberty, than to abandon the cause of my suffering brethren, and forsake my native country, and those who by conjugal and kindred ties were dearer to me than my own life. With these sentiments buoying me up, and burning like quenchless fire upon the mean altar of my heart, I would have stood my ground and hazarded all consequences, but for the fact that my personal liberty had been some time threatened, and from the earnest entreaties of my wife and four children,[4] from whose presence I am driven, as well as my esteemed and faithful friends, who placed a higher estimate upon my life and freedom than I was disposed to do.

It was ordered by an all-wise Providence, that watches over the falling sparrow and numbers the very hairs of our head, that I should visit again this glorious land of refuge about the time that some of my fellow-sufferers in freedom's cause were being arrested at Syracuse; but be it known that I am not here, sheltered under the protecting aegis of her Majesty's powerful Government, as a felon or a fugitive from justice—for I have committed no crime—but the fiendish machinations of the merciless slave-hunters, and their equally guilty, but infinitely meaner and more contemptible Northern abettors (officials and non-officials), with the fear of flagrant injustice, have driven to these shores. Having thus defined my position, and explained my circumstances, I am now prepared, as a man and a Christian minister in exile, to ask your Excellency the following questions:

1st. Is the Fugitive Slave enactment, by the American Congress, in such a sense an *ex post facto* law, that it can endanger the liberty of an American citizen who, for twenty years before it was enacted, has stood upon free soil, inhaling and exhaling the air of freedom?

2nd. Will your Excellency, in the name and on the behalf of the sovereign State of New York, guarantee to me that protection which belongs of right to an American citizen, if I will voluntarily return to Syracuse, and stand trial as indicted for the crime of loving liberty?

A satisfactory reply to these queries would do much to influence my future course.

In regard to the rescue of *Jerry*, at Syracuse, it does not become me at present to say whether I took part in the transaction or not; but I have no hesitancy in saying, that the bill of indictment found against me, in Buffalo, is based only on mistaken or perjured testimony; as I am prepared to prove myself innocent of any violation of law, by substantial witnesses. This I claim the right, and crave the privilege of doing, whenever and wherever it can be done without exposing my person to rapacious slave-hunters.

I wish, sir, to assure your Excellency, that I possess the feelings of a Christian and a man of honor. I do not understand precisely on what grounds I am indicted. If I am charged with having made use of violence of any kind for the purpose of impeding or preventing the execution of just and equitable laws, I have only to say, before God and man, that I am innocent, and am prepared to establish my innocency. But if the irrepressible heavings of a bosom fraught almost to bursting with love of freedom, and the free tribute of my voice to that of thousands under like condemnation, rending the vault of heaven with shouts of triumph, and shaking the earth beneath, was treasonable, then I was a great transgressor.

While at Syracuse, on the memorable 1st of October, the volcanic fires of liberty were expanding and flaming up to heaven: although I was not an incendiary, neither was I active in throwing water, my curiosity having been a little excited in favor of witnesssing so magnificent a conflagration, until it could be extinguished by some 'Union Safety Committee,'[5] or other proper authority. That your Excellency may be the better informed respecting my character and standing as a confiding applicant, not for Executive clemency, but for the shield of protection in the free course of Justice, I am happy to refer you to the following gentlemen, who are well-known in the city of Syracuse and vicinity:

John Wilkinson, Esq., President of the Syracuse and Utica Railroad Company;[6] Charles B. Sedgewick, Attorney at Law;[7] Hon. E. W. Leavenworth, ex-Mayor of Syracuse;[8] Horace Wheaton, Esq., present Mayor;[9] Rev. R. R. Raymond[10] and Rev. S. J. May,[11] of Syracuse; and Gerrit Smith, Esq., of Peterboro.

Hoping that your Excellency may enjoy the unabated confidence of an enlightened and grateful people, in following the footsteps of your illustrious predecessors, especially the noble-minded ex-Governor Seward,[12] and be crowded with the smiles of Heaven, I have the honor to be, dear sir, Your faithful servant,

J. W. LOGUEN[13]

Liberator (Boston, Mass.), 14 May 1852.

1. Washington Hunt (1811–1867), a New York jurist, served as a Whig in Congress, where he opposed proslavery legislation, from 1842 to 1849. He was narrowly elected Democratic governor of New York in 1850. After losing his reelection bid two years later, he remained active in state and national party politics for another decade. *DAB*, 9:395–96.

2. Louis Kossuth (1802–1894), the leader of the Hungarian independence movement, rose to prominence during the European revolutions of 1848. After initial political and military successes, the nationalist movement was crushed by the Austrian and Russian armies, and Kossuth was forced into permanent exile. England and the United States welcomed him during 1851–52 as a spokesman for democracy and human rights. But abolitionists turned on Kossuth after failing to enlist his aid in the antislavery struggle. He later resided in England and Italy. Donald S. Spencer, *Louis Kossuth and Young America: A Study of Sectionalism and Foreign Policy, 1848–1852* (Columbia, Mo., 1977).

3. Loguen refers to the fact that, throughout the antebellum period, southern laws required free blacks to carry papers documenting their freed status. Berlin, *Slaves Without Masters*, 93.

4. In December 1851, Loguen's family consisted of himself, his wife, Caroline

Storum Loguen (1817–1867), and four children—Sarah Marinda, Amelia, Cora, and Garret Smith. A fifth child, J. William, was born the following year. Sarah Marinda graduated from the Syracuse Medical School in 1876 and lived in the Dominican Republic until 1902. Amelia married Lewis E. Douglass, Frederick Douglass's son. Cora and J. William lived in Cleveland during the 1880s. Garret Smith Loguen gained prominence as an artist and as deputy recorder of deeds in Washington, D.C. (1887). *PA*, 5 October 1867; *CG*, 16 February, 10 May, 5 July 1884; *DANB*, 404; Theresa D. Cederholm, *Afro-American Artists: A Bio-bibliographical Directory* (Boston, Mass., 1973), 73; E. Franklin Frazier, *The Negro Family in the United States* (Chicago, Ill., 1939), 52–53, 69, 76.

5. The Union Safety Committee was established on 23 October 1850 at a mass meeting of New York City merchants, who, fearing that continued agitation over slavery would destroy the Union, endorsed the Compromise of 1850 as a final settlement of the slavery question. The merchants instructed the committee to facilitate the enforcement of the Fugitive Slave Law and to convert New Yorkers to their beliefs. The predominantly Whig group, composed of one hundred prominent businessmen, vigorously pursued the task by successfully soliciting and publishing pro-Compromise statements from local clergymen, entering the political arena, and supporting the January 1851 case against the fugitive slave Henry Long. Philip S. Foner, *Business and Slavery: The New York Merchants and the Irrepressible Conflict* (Chapel Hill, N.C., 1941), 49, 55–87; Campbell, *Slave Catchers*, 73–75, 116–17.

6. John Wilkinson (1798–1862), a New York lawyer, business executive, and civic leader, became the first postmaster of Syracuse in 1820. He later served as president of the Utica and Syracuse Railroad, the Michigan Southern Railroad, and the Bank of Syracuse. Dwight H. Bruce, ed., *Memorial History of Syracuse, New York* (Syracuse, N.Y., 1891), Part 2, 75.

7. Charles B. Sedgwick (1815–1883) was born in Pompey, New York, and educated at Hamilton College. After settling in Syracuse in 1848, he practiced law and became involved in Free Soil politics. He later served as a Republican congressman (1859–63) and as a naval affairs administrator (1863–65). *BDAC*, 1674.

8. Elias W. Leavenworth (1803–1887) was born in Canaan, New York, and studied at Yale and Litchfield Law School. He established a law practice in Syracuse in 1827. Leavenworth became active in Whig politics and held various municipal posts, including mayor, and served in the state legislature and as New York secretary of state (1854–55). He sat in Congress (1875–77) as a Republican. *BDAC*, 1274.

9. Horace Wheaton (1803–?), a successful Syracuse merchant, became active in Free Soil politics, served on the town council, and was appointed mayor of Syracuse in 1851. United States Census, 1850; *Lib*, 17 October 1851; *PFW*, 22 May 1851.

10. Robert R. Raymond (1818–?), a New York clergyman, was pastor of the Syracuse First Baptist Church from 1847 to 1852. He also edited the *True Democrat* in Syracuse and used both press and pulpit to raise antislavery issues. Bruce, *Memorial History of Syracuse*, 478; United States Census, 1850; *PFW*, 23 October 1852.

11. Samuel Joseph May (1797–1871) was born in Boston and attended Har-

vard College and Harvard Divinity School. From 1822 until 1867, May served several Unitarian congregations and, at the request of educational reformer Horace Mann, served as principal of the normal school at Lexington, Massachusetts. May's interests included international peace, temperance, equal rights for women, and public education. He attended the organizational meetings of the American Anti-Slavery Society at Philadelphia in 1833 and acted as general agent and secretary of the Massachusetts Anti-Slavery Society, but he did not consider himself a Garrisonian in antislavery attitudes. He strongly supported black education, counseled resistance to the Fugitive Slave Law of 1850, was involved in the Jerry rescue case at Syracuse, New York, in 1851, and was active in the underground railroad. *DAB*, 6(2):447–48.

12. Loguen refers to William Henry Seward (1801–1872), who was born in Florida, New York, graduated from Union College, and practiced law in Auburn. He was elected governor of New York in 1838 and went to the U.S. Senate in 1848. He was a leading antislavery spokesman in the Senate. Seward unsuccessfully sought the Republican presidential candidacy in 1856 and 1860. As secretary of state in the administrations of Abraham Lincoln and Andrew Johnson (1861–69), he coordinated the delicate Civil War diplomacy with European nations and negotiated the 1867 purchase of Alaska from Russia. *DAB*, 16: 615–21.

13. Jermain Wesley Loguen (1813–1872), a noted black abolitionist, underground railroad agent, and African Methodist Episcopal Zion clergyman, was born in Davidson County, Tennessee. His slave name was Jarm Logue. He was the son of a slave mother and a white slaveholder, David Logue. When Logue sold mother and son to a brutal master, the slave determined to obtain his freedom. About 1835 Quakers in Kentucky and southern Indiana helped him escape to Hamilton, Upper Canada. There he learned to read and worked for a time as a lumberjack, hotel porter, and farmer before settling in western New York State. After studying at the Oneida Institute for three years, he opened schools for black children in Utica and Syracuse. Loguen was ordained into the AMEZ clergy in 1842. About that time, he changed his name, adopting Wesley in honor of the famous Methodist leader. During the following decade, he became a leading AMEZ preacher and founded six new churches in western New York. In the 1850s, he also did itinerant preaching throughout the region with American Missionary Association support. During the early 1840s, Loguen began to work closely with Frederick Douglass to aid and protect fugitive slaves escaping through the area. He managed underground railroad activities in Syracuse in the latter part of the decade and stepped up this work after passage of the Fugitive Slave Law of 1850. Indicted for his participation in the October 1851 fugitive slave rescue of William "Jerry" McHenry at Syracuse, Loguen fled to St. Catharines, Canada West. He did missionary work and temperance lecturing among the fugitive slaves there under the direction of Hiram Wilson. The Anti-Slavery Society of Canada also engaged him to give several antislavery speeches in Toronto. Loguen returned to Syracuse in late 1852 and resumed his underground railroad activities. He managed the Fugitive Aid Society, a local vigilance committee, throughout the 1850s and devoted all his time to this work after 1857. His pleas for international assistance generated nearly $400 a year for the society from British

antislavery women. He claimed to have assisted nearly 1,500 fugitive slaves in the decade before the Civil War.

Loguen was an outstanding antislavery orator and a leading black activist. Originally a Garrisonian moral suasionist, he moved toward support of political antislavery by the late 1840s. He joined the Liberty party remnant about 1850, helped direct its work through 1854, and two years later abandoned it for the Radical Abolition party. After passage of the Fugitive Slave Law, he became more militant, urging local abolitionists to resist that law at any cost and to make Syracuse an "open city" for fugitive slaves. By 1854 he openly supported use of violent means to end slavery, and he eventually recruited men for John Brown's Harpers Ferry raid, although no evidence exists to indicate that he was involved in the planning of the raid. Loguen was a reformer of broad vision, as evidenced by his concern for temperance and women's rights and his work among the poor and prisoners in Syracuse. He summarized his antebellum activities in *The Rev. J. W. Loguen, As a Slave and as a Freeman* (1859), which was well received by the abolitionist community. After the Civil War, he concentrated his efforts on doing missionary work and establishing AMEZ churches among southern freedmen. Elected to an AMEZ bishopric in 1868, he directed denominational efforts in the upper South and border states during the middle years of Reconstruction. In 1872 Loguen was named to take charge of AMEZ missionary efforts on the Pacific coast, but he died in Saratoga Springs, New York, before leaving for the new position. *DANB*, 404–5; *NYT*, 1 October 1872; Walls, *African Methodist Episcopal Zion Church*, 573–74; Pease and Pease, *They Who Would Be Free*, 235, 293n; Hiram Wilson to George Whipple, 24 November 1851, AMA-ARC; Pemberton, "Anti-Slavery Society of Canada," 39; Quarles, *Black Abolitionists*, 80, 93, 154, 157–59, 178, 188, 210–11, 238.

29.
Editorial by Henry Bibb
3 December 1851

Henry Bibb pressed ahead with the emigrationist agenda developed by delegates to the North American Convention. He used his *Voice of the Fugitive* to spread the emigrationist message, to refine concepts, and to answer his critics. That proved to be a hazardous business, as anti-emigrationists charged that emigration was akin to abandoning the slave and to embracing white-sponsored Liberian colonization, which had been rejected by a majority of blacks in the 1830s. Bibb and his allies insisted that their movement was not cut from colonizationist cloth. They reminded potential converts that immigration to Canada West and Jamaica brought blacks the benefits of living under the British government. And Bibb explained in a 3 December 1851 editorial that black farmers who settled in those two countries would be aiding the slave: a black, agricultural economy in either of those locations would further the antislavery cause by contributing to the free produce movement—an abolitionist theory that held that slavery could be made unprofitable, and eventually eliminated, by boycotting slave-produced goods and purchasing products raised by free laborers.

No. 2

Emigration to Canada and Jamaica

In our last article,[1] we promised to examine this subject in several particulars, among which was its commercial, agricultural, social and political advantages.

While we affirm that the world is the colored man's home, and that any attempt on the part of human legislation to restrict his boundary, or to circumscribe his field of locomotion, is a gross violation of the fundamental principles of right and justice; it is plainly to be seen that there are certain fields of enterprize open to us, under the British Government, which will enable us to do far more for the abolition of slavery, and the elevation of the colored population in North America, than we can ever effect by remaining in the United States or being coaxed off to Liberia by the American Colonization Society. Those fields, in our judgment, are Canada and Jamaica. We say Canada first because it is the most convenient refuge for the American slave; and in fact the only spot on the American Continent upon which the hunted fugitive can find a protection by law for his liberty. Again we say Canada, because it is known to be one of the best agricultural countries on this continent, or at least a large portion of it, notwithstanding it was long looked upon and spoken of as being equally as cold and barren as Greenland itself. She can now boast of being one of the best wheat growing countries in America—with beautiful forests of the most valuable timber—and inexhaustible mines of lead, iron, coal and copper; with some of the best harbors and fisheries also in the known world. And we are proud to say, that under this Government, all of these resources are as open to enterprizing colored men as to any other class. All this mineral and agricultural wealth is soon to be developed by the enterprizing yeomanry of the country, and should be brought into direct competition with American slavery.

This can be done more effectually, however, by the formation of a commercial and agricultural league[2] between the colored population of North America and the inhabitants of the island of Jamaica.

But before entering upon the commercial and agricultural advantages to be derived by and through this league, which is already in vogue, and will, we trust, by the Divine blessing, soon be in successful operation, it might be well to remind our readers of the fact that the Island of Jamaica is now owned and governed chiefly by the colored population, many of whom were held and worked there not longer than 14 years ago as slaves. At the present time the population of Jamaica is about 600,000, 16,000 of whom are white, and the rest are colored. Morally, socially and politically they are on an equal footing with the whites, and prejudice against color is a thing unknown among that people since the abolition of slavery.[3] From the proximity of Jamaica to Canada and the United States, a voyage across from the City of New York or Montreal is only about six days' sail, so that there can be no reason why a gentleman might not own a plantation in Canada and Jamaica also, and gather a harvest from both during the same year.

Their principal crops are sugar, cotton, rice, tobacco, coffee, ginger and indigo, which are the commercial products of all tropical climates.

In Jamaica they have perpetual summer—no chilling winds—no blighting frosts; and it is not an uncommon thing for persons to raise two and three crops in one year from the same field of land. Its climate is known to be mild and genial, and from its commercial, agricultural, and geographical position, Jamaica might with propriety be called the Italy of the Western World. And shall we, as colored Americans, oppressed and driven as we are in the United States, like the partridge on the mountain's brow, shut our eyes against Jamaica with all her natural advantages and rich treasures of undeveloped wealth which is now offered to us, say that we will be content to be hewers of wood and drawers of water for the white man; or shall we burst the chains of indolence, which have so long bound us, and take possession of these new fields of enterprize?

We speak of this subject, not as a scheme of colonization, but as a great commercial and agricultural enterprize, possessing, in itself the elements for breaking down the system of American slavery. We believe that the time has now fully come when the watchword of every colored American should be FREE LABOR FOR FREE MEN.[4]

Let us at once organize the anticipated commercial and agricultural league among the colored population of North America and the West Indies, and, through it, stab American slavery to its vitals. Let there be free labor stores established all through Canada and the West Indies, and the United States, in order that the friends of liberty may have an opportunity of supporting free labor and excluding slave labor products (which are the price of blood).[5]

The principal part of the flour, pork, &c., now consumed in Jamaica, is furnished from the United States, when it could and ought to be furnished by the colored population of Canada, who should receive in return for it, free labor cotton, sugar, rice, &c., produced by colored men in Jamaica. What a wonderful check this would prove to American slavery in a commercial point of view!

In our next number we shall continue our remarks on this subject.[6]

Voice of the Fugitive (Windsor, Canada West), 3 December 1851.

1. "No. 1—Emigration to Canada and Jamaica," an article by Bibb in the 19 November 1851 issue of the *Voice of the Fugitive*, introduced a series of forthcoming articles by Bibb that proposed to outline the advantages of black settlement in the two British colonies. Because of slavery and racial prejudice in the United States, Bibb encouraged black immigration to these two areas. *VF*, 19 November 1851.

2. Bibb refers to the North American League.

3. Bibb was apparently misinformed about conditions in Jamaica. Race remained a significant factor in the colony's affairs long after the Emancipation Act of 1833. Even after the apprenticeship system ended in 1838, planter interests exercised inordinate control while an isolated black peasantry developed. Equal rights were frequently abridged, poor blacks were excluded from the franchise (by taxation), and blacks who were free prior to emancipation and who held a majority of the minor offices by 1849 did not necessarily share common interests with the former slaves. Samuel J. Hurwitz and Edith F. Hurwitz, *Jamaica: A Historical Portrait* (New York, N.Y., 1971), 121–51; Green, *British Slave Emancipation*, 295–326, 355–79.

4. During the 1850s, the free labor concept provided an ideological base for political antislavery in the northern United States and became a popular alternative to the moral arguments of abolitionists. Rooted in the Protestant ethic and northern capitalist culture, it posited a harmony of interests between capital and labor that allowed wage earners to control the fruits of their labor, to have economic choices, and to work their way into a position of economic independence. According to free labor proponents, northern society exemplified the dynamic possibilities of free labor while southern society perpetuated a rigid hierarchy and a stagnant economy devoid of opportunities. Slavery, they argued, degraded all labor, black and white, and left the people of the South lazy and inefficient. Eric Foner, *Free Soil, Free Labor, Free Men: The Ideology of the Republican Party before the Civil War* (Westport, Conn., 1983).

5. Proponents of the free produce movement theorized that the organized boy-

cott of slave-produced goods would reduce the profitability of slavery and thus destroy the institution. The concept arose among American Quakers during the late eighteenth century but had its earliest success with the British boycott of slave-produced West Indian sugar. Encouraged by the British efforts, the American Anti-Slavery Society, the American and Foreign Anti-Slavery Society, and many local societies approved the technique between 1833 and 1840. The movement eventually failed in America in no small measure because the lack of readily available free labor goods destroyed abolitionist enthusiasm. Mabee, *Black Freedom*, 185–204; Ruth Ketring Nuermberger, *The Free Produce Movement: A Quaker Protest against Slavery* (Durham, N.C., 1942); Quarles, *Black Abolitionists*, 74–75.

6. Bibb's third article in the series, entitled "No. 3.—Agricultural League," appeared in the 17 December 1851 issue of the *Voice of the Fugitive*. It called for the creation of the proposed North American League, also known as the Agricultural League. Bibb suggested that such a league could encourage purchases of free produce from the Canadas and Jamaica and enforce economic sanctions against slave produce. He believed that, in this way, it would contribute to the abolition of slavery. *VF*, 17 December 1851.

30.
Henry Bibb to William Still
15 January 1852

The underground railroad was seldom the complex, secretive network that slaveholders charged but often consisted of haphazard, localized, and semipublic efforts by free blacks, Quakers, and other abolitionists to aid fugitive slaves who came to them for sanctuary, information, food, money, clothes, shelter, and, occasionally, weapons. After the passage of the Fugitive Slave Law, workers on the underground railroad encouraged fugitives to continue on to Canada West rather than remain in the North. But they needed reliable information about what routes were safe, what supplies were needed, and what to expect once there. They looked to Canadian blacks for that. Henry Bibb regularly responded in the *Voice of the Fugitive* to such queries, including two from William Still, the black abolitionist who directed Philadelphia's aggressive vigilance committee. Much of this information anticipated long-term settlement and was equally useful to the free blacks who considered Canadian immigration in the wake of the Fugitive Slave Law. *VF*, 1, 15 January, 12 February 1852 [7:0320, 0348, 0408].

Moving to Canada

TO WM. STILL, ESQ.[1]
My Dear Sir:

We published your very kind and appropriate letter of inquiry in our last,[2] but had not time then to write a reply, but shall now proceed to do so in as few words as we can.

It affords us great pleasure to be able to give you the information which you asked for in behalf of your friend, and at the same time we can answer the request of several other persons who have asked us for information on the same subject.

First, The most direct and cheapest route from Philadelphia to this part of Canada is, to come by steam to New York, thence to Detroit, Michigan, by the way of Dunkirk, after the opening of navigation.

Second, We would not advise persons to bring with them beds or any very heavy luggage so long a distance, because it is liable to be injured by moving, and the freightage thereon would cost about as much as ordinary furniture would be worth; and not only so, all such things can be bought here in Canada, or Detroit, Michigan, as cheap as they can be there, we presume.

Third, There is no duty to pay on any of the household furniture, cattle, horses, wagons, &c., of emigrants to this country, if they bring them all with them. They have simply to pay at the custom house an entrance fee of 25 cents. We would think it advisable to bring along good wearing apparel and bed-clothing, and sell all the rest if they have a long distance to come, and bring the money, and they will find no difficulty in getting anything they need at a reasonable price.

Good farming land may be bought within ten miles of Detroit, on the Canada side, at from $2 to $40 per acre. Persons within 7 miles of this place with a log house &c., and with from ten to twenty-five acres cleared, can be purchased for the sum of $7 per acre, lots containing from 50 to 100 acres, and all the timber from this land may be converted into cord wood, and sold for cash.

After directing your attention to an article in our last, addressed to Peter Clark,[3] of Cincinnati, Ohio, which we think will answer or include all your questions of inquiry, we trust, sir, that you will overlook the brevity of this article on the subject.

Voice of the Fugitive (Windsor, Canada West), 15 January 1852.

1. William Still (1821–1901) was born in New Jersey, the youngest of eighteen children of a former slave, Levin Steel, who changed his name to Still to protect his fugitive slave wife, Sidney. William Still moved to Philadelphia in 1844 and worked as a mail clerk and a janitor for the Pennsylvania Society for the Abolition of Slavery. Still's continued efforts for self-education, his commitment to antislavery, and his concern for fugitive slaves led to his increasing responsibilities in the society and to his appointment in 1852 as chairman of the General Vigilance Committee of Philadelphia. Still reorganized and reinvigorated the committee by building a network of safe hiding places for fugitives in the city's black community, by effectively raising funds for fugitives, and by carefully monitoring the activity of slave catchers in Pennsylvania. Under Still's direction, the committee aided almost eight hundred fugitive slaves by the beginning of the Civil War. Still maintained close contacts with Canadian black leaders, such as Mary Ann Shadd Cary, and traveled in Canada West to examine black communities (1855) and to rebut charges that blacks failed to cope with freedom. Still's organizational and managerial achievements were based on his attention to detail and his careful accumulation of statistics. As chairman of the vigilance committee, he recorded the personal history of each fugitive slave he assisted and later used this information to write *The Underground Railroad* (1872), an investigation of slave rescue efforts that emphasized free black participation in the process and the courage of fugitives themselves.

Still was a voice for change and progress among Philadelphia blacks. In 1859 he initiated a successful eight-year struggle to end discrimination on Philadelphia streetcars. Two years later, he helped found and finance the Social, Civil, and Statistical Association of the Colored People of Pennsylvania to sponsor cultural events and collect accurate information about the city's black community. After the Civil War, he achieved success as a businessman, was active in local Presbyterian churches, helped establish the Mission Sabbath School and a black Young Men's Christian Association, served on the Philadelphia Board of Trade and as a director of institutions for the black aged and for black orphans, and was a member of the Freedmen's Aid Commission. *DANB*, 573–74; Larry Gara, "William Still and the Underground Railroad," *PH* 28:33–43 (January 1961).

2. Bibb published William Still's 15 December 1851 letter in the 1 January 1852 issue of the *Voice of the Fugitive*. In the letter, Still inquired about the safest routes to Canada West, the quantity and type of provisions needed for the journey and the initial period of settlement, and the duties and taxes to be paid on goods brought into the province. He intended to relay this information to fugitive slaves he encountered through his work for the Vigilance Committee of Philadelphia. *VF*, 1 January 1852 [7:0320].

3. Bibb refers to an article in the 15 January *Voice of the Fugitive*, which responded to questions raised by Peter Humphries Clark (1829–1925) about Canada West. Clark queried Bibb about a variety of issues, including black morality, black intelligence, racial prejudice, legal equality, church and school segregation, taxation, land quality, and commercial markets in the province. Clark, born to a free black family in Cincinnati, Ohio, was educated at Rev. Hiram S. Gilmore's high school (1844–48). In 1849 he began a long but erratic association with Cincinnati's black schools as a teacher and administrator. During the early 1850s, Clark promoted emigration. For a time, he favored a black exodus to another part of the North American continent as a means for improving the condition of black Americans, but by mid-decade, he condemned proposals for mass emigration. Clark believed that black Americans could improve their condition in the United States by obtaining a fair share of the country's wealth, by becoming educated and by facing their oppressors with a united front. He was dismissed from his teaching position in 1853, ostensibly because of his Unitarian religious views, but more likely because of factionalism within the city's black school board and because of his antislavery activities and attendance at national and state black conventions during the early 1850s. During the next few years, he operated a grocery, established and edited the short-lived *Herald of Freedom* (1855), briefly edited a Free Soil paper in Newport, Kentucky, and assisted Frederick Douglass with his paper (1856). In 1857 he returned to teaching in Cincinnati, where in 1866 he helped organize and became principal of Gaines High School, the city's first black public secondary school. Clark's commitment to abolitionism and equal rights attracted him to the Republican party in 1856, but he soon recognized its limitations, expressed his dislike for its conservatism, and charged it with being more interested in land speculation than in antislavery. Further discouraged by the party's postwar abandonment of the equal rights cause, Clark urged blacks to follow a politically independent course, and in 1877 he became a proponent of the Workingmen's party and democratic socialism. Although he returned to the Republican party in 1879, he urged Ohio blacks to support Democratic candidates during the early 1880s in an attempt to force Republicans to pay attention to black demands. His tactics were successful, but as a result, a Republican board of education removed him from his principalship in 1886. After a brief tenure as principal at a black industrial school in Alabama, he moved to St. Louis and taught high school until his retirement in 1908. *VF*, 12 February 1852 [7:0408]; *FDP*, 5 February 1852, 20 October 1854 [9:0160]; *ASB*, 3 September 1853, 4 December 1858 [8:0433, 11:0432]; *PFW*, 24 March 1855 [9:0505]; Lawrence

Grossman, "In His Veins Coursed No Bootlicking Blood: The Career of Peter H. Clark," *OH* 86:80–95 (Spring 1977); Herbert G. Gutman, "Peter H. Clark: Pioneer Negro Socialist, 1877," *JNE* 34:413–18 (Fall 1965); William J. Simmons, *Men of Mark: Eminent, Progressive and Rising* (Cleveland, Ohio, 1887; reprint, New York, N.Y., 1968), 374–83.

31.
Constitution and Bylaws of the Refugee Home Society
29 January 1852

The growing number of destitute fugitive slaves in Canada West after 1850 concerned the antislavery community. Black and white abolitionists and philanthropists in Canada and the United States attempted to meet the needs of the new arrivals. The Refugee Home Society was one of the more ambitious attempts at organized assistance. Formed in the spring of 1851 by a Michigan antislavery group, the RHS bought tracts of land in southwestern Canada West and resold parcels on convenient terms to fugitive slaves. The idea of turning fugitives into prosperous freeholders conformed to American abolitionists' goal of black uplift. With support from white philanthropists and prominent Canadian blacks—Henry and Mary Bibb, James T. Holly, and others—the RHS met on 29 January 1852 to issue its constitution and bylaws. These documents included stringent ownership requirements meant to enforce sobriety, industry, and stability in the settlements. Pease and Pease, *Black Utopia*, 109–13; *VF*, 1 June 1851 [6:0961].

Whereas it is supposed that there are, at the present time, between thirty-five and forty thousand refugee slaves in Canada, whose number has been constantly increasing since the passage of the Fugitive Slave Bill.

And whereas, on their arrival, they find themselves in a strange land, uneducated, poverty-stricken, without homes, or any permanent means of self-support; however willing they may be to work, they have neither means to work with, nor land to work upon; and the sad story of the numerous fugitives who have been dragged back into perpetual slavery by the strong arm of the American Government, is a sufficient proof that there is no protection for the slave this side of the Canadian line. The only protection for their liberty on the American Continent is emphatically under the shadow of the British throne.

In view of the above facts, the friends of humanity in Michigan, in May 1851, organized a Society which has undertaken the purchase of 50,000 acres of farming land, in Canada, on which to settle refugees from slavery.

This Society would therefore represent to the refugees from Southern slavery, who are now in Canada destitute of homes, or who may hereafter come, being desirous of building themselves up in Canada, on an agricultural basis, and who do not buy, sell or use intoxicating drinks as a beverage, shall, by making proper application to this society, and complying with its Constitution and By Laws, be put into possession of 25 acres of farming land, and their children shall enjoy the blessings of education perpetually.

The following Constitution and By Laws have been ordained and established by the Society, for the government of their future action.

CONSTITUTION

Article 1. The title of this Society shall be known as the Refugees' Home Society.

Article 2. The object of this Society shall be to obtain permanent homes for the refugees in Canada, and to promote their moral, social, physical, intellectual, and political elevation.

Article 3. The officers of this Society shall consist of President, Vice-President, Recording Secretary, Corresponding Secretary, Treasurer, and an Executive Committee of at least five persons, two of whom shall constitute a board of trust.

Article 4. It shall be the duty of the President to preside over all meetings of the Society; in his absence, it shall be the duty of the Vice-President to preside; and in the absence of both, the Society shall appoint a president *pro tem.*

Article 5. It shall be the duty of the Recording Secretary to record in full the proceedings of the Society's meetings in a book provided by the Secretary for that purpose, and to do such other business as usually devolves on such officers.

Article 6. It shall be the duty of the Corresponding Secretary to correspond for the Society with other kindred societies, and private individuals who are interested in our cause, and to preserve and report such communications to the Society.

Article 7. It shall be the duty of the Treasurer to receive and deposit all funds collected for the Refugees' Home in the Savings Bank of Detroit,[1] to the credit of the Executive Committee, no part of which shall be drawn therefrom except it be by an order which shall be signed by at least three of the Executive Committee.

Article 8. It shall be the duty of the Board of Trust to hold property for the Society, and to deed the same to settlers thereon, when directed so to do by the Executive Committee.

Article 9. It shall be the duty of the Treasurer, and of all agents who collect funds for the Society, to report the result of their collection in detail, at least once in every month, through the Society's organ.

Article 10. It shall be the duty of the Executive Committee to appoint agents to collect funds and to transact all other necessary business for the Society, and to have a written annual report for the Society, in which its pecuniary and business transactions shall be fully set forth and published to the world.

Article 11. This Society shall not deed land to any but actual settlers who are refugees from Southern slavery, and who are the owners of no land.

Article 12. All lands purchased by this Society shall be divided into 25-acre lots, or as near as possible, and at least one-tenth of the purchase price of which shall be paid down by settlers before possession is given, and the balance to be paid in equal annual instalments.

Article 13. One-third of all money paid in for land by settlers shall be used for educational purposes for the benefit of said settlers' children, and the other two-thirds for the purchase of more land for the same object, while chattel slavery exists in the United States.

Article 14. Any person can become a life-member of this Society by paying into its treasury, at one time, the sum of $5.

Article 15. No land bought by individuals from this Society shall be sold or transferred by them to any other person or persons, except it be to their heirs, the wife, husband, or children, as the case may be, otherwise it shall fall back to the Society.

Article 16. This Society shall meet for the transaction of business at least twice per year, and extra meetings may be called by the Executive Committee, if the business of the Society should require it.

Article 17. When a settlement under the supervision of this Society shall increase to as many as six families or more, they shall erect a school for the instruction of their children.

Article 18. Any society may become auxiliary to this Society, by contributing to the funds of the parent institution.

Article 19. This Constitution may be altered or amended by a majority of two-thirds of the votes of its members present, if due notice shall have been given for such alteration or amendment, three months previous to its being voted upon.

BY LAWS

Article 1. No person shall receive more than five acres of land from this Society at less than cost.

Article 2. No person shall be entitled to a free grant of land from this Society, except they are widows, men with families, or aged persons: and in all cases they shall clear off that portion of the land which the Society proposes to deed to them free of cost, within two years from the time they enter it, unless prevented by casualties, otherwise they shall pay the Society for it just what it costs.

Article 3. This Society shall be under no obligation to hold in reserve any lot for those who shall not have settled on it, or commenced improvements within three months from the day they make the first payment.

Article 4. No person shall be allowed to remove any timber from said land until they have first made payment thereon.

Article 5. All matters of difficulty arising among settlers on said land, where the laws are violated which are intended to regulate the settlement, shall be left to arbitration with the Executive Committee, and by whose decision the parties shall abide.

Article 6. All applications for lots of land shall be to the Executive Committee.

Article 7. No dwelling-house can be erected on said land by settlers containing less than two rooms, nor shall they have chimneys of wood and clay, but of brick or stone.

Article 8. Any settler who shall willfully violate the Constitution or By Laws of this Society, shall forfeit and pay to the aggrieved party according to the nature of the offence, which shall be left to the decision of the Executive Committee, and if the same offence is repeated, the fine shall be doubled; and repeated the third time, the offender shall be expelled from the settlement or said lot of land, receiving such compensation as the Executive Committee shall decide his improvements entitle him to.

Voice of the Fugitive (Windsor, Canada West), 12 February 1852.

1. The Detroit Savings Fund Institute was chartered in March 1849. After being reorganized in 1871, it was renamed the Detroit Savings Bank. The bank merged with three other firms in 1956 to become the present-day Detroit Bank and Trust. Arthur M. Woodford, *Detroit and Its Banks* (Detroit, Mich., 1974), 69–87, 106–7, 137–47, 184, 211–27.

32.
Thomas H. Jones to Daniel Foster
15 July 1852

Flights to freedom frequently separated fugitive slaves from their families. After reaching safety, many refugees went about the difficult task of freeing those left behind. Some fugitives returned south to spirit away their loved ones, thereby enlarging the mystique of the underground railroad. Others tried to purchase the freedom of their family members and sought the assistance of the abolitionist community with that process. Thomas H. Jones's 15 July 1852 letter informed Massachusetts abolitionist Daniel Foster, his friend and benefactor, about his efforts to purchase his son out of slavery. Jones had left Edward, his eldest son, behind when he escaped from slavery in North Carolina in 1849. During early 1852, Edward's owner informed Mary Jones, Thomas's wife, that the son could be purchased for $850 if the money could be raised quickly. Mary Jones immediately sought funds in the Boston area, while Thomas Jones solicited contributions in the Maritime Provinces. By the time that Jones wrote to Foster, they had collected $324. But subsequent contributions came in slowly. Thomas Jones considered a fund-raising tour of England that never materialized; he continued to collect donations in the Maritimes and New England through 1854, selling copies of his slave narrative, *The Experience of Thomas Jones* (1854), as part of the effort. Jones, *The Experience of Thomas Jones*, 33–43 [8:0551–56]; *Lib*, 18 August 1854.

LIVERPOOL, N[ova] S[cotia]
July 15, 1852

REV. AND MUCH REVERED SIR:

When I call to mind, which is not unfrequent, your generosity and brotherly kindness to me, an unworthy creature, I am constrained by such recollections to address a few words to you, merely to inform you where I am, and how I came to be here. Last autumn, when I came to Halifax, I found that my health was not as good as usual; that I was much debilitated. After a little time spent in and about Halifax, I came to this place, where I have tarried almost ever since. I have visited several villages in this (Queen) county. At times, I have been quite indisposed; but now, thank God for it, I am enjoying tolerably good health. My wife and one child are here with me. She came here to visit me, because I could not or dare not go to her in Boston.

O, my worthy brother in the Lord, pardon my freedom! How hard is the lot of the man, whose misfortune it is to be born of my color—though the great Creator has thought proper that it should be so. I therefore will submit, for it is his righteous will. I dare not proceed further on such a subject, lest I am found to murmur.

My wife has received a letter from a lady in North Carolina, stating that she has my wife's son, and will sell him for $850, provided the money can be made up soon. She has been offered $1000 for him, but has been kind enough to make this offer to us.

I have succeeded, through my wife's exertions in and near Boston, and my own in this country, to realize $324.00 towards making up the sum. Sometimes I get quite discouraged, and again I rally and strive on. If I can but get him freed from bondage and slavery, I think I could endure any thing in the shape of hardships in this life, to the end of my earthly career. I intend to go to old England, and state his case there, before I will give up all hopes of such comfort as the redemption of our son from all human, or rather inhuman, bondage. When I look at the kind recommendations you were pleased to give me, together with others, I am thereby stimulated to persevere.

Pardon, dear Sir, my liberty in thus addressing you. May God Almighty bless you and yours, even in this present life, is the sincere prayer of Your unworthy brother in Christ,

THOMAS H. JONES

P.S. Dear brother Foster, before I quite close up this letter, I want to make a few more remarks. I am now under the roof of an esteemed friend, at Mill Village, William H. Whitman, whose home has always been an asylum to the poor fugitive slave, who had recently escaped from the land of boasted liberty. He has, in these respects, obeyed the commands of the dear Redeemer. When I was a stranger, he took me in; if hungry, he fed me—thirsty, he gave me drink; and when weary and faint, I would find myself rested and refreshed at his residence. But, thank God, the best of all is, that so soon as a slave lands on British soil, his shackles fall off. Since I have been on British ground, I find more time to study, and to learn the evils of slavery, than I could ever find in all my life previous to my coming here. Now it seems to me I can see our noble friend, WM. LLOYD GARRISON, and his noble band, on the platform and in the pulpits, pleading for the poor oppressed and down-trodden slave. I see that the old missionary has visited the British Provinces, and wherever that missionary goes, converts are made. I mean the old *Liberator*, 21 *Cornhill*. I have received several copies from the Agent, Mr. Wallcut.[1] I have sent some to the West Indies, where converts have been made—thanks be to God for it! I hope, Sir, that there will not be a lady or a gentleman of color who may have the means, but will subscribe for that excellent paper; and if they do not want it themselves, let them send it across the water to British subjects. I have frequently lectured on slavery, and exhibited the handcuffs, collar, chain, cowhide, and the paddle, showing many friends in this country what constitutes the liberty of the United States of America. Yours, &c.,

T. H. J.

Liberator (Boston, Mass.), 13 August 1852.

1. Jones refers to Robert F. Walcutt (1797–1884), who was born on Nantucket Island, Massachusetts, and educated at Harvard, where he was a member of the famous "abolition class" of 1817. Walcutt briefly served as pastor to a Cape Cod Unitarian congregation but was dismissed for his antislavery views. A lifelong friend and associate of William Lloyd Garrison, Walcutt joined the New England and American antislavery societies and adopted Garrison's nonresistance and anti-Sabbatarian views. From 1846 until 1865, Walcutt was the general agent for the *Liberator*, a position that made him one of antislavery's most important administrators. Wendell Phillips Garrison and Francis Jackson Garrison, *William Lloyd Garrison, 1805–1879: The Story of His Life*, 4 vols. (New York, N.Y., 1885–89), 1:213, 2:209, 236–37, 422, 3:221, 353, 481, 4:58, 137, 306; Merrill and Ruchames, *Letters of William Lloyd Garrison*, 3:342–43, 516, 531–32, 598, 4:37, 64, 199, 206, 263, 275, 305, 433.

33.
Samuel Ringgold Ward to George Brown
27 July 1852

Blacks recognized the importance of refuting racial bias in newspapers as a way to combat prejudice in Canadian society. They monitored the local press and, when they found bias, responded with letters and editorials. Samuel Ringgold Ward was particularly skilled at this practice. In a 27 July 1852 letter to George Brown, the abolitionist editor of the Toronto *Globe*, Ward corrected erroneous newspaper reports of an incident of racial violence in St. Catharines, Canada West. On 28 June, local militiamen had gathered at St. Catharines's parade grounds for their annual militia exercises. Among them was the Coloured Company under the command of a Captain Clarke. During the drills, whites taunted the black militiamen, and a scuffle ensued. About the same time, a local ruffian knocked a black man named Harris off a fence near the parade grounds. Harris appealed to several local magistrates for redress but obtained none. Harris and his friends later found the offender at a local tavern and assaulted him. A second melee broke out. Incorrect rumors reached members of the fire brigade that two of their number had been killed by blacks. They responded by mobbing the black settlement, destroying several houses, and driving black residents into nearby woods. Local papers reported the incident at length and, Ward believed, reported it unfairly. The *Globe* reprinted reports of the incident from the St. Catharines papers and published Ward's corrections in its 31 July issue. By that time, a "just and honorable . . . settlement" of the matter had been made: several rioters were arrested, and the black property destroyed was repaired at the expense of the white rioters. *TG*, 3 July 1852; *SCJ*, 1 July 1852; *FDP*, 16 July 1852; Murray, "Canada and Anglo-American Anti-Slavery Movement," 326.

Toronto, [Canada West]
July 27, 1852

To the Editor of the Globe[1]

MR. EDITOR:

Your well known impartiality and justice to all parties, as a journalist, embolden me to hand you the following account of the origin of the St. Catharines' difficulties. You will see that the matter differs somewhat from the published accounts of it. I have the facts from a reliable source (a gentleman who was an eye-witness) of undoubted veracity.

After the Militia drill, the Colonel spoke in terms of commendation and encouragement of the black corps, whereupon several of the white soldiers began to throw the most disgusting and filthy substances upon the blacks. The latter appealed to Captain Clarke for protection against this outrage. Capt. C. promptly rebuked the whites, who for awhile obeyed his orders. Subsequent to this, a black man, named Harris was sitting upon a fence, near the parade ground; a white man, without provocation, knocked Harris from the fence with a stone. Harris went to several Justices of the Peace for redress, but sought justice from them in vain. He then, in the heat of passion repaired to Stinson's tavern, where this white man was, and flogged him. Thence arose the general *melee*. Upon the request of several leading white persons, the blacks gave up the clubs with which they were defending themselves against superior numbers of whites, while the latter continued their assault upon the former. Then the blacks resorted to stones, with which they fought, until the whites were reinforced by the fire brigade.

The damage done to the property of the blacks was done by the firemen alone.

The difficulty was finally adjusted by the whites agreeing to repair all damages done to the property of the blacks, which they have promptly and honourably done.

It is gratifying to know, that the riot did not commence with the blacks; that the officers of the regiment behaved impartially; that the blacks resorted to no violence until provoked beyond endurance; that they gave up their weapons when requested to do so; and that so just and honourable a settlement of the matter was made. May it prove to be a "finality!" Your obedient servant,

S. R. Ward

Globe (Toronto, Canada West), 31 July 1852.

1. George Brown (1818–1880) emigrated from Scotland to the United States in 1837. After he and his father, Peter Brown, had operated a small, dry goods shop in New York City for several years, they began publishing the New York *British Chronicle* in 1842; one year later, they relocated it in Toronto as the *Banner*. The younger Brown's interest in Reform politics attracted financial backing, and he founded the Toronto *Globe* in 1844. With innovative publishing techniques and forceful political commentary, the *Globe* became the largest, most influential paper in the British North American Provinces. Brown sat in the Canadian parliament during the 1850s and 1860s and played an indispensable role in Canadian unification. He adopted his father's abolitionist sentiment; both participated enthusiastically in the Anti-Slavery Society of Canada and the Elgin Association. *DCB*, 10:91–103.

34.
Henry Bibb to Albert G. Sibley
23 September 1852
7 October 1852

Black abolitionists occasionally wrote public letters to their old masters, an act that had broad implications. There was a clear personal and emotional dimension when former slaves confronted the people who had owned them. Such letters served an antislavery purpose: they demonstrated the intellectual advancement that came with freedom, they challenged notions of black inferiority, and they provided a forum for addressing specific antislavery issues. In the fall of 1852, sixteen years after escaping from slavery, Henry Bibb wrote a series of four letters to his old master, Kentucky planter Albert G. Sibley. The letters are a mixture of abolitionist theology (the hypocrisy of slaveholding Christians), personal anger ("you sold my mother"), ridicule (Bibb accused Sibley of stealing hogs and sheep), and defiance ("If you do not answer this soon you may expect to hear from me again"). There is no evidence that Sibley responded. *VF*, 23 September, 7 October, 4 November 1852 [7:0739, 0767, 0813].

A Letter to my Old Master

[No. 1]

Windsor, [Canada West]
Sept[ember] 23, 1852

MR. ALBERT G. SIBLEY[1]
SIR:

It has now been about sixteen years since we saw each other face to face, and at which time you doubtless considered me inferior to yourself, as you then held me as an article of property, and sold me as such; but my mind soon after became insubordinate to the ungodly relation of master and slave; and the work of self-emancipation commenced and I was made free.

I have long felt inclined to open a correspondence with you upon this subject, but have refrained from doing so, until now, for two reasons; first, I knew not your post office address; and secondly, you then held in bondage several of my mother's children, of which you robbed her when you left the State of Kentucky in 1836. But as those obstacles are now both removed out of the way, I can venture to address you.

For more than twenty years you have been a member of the Methodist Episcopal Church—a class-leader and an exhorter of that denomination; professing to take the *Bible*, as your standard of christian duty. But sir know ye not that in the light of this book, you have been acting the hypocrite all this while? I feel called upon as a christian to call your attention to a few facts with a regard to it. But before doing so, I am happy to inform you that my brothers, John, Lewis and Granville, whose legs brought them from your plantation, are now all at my house in Canada, with our dear mother, free and doing well on British soil:[2] so you need not give yourself any trouble about advertising or looking for them. They have all served you as slaves for 21 to 30 years without compensation, and have now commenced to act for themselves. Is this incompatible with the character of a Bible christian? And yet I suppose that you, with your man robbing posse have chased them with your dogs and guns, as if they were sheep-killing wolves upon the huge mountain's brow, for the purpose of re-capturing and dragging them back to a mental graveyard, in the name of law and slaveholding religion. Oh! what harmony there seems to be between those two twin sisters; the Fugitive Slave Law and the Methodist E. Church.[3] Listen to the language of inspiration: "Feed the hungry, and clothe the naked:" "Break every yoke and let the *oppressed go free*:" "All things, whatsoever ye would that men should do unto you, do ye even so unto them, for *this is* the law and the prophets."

While on the other hand your church sanctions the buying and selling of men, women, and children: the robbing men of their wives, and parents of their offspring—the violation of the whole of the decalogue,[4] by permitting the profanation of the sabbath; committing of theft, murder, incest and adultery, which is constantly done by church members holding slaves and form the very essence of slavery. Now Sir, allow me with the greatest deference to your intelligence to inform you that you are miserably deceiving yourself, if you believe that you are in the straight and narrow path to heaven, whilst you are practising such abominable violations of the plainest precepts of religion.

The fellowship of no number of professing christians, however extended nor the solemn baptism and silent toleration of all the Reverend time serving ministers in creation, can make you really a christian, or dispense with the binding force of the Gospel of Jesus Christ, as the rule of your life and practice; and whilst you continue in such an unhallowed course of conduct, your prayers, your solemn fasts and ordinances are an abomination to the Lord, from which he will turn his face away, in disgust, and will not hear or look upon.

I must here conclude for the present, but as this subject is fraught with such vital importance to your eternal interest and as I have once maintained an intimate relation to you, I shall feel bound as a christian to interest myself in calling your attention to it again. Yours with becoming respect,

HENRY BIBB

No. 2

MR. ALBERT G. SIBLEY
SIR:

At the close of my last I promised to call your attention to this subject again—and in doing so my object is not merely to convince you that I have acquired the art of communicating my thoughts intelligibly on paper to be read by tyrants, notwithstanding they with yourself have done their best to keep me in perpetual bondage and ignorance—but it is to warn you of the great danger to which you are exposed while standing in the attitude of an incorrigible slaveholder. I mean that you shall know that there is a just God in heaven, who cannot harmonise human slavery with the Christian religion: I mean that you shall know that there is a law which is more binding upon the consciences of slaves than that of Congress, or any other human enactment—and I mean that you shall know that all of your slaves have escaped to Canada, where they are just as free as yourself, and that we have not forgotten the cruel treatment which we received at your hands while in a state of slavery. I have often heard you say that a slave who was well fed, and clothed, was far better off than a "free Negro," who had no master to provide for and take care of him.

Now with all candour in answer to this proslavery logic, let me ask who is it that takes care of the slaveholders and their families? Who is it that clears up the forest, cultivates the Land, manages the stock, husbands the grain, and prepares it for the table? Who is it that digs from the cotton, sugar, and rice fields the means with which to build southern Cities, Steam boats, School houses and churches? I answer that it is the slaves, that perform this labor, and yet they or their children are not permitted to enjoy any of the benefits of these Institutions: your former slaves who are now British subjects, are about trying the *dangerous experiment* of taking care of themselves—which has so far proved to be a very successful one. Their services are worth to them here upon an average one dollar per day—they are also attending a night School for the purpose of learning to read and write.[5] With the above facts before me, I am led to the conclusion that the slave who can take care of himself and master both can certainly take care of himself alone, if he is only given a fair chance. Oh! tell me not then Sir, that a man is happier and better off in a state of chattel bondage than in a state of freedom. The idea of a man being a slave—of being subjected to the will and power of a master, is revolting to his very nature. Freedom to act for ones-self though poorly clad, and fed with a dry crust, is glorious when compared with American slavery, even if it should, appear dressed in broad cloth, and fed with all of the luxuries which the human appetite could desire. This right is highly appreciated by the wild beasts of the forest and the fowls of the air. The terrific screech of the hooting night owl is animating to himself and musical to his kind as he goes through the tall forest, from the hill top, to the valley. Not so, with the miserable little screech owl, while he is tied by the leg, or boxed up in a cage though well fed he is made the sport of children. The startling scream of the wild panther, or the roar of the lion—it is majestic and independent in their native desert. Not so when they are chained in a cage to be fed by a "kind master," on Johnny cake,[6] roast beef, or no beef just as he chooses. But my illustrations are inadequate to describe the injustice, and my abhorrence of slaveholding.

Again I call your attention to the moral bearing of this subject, as it applies to yourself. You profess to be a christian—a leader in the M. E. Church, and a representative of the Lord Jesus Christ, and yet you sold my mother from her little children, and sent them away to a distant land—you sold my brother George from his wife and dear little ones,[7] while he was a worthy member, and Clergyman, of the same Church, to which *you belong*. In early life you also compelled me to cheat, lie and *steal* from your neighbours. You have often made me drive up sheep, and hogs, which you knew to be the property of your neighbours and slaughter them for market and the use of your own table.

The language of Holy writ is that "thou shalt not steal," "let every man have his own wife, and every woman her own husband," and parents are strictly required to train up their children in the fear and admonition of the Lord. Every one of these Holy injunctions you have wickedly, and willingly broken. Oh! what hypocrisy is this? A Methodist class leader, selling a Methodist Minister—a Methodist class leader, separating husbands, and wives—a Methodist class leader, stealing and slaughtering his neighbours sheep and hogs. Vain is your religion—base is your hypocrisy. We have no confidence in your sheep stealing, and man robbing religion. My brothers Granville, John, and Lewis, all unite in corroborating the above facts: and if you dare to deny a single word of it let us hear from you and we will furnish undoubted proof. Yours with due respect,

H. BIBB

P.S. If you do not answer this soon you may expect to hear from me again.

Voice of the Fugitive (Windsor, Canada West), 23 September, 7 October 1852.

1. Albert G. Sibley (1808–?) was born in Virginia but settled in Bedford, Kentucky. He acquired ownership of Henry Bibb through marriage to Harriet White, the daughter of Bibb's original owner, David White. In 1836 Sibley sold Bibb to his brother John Sibley for $850. He later resettled on a 2,800-acre farm in Clark County, Missouri. Bibb, *Narrative of Henry Bibb*, iv, 14, 41, 203; United States Census, 1850.

2. Henry Bibb and his brothers John, Lewis, and Granville were among the seven sons of Mildred Jackson, a Kentucky slave. Prior to 1836, Bibb, his brothers, and his mother were owned by Albert G. Sibley. Jackson's free black husband arranged to purchase her freedom but was killed in a steamboat explosion before

making full payment. When Sibley moved to Missouri in 1836, he sold Jackson and her youngest son to George Ray of Bedford, Kentucky. After working six years in Ray's service as a tavern cook, she was freed and her youngest son was sold to a slave trader. During the winter of 1845, Bibb—then a fugitive in Madison, Indiana—hired a white man to bring her out of Kentucky. Jackson moved with Bibb, her eldest son, to Michigan, then in 1850 to Windsor, Canada West, where she became an active member of the Anti-Slavery Society of Windsor. Sibley took Bibb's other five brothers—including John, Lewis, and Granville—to his Clark County, Missouri, farm in 1836. He soon sold Granville to another Missouri slaveholder but kept John and Lewis. In December 1851, Granville escaped from his new master and returned to the Sibley plantation to find John and Lewis before departing for Canada West. A few months later, John and Lewis coincidentally followed Granville's escape route along the underground railroad. They located Granville in Windsor in September 1852 and were reunited with Bibb and their mother. Bibb later reported that his brothers acquired farms in the Windsor area. Bibb, *Narrative of Henry Bibb*, 14, 189; *VF*, 22 September, 7, 21 October, 4 November, 2 December 1852.

3. Although the Methodist church had an antislavery heritage, it had accommodated itself to the institution of slavery by the end of the 1820s. The rise of militant abolitionism in the 1830s reawakened concern among some northern Methodists, placed southern members on the defensive, and nurtured controversy that led to a schism along sectional lines in 1845. The Methodist Episcopal Church, South, was subsequently founded and confirmed slavery as a biblically supported positive good. Donald G. Mathews, *Slavery and Methodism: A Chapter in American Morality, 1780–1845* (Princeton, N.J., 1965).

4. The decalogue refers to the Ten Commandments, a basic outline of ancient Jewish law found in Exodus 20:2–17 and Deuteronomy 5:6–21.

5. Bibb refers to the Refugee Home Society school, which was established in September 1852. Laura Smith Haviland, a Michigan abolitionist and underground railroad agent, was hired to teach day and evening classes. During the first year, the school reported between sixty and eighty students in attendance. Carlesimo, "Refugee Home Society," 128–30; Pease and Pease, *Black Utopia*, 13, 112–22; Winks, *Blacks in Canada*, 242–44, 364–71.

6. Johnnycake is a bread made of cornmeal mixed with salt and water or milk and either baked in a pan or dropped onto a hot greased griddle.

7. When Albert G. Sibley moved from Kentucky to Clark County, Missouri, in 1836, he took Henry Bibb's brother George with him. Once in Missouri, Sibley sold George to another slaveholder. *VF*, 22 September 1852; Bibb, *Narrative of Henry Bibb*, 14, 189.

35.
Constitution of the Anti-Slavery Society of Windsor
18 October 1852

Blacks dominated the Canadian antislavery movement. They held key positions in the Upper Canada Anti-Slavery Society and the Anti-Slavery Society of Canada, and they formed numerous black societies. On 18 October 1852, a large number of Windsor residents met at "the Barracks" and established the interracial Anti-Slavery Society of Windsor, an ASC branch. The meeting, which was chaired by Coleman Freeman, a local black, also adopted a preamble and a constitution for the new organization. The society's primary objectives were promoting the "right principles upon the subject of Slavery," cooperating "with similar societies . . . to awaken greater zeal" in the antislavery cause, and relieving "the wants of the newly arrived fugitives." Henry Bibb was elected as its first president. Society members, mostly black, included notable black Canadians such as Freeman, Mary E. Bibb, and Mary Ann Shadd Cary. Within two months of its founding, the society came under Cary's dominant influence. *VF*, 21 October, 18 November 1852 [7:0788, 0829]; Pemberton, "Anti-Slavery Society of Canada," 52–53.

Whereas we regard American Slavery, to be the sum of *all* villanies—holding as it does about three and a half millions of our fellow men in the condition of chattles, many of whom are our own kinsmen according to the flesh. And whereas we feel bound by the law of God and humanity to do all that is in our power morally and legally to effect their emancipation, and secure their elevation in the scale of being, therefore.

Resolved, That we do now constitute a Society which shall be a branch of the Anti-Slavery Society of Canada,[1] the leading object of which shall be the abolition of chattle Slavery, and the elevation of the colored population of North America, under the following.

CONSTITUTION

ARTICLE 1. This Association shall be called "THE ANTI-SLAVERY SOCIETY OF WINDSOR," and have for its object the promotion of right principles upon the subject of Slavery, and co-operation with similar Societies already formed, in diffusing information, and seeking to awaken greater zeal in religious bodies in regard to this momentous question.

ART. 2. That all persons paying Two Shillings per annum shall be entitled to be Members of the Association.

ART. 3. That the Society shall hold an Annual Meeting, at which the proceedings of the past year shall be reported, and the account of Funds received and disbursed shall be submitted.

ART. 4. That the business of the Society shall be conducted by a Committee appointed by the Annual Meeting.

ART. 5. That the Committee shall meet on the first Monday of each Month for the prosecution of business, such Meeting to be announced previously by the Secretary: who may also, with the consent of the President, or in his absence, of his own accord, convene Extraordinary Meetings of the Committee, as occasion may require; there to form a quorum.

ART. 6. That application for Subscriptions be made to the friends of this cause, in Windsor, and elsewhere, as soon as the Society may deem it proper.

ART. 7. That a Course of Lectures be delivered Annually by Ministers of the Gospel and others, on the subject of SLAVERY, so as to meet prevalent fallacies on the question, opposed to Scripture as well as humanity.

ART. 8. That these Rules shall not be altered or amended, unless after notice of such proposed alteration or amendment has been given One Month previously.

Voice of the Fugitive (Windsor, Canada West), 21 October 1852.

1. The immediatist Anti-Slavery Society of Canada was founded during February 1851 in Toronto, Canada West, in response to passage of the Fugitive Slave Law of 1850. Initially a local Toronto organization, its principal support came from Protestant clergy, liberal business and professional circles, and black abolitionists. Rev. Michael Willis (president), Thomas Henning (secretary-treasurer), and Toronto *Globe* editor George Brown guided the society until the Civil War. During 1852–53, it grew to a national organization with auxiliary societies in Kingston, Hamilton, Windsor, London, Grey County, and St. Catharines and with fourteen vice-presidents from various Canadian towns, including Montreal. The society assisted fugitives in the western region of Canada West, urged them to become farmers, and endorsed communities such as Dawn and the Refugee Home Society. Between 1851 and 1857, the society's women's auxiliary—the Toronto Ladies' Association for the Relief of Destitute Colored Fugitives—assisted hundreds of fugitives with clothing, money, and employment. Samuel Ringgold Ward, the society's itinerant agent, raised £ 1,200 in Britain between 1853 and 1855 to aid Canadian fugitives. Although considerably less active after 1857, the society revived briefly during the John Anderson extradition case of 1860–61 and the period following the Emancipation Proclamation. It disbanded by 1867. Pemberton, "The Anti-Slavery Society of Canada" 17, 20–27, 34–40, 48–55, 69, 77, 80–84, 99, 122, 126, 135; Robin W. Winks, "A Sacred Animosity: Abolitionism in Canada," in *The Antislavery Vanguard*, ed. Martin Duberman (Princeton, N.J., 1965), 323–29.

36.
Samuel Ringgold Ward and Canadian Racism

Samuel Ringgold Ward to Henry Bibb and James Theodore Holly
October 1852

Editorial by Samuel Ringgold Ward
24 March 1853

The flood of fugitive slaves arriving in Canada West during the early 1850s brought a corresponding rise in racial tensions. Samuel Ringgold Ward frequently wrote about the origins and nature of Canadian racism. Ward believed that racism in Canada was a reaction to the idea and practice of black equality; it did not evolve directly from slavery as in the United States. He worried that black Canadians reinforced these prejudices by establishing separate institutions, by ignoring Victorian social mores, and by failing to see the urgency of the antislavery movement once they were safe in the Canadas. Ward reminded the public that the tentacles of American slavery reached well beyond the slave states, and he urged blacks to combat these influences. "So long as these facts exist," he observed, "we shall want anti-slavery labors, organizations, agitation, and newspapers." Ward's writings on the character of Canadian society and on separate black institutions reveal his vision for the black Canadian community—free, educated, prosperous, staid, and socially integrated. *VF*, 9 September, 21 October, 4 November 1852 [7:0733, 0784, 0815]; *PFW*, 24 March 1853 [8:0172].

Canadian Negro Hate
No. 3

MESSRS. BIBB & HOLLY
Gentlemen:

I do not pretend to deny, that in Canada, in general, and in the old Western District, in particular, there exists negro hate, such as Mr. Larwill,[1] and his fellow petitioners describe.[2] Very far am I, from making any such denial. That the representatives of that district should have sent to the Governor General[3] such a petition as that I have been considering, is evidence enough, of the existence of this feeling on *their* part, at least. But I do deny that such a feeling, is, or ever was so general, so universal, as those gentlemen represent it, or as they would like to have it.

In the present paper, I wish to state some facts showing how it operates, in Canada, and pointing out some of its differences from the negro hate of the United States.

A friend of mine, residing in Brantford, Rev. Peter O'Banyan published last winter, how he and his lady were denied entertainment, in different taverns, in the Niagara District, on the coldest night of last January.[4] Weeks, the Yankee Hotel keeper of Hamilton,[5] treated me in like manner, last December. Capt. Kerr, of the Steamer *Admiral*, plying between Rochester and Toronto, abused my family in November last, by forbidding them having a cabin passage.[6] The *Plough-boy*, and the *Brothers*, plying between Windsor and Chatham, invariably deny to black people, a cabin passage, and sometimes the officers of those boats will even descend to the use of brute force, upon *unresisting women*, to eject them from the cabin or the table. A Methodist minister residing near Dresden, in the Gore of Camden,[7] invited Mr. Vick,[8] a black brother, to his house to aid in some work. The good(?) priest called on brother Vick, to pray at family worship, but when meals were ready brother Vick must not eat at the same table, with this reverend preacher of a "free salvation." Another Methodist minister, a gentleman, thank God, of very different spirit, Rev. Mr. Clements,[9] now of Paris, C.W. riding his circuit, in your district, and approaching the residence of one of his members, on a dark, cold, stormy evening, proposed to spend the night with him. Brother Clements, was promptly denied admittance into his parishioner's house. Upon enquiring the cause, he learned that this man, a Scotch Highlander, refused to entertain his Pastor, for what reason think you? Because he had been informed, that Mr. Clements had eaten at a table where a black person ate, at the same time!!! Rev. E. E. Kirkland,[10] of New Canaan, Colchester, told Mrs. Bibb and me, in August last, that there were persons in their vicinity, who would not receive Mr. K. or any of his family at their tables, because he received the black people, among whom he is laboring, at his table. In Simcoe, Norfolk Co. and in Norwich, Oxford Co. black children are shut out of the common schools. The same is true in Chatham. Dennis Hill, Esq. of the Gore of Camden, a black gentleman owns the largest farm, and has the best education of all the rate payers in his own school section. The trustees of that section (No. 3), by a majority of two to one, deny to Mr. Hill's son, the right of attending the common school, solely on the ground of his complexion.[11] Rev. Mr. Clark,[12] formerly of Simcoe, now of Dresden, attended and occupied the chair at an anti-slavery meeting, near Dresden also attended quite numerously by black persons, and addressed by the undersigned. For so doing Mr. C. was forbidden to preach in a school house in Dresden village. Facts of this sort are abundant. But you have enough.

I now proceed to my second point, the comparing of Canada, with Yankee negro hate.

1. Canadian Negro Hate, is incomparably MEANER than the Yankee article. The parties who exhibit most of this feeling, are as poor, as ignorant, as immoral, as low, in every respect as the most degraded class of

negroes. In numerous instances, are they very far below them. No one can visit Canada, or any part of Canada, without seeing this, if his eyes be open. Our recently arriving slaves, are, in all respects quite equal to our newly arrived emigrants from Europe, and the free blacks coming from the United States are quite comparable to any class of whites, coming from the same country. The meanness of negro hate, therefore, is greater and lower, than that of the United States, as it is the setting up of one class of poor ignorant people, against another, by themselves, with just nothing under the moon, to boast of. In the United States, we are slaves, and but demi-freemen, if not all slaves. Here we all stand on a legal and political equality. The blacks [are] as free as the whites, and in law and in fact quite equal to them. Hence the greater meanness of Canadian than American Negro Hate.

Again Canadian Negro Hate is NOT ORIGINAL. Copied aped deviltry is always meaner than the original diabolism. But the negrophobia of Canada, is a poor pitiable, brainless, long eared imitation of Yankeeism, certain parties, go to Yankeedom to work. They return with Yankee cash, and Yankee ideas, and deal out both, in small quantities around their respective neighborhoods. In other cases, Yankees come here to reside. They bring their negrophobia with them. Canadians of the smaller sort catch the infection, straight way, go to aping their Yankee neighbors in this thing, in an awkward manner, and upon a very small scale. All they know is what they have heard, all they feel is second-handed. A meaner set of negro haters, God in his inexplicable mercy, does not suffer to live, than these poor fools of Canadian second-handed imitations.

But the greater meanness of this feeling, here, is also, in the fact that it is *gratuitous*. The whole world despise[s] gratuitous deviltry. A Yankee, commends himself to his richer more aristocratic neighbors, by his negrophobia. He puts himself on the side of Yankee fashion, by it. He sells more of his wares, in this way: he gets trade with men-stealers, and women-whippers, and human flesh mongers by it. If he be a priest he renders himself more acceptable to the occupants of the *front pews*, by it. If a politician he gets more votes, because he better pleases his slave-holding masters, by it. It is to him, therefore, a fair matter about which to "*calculate*." But not one word of this, applies to the Canadian. All he does, in this matter, is gratuitous: a devil serving without reward, in any possible shape. Bad and mean as is Yankee Negro Hate, it cannot be called as the Canadian article can *disinterested deviltry*. Be sure, as Hiram Wilson says, "it came from Hell by way of the United States," but it was *damaged* terribly in the passage hitherwards.

It should be added that the Yankees who bring this thing with them, and *peddle* it about the province appear meaner than they do at home, inasmuch as they come here for the same reason as we blacks come, to better our conditions. I look upon them just as I look upon an Irishman in the United States, who tramples upon blacks who helped to fight for the very liberties which these Irish paupers enjoy, and of which they seek to deprive the blacks.[13]

2. Unlike the Yankee product of the same name, Canadian Negro Hate, here has neither the current religion, nor the civil law, to uphold it. Steam-boat Captains, and Hotel keepers referred to above would be fined if brought before our courts, for their maltreatment of black persons. The British law knows no man by the color of his skin. In Yankeedom, negroes have no legal protection against such outrages. I never knew of but one instance, of a colored person receiving damages against a Steam-boat, for maltreatment in the United States. Instances here are numerous. A Hotel in Canada, forfeits its licence by treating a man as Mr. O'Banyan was treated. Trustees, who deny a black child the right of attending school, forfeit £ 5, each, and lose the Government money for their school.[14] In Boston, no such punishment can be brought upon the white trustees, who exclude black children from the school.

Not a single denomination, have we in Canada, where ministers uphold or sanction this illegal and unchristian treatment of black persons.[15] I have travelled much, and mingled freely with all sects, and I find it invariably true that in their places of worship and in their religious devotions whites and blacks, are on a common footing. The Holy Trinity, is the richest Episcopal church in Canada, equality—prevails there.[16] Knox's church is the largest Free Presbyterian church in Canada,[17] the same is true there. So in the Congregational church, so in the Methodist, so also in the Roman Catholic. Individuals belonging to each of these communions, ministers and laymen, may and do *enjoy* this beautiful brotherly negro hate. But the thing is far from being general. Indeed on this part of all denominations I have received uniformly, the treatment of a christian gentleman. There are not one dozen places in the United States, where so much can be said.

You will readily judge from the last point, that Canadian Negro Hate can not be eternal. The labors of the anti-slavery society, the improvement, progress, and good demeanor of the black people will, in a very short time, undermine and destroy this abomination, unless, certain things, to which I shall presently refer, exert an unhappy influence. Having law, religion, and British example at headquarters against it, Canadian negrophobia, cannot long abide. When publicly attacked, it hides its head from the indignant gaze of a condemning community. The pulpit, in ninety-nine cases of an hundred could be marshalled against it, at any time. The Press (which in too many instances is far from being what it should be) condemns it, through the most influential papers in our Province. It is therefore, quite destitute of the influences which keeps it alive in our native land, let a hundredth part, of as much be done, here, against it as in the United States, in the shape of direct attack and it would disappear altogether.

There is this to be said, however, touching this feeling here. Ours is an aristocratic country. We make here, no pretentions to "social equality," "Republicanism," "Democracy" all that. Many blacks come here, and finding that they are not treated as equals by the better classes, attribute the treatment they receive, to the prejudice. The mistake, is [i]n not looking at society as it really is. A black gentleman of good education, polite manners, and courtly address, would be received as a gentleman, while a white man destitute of these would not be so received. Then too, as wealth enters largely into a man's position, here, it is not to be wondered at, that our people should be treated, in Canada as are other poor people.

Happily for us, now, we are receiving some very valuable accessions to our black population, heretofore, very much needed. Such men as William Watkins Esq. of Baltimore formerly,[18] Rev. John B. Smith, late of Providence R.I.,[19] Marcus Sarsenett,[20] once of Ontario Co. N.Y. now settling among us, help to give us better character, and widen the circle of good society, among us.

The only thing to be feared, is, that some of the black people will act in such a manner as to increase, rather than diminish the prejudice against us. We have separate and distinct black churches, schools and preachers, whose existence and influence are much against us. Some of our preachers of the Methodist and Baptist denomination, are really too ignorant to instruct any body.[21] The noisy behaviour of some women among whom was a female preacher in one of the Toronto churches not long since, was any thing but creditable or elevating. But if we act rightly, all will be well.

S. R. WARD

Voice of the Fugitive (Windsor, Canada West), 4 November 1852.

Relations of Canada to American Slavery

Do we need anti-slavery labor in Canada?

We say, Yes; and to us

"The why is as plain as [the] way to parish church."

And that is, because this Province and its inhabitants bear very important relations to American slavery. Hear us, good readers, while we discourse a little about some of these relations. We shall now speak of two, viz., the antagonistic and the friendly.

1. The fact that this is a British Province, and that slavery has no existence on British soil—the fact that this soil never was polluted by slavery—and the fact that since the ever memorable Somerset decision, the slave of another country became a freeman by touching our soil[22]—place us in relations of antagonism to slavery. This was early seen and felt by the

slave, and as early seen and felt by the slaveholder. Accordingly, so early as 1825, the attention of the U.S. Government was directed to this point. In the month of May, of that year, the House of Representatives passed a resolution calling upon the President to enter into correspondence with the British Government, for the recovery of slaves who had escaped into Canada. The reply of President Adams, to this resolution was, that his Excellency had, of his own accord, commenced such a correspondence some ten or fifteen days before. (See Jay's View.) From that time to 1842, the number of slaves escaping to Canada constantly and rapidly increased. Then, when a treaty was made between the two Governments, called the Ashburton Treaty, it was most earnestly sought on the part of the United States' Government, first to have an article inserted which should authorize slave-catching in Canada; and, secondly, so to interpret the tenth article of that treaty so as to make it a slave-catching article; but the Court of St. James promptly refused, in 1825, to allow the American slaveholder to use Canada as a park to chase human game in. So they decided the tenth article of the Ashburton Treaty not to include slaves among "fugitives from justice," nor slaves as "felons," though they should use a horse or a boat to convey them on their way Canada-wards, or though they should strike a blow to prevent some slaveocrat's impeding their progress. Canada, therefore, from her connection with the British Crown, is legally and constitutionally in an attitude of antagonism to American slavery.[23] She offers and secures to the American slave the moment he arrives here, Freedom—British Freedom—impartial Freedom. And when he has stood his seven years' probation, and taken the oath of allegiance, Canada secures to him, at home and abroad, in law and in equity, all the rights and immunities of a British subject.

But there is another view of our relations to this subject—it is painful to admit it—it is a deep disgrace to us; it is true, but disgraceful as it is, it is useless to conceal it—friendliness to slavery is to be found in this Province in more forms than one.

1. There are some parties here who practised slave-driving in the South. They love slavery as they love the gain they derived from wielding the whip over its victims. A sprinkling of such customers is to be found here and there, the Province over.

2. There are others, too, who have married heiresses to slave estates. Having received their wives and slaves by the same act of matrimony, they are strongly tempted to regard slavery to be as sacred as marriage itself.

3. Then there are persons resident in Canada who were once slaveholders in the West Indies. The glorious people of Great Britain, determined to have the great principle of British freedom applied practically to the enslaved, as well as to all others, like Job, they, through the Government, "broke the jaws of the wicked, and delivered the spoiled out of their teeth."[24] But these ex-slaveholders were never convinced of the *sin* of

slaveholding—or, if *convinced* of it, they never were *converted from* it. Hence they are in spirit now, what they were in practice before the Act of '32.[25] The influence of these parties is as deeply and wickedly pro-slavery as that of the vilest slaveocrats of New York, Boston, Philadelphia, or Baltimore.

4. As a born Yankee, we are ashamed of it, but it is true that too many of the natives of the United States have brought their pro-slaveryism with them, from the other side. Like the refugee slaves, they come here to enjoy an improvement of their condition, and like them, too, they enjoy the prote[c]ting care of this good British realm; but they turn scornfully upon the black man, and do what in them lies to rob him of the rights to which the latter is as fully entitled as themselves. From sympathy with their native country, and from their own negro-hate, they maintain a constant and growing pro-slavery influence wherever they are settled. There are but very few exceptions to this rule, for it is a rule; and most safely may it be said, that while the Yankees are far from being the only negro-haters, or pro-slavery parties whose principles disgrace our country, it is nevertheless true that the mass of them are the most decided slaveocrats in the land; and what is more, they most industriously spread and promulgate their sentiments, and seek to make them prevalent and controlling, even to the violation of Her Majesty's laws. We could give abundant illustrations of this.

5. It remains to be said that the prejudice against negroes, so prevalent in various parts of the Province, as maintained by many persons of all nations, including, of course, native Canadians, is one of the strongest pro-slavery influences that disgraces and degrades our fair country; it does more to place us side by side with American oppressors than any other thing. Every body knows that it is the North and not the South that supplies the power of public opinion, of the pulpit, the press, commerce, manufactures, literature, religion, politics, everything that keeps slavery alive. Now the sentiment—the controlling sentiment of the people of the North, that renders them the volunteer body-guard of slavery, is their negro-hate. The maintenance of a like negro-hate here, of course, encourages the same feeling there, and aids it in doing its very worst work. Every Canadian negro-hater is a volunteer British slaveocrat. Every such one is a strengthener of the slave system, and we repeat, that there should be such, is one of the worst facts—the foulest disgrace—the deepest degradation—in all our history.

So long as these facts exist, we shall want anti-slavery labors, organizations, agitation, and newspapers in Canada. Our humble life shall be devoted to the counteracting of the pro-slaveryism of our adopted country. It is for this reason that we leave our own hearthstone, and expose ourselves to so many disagreeables, as a lecturing agent of the Canadian Anti-Slavery Society. Hence it is we consent, without pay, to scribble for the *Provincial Freeman*.[26] And we do believe that the education and improvement of our own people will lay this enmity to liberty and humanity—this friendship for despotism—low, in a death and burial that shall know no resurrection, and that at no very distant day. At any rate we shall labor on in hope.

Let the pro-slaveryism of Canada be overcome, and let the anti-slavery influence of our laws, constitution, and position be fully and freely exerted, and there is no portion of the British Empire whose influence against slavery would be so healthful and so potent as that of Canada. "A consummation most devoutly to be wished for."

Provincial Freeman (Windsor, Canada West), 24 March 1853.

1. Edwin Larwill, an English-born tinner, land speculator, and Conservative politician, settled in Chatham, Canada West, in 1841. He obtained his first public position—school commissioner for Raleigh township—the following year. As editor of the *Chatham Journal* during the mid-1840s, he gained sufficient notoriety to win seats on the Western District Council and in the Canadian Legislative Assembly. While in the assembly, he promoted immigration restrictions, racial segregation, and black laws. He also organized local white opposition to William King's proposed Elgin settlement in 1849. Larwill's blatant racism antagonized the Conservative black voters of Kent County, who turned against him in 1857 and helped elect Archibald McKellar, the Reform party candidate. Winks, *Blacks in Canada*, 213–15; Pease and Pease, *Black Utopia*, 103–6; Simpson, "Negroes in Ontario to 1870," 157, 334, 474.

2. Ward refers to a petition adopted by the Western District Council on 8 October 1849. Council members, including Edwin Larwill, prepared a lengthy resolution to the governor-general of the Canadas that opposed William King's plan to establish the Elgin settlement. Larwill appears to have surreptitiously amended the resolution to include complaints about alleged black misconduct and a call for the enactment of restrictive black laws. *VF*, 9 September 1852; William H. Pease and Jane H. Pease, "Opposition to the Founding of the Elgin Settlement," *CHR* 38:202–18 (September 1957).

3. Ward refers to James Bruce (1811–1863), the eighth earl of Elgin and twelfth earl of Kincardine. He was educated at Eton and Christ Church, Oxford, was elected to Parliament from Southampton in July 1841, and, in March 1842, was appointed governor of Jamaica. His efforts at modernizing Jamaican agriculture and improving educational opportunities for blacks were successful; his administration was so satisfactory that in 1846 the Whig party appointed him governor-general of Canada, where he remained until late 1854, despite difficulties. He was primarily responsible for negotiating the Canada–United States Reciprocity Treaty of 1854. In 1855 Elgin declined several key positions and spent most of the remainder of his life in Asia in government service. *DNB*, 3:104–6.

4. Ward refers to a 30 January 1852 letter written by Peter O'Banyan (1796–?), which appeared in the 26 February issue of the *Voice of the Fugitive*. The letter described O'Banyan's mid-January journey with his wife Sophia (1816–?) from Brantford, Canada West, to Buffalo, New York. During the trip, they were forced

to accept inferior accommodations at a Canboro hotel because of their color and were refused lodging at hotels in Drummondville and Niagara Falls. O'Banyan, a Kentucky-born mulatto, was pastor of an African Methodist Episcopal congregation in Brantford during the 1840s and early 1850s. Although described as "a man of wealth and high moral standing among the citizens" in the local community, he was regularly criticized by AME officials for his lack of interest and involvement in the affairs of the denomination's Canada Conference. About 1856 O'Banyan led his congregation into the new British Methodist Episcopal church, but later in the decade, accusations of misconduct and mismanagement against him divided the congregation and led to his dismissal. He was the father of Josephus O'Banyan, a noted BME minister after the Civil War. *VF*, 26 February, 12 August 1852; Census of Canada, 1851; Simpson, "Negroes in Ontario to 1870," 803–4.

5. William Weeks, an American, purchased Peest's Hotel in Hamilton during the mid-1840s. Weeks first renamed it the American Tavern and later, in the mid-1850s, the Hamilton House. The hotel was reputed to be one of the finest in Canada West and primarily served an American clientele. Guillet, *Pioneer Inns and Taverns*, 3:184.

6. Ward refers to Robert Kerr, captain of the steamer *Admiral*, which traversed Lake Ontario between Rochester, New York, and Toronto. Kerr typically allowed no blacks to obtain passage on his boat. Following Kerr's lead, on 13 November 1851, a cabin maid and purser on the *Admiral* ordered Ward's wife, Emily, and children (including son Samuel and daughters Emily and Alice) from their staterooms, and they spent the cold night huddled on deck. Shortly thereafter, Kerr became captain of the steamer *America*. *FDP*, 11 December 1851.

7. The term *gore* connotes an unorganized section of land, usually part of a county or other political subdivision. Ward refers to the immediate area surrounding the village of Camden, Canada West, which was located between the Thames and Sydenham rivers.

8. Newett Vick (1807–?), a Virginia-born black farmer, resided near Chatham, Canada West, where he owned fifty acres of farmland and woodland. A Wesleyan Methodist, he was the victim of a well-publicized incident of racial prejudice near Dresden in the early 1850s, when, as the guest of a local white Methodist clergyman and his family, he was allowed to join the group in prayer but was later requested to dine alone in the kitchen, away from his white hosts. News of the incident was frequently carried in abolitionist newspapers to demonstrate the existence of Canadian racial prejudice. Census of Canada, 1851, 1861; *VF*, 4 November 1852 [7:0815].

9. Edwin Clement (1819–?) was a Methodist clergyman in Paris, Canada West, during the 1850s. Although born in England, he lived for a time in the United States before settling in Canada West in the late 1840s. Census of Canada, 1851.

10. Elias E. Kirkland, a Wesleyan Methodist minister, began missionary duties at Dawn in 1843 but shifted his work to the Queen's Bush later in the decade. In 1851 Kirkland received an American Missionary Association appointment to work at the black New Canaan settlement near Colchester. He attended the organizational meeting of the Refugee Home Society in Detroit in May 1851. Kirkland, discouraged by the controversy surrounding the RHS and by the increasing black resistance to the presence of white missionaries, resigned his posi-

tion with the AMA's Canada mission and returned to the United States in 1853. *AM*, December 1851, November 1853; *Lib*, 17 March 1843; *NSt*, 29 November 1848; Johnson, "American Missionary Association," 329–52; Murray, "Canada and Anglo-American Anti-Slavery Movement," 68, 404, 411, 436; *VF*, 26 March 1851.

11. Dennis Hill apparently settled in the black community surrounding Dawn during the 1840s. By 1852 he owned a three-hundred-acre farm in the gore of Camden, with eighty acres under cultivation. Samuel Ringgold Ward called Hill "one of the best educated yeomen in Canada." Despite Hill's financial and educational status, local school trustees denied his son admission to the local public school by a two-to-one majority in 1852. Hill protested the decision to Egerton Ryerson, superintendent of common schools for Canada West, who advised him to seek a legal remedy. One year later, when he had two children of school age, both of whom were refused admission to the common schools, Hill pursued the matter. In the case of *Hill* v. *The School Trustees of Camden and Zone* (1853), Chief Justice John Beverly Robinson of the Court of Queen's Bench ruled that, in the Common School Act of 1850, the legislature had intended that black students would be required to attend separate schools for nonwhites (public or private) where they were established. The ruling sanctioned segregated education in the province. Despite this setback, Hill remained prominent in the Canadian black community and maintained his advocacy of black self-help ventures. In 1854 he was elected a vice-president of the Provincial Union Association. The following year, he served as local subscription agent in Dresden for the *Provincial Freeman*. During the late 1850s, Hill chaired several meetings and sat on several committees investigating the Dawn Institute and the condition of fugitives in Chatham. Ward, *Autobiography of Fugitive Negro*, 193–94; *VF*, 4 November 1852 [8:0441]; Winks, *Blacks in Canada*, 373; *PFW*, 19 August 1854 [9:0017], 7 April–30 June 1855; *WAA*, 23 July 1859 [11:0876]; *CTWP*, 10 November 1859 [12:0203].

12. William F. Clark, a Congregational clergyman active in the antislavery movement, later served a church in London, Canada West. He became a director of the London Anti-Slavery Society in 1852, and one year later, the Amherstburg Convention appointed him to a committee created to monitor fugitive relief efforts in London. Fred Landon, "Fugitive Slaves in London before 1860," *Trans* 10:35 (1919); *Minutes of Convention in Amherstburg*, 9 [8:0301].

13. Between 1830 and 1865, more than 1.5 million Irish immigrants entered the United States. Confronted with the anti-Irish prejudices of native white Americans, these new arrivals frequently directed their anger and frustration against the free black community. Racial violence erupted regularly between Irish immigrants and blacks during the 1840s, especially in northern cities like Philadelphia and New York City where the two ethnic groups competed for menial and semiskilled employment. In the two decades preceding the Civil War, unskilled Irish immigrant labor flooded the work force, depressed wages, and displaced black competitors in numerous service occupations, which included barbers, domestic servants, cooks, coachmen, and stevedores. Litwack, *North of Slavery*, 159, 163–66.

14. Ward refers to penalties specified in the Common School Act of 1850.

15. Throughout the period of nineteenth-century black immigration to the

British North American Provinces, Canadian churches took varying positions on the slavery issue and displayed a mixture of attitudes toward the growing black population in their midst. This inconsistency translated into a range of behavior—much of it discriminatory—toward black men and women. Winks, *Blacks in Canada*, 219–31.

16. Holy Trinity Anglican Church, a cross-shaped Gothic structure located on Trinity Square in central Toronto, was constructed in 1847. *St. Lawrence Hall*, 30–31; C. P. Mulvany et al., *History of Toronto and County of York, Ontario*, 2 vols. (Toronto, 1885), 1:310–12.

17. The Knox Free Presbyterian Church, a white-brick structure located on Queen Street in central Toronto, was erected in 1847. Abolitionist Robert Burns was the pastor from 1845 to 1856. *St. Lawrence Hall*, 30–31; Mulvany, *History of Toronto and York*, 1:314; *DCB*, 9:105–7.

18. William Watkins (1801–1858) was born to free parents in Baltimore. He received his early education at a school operated by Rev. Daniel Coker, a prominent black Methodist clergyman, at his Sharp Street Church. At age nineteen, Watkins established his own school. The Watkins Academy offered courses in grammar, reading, writing, natural philosophy, music, and mathematics to local black children for twenty-five years. Watkins's oratorical and leadership skills placed him at the forefront of Baltimore's black community from the late 1820s to the early 1840s. Having studied medicine, he frequently prescribed treatments for black patients; he regularly ministered to black parishioners at the city's Sharp Street, John Wesley, Orchard Street, Asbury, and Centennial congregations; and he helped organize a local black literary society. But Watkins is best remembered for his antislavery work. He first attracted attention in late 1826 when he publicly refuted the notion, purported by the American Colonization Society, that free blacks wanted to settle in West Africa. He chastised colonizationists for their patronizing and selfish attitudes, criticized white churches and white clergymen for urging black Christians to settle in a "heathen land," and argued that blacks thought of themselves as Americans, not Africans. Watkins urged blacks to "die in Maryland, under the pressure of unrighteous and cruel laws [rather] than be driven like cattle to the pestilential clime of Liberia." He personally dissuaded many local blacks from emigrating. Watkins penned numerous anticolonization and antislavery essays, which were published in Benjamin Lundy's *Genius of Universal Emancipation* and William Lloyd Garrison's *Liberator* under the pseudonym "A Colored Baltimorean" during the late 1820s and 1830s. He also served as a local subscription agent for the *Liberator* and frequently corresponded with Garrison, thus serving as a conduit linking Baltimore blacks with the broader antislavery movement. After the mid-1830s, Watkins turned his attention from colonization to black education, frequently writing on that subject for the *Colored American*. Although never prominent in the black convention movement, he was a charter member of the American Moral Reform Society that emerged from the movement in 1836. He endorsed all of the AMRS's objectives—education, temperance, economy, and universal liberty—but he paid particular attention to the society's educational work. Watkins severed his relationship with the AMRS two years later because he believed that members paid too much attention to semantic questions rather than to antislavery work. Watkins's stature and credibility in the antislavery movement was destroyed when he became attracted to the mil-

lennialist ideas of Adventist preacher William Miller in 1844 and believed that the world was coming to an end. Baltimore's worsening racial climate prompted Watkins to settle in Toronto, where he opened a grocery in September 1852. He continued to write occasional antislavery essays, publishing them in *Frederick Douglass' Paper* under the pen name "A Colored Canadian." Watkins was the father of William J. Watkins and the uncle of antislavery lecturer Frances Ellen Watkins Harper. Bettye J. Gardner, "William Watkins: Antebellum Black Teacher and Anti-Slavery Writer," *NHB* 39:623–25 (September–October 1976); Leroy Graham, *Baltimore: The Nineteenth Century Black Capital* (Lanham, Md., 1982), 93–146.

19. John B. Smith (1819–?), a black antislavery activist, left Providence, Rhode Island, for Canada West in 1852. He settled in Toronto, where he pastored a Baptist congregation and did missionary work among fugitive slaves. In late 1854, the Anti-Slavery Society of Canada established a permanent office in Toronto and named Smith as office agent. But Smith's frequent disagreements with ASC secretary Thomas Henning and the criticism he received in the *Provincial Freeman* prompted him to abandon the field by May 1855 and return to New England. For the next few years, he again labored for the antislavery cause in Rhode Island and Massachusetts. As the decade drew to a close, Smith became increasingly pessimistic about black prospects in the United States and turned to the emigration movement. He lectured in Toronto for the African Civilization Society during the winter of 1860. The following year, he became an agent for James Redpath's Haytian Emigration Bureau. He toured throughout the eastern United States and the Maritime Provinces, lecturing and recruiting blacks willing to settle in Haiti. Smith frequently corresponded with the *Pine and Palm* and composed detailed accounts of life in the black communities he visited. He traveled to Haiti in the spring of 1862 and, upon his return, continued to lecture for the Haitian cause. When the movement collapsed late in the year, Smith settled in Boston. After the Civil War, he served as general agent for the National Lincoln Monument Association, a black effort to memorialize the fallen president. An eloquent and informed speaker, Smith was well respected in the antebellum abolitionist community, even by his critics. Winks, *Blacks in Canada*, 258, 491; *VF*, 4 November 1852 [7:0815]; *FDP*, 30 June 1854, 1 February 1856 [10:0040]; *PFW*, 24 March 1853, 17 June, 1 July, 9 September 1854, 7 April 1855, 21 March 1857 [8:0175, 0880, 0907, 9:0077, 0523, 10:0588]; Pemberton, "Anti-Slavery Society of Canada," 76; *Lib*, 22 February 1861 [13:0348]; *PP*, 8, 29 June, 13 July, 3, 17 August, 7 December 1861, 18 February, 22 May, 31 July 1862 [13:0588, 0609, 0621, 0679, 0690, 0955]; *WAA*, 17 December 1859, 30 June, 15 December 1860 [12:0297, 0850, 13:0038]; *AAN*, 12 August 1865 [16:0058].

20. Ward apparently refers to Marcus Sargnett, who was a black saloon-keeper in Hamilton, Canada West, during the 1850s. *Hamilton City Directory*, 1853.

21. Ward based his critical remarks about black preachers in Canada West upon personal observations in several Toronto churches, particularly that of Rev. Jeremiah Taylor, an African Methodist Episcopal clergyman. Ward was appalled by Taylor's use of "disgusting, abusive, indecent language" and "semi-theatrical gestures" in his sermons. He argued that such enthusiastic, emotional behavior by black preachers and congregations fostered antiblack prejudice. Ward urged black churches to engage in serious, systematic study of the Bible and Christian

doctrine, but he also understood that most black Canadian clergymen lacked formal education. In 1854 the Colonial Church and School Society reported that "colored preachers, with some few exceptions, are uneducated and incompetent . . . scarcely able to read." From the 1840s through the 1860s, the Canadian Conference of the AME, the British Methodist Episcopal church (after 1856), and the Amherstburg Baptist Association voiced concern about the poor education of black Canadian preachers. But not until the BME's Nazrey Institute (Chatham) was incorporated in 1870 was a remedy found. A major hindrance to the development of an educated black clergy was the belief of many black Methodists and Baptists that conversion and calling experiences, not knowledge of the Bible, theology, and ancient languages, qualified one to preach. *VF*, 17 December 1851 [7:0224]; Simpson, "Negroes in Ontario to 1870," 123–28.

22. Ward correctly notes that, under most circumstances, a fugitive slave was free upon arrival on British soil. Slavery had existed in Britain and her colonies, including the Canadas (although provincial legislation and judicial decisions limited it there by 1803), until the Emancipation Act of 1833 ended the institution in the Empire. Yet throughout the late eighteenth century and the first half of the nineteenth century, British and American abolitionists incorrectly regarded the Somersett decision (1772) as the definitive judicial statement on the illegality of British slavery. In that famous case, Lord Mansfield, chief justice of the Court of Kings Bench, freed James Somersett, a slave who had refused to return to the American colonies with his master. But Mansfield did not rule on the legality of English slavery. Instead he applied the country's long-standing laws of villenage, particularly the law requiring a master to respect his servant's attachment to place. Jerome Nadelhaft, "The Somersett Case and Slavery: Myth, Reality, and Repercussions," *JNH* 51:193–208 (July 1966).

23. During the 1820s, Kentucky and Virginia slaveholders pressured the federal government to arrange a treaty with Britain that would permit recovery of fugitive slaves from the British North American Provinces. Acting on instructions from Secretary of State Henry Clay, the American ambassadors to Britain, Albert Gallatin and James Barbour, repeatedly approached the British Foreign Office with slave extradition proposals between 1826 and 1828. These overtures were consistently rebuffed. Finally, on 10 May 1828, the U.S. House of Representatives instructed President John Quincy Adams to personally open negotiations on the topic with Britain. He later provided Congress with documentation drawn from the Gallatin-Barbour efforts to demonstrate that such a correspondence had already been initiated. Adam's diplomacy also failed. The Webster-Ashburton Treaty (1843) finally settled the slave extradition question but not to the satisfaction of southern slaveholders. Although slaveholders called for a slave extradition clause in the treaty and then interpreted Article X—a criminal extradition clause—as meeting their objective, British officials observed that criminal acts necessarily related to flight from bondage would not be treated as extraditable offenses. William Jay, *View of the Action of the Federal Government in Behalf of Slavery* (New York, N.Y., 1839), 47–49; Roman J. Zorn, "Criminal Extradition Menaces the Canadian Haven for Fugitive Slaves, 1841–1861," *CHR* 38:284–91 (December 1957).

24. Ward quotes this Old Testament phrase from Job 29:17. It is attributed to the patient and long-suffering character for whom the book is named.

25. Ward refers to the Emancipation Act of 1833, which ended slavery in the Canadas and other areas of the British Empire.

26. After printing an earlier sample issue, the *Provincial Freeman* began regular, weekly publication in March 1854 in Toronto, Canada West. Although devoted to "Anti-Slavery, Temperance, and General Literature," a wide range of interests and issues found expression in the paper. Samuel Ringgold Ward was nominal editor the first year, but Mary Ann Shadd Cary performed most editorial labors, and readers soon addressed letters to the editor, "Dear Madam." In March 1855 the paper became the *Provincial Freeman and Weekly Advertiser*. Three months later, Cary began a lecture tour to raise subscriptions and relinquished the editorship to William P. Newman. The following month, the *Freeman* permanently moved to Chatham. Newman left the paper in January 1856, and by May, editorial responsibilities were divided between Cary, her brother Isaac Shadd, and H. Ford Douglas. This circle, which also included coproprietor Louis Patterson, determined editorial policy for the next two years. The paper initially opposed emigration and reported, with relish, the internal conflicts within black Canadian settlements, particularly Dawn and the Refugee Home Society experiment at Windsor. But after the disintegration of the latter in the mid-1850s, the *Freeman* shifted its position, endorsed the emigration movement, and became the official organ of the 1856 National Emigration Convention at Cleveland. It also informed readers of Canadian affairs (endorsing first Reform, then Conservative, candidates) and frequently chastised the Anti-Slavery Society of Canada. The *Freeman* evidently suspended publication in late 1857, but Isaac Shadd revived it the following year. When Shadd was arrested in late 1858 for his part in a fugitive slave rescue, publication of the paper was again halted. By July 1859, Shadd was publishing the *Provincial Freeman and Semi-Monthly Advertiser* in Chatham. The paper's date of demise is uncertain, but it advertised in the *Weekly Anglo-African* through July 1860. By September 1861, the paper was defunct. Alexander L. Murray, "The *Provincial Freeman*: A New Source for the History of the Negro in Canada and the United States," *JNH* 44:123–35, 135n (April 1959); *PFW*, 24 March 1853, 25 March, 9 September 1854, 10 March, 23, 30 June, 22 September 1855, 2, 23 February, 29 March, 10 May, 14 June 1856; Miller, *Search for Black Nationality*, 157–60, 166; W[illiam] H[oward] Day to Gerrit Smith, 21 June 1858, Gerrit Smith Papers, NSyU [11:0253–54]; *GSB*, 28 October 1858 [11:0393]; *WAA*, 30 July 1859, 14 July 1860; *PP*, 28 September 1861 [13:0774].

37.
Samuel Ringgold Ward to Benjamin Coates
[October 1852]

Some abolitionists feared that the United States would annex the Canadian provinces. The most substantial Canadian annexation movement peaked in the late 1840s on the eve of an increase in black migration to Canada West. Blacks who viewed the British North American Provinces as a sanctuary for fugitive slaves and as their new home opposed annexation. Others, particularly white colonizationists and blacks who advocated black resettlement in West Africa or the Caribbean, used the fear of annexation to discourage black immigration to Canada. They warned that annexation would again make blacks victims of American prejudice, the Fugitive Slave Law, and slavery. In an October 1852 letter to white colonizationist Benjamin Coates of Philadelphia, Samuel R. Ward explained why he believed that annexation would never take place. Careless, *Union of Canadas*, 127–31; Winks, *Blacks in Canada*, 165–69; *FDP*, 19 November 1852 [7:0834].

BENJAMIN COATES, Esq.[1]
PHILADELPHIA, U.S.
MY DEAR SIR:

I said, in my hasty reply to your doubly welcome note of May last, that a portion of your letter should receive, as it deserved, a more extended reply. From that time to the present, my engagements have been such as to forbid my paying the attention to the subject, to which it was entitled. Besides, in order to reply to something you referred to, I needed to acquaint myself more intelligently with some facts in relation to my adopted country, Canada.

In the first place, allow me to say that the annexation of Canada to the United States by treaty, or otherwise, is an event of which there is, so far as I can learn, not the most distant prospect.[2] There are Americans residing in Canada who desire it. There are also British subjects who desire it. From such, when in Toronto, I presume you got information as to its being prospective. With such, "the wish is father to the thought." Indeed, I do not doubt that there are members of our Parliament, of both political parties, who entertain annexation hopes and opinions. The day was, when this feeling found utterance and advocacy in numerous quarters. But from all I can gather, there is now no considerable number of persons who avow any such opinions—no newspapers advocating them, and no political party favoring them as such; and at a general election, no candidate regards annexationism to be popular enough for him to risk the chance of an election by the avowal of feelings or tendencies in that direction. Indeed, I am told by those whose means of knowing are superior to mine, that of our two millions of population, there are not ten thousand annexationists.

This feeling has been greatly exaggerated. And now it is rapidly disappearing. But should the measure ever be fully and fairly discussed, as it must be, ere it could receive the sanction of the people, a very few facts would settle the question at once, and forever, against annexation. For example, the passage of the Fugitive Slave Bill has disgusted so many who *were* annexationists, that they now rejoice to change their sentiments; and they prefer to remain forever disconnected with a country whose government enacts so odious and inhuman laws. Very many with whom I have conversed on this subject, tell me frankly, that the enactment of that law was so abhorrent to them as to entirely change their views of the expediency of a union with our native country. I think it may be fairly and truly said, that nine tenths of those who favored annexation previous to September, 1850, do now, because of the Fugitive Law, prefer altogether, another line of policy.

Canadians see, too, in the passage of the Fugitive Law, how manifest are two great facts in the history and attitude of the United States, viz: The South rule and control the country at will; and, The North are perfectly and almost unanimously subservient to Southern dictation.[3] The more clearly these two facts are seen, the more abhorrent will annexation appear to us all. For one of the chief reasons why annexation has been desired by many, is the aversion to the controlment of the British government. But when they shall see that by annexation they would only exchange British governmental controlment for mere subjection to a slaveholding oligarchy, they will readily spurn the latter. Every legislative fact in the history of the United States government is full of evidence that such an exchange would be made; and that we should, if annexed to the United States, be brought under the heel of that worst of all despotisms, the American slave power. In connection with this, the fact that you northern people are so lacking in manliness as to hasten to do the bidding of your slaveocrats to any extent, and at whatever sacrifice of conscience, principle, patriotism, republicanism, or religion, when fairly seen, as investigation would make it appear, would forever stop all tendencies towards annexation on the part of our people. We never could subject ourselves to the American slave power, nor could we ally ourselves with a people who welcome and rejoice in, and perpetuate the encroachments of that power. In private conversation with persons favoring annexation, in different parts of the province, they have invariably scouted the idea of yielding up their freedom upon such an altar, for any consideration.

Besides, it is quite well known, that the chief object in view by your government, in favoring annexation, is the subjection of Canada to the Fugitive Slave Law, for the purpose of making one free province a park to hunt human deer in. Obviously, the negro-catching act would cover Canada, should a union take place. Thirty thousand negroes, worth five hundred dollars each, would never be suffered to remain free from the piratical grasp of American man-mongers, with their consent. And Canada, once subject to the American government, whose first, greatest business is the securing of slavery at home and abroad, no obstacle would by that government be placed in the way of having free range among our blacks. To this, no class of Canadian citizens would for one moment submit, on any terms.

But the negro population of Canada is now large, and daily increasing. When they come fresh from slavery, bearing the marks of their worse than barbarous treatment, by their *Christian republican* masters, the sight of them helps to fix in the minds of the thinking and humane a deeper hatred to American slavery, and a more intimate acquaintanceship with the qualities of American character. They enjoy the sympathies of all whose good will is worth having. The dragging of them back into bondage, would drench our streets with blood: aye, over the attempt to do it, would be the signal for a most fearful, bloody commotion. We blacks, having tasted of the genial sweets of true British freedom, would no more comment or submit to be made bondmen again, than we would deliberately jump into perdition. We would see every slaveholder in the bottomless pit, before we could, or would submit to such a thing. Some of us fought in the wars of our native country: others fought in defence of our adopted government, fourteen years ago;[4] all of us would fight till our last blood was spilt, before we should be subjected again to the tender mercies of American barbarism. Honest Irishmen, Scotchmen, Englishmen, and Canadians would not stand by and see us struggle alone. And the blood and carnage following them would be horrible to contemplate. And yet, this must be one of the inevitable results of annexation. There is not one thousand—not one hundred men—nay, not even including the black and the white slaveholders amongst us, who would dream of annexation upon such terms. Still, I repeat, annexation and civil war are inseparable.

Some reply to this, that any party which should be made for annexation, would secure the right of all Canadians. But who would trust a nation who violate their solemn Declaration of Independence, their Bill of Right, their Federal Constitution, their Puritan Faith, the right of Jury Trial, the Habeas Corpus—who have passed the Fugitive Slave Law?[5] Such a people may almost be said to have lost the power—the moral power—of keeping a treaty. No, no; this fair province once under the rule of the slave power, and we blacks would be re-enslaved just so surely as slaveholding, slave-trading, and slave-breeding are, practically, great American principles.

Have no fears, then, I beseech you, my dear Sir, about annexation. The facts in American history would, upon a discussion of this question, cure the most rabid of any remaining symptoms of this mania.

The adoption of Canada to black people, in preference to Liberia, I will treat in my next. Meanwhile, I am Your obedient servant,

SAMUEL R. WARD

Frederick Douglass' Paper (Rochester, N.Y.), 19 November 1852.

1. Benjamin Coates (1806–1887), a Philadelphia wool merchant, was active in both the colonization and antislavery causes. He wrote *Cotton Cultivation in Africa* (1858) to generate interest in black agricultural settlement in West Africa, was a prominent member of the American Colonization Society, and supported Martin R. Delany's Niger Valley Exploring Party and Henry Highland Garnet's African Civilization Society. Merrill and Ruchames, *Letters of William Lloyd Garrison*, 4:598n; *FDP*, 17 September 1858; *FI*, 7 May 1887.

2. Annexation of the Canadas by the United States was rumored throughout the early nineteenth century. But a serious annexation movement emerged in the Canadas in the late 1840s, prompted by economic hard times and Britain's abandonment of the old preferential colonial system. The movement appealed primarily to embittered Conservatives and young French-Canadian nationalists and was particularly strong in Montreal, where local merchants, four English-language newspapers, and the Annexation Association backed the annexationist cause. The movement reached its zenith in October 1849, when the Annexation Association issued a manifesto calling for peaceful separation from Britain and union with the United States. It was signed by a large segment of Montreal's political and business elite. But reaction in the Canadas was mixed. Some American border groups rallied to the manifesto, but the federal government was decidedly cool toward annexationist overtures. British opposition, anti-American feeling resulting from passage of the Fugitive Slave Law of 1850, and enactment of Canadian-American trade reciprocity soon extinguished the Canadian annexation movement. Expansionist interest in the Canadian West prompted a wave of annexation sentiment in the United States during the Civil War, but this, too, was short-lived. Blacks who favored immigration to Africa, the West Indies, or Central or South America used the threat of annexation to discourage Canadian immigration. Careless, *Union of Canadas*, 127–31, 136, 138; Robin Winks, *Canada and the United States: The Civil War Years* (Baltimore, Md., 1960), 165–69.

3. Ward's reference is to what, throughout the antebellum period, abolitionists termed the *slave power conspiracy*; for them the conspiracy explained what they saw as the concerted efforts of proslavery southern leaders and northern sympathizers to use their political influence to preserve and expand the institution of slavery. According to abolitionists, the slave power conspiracy had guaranteed slavery in the Constitution, extended the slave trade for twenty years, and added numerous slave states to the Union. During the late 1840s and 1850s, this abolitionist vision of a carefully designed plan to overturn freedom in the United States was confirmed by the proslavery expansionist demands of the South and repeated federal legislation and legal decisions that supported slavery. David Brion Davis, *The Slave Power Conspiracy and the Paranoid Style* (Baton Rouge, La., 1970).

4. Ward refers to black participation in the American Revolution, the War of 1812, and the Rebellion of 1837. Several thousand free blacks and slaves fought in the American Revolution. Although blacks were initially excluded from the Continental army and state militias, this policy was later abandoned when the

colonial rebels faced a recruitment crisis while thousands of slaves—responding to promises of freedom—were escaping to British lines. Most black recruits were from the northern colonies and joined integrated regiments and naval crews. Only a few black companies were formed. Blacks served primarily as military laborers and guides. Many of the slaves that enlisted received their freedom after the war. A smaller number of black Americans fought in the War of 1812, yet they made notable contributions to the American victories on Lake Erie and at the battle of New Orleans. Meanwhile, blacks in Upper Canada helped defend the Canadian border against invading American forces. Black Canadians also fought in the Rebellion of 1837, when separatists and republicans, supported by sympathetic Americans along the border, challenged the colonial government in the winter of 1837–38. The armed insurrection failed to garner popular support and was quickly suppressed. But the threat of American filibustering gave the crisis extended life. Fear of American designs on the British North American Provinces and a desire to demonstrate their loyalty to crown and country brought the Canadian black community to the side of the government. Hundreds of blacks volunteered for armed service when the uprisings began, and five black companies were authorized during the rebellion. Black troops patrolled the Canadian-American border and rivers, guarded American prisoners, and manned work details. John Hope Franklin, *From Slavery to Freedom: A History of Negro Americans*, 4th ed. (New York, N.Y., 1974), 89–96, 123–26.

5. Ward, like many abolitionists, frequently underscored the contradiction between American denial of civil rights to blacks and the principles of equality and freedom embodied in the Judeo-Christian tradition and in the American democratic credo.

38.
Dennis Hill to Egerton Ryerson
22 November 1852

Segregated education was the sole vestige of legal racial discrimination in the Canadian provinces. Racially separate schooling existed before 1850, but the Common School Act of 1850, which was intended to protect parochial education, was used to give legal sanction to segregated schools in southwestern Canada West. Dennis Hill, a Kent County farmer, mounted the first legal challenge to segregated education. Rather than send his son to a black school four miles away, he applied to a nearby white school and was refused. He then appealed to Egerton Ryerson, the superintendent of education for Canada West, who recommended that Hill pursue redress through the courts. Hill's complaint eventually reached the Court of Queen's Bench in Canada West. In *Hill* v. *School Trustees of Camden and Zone*, Chief Justice John Beverly Robinson ruled that, where separate schools for blacks existed, blacks must attend them rather than a white school. What had been an unintentional outcome of the Common School Act attained judicial sanction. Subsequent court rulings and economic conditions discouraged separate schools, but de facto segregation persisted for several decades. Winks, *Blacks in Canada*, 362–89; Silverman and Gillie, "Pursuit of Knowledge Under Difficulties," 95–112.

Dawn Mills, C[anada] W[est]
Nov[ember] 22nd, 185[0]

Rev. E. Ryerson, d.d.[1]

You will please pardon me for the liberty I have taken in appealing to you for redress for the base treatment I have receiv'd. from the majority of the trustees of School Section No. 3 in the Township of Camden County of Kent. I have used every respectful effort in my power with them, to have my son eleven years of age admitted into the above named school, but all to no purpose; they say that I am a Black Man and that it would be presumtion in me to contend for my son to go to school among white Children, though I am among the largest Tax payers in the said school section. The amt. of Taxes that I am charged with and have paid this year was $17 or less a few pence. Besides 12 Days statuted Labour.[2] I am the owner three hundred acres of land of which between 80 & 90 acres under cultivation situated nearly in the centre of said school section, and to be debarr'd from my Rights of school privilege for no other crime then that my skin is a few shades darker then some of my neighbours, I do think it unfair and at the same these same Trustees have invited white Children, out of the Township and they went as far as invite some whites of the adjoin[in]g county to attend the said school and do enjoy the privileges of sending as many scholars as they please, and the whole of that party put together do pay but a little more taxes then I do. The above are facts. Therefore will you be so kind as to instruct me how to proceed & How I shall arrange matters so as to give my Children their education, for I cannot Let them grow up in ignorance. Be so good, Most Rev. (sir) as to let me here from you by the earliest opportunity. Your most Humble and obedient ser't.,

Dennis Hill

P.S. Address Dawn Mills, Canada West.

Egerton Ryerson Papers, Archives of Ontario, Toronto, Ontario. Published by permission.

1. Adolphus Egerton Ryerson (1803–1882) was a Canadian-born Methodist minister and educator. He edited the *Christian Guardian* in the 1830s and afterward served as administrator-principal for Victoria College. Ryerson served as superintendent of schools in Upper Canada from 1844 until 1876. Although a conservative, dogmatic administrator, he promoted a liberal program of free, nonsectarian schools and compulsory attendance and became the chief architect of Canada's public education system. *DCB*, 11:783–95.

2. During the nineteenth century, local governments frequently mandated by statute that property owners perform several days of labor each year on public projects, usually road repair. This functioned as a form of property taxation.

39.
Mary Ann Shadd Cary to George Whipple
28 December 1852

Controversies over the objectives and leadership of the Refugee Home Society divided the Canadian black community. Mary Ann Shadd Cary and Samuel Ringgold Ward spoke for those who opposed the RHS, and they were particularly agitated by the fund-raising tours conducted on its behalf. Such "begging" campaigns, they charged, characterized black Canadians as destitute and starving and did little to demonstrate black self-reliance or to encourage Canadian immigration. Henry and Mary Bibb, James T. Holly, and others associated with the RHS defended the society. As the debate became more acrimonious and personal, both sides turned to the broader American and Canadian antislavery movements for support. The *Liberator* and *Pennsylvania Freeman* provided public forums for the combatants. This publicity created a dilemma for George Whipple, secretary of the American Missionary Association. The AMA had close ties with the RHS but at the same time subsidized Cary's Windsor school. When Whipple expressed his concern to Cary, she responded by refuting allegations made against her by Henry Bibb and Charles C. Foote and by describing RHS abuses and the misconduct of its leadership. As Cary's letter to Whipple suggests, the RHS controversy was both philosophical and personal. *Lib*, 15, 29 October, 10 December 1852; *PF*, 18 November 1852, 6, 20 January, 17 March 1853.

Windsor, C[anada] W[est]
Dec[ember] 28, [18]52

Professor G. Whipple
Dear Sir-

Yours of the 15th has been received for which and the enclosed draft you will please accept my thanks.

I am not at all surprised that your attention should be called to my case, indeed the many assertions made by Mr. and Mrs. Bibb, publicly and privately, of my being "nearly down [now]" with the certainty of a still more dishonorable position, and over all, the confident way in which they expressed themselves, made their dishonorable actions both in supplying Rev. C. C. Foote[1] with falsehoods concern[ing m]e, and in endeavoring to make my residence here an impossibility too apparent. I am surprised though that the Rev. C. C. Foote should accuse me of "outrageous slanders."

Had your letter reached me two weeks, before I would have answered in person and given that gentleman an opportunity of putting before you his evidence that I have slandered him or any person; but as the boats

5. Mary Ann Shadd Cary
Courtesy of Public Archives of Canada/C 29977

have stopped running, I can give you but an imperfect idea of the matter by letter.

I will proceed to take up Mr. F.'s charges in their order, and in the outset deny ever having written "slanderous letters to abolitionists concerning their society and agents.["] I have written truthful private letters to friends, to which his attention has been called, and which contained just what Rev. C. C. Foote knew to be true. I have not given my opinion merely, but have given facts; when it was a matter of opinion, only, I said nothing.

In "affirming that the ~~fugitises~~ fugitives do not need help" there is no slander, but a fact known to every one who knows much about them, and continually insisted upon by fugitives themselves. I will here call your attention to a large meeting held, in this place, by fugitives on this very subject:[2] it was one of a number of the same kind held in different parts of the province. "That they get but little of what is raised" is no slander, but is strictly true, whether it refers to begging for old and new clothes, money &c., or for the Refugees Home Society. Agents of the clothes and money, in most cases give out very little to destitute fugitives, and fugitives in this district, never heard of money being given to them—some have had it taken away. Henry Bibb denied ever having received "one shilling" for fugitives when talking to them, although dollars have been acknowledged through the *Voice* as having been sent for that purpose. It may be asked why publish and then deny the receipts?[3]

'Few take the *Voice* and its contents are not generally known' is the opinion of many when trying to account for that fact.

Mr. Foote knows that at a subsequent meeting of the R.H.S. to the one held Aug. 25th, every agent but himself was discharged for taking too large a percentage; he did not take quite so much as the others, and was therefore [word crossed out] retained. However, that he is solely absorbed in this money question, the points raised by him in the meeting of the 25 Aug., have no doubt. They were 1st: Twenty-five acres were ample, as many who contribute had not more land themselves, and were not willing to give for more acres to others than they possessed. 2nd: If the retension and other objectionable clauses contained in the Constitution were omitted, people would not give.[4]

Again: the name of Hon. Joshua R. Giddings should not be on the Ex. Committee, as many persons who gave, and would give, were opposed to Mr. Giddings and would withhold contributions were he appointed.[5]

I deny ever having said or written that the Society was "got up" for the benefit of the agents, and declare that to be gratuitous on the part of Mr. Foote, as is the assertion of my having sent seven pages of scandal after him. I believe a few of the officers are anti-slavery men and that many who contribute to support it are genuine abolitionists. I do not know that it was gotten up only for the benefit of the agents and officers, but I believ[e] it is for their benifit now only; I know that if the agents have not been benefitted, the black people have not. Let it be "got up" for whatever purpose, it is not at present answering any good one.

The average amount taken by agents has been [~~53~~] 63 percent; Mr. Foote knows that, and a school boy can tell how much has been collected when told that three thousand and a few hundred dolls., the amount they report make 37 percent of a number.

Theodore Holly, junior editor of the *Voice*, told me several months since that more than ten thousand dolls. had been received, and intimated that Henry Bibb was his authority: when told of the fraud, he also said that Horace Hallock and the other members in Detroit,[6] had free access to the funds, by which they carried on extensive business operations, and he was glad a colored man (H. Bibb) could have the same. He said Bibb was the originator of the [~~same~~] scheme—that Hallock and the rest "stol[e] his thunder," (Mr. B. and wife have told me the same,) and that it was gotten up on the principle that the whites owed the blacks, and would never be done paying them. Mr. George Cary a member of the Ex. Committee told me the agents had acted dishonestly, and made no exception—that he distrusted most of the officers—they were not anti-slavery men; but they insisted on buying lands in one locality, as there was the prospect of increased value from the vicinity of the Great Western Railroad.[7] He said that H. Bibb and himself held a Deed of the first two hundred acres purchased, and that they had not transferred it to the Society (though asked to do so) and never would, as from the movements of the men he was convinced they were not honest. The fact is (and I can bring the evidence,) the black men in the Society distrust the white men, and they in turn distrust them. A prominent member of the Ex. Committee (Mr. S. A. Baker)[8] told me I could assure fugitives, that H. Bibb would have nothing to do with the Deeds. C. C. Foote who with E. P. Benham[9] (one of the formerly discharged agents, but now reinstated) counselled the doing away of the Farmington organization,[10] as perfected by H. Bibb, thought "abler hands" might be at the helm. He will recollect of [visits] to a prominent gentleman in Canada, made by himself, to know if the purchasing of lands would not be made by him instead. I know that, then H. Bibb threatened to "blow up" the whole scheme.

That many thousands of dollars have been collected is evident, prominent members of the Ex. Committee say so—they also say that agents took 63 percent—they also say that if the blacks make "a time" about the scheme, they will keep the land; members of the Committee living in Detroit, said so to men who went to inquire about the land, & George Cary of Dawn repeated it in my hearing to fugitives here.

The prominent objections to the Society are: It is not needed at all as Government offers land cheaper and on better conditions: many families of fugitives own farms near the Refugees Home, and not one of whom gave as much per acre as the Society charges; it [arrays] the whites against the blacks, because of the superior political privileges sought to be given to ignorant men, by which in petty elections, black men may control, when the provisions made by Government affect all alike.

It keeps active the begging system, and thus diverts the gifts of benevolent persons from their proper course. By claiming to be a "Missionary Society," funds are diverted from efficient missionary organizations. It fosters exclusive institutions, making a line between black men even. Though one half is said to be applied to educational and religious purposes, fugitives only may be so benefitted, if it can be called a benefit in such a case. Thousands of dollars are collected on the plea that much is being done for fugitives, with them, when the Society's organ, the *Voice*, actually advertises lots as ready for settlers, so indifferent are the people about them; and of the few lots taken, of the thousand acres now held by the Society, but eight families live thereon, although funds have been accumulating for more than one year. Instead of the settlers being men of "good character," as at Mr. King's,[11] the testimony of respectable fugitives is that they come to [word crossed out] town whenever they can get a few shillings, spend them in the liquor stores for whiskey, and depend upon borrowing a little meal etc., from their neighbors. The Home is looked upon as a lounging place for worthless thriftless men, and is calle[d] "Bibbs plantation," "Nigger quarter" and other names indicative of their hatred of oppression. In calling attention to what he is pleased to call my slanders, Mr. Foote should have said what he knew of the hostility to the Society entertained by fugitives, at whose request I have written such parts of the private letters as touch on the ~~subject~~ Home, and also a letter for the *Liberator* which is in that paper of the 10th inst.—also a letter to the *Freeman*, not [word crossed out] out. The Editors asked questions after reading the minutes of the meeting held here, and fugitives hold the views expressed in the answer[s].[12]

It is no slander to say that Henry Bibb has hundreds of dollars belonging to fugitives—probably thousands would be nearer the truth. Henry Bibb is a dishonest man, and as such must be known to the world. To expose him is a duty which though painful, involving as it does loss of confidence, in colored men, who assume to leaders of their people must nevertheless be performed, and that event Rev. C. C. Foote has no power to prevent. True, he may partly [word crossed out] succeed in crushing a mere woman like myself, but I have the certainty that it will be done; and I will here say in passing, that it may be wisdom, but it is certainly not brave neither is it christian-like in Mr. Foote, because of his love of the dollar, to pounce upon one he thought easy to crush, and cautiously avoid allusion to able and weighty men, whom he knew to be actively opposed to his scheme, and who in reality spoiled his prospects in Philadelphia.[13]

C. C. Foote does not believe Mr. Bibb to be strictly honest, else why not let the purchasing of land remain in his hands? Not one of the Officers of the R.H.S. can give a good title to land excepting probably, Mr. Cary, he being the only British subject connected with the society—for according to the laws here aliens cannot hold real estate without a risk. Bibb who is not yet a subject, could have given as good a title as Mr. Foote or those who now give. No, sir Mr. Foote distrusts him, and seeks to get land purchasing out of his hands and succeeds too. Prominent abolitionists in Illinois say that Bibb's appeals for axes, hoes, seminaries, etc., after the passage of the fugitive Law, obtained for him several hundreds of dollars, and there are men here who gave to him for that purpose, and who were surprised to learn that fugitives had never heard of the money. Abolitionists in Indiana whose names I have, told fugitives now here, that Henry Bibb had money sent him by them and others for fugitives—that friends sent to him liberally for that purpose, and recommended to them to call on him for funds to start business. They further add their testimony to others of veracity, that he took up collections frequently West, for the fugitives, but he denies it. Within the present year, and during the time he has been asking for "donations" etc. to help him out of difficulty, he has built a house, bought a vessel, bought a house and lots ~~leased~~ on which he lives, leased another, and Mrs. Bibb has purchased a farm, and there are other business operations I can mention, besides the paper and being in receipt of several hundreds per annum for buildings and lots in Detroit. This is the man who is "making sacrifices" for the fugitives. The man who travels West with toes and elbows out, to create sympathy—who has a smile a prayer or billingsgate ready on the instant, and who at home, wraps up in purple and fine linen by warm fires, and sends from his door naked fugitives, on the plea that "abolitionists have left it discretionary with him to give or not." Fugitives have come to me to inquire what steps must be taken to secure money given to them by friends in his house and withheld by him, on the pretence that they would not know how to expend it. I have seen the miserably clad fugitive fresh from a southern plantation sent away empty, when in the cellar under our feet were cloth clothes rotting; and have helped un-head barrels of new and excellent clothing of all description.

Fifty persons, hereabouts, will testify to flat denial when needy, or abuse and rags. His chickens have been comfortably roosting on good fugitive clothes the entire season, a fact I called his attention to on the evening of Dec. 1[5] and which resulted in their removal from the poles the next day. Within a month I have heard a prominent Western abolitionist (Rev. A. St. Clair)[14] say in the [presence] of several others that it was well understood, by the leading men in Michigan, that Henry Bibb was not to be "trusted in money matters." He and wife are at one in this matter. Under advice from her, appeals can be made to abolitionists to help sustain an objectionable paper, on the pretence of doing much for the fugitives; sacrifices are reported—great pecuniary disadvantages—mortgages etc., when at the same time he and she both, buy and build and carry on more extensive operations by land and water, than any colored people within fifty miles on either side of the river. The "seven pages of scandal" spoken of, was the reply to an article in the *Pa. Freeman* written too by request of fugitives[15] and in which C. C. Foote's name does not occur; but which was received when Mr. Foote was in the city. I have a letter from Philadelphia dated Dec. 6th which ~~says~~ contains this passage: "He (Mr. Foote) bestowed any amount of praise on Bibb and wife—said they were held in universal 'respect in Canada to his certain knowledge;' but you were looked upon in a different light.["]

He also intimated that ambitious motives led "you to Canada, but finding yourself inadequate" to compete with [Mrs.] Bibb, it naturally excited "your ire. Such stuff and much more was let off" by Mr. Foote. I [th]ink I might with truth retort and charge Mr. Foote with slandering me. He has certainly done his best both in Pennsylvania and in New England to give me bad eminence, by saying what he knew was false, but Mrs. Bibb has said the same [just here] and also that your Society would not sustain me. I have no fear that the Refugees' Home Society will succeed—it must ultimately go down. God's approbation may not be looked for of a scheme whose advocates as a last resort, are driven to make a wreck of private character to sustain it.

In conclusion I can only say I have endeavored to do my duty here as your teacher, and have studiously sought to so act as not to bring contempt upon our Lord's cause. I have spoken out what I and others know of the Refugees' Home Society, and of Henry Bibb, but not until silence was no longer safe nor right. Foreseeing what must inevitably result should I remain here, I asked to leave this field last summer, though against the wishes of the people and not in accordance with my desire to serve them. I wished to avoid direct collision with the Bibbs. But you intimate that permanency was desirable, and I made no effort to provide for the future. In doing what I have done I repeat no one has been slandered; facts and statements made by persons of veracity have been given; and I trust the cause of truth has been subserved and the interests of fugitives promoted measurably.

May God and not man decide for you in this matter, that exact justice may be given to all parties. Yours very respectfully,

Mary A. Shadd

P. S. Several officers of the R.H.S. make no pretensions to being anti-slavery men—that is [especially] true of the purchasing committee, as told me by an officer; one cause of complaint against H. Hallock is, that he steadily refuses to give security for the funds entrusted to him.

M.A.S.

American Missionary Association Archives, Amistad Research Center, New Orleans, Louisiana. Published by permission.

1. Charles C. Foote (1811–?), a New York Presbyterian clergyman, was active in Liberty party politics during the 1840s. By mid-decade he had settled in Michigan, where he served a White Lake congregation until 1862. Foote was the principal agent for the Refugee Home Society during the early 1850s. In this capacity, he toured the northern United States, promoting the RHS, raising funds to buy land for blacks in Canada West, and collecting and distributing clothing and other supplies for Canadian fugitives. His well-publicized "begging" activities for the RHS and his patronizing attitude toward blacks made him a special target for criticism by Mary Ann Shadd Cary, Samuel R. Ward, and other black abolitionists. While in Michigan, Foote remained involved in politics. A Liberty party faction in New York state nominated him for vice-president in 1847; he attended the founding meeting of the Michigan Republican party in 1854. The American Missionary Association appointed Foote to a Livonia, Michigan, mission in 1860, although he continued to reside in Detroit. Richard Sewell, *Ballots for Freedom: Antislavery Politics in the United States, 1837–1860* (New York, N.Y., 1976), 119; *Lib*, 24 December 1852, 2 March 1860; *AM*, April, September 1854, September 1860; *PFW*, 24 March 1853, 18 April, 4 July 1857; *FDP*, 14 January 1853; *PF*, 6 January 1853; Carlesimo, "Refugee Home Society," 23, 100–110.

2. Cary refers to a meeting of local blacks held in the Windsor army barracks on 27 September 1851. Peter Poyntz chaired the meeting, which was called to inquire into fugitive slave grievances against the "*begging system*." Cary and Elisha Robinson acted as secretaries. Those in attendance adopted a series of resolutions by Thomas Jones, which expressed opposition to fund raising except for "gospel and educational purposes," criticized the Refugee Home Society and its agents for perpetuating the practice, and asked abolitionists to refrain from sending money and clothes for the fugitives in Canada West. There were only four dissenting votes—three of them were cast by Henry and Mary Bibb and James T. Holly. *Lib*, 15 October 1852.

3. Although Henry Bibb denied having personally received contributions for Canadian fugitives, many issues of the *Voice of the Fugitive* carried reports of the results of fund raising by agents of the Refugee Home Society. During 1852 these detailed reports frequently listed the names of individual donors, their place of residence, the date the contribution was made, and the amount contributed. Rev. C. C. Foote consistently collected the bulk of these contributions. From April through July, for example, the *Voice* reported that these agents had collected $1,283; Foote had collected $1,102 of that sum. The *Voice* stopped publishing these reports in August. *VF*, 26 February, 12, 26 March, 9, 23 April, 21 May, 13 August, 24 September 1851, 8, 22 April, 6, 20 May, 3, 17 June, 1, 29 July 1852.

4. The 25 August 1852 meeting referred to was held in Detroit's First Presbyterian Church for the purpose of revising the Refugee Home Society's constitution and bylaws. It was attended by Henry Bibb, Horace Hallock, C. C. Foote, and other leading members of the society. Samuel Ringgold Ward, Mary Ann

Shadd Cary, Rev. S. A. Baker, and other opponents of the society's begging practices also attended. Several revisions in the RHS constitution addressed land questions. These were "the retension and other objectionable clauses" referred to by Cary. Article 5 of the constitution granted each family accepted into the society five additional acres of land once they had purchased an initial twenty acres in nine annual installments. Only when the land purchase was completed and all necessary improvements made would the title be transferred to the family. The RHS retained possession of land not paid for in the designated time or lacking the proper improvements. Article 15 restricted RHS members from selling or transferring title on their land for a period of fifteen years; even after that, owners could only sell or transfer land to family members. In all other cases, ownership of the land automatically reverted to the RHS. At a second session, held within the two weeks following the first meeting, Foote and Rev. A. N. McConoughey were designated the RHS's sole authorized fund-raising agents. A 9 September 1852 notice in the *Voice of the Fugitive* noted that no other agents but Foote and McConoughey were authorized to accept contributions to the RHS without the written permission of six members of the executive committee. Bearden and Butler, *Shadd*, 102–3, 105, 119; Carlesimo, "Refugee Home Society," 183–84; *VF*, 9 September 1852.

5. Joshua Reed Giddings (1795–1864) was suggested as a potential member of the Executive Committee of the Refugee Home Society. The committee rejected Giddings in early 1853 from fear that his political antislavery position might alienate potential donors. Giddings was born in Bradford County, Pennsylvania, and for twenty years (1838–58) represented Ohio as a militant antislavery Congressman, being elected successively as a Whig, a Free Soiler, and a Republican. He opposed the spread of slavery, fought for preservation of the Union, and proposed that presidential power be used to free the slaves in event of war. In 1861 Lincoln appointed him consul general to Canada, a post Giddings held until his death. *DAB*, 7:260–61; Carlesimo, "Refugee Home Society," 45.

6. Cary evidently refers to officers and members of the executive committee of the Refugee Home Society who resided in Michigan towns. Detroit residents included Horace Hallock, J. Nathan Stone, Samuel Zug, Francis Raymond, Silas M. Holmes, Edward C. Walker, S. A. Baker, and H. D. Kitchell. Abraham L. Power, Nathan Power, and Elias P. Benham of Farmington, Charles C. Foote of Commerce, and Robert Garner of White Lake were also active in the society. Horace Hallock (1807–?), although originally from New York, settled in Detroit in 1831 and established a dry-goods business. There he became active in the local temperance movement, the Presbyterian church, and served as treasurer of the Michigan Anti-Slavery Society. Hallock worked closely with Laura Haviland in assisting fugitive slaves escaping through Michigan to Canada West. As treasurer of the Refugee Home Society during the 1850s, he was at the center of many controversies created by that organization. During the 1860s, Hallock was a vice-president of the American Missionary Association. *VF*, 6 April, 9 September 1852; Carlesimo, "Refugee Home Society," 21–25; United States Census, 1850.

7. The London and Gore Railroad was chartered in 1834 and rechartered in 1845 as the Great Western under President Allan McNab. By 1855 the railroad spanned southern Ontario, linking Windsor, Sarnia, and Hamilton with the

Niagara River. The Great Western merged with the Grand Trunk Railroad in 1882. G. P. de T. Glazebrook, *A History of Transportation in Canada* (Toronto, 1938), 165–67, 186–87, 289–90, 294.

8. S. A. Baker was a Detroit-area Methodist clergyman and editor of the *Wesleyan Evangelist.* When the Refugee Home Society reorganized in 1852, Baker was named to a newly formed, nine-member executive committee that supposedly exercised complete control over the society's finances. Baker presided over the Michigan conference of the Methodist church during 1854–55. *VF*, 9 September, 21 October 1852; *PFW*, 24 March 1853; Carlesimo, "Refugee Home Society," 22.

9. Elias P. Benham, a Farmington, Michigan, resident, served as corresponding secretary and fund-raising agent for the Refugee Home Society during the early 1850s. He also acted as a subscription agent for the *Voice of the Fugitive* and participated in emergency relief efforts among black refugees in Canada West. *VF*, 1 February, 1, 18 June, 17 August 1851, 29 January 1852.

10. The Farmington organization, as referred to by Cary, is another term for the Refugee Home Society during its developmental period.

11. Cary refers to the Elgin settlement founded by William King (1812–1895) in southwestern Canada West. King, an Irishman educated at Glasgow University, immigrated to the United States in 1833 and became headmaster of a Louisiana academy. Through marriage to a planter's daughter, he acquired several slaves. King returned to Scotland in 1844; after being ordained into the Presbyterian clergy, he left to do missionary work in Canada West. In 1849 he founded the Buxton Mission under the auspices of the Toronto Presbyterian Synod. About that time, King manumitted his Louisiana slaves and settled them near the mission. This became the nucleus of the Elgin settlement, a model black agricultural community named for Lord Elgin, the governor-general of the Canadas. The Elgin Association, a joint-stock company, directed the settlement's financial and legal affairs, purchased government land, and resold it to the settlers in fifty-acre parcels. Local opposition stimulated by racist politician Edwin Larwill threatened the venture, but, with the support of other prominent local residents, King overcame white resistance. Under his close supervision, the Elgin experiment became the most successful planned black settlement in the province. King carefully screened potential settlers to ascertain their character, and he encouraged temperance, industriousness, and high moral standards. Regulations at the settlement required uniform property improvements and minimum housing standards. Landowners were bound by an agreement restricting transfer of deeds. But despite King's paternalistic rule, black Elgin residents regulated their own daily lives. By 1861 three hundred families resided at the ten-thousand-acre Elgin settlement. In addition to agriculture, residents plied various trades and established a potash and pearl ash factory and a sawmill. The settlement boasted two hotels, a general store, and a post office. King's mission sponsored a church and a common school. Even with inadequate facilities and meager financial support, the school thrived and attracted white students from the surrounding area. By the mid-1850s, Elgin supported three integrated schools with a total enrollment of nearly 250. Settlers founded Baptist, Methodist, and Roman Catholic congregations. Elgin flourished until the Civil War, but then a decline in the number of black settlers and the growth of the local white population ended the experiment. The Elgin Associa-

tion issued its last report in 1873. King continued his missionary work until 1880, then retired to Chatham. His remarkable life provided the model for the fictional character Edward Clayton in Harriet Stowe's *Dred, a Tale of the Dismal Swamp* (1856). Pease and Pease, *Black Utopia*, 84–108; Winks, *Blacks in Canada*, 208–18; Victor Ullman, *Look to the North Star: A Life of William King* (Boston, Mass., 1969), 146–62, 166–67; *MDCB*, 413.

12. In late 1852, Cary wrote two letters to the *Liberator* and *Pennsylvania Freeman* that criticized the Refugee Home Society. One of these—signed "The Officers of the Windsor Meeting"—was published in the 10 December issue of the *Liberator*. In the 20 January 1853 issue of the *Freeman*, the editors printed an extract of a letter from "a trustworthy colored woman in Canada" (probably Cary) to a Philadelphia friend. But the author was not identified, and the complete text was never published. *Lib*, 10 December 1852; *PF*, 6, 20 January 1853.

13. Rev. Charles C. Foote arrived in Philadelphia in late 1852 to raise funds for the Refugee Home Society. But he found that letters by Cary and Samuel R. Ward had preceded him and had raised doubts in the minds of potential donors. When he visited the local antislavery office, he was advised "to go to the outsiders" rather than solicit among abolitionists. Bearden and Butler, *Shadd*, 121; *PF*, 20 January 1853.

14. Alanson St. Clair (1804–1877), a Massachusetts Congregationalist minister, became an agent for the American Anti-Slavery Society in 1839 but soon broke with the Garrisonians over political and religious issues. After serving briefly as editor of the New Hampshire *People's Advocate*, he entered Liberty party politics in the western states. In 1848 he founded and edited the abolitionist *Iowa Freeman* in Fort Madison. Merrill and Ruchames, *Letters of William Lloyd Garrison*, 3:25–26, 210n, 308–10, 508–9; Garrison and Garrison, *William Lloyd Garrison*, 2:61; Theodore Clark Smith, *The Liberty and Free Soil Parties in the Northwest* (New York, N.Y., 1897), 95, 137, 321.

15. The "seven pages of scandal" to which Cary refers is undoubtedly her late 1852 letter to the *Pennsylvania Freeman*. It was never fully published, but Foote must have read it or been told of its existence when he visited the *Freeman*'s offices.

40.
Report by Samuel Ringgold Ward
24 March 1853

A shared belief in human progress animated the antebellum reform movement, particularly abolitionism. Radical abolitionists contradicted proslavery theorists by insisting that blacks were not inferior but merely degraded by slavery and prejudice and lacked only the opportunities of an egalitarian society to demonstrate their fitness for freedom. Many considered black success or failure in Canada West to be a test of that theory. Recognizing that fact, black abolitionists regularly published and circulated positive reports about black life there. During the winter of 1853, Samuel R. Ward completed a six-week, 565-mile tour through southwestern Canada West for the Anti-Slavery Society of Canada. His report of the tour, which appeared in the *Provincial Freeman*, combined sociology, folksy news, and antislavery rhetoric in an explanation of the redemptive value of Canada West. He concluded: "Our tour satisfied us abundantly that the colored people of Canada are progressing more rapidly than our people in the States—that the liberty enjoyed here makes different men of those once crushed and dispirited in the land of chains." Pemberton, "The Anti-Slavery Society of Canada," 55; *PFW*, 24 March 1853 [8:0175].

A Recent Tour

On the 11th of January last we started upon a tour of some six weeks time, and some 565 miles travel, in the western and frontier districts.

At Hamilton, on the 11th of January, we found a protracted meeting in progress, under the charge of Elders Hawkins and Brown, aided by Elder Garrett. This was in the colored Baptist Church.[1] Arriving at St. Catharines on the 12th, we were a little curious, not to say anxious, to see for ourself what is the state of negro hate in that town. We stopped at the St. Catharines House,[2] and found that the servants, landlord, and all others, were both polite and kind.

At the invitation of the Rev. Hiram Wilson, whose guest we had the pleasure to be, we attended a temperance meeting, addressed by the eloquent Elder Ryerson, of the Baptist Church.[3] After Mr. R. had finished his very able discourse, we were invited to say a few words, which we consented to do, though our awkwardness, in contrast with our predecessor, must have been apparent to all.

On the 13th, Brother Wilson introduced us to Hon. Mr. H. Meritt,[4] His Worship the Mayor, Mr. Adams,[5] of the Custom House, and several other gentlemen of prominence. We lectured, that evening, in the Town

Hall,[6] to a large audience, who seemed to evince a good degree of interest in our cause, enough, at any rate, to request us, by a unanimous vote, to speak again the next evening. The meeting of the 14th was also a large one, and, at the close, a vote of thanks was offered us by Rev. Mr. Ryerson, and carried unanimously. In company with our excellent friend, Wilson, we went to Niagara on the 15th, where, through the activity of William Barr, Sen., Esq., a large assemblage was ready to hear us at the appointed hour. Mr. Barr occupied the chair with great ability. A most encouraging meeting was that at Niagara. Returning the same night to St. Catharines, we accepted the invitation of Rev. Mr. Cooke, of the American Presbyterian Church, to preach for him. We spoke, the same day, in the two colored churches, Rev. Mr. Helmseley's[7] and the Baptist.

We must confess that we found things better in St. Catharines than we had feared. The prejudice against our people, was not so strong, so prevalent nor so unprovoked as we had thought, from what we had heard. Personally, we were treated by persons of all classes as well as we ever were, anywhere. Our people in St. Catharines are not the poorest in the town, by a good deal. Many of them own little houses and lots, and enjoy a comfortable maintenance. Mr. J. W. Lindsey[8] and Mr. James Harris live as comfortably as any one needs to live. Each of them has a good team, and they are making as rapid progress, in worldly weal, as the majority of their white fellow-subjects. As much may be said of Mr. J. W. Taylor[9] and others, on whom we did not have time to call. The "Negro Village," of which so much has been said, we expected to find in a swamp or a mud-hole. But the settlement, if such it may be called, is on a street running parallel with the main street, and within one hundred rods of it. The site is good, the property valuable, the part of the town respectable, and whites live in the most immediate vicinity of it. Some foolish actions of our people have given occasion for some prejudice, and there are too many who would rather cringe than contend for what law and right entitle them to. It is true too, that there are some natives of the U.S. there, who act the part of fools and knaves towards our people. Having aided in trampling negroes under foot at home, they seek to engraft their pro-slavery negro hate upon British stock. It is also true, that they now and then find a Canadian soft sapling that will bear innoculation; but we are quite convinced that when our people shall have done all they ought to do, in St. Catharines, towards their own elevation, the whites will be right enough. We had a most tedious, comfortless journey from St. Catharines to London. Our business at the latter place was, to attend the anniversary of the London Anti-Slavery Society.[10] But all the anniversaries had been postponed a week later than we had supposed, and that week we must wait. In the meantime we held meetings in the vicinity.

The London anniversaries embraced the Bible, Tract, Sabbath Schools,

Temperance, and Anti-Slavery Societies. How unlike Yankeedom! Besides, the same gentlemen who are officers of the other benevolent societies, are officers of this. Again, how unlike Yankeedom. Then again, the Anti-Slavery Anniversary was the most numerously attended, and the best patronized of all the anniversaries.[11] Captain Gardner, of the Royal Artillery[12] was on the platform, and he seconded one of the resolutions. The Captain sat side by side with A. B. Jones, Esq.,[13] a gentleman as black as ourself. It did look like an European meeting, that anniversary.

At the same meeting it was announced, that William Horton, Esq.,[14] would address a meeting the following Monday evening, and that, in the afternoon of that day, the agent of the Canadian Anti-Slavery Society would address a meeting of ladies, preparatory to the formation of a Female Anti-Slavery Society.[15] Both meetings were largely attended, and Mr. Horton's debut was most triumphant. A most valuable accession to our cause is Mr. H.

On the evening of Feb. 1st, we went to Soho, in company with my excellent host and hostess, Mr. and Mrs. A. B. Jones and a few other friends. The meeting was one of the best country meetings we ever attended. Rev. Mr. Turner[16] was in the chair. The [black] people in Soho are doing as well as the [farmers] of Middlesex generally.

In London the blacks are as well off as their neighbors. A. B. Jones could, at any time, retire from business, live in the style of an amateur farmer, and [his] property in town would yield an income [that] would support his family. A. T. Jones is progressing as fast as any other young druggist in that town.[17] Nelson Moss is doing as good a business, as a cordwainer,[18] as any man need do. Moses B. Smith[19] and Henry Garrett,[20] get on, as bakers, equally as well as others who follow the same business. Energy and enterprize are all that our people need in London to enrich themselves. Those now doing well are the artificers of their own fortunes, so might others be if they choose. We know of no town where a black mechanic or artizan could do better than in London. He would find some of the meaner sort of whites there, but they are as near akin to nobody as you can imagine. Folks who are folks, in London, are as free from negro hate as any people we ever saw.

We went from London, at the invitation of the Rev. Mr. Dawson,[21] to Chatham, thence to Buxton. In these two places our people are making rapid progress. In Chatham there is a constant increase of the numbers of our people, and among them are some of the best mechanics and artizans in the county of Kent. J. M. Jones stands head and shoulders above any gun-smith west of London.[22] Thomas Bell, as a builder;[23] J. C. Brown, as a mason;[24] R. Charrily, as a cordwainer;[25] W. Moore, as a chandler; Mr. Smith, as a blacksmith,[26] need fear comparison nor competition with any of the same crafts in that part of the Province. Then we see more buildings, new ones, too, than we saw last September, owned by black men. We asked one old man, who ran away from slavery a few years since, what he could get for his property? He said he had been offered £ 300; he confessed that it cost him but £ 30. The advance in the price of property was no greater in that, than in several other instances, in the same town. We spoke twice in Chatham, and most nobly did the brave blacks of Chatham stand by the cause.

Buxton, in more points than one, is the model settlement,[27] not only of the colored people, but of Canada. There are 120 families there, and almost every family is settled on land in their own possession. In clearing, building and improving, most commendable progress is being made by them. Generally they came in poor—they are making their way to independence with zeal and perseverence. They beg no old clothes from the States, they receive none begged by others professedly for Canadians. They lately held a bazaar to raise money to aid their own poor. They have been there but three years, and they are doing all that any people could do, in the same time. But the efforts of those settlers to educate themselves and their children are most praiseworthy. In the day-school you find both children and adults, in some instances, parents and children, earnestly intent upon the acquisition of knowledge. The evening school is attended by parties who walk miles through the forest by torch-light, but they are determined; they have counted the cost, and they will rest nothing short of what they desire. In morals the settlement has no superior. There is not a drunkard in the settlement, and, if any habitual drinking, they keep it to themselves. No person sells—no person is allowed to sell—the accursed stuff. The Maine Law is in full force in Buxton.[28] We spoke twice in Buxton, preaching, on Sunday, for Rev. Mr. King, and speaking in a public meeting, Mr. West[29] in the chair. The day is not far distant when that settlement will contain 1000 inhabitants, and when the land for which they pay 12s. 6d. per acre, will be worth £ 6 per acre.

But for our illness we should have gone to Dresden, but must defer our visit thither till some future day. Our tour satisfied us abundantly that the colored people of Canada are progressing more rapidly than our people in the States—that the liberty enjoyed here makes different men of those once crushed and dispirited in the land of chains—that along with the other poor classes who come here, and improve themselves in wealth and status, the black people will also arise, in some cases, very rapidly, but generally slowly, though surely—that the day is not far distant when we shall put to shame the selfish, systematic charity seekers who go to the States, *and some of them to the South*, to beg, partly for fugitives, but chiefly for their own pockets—that more money has been begged, professedly in behalf of Canadian blacks, than said blacks ever did, or ever will receive, by a thousand fold—that unless persons going to the States, begging for us, are the accredited agents of some duly organized society, with honest, unselfish men at its head, our friends should hold them at arm's length—that what the recently arrived refugee most needs, is not land-buying societies, not old clothes, not any substitute for labor, but stimulation to *self-development.*

Provincial Freeman (Windsor, Canada West), 24 March 1853.

1. The meeting to which Ward refers took place in Hamilton's Coloured Baptist Church and was directed by Rev. A. Brown, pastor of the congregation during the 1850s. He was assisted by Rev. Horace H. Hawkins, a Chatham clergyman, and Henry Garrett, a local lay preacher. The congregation was founded by Washington Christian during the late 1830s, and by 1848 it had joined the Amherstburg Baptist Association. About forty members belonged to the church until 1860, when it experienced rapid growth. Hill, *Freedom-Seekers*, 145; Simpson, "Negroes in Ontario to 1870," 416, 849–50.

2. The St. Catharines House was a hotel located on Ontario Street in St. Catharines. Guillet, *Pioneer Inns and Taverns*, 4:8–9.

3. J. E. Ryerson was a Baptist clergyman of St. Catharines. Assessment Roll, St. Catharines, 1854.

4. William Hamilton Merritt (1793–1862) was an American-born merchant and politician of St. Catharines, Canada West. Merritt was a major promoter of Canadian transportation and Canadian-American trade reciprocity who advanced his ideas through Canadian politics, particularly through long service in the Canadian legislature, the executive council, and as chief commissioner for public works during the early 1850s. Merritt was a member of the Refugee Slaves' Friends Society, which aided black fugitives in Canada during the 1850s. *DCB*, 9:544–48.

5. Elias Smith Adams (1800–?) was the first mayor of St. Catharines, Canada West. Like several of his colleagues at the local customhouse, Adams was a founder of the interracial Refugee Slaves' Friends Society in St. Catharines in 1852 and played an active role in the society's efforts to assist American fugitive slaves. *DCB*, 11:559; *VF*, 6 May 1852 [7:0571]; Winks, *Blacks in Canada*, 258; Assessment Roll, St. Catharines, 1854.

6. In 1853 the St. Catharines Town Hall was located on the corner of King and St. James streets. John N. Jackson, *St. Catharines, Ontario: Its Early Years* (Belleville, Ontario, 1976), 318.

7. Alexander Helmsley (ca. 1795–1855) was born a slave in Queen Anne County, Maryland. At age twenty-three, he escaped to New Jersey. He was arrested there in 1836 and faced extradition until freed by a ruling of the New Jersey Supreme Court. Fearing further threats from slave catchers, Helmsley settled himself, his wife, and three children in St. Catharines, Canada West. He pastored AME congregations in the province until 1854. Helmsley represented St. Catharines at the Drummondville Convention (1847). Drew, *North-Side View of Slavery*, 32–40; Payne, *History of the AME Church*, 359–60; *Convention of the Colored Population*, 5.

8. John W. Lindsay (ca. 1810–?) was born to free black parents in Washington, D.C. As a child, he was kidnapped, taken to western Tennessee, and sold into slavery. About 1835 he escaped to Pennsylvania, where he passed for white and worked as a blacksmith. Lindsey eventually settled in St. Catharines and took an

active role in the local black community. He represented St. Catharines blacks at the Drummondville Convention (1847). He served as an officer of the local AME church, helped lead a regional movement to abolish separate schools, and participated in fugitive relief efforts. During the mid-1850s, he was selected to the Dawn Investigating Committee, a group organized by local blacks to resolve financial and managerial controversies at the Dawn settlement. Lindsey later supported his family by farming, teaching, and operating "a small beer business." John W. Blassingame, *Slave Testimony* (Baton Rouge, La., 1977), 396–405; Simpson, "Negroes in Ontario to 1870," 828; Drew, *North-Side View of Slavery*, 77–78; *PFW*, 29 August, 15 September, 3 November 1855, 20 May 1856; *VF*, 6 May 1852; *Convention of the Coloured Population*, 5.

9. J. Williamson Taylor, a black resident of St. Catharines, was a local subscription agent for the *Provincial Freeman* and a deacon of the Zion Baptist Church during the 1850s. He helped organize the Amherstburg Convention (1853). *PFW*, 24 March 1853, 15 April 1854; *VF*, 6 May 1852.

10. The London Anti-Slavery Society, an affiliate of the Anti-Slavery Society of Canada, was founded in September 1852 following a visit to London by ASC agent Samuel R. Ward. The primary figure behind the society's organization was William McClure, a Methodist clergyman and secretary of the ACS. McClure was elected president of the London organization, and Rev. Robert Boyd, a Baptist minister, became its secretary-treasurer. Among the society's seven directors were two other local clergymen, Rev. William F. Clark and Rev. John Scott, and A. B. Jones, a London black. The society's major accomplishments included opening a fugitive slave chapel in London and coordinating local fugitive slave relief efforts. The London Anti-Slavery Society apparently lapsed into inactivity following McClure's transfer to a Hamilton parish in 1854. Pemberton, "Anti-Slavery Society of Canada," 93; Winks, *Blacks in Canada*, 258; Landon, "Fugitive Slaves in London," 455.

11. The London, Canada West, anniversaries were similar to the annual gatherings of American benevolent and reform societies, but on a smaller scale. Between the 1830s and 1870, major American anniversary weeks were held by such societies in both New York City and Boston during May of each year. Anniversaries brought together health reformers, evangelicals, pacifists, school and prison reformers, abolitionists, and colonizationists, and provided organizations with an opportunity "to compare notes, hold meetings, and raise money." Although these diverse societies initially shared a common leadership, growing conflict between immediatist abolitionists, colonizationists, and evangelicals ended this practice by the 1840s. As Ward notes, the societies represented at the London anniversaries retained their common leadership. Ripley et al., *The Black Abolitionist Papers*, 96.

12. Captain Gardner apparently was an officer of the Twenty-third Royal Welsh Fusiliers, an artillery unit garrisoned at London from 1843 through 1845 and 1849 through 1853. Campbell, *Pioneer Days in London*, 115.

13. A. Beckford Jones (1803–?), a Kentucky slave, purchased his freedom at the age of thirty. He settled in London, Canada West, established a grocery business in the early 1840s, and eventually acquired substantial property holdings. Jones's Horatio Alger experience was frequently cited by abolitionists as an example of what blacks could achieve in the Canadian provinces. The most promi-

nent figure in London's black community during the 1840s and 1850s, he led a black protest against local school segregation and financed the construction of London's black Second Baptist Church. He actively participated in the Canadian antislavery movement during the early 1850s, serving as one of three black vice-presidents of the Anti-Slavery Society of Canada and as a director of the London Anti-Slavery Society, a local ASC affiliate. He was also a leading member of the Canadian Anti-Slavery Baptist Association. Jones supported the editorial position of the *Provincial Freeman*, particularly on the begging question. He became one of the paper's principal patrons, buying advertising space in nearly every issue, serving as a local subscription agent, contributing copy, and helping to lead the Provincial Union Association—a black self-help organization that generated financial support for the *Freeman*. Despite his advocacy of black assimilation into Anglo-Canadian society, Jones paid considerable attention to the work of the organized black settlements in Canada West. He was an Elgin Association stockholder, and during the mid-1850s, he became involved in black efforts to reassert control over the British-American Institute property at the Dawn settlement. Drew, *North-Side View of Slavery*, 149–52; Winks, *Blacks in Canada*, 255; *VF*, 13 August 1851, 21 October 1852 [7:0068]; *PFW*, 24 March 1853, 25 March, 29 July, 19 August 1854 [8:0175, 0949]; A. Beckford Jones et al., Memorial of the Colored Inhabitants of London and Wilberforce, Canada West, 10 October 1842, Fred Landon Papers, CaOLU [4:0475].

14. William Horton, a London attorney, entered the profession in 1839 and had an active and respected legal practice in the city for several decades. Horton provided legal counsel to blacks in Canada West in several cases opposing separate schools during the 1850s. Campbell, *Pioneer Days in London*, 78–79; Simpson, "Negroes in Ontario to 1870," 642, 780–81.

15. The London Female Anti-Slavery Society was an auxiliary of the London Anti-Slavery Society and a local female affiliate of the Anti-Slavery Society of Canada.

16. Daniel Turner (1805–1860) was born in Baltimore. A sailor and caulker turned evangelist, he joined the Wilberforce settlement in the early 1830s and was prominently involved in the development of a black Baptist congregation there. Wilberforce's First Baptist Church was built on a section of Turner's farm. After Benjamin Paul's death in 1836, Turner pastored the congregation until the mid-1840s. During the 1840s, he also did itinerant preaching among the developing black communities throughout southwestern Canada West. Turner's later years were spent as minister of the Second Baptist Church at London, Canada West. Landon, "History of Wilberforce Refugee Colony," 42; Simpson, "Negroes in Ontario to 1870," 354, 366, 372.

17. Alfred T. Jones (1810–?), a Kentucky slave, escaped to Upper Canada in 1833 after an unsuccessful attempt to purchase his freedom. He lived briefly in St. Catharines, then resettled in London and established a successful pharmacy. By the mid-1850s, he had accumulated property valued at $45,000. Like his older brother, A. Beckford Jones, he became a prominent member of London's black community. He helped organize black protests against local school segregation efforts in the early 1840s and again in 1860. Winks, *Blacks in Canada*, 371; Drew, *North-Side View of Slavery*, 152–53; *PFW*, 24 March 1853 [8:0175]; A. Beckford Jones et al., Memorial of the Colored Inhabitants of London and

Wilberforce, Canada West, 10 October 1842, Fred Landon Papers, CaOLU [4:0475].

18. Nelson Moss (1810–?), a Virginia slave, escaped to Pennsylvania in 1848. Following the passage of the Fugitive Slave Law of 1850, he settled in London, Canada West, and established "a boot and shoe business." Drew, *North-Side View of Slavery*, 153–54.

19. Moses B. Smith appears on subscription lists for the *Voice of the Fugitive*. *VF*, 15 July 1852.

20. Henry Garrett, a former Virginia slave, evidently settled in Brantford, Canada West, during the 1840s. By the early 1850s, he was active in black affairs in the province as a charter member of the Elgin Association and a signer of the call for the black North American Convention, which was held in Toronto in 1851. About 1852 Garrett moved to London, Canada West, where he operated a bakery and became a self-styled Baptist preacher. He gained notoriety in 1855 when he advocated a plan to raise funds for the compensated emancipation of slaves in the South. During the fall of that year, Garrett invested considerable energy in promoting his scheme, publishing a circular describing it, and speaking to audiences in Windsor, Chatham, and Toronto. But the plan was poorly received by black Canadians. Garrett contemplated going to England (and possibly the continent) to promote his compensated emancipation idea and to "shake the Queen's hand," but he evidently changed his mind. He soon disappeared from public prominence. *PFW*, 24 March 1853, 29 August, 22 September, 6 October, 1, 8 December 1855 [8:0172, 9:0808, 0837–38, 0864, 0866, 0970, 0976, 0978]; *VF*, 13 August 1851 [7:0054]; *Fifth Report of Elgin Association*, 15; Simpson, "Negroes in Ontario to 1870," 757; Murray, "Canada and Anglo-American Anti-Slavery Movement," 278.

21. Henry W. Dawson arrived in Canada West in the early 1840s. He was ordained a deacon in the African Methodist Episcopal church in 1851 and was assigned to congregations in the Hamilton and Chatham districts. Later in the decade, he moved to London, where he taught Sunday school and worked for the local Anglican mission of the Colonial Church and School Society. About 1859, unable to find further employment in London, Dawson left Canada West and settled in Victoria, Vancouver Island. A. Beckford Jones et al., Memorial of the Colored Inhabitants of London and Wilberforce, Canada West, 10 October 1842, Fred Landon Papers, CaOLU; *VF*, 12, 26 August 1852; *PFW*, 23 February 1856; *PA*, 2 May 1863; Simpson, "Negroes in Ontario to 1870," 772; Payne, *History of the AME Church*, 257–59.

22. James M. Jones (1811–?) was a black gunsmith in Chatham. He was born in the United States. Census of Canada, 1861.

23. Thomas Bell (1812–?), an American-born mulatto, worked as a plasterer in Chatham. He was a member of the Methodist church. Census of Canada, 1861.

24. Ward refers to James C. Brown.

25. Ward probably refers to a member of the Charity (also spelled Charrity) family of Chatham. James Henry Charity (1822–?), a bootmaker, was born in Virginia but settled in Canada West by 1850. He built and leased the brick building on King Street in Chatham that housed the *Provincial Freeman* offices and other black-owned businesses. He also opened a store in Dresden and owned a commercial boat, the *Industry of Detroit*. His Maryland-born wife, Rebecca

(1829–?), apparently assisted him with the family enterprise. They immigrated to Haiti in January 1862. Cornelius H. Charity (1828–?), James's brother, operated his own bootmaking business in Chatham, where he was an active member of the First Colored Baptist Church. His wife, Martha (1827–?), was born in Virginia and worked as a shoebinder. They later settled in Victoria, Vancouver Island. In her later years, Martha resided in Oakland, California. Hill, *Freedom-Seekers*, 171; *PFW*, 3 November 1855, 17 May [10:0158], 26 July 1856, 8 August 1857; *PP*, 8 May 1862; James W. Pilton, "Negro Settlement in British Columbia, 1858–1871" (M.A. thesis, University of British Columbia, 1951), 207; Abajian, *Blacks in Selected Newspapers*, 1:383; Census of Canada, 1861.

26. Several blacksmiths named Smith lived in the black community at Chatham during the early 1850s. Ward probably refers to George Smith (1819–?) or Andrew Smith (1824–?). Little is known about George Smith, who settled in Canada West in 1841. Andrew Smith was originally a blacksmith but by 1855 operated a grocery in Chatham. He also participated in several local black organizations; he was a founding member and vice-president of the Provincial Union Association, attended the Amherstburg Convention (1853), and chaired the Dawn Investigating Committee—which inquired into charges of mismanagement at the Dawn settlement—in 1857. Census of Canada, 1851; *PFW*, 19 August 1854 [9:0018], 29 August 1855, 24 January, 28 February 1857; *Minutes of Convention in Amherstburg*, 2–3.

27. Ward refers to the Elgin settlement at Buxton.

28. The Maine Liquor Law (1851) prohibited the sale and manufacture of alcohol except by licensed agents for medical and industrial use. As the first state prohibition law, it provided a model for temperance advocates nationwide. Eleven states enacted similar laws between 1851 and 1855. The Elgin settlement followed the Maine example. Jack Kobler, *Ardent Spirits* (New York, N.Y., 1973), 76–91.

29. Alfred H. West, a black resident of Buxton, Canada West, operated a temperance hotel and helped organize the First Baptist Church of Buxton. Hill, *Freedom-Seekers*, 84; *PFW*, 10 January 1857.

41.
Founding the *Provincial Freeman*

Editorial by Samuel Ringgold Ward
24 March 1853

Resolutions by a Meeting of Sandwich Blacks
Sandwich, Canada West
26 March 1853

The *Provincial Freeman* published its first issue on 24 March 1853. "Introductory," an editorial written by nominal editor Samuel Ringgold Ward for the inaugural issue, aligned the paper "on the side of the great principles of British Progress" and introduced readers to the paper's objectives. The *Freeman* advocated antislavery, temperance, and black self-reliance, opposed separate black schools, churches, and settlements, and urged blacks to assimilate into Anglo-Canadian society. Ward was assisted by publication agent Mary Ann Shadd Cary and a committee of publication composed of seven notable Canadian blacks. Under their guidance, the *Freeman*, which began regular weekly publication in Toronto on 25 March 1854, became a voice for black Canadians. Henry Bibb and James T. Holly hastily organized a protest meeting in response to the *Freeman*'s first issue. The 26 March gathering defended the Refugee Home Society, endorsed Bibb's *Voice of the Fugitive*, argued that there was no need for a rival black newspaper in Canada West, and condemned the factionalism generated by Samuel Ringgold Ward and his allies. In an implicit acknowledgment of Ward's criticisms of the RHS, the Sandwich meeting addressed the "begging" issue by denying that there was urgent need for fugitive relief and instead emphasized the importance of providing homesteads and education for the fugitive slaves in the province. Frederick Douglass, an opponent of emigration, carried the Sandwich resolutions in his newspaper. He lamented the discord among black Canadians, chided Bibb for being oversensitive to the appearance of the *Freeman*, and applauded Ward's endeavor to establish a new black newspaper in Canada West. The *Freeman* was Ward's second editing venture; he had earlier published the *Impartial Citizen* (1849–51) in Syracuse and Boston but was forced to suspend publication and declare bankruptcy. Hill, *Freedom-Seekers*, 187–89; *PFW*, 24 March 1853, 25 March 1854; Burke, "*Impartial Citizen*," 759–60; *FDP*, 8 April 1853 [8:0202].

INTRODUCTORY

IT was my intention not to connect my name with the Press ever hereafter. A very severe and painful experience had induced me to this conclusion. But the earnest solicitations of numerous friends, and the consideration of the very great necessity of such a paper, led me to consent to edit a paper for one year, without fee or reward, as my humble share in the promotion of an object, in which I am unable to invest a single penny. It is to be hoped, that after a year shall have expired, the friends of the paper, and the committee of publication will be able to find some person much more competent than myself, to discharge the duties I now reluctantly assume.

The *Provincial Freeman* will be devoted to the elevation of the Colored People; and in seeking to effect this object, it will advocate the cause of TEMPERANCE, in the strictest and most radical acceptation of that term. Partly, because such are the well-known sentiments of its Editor,[1] and, partly, because there is no such thing as the elevation of any people without it. For like reasons, the *Freeman* must be a straightforward, outspoken ANTI-SLAVERY PAPER. Its voice shall ever be heard in denunciation of the chattelizing of human beings, and of all systems and sentiments akin to it, and tending towards it. The refugees from the southern plantations shall be made welcome and pointed to means and measures for such improvement and development, as shall make them independent, self-sustaining laborers, justifying the impartial freedom they here enjoy, and contributing by their energy and industry, to the weal of their adopted country. Thus a reflex influence upon the slavery of the neighboring republic will be exerted, which can neither be gainsayed nor resisted.

The religious influence of this Journal shall be free from sectarianism. The broad, Catholic principle of the Protestant Faith, shall here find an advocacy, for there is no true moral and social elevation apart from the Religion of Jesus. It is not to be concealed, however, that the Editor is a Congregationalist, and that as fully and as freely as *he* shall deem best, he will give, among other religious information, intelligence in respect to the public proceedings, the progress and the prospects of his own denomination.

The news of the day, the state of the markets, foreign and domestic intelligence, shall each have its place in the columns of the *Freeman*.

As to politics, the *Freeman* is the organ of no party. But, as a free, untrammeled journal, it will, from time to time, take note of what is done in Parliament, and elsewhere, and make free comments thereon, wielding what of influence it may have, on the side of the great principles of *British Progress*, as the Editor shall understand them.

The present number is issued from Windsor, where the determination to start such a paper originated. The place of future publication will either be London or Toronto, as the Committee shall decide. The regular weekly issues will commence just so soon as the number of *cash subscribers* shall justify it. May it not be hoped, that the need of a family newspaper, uncommitted to any clique, sect or party—that is a population as large as ours in Canada—and from among so many real, tried earnest friends, as we have over the length and breadth of the land, that such a Journal as this will find a living support?

SAMUEL R. WARD

Provincial Freeman (Windsor, Canada West), 24 March 1853.

Resolved, That as we believe "Union is strength," and that it is the only way for our elevation, we do not sympathise and have not participated in the discussions, strife, and personal envy that has been fomented, by a faction in the village of Windsor, under cover of opposition to the Refugees' Home Society, and we therefore deprecate and condemn their proceedings as highly injurious to our cause.

Resolved, That we regard the Refugees' Home Society, the Elgin Settlement and the Sandwich Institute, from their similarity of design as occupying common ground; and we believe them to be benevolent in their objects and aims for the elevation of the colored people in Canada, salutary in their operations, and deserving the sympathy and support of all well wishers of humanity.

Resolved, That the *Voice of the Fugitive*, was the first standard unfurled on the free soil of Canada, especially devoted to the anti-slavery cause, at that trying hour, when the atrocious fugitive slave bill was scattering confusion and dismay over the colored population of the United States; and that it is in charge of a noble and well tried Refugee from American slavery, and that it has been a faithful exponent and monitor of their interests, and is therefore worthy of the support of the colored people and their friends.

Resolved, That as the *Voice* is not as extensively patronised as its merits demand, there is no necessity for another paper devoted to the interests of the colored people of Canada, and therefore the rival paper about being established to supercede, or divide the interest of the *Voice*, especially as [it] is the creation of the factionists alluded to above, is unworthy of the support of the well wishers of our race.

Resolved, That the collection and distribution of old clothing should be discouraged as discreditable to the self-respect of the colored people, except in the special case of newly arrived fugitives destitute of decent apparel, and that donors of these charities should deposit them with such persons on whose judgments they can rely for a judicious distribution of the same.

Resolved, That the circumstances of many of the colored people in Canada are not such as place them above the need of assistance; but on the contrary there is a necessity for aiding them to obtain permanent Homes and for Religious and Educational purposes.

Resolved, That the delegates be furnished with statistics of the Churches, Schools and Temperance Society,[2] among the colored people of this country seat to be reported to the Convention.

Resolved, That the Chairman, and Secretary, of this meeting be a committee to collect these statistics forthwith, and furnish the same to the delegates; and publish a copy of them with the proceedings of this meeting in the *Voice*.

Resolved, That the Boston *Liberator*, *F. Douglass' Paper*,[3] *Am. Baptist*,[4] *Pa. Freeman*,[5] *Telegraph & Temperance Journal*,[6] and other Anti-Slavery papers be requested to notice the proceedings of this meeting.

Frederick Douglass' Paper (Rochester, N.Y.), 8 April 1853.

1. Ward contended that "Rum and Negro-hate" were the two greatest evils degrading North American blacks. He sought to eliminate both. He argued that temperance would permit black men to spend a larger portion of their income on their families and businesses, thus alleviating the need for "begging" to assist the black communities in Canada West. Ward perceived that alcohol consumption was far too common among blacks and called for statistics on alcohol consumption and temperance to be generated and presented to the Colored National Convention (1853) in Rochester. He also publicized black communities that practiced temperance, such as the Elgin settlement, in the hope of persuading other blacks to adopt the practice. *VF*, 24 September, 5 November 1851, 12 February 1852; *PFW*, 24 March 1853, 25 March 1854; *PtL*, 27 June 1853; *NC*, 29 June 1853.

2. The moral improvement of fugitive slaves through religious training, education, and the practice of temperance was among the objectives of the Refugee Home Society. Several religious and educational organizations and institutions tended to those responsibilities. At different times, RHS settlers supported Baptist, Methodist, Presbyterian, African Methodist Episcopal, and British Methodist Episcopal congregations, many of which met in private homes. A Union Sunday school was established near Sandwich in 1851. During 1852–53 white abolitionist Laura Smith Haviland founded the interdenominational Christian Union Church near Puce River. The American Missionary Association had the most widespread religious influence. It operated several mission churches near Sandwich and Puce River. Two schools of note were founded at the RHS. Haviland opened one near Little River in 1852 at the urging of Henry Bibb, C. C. Foote, and Horace Hallock. Mrs. David Hotchkiss opened the second in 1857 at Puce River. The RHS constitution maintained that when six or more families settled in a given area, a school should be established. It also included temperance provisions. No alcoholic beverages were to be bought or sold and their consumption was discouraged. Drunkenness was explicitly prohibited. Violation of the temperance regulations resulted in punishment ranging from a warning to forfeiture of land claims. Carlesimo, "Refugee Home Society," 125, 128–130; Pease and Pease, *Black Utopia*, 109–15.

3. *Frederick Douglass' Paper* was an antislavery weekly edited and published by Frederick Douglass in Rochester, New York, from 30 June 1851 to July 1860. It succeeded Douglass's first newspaper, the *North Star*, which began publication on 3 December 1847. *Frederick Douglass' Paper* was formed when the *North Star* merged with the *Liberty Party Paper*, a Syracuse weekly edited and published by John Thomas, who briefly became Douglass's assistant editor. The paper met its expenses for the first two years, largely through subsidies from Gerrit Smith, but after 1853, it suffered continual financial problems. Despite a readership in excess of four thousand, delinquent subscribers made Douglass dependent upon external sources. British abolitionist Julia Griffiths, the paper's business manager, regularized its finances, sponsored fairs, mailed personal appeals, developed the Rochester Ladies Anti-Slavery Society into a support group for the paper, and produced an antislavery giftbook, *Autographs for Freedom* to raise funds. In 1857 she returned to Britain to generate donations to the weekly. Douglass also tapped a variety of black sources for support, including women's groups, public meetings, and several talented but unpaid local correspondents. He also spent over $12,000 of his own to subsidize the paper. To counter mounting debts, he began publishing *Douglass' Monthly* for British subscribers in June 1858 and reduced the size of *Frederick Douglass' Paper* in 1859, but he was forced to cease publication one year later. Douglass continued to publish the *Monthly* through August 1863. Philip S. Foner, *Frederick Douglass*, 2d ed. (New York, N.Y., 1969), 82–91, 218; Quarles, *Black Abolitionists*, 87–88.

4. The *American Baptist* was founded in Utica, New York, in 1845 by the American Baptist Free Mission Society. The weekly "religious family newspaper" championed antislavery, temperance, and women's rights; during the 1860s, it advocated black and women's suffrage. The paper was moved to New York City during the mid-1850s. Nathan Brown and John Duer edited the *Baptist* for much of its existence. It was superseded by the *Baptist Weekly* in 1872.

5. First published on 3 August 1836 as the *National Enquirer and Constitutional Advocate of Universal Liberty*, this paper was renamed the *Pennsylvania Freeman* when the editorial reins passed from Benjamin Lundy to John Greenleaf Whittier in March 1838. Subsequent editors of the Philadelphia abolitionist weekly included Charles C. Burleigh, James Miller McKim, Mary Grew, Oliver Johnson, and Cyrus M. Burleigh. The *Freeman* followed the Garrisonian lead on most antislavery issues, but its moderated editorial tone reflected the tempered views of the Pennsylvania Anti-Slavery Society's Hicksite Quaker membership. At its height, the paper's circulation reached about two thousand copies. Financial problems forced suspension of the *Freeman* from December 1841 to January 1844; the last issue appeared on 29 June 1854. Robert Stephen Hochreiter, "The *Pennsylvania Freeman*, 1836–1854" (Ph.D. diss., Pennsylvania State University, 1980), 123–52, 160–81; John W. Blassingame, Mae G. Henderson, and Jessica M. Dunn, *Antislavery Newspapers and Periodicals*, 5 vols. to date (Boston, Mass., 1980–), 3:61–64.

6. The resolution refers to the *Telegraph*, a short-lived temperance journal published in Albany, New York, by Stephen Myers, agent of the Delevan State Temperance Union of New York, Foner and Walker, *Proceedings of the Black State Conventions*, 1:59.

42.
Report of the Committee on Emigration of the Amherstburg Convention
Presented at the First Baptist Church, Amherstburg, Canada West 17 June 1853

Canadian blacks gathered in Amherstburg, Canada West, in June 1853 for a general provincial convention. Called and controlled by supporters of Henry Bibb and James T. Holly, the meeting sought to continue the work started two years earlier at the North American Convention, particularly that of reviving the North American League—an organization designed to promote cooperation and commercial activity between blacks in North America and the British West Indies as an instrument of continental black unity and progress. The convention approved more than twenty-five resolutions, most of them concerning life in Canada—praising Her Majesty's government, urging blacks to be loyal subjects and good citizens, controlling fraudulent fund raisers, and encouraging agriculture, mechanical trades, and commerce as paths to black elevation. But the report of the emigration committee was the main order of business and the primary reason for the convention. Holly, Coleman Freeman, and Lewis Clarke constituted the committee, but Holly's religious fervor, emigrationist philosophy, and growing militancy dominated the report. The committee concluded that slavery and oppression in the United States left black Americans with two alternatives—revolution or emigration. While revolution was "the most glorious" alternative, it was not practical; instead the committee urged blacks to leave the United States. They recommended Canada or the British West Indies (as a "first consideration"), Haiti (as a black republic), or specific sites in Central or South America (as points of "secondary interest") but insisted that blacks must leave the United States. The report represents one of the few instances when black abolitionists publicly endorsed the concept of revolution as an alternative to slavery and racial oppression. *Minutes of Convention in Amherstburg* [8:0297]; Miller, *Search for Black Nationality*, 111–12.

Report on Emigration

Your committee to whom was referred the subject of Emigration beg leave to submit the following report.

Emigration is emphatically one of the most important subjects that can engage the attention of an oppressed and denationalized people, as a means for to accomplish their elevation; and it is a subject that peculiarly addresses itself to the free colored American at this time, demanding of him in the name of posterity, in the name of the future greatness of the Africo-American race, and in the name of the great Jehovah to give it his earnest attention.

And were it in our power we would sound a trumpet long and loud, that would vibrate from the St. John's to the *Rio Grande*, and from the Atlantic to the Pacific, in order to arouse the slumbering attention of our people, and bid them give this subject the attention it demands at their hands.

The free colored man in the United States, finds himself divested of every right that a freeman holds dear in two thirds of the sovereignties of the American Union, and but a menial and pitiable outcast socially, in the other third. Every thing that tends to endear the land of his birth to the colored man, and make him proud of a beloved country are denied to him, and he rendered an out and out alien on the very soil that gave him birth. Nor is this the result of a mere temporary or accidental policy, or just punishment for any real or imaginary treasonable conspiracy on the part of those so cruelly proscribed. But it is a systematic, well digested and long pursued course of oppression, commencing in the very cradle of the American Republic, in the Hall of the Continental Congress at Philadelphia, and followed up with increased vigor and rigor ever since, until the present time, and probably will be for all coming time, and that too upon the most unoffending portion of their population, a people, who notwithstanding their oppression at home, have bravely shed their blood in defence of that home, on every battle field, and on every sea, where the American hosts have met in deadly combat with a hostile foe.

Considering therefore so much forbearance and self-sacrifice on the one side, and the studied cruelty and ingratitude on the other, we hesitate not to solemnly pronounce in the name of God, that the colored Americans in the U.S. owe that Government no allegiance, but interminable hatred, that there should not be any endearment of Country on a soil, whose every concomitant recollection, are chains and slavery; that there is no religion, no manhood, no magnanimity, in any longer professing this allegiance to an infernal Government, and a love for such an accursed land of nativity, but on the other hand the curse of God, and the execration of mankind in all coming time, must and will rest upon such a puerile and insignificant people, if they continue longer to hug their chains, under the delusive phantom, that by whining appeals, in this utilitarian age of action, they will be elevated, instead of adopting a bold and decisive course to place themselves upon the pinnacle of fame, despite their oppressors. The question then in short is what is to be done? To this we will answer, there are but two alternatives that can be presented to a people, in the circumstances of the colored Americans. Those are Revolution or Emigration. Revolution is the boldest and probably the most glorious alternative, it is the right of the colored Americans, and if they could count man for man with their oppressors, if they could have free communication with each other so as to insure concert of action, and if there was but one day in the year that every slave could call his own, on such meagre conditions alone, without any of the advantages of civilised warfare we would say strike! for God is with you, and leave the consequences with him for he is as strong as an army with all the paraphernalia of battle; and what though you be defeated by the overwhelming odds in favor of the devil, and you all are massacred—then *die—die manfully*, for in such an alternative, you had better be *dead* FREEMEN, than *Living* SLAVES. But we have not either of the three meagre conditions referred to above, to count upon in the sacred cause of Revolution, and therefore, Emigration is our alternative. But before pointing out the most eligible points of Emigration, we will remark here that a great portion of our people can never be reached by any argument to be incited to praiseworthy action, it is so with a similar portion of all races of people—they are the cyphers of humanity, who are inert under any phase of political and social commotion that may take place in society; and if we did not see in this seeming stupor an organic law of God, favorable as a general rule to the stable development of man, when placed in proper circumstances, it would indeed be a sad commentary on the idea of popular Governments, and the strongest argument that could be adduced to prove the natural depravity of mankind. This class of beings we must leave to wither and die under their oppression—the eternal laws of their being decree it. We will not contend with the fates. But to those who are favored with a more noble organization, who are restless under their chains, we shall endeavor to point out the fields of their development.

CANADA

Canada is the first place that presents itself to our consideration. Here is the Asylum of the Refugees from American Slavery, and here the impartial laws of Great Britain have full sway. Here is a vast unoccupied area of soil, equal to the best Agricultural lands in the Western States of the American Union, and here are plenty of irrigating and navigable streams. Under the hands of enterprising industry this Province is susceptible of an incalculable development of Agricultural Manufacturing, and Commercial resources. No laws prohibit the colored man of availing himself of these advantages, his color is no bar to his naturalization after a proper period of residence here according to the laws, at which time he becomes entitled to all the privileges and immunities of any other naturalized citizen. He may educate his children for any of the learned professions, and when they grow up, there is nothing to prevent them standing side by side with their white fellow-citizens in public affairs if their qualifications are equal. By settling here in large numbers, and availing ourselves of all the advantages that the laws afford us, we may do much to counteract the tendency to annexation to the American Union, deemed by some to be inevitable, and if it must take place, if we are here in large numbers, we may be able to give character to the terms of annexation so as to preserve inviolable our vested rights; or if not to afterwards make this the germ of a commotion that shall shake into atoms the proud Anglo-American confederacy. At any rate whatever may be the future destiny of Canada our fate by no possible chance can be worse than what it would be in the States, and there is every probability, that it will be better. We urge this Province upon the attention of the colored people of the U.S. in preference to any other, because of its proximity to that country. Here men of families with limited means can come, when it would be out of the question for them to go to a more distant abode, here the panting fugitive has come, is coming, and will come, by means of the Underground Railroad, for they all know the way. Here we can literally hang as a threatening *black* cloud over the American Union, waiting and praying for the Lord's day of vengeance, when we may be the humble instruments in his hands, to do the terrible work, of his settling, for centuries of oppression, wrong and blasphemy. These are important things that cannot be over-looked by the intelligent colored American. They offer too great inducements to himself and posterity to be disregarded. They place in his hands a key to the prison door of the slave, and bid him deliver the captive. It is these things that make Canada a more beautiful country to the refugee from the plains of Carolina than the sunny home where he has left his chains, and though our goodly heritage here was as cold and bleak as the rugged hills of Greenland, these considerations above would render it as pleasant to the mind as the sunny clime of delightful Italy. But we can thank God, that our Province is no unhospitable place. A pleasant temperate climate, and a fertile soil invites the honest toiler to abundant rewards.

BRITISH WEST INDIES

The British West Indies present other very interesting points, inviting the attention of the colored Americans. The Colonial Governments, and their most prominent citizens, are very desirous, that emigrants from the United States should settle among them. Several attempts have been made to induce emigration thither without much success. Our enterprising men have not counted the value of settling in those Islands, or they would not need much persuasion to go. Jamaica, is probably the most important of all the Islands to which our attention can be directed. Already there is an Agent in New York city setting before our people the advantages of that Island. This man is a colored man who went from South Carolina to Jamaica to settle, he has been there two years, and has made himself acquainted with the advantages and resources of the Island; and from his knowledge of his own people in the States he knows Jamaica is a good place for their development. Besides it is under the free laws of Britain as well as Canada, and from the large preponderance of the colored population over the whites, being 36 to 1, colored men hold the most of the local official functions.[1] This and its sister Islands are but a few days sail from the Southern coast of the U.S. and they stand as great beacon lights to the slave, and are destined to play an important part in the settlement of the final destiny of the Africo-American race on the continent. We would therefore encourage the mission of Mr. Harrison, the agent from Jamaica,[2] and recommend all colored Americans who can go to that Island, by all means to do so.

HAYTI

This Empire as is well known is wholly in the hands of colored men and forms the grandest centre of attraction for our race wheresoever scattered around the globe. It is the first nationality established by our race, sacred through the means of revolution against tyrannical oppression. It was the second independent government established in America. And that independence has been creditably maintained ever since under the most adverse circumstances, and that too by a people just emerged from slavery, and wholly unacquainted with the arts of political administration. In 1824 President Boyer offered great inducements to the colored Americans to settle in that country, and several thousands did go from the U.S.[3] But it is a matter of surprise that this emigration entirely ceased after a few years duration, and a knowledge of the existence of such a country has become almost entirely obscured. Every colored man should feel binding upon himself the duty to sustain the national existence of Hayti, intact against the intervention of any or all powers whatsoever, and should pursue a policy to that end. Emigration there in large numbers on the part of the colored Americans would do much to strengthen the hands of that Government, and forward in an incalculable degree the cause of our elevation in America. From that point we could watch the fate of our brethren in Cuba, and prepare ourselves to lend them a helping hand when the day of their reckoning shall come.[4]

CENTRAL & SOUTH-AMERICA

Guatemala, Guiana, and New Grenada are also important points, of secondary interest to those we have named above, that open a field for the development of the colored race, and to which we must turn our attention, in the great work before us.

It is not too soon for us to take them into our account now, in calculating our future destiny in America, and the emigration of a few companies of enterprising men in these directions, would not be amiss, and would meet our hearty approbation.

In conclusion your committee beg leave to recapitulate the important points of emigration, Canada, British West Indies, Hayti, Central and South-America. We have presented so many different points, in order to suit the various minds, and the available capacity of all who are calculating to emigrate. We have no doubt but that Canada for the reasons we have stated when referring to it, will for the present claim the first consideration. After Canada the British West Indies appear to be the next available point[s], but we have no doubt as our cause rolls on to the great issue that awaits our destiny on the continent, no points will figure more conspicuously in our considerations than Hayti, Central and South-America. We have taken no other places into our account but places on this Continent and the adjacent Islands. The reason of this is because we regard all measures calculated for our elevation, in order to be immediately practicable, must be strictly confined to a continental policy.

We know there are millions of our race in the Eastern world that have claims on our considerations, but our own claims are prior, and must take precedence.

In a future age when we shall have achieved an honorable destiny for ourselves in America, and wiped out from the whole western continent the stain of slavery. We confidently trust that there will be enough of christianity, philanthropy and civilization, among our descendants of that day to send missionaries to Africa in common with other christian races, to re-kindle the flames of her ancient christian civilization. We cannot close this report without urging the Convention to re-adopt the policy of the Toronto Convention in relation to a Continental League of the Africo-American[5] race, and to take measures to place it in practical operation forthwith. For a systematic combination should go hand in hand with every band of emigrants wheresoever they may go on the continent, uniting them in co-operative efforts with those they leave behind, or who may be scattered throughout its different parts.

J. T. Holly
C. Freeman[6]
Lewis Clark[7]

Minutes and Proceedings of the General Convention for the Improvement of the Colored Inhabitants of Canada, Held by Adjournments in Amherstburgh, C.W. June 16th and 17th 1853 (Windsor, Canada West, 1853), 11–16.

1. According to the 1844 Jamaican census, the island's population consisted of 15,785 whites, 293,128 blacks, and 68,520 "coloureds" (mulattoes). One observer reported in 1851 that nonwhites held four-fifths of Jamaica's public offices. Although those figures may be inflated, more cautious modern estimates suggest that "coloureds" filled a "great majority" of the less prestigious offices by 1849. Green, *British Slave Emancipation*, 13–14, 316, 357.

2. J. Wesley Harrison, a South Carolina black, immigrated to Jamaica in 1851. He returned to the United States two years later to refute antiemigrationist charges of slavelike conditions in Jamaica, to testify that he had improved his condition by immigrating there, and to recruit free black immigrants to Jamaica. He

had been authorized by a Jamaican planter to sell land on the island at $1 per acre. But few blacks responded. Foner, *History of Black Americans*, 159; *FDP*, 10 June 1853.

3. Haiti was the first black republic and, after the United States, the first independent nation in the Western Hemisphere. Led by Toussaint L'Ouverture, a former slave, Haitian blacks struggled for more than a decade before winning independence from France in 1804. Jean-Jacques Dessalines, the country's first president, was assassinated two years later, and the nation was divided by two political rivals. Jean-Pierre Boyer (1787–1850), a French-educated mulatto, became president of Haiti in 1818. He reunited Haiti, extended government control over the entire island of Hispaniola, and won diplomatic recognition from the French. In 1824 Boyer invited black Americans to settle in Haiti and offered transportation and land grants to any who came. An 1843 coup forced him into exile. Haiti continued to be troubled by repression, internal turbulence, and frequent coups throughout the nineteenth century. Perusse, *Historical Dictionary of Haiti*, 10, 17–19, 27–28, 50–52, 79–80, 99–100; Miller, *Search for Black Nationality*, 76–77.

4. The committee refers to the existence of slavery in Cuba. Slavery was introduced into Cuba during the era of the *conquistadores*, and the later growth of the sugar cane industry made slave labor a prevalent characteristic of the island's economy. In the late 1700s, Spain granted the colony the right of free and unrestricted importation of slaves, and black Cubans—free and slave—soon constituted a majority on the island. By 1872 there were more than 286,000 slaves on the island. Spain implemented a plan for the gradual emancipation of Cuban slaves in 1879, and slavery was officially abolished in 1886. Jaime Suchlicki, *Cuba: From Columbus to Castro* (New York, N.Y., 1974), 49, 70–71n.

5. The committee refers to the North American Convention held in Toronto on 11–13 September 1851 and its resolution to form the North American League; the league of black residents of North America and the West Indies was designed to promote the abolition of slavery, the protection of black rights, and the improvement of the race. The proceedings of the convention are printed as document 23 in this volume.

6. Coleman Freeman originally lived in Ohio, but the degrading effect of the state's black laws prompted him to resettle his family along the Detroit-Windsor frontier during the early 1840s. A modest farmer with a reputation for honesty and charity (he adopted four orphaned children), he involved himself in the religious, educational, benevolent, and antislavery concerns of the local black community. He served for a time as a trustee of an African Methodist Episcopal church in Detroit. Freeman supported Mary Ann Shadd Cary's efforts to maintain a black school in Windsor and participated in local fugitive relief efforts, opening his home to new arrivals from slavery and distributing food and clothing received from the United States. Much of this latter work was performed in conjunction with his position on the executive committee of the Refugee Home Society. Freeman's interest in Canadian immigration led to his involvement in the black convention movement; he was a prominent participant in the North American Convention (1851) and the Amherstburg Convention (1853). He also became a leading member of the Anti-Slavery Society of Windsor and presided over its orga-

nizational meeting in 1852. Freeman was appointed treasurer of the ASSW, and his wife, Anna, sat on the society's executive committee.

Freeman exemplified the many black Canadians who initially supported the RHS, then became increasingly disillusioned with it, and eventually embraced the views of Mary Ann Shadd Cary, Samuel R. Ward, and other critics of the society. During the early 1850s, Freeman protested against the "begging" activities of RHS agent Charles C. Foote. In 1854, to indicate his concern for black self-reliance, he refused a three-ton shipment of clothing that had been forwarded from the United States for fugitive relief. He served as a vice-president of the self-help-oriented Provincial Union Association and acted as a local subscription agent for the *Provincial Freeman*. In August 1855, he was appointed to a committee charged with resolving a dispute over control of the British-American Institute property at the Dawn settlement. Later in the decade, Freeman served as a trustee of the short-lived Agricultural, Mechanical, and Educational Association of Canada West. Drew, *North-Side View of Slavery*, 330–33; *E*, 14 May 1846 [5:0219]; *VF*, 12 February, 12 March, 13, 27 August 1851, 29 January, 11 March, 20 May, 21 October 1852 [6:0816, 0847, 7:0068, 0588, 0788, 0864]; *PFW*, 15 April, 3 June, 19 August, 9 September 1854, 30 June, 15 September 1855 [9:0017, 0833]; *Lib*, 4 March 1853; *FDP*, 10 February 1854 [8:0645]; *Minutes of Convention in Amherstburg*, 3, 5, 11–16 [8:0297]; Proceedings of a Public Meeting Held at Windsor, Canada West, 20 July 1852, AMA-ARC [7:0666]; Lewis Clark[e] et al., *The Agricultural, Mechanical, and Educational Association of Canada West* [Sandwich, Canada West, 1859], 5 [11:0627].

7. Lewis George Clarke (1815–1897), the son of a mulatto slave woman and a white Revolutionary War veteran, was born a slave on his maternal grandfather's plantation in Madison County, Kentucky. The grandfather promised to emancipate the entire Clarke family by a provision in his will, but upon his death, the document could not be located, and the family was sold at auction. Sixteen-year-old Lewis, already separated from his family for ten years, became the property of a tobacco farmer, who allowed him to hire out his time. When that master died, Clarke ran away to avoid being sold to Louisiana. In August 1841, after one abortive attempt, he gained his freedom. After a short stay in Canada West, he joined his brother Milton in Ohio and, in July 1842, helped his youngest brother Cyrus escape from slavery. During the 1840s and 1850s, Clarke devoted much of his time to the antislavery lecture circuit. He compared African colonization to the slave trade for its adverse impact on black families, and he criticized New England ministers who claimed to be abolitionists while they apologized for slaveholders and failed to pursue antislavery measures. Clarke returned to Canada West in the early 1850s, settled in Sandwich, acquired several parcels of land, and remained active in the abolitionist movement. On 1 March 1859, he helped found the Agricultural, Mechanical, and Educational Association of Canada West, a short-lived organization designed to aid fugitives in their transition to freedom; Clarke served the association as a trustee and general traveling agent. Later that same year, at the New England Colored Citizens Convention, he praised Canada as a land of opportunity and freedom for blacks and urged black parents to separate their sons from the bad influence of the cities in favor of the wholesome environment of the countryside. Clarke had sold his Canadian land-

holdings by 1874, and, after his wife died, he moved with his children to Oberlin, Ohio. In the late 1870s or early 1880s, he returned to Kentucky. At the request of a group of planters, he lectured black agricultural laborers in the state not to immigrate to Kansas. He died in his native state and was buried at Oberlin. Jean Vacheenas and Betty Volk, "Born in Bondage: History of a Slave Family," *NHB* 36:101–6 (1973); *DANB*, 116; *SL*, 9 January 1843 [4:0523]; *E*, 11 May 1843 [4:0567]; *Lib*, 26 August 1859 [11:0966]; *BT*, 7, [14?] December 1895; *NYSu*, 9 December 1900; Clark[e] et al., *Agricultural, Mechanical, and Educational Association* [11:0625].

43.
Mary Jane Robinson to Sarah Ann Harris
23 March 1854

Professional black abolitionists were not the only proponents of Canadian immigration. Information informally passed by word of mouth and personal correspondence also enhanced Canada's image among black Americans. In a 23 March 1854 letter, Mary Jane Robinson, a New York City laundress, offered a fellow laundress an informative account of her family's move to Buxton, Canada West. The Robinsons' choice of Buxton was fortuitous. It was there that Presbyterian missionary William King established Elgin, the most successful of the black Canadian settlements, which offered economic and educational opportunities unavailable to blacks in the United States. Robinson described life at Elgin in almost idyllic terms—a sharp contrast to the conditions of blacks in the urban North. Her letter was one of scores of personal testimonials that contributed to black migration to Canada. Pease and Pease, *Black Utopia*, 84–98; *New York City Directory*, 1852–58.

BUXTON, Canada West
March 23, 1854

Mrs. Sarah Ann Harris
Weeksville
Care of W[illia]m Dolly
Zion's Church[1]
New York
MY DEAR MRS. HARRIS:[2]

I take up my pen to write you a few lines, after so long a delay. I suppose you all thought that we were all dead, but it is not so, I can assure you, although we have been quite sick since we arrived in Canada. I have been quite ill with the pleurisy, and, in the Fall, we all had the dumb ague and fever; but now we are enjoying good health, except my son John; it left him feeble and a pain in the side; but he never was strong in health. This is a healthy place—but little sickness except the ague and fever. We arrived in Chatham on the 13th May, after a pleasant journey. It's really beautiful to travel in the Spring, and to behold the different faces of nature's beauty. In the steamboat we went to Troy; then took the cars to Buffalo, and there we put up until Monday from Friday, and I found Buffalo a very pretty place indeed; then we took the steamboat for Detroit—a beautiful sail across the Lake—Erie—and out of sight of land, it seems to me as on the sea; and then we took the steamboat again for Chatham—then we were done and at our journey's end. Now, Chatham is a fine place indeed, a town pleasantly situated on the banks of the

Thames; and there we kept house six weeks—we had a small house—much cheaper than to board; and then my husband went to Buxton, to the coloured settlement,[3] a distance of six miles, and purchased a farm of fifty acres, with nine acres cut down and one all cleared. The man who had taken it has to give it up, or build; it's a pleasant place. So, my husband liked it, and bought it and paid the money on the spot. He had to pay for the improvements and the balance of the ground—but if you buy a farm with no improvements on it, then it is two dollars and a half an acre. And he hired his house put up, and on the first of July, we moved on our farm. O, my dear friend, how I do want to see you again; I do wish you would try and come to Buxton, Canada West. *Come to a land of liberty and freedom, where the coloured man is not despised nor a deaf ear turned to them. This is the place to live in peace and to enjoy the comforts of life.* In September, we got a fine cow, with a heifer calf ten months old. So I have been quite a country-woman. I both churned my own butter and milked my own cow. We have got three nice sows, and, by and by, I shall have some geese, and chickens, and ducks, and all those things. Here is nine thousand acres of land now taken up by coloured people in Buxton, where we live; and Mr. King,[4] the government agent, who sells the land, has purchased eight thousand more to sell at the same rate; and the people are coming in from all parts, and the place is filling up fast. I hear that OLD FILLMORE *is a screwing you all up tighter still,*[5] but don't stay there, come to *Queen Victoria's land, where they are not making laws to oppress and to starve you.* I raised a fine sight of tobacco. We had turnips as big as the crown of your husband's hat, and cabbage as large as a water-pail. O, don't laugh, for it's a fact—for the ground is so rich it raises everything up in no time. We were late, so we had only Fall things. There is a saw-mill and a grist-mill building in Buxton, and a school now here, with seventy or eighty scholars. *O, we are just beginning to live well enough without the white man's foot on our necks. Away with your King Fillmore, I am for* QUEEN VICTORIA. GOD SAVE THE QUEEN. We have all kinds of game, deer, raccoon, ground-hogs, black-squirrels, hens, pheasants, quails, wild turkey, wild duck, woodcock and red-headed woodpeckers, and sapsuckers, wild red raspberries and plumbs, crabapples and wild gooseberries, and all kinds of nuts. *Not as cold as I thought.* We have Methodist, Baptist and Presbyterian meetings, too.[6] We are to have a log-rolling soon, and then we will have ten acres cleared. They (the people) all will help you to raise and log, and you help them again. Whatever you raise in the ground, you can sell it in Chatham, six miles from here. My husband walks up and down once or twice a-week, and thinks nothing of it; but I hope soon we'll have a team of our own. There is a number come from Toronto to this place, as land can be got cheaper—20*s.** an acre and ten years to pay it in, and land that will bring anything you plant just as I did in Weeksville[7] (only it wanted more manuring); only put in the seed and *pray to the Giver of rain*, and they will come up. O, dear, how I want to see you again. Do come to Buxton, Canada West.

MARY JANE ROBINSON[8]

* York Shillings.

Provincial Freeman (Toronto, Canada West), 13 January 1855.

1. Dolly was affiliated with the Zion Baptist Church of New York City, a black congregation formed in 1832. Rev. John T. Raymond served as its pastor through 1839. Thereafter, a succession of preachers, white and black, filled Zion's pulpit until Rev. Stephen Dutton arrived in 1843. The congregation grew rapidly under Dutton's guidance, reaching a membership of 444 by the time he left in 1848. After that, membership declined, largely as a result of the Fugitive Slave Law of 1850. By 1860 the congregation claimed only 118 members. Zion was one of three black churches that organized the quasi-national American Baptist Missionary Convention (1841), and it remained an active member of the association. Walker, "Afro-American in New York City," 136–37; Sobel, *Trabelin' On*, 267, 364.

2. Sarah Ann Harris, a black laundress, lived in New York City during the 1840s and 1850s. *New York City Directory*, 1842, 1859–60.

3. Robinson refers to the Elgin settlement at Buxton.

4. William King.

5. Robinson refers to President Millard Fillmore's vigorous enforcement of the Fugitive Slave Law of 1850.

6. Religion played an important role in the life of the Elgin settlement. In 1849 William King, the founder of the settlement, established the Buxton Mission. It was sponsored by the Toronto Presbytery and supported by contributions from local churches and Anglo-American philanthropists. The religious life of the community initially centered around the mission, but other churches soon developed. A First Baptist church was organized in 1853, a British Methodist Episcopal congregation was established in 1855, and a small Roman Catholic congregation was also formed. By 1857 a majority of the settlers associated with the local Baptist and Methodist churches. In 1858 the Buxton Mission was officially organized as St. Andrew's Presbyterian Church. Establishment of a local branch of the Upper Canada Bible Society in 1861, the practice of sending missionary trainees from Knox College to work at the settlement, and the creation of a mission library of over five hundred volumes all testify to the religious ferment at the settlement. Winks, *Blacks in Canada*, 211–12; Pease and Pease, *Black Utopia*, 99–100; Ullman, *Look to the North Star*, 163–77.

7. Weeksville, situated in the Bedford-Stuyvesant section of Brooklyn, New York, was a distinct community of property-owning free blacks prior to the Civil War. Acknowledged as a distinct black neighborhood by the 1840s, Weeksville contained a number of prominent Afro-American institutions, including the Bethel African Methodist Episcopal Church, the Howard Colored Orphan Asylum, the Zion Home for Aged Colored People, and the African Civilization Society offices (after 1865). By the 1870s, white encroachment had caused the community to lose much of its distinctive black character and its discrete neigh-

borhood status. Harold X. Connolly, *A Ghetto Grows in Brooklyn* (New York, N.Y., 1977), 8, 10, 30–31.

8. Mary Jane Robinson was a black laundress in New York City during the 1850s. She and her husband Leander Robinson lived briefly in Canada West in 1854. *New York City Directory*, 1852–58.

44.
Editorials by Mary Ann Shadd Cary
25 March 1854
27 May 1854

Black abolitionists constantly reminded themselves, and their white colleagues, that their primary objective was to free the slave, and they were critical of anything that impeded the antislavery cause. When Mary Ann Shadd Cary outlined the *Provincial Freeman*'s editorial position during the spring of 1854, she insisted that the paper would avoid the factionalism that plagued the American antislavery movement, particularly the cliques that had formed around competing ideologies and the dominant personalities of such leaders as William Lloyd Garrison, Lewis Tappan, and Frederick Douglass. She believed that slavery's existence in the United States and its absence in Canada made the antislavery movements in the two countries quite different. American abolitionists could use a variety of means to strike at slavery, including political action. Canadian abolitionists had to work to turn international public opinion against slavery through arguments based on higher law, not on politics. Cary's editorial critiques also revealed the subtler forms of racism at work in the antislavery movement. "The Humbug of Reform," her 27 May 1854 editorial, examined the economic, political, and racial considerations that defined the movement. In it she questioned the motives of the movement's white leadership and argued, with considerable irony, that white antislavery paternalism reinforced the proslavery myth of black dependence. Cary urged white abolitionists to remember that their first allegiance was to the slave. *PFW*, 25 March, 3, 10 June 1854, 31 January, 30 May 1857 [8:0701–2, 0858, 10:0522–23, 0701]; Bearden and Butler, *Shadd*, 232–33.

ANTI-SLAVERY RELATIONS

As a new, though humble instrumentality in the anti-slavery field, it is necessary to state clearly the position of the *Provincial Freeman*, and the relation it holds to the great anti-slavery bodies of America; 1st, that there may be no doubts in the minds of the public as to its real position; and 2d, by way of reply to questions already propounded.

As a matter of curiosity, growing out of the establishment of a paper devoted to the measures it is proposed to advocate, the inquiry has been made by friends in the U.S. as to the "bearings" of the *Freeman*; "whether towards Garrisonianism, Lewis-Tappanism, Douglassism, Free-Soilism, or what?" In other words, will this journal be committed to the distinguishing doctrines of any one of the above schools exclusively?[1]

No, friends, no! In the United States, the centre of operations of American Slavery, and hitherto the field of active anti-slavery [operat]ions on this continent, circumstances not directly affecting us, have divided abolitionists into several classes; each of which has in its particular way, and with especial deference to the peculiar tenets held, endeavored to lead the growing liberal sentiment of the people. The national relations of abolitionists in the U.S., the peculiarity of the civil and religious polity under which they live, and their present local position in the Northern division of the country, no doubt, determine the phase of anti-slavery effort with them; but with Canadians, as with British subjects everywhere, the case is quite different.

Living in a country in which chattel Slavery is not tolerated; in which this man's origin or that man's peculiarities of feature, complexion, &c., are not made subjects of special legislation, and do not militate against him, it is not thought to be either practicable or necessary to insist, *solely*, upon a political view of the matter.

We wish to help create a sentiment in Canada, and out of Canada, that shall tell against Slavery; and to point out, so far as we can see it, the course that people in this country should pursue to that end.

The matter of political action to affect Slavery[2] should, we think, be left for the consideration of abolitionists, in those communities in which it is legalized; to them properly belongs the right to adopt whatever course of action therein, a knowledge of its practical bearings may suggest. It is not for us to say, Do this or do that to remove the evil from among you; but, Be just and untiring in your efforts to speedily accomplish your object; leaving to ourselves the right at the same time to prefer this or that course as a matter of opinion. But we do claim for Canadians the right to say how they will work.

With British subjects, then, whether by birth or adoption, the question assumes and can assume only a moral phase. Having no slaves (the southern U.S. assertion to the contrary notwithstanding), extending to each class the immunities of freemen, it is important to aid in fashioning public opinion on the question of Slavery by insisting on a strictly Scriptural course of conduct between man and man; on the part of governments towards individuals; on the part of individuals to *preserve* their freedom, that the enormities of a system such as American Slavery and its cognates, Russian despotism and Italian and Austrian oppression, may be clearly understood and destroyed.[3]

The precaution of exposing to the moral, religious and immoral, the immoral, irreligious, revolting features of any system of oppression however mild (?) is indispensable to the preservation of liberty in this country, contiguous as it is, to a powerful nation in various parts of which Slavery is not only invested with the sanctity of lawful protection, and made the distinguishing feature of political preferment; but in which the general polity, is, by contrast with the long tried and approved axioms of the most liberal government of Europe[4] and our own country, suggestive of exciting change; where the deceptive glare made by the cry of "equality! progress! toleration!" obscure the evils inflicted upon all classes, too surely resulting from despotism practised upon one class.

Our crusade, then, must be a moral one. If a sound moral and religious influence, when exerted by individuals, can accomplish great good, surely the influence of large communities, such as this, for instance, in its character of a liberal, powerful, well sustained Province, can do more. If Slavery is better than freedom in its general features, to individuals, it is also in particulars; if better for individuals or classes in a country it is for the people at large. If Slavery is the better condition, the relation is a moral one, its results to the enslaved are elevating, and the idea that freedom is desirable is nothing more than a wild hallucination of disordered intellect. But it is not so. The experience of mankind, whether they will confess it or not, is, that Slavery works positive evil; and, it is not unimportant to observe that the moral sense of mankind, formed, sustained, enforced by Christian teaching and example, is opposed to it. Then, duty requires that it be destroyed; sympathy for those who cannot of themselves break its iron grasp requires it; and as the influence of nations is not sectional but world wide, and as among those of America, our own is preeminently gaining importance, from position, relation to European governments and national origin, it is of the first moment that a strong moral feeling shall be created here.

The British government and people possess a power, determination and influence, hardly equalled by any other nation; and it is very clear that efforts made in this part of Her Majesty's dominions to countenance the despotism in the U.S., at the same time that they deeply injure us, have a direct influence in retarding the period of emancipation. These remarks will, it is hoped, satisfy all that it is neither our duty nor inclination to be the advocate of any particular school; but at the same time that we endeavor to enforce the broad and comprehensive ground of the moral bearings of the question, so firmly insisted upon by British anti-slavery men every where, we shall accept whatever we understand to be anti-slavery, in spirit and tendency, in the views and doctrines held forth by the different schools of the United States.

Provincial Freeman (Toronto, Canada West), 25 March 1854.

THE HUMBUG OF REFORM

"This is a great age," we are often told, and undeniably it is; great in moral progress—great in the inventive genius displayed, and great in the facilities it offers to invest vice with the semblance of virtue.

The disposition to make black appear white, is the most prominent feature of the times. It is not confined to projects of doubtful propriety either; but is as true of the most necessary reforms as of other, and less important projects. We pass over the different schemes for this great purpose or the other, which are, in some degree, made to contribute their quota to the general fund of deception, and come at once to the most important movement now engrossing the attention of the people of America—the abolition question. This project which has for its object the emancipation of the slave, is not an exception.

It is a difficult matter for an American to take a liberal view on subjects involving the interests of colored Americans, disconnected from the selfishness of *individual* gain, personal or pecuniary. The position assumed by the majority who oppose Negro Slavery, is, that it works positive evil to the white classes, and, for our own profit, it should be abolished; the inherent wickedness of the system is lost to sight, but "*our*" interests as white *freemen*, may not be subserved by its continuance.

All around, we hear much of Anti-Slavery. Men now have a measure of *glory* in being abolitionists, since the thought of security against "any more ebony additions on this continent," is prevailing, the thousands who flock to the standard, are only required to use the Shibboleth abolition, in order to be received into the household of Anti-Slavery faith; such proselytes are not to be relied upon, much less should they be tolerated as orthodox on a subject of such great importance. Some of the most miraculous changes of the present time, have been wrought among them, first, *violently* in favor of freedom for the poor negro, and as quick, and with no perceptible intermediate change, as decidedly in favor of his expatriation or his continuance in servitude. A man in haste to be popular, sets out with the opinion that Slavery is encroaching upon his rights—at once a love for all men is announced, but, as there is an intervening obstacle in his progress, the brotherhood of the race is a "fixed fact": there is a surplus of affectionate consideration for the black brother; wondrous things are to be done for him, and that in the twinkling of an eye.

In fact, being so blind that he cannot see to advantage, the seeing must be done for him. He cannot hear either, except that which has first been tried, and found to be safe for his delicate organs; the consequence is, that after many "convictions" and "opinions" a [word illegible] puzzle induced by his decidedly progressive course, in spite of the tutoring and watching he gets, he is thought to be just what his barefaced oppressors have all along asserted of him—"an undesirable part of the *free* population." The land of his forefathers would be the best country for him, could it only be "fixed up a bit"—say a few missions and some republics; at all events, America is wanted for those whom Sojourner Truth[5] delights in calling the "Shaxon race."

Why is it that many reflecting men will not be influenced by appeals when made to them by popular reformers, but that their true principles will out, although they cautiously try to conceal them? Sensible people will not allow themselves to be caught with the chaff of an empty profession, made by men calling themselves abolitionists, who, in addition to this, wrangle about this trifle or the other, connected with their particular creed, and so lose sight of the shadow of their aim.

We are an abolitionist—we do not want the slave to remain in his chains a second; whether the master gets paid or not, is a point of no importance to us whatever; strictly speaking; however, he has no claim to him and should not, therefore, have pay for that to which he has no shadow of right!

We go further, we want that the colored man should live in America—should "plant his tree" deep in the soil, and whether he turns white, or his neighbors turn black by reason of the residence, is of no moment. He must have his rights—must not be driven to Africa, nor obliged to stay in the States if he desires to go elsewhere. We confess to their views as objectionable, as we know them to be, but this does not close our eyes against the "humbug" connected with this abolition reform, some phases of which would cause a worm-eating New Hollander to hide his head from very disgust.

Provincial Freeman (Toronto, Canada West), 27 May 1854.

1. Cary refers to major divisions that existed in the American antislavery movement for a variety of ideological and personal reasons. The American Anti-Slavery Society, led by William Lloyd Garrison, dominated the movement in the 1830s. It advocated immediate abolition of slavery, nonresistance, anticlericalism, and women's rights. But Garrison's immediatist hegemony was sundered during the 1840s. Some AASS members advocated a more moderate route than Garrison offered and, led by Lewis Tappan, broke from the society in 1840. They established the American and Foreign Anti-Slavery Society and the Liberty party to advance antislavery through political means. Those organizations soon became moribund, but Tappan and his followers created the American Abolition Society and the Radical Abolition party in 1855 for the same purpose. After the death of the Liberty party, some disaffected Democrats and old Liberty party members formed the Free Soil party in 1848 to oppose the extension of slavery. But Free Soilers, who did not demand immediate abolition, were anathema to Garrisonians and many Tappanites. White Garrisonians also alienated many black abolitionists by their paternalistic attitudes and their criticism of Frederick Douglass. Relations between Garrisonians and Douglass were strained in 1847 when Douglass established the *North Star* in Rochester, in opposition to Garrison's advice. The final break came in 1851 when Douglass accepted the legitimacy of political antislavery action. William H. Pease and Jane H. Pease, "Boston Garrisonians and the Problem of Frederick Douglass," *CJH* 2:29–48 (September 1967).

2. The political antislavery crusade can be divided into three general phases between 1840 and 1860. During the first phase (1840–46), political abolitionists founded the Liberty party, a single-issue organization committed to emancipation and black civil rights. The party moved the American antislavery impulse into

political channels, but it failed to attract popular support and was soon abandoned by its leaders. Moderate party men then tried to link political antislavery to a broader political platform, and as part of that process, they abandoned immediate emancipation in favor of the less threatening nonextension of slavery. The second phase (1846–54) of political antislavery activity began when many political abolitionists joined a coalition of disgruntled Whigs and Democrats to form the Free Soil party. The Free Soil party was defeated by northern nativists and temporary national reconciliation. But passage of the Kansas-Nebraska Act (1854) shattered the illusion of sectional harmony, prompted the reemergence of the Free Soil coalition as the Republican party, and ushered in the third phase (1854–60) of political antislavery action. The Republican party attracted moderate political antislavery men as well as radical political abolitionists, who viewed nonextension of slavery as the first step in the struggle for emancipation. The presence of these radicals insured that the Republican party maintained antislavery as one of its guiding principles. Sewell, *Ballots for Freedom*; Foner, *Free Soil, Free Labor.*

3. Cary probably refers to the autocratic rule of Nicholas I in Russia and to the crushing of the revolutions of 1848 in Hungary and Italy by Austrian forces.

4. Cary refers to Britain.

5. Sojourner Truth (ca. 1797–1883) or Isabella Van Wagener, as she was known during the early part of her public career, was born a slave in Hurley, Ulster County, New York. She had several owners before she ran away in 1827, the year preceding the emancipation of New York's slaves. About 1829 she arrived in New York City, worked as a domestic, and began having mystical experiences. She assisted the ministry of an unorthodox preacher named Elizah Pierson. In 1833 she joined Robert Matthew's Zion Hill in Sing Sing, New York, and resided there until a scandal disrupted the commune. She returned to domestic work in New York City for eight or nine years until mystical experiences once again drew her into preaching. In 1843 she took the name Sojourner Truth, became a traveling preacher, and discovered abolitionism. In 1850 she moved to Salem, Ohio, making the office of the *Anti-Slavery Bugle* her headquarters. That same year, she published her narrative, which she sold during her lecture tours, and was introduced to the women's rights movement, a cause she continued to champion after the Civil War. In the mid-1850s, she settled in Battle Creek, Michigan. During the Civil War, she solicited supplies for black troops and, in December 1864, became the National Freedmen's Relief Association counselor at a refugee settlement at Arlington Heights, Virginia. Her experience there prompted her to pursue the establishment of an all-black state, and in 1870 she petitioned President Ulysses S. Grant for government assistance to settle blacks on western public lands. The president did not accommodate her request, but she probably helped stimulate the exodus of blacks to Kansas and Missouri during the late 1870s. Sojourner Truth continued to preach religion, black rights, women's suffrage, and temperance to white audiences until 1875, when she returned to Battle Creek, where she remained until her death. *NAW*, 3:479–81.

45.
Editorial by Mary Ann Shadd Cary
3 June 1854

Black abolitionists and antislavery women were largely responsible for the success of the antislavery bazaar, an event at which clothes, household articles, books, ornaments, and other items were sold to support antislavery activities. During the 1850s, the Rochester Ladies Anti-Slavery Society sponsored an annual bazaar to help support *Frederick Douglass' Paper*. Following the 1854 event, many goods donated by British abolitionists remained unsold. The Toronto Ladies' Association for the Relief of Destitute Colored Fugitives agreed to sell these goods at a Toronto bazaar. News of this arrangement angered the editors of the *Provincial Freeman*. They perceived that Canadian abolitionists were ignoring the financially strapped *Freeman* in favor of Douglass's paper. An indignant Mary Ann Shadd Cary responded with a series of vitriolic editorial broadsides. Subsequent attempts at mediation by Thomas Henning, secretary of the Anti-Slavery Society of Canada, proved useless. The *Provincial Freeman*'s editors continued to rail against the alleged favoritism and patronizing attitude of the Toronto antislavery societies. Ripley et al., *The Black Abolitionist Papers*, 101–2; Murray, "Canada and Anglo-American Antislavery Movement," 395–98; *PFW*, 3, 10, 24 June, 1 July 1854.

A Bazaar in Toronto for *Frederick Douglass' Paper*, &c.

Since writing the remarks to be found in another column, proposing a Bazaar[1] for the *Provincial Freeman*, we see it announced that Miss Julia Griffiths, an English lady, Secretary to the Rochester Female Anti-Slavery Society, and assistant in the office of *Frederick Douglass' Paper*, will open a Bazaar in Toronto, about the middle of this month, under the patronage of the Toronto Anti-Slavery Society, to dispose of the unsold English and Irish goods of the Rochester Fair.[2]

A lucky paper, that! The Rochester Bazaar is held every year for its support. It has, we are informed, a paying subscription list, numbering thousands. The first instalment of the UNCLE TOM FUND, was given by MRS. STOWE for its support.[3] It has private patronage incredible, besides, very recently, an addition to its coffers has been made, called the "Thousand Dollar Fund"—a sum contributed by one hundred persons, and gotten up, mainly, we are told, by a great effort on the part of Miss Griffiths, and now, Toronto must pay her golden tribute, by solicitation of the same untiring Miss Griffiths.

Barnum is distanced, and no mistake, in this, succession of brilliant efforts to get the "tin!"[4] But how is it that the wire-workers of a paper opposed to emigration to Canada, are making arrangements to hold a Bazaar for its support in the country? Are the abolitionists of Canada, or, rather of the Toronto Society, opposed to free colored people coming into the Province to settle? and are these the initiatory steps to a public endorsement of Anti-emigration views?

We know that such is the opinion of a portion of the citizens here, but may they not be mistaken? We do not wish to be liable to a silent imputation of mis-representing the *great* people engaged in this movement—humble as we are, we would like to know more of the facts, as well to satisfy our minds, as to enlighten the public. We have had many inquiries made of us, recently, as to the movements of the Toronto Anti-Slavery Society, not one of which we could answer, of course, not knowing where to find it, to get any information. We think, however, that as there is a prospect of its being found about the "middle of June," anxious inquirers will then be able to see and hear to their satisfaction. Should they conclude not to lose a moment in the search, we would suggest an application to the parent Society, in New York City, U.S., through Lewis Tappan, Esq., the great embodiment of Anti-Slavery Society tactics for the States and the Canadas.[5]

The Toronto Anti-Slavery Society have had Rev. Samuel R. Ward in England and other parts of Britain, collecting funds for newly arrived fugitives—because the necessary amount was difficult to raise here in a reasonable time for those needy ones. Now in the name of honor and humanity, what is the state of the case? Are those funds to be lavished on favorites in Yankeedom, because Mr. Ward has unfortunately fallen into disgrace with Lewis Tappan, Esq.,[6] and the right wing of the Toronto Society, for his devotion to the interests of colored Canadians, and his manly determination not to bow down sufficient-low, to please this one or that, who may have the shadow, but not the substance of anti-slavery? Poor fugitives! We trust that you may not have to content yourselves in the coming and future winters with only the crumbs that may be left from the £ 1500 ($6,000) raised by Mr. Ward[7] for you. And poor people of another class, who blow the trumpet for, and 'prostrate yourselves['] at the feet of other people!

Well after all this array of facts and opinions, it may be well to look at the bright side: the coming "elephant" may be but a precursor of the "good time," when the 'distinguished organ['] of Anti-Emigration in the U.S.,[8] will cease its opposition to colored freemen who wish to settle in Canada—will emigrate hither instead of simply coming over to take away the money before our "hard" winter sets in, and pour forth its "clarion notes" as the organ of the Toronto Anti-Slavery Society, until the *globe*[9] shall be shaken by the "awful sound."

But will not Miss Griffiths leave a few coppers behind? The Underground emigrants[10] come on in great numbers, and may "need" a little of something in the cold weather, *besides*, we know that the friends of Mr. Ward, and of the *Provincial Freeman*, talk about holding a Huzza for this paper about the same time!

Provincial Freeman (Toronto, Canada West), 3 June 1854.

1. The antislavery bazaar, an event at which clothing, ornaments, books, and other items were sold to raise funds to support antislavery activities, was conceived by members of the Boston Female Anti-Slavery Society in 1834. By the mid-1840s, the annual Boston bazaar served as a source of power and influence for women abolitionists, who supported the Massachusetts and American societies, assisted black institutions, and sponsored lectures, legal actions, and abolitionist publications like the *Liberator* and *National Anti-Slavery Standard*. Numerous abolitionist societies throughout the United States, Britain, and Canada took their cue from the Boston society and held similar bazaars. Antislavery bazaars remained popular into the 1860s. Merrill and Ruchames, *Letters of William Lloyd Garrison*, 3:136, 517; Benjamin Quarles, "Sources of Abolitionist Income," *MVHR* 32:63–76 (June 1945).

2. Julia Griffiths, an English antislavery advocate, first met and befriended Frederick Douglass during his 1846 tour of Britain. She settled in Rochester in 1848, lived in the Douglass household, and provided editorial and managerial expertise for Douglass's antislavery publications. She devised a number of means to keep the *North Star* and *Frederick Douglass' Paper* financially solvent. Direct appeals were one method. In late 1853, Griffiths collected $1,000 in $10 donations by sending letters of solicitation to antislavery friends. The Rochester Anti-Slavery Bazaar, conducted by the Rochester Ladies' Anti-Slavery Society, was another successful fund-raising device. As the society's permanent secretary, Griffiths organized the annual affair, solicited donations of goods from British antislavery women, and edited *Autographs for Freedom*—an antislavery gift book sold at the bazaar. Proceeds from the bazaar netted between $200 and $300 each year. Unsold goods were shipped to Toronto and disposed of there. Griffiths also joined Douglass in assisting fugitive slaves. Their close relationship sparked rumors of impropriety that exacerbated the developing schism between William Lloyd Garrison and Douglass. Griffiths returned to England in 1855 and toured the country raising funds for Douglass and organizing women's antislavery groups. She married H. O. Crofts, a Halifax clergyman, in 1858. In later years, she conducted classes for young women. Foner, *Frederick Douglass*, 87–92, 132–50; Merrill and Ruchames, *Letters of William Lloyd Garrison*, 4:391–92n; Benjamin Quarles, *Frederick Douglass* (Washington, D.C., 1948), 92–93.

3. Cary refers to Harriet Beecher Stowe (1811–1896), a leading American novelist during the nineteenth century. Stowe's antislavery trilogy—*Uncle Tom's Cabin* (1852), *A Key to Uncle Tom's Cabin* (1853), and *Dred* (1856)—profoundly influenced public debate about slavery. In 1853 Stowe decided to use part of the proceeds from the sale of *Uncle Tom's Cabin* to establish a black school. She initially intended to assist the American Industrial School, a black manual labor college planned and promoted by Frederick Douglass and others; Douglass expected that she would donate $1,500 to the school from an Uncle Tom Fund collected in Britain. But in 1854 Stowe lost interest in the school and refused to finance it,

probably due to Garrisonian opposition to the project. Although Stowe undoubtedly encouraged and assisted *Frederick Douglass' Paper* in minor ways, Cary wrongly assumes that she was a major contributor. *DAB*, 18 : 115–20; Pease and Pease, *They Who Would Be Free*, 141.

4. Cary's reference implies that Julia Griffiths's behavior exceeded that of Phineas T. Barnum (1810–1891), the American showman and circus entrepreneur. Barnum was noted for his aggressive and suspect business practices.

5. Cary reprimands the Anti-Slavery Society of Canada by comparing it to the virtually defunct American and Foreign Anti-Slavery Society. The AFASS was founded in May 1840 by Lewis Tappan and other disaffected American Anti-Slavery Society members, including several leading black abolitionists. The association hoped to expand the arena of abolitionist activity by endorsing the idea of antislavery political action. Although the AFASS met annually throughout the 1840s, the society did not flourish. The organization was administratively top-heavy, lacked vigorous local affiliates, was financially troubled, did not sharply define its goals, never developed an effective newspaper, and failed to attract a large membership. The AFASS's white leaders divided over whether or not the organization should attach itself to a political party. Black leaders were alienated by the association's eventual support for a third political party and its 1852 endorsement of African settlement. In 1855 Tappan abandoned the AFASS to help form the American Abolition Society. Wyatt-Brown, *Lewis Tappan and Evangelical War*, 193–200, 213, 215, 249, 252, 279, 282, 315, 332, 516; Aileen S. Kraditor, *Means and Ends in American Abolitionism: Garrison and His Critics on Strategy and Tactics* (New York, N.Y., 1969), 7, 52–57, 63, 107, 118, 129, 141, 142, 148, 152.

6. Lewis Tappan (1788–1873), a successful New York City businessman and philanthropist, was a primary figure in a variety of antebellum religious and social reform movements. During the 1830s, he befriended William Lloyd Garrison and helped organize the New York Anti-Slavery Society and the American Anti-Slavery Society. Tappan helped fund several antislavery newspapers, including the *Liberator* and the *Emancipator*. He broke with Garrison in 1840 over the participation of women in the movement and the use of political action and joined other anti-Garrisonians in founding the American and Foreign Anti-Slavery Society and supporting the 1840 Liberty party campaign. As AFASS corresponding secretary, Tappan maintained close ties with British abolitionists during the 1840s. Tappan also filled executive positions with the Amistad Committee and the American Missionary Association. In 1855 he abandoned the AFASS to join the more radical American Abolition Society. After the Civil War, he published *Is It Right to Be Rich?* (1869), an apologia for his philanthropic endeavors, and *The Life of Arthur Tappan* (1870), a biography of his brother. Merrill and Ruchames, *Letters of William Lloyd Garrison*, 2:xxix; *DAB*, 18 : 303–4.

7. Samuel Ringgold Ward (1817–ca. 1866) was the second son of slave parents who fled to freedom in 1820. The Ward family lived in New Jersey for six years until the threat of kidnapping by slave catchers prompted them to resettle in New York City. Ward received the rudiments of an education from his father, attended New York's African Free School, and clerked for two leading black activists, David Ruggles and Thomas L. Jennings. He moved to Newark, New Jersey, in

1835 and taught school until 1839; he and his wife then relocated in Poughkeepsie, New York, where he was employed at the Colored Lancastrian School. That same year, Ward became a licensed minister in the New York Congregational Association. At the end of the year, his growing reputation as a forceful and articulate antislavery spokesman earned him an appointment as lecture agent for the American Anti-Slavery Society. When the society divided in 1840, Ward left his agency and joined the American and Foreign Anti-Slavery Society because he believed slavery should be attacked with political weapons as well as moral suasion.

Throughout the 1840s, Ward led New York blacks in their efforts to acquire the right to vote. He returned to the ministry, first as a pastor of a church in South Butler, New York (1841–43), and then as leader of a white congregation in Cortland, New York (1846–51), while continuing his antislavery activity. Perhaps more than any other black abolitionist, Ward was angered by the hypocrisy of white reformers, and he often cautioned his listeners that there were many abolitionists "who best love the colored man at a distance." Ward founded and edited several reform newspapers: first the short-lived *True American* in 1847–48 and later the more successful *Impartial Citizen*, which lasted from mid-1849 until well into 1851 and which allowed Ward to display his Liberty party commitment and his interpretation of the American Constitution as an antislavery document.

He joined the Syracuse Vigilance Committee, Gerrit Smith, and his longtime friend, black minister Jermain W. Loguen in rescuing the fugitive slave William "Jerry" McHenry from federal officers in October 1851. Difficulties resulting from the Jerry rescue sent Ward to Canada, where he remained for over two years, serving as an agent for the Anti-Slavery Society of Canada. Early in 1853, he founded the *Provincial Freeman*, a newspaper meant to serve the Canadian black community. A few months later, he accepted a commission from the society to seek British funds for Canadian fugitives, and he remained abroad for two-and-a-half years, touring successfully (he impressed British audiences with his eloquence, humor, and imposing black presence) and publishing his narrative, *Autobiography of a Fugitive Negro: His Anti-Slavery Labours in the United States, Canada and England* (1855).

When Ward left England, he sailed not to Canada, but to Jamaica, where he ministered to a Kingston congregation for the next five years. In 1860 he settled on a small piece of land he had received as a gift while in England. In the wake of the Morant Bay Rebellion in Jamaica (October 1865), Ward wrote *Reflections on the Gordon Rebellion* (1866), a critical examination of George William Gordon, the leader of the island's black revolutionary forces. Ward, *Autobiography of a Fugitive Negro*; Ronald Kevin Burke, "Samuel Ringgold Ward, Christian Abolitionist" (Ph.D. diss., Syracuse University, 1975), 12–98; Winks, *Blacks in Canada*, 206–7, 218, 227, 235, 241, 249, 255–59, 265–66, 361, 441; *NASS*, 2 July, 10, 17 September 1840, 11 March 1847 [3:0478, 0612, 0619, 5:0391]; *IC*, 14 March, 11 April, 27 June 1850, 13, 20 February 1851 [5:1003, 1054, 6:0021, 0023, 0398, 0404]; *NSt*, 27 June 1850 [6:0526]; *WAA*, 20, 27 August 1859 [11:0944, 0972]; *DANB*, 631–32.

8. Cary refers to *Frederick Douglass' Paper*.

9. Cary evidently refers to the Toronto *Globe*, George Brown's Reform party newspaper. The *Globe* was sympathetic to antislavery and to black concerns,

which earned it the respect of Canadian blacks. Nevertheless, Cary and the other editors of the *Provincial Freeman* occasionally chided the *Globe* for its patronizing attitude and lack of abolitionist zeal. *PFW*, 29 September, 6 October 1855 [9:0855–56, 0868–69].

10. Cary refers to the underground railroad.

46.
Address to the Queen
Presented by George Dupont Wells at the Government Grounds Toronto, Canada West 1 August 1854

Emancipation Day celebrations gave black Canadians an opportunity to commemorate the Emancipation Act of 1833, which ended slavery throughout most of the British Empire, and to affirm their allegiance to their new homeland. The 1 August 1854 activities in Toronto began with a prayer service at the black Sayer Street African Methodist Episcopal Church. Celebrants then proceeded to the Government Grounds, where Thomas Smallwood, a local black who had been elected president of the day, addressed the gathering. He welcomed the audience assembled to celebrate the day that Britain "swept the bonds from 800,000 bondsmen, and made them free." About noon the crowd adjourned to St. James Anglican Church to hear an Emancipation Day sermon by Rev. Henry James Grasett. Following that, the festivities returned to the Government Grounds, where a banquet was served and antislavery speeches made. George Dupont Wells, a local white attorney, was asked to rise and read an "Address to the Queen" that had been drafted by Toronto blacks. The address thanked the British monarch, Queen Victoria, for her nation's efforts to abolish slavery. *PFW*, 5 August 1854 [8 : 0994]; *Toronto City Directory*, 1850.

To Her Most Gracious Majesty, Queen Victoria

MAY IT PLEASE YOUR MAJESTY:

WE, the Coloured Inhabitants of Canada, most respectfully, most gratefully and most loyally approach your Gracious Majesty, on this, the anniversary of our *death* to *Slavery*, and our *birth* to *Freedom*. With what feelings, or what words can we adequately express our gratitude to England for such a boon?

Our hearts are wholly your Majesty's; and if the time should ever come when your Majesty might need our aid, our lives would be as they are, *at your service*.

What a happy, what a proud reflection it must be to your Majesty, to know that the moment the poor crushed slave sets foot upon any part of your *mighty* dominions, his chains fall from him—he feels himself a man, and can look up. Can it be conceived that he would not on that same spot turn, and whilst defending the hallowed soil, that memory would not fire his brain, and gratitude nerve his arm! Can your Majesty imagine that from such a people, loyalty could be an *empty name*, or *devotion be a dream!* Faults of commission may be urged against us by those who grudge us our Freedom; but we carefully watch that such faults shall be the exception and not the rule; at the same time, we pray your Majesty in your judgment of us, to remember that whilst the invigorating food of education was jealously withheld from us, the brutalizing cup of Slavery was forced between our lips until we drained it to the very dregs.

The effects, more or less, must have been a moral stupor, for which the hand of time and kindness can alone provide the cure. But amid all our trials, we beg your Gracious Majesty to believe we yet thank the Most High that he has granted us the privilege of teaching our little ones to join us in praying that the God of battle may give victory to your Majesty's arms[1]—that He will continue to bless your Majesty as a Queen, bless you as a wife, bless you as a mother; and that it will please Him in his infinite wisdom and mercy, long "to put back the time" of removing you from your Earthly to your Heavenly crown. And as in duty bound, We will ever pray.

Toronto, Canada Wes[t]
August 1st, 1854

Provincial Freeman (Toronto, Canada West), 5 August 1854.

1. The authors refer to Britain's participation in the Crimean War (1854–56). Britain joined France and the Ottoman Empire in a war against Russia to settle territorial and religious questions in the Balkans and Asia Minor.

47.
Proceedings of a Meeting of St. Catharines Blacks
Convened at the North Street Methodist Church, St. Catharines, Canada West 4 August 1854

When confronted with white Canadian racism, blacks often took vigorous action. During early 1854, the drivers of public coaches owned by two hotels in St. Catharines refused to accept black passengers, including two bishops of the African Methodist Episcopal church. On the evening of 4 August, local blacks met in the North Street Methodist Church to protest the practice and to develop a strategy to end it. At the meeting, black waiters employed at the American Hotel and the St. Catharines House resolved to leave their jobs unless blacks were allowed to ride in the coaches. The boycott had the desired effect. By late August, local missionary Hiram Wilson reported that the owner of the St. Catharines House had relented, and the owner of the American Hotel seemed prepared to follow suit. The incident and the resulting black response attracted considerable attention in the Canadian-American press. Murray, "Canada and Anglo-American Anti-Slavery Movement," 321–22; *Lib*, 25 August 1854; *PFW*, 2 September 1854.

Indignation Meeting

A meeting of the colored citizens of St. Catharines, including the waiters at the principal hotels of the place, convened this evening at the Methodist Chapel on North Street, to take into consideration their aggrievances from certain innkeepers and their hirelings who drive their omnibusses.

The meeting was opened with prayer, after which the Rev. Nelson Countee was appointed President;[1] Emanuel Morris, Vice-President, and David Baxter, Secretary.[2]

The President rose and addressed the meeting, and stated the object for which it was called, viz., to take action against the cruel prejudices which deny to coloured persons, however respectable, the use of public conveyances to and from the Railroad station and the steamboat.

Mr. Dyke, the head waiter of the American Hotel,[3] was called to express his sentiments, which he did in an appropriate manner. It was his settled determination to quit the hotel, and urged others to do the same rather than be compelled to witness such treatment as had lately occurred; that he could stand it no longer.

Mr. Morris, the head waiter of the St. Catharines House, was called on to express his sentiments, which he did in a brief but decided manner.

He said that he considered the insults and outrages heaped upon his brethren, on account of prejudice, as committed against himself. He could endure such outrages no longer; and made a stirring appeal to all present to respect themselves, and their rights as a people, and submit no longer to such degrading treatment. The head waiters were followed by quite a number of other persons, most of whom were employed at the hotels above named. The meeting was one of great harmony, and all were united in giving utterance to manly indignation towards the guilty parties who had injured and insulted them repeatedly, by excluding from conveyances persons of colour; men of the highest respectability, and in one or two instances, using violence to effect their nefarious purposes.

The following resolutions were presented, and passed unanimously; the latter more particularly, by the waiters of the two leading hotels:

> *Resolved*, That, in this glorious land of Freedom, and under this equitable and powerful Government, *man is man*, without respect to the colour of his skin, and that we, as men, will not submit to degrading terms of service, nor see our brethren treated with indignity by public conveyances, or excluded therefrom, without showing a manly spirit of resentment.
>
> *Resolved*, That, as waiters, at the public hotels, of St. Catharines, we will not continue in the service of our present employers, unless, in the management of their conveyances, they henceforth treat ourselves and our people with that respect and civility, to which we are entitled, as men.

It was unanimously resolved that the proceedings of this meeting be published.

NELSON COUNTEE, President
DAVID BAXTER, Secretary
St. Catharines, C[anada] W[est]
August 4, 1854

Provincial Freeman (Toronto, Canada West), 12 August 1854.

1. Nelson Countee (1815–?), a black cooper, left the United States and settled in Canada West in the early 1840s. He entered the African Methodist Episcopal ministry in 1844 and resided in St. Catharines. Countee represented St. Catharines at the Drummondville Convention (1847) and was involved in local fugitive relief efforts during the 1850s. As president of the Emigration Club in Hamilton, he advocated Haitian immigration during the early 1860s. Payne, *History of the AME Church*, 178; Census of Canada, 1861; *Convention of the Colored Population at Drummondville, 1847*, 5; *PFW*, 10 May 1856 [10:0147]; *PP*, 7 September 1861.

2. David Baxter (1828–?), a black laborer, left the United States and settled in

St. Catharines, Canada West, by 1843. He owned some property and livestock there. Baxter was married to an Irishwoman; they had two children. Census of Canada, 1861.

3. The American Hotel was located on St. Paul Street in St. Catharines. Jackson, *St. Catharines, Ontario*, 318.

48. Report of the Business Committee of a Meeting of Toronto Blacks

Presented at the Sayer Street African Methodist Episcopal Church Toronto, Canada West 25 September 1854

Black abolitionists rarely tempered their antislavery and civil rights principles, even if that meant criticizing abolitionist friends. Officials of the Colonial Church and School Society, an English-based missionary association, became aware of that during 1854. In August the CCSS sent Rev. Marmaduke Dillon and three black assistants to Toronto, Canada West, to establish a school for fugitive slaves. Black leaders favored the plan until it became clear that Dillon intended his new school to be exclusively black. Offended blacks met on 25 September at the Sayer Street AME Church in Toronto to consider the matter. Wilson R. Abbott, a local black businessman, chaired the meeting. After preliminary discussions, a business committee presented a preamble and several resolutions to the gathering, which included Dillon and CCSS supporters. The preamble contradicted CCSS assumptions about the extent of Canadian racial prejudice, the moral condition of fugitive slaves, and the impact of Christian education on slavery. The resolutions argued that CCSS schools were unneccessary, that schools should not be established without black support, and that they should make no "*distinction on account of color*." Black leaders vigorously debated these resolutions with Dillon and a few of his advocates, then approved them "with much enthusiasm." This expression of black resolve so impressed Dillon that, when the CCSS mission school was finally opened in London, Canada West, he allowed both blacks and whites to attend. *PFW*, 16, 23 September, 14 October 1854 [9:0139]; Murray, "Canada and Anglo-American Anti-Slavery Movement," 486–98.

Your Committee, to whom was submitted the business of drafting resolutions for this Meeting, beg leave to report, as follows:

Whereas, the "*Colonial Church and School Society*"[1] have sent out Missionaries and Teachers to this country, for the purpose of "*Evangelizing the Colored Settlers*" by the means of Normal Schools, for us, as a *distinct class*. And, whereas, the said effort is to be made, because of a *misconception* of our true condition, as Her Majesty's loyal subjects in this country, where *no distinction is made on account of color*, we deem it a duty to ourselves, and to our white fellow-citizens, to say, that the

Report which gave rise to the before-named mission, as published in the "Seventeenth Annual Report of the Colonial Church and School Society," is entirely *untrue*; and especially that part of it that says, that "*They*—we the colored people of Canada—*are in the* LOWEST *state of ignorance of* RELIGION, *and even of secular knowledge; and according to accounts that have been received, utterly neglected by all around them; and, though permitted to live in freedom, to a great extent, it is to be feared are as much the victims of Popular Prejudice as their brethren in BOSTON AND NEW YORK.*"

And whereas, the "Colonial Church and School Society" *has been credibly informed, on the authority of persons conversant with the views and feelings of the SOUTHERN PLANTERS that the spectacle of a large body of the NEGRO RACE, elevated in a social and religious condition, and WALKING LIKE CHRISTIAN MEN in the light of the Gospel, would do more to TRANQUILIZE THEIR FEARS, and to effect a general, if not an universal manumission THAN ANY PLAN yet devised in England or America;* it seems proper that we should express our opinion, and say that *OUR EXPERIENCE TEACHES US, that just the opposite result would be true*: for it is a notorious fact, that the more the *NEGRO RACE* on this continent have "*walked like CHRISTIAN MEN, in the light of the Gospel,*" the *LESS* have slaveholders' fears been *TRANQUILIZED*; hence the internal scheme of Colonization, &c., &c.; and it is especially true, that the more the Negro race, who are slaves, and those who are nominally free, in slave States, ["]have walked like Christian men," the more have they been oppressed; and hence the legal regulations, in nearly every slave State, to prevent them *FROM walking like Christian men* in the light of the Gospel, the use of the Scriptures and other Religious means."

We recommend the adoption of the following Resolutions, by this Meeting, to wit:

1. *Resolved*—That we assure our friends in England, and especially the "Colonial Church and School Society," that we are truly grateful for their sympathy with, and regard for us, as an exiled and wronged people; and that we can but hope that their efforts for our good may be directed otherwise than through *Normal Schools* of which there is *no need*, in this country, since such schools here, are open to us, in common with all other citizens.

2. *Resolved*—That should such schools be opened, and efforts made by the "Colonial Church and School Society," contrary to our expressed wish and interest, we cannot, consistently, and *will not, as colored citizens*, give them our support.

3. *Resolved*—That we caution *our* people throughout the Province to be careful, as to how they give their influence and support to institutions

and efforts, whether established and made by friend or foe—*white* or *black*—that tend to make *distinction on account of color*, and to destroy the foundation of our liberties.

Committee
W. P. NEWMAN[2]
W. R. ABBOTT[3]
R. M. JOHNSON[4]
A. H. JUDAH[5]
THOS. SMALLWOOD

Provincial Freeman (Toronto, Canada West), 14 October 1854.

1. The Colonial Church and School Society, an evangelical Anglican missionary organization, was created in 1851 when the Colonial Church Society merged with the Newfoundland School Society. The CCSS attempted to meet the spiritual needs of British emigrants and, eventually, English-speaking sailors and craftsmen in European seaports and towns. A network of committees in Britain and the colonies supported the society. The CCSS's Canadian mission to fugitive slaves was the particular project of the West London Ladies' Association. Despite its controversial debut in Toronto, the mission prospered after it shifted its effort to general education without explicit reference to race. Following emancipation, interest in the mission declined; the association disbanded in 1869. The parent organization, known after 1861 as the Colonial and Continental Church Society, continued to function and was instrumental in establishing Anglicanism in midwestern Canada during the late nineteenth century. Francis Warre Cornish, *The English Church in the Nineteenth Century*, 2 vols. (London, 1910; reprint, New York, N.Y., 1977), 2:211; Murray, "Canada and Anglo-American Anti-Slavery Movement," 486–516.

2. William P. Newman (1815–1866) was born a slave in Richmond, Virginia, but escaped from bondage in the 1830s. He eventually settled in Ohio and, after a year of study at Oberlin College (1842–43), was ordained a Baptist clergyman. During the next two years, he pastored the Union Baptist Church in Cincinnati and did itinerant preaching in Zanesville and Chillicothe. About this same time, he became involved in Ohio antislavery activities, attended two black state conventions, and served as a subscription agent for David Jenkins's *Palladium of Liberty*. In 1845 Newman accepted an appointment in Canada West from the American Baptist Free Mission Society. Arriving at the Dawn settlement in June, he took charge of the British-American Institute and assumed secretarial duties on the Dawn executive committee. His insistence on financial accountability led to confrontations with Dawn agents Hiram Wilson and Josiah Henson. Frustrated by affairs at Dawn, Newman resigned in September 1846 and returned to Cincinnati, where he again served his old congregation and briefly acted as an agent for the Colored Orphan Asylum. But he continued to criticize the conduct of Wilson and Henson and brought Dawn's condition to public attention. When responsibility for Dawn fell to the ABFMS in 1850, Newman returned to Canada West and assisted Rev. Samuel H. Davis in managing the British-American Institute. His

work at Dawn ended when British abolitionist John Scoble assumed control of the institute in 1852. Newman then settled in Toronto and pastored Baptist congregations there for the next seven years. But he also found time for antislavery and civil rights work. He served as secretary of the Canadian Anti-Slavery Baptist Association and the Provincial Union Association and helped lead the black struggle for equal access to the province's public schools. In 1855 Newman accepted the editorship of the *Provincial Freeman*, a position that gave him a forum to express his political conservatism, his opposition to begging practices, and his militant abolitionism. He remained at that post for one year.

Newman became pessimistic about black prospects in Canada West during the late 1850s. Black minority status, the persistence of racial prejudice, and the Canadian climate convinced him that the Afro-American destiny lay beyond the North American continent. Unimpressed by Martin R. Delany's Niger Valley venture, he looked to the Caribbean and traveled to Haiti as an ABFMS missionary in 1859 to investigate the feasibility of black immigration there. His initial reports were positive, but by the summer of 1860, he offered a more skeptical assessment, criticizing Haiti's military government, Catholic faith, and liberal social customs. By the time Newman returned to Canada West in late 1861, he was a staunch opponent of Haitian settlement. Believing that blacks had no stake in the outcome of the Civil War, he promoted Jamaican immigration during the early war years. But by 1864 he had returned to his old position at the Union Baptist Church in Cincinnati, enthused by the new opportunities that Reconstruction offered. He attended the National Convention of Colored Men (1864) and served as an officer of the National Equal Rights League. Newman led an attempt to merge black and white Baptists into an interracial, egalitarian denomination, but this ambitious work had only begun when he died of cholera in 1866. James Melvin Washington, "The Origins and Emergence of Black Baptist Separatism, 1863–1897" (Ph.D. diss., Yale University, 1979), 33, 43, 53, 62, 70, 72–74, 79–83; *E*, 1 September 1842; *P*, 18 October 1843 [4:0685]; *PL*, 27 December 1843, 1 May, 16 October 1844 [4:0712]; *CF*, 27 November 1845 [5:0114]; Winks, *Blacks in Canada*, 164–65, 196–203; Pease and Pease, *Black Utopia*, 71–77; *ASB*, 21 January 1848 [5:0559]; *NSt*, 22 December 1848, 9 March 1849, 21 October 1852 [5:0862]; *WC*, 29 October 1850 [6:0654]; *VF*, 15 January, 9 April 1851, 23 September, 21 October 1852 [6:0878]; *Lib*, 4 March 1853 [8:0154]; Simpson, "Negroes in Ontario to 1870," 868–69; *PFW*, 24 March 1853, 15, 29 April, 24 June, 1 July, 9 August, 2, 23 September, 14 October 1854, 13, 20 January, 30 June, 22, 29 August, 15, 22 September, 22 December 1855, 19 April 1856 [8:0175, 9:0018, 0110, 0139, 0787, 0807, 0833]; William P. Newman to Egerton Ryerson, 7 March 1852, 13 January 1856, Ryerson Papers, CaOTAr; *WAA*, 23 July 1859, 23 June 1860, 31 August, 30 November 1861, 4 January, 29 March 1862 [11:0865, 12:0807, 13:0718, 0942, 14:0058, 0203]; *PP*, 31 August, 14 September 1861 [13:0715, 0753]; *CP*, 19 July, 20 December 1859, 22 March, 21 June 1860 [11:0862, 12:0304, 0583, 0804]; *Proceedings of the National Convention of Colored Men . . .* (Boston, Mass., 1864), 6.

3. Wilson Ruffin Abbott (1801–1876) was born in Richmond, Virginia, the son of a Scotch-Irish father and a free black mother. After working as a carpenter's apprentice, he left Virginia at age fifteen, became a steward on a Missis-

sippi riverboat, and eventually married and opened a grocery in Mobile, Alabama. He remained there until 1834, when sentiment against free blacks forced him and his family to flee to New York State. During the winter of 1835–36, he moved to Toronto, Upper Canada. He became a successful businessman there, making his fortune in real estate and accumulating a substantial amount of property. Once in Canada, Abbott devoted much of his energy to his new home and its black community. He served in the militia during the Rebellion of 1837. In 1838 he was among the founders of Toronto's Colored Wesleyan Methodist Church, an enterprise he hoped would encourage black émigrés to consider Canada their permanent home. During the early 1840s, he joined other black residents in petitioning city officials to stop the production of racist theatrical performances in Toronto. Abbott regularly participated in various antislavery and self-improvement meetings. He was a longtime director and stockholder of the Elgin Association, a founding member and a local vice-president of the Anti-Slavery Society of Canada (1851), and a contributor and founder of the Canadian Mill and Mercantile Association (1852)—an organization that proposed to establish a sawmill, gristmill, and country store in Buxton to encourage black business enterprise. In 1854 he helped organize the Provincial Union Association, a self-help association that encouraged equal rights and loyalty to the Queen. During the same year, he served on a committee that represented the black community's objection to the Colonial Church and School Society's proposal to establish a separate normal school for blacks. Abbott later served on the Toronto City Council and on the central committee of the Reform party in Canada West. *DCB*, 10:3; Winks, *Blacks in Canada*, 211, 212, 226, 255, 328–29, 366–67; Wilson R. Abbott et al. to Mayor of Toronto, 20 July 1840, 14 October 1841, 9 May 1842, 21 April 1843, CaOTCi [3:0531, 4:0253, 0431, 0562]; *VF*, 22 April 1852 [7:0532]; *PFW*, 19 August, 23 September, 14 October 1854 [9:0017, 0110, 0139].

4. Robert M. Johnson was a clergyman in the Indiana conference of the African Methodist Episcopal church during the early 1850s. Appointed to raise money to establish a seminary for the conference, he failed to secure the necessary funds. He became pastor of an AME congregation in Cleveland in 1852 but resettled in Toronto within two years. There he was active in the Toronto Literary Association and served as a subscription agent for the *Provincial Freeman*. Johnson apparently served BME congregations in Bronte and Collingwood, Ontario, during the 1860s and 1870s. Smith, *African Methodist Episcopal Church*, 23, 38–39; *PFW*, 23 September 1854 [9:0110], 7 April, 9 June 1855, 1 March 1856; Simpson, "Negroes in Ontario to 1870," 892.

5. Adolphus H. Judah (?–1888), a black Toronto carpenter, became involved in the antislavery movement when he helped organize the British-American Anti-Slavery Society in the late 1840s. The brother-in-law of Wilson R. Abbott, a wealthy Toronto black, he joined the city's black elite and assumed a prominent role in local and provincial black affairs during the early 1850s. Judah was an Elgin Association stockholder and petitioned the Canadian parliament to approve the association's charter. He was the founding secretary of and a stockholder in the Provincial Union Association, a black self-help organization. Intensely interested in local politics, he publicly endorsed Conservative candidates. Judah served as treasurer and trustee of the Toronto-based Provincial Association for the Education and Elevation of the Colored People during the early 1860s.

TET, 17 May 1911; *Toronto City Directory*, 1860; *ASRL*, 1 April 1858; *NSt*, 1 December 1848 [5:0838]; *I*, 12 January 1850 [6:0352]; *PFW*, 17 June, 19 August, 23 December 1854, 3 November 1855, 20 June 1857 [9:0018, 0916, 10:0733]; *WAA*, 7 April 1860, 16 February 1861 [12:0622, 13:0326]; *CTWP*, 21 December 1857; *TG*, 3 March 1860 [12:0542]; Simpson, "Negroes in Ontario to 1870," 868.

49.
Officers of the True Band Society of Amherstburg to Mary Ann Shadd Cary
13 March 1855

Some black abolitionists viewed persistent fund-raising efforts for black Canadian settlements and institutions as detrimental to the goal of black self-reliance. The arguments of Samuel Ringgold Ward and Mary Ann Shadd Cary were particularly persuasive. By the mid-1850s, blacks in communities throughout Canada West began to form true band societies—organizations designed to encourage black self-help and mutual aid and to oppose black fund-raising (or "begging") schemes. Amherstburg blacks formed the first true band society in the fall of 1854. The True Band Society of Amherstburg attacked begging, administered an emergency fund for blacks, and arbitrated disputes between blacks to keep them from becoming public issues, particularly in the press. The organization's 13 March 1855 "Report and Circular," which was published in the *Provincial Freeman*, outlined its specific objectives. The society grew quickly. By June 1855, it claimed nearly two hundred members; one year later, membership reached six hundred. Blacks organized thirteen other true band societies in the southwestern part of the province by 1856. Toronto blacks formed the Provincial Union Association, which worked toward the same goals. But the true bands achieved mixed success. Some generated sufficient operating revenue in the black community; others violated their antibegging principles and became dependent on fund-raising efforts. Winks, *Blacks in Canada*, 226–27; Hill, *Freedom-Seekers*, 180–81; Simpson, "Negroes in Ontario to 1870," 218; *PFW*, 22 August 1855.

Amherstburg, [Canada West]
March 13, 1855

To the Editor of the Provincial Freeman
DEAR MADAM:

Please publish the following Report and Circular, in behalf of the True Band Society of Amherstburg, C.W., and vicinity, for the benefit of the Colored people in Canada, and to invigorate the panting Fugitive, who is now fleeing before the baying bloodhounds of the slaveholder, and the more cruel minions and slave-catchers of the "Fugitive Slave Bill":

> We, the colored people of Amherstburg, have the most of us fled from American Slavery—'the vilest that ever saw the light'—where we have been robbed of all our earnings, crushed in our intellects, denied education, under the debauch system of Slavery; where we have been chattels and goods in the hands of our masters, and resistance to white men is made crime by the slave law; where virtue is

necessarily (under such laws) crushed in the dust, and the slave is a victim to the lust and avarice of the oppressor. But, through the good Providence of God, and by means of *friends*, the North Star, and underground railroad, we have sought for freedom and found it in Canada, under Her Majesty; and when many of us arrived here, we were literally naked, hungry, and penniless; the country being new, and but little cleared up, we have necessarily been very poor. Appeals have been made to our friends, the Abolitionists, in the States, and we have, in common with other fugitives, received some temporary relief through their *benevolence*, for which we are thankful.

But, while we have received such relief, the goodness of our friends has been imposed upon; and a system of 'begging' has been got up, and agents have been going out through the States, constantly telling of our suffering and poverty, and asserting that we cannot *sustain ourselves*, after so many years of freedom: at the same time, those agents are living upon the spoils of beggary, neglecting to work with their hands—one dollar per day being a common price allowed to begging agents.

Now, brethren, this begging brings us no permanent good; but degrades us in the eyes of the world. And the people of the United States, and the slaveholders, have cause to say, and in fact do say, 'the slaves can't take care of themselves. The blacks were made for slaves, and freedom is a curse to them.' We, the True Band of Amherstburg, repudiate the whole system of begging in behalf of the fugitives in Canada; and by an unanimous vote, in our last meeting, we passed a solemn resolution to that effect. The resolution passed was:

'Under God we can take care of ourselves.'

Our True Band Society was formed and organized the 13th day of Nov. (A.D.), 1854, for the following purpose: First, to form a Union among ourselves. Second, for our intellectual improvement. Third, to increase our benevolent feelings (the most ennobling principle of the human mind) and to prove that truth of Scripture, 'It is more blessed to give than to receive.' Fourth, to raise funds to assist the fugitive on his way to Canada; and also, after getting here, those who have not the means to support themselves until they can get employment. Fifth, to get them into good business as soon as possible, and to encourage them to improve their talents, to live by the sweat of their own brows, and make themselves useful men and women amongst us. Sixth, to encourage all to escape the 'yoke of bondage' for freedom; and those in the Northern States exposed to the Fugitive Slave Law, to make sure their liberty.

We have a Constitution and By-laws, by which we are governed.

Our officers are: a President, Vice-President, Recording and Corresponding Secretary, a Treasurer, two Auditors, and a Board of Managers, consisting of five. The Society has been in operation four and a half months, and has paid out 13s. 9d. ($2 75c.). Cash in the Treasury, £5.4s. 1½. ($22 85c.). The terms of membership are—for males, 12½ cents; females, 6¼ cents.

We meet on the first Tuesday evening in each month, in the Baptist Church,[1] without regard to sect. By order, and in behalf of the Society,

MAJOR STEPHENS, *President*[2]
FOUNTAIN BUSH, *Vice-President*[3]
ABRAM TOLES, *Auditor*[4]
EMANUEL BURNETT, *Auditor*[5]
N. W. BROWN, *Cor. Sec.*[6]
L. G. SPEARS, *Rec. Sec.*[7]
Board of Managers:
WILSON BATTLES
JOHN HATFIELD[8]
LEVI FOSTER[9]
GEORGE YOUNG[10]
JAMES SMITH[11]

Provincial Freeman (Toronto, Canada West), 7 April 1855.

1. Finding their presence unwelcome in local white Baptist churches, fugitive slaves, under the leadership of Rev. Anthony Binga, established the First Baptist Church of Amherstburg between 1838 and 1841. The congregation then helped found (and served as the "mother church" for) the Amherstburg Baptist Association, which became the central administrative body for Canada West's black Baptist churches. The First Baptist Church supported antislavery, advocated temperance, and aided fugitive slaves. Its Sunday School taught reading and writing as well as religious doctrine. The congregation reported nineteen members in 1841, but passage of the Fugitive Slave Law greatly increased that number. Under the enthusiastic direction of Rev. Horace Hawkins and Rev. William Troy, Amherstburg's First Baptist Church maintained a membership of nearly two hundred persons until after the Civil War. The congregation remained active into the 1890s. Hill, *Freedom-Seekers*, 54, 104, 140, 142; Lewis, "Pioneer Coloured Baptist Life," 243–73; James K. Lewis, "Religious Nature of the Early Negro Migration to Canada and the Amherstburg Baptist Association," *OntH* 58:117–22 (1966); Simpson, "Negroes in Ontario to 1870," 112–14, 120–21, 169, 489, 571.

2. Major Stephens (1803–?), a black laborer, emigrated from the United States and settled in Amherstburg, Canada West, by 1841. His marriage to an Englishwoman produced two sons. Stephens was a deacon and officer of the Amherstburg

First Baptist Church, an active member of the Amherstburg Baptist Association, and a participant in local, black self-help organizations, including the True Band Society of Amherstburg. He attended the Amherstburg Convention (1853). *VF*, 26 February 1852; Census of Canada, 1861; *Minutes of Convention in Amherstburg*, 2 [8:0298].

3. Fountain Bush (1810–?), an American-born black laborer, settled in Amherstburg, Canada West, sometime after 1836. He was married and had two sons. Census of Canada, 1861.

4. Abram Tolls (1823–?), a black resident of Windsor, was originally from the United States. Tolls was married and employed as a whitewasher. Census of Canada, 1861.

5. Emanuel Burnett (1781–?), a black Amherstburg laborer, was born in the United States. He was a member of the Baptist church. Census of Canada, 1861.

6. Nelson Brown (1810–?) emigrated from the United States to Amherstburg, Canada West, sometime after 1833. There he worked as a laborer and was a member of the local Baptist church. Census of Canada, 1861.

7. L. G. Spears was the clerk of the Amherstburg First Baptist Church during the mid-1850s. *PFW*, 17 June 1854, 7 April 1855, 7 February 1857 [8:0800, 9:0522, 10:0536].

8. John Hatfield of Amherstburg was a free black from Pennsylvania. He lived for a time in Cincinnati, working as a barber on an Ohio riverboat and opening his home to fugitive slaves escaping through the city. During the 1830s, Hatfield joined the exodus of Ohio blacks to Upper Canada. He settled in Amherstburg, where he took part in fugitive slave relief efforts and served as a subscription agent for the *Provincial Freeman*. Drew, *North-Side View of Slavery*, 363–66; *PFW*, 23 June, 12 August 1854 [8:0880].

9. Levi Foster (1811–?), a fugitive slave, settled in Amherstburg, Upper Canada, about 1840. He established a successful livery business and winter stage line between Amherstburg and Windsor. A visible participant in the local black community, Foster was a subscription agent for the *Voice of the Fugitive* and the *Provincial Freeman*, a member of fugitive slave relief committees, an officer of the Provincial Union Association, and an advocate of temperance and moral improvement. *VF*, 1 January, 27 August 1851; *PFW*, 12 August 1854, 30 June 1855, 12 July 1856 [7:0722, 0725]; *PP*, 7 December 1861 [13:0954]; Census of Canada, 1861.

10. George Young (1820–?), a black U.S.-born resident of Amherstburg, Canada West, was a laborer and Baptist church deacon. He attended the 1853 Amherstburg Convention. Census of Canada, 1861; *Minutes of Convention in Amherstburg*; *VF*, 26 February 1852.

11. James Smith (1825–1861), an Amherstburg grocer, was born a slave in Pendleton County, Virginia. The son of an English father and a mulatto mother, Smith frequently passed for white. He escaped to the free states in 1847 and settled in Canada West in 1850. Drew, *North-Side View of Slavery*, 351–53; Census of Canada, 1861.

50.
John W. Lewis to Frederick Douglass
20 March 1855

After completing an antislavery lecture tour in Vermont, black clergyman John W. Lewis, a traveling agent for *Frederick Douglass' Paper*, began a tour of Canada East in late February 1855. He recruited subscribers and gave several well-received lectures in the province. Lewis wrote a 20 March 1855 letter to Frederick Douglass describing his tour and informing readers of his perceptions of Canada East. Lewis challenged the commonly held belief that the province was "a cold, bleak, out-of-the-way part of the world," but he suggested another reason why it might be uninviting to fugitive slaves. He complained that many Canadians in the southern part of the province had "become so Americanized and Yankeeized" that they did not welcome black refugees with the same "noble spirit of philanthropy" that characterized residents in Canada West. His observations on Protestant treatment of French Catholics in Canada East provide a telling example of the nativism he encountered. Lewis thought it was similar to that which he had seen in northern New England. He left the province and returned to Vermont by mid-April. *FDP*, 16 February, 16 March, 4 May 1855 [9:0447, 0487, 0576].

STANSTEAD, C[anada] E[ast]
March [2]0, [18]55

MY DEAR DOUGLASS:[1]

For a colored man to hail from Canada would naturally incline the mind of a reader to suppose him to be in a position to breathe freely, and act like a man. I always feel a peculiar sensation in crossing the line between the two countries, not that I feel myself any more of a man when I get into Canada, yet I am in a place where the rights of men are more respected; and my sympathy with my poor brother is such, I love to feel his wrong, my wrong, and his right and my right. When on the soil of the American Republic, he is bowed down by the proscriptive influence of proslavery—a legitimate offspring of despotism—I love to sorrow with him; and when he stands up as a man among men, on British soil, my free spirit bounds in pleasure among the Canadian hills, and over plains—"for I am a man, and whatsoever concerns men interests me."

But, sir, there is some difference in the appearance of things, in stepping out of the States into Canada West; but the difference is not so great in Canada East. Here, one would hardly know that he is out from under the flag of stripes and stars, in going over Derby line,[2] until he had journeyed far up into the province. The fact is, Canadians, in the border towns, on the part near the United States, have become so Americanized and Yankeeized, they do not manifest that noble spirit of philanthropy in all respects, that is seen and felt in the Western townships. This, no doubt, may account for the few fugitives coming into the Eastern,[3] while so many crowd into the Western townships; yet, still the poor panting fugitive is safe, be he in the Eastern or Western province. People have a wrong idea about Canada. Some imagine it to be a cold, bleak, out-of-the-way part of the world, solitary and uninviting. This is a mistake. I have never been more interested in any section of country. Good roads, beautifully located farms, forming some delightful rural districts; and interspersed all through the country are some as pleasant, thriving villages as can be found in any other country. One of those villages is Coaticook, a flourishing village on the Portland and Montreal Railroad.[4] I spent the Sabbath there (March 11th), and spoke to an immense congregation day and evening. I met some of the noblest specimens of humanity among them—deacon Ham, brother Levi Baldwin, and brother William Stoddard, with their families. I can assure passengers on the U.G.R.R.,[5] who wish to come into the province, by way of the East, through Portland, they would meet with all the hospitable kindness that heart could wish, in the village and vicinity of Coaticook. It is the first depot of any importance after crossing the line from Maine into the province.

There is a considerable sensation felt in this community where I now write, caused by the movements of the Catholics, in the erecting of a Convent. The Americanized Canadians, and Yankees on the other side of the line, begin to feel their blood running up to fever heat, in excited opposition. I was spending the night in the family of a good Protestant friend, right on my tour here. In the evening, quite a respectable traveller came in and asked to be accommodated over night. He was a well dressed, respectable looking Frenchman. Much pains was taken to ascertain if he was a Catholic. The lady of the house said if he was, not one mouthful should he eat from her table, let him be ever so hungry. Well, now, if all our Yankee matrons would all hate slavery with as much holy horror as this one did the Catholics, the great work of reform would go on at a more rapid rate. This straining at a gnat, and swallowing a camel, is not good Christian policy. But the inconsistency of the Protestant American Church, has always made the work of reform drag along; yet, one thing is encouraging, though slow, yet sure, has been the progress of the antislavery cause.

I have been looking with some impatience for the mail to bring us intelligence of the New Hampshire election. Thank God it has come to us this morning. New Hampshire, the bulwark of old Hunker Democracy, has at last fallen before the genius of liberty, in the march of republican reform. The Pierce dynasty has received another rebuke that must make it quail. Mr. Metcalf, the Know Nothing candidate for Governor, is elected by a large majority, also the anti-Administration candidates to Congress, with two thirds of both branches of the Legislature. It is understood that Mr. Metcalf is an anti-Nebraskaite, and a strong opposer of the Pierce slavery-ridden Administration. This drew to him almost the entire liberty vote of the State. If Governor Metcalf, of New Hampshire, on the Know Nothing platform, with his party, is as true to freedom as Governor Gardner, of Massachusetts, and the majority of the Know Nothings, then the New Hampshire election will be a glorious triumph for liberty.[6] I cannot feel that exultation in a liberty victory, through another channel, as when it is gained on its own merits, free from other agencies; yet, after all, I can say, with the good apostle, some preach through envy and strife, and some of good will, and some of love; but, whether of either, he rejoiced that the Gospel was preached.

I feel happy informing you that your paper meets with much approval in this State, in places where I have introduced it. I have no doubt but as soon as the season of bad travelling is over, and tight times lets go his grip on the financial interest of the community, I shall be able to do considerable for it. I hope, by exertion, to get quite a good list in this State during the spring and summer. The people here like its independent tone and spirit on reform. Yours as ever,

JOHN W. LEWIS[7]

Frederick Douglass' Paper (Rochester, N.Y.), 27 April 1855.

1. Frederick Douglass (1817–1895) was born in Maryland and was named Frederick Augustus Washington Bailey. Douglass (the name he assumed after escaping slavery) was the son of an unknown father (possibly his master) and a slave mother, Harriet Bailey. In 1825 Douglass was sent to Baltimore, where he was employed first as a house servant and later as a ship's caulker. During his years in Baltimore, Douglass acquired the rudiments of an education. Early in September 1838, on his second attempt, he escaped slavery, traveled to New York City, married Anna Murray, a free Baltimore black who had encouraged his flight, and settled in New Bedford, Massachusetts.

Late in 1841, Douglass was appointed as a lecture agent for the Massachusetts Anti-Slavery Society, and he began a long and sometimes controversial career in antislavery reform; eventually he was regarded by many as the leading black abolitionist spokesman in the United States. Douglass's rapid development as a gifted orator and his growth as an antislavery thinker during the first four years of his career (1841–45) led many to doubt his slave origins. To allay their doubts, Douglass wrote *The Narrative of the Life of Frederick Douglass* (1845), the first of three autobiographies and the most widely read and highly acclaimed piece of slave literature in the nineteenth century. After publishing it, Douglass made a well-received tour of Great Britain (1845–47) and, during the tour, acquired funds to purchase his freedom and to begin an antislavery newspaper. In spite of contrary advice from many Garrisonians, Douglass founded the reformist weekly the *North Star* (1848–51), a journal that was succeeded by *Frederick Douglass'*

Paper (1851–59) and *Douglass's Monthly* (1859–63). Between 1848 and 1853, Douglass continued to refine his abolitionist thinking and parted with essential Garrisonian doctrine by advocating political antislavery and by interpreting the United States Constitution as an antislavery document. Like many of his black colleagues, Douglass called for resistance to the Fugitive Slave Law of 1850 and rejected the Dred Scott decision (1857). He was one of the few abolitionists to support John Brown's attempt to stir an insurrection at Harpers Ferry, Virginia. Although Douglass had criticized blacks who advocated emigration during the 1850s, he briefly embraced the idea in 1860.

At the start of the Civil War, Douglass urged Lincoln to enlist black soldiers in the Union army and to emancipate slaves as a war measure. He became a recruiting agent for the Massachusetts Fifty-fourth and Fifty-fifth regiments. During the 1870s, Douglass moved to Washington, D.C., edited the *New National Era* (1870–74), became an active member of the Republican party, and served as the district's marshal (1877–81). He also continued to address the major issues of racial injustice that faced black Americans. During the 1880s, Douglass served as the city's recorder of deeds (1881–86) and, at the end of the decade, was appointed consul general to Haiti (1890–91). *DANB*, 5:406–7.

2. Derby Line, Vermont, is located in Derby County on the Vermont-Quebec border.

3. Although some noted fugitives, like Frederick "Shadrach" Wilkins, reached Montreal's black community, few fugitive slaves settled in Canada East (sometimes called the "eastern townships") in the decades preceding the Civil War. The 1844 census reported only 266 blacks in the province; the 1861 enumeration included no more than 190. But the actual black presence, while limited, was undoubtedly larger. The censuses, particularly the one conducted in 1861, were unreliable and frequently underenumerated racial and ethnic minorities. The *Montreal Gazette* asserted in 1861 that there were ten times more blacks in the city than the census takers had found. Winks, *Blacks in Canada*, 247, 486, 489.

4. The Montreal-Portland line was reputedly the world's first international railroad. The St. Lawrence and Atlantic Railroad, which was chartered in 1845 and promoted by Alexander T. Galt, constructed the line to allow Montreal year-round access to the Atlantic. In the early 1850s, the Grand Trunk Railroad took control of the line on a 999-year lease. Glazebrook, *History of Transportation in Canada*, 153, 161–64, 169.

5. Lewis refers to the underground railroad.

6. The Democratic party suffered heavy losses in the New Hampshire state elections held on 13 March 1855. A coalition of Know-Nothings, Whigs, and Free Soilers gained 221 of the 300 seats in the state house of representatives and 10 of the 12 available seats in the state senate. Know-Nothing candidates won all three seats in the U.S. House of Representatives, and a Free Soiler and a Whig were selected to the U.S. Senate. Ralph Metcalf (1798–1858), a lawyer, was elected governor on the Know-Nothing ticket. As an "anti-Nebraskaite," Metcalf opposed the provisions of the Kansas-Nebraska Act (1854) that permitted the extension of slavery into the western territories.

The Know-Nothing (or American) party was particularly successful in the 1855 elections. Dubbed Know-Nothings because of their secretiveness, members generally endorsed antiemigration, anti-Catholicism, and temperance. Formed in 1849, the organization grew rapidly; by 1854 it had between 800,000 and 1,500,000 members—most were disaffected Whigs, former Democrats, and native-born workers fearful of competition from poorly paid immigrants. During 1854–55 the party surfaced as a major political force, sweeping to power in four New England states (including Massachusetts and New Hampshire), Maryland, Kentucky, and Texas. Many Know-Nothings held moderate antislavery views, and abolitionists initially viewed them as allies against the proslavery policies of President Franklin Pierce and other conservative northern (or "Hunker") Democrats, who supported unionist principles over abolitionism. Abolitionists pointed to Metcalf and Henry Joseph Gardner (1818–1892), a Boston merchant who was elected governor of Massachusetts on the 1854 Know-Nothing ticket, as potential leaders in the political antislavery struggle. But the Know-Nothing movement soon proved a disappointment to political abolitionists. Northern and southern Know-Nothings split in 1856 over the question of slavery in the territories, and the party soon declined. *NYTi*, 19 March 1855; *BDAC*, 165, 576, 794, 1545, 1790; *BDGUS*, 3:960–61; John W. Blassingame, ed., *The Frederick Douglass Papers*, series one, 3 vols. to date (New Haven, Conn., 1979–), 2:363n; *DAB*, 7:142.

7. John W. Lewis (1810–1861) of Providence, Rhode Island, was ordained into the African Methodist Episcopal Zion ministry in 1832, but he later served local Freewill Baptist congregations. An amateur denominational historian, he wrote biographies of several Freewill Baptist clergymen, most notably *The Life, Labors, and Travels of Elder Charles Bowles* (1852), a book with antislavery overtones. Lewis established and taught at the black New England Union Academy in Providence during the mid-1830s but thereafter devoted most of his energy to antislavery, temperance, and other reform causes. Increasingly concerned about the use of alcoholic beverages among the northern, urban black population, he organized the Providence Temperance Society and called for the formation of the New England Temperance Society in 1836; he served as the latter organization's president during its first three years. He urged blacks to adopt temperance practices as an avenue to both economic survival and moral salvation. Lewis first attracted the attention of white abolitionists in 1837, when a series of his letters to the Concord (New Hampshire) Juvenile Anti-Slavery Society was published in the *Herald of Freedom*. The pro-Garrisonian New Hampshire Anti-Slavery Society employed him as a lecturing agent by 1839; he lectured and solicited funds for the society throughout the state. When the antislavery movement splintered in 1840, Lewis, a moral suasionist, initially supported the Garrisonians; but he later informed the NHASS Executive Committee that he planned to avoid antislavery infighting and considered it his "duty to make the advocacy of the [slave's] cause the paramount question." The NHASS responded vituperatively, questioning Lewis's antislavery commitment and charging him with keeping a portion of the funds he had raised for the society. Lewis resigned and for the next few years was a traveling agent for the Albany *Northern Star and Freeman's Advocate* and the *Colored American*, two black papers. Then throughout the late 1840s and early 1850s, he did independent antislavery lecturing throughout northern New England. Lewis moved to St. Albans, Vermont, by the early 1850s. In 1855 he was appointed a traveling agent for *Frederick Douglass' Paper* and solicited subscriptions throughout

northern New England, upstate New York, and southern Canada East. He proved to be an indefatigable lecturer.

Lewis had favored the formation of a black national organization as early as 1840, and in the 1850s, he played a role in attempting to form such an organization. He entered the black convention movement and served on the National Council of the Colored People—a national black coordinating body formed at the 1853 Colored National Convention in Rochester. About the same time, he abandoned his moral suasionist ideals and joined the Liberty party remnant. Lewis moved to New York City around 1860 but soon became disillusioned by black prospects in the United States. Believing that blacks could "better develope [sic] their manhood" in a black nation, he became attracted to the Haitian immigration movement. In February 1861, shortly after the death of his wife, he sailed to Haiti as minister and leader of the black Lawrence Association colony. Lewis settled near St. Marc but died of neuralgia and inflammation of the kidneys within six months of his arrival. *PP*, 26 October 1861; *Lib*, 7 July 1832, 27 August, 3 September, 29 October, 26 November 1836, 15 September 1837, 14 September, 5 October 1838 [1:0698, 0701, 0723, 0741, 2:0185, 0585, 0604]; *HF*, 3, 24 June 1837, 11 January 1840, 1 January, 30 July 1841 [2:0067, 0086, 3:0322, 4:0132]; Pease and Pease, *They Who Would Be Free*, 33, 77–78, 126; *Minutes of Convention of People of Color, for the Promotion of Temperance in New England* (Providence, R.I., 1836), 3 [1:0710]; *CA*, 25 July 1840, 30 January, 3 July, 4 September 1841 [3:0533, 4:0093]; *NSFA*, 10 February, 8 December 1842; *FDP*, 2 December 1853, 5 May, 28 July 1854, 16 February, 30 March, 27 April, 8 June 1855 [8:0770, 0941, 9:0560, 0686]; Foner and Walker, *Proceedings of Black State Conventions*, 2:207–8, 217, 224–25; John W. Lewis to Gerrit Smith, 20 December 1860, Gerrit Smith Papers, NSyU [13:0049]; John W. Lewis to George Whipple, 30 January 1861, AMA-ARC [13:0250]; *WAA*, 2, 9 February, 4 May 1861 [13:0256, 0502].

51.
James C. Brown to the Dawn Investigating Committee
12 April 1855

British abolitionist John Scoble assumed control of the Dawn settlement in 1852 amidst a good deal of optimism. His arrival quieted a public controversy over the settlement and convinced many observers that Dawn would thrive once again. But that proved not to be the case. Presbyterian minister Robert Burns visited Dawn and reported that conditions were deteriorating under Scoble's leadership. He was particularly concerned about the absence of financial accountability and the dilapidated state of school buildings. Burns's report rekindled the dispute over control of the property of the British-American Institute. Critics who had previously attacked Josiah Henson now turned against Scoble. James C. Brown, one of the original black trustees of the institute, challenged Scoble's leadership on the principle that the "Dawn Institute belongs to the People of Colour in Canada generally." During the spring and summer of 1855, concerned blacks in Toronto and Chatham organized Dawn investigating committees. Brown wrote an open letter, apparently to the seven-member Toronto committee, to level allegations against Scoble. He charged Scoble with surreptitiously taking control of Dawn, and he called for a black convention to address the controversy. Brown's letter offers some indication of the leadership problems endemic to black Canadian settlements. The Dawn controversy persisted well into the 1860s. *PFW*, 25 August, 4 November 1854, 7, 14 April, 9 June, 22 August 1855; Murray, "Canada and Anglo-American Anti-Slavery Movement," 466–74; *Convention of the Colored Population*, 11.

Chatham, C[anada] W[est]
April 12, 1855

To the Members of the Investigating Committee

GENTLEMEN:

As you have been appointed to get at the true state of the Dawn Institute, allow me to make some remarks and to propose some questions to you, which if asked by you and answered, will serve you as a key to the information you want. How long shall they ask and not get an answer, or are the Trustees of the Dawn Institution dumb or deaf? The Press has asked in vain what has become of the money that was laid out for the Fugitives in Canada? Secondly, whose hands is that property got into now? if they are carrying out the Manual Labor School or not, or if a few individuals have converted it to their own uses? Ask the Rev. John Roaf,[1] of Toronto, if he and George Johnson[2] did not pay the debts to Josiah

Henson and Peter B. Smith,[3] which they said they owed some six years ago? I refused to pay the said debts, because the Committee[4] did not audit up their book accounts, as Mr. Roaf stated, to that Committee, that he would pay no debts contracted by them, not one dollar; for they should be responsible for their own debts. Ask Josiah Henson if the debts were not paid to him and Peter B. Smith by the Trustees? or who sent him to England, there to represent himself to the good people on that Island, and that the Trustees at Dawn had sent him out as their good, faithful, and tried servant (Josiah Henson), to beg money to pay a debt when he well knew that it was already paid off? Ask him if he will deny this. Ask Mr. Roaf for what reason he turned off the Free Mission Baptist,[5] when, at the same time himself and the Trustees acknowledged that they had faithfully done their duty to the pupils, as Teachers and Ministers, and told them to go on, good and faithful servants, "I bid you God speed in your work of charity?" The scenes have all changed. One Mr. John Scoble came over from England that evening; truthful were the words that Dr. Burns[6] wrote, that these were the sunny days of Dawn, under the care of the Mission. Please to ask Mr. Roaf if he did not hold informal meetings, one at his house in the country, and the other next morning in the basement story of his church? I was one of the Trustees, and happened to be sent from Chatham to the North American Convention held in Toronto, or I would have known nothing about the plans that were concocted. Please to know of Peter B. Smith, did he sign over his trust to Mr. Scoble in the Dawn Institution, and whether the said Scoble was to carry out the spirit and letter of the Declaration of Trust,[7] which he jointly agreed with other Trustees to carry out?

It would be well for you to know of Mr. George Johnson, whether he signed his trust to Mr. Scoble in the basement story of Mr. Roaf's church,[8] or was he induced to sign away on the highway?

Mr. Frederick Stover,[9] one of the Trustees, had signed away his trust in the said Institution, by a written document, given to the remaining Trustees some eight years ago. Ask Mr. Henson if he was not sent by some one to induce Mr. Stover to sign away a right he had no control over, to Mr. John Scoble? And ask Mr. Henson, why he should make himself so interested, as he never was a Trustee? All the figure he acted upon the stage of Dawn was that of a beggar for it. Ask him if he knows who took forcible possession of the Dawn, and if so whether, when doing so, any locks were forcibly broken, and if so, who by? Ask him if Mr. John Scoble is not walking in there and enjoying the property given to the Fugitives? You will do well to ask the Rev. Hiram Wilson, who was first resident of Dawn, if he signed over to Mr. John Scoble a deed of one hundred acres of land, belonging to the Fugitives, for which he and his wife[10] had signed one jointly before, to all of the Trustees? if so, who of the Trustees authorised him to do so? The Rev. Mr. Roaf promised George Johnson and myself, if we would sign over to John Scoble our trust in the Institution, he would see the Free Mission Baptists satisfied for all the expenses during their removal there; "if so, good; if not, they will prove a great obstacle in our way in trying to raise up Dawn!" as they are our true friends through America, in particular would they be when sending out agents, for we might find them as Noah did the raven.

A word, Gentlemen, as to Dawn at present. Instead of carrying out the Manual Labor School, agreeable to promise, Mr. Scoble has got the Institution, with hired men cutting a grove, which the Trustees had reserved for a Methodist Camp Ground and Students Pleasure Grounds. He is having some hundred cords of wood cut; I am in hopes he will not turn out as Henson did, get all the Fugitives fine walnut logs. Where are the Trustees that ever knew of the income of one dollar? Call upon the colored people of the Province to rally, as one man, to select two or three of your most intelligent men in the different districts to meet at the School house at Dawn, the day before the last Wednesday in August, 1855, to appoint six Trustees, and augment their number up to twelve;[11] this is in accordance with the Declaration of Trust. We read that many who are not thought of come to wear crowns. Education is the greatest blessing to man, strive to encourage it then by promoting its Institutions; if you raise up your children without education, at least one-half will go down to the tomb of oblivion, or bring shame and disgrace upon you. Educate your children, and they will prove a blessing to their country, an honor to themselves, and to you, and it will be a consolation in death.

J. C. Brown

Provincial Freeman (Toronto, Canada West), 12 May 1855.

1. John Roaf (1801–1862), a Congregational minister, was born in Margate, Kent, England, and went to Upper Canada in 1837 as an agent for the Colonial Missionary Society. There he founded the Zion Church of Toronto, organized Congregationalism in the province, and worked to reorganize the Congregational Union of Canada. Roaf actively supported the temperance movement and the creation of nondenominational public schools. Controversy, created by church financial problems, led to his removal as missionary agent and retirement in 1856. *DCB*, 9:663–64.

2. George Johnson lived in the Toronto black community during the early 1840s. He was an original trustee and treasurer of the British-American Institute at the Dawn settlement. Johnson settled near Dresden by 1850. There he served as a Baptist deacon and actively supported the *Provincial Freeman*. *PFW*, 22 July 1854, 29 September 1855 [8:0935, 9:0854]; *Lib*, 14 November 1845 [5:0112]; *CF*, 27 November 1845 [5:0114]; *CTWP*, 10 November 1859 [12:0203]; Winks, *Blacks in Canada*, 180; Wilson R. Abbott et al. to the Mayor of Toronto, 21 April 1843, CaOTCi [4:0562].

3. Peter B. Smith (1809–?) was born in Kentucky and lived in Indiana before settling in Upper Canada with his wife and children during the late 1830s. A

farmer and blacksmith, he eventually acquired 366 acres of land near Chatham. Smith became a deacon in the African Methodist Episcopal church in 1844. One of three blacks among the original trustees of the British-American Institute at the Dawn settlement during the 1840s, he shared responsibility with Josiah Henson for the settlement's sawmill. But he became embroiled in the controversy that plagued the settlement during the 1850s. A founding member and vice-president of the Provincial Union Association, Smith supported the *Provincial Freeman*'s campaigns for black self-help and against begging. He immigrated to Haiti in late 1861. Census of Canada, 1851; *PFW*, 22 July, 29 July, 19 August 1854 [8:0935, 9:0018]; *CTWP*, 10 November 1859 [12:0203]; *CF*, 27 November 1845 [5:0114]; *NASS*, 11 November 1847 [5:0513]; Payne, *History of the AME Church*, 144, 178–79; Simpson, "Negroes in Ontario to 1870," 352, 719; Winks, *Blacks in Canada*, 180; *PP*, 8 May 1862.

4. Brown refers to the executive committee of the British-American Institute at the Dawn settlement, which was responsible for the daily direction of the school and related community concerns. Committee membership—which changed frequently during the 1840s and 1850s—included Peter B. Smith, George Cary, and George Johnson; William P. Newman, secretary of the committee; and Josiah Henson, a cofounder of Dawn. *NASS*, 11 November 1847; *CF*, 27 November 1845; Pease and Pease, *Black Utopia*, 71–73.

5. The American Baptist Free Mission Society managed the British-American Institute at Dawn, Canada West, from 1850 to 1852. John Scoble arrived at Dawn in 1852, announced that he would take charge of the institute, and convinced Rev. John Roaf and the other Dawn trustees to ask the ABFMS to abandon the settlement. The ABFMS was established as the American and Foreign Baptist Mission Society in 1843 by members of the American Baptist Anti-Slavery Convention. Renamed in 1846, the society represented about 6 percent of the northern Baptists. Seeking "no fellowship with slaveholders," the organization carried on an extensive antislavery campaign within the Baptist churches. In addition to its evangelizing and publication functions, the ABFMS helped found two interracial colleges—New York Central College and Eleutherian College. After the Civil War, the ABFMS merged with other northern Baptist organizations. John R. McKivigan, "The American Baptist Free Mission Society," *Found* 21:346–49 (October–December 1978); Pease and Pease, *Black Utopia*, 68–77, 176n; Murray, "Canada and the Anglo-American Anti-Slavery Movement," 465–66.

6. Brown refers to Robert Burns (1789–1869), who was born in Barrowstowness, Scotland, and ordained a Presbyterian minister in 1811. He left the Church of Scotland in 1843 for the Free Church. Active in Scottish missionary organizations and publications, he accepted an 1845 call to preach at Knox Church, Toronto, Canada West, and to teach theology at Knox College. He became a leader of several Canadian reform causes, including home missions, temperance, opposition to the clergy reserves, and antislavery. He accompanied William King on an 1860 fund-raising tour of Britain on behalf of Canadian blacks. *DCB*, 9:104–8.

7. The Declaration of Trust, a document signed by the six original trustees of the Dawn settlement, described the nature and purpose of the settlement and outlined the responsibilities of its trustees and managers. Although Scoble apparently had not signed the declaraton, Brown implies that he had agreed to its provisions

when he assumed trusteeship of Dawn in 1852. *PFW*, 25 August 1854, 15, 22, 29 September 1855.

8. John Roaf was the pastor of Zion Congregational Church, which was located at the intersection of Adelaide and Bay streets in central Toronto. *St. Lawrence Hall*, 30–31.

9. Frederick Stover, representing Ohio and Indiana annual meetings of the Society of Friends, went to Canada to purchase eight hundred acres of land for the Wilberforce settlement in 1830. He settled on a farm near Norwich, Upper Canada, and later served as a trustee for the Dawn Institute (1842–48). Steward, *Twenty-Two Years a Slave*, 117; Winks, *Blacks in Canada*, 156, 180; *PFW*, 20 October 1855 [9:0901].

10. Brown refers to Hiram Wilson's first wife, Hannah Maria Hubbard (?–1850), a Presbyterian abolitionist from Troy, New York. She married Wilson in 1838 and afterwards assumed a significant share of his missionary responsibilities in Canada West. She also organized and conducted a school for women at the Dawn settlement during the 1840s. Plagued by chronic ill health, she died at Dawn in 1850. After her death, Hiram Wilson resettled in St. Catharines, remarried, and conducted independent relief work among the black fugitive slaves there. *CA*, 22 September 1838; *Lib*, 2 August, 13 December 1850; *PFW*, 22 March, 4 May, 5 October 1856; Daniel A. Payne, *Recollections of Seventy Years* (Nashville, Tenn., 1888; reprint, New York, N.Y., 1969), 65–66.

11. Brown's call for a meeting on the "day before the last Wednesday in August" was not arbitrary. During the settlement's early years, its trustees met annually on that date. But delegates to the 29 August 1855 session found themselves locked out of the Dawn schoolhouse by John Scoble; they assembled instead at the nearby Methodist church. The delegates resolved to file suit against the six original trustees for "non-performance of their duties," and to petition the legislature not to act on a request to incorporate Dawn while control of the settlement was being litigated. A committee of fifteen was elected to carry out the resolutions. Six new trustees—Weldon Harris, Joseph C. Lewis, John W. Lindsay, George Francis, A. B. Jones, and Peter J. Jackson—were also selected. *PFW*, 15, 22 September 1855.

52.
Resolutions by a Meeting of Chatham Blacks
Convened at the First Baptist Church, Chatham, Canada West
23 June 1855

Blacks who considered Canada their permanent home recognized the importance of turning away from the United States and embracing British values and institutions. They affirmed their Anglo-Canadian identity with regular displays of patriotism and loyalty to the British crown, including military service during the War of 1812 and the Rebellion of 1837. The outbreak of the Crimean War between Russia and Britain provided another occasion for patriotic demonstrations. Blacks in Chatham, led by Isaac D. Shadd and Harvey C. Jackson, expressed their support of Britain and offered their services to the crown at a public meeting held in Chatham's First Baptist Church on 23 June 1855. The resolutions, although addressed to the Queen, were intended to remind all black Canadians, especially recent arrivals from slavery, of the benefits of their adopted homeland. *PFW*, 5 August 1854 [8 : 0994], 30 June 1855.

1. *Resolved*—That we, the Colored people of Kent County, Canada West, assembled in Mass Meeting, this 23rd of June, feeling indebted to Her Most Gracious Majesty, and Her Government, make known our willingness and determination to assist in arresting the usurpations of Russia or any other power.

2. *Resolved*—That after having been subjected to the iniquitous system of Yankee oppression, and having the privilege of a home on British Territory extended to us, in common with all others of Her adopted subjects, the duty devolves upon us to aid in any and every case where we would be in any way serviceable.

3. *Resolved*—That in consideration of the difficulties existing between Her Majesty's Government and the Government of Russia, and forming as we do a portion of the subjects of the former, we deeply sympathize with Her Most Gracious Majesty in the loss of those brave and gallant troops who waded in the blood of thousands with invincible courage, to break the iron arm of Russian oppression.

4. *Resolved*—That it is the duty of every man to act up to the above Resolution, and each and every one who is not willing and does not feel it to be his duty to stand in defence of the Government that shields him from oppression, is not worthy of the esteem of the Canadian people, and should not be allowed the privileges of British subjects.

Provincial Freeman (Chatham, Canada West), 30 June 1855.

53.
Editorial by William P. Newman
22 September 1855

Participation in the Canadian political process presented blacks with opportunities nearly unknown in the United States. The major electoral issue confronting black Canadians was determining which political party to support. In a 22 September 1855 letter to the *Provincial Freeman*, black Baptist minister William P. Newman argued in favor of the Conservative party. For Newman, political conservatism meant loyalty to the British Crown. He believed that Anglo-Canadian identity afforded black Canadians the best protection against American influence and annexationist designs on the Canadian provinces. Conservatism, he perceived, hewed to traditional political principles and concern for the commonweal, which protected minorities from the excesses and prejudices of the majority. Newman emphasized that his arguments were not derived from abstract propositions or political theories but actual historical comparisons—especially between the condition of blacks in the republican United States and in conservative-monarchical Canada.
His prediction that blacks in Kent and Essex counties would soon hold the "balance of political power" proved overly optimistic. But during the 1850s, the black vote was instrumental in the electoral defeat of two racist candidates in Kent County—Edwin Larwill and John Prince. Ironically, both were Conservative politicians. Winks, *Blacks in Canada*, 214–15; *PFW*, 22 September 1855.

The Colored People and the Conservative Party

Within the next five years, the colored men of the Counties of *Kent & Essex*, C.W., will have doubtless the *balance of political power*. They have it in several *municipalities* now. God be praised for it! May they have wisdom to use that power aright! My brethren, look around you, and mark well the *demagogue*. He has noted *you* as his prey. His plans are laid. This is quite clear from some things which have come to sight. It is really amusing to see and hear some of our *long-face Reformers*.[1] O! how they love their *colored* friends! What evidence they *have* given of the fact! The greatest abundance, and *no* mistake! Why you, brethren, have had as much proof of it, as you have that "Old Nick" is dead.[2] You have had it, on the *steamboat*, when *you* and *he* sat together, at the dinner table. You have had it, in the *Hotel*, when you and he had a little "chit chat," in the parlor, where there were a few Southern nabobs. You have had it in the *Stage Coach and Railway Cars*, as you and he journeyed over plank roads, or fled on iron, through our envied country. You have had it, in the past *municipal* arrangements and "*Common School*" doings. And you had it, no doubt, to your heart's content, in the general *Social* circle of your friends—the Reformers. We do not mean to insult you! But you should *not* forget all *this evidence* of the Reformer's love for you and your interest. Shall we say, *their profession* of love for us, as a people, is hypocrisy? There are noble exceptions—*but* . . . our friends are the *Conservatives.*[3]

We allow, it has been truly trying to us, to meet now and then a cold shoulder from *certain* Conservatives; but still the *theory* and *practice* of the party are such as to give us hope; and as a people, we could not lose sight of the fact, that the *principles* of Conservatives are *loyal* and *true*, and that with them, is *inseparably* connected our weal or woe. And besides, the party is a combination of such men and means, as will ultimately destroy those elements and influences among us, which are the legitimate off-springs of "*Red Republicanism*"[4]—the worst enemy, in existence, to the colored race, and a general curse to society. *Any* government *unsuited* to the condition of the people, is a curse, and such, hitherto *Republican governments* have proved themselves to be, as their history abundantly attests.[5] We do not mean principle *abstractly* considered, but *concretely*. The colored people should never lose the truth, that the Conservative party is composed, in the main, of materials, that are *incapable* of a general course of procedure, that will favour *caste*, because of *complexional* differences.

We say once for all, that the Conservative party is the *Constitutional* party of our much envied country—it is *true* to the general interest, and *loyal* to the Crown. It seeks the *Union* of the North American Colonies and a Representation in the Imperial Parliament[6]—the means necessary to *maintain pure allegiance* to the Crown. Its principles are fixed in virtue, and must result in intelligence, freedom, and happiness.

Provincial Freeman (Chatham, Canada West), 22 September 1855.

1. Newman refers to members of the Reform (or Radical) party, which was inspired by the English and American democratic reform movements of the 1830s. Reform leaders—Protestant Nonconformist clergy, businessmen, and professionals—campaigned for "responsible government" and other reforms aimed at reducing the power of the Conservative oligarchy. Gerald M. Craig, *Upper Canada: The Formative Years* (London, 1963), 188–209.

2. Old Nick, a name of uncertain origins, refers to Satan or the devil.

3. The Conservative (or Tory) party represented the established English oligarchy in the Canadas. Until the mid-nineteenth century, Conservatives dominated the political and economic life of the country through the appointed executive and legislative councils. They were predominantly Anglican, loyal to the empire, anti-American, and suspicious of any democratic or "leveling" tendencies in society. Craig, *Upper Canada*, 106–23.

4. Newman refers disparagingly to the more radical, political tenets of republican ideology. During the nineteenth century, "red republicanism" came to con-

note political subversion in a fashion similar to socialism and anarchism. Mitford M. Mathews, ed., *A Dictionary of Americanisms* (Chicago, Ill., 1951), 2:1372.

5. Newman evidently alludes to the dangers faced by minorities in republics when they are subjected to the will of an irresponsible, prejudiced majority. He may have had in mind slaveholding republics like ancient Greece and the United States.

6. Newman's statement is inaccurate. In 1855 the Conservative party was divided on the idea of confederation, and no political party in the British North American Provinces advocated Canadian representation in the British Parliament. Careless, *Union of the Canadas*, 185–213.

54.
Editorial by William P. Newman
10 November 1855

Religion was an essential part of the antebellum reform vision. Christian belief animated many reformers; Christian teachings often defined the nature of reform. In "The Way to do Colored Canadians Good," Baptist minister William P. Newman discussed the role of religion in the progress of blacks in Canada West. He chided Baptists and Methodists for ignoring their black Canadian members and leaving the missionary field open to the well-intentioned but largely ineffective white Presbyterians and Congregationalists. Newman suggested that white missionaries and philanthropists had failed in their efforts to improve the condition of black Canadians because they had neglected the religious foundation on which genuine self-help was based. He insisted that, within the proper religious context, the black Canadian community could develop an ethic emphasizing familial, civic, and religious duty; human dignity; and personal industry. For this reason, Newman called for more extensive religious and vocational education for blacks in the province. Ronald Walters, *The Antislavery Appeal: American Abolitionism After 1830* (Baltimore, Md., 1976), 37–53; *OE*, 30 August 1848 [5:0761]; *PFW*, 20 October 1855, 1 December 1855, 22 December 1855 [9:0902, 0969, 0989].

The Way to do Colored Canadians Good

We have long thought of, and been deeply oppressed with what, seems to us, to be the *cause* of failure, to do the colored people, of Canada, good, by the efforts of their friends.

It is very clear to us, that God's plan to benefit a certain people, or our race, as a whole, is the *very best one* that can possibly be adopted, to secure that end. We attribute the failure of our friends, to do us as a people, the good, they intended to do us, to *their* oversight to adopt *God's* mode to accomplish the work. It seems to us, that their FIRST efforts should have been to *convert the people to Christ*, instead of the mere *intellectual* education of them. Had they succeeded in that, and it is certain that they might have done so, then, the people themselves would have become *fellow-helpers* to the work, which, to us, is indispensably necessary to success to any great degree. Such conversion would have fixed erasably upon them a sense of their own *obligation*. It would induce them to act from *principle*. Their acts would have been consistent, progressive, and beneficial. We do not mean to say that so much has not been true to some extent, but only, that, it would have been more so, in view of the end that *ought* to be attained. To accomplish such an end, too, teachers should have been selected from the *religious denominations*, TO WHICH THE PEOPLE BELONGED, among which they were to labour. It is a fact, that the colored people, of Canada, are almost entirely of the Baptist or Methodist persuasion, and nearly all the teachers sent among them have been either Presbyterians or Congregationalists.[1] No one need wonder at their failure, since *black* people have *conscientious* conviction of their duty, as well as *white* ones! We thank our Presbyterian and Congregational friends for what they *intended to do*, for us. They meant well! But we must admonish our Baptist and Methodist friends, that they are sadly in fault, since they neglected their duty, and done but little or nothing for us, when they have been *earnestly entreated* to do something; nor are our "*Free Mission Baptist*" friends, even to be excused, in this case.

The SECOND great truth that our people need to be taught is the *nature, value, and dignity of humanity*. We must know its *nature*, to properly appreciate it! We must know its *value* to be induced to take suitable care of it! We must know its *dignity* to lead us, to develop, adorn, and sanctify it! Ignorance of such a subject has wrought nearly the ruin of more people than the colored people. To it may be attributed nearly all the demoralizing influences, to which, human nature is subjected. To leave us, in the road to *ruin*, and while in it, we must be careless, restless, and degraded.

The THIRD point of instruction, we need, is on the *duties* growing out of the *relations*, we sustain to God, our families, to the church and state! Let us *know* the relation, we sustain, and we will *respect* the duty arising from it. Whatever may be true of the *Sovereignty* of God, and the *destiny* of man, still, to us, it is clear, all must turn upon OUR DUTY DONE, OR NOT DONE. It is *fatal* to any people, to be ignorant of the relation, *they* sustain to their Creator, Redeemer, and King, and the *ruins*, of duty not done, *must* follow, in the absence of such information. There is but little hope of family success, until its member[s] understand *their* relations to it, and be induced, by the *obligation*, they impose, to discharge their duties in it. The mission of the church, in our world, is too important, for us, not to know our relations to it. Its existence, on earth, will depend upon its members doing their duty. What would our world be without a Christian church in it? and is that *a Christian* church, in which its members perform *not* their duty? Our relations to our country are various, and the duties, from such, are many and onerous. To be patriots, or lovers of our country, we must know it, and our relations to it. To have our country love us, we must do our duty to it. We must at least help to refine its society, develop its resources, and defend its interests!

We are firm believers in the *spirit-world*, and in "*things eternal and unseen*." Hence, the FOURTH point of importance, to us, is, to give us such information as *is revealed* respecting these things, and not the *fancy* of a prolific imagination when religiously excited, as has been too frequently the case with our religious teachers. The things that belong to immortality, and eternal life, we would know, and be guided to obtain them. We need instruction about heaven, while on earth, and how to use the latter to obtain the former.

Who among the saints below,
That to the church their time has given,
Will to us, the needed show,
The use of earth, and way to heaven?

We hold that *intellectual education* is to be subservient to such an end, or it is worse than no education at all; hence, with us, the FIFTH point of great interest, is, a *physical* education. Mark! the *fifth* point, not the *first* one! The great error of our friends has consisted in making it FIRST. It is the error of *missionaries generally* TO EDUCATE THE HEATHEN FIRST, in order to their becoming *Christians*, when they should make their Christians first, in order to their being *properly* educated. Such a plan does not meet with God's approbation, and there should not be much regret at its failure! Such a plan will do for heaven, not earth, in its present state, and especially that part of it called *Canada*! We want laborers among us of the right sort, and who will commence their work in the right way. Such persons will do us good. We ask our friends in the name of God, and our wronged humanity, shall we have them?

Provincial Freeman (Chatham, Canada West), 10 November 1855.

1. By the 1850s, most black Canadians were members of black Baptist and Methodist congregations. But a majority of the missionary teachers in Canada West were sponsored by other religious organizations, particularly the Congregationalist-dominated American Missionary Association and the Colonial Church and School Society, an Anglican group. Several were Presbyterian, and a sizeable minority were Baptist or Methodist. The American Baptist Free Mission Society sponsored teachers at Dawn, Chatham, Hamilton, and the Queen's Bush during the 1850s. Among AMA teachers, David Hotchkiss, Elias E. Kirkland, and their wives were Wesleyan Methodists; blacks Lewis C. Chambers and Mary Ann Shadd Cary belonged to the AME church; and Mary Teall was sponsored by a Baptist congregation in Albany, New York. Even a few CCSS missionary teachers were Methodist. Winks, *Blacks in Canada*, 224–30; Hill, *Freedom-Seekers*, 130–45, 151-53.

55.
Editorial by William P. Newman
17 November 1855

Abolitionism and support for amalgamation were practically synonymous in the antebellum popular mind. Although abolitionists urged the repeal of state laws outlawing interracial sex and marriage, few of them—black or white—encouraged either practice. White abolitionists avoided the amalgamation issue in an attempt to counteract antiabolitionist criticism. Many black abolitionists opposed amalgamation because they believed that it would destroy racial pride; others simply remained silent on the issue. Only a few black abolitionists, like Henry Highland Garnet and William P. Newman, embraced amalgamation without qualifications. Garnet predicted that the "western world is destined to be filled with a mixed race." Newman, a Baptist clergyman and the editor of the *Provincial Freeman*, saw amalgamation as the solution to the twin evils of American slavery and racism. He attempted to convince Canadian blacks of this in a 17 November 1855 editorial in the *Freeman*. It would, he believed, "annihilate unbecoming distinctions" and make of all peoples "one blood." Quarles, *Black Abolitionists*, 38–39; Pease and Pease, *They Who Would Be Free*, 105, 163.

Amalgamation

The imperfection of human nature is seen in nothing more clearly than in the *un*natural prejudices which exist among the several nations of the earth.

There is nothing about which they are more sensitive than the subject of amalgamation. There is nothing that excites their unmitigated wrath more than the permanent union of their kith and kin with one, whom they regard as an *inferior*. We say *permanent* union, because, an illegitimate one does not effect them in the same way. To illustrate the fact. In Southern society of the American Union, colored females are forced into such an union *publicly*, by white men; and white females of the highest standing form such unions with colored men *secretly*, to escape the family's indignation and the odium of public opinion.[1] In the Northern portion of the same country, there is but little difference, in the case, except in the *morality* of it. We remember, some eight years since, that nearly every member of a rich and distinguished family came well nigh dying, from the anguish produced by the elopement with and marriage of a young lady, a relative, and heiress, to an *Irishman*, who was the family's coachman. This single case indicates the fact generally there. The inhabitants of our country are by no means free from the like imperfection. It pervades the bosom of every class among us. The descendants of Shem,

Ham, and Japhet, in Canada, are alike possessed with an *un*natural prejudice, on account of national distinctions, and are equally horrified at the idea of amalgamation![2] Doubtless such is common to some extent to all nations, but it is awful indeed, to see it increase with what is called civilization and the spread of christianity. Is it not apparently true, that those, who are the most devoted religionists, give it the greatest power? Indeed, it would seem, as though it had become a cardinal feature in their religious creed. We need not say, that such piety must be spurious since it produces what positively *un*natural; and piety against *nature*, is NO PIETY!

Amalgamation is proper, and its results most happy. It is a part of the divine arrangement, and hence the different nations should practice it. It is the blending of the beauties of nature. It is the imparting of force and dignity to man and beast. It adds to those, who practice it, those varieties which may be regarded as the spice of life.

Happy will be the world, the day its principles shall be general! It will annihilate unbecoming distinctions. It will bring a wor[l]d-wide peace, and war will be known no more. It will take the slave from among the *beast*, and put him among *men*—despotism will be done, and the world will be free! The feelings produced by amalgamation, *must* bring about such results. Such has been the tendency whenever and wherever practised. Why do the whites of Southern States of America *love the mulattos* more than the blacks? and the *blacks* more than whites of the Northern States do the colored people generally? Happy will it be for Europe, when her nations learn this lesson, and for the slave, when the tendency of Southern society to amalgamate becomes perfect! The hope of the world is in the amalgamation of nations, for the *Gospel of Christ is in the doctrine of* ONE BLOOD!

Provincial Freeman (Chatham, Canada West), 17 November 1855.

1. While interracial marriages were often illegal and seldom acceptable in American society, miscegenation, or the interbreeding of two races, was common from the seventeenth century. The process frequently involved white planters and black slaves, a circumstance that contributed to the growth of a mulatto population. By 1850 southern mulattoes numbered 350,000 and comprised 3.6 percent of the region's population. Berlin, *Slaves Without Masters*, 265–68; Joel Williamson, *New People: Miscegenation and Mulattoes in the United States* (New York, N.Y., 1980), 5–91.

2. Shem, Ham, and Japheth are the names given in Genesis 10:1 to the three sons of Noah. According to tradition, Shem was the father of the Semitic peoples, Ham's descendants became the black race, and Japheth was the progenitor of the Medes and Greeks. Newman evidently uses Shem and Japheth in reference to white Canadians of various European ethnic backgrounds.

56.
Report of a Committee Appointed to Consider Henry Garrett's Compensated Emancipation Plan
Chatham, Canada West
20 November 1855

Most black antislavery lecture tours in the British North American Provinces were well-received. Frederick Douglass, Samuel Ringgold Ward, Jermain W. Loguen, Thomas H. Jones, Mary Ann Shadd Cary, and H. Ford Douglas were among those who addressed enthusiastic audiences. Yet an occasional tour proved controversial. This was the case with Henry Garrett's 1855 excursion through Canada West. Garrett—a former slave, black activist, and self-styled Baptist preacher—promoted a plan for the compensated emancipation of slaves in the South. He introduced his scheme in Detroit, where it was applauded. But it was attacked throughout Canada West. The Chatham *Planet* dismissed the fund-raising proposal on the grounds that it would take $1.35 billion to free the estimated three million slaves in the South. The *Provincial Freeman* characterized Garrett as a puppet of American politicians and urged abolitionists in Britain, Canada, and the United States to reject the plan. On 19 November 1855, Chatham blacks met at the Second Baptist Church to hear Garrett. After he completed his lecture, the disapproving audience appointed a committee to respond to the scheme. The committee, which consisted of local blacks John A. Warren, R. M. Duling, Alfred Whipper, Horace H. Hawkins, Henry J. Young, J. Kelly, and George W. Brodie, met late the following afternoon and completed their work. Their resolutions, which were published in the 8 December issue of the *Provincial Freeman*, supported immediatist abolitionist methods—moral suasion, political antislavery, black education, and the underground railroad—and rejected Garrett's alternative. *PFW*, 29 August, 22 September, 6 October, 1, 8 December 1855 [9:0808–9, 0837, 0864, 0866, 0970, 0976, 0978]; Murray, "Canada and Anglo-American Anti-Slavery Movement," 278.

At a meeting appointed by Committee to consider the above mentioned scheme, by Henry Garrett, on emancipation, it was, on motion:

Resolved, That we do denounce the said scheme as being unholy, unjust, and impracticable, fraught with the greatest evil.

1st. It acknowledges the right of property in man.

2nd. It shows to every intelligent mind, that it would be wrong for the Slaveholder to emancipate his slave without an equivalent for said slave.

3rd. It shows that such a scheme will not only augment the slave States, but increase the trade; because the money acquired by such a course, would not change the disposition of the Slaveholder; but increase his desire to carry on the nefarious traffic in those States and Territories now free.

Your Committee would, therefore, highly commend the various plans now in operation in the States for the abolition of slavery (to wit): Moral suasion, the power at the ballot box, the power of education, and the happy force of the underground Rail Road.

Your Committee would, therefore, beg to suggest, the sending of missionaries of the cross of Christ, to the Master and slave, to enlighten and christianize them.

COMMITTEE
John A. Warren[1]
H. H. Hawkins[2]
R. M. Duling[3]
H. J. Young[4]
A. Whipper[5]
J. Kelly
G. W. Brodie[6]

Provincial Freeman (Chatham, Canada West), 8 December 1855.

1. John A. Warren (?–1870) was an African Methodist Episcopal clergyman. Born in Baltimore, he moved to Philadelphia as a young man. In 1848 he became one of the first AME preachers to do missionary work west of the Allegheny mountains. After serving briefly in the Indiana conference, Warren was transferred to the Ohio conference in the early 1850s. He served churches in Ohio, Michigan, and Canada West until shortly before his death. Warren was transferred to Baltimore in 1870 and died soon after his arrival. *CR*, 25 June 1870; Payne, *History of the AME Church*, 338; Smith, *African Methodist Episcopal Church*, 61, 91, 101; Wayman, *Cyclopaedia of African Methodism*, 172.

2. Horace H. Hawkins (1819–?) was the son-in-law of noted clergyman-abolitionist Benjamin Paul of Wilberforce. Born into slavery in Kentucky, Hawkins escaped to Upper Canada in 1835. After working in an Amherstburg tobacco factory during the winter of 1835–36, he moved to New York State, where he obtained an education at Geneva and the University of Rochester. He also became active in the antislavery movement, cofounding and serving as president of the Geneva Colored Anti-Slavery Society (1836), a New York Anti-Slavery Society affiliate. Hawkins returned to Canada West in the early 1840s and did missionary work among the fugitives for three years under the sponsorship of the New York State Baptist Convention. He became pastor of the First Baptist Church of Chatham in 1844 and was ordained the following year. About that same time, the Amherstburg Baptist Association appointed him as its traveling minister to serve member congregations too small and too poor to support a clergyman of their

own. He visited ABA churches throughout the province, observing congregational life, serving communion, baptizing, and preaching. Hawkins remained a leading figure in the ABA through the early 1850s and served as secretary of the organization in 1852. Also during the early 1850s, he pastored a black Baptist congregation in Amherstburg. While there he acted as corresponding secretary for a Sandwich antislavery society (1851) and became a fervent temperance advocate. Hawkins returned to his Chatham congregation in 1852. A recognized Canadian black leader, he attended the Amherstburg Convention (1853). From 1855 through 1857, Hawkins served a controversial pastorate at the Zoar Church in Chicago, where he expelled twenty-one former slave members for their allegedly unchristian behavior. He later returned to Canada West, where he continued his ministry into the 1860s. Blassingame, *Slave Testimony*, 442–44; Simpson, "Negroes in Ontario to 1870," 114, 333, 489, 571, 679; *CA*, 4 March 1837 [1:0991]; Lewis, "Religious Nature of Negro Migration," 124; *VF*, 1 January, 26 February 1852; Hill, *Freedom-Seekers* 142; *PFW*, 29 August 1855; *Minutes of Convention in Amherstburg*, 2; Sobel, *Trabelin' On*, 241, 276.

3. R. M. Duling, a black antislavery activist, lived in Harrisville, Ohio, before settling in Canada West during the early 1850s. A resident of Chatham, he served as secretary for black meetings in both Chatham and Windsor during 1852. Duling urged black self-help as the best means to achieve emancipation. *ASB*, 10 August 1850; *VF*, 15 July 1852.

4. Henry J. Young (1819–1874) was born to free black parents in Delaware. Converted to Christianity in 1830, he was licensed to preach in the Methodist Episcopal church (South) later in the decade. Young joined the African Methodist Episcopal church in 1840 and preached in local AME churches until 1848, when he was ordained and joined the Philadelphia conference. Young immigrated to Canada West in 1853. After ministering to the Sayer Street AME Church in Toronto for a time, Young moved to Chatham in 1855 and pastored a British Methodist Episcopal congregation there for the following decade. During his Chatham years, he acted as a subscription agent for the *Provincial Freeman*, participated in vigilance committee efforts, hosted antislavery bazaars, presided over the United Daughters of Zion, and sat on a committee appointed to investigate the British-American Institute at Dawn. After the Civil War, he returned to the United States, established AME congregations in Cincinnati and Louisville, and became a well-respected elder statesman of his denomination. From 1870 until his death, Young was pastor of Bethel Church—the AME mother church—in Philadelphia and the Sullivan Street Church in New York City. Wayman, *Cyclopaedia of African Methodism*, 188–89; *ESF*, 12 December 1874; Simpson, "Negroes in Ontario to 1870," 439, 694; Payne, *Recollections of Seventy Years*, 365; *PFW*, 3 June, 18 November 1854, 30 June, 20 August, 20 October, 1, 8 December 1855, 21, 28 June 1856; Smith, *African Methodist Episcopal Church*, 61, 90–95, 110; *CR*, 3, 17 December 1874, 5 January 1875.

5. Alfred P. Whipper (1830–?), a Philadelphia-born black, was the younger brother of noted black abolitionist William Whipper. Although only a teenager at the time he started out in business, the younger Whipper operated a clothing store in the city between 1847 and 1852. He joined the antislavery movement after the passage of the Fugitive Slave Law of 1850, becoming a vocal opponent of the measure, which he saw as a violation of both the Constitution and "God's

Law." Disgust with conditions in the United States eventually prompted Whipper to immigrate to Chatham, Canada West, in 1852. He became a teacher there, first at the Free Mission School, a small private institution, then, after 1856, in the local black public schools. During these years, Whipper served as a subscription agent for the *Provincial Freeman*; he married, accumulated property, converted to Anglicanism, and participated in the local black Odd Fellows Lodge. But he was less than satisfied with white Canadian treatment of blacks, and he joined the black emigration movement in the late 1850s. At the National Emigration Convention in Chatham (1858), he was elected auditor of the movement's General Board of Commissioners. He also participated in John Brown's Chatham Convention that same year, and supported the session's plan to establish a black republic in the southern Appalachians. Whipper became the focus of a controversy in the Chatham community in 1860, when he was forced to yield his teaching position to Peter Nicol, a better-educated white teacher. Black parents objected, expressing their desire for a black role model for their children, and Whipper was rehired. He moved to Windsor during the Civil War and again found employment as a teacher, first at the local black public school, then at a Colonial Church and School Society institution. He evidently remained in Ontario after the war and died there sometime before 1876. Census of Canada, 1861; Richard P. McCormick, "William Whipper: Moral Reformer," *PH* 43:24, 40, 44 (January 1976); *Philadelphia City Directory*, 1847–52; *Lib*, 8 November 1850 [6:0662]; *PFW*, 3 January, 29 December 1855; Hill, *Freedom-Seekers*, 21, 154; Simpson, "Negroes in Ontario to 1870," 668, 671, 686, 710, 748; Victor Ullman, *Martin R. Delany: The Beginnings of Black Nationalism* (Boston, Mass., 1971), 193; *AA*, 20 June 1863.

6. George W. Brodie was born in Kentucky and received his schooling from Cincinnati clergyman John W. Alvord during the 1830s. Little else is known about his early life. By the early 1850s, he had settled in Chatham, Canada West, where he operated a grocery with William Sterritt and used his storefront as a real estate office. Brodie was active in local black affairs. He endorsed the *Provincial Freeman*'s antibegging stance and supported the paper through his business advertisements. As a member of the Chatham Vigilance Committee, he helped mobilize public support for those arrested in the Sylvanus Demarest rescue (1858). In the late 1850s, he was corresponding secretary for the Dawn Committee—a group of Chatham blacks who litigated for control of the British-American Institute property—and was secretary to the General Board of Commissioners of the National Emigration Convention at its 1858 Chatham convention. Brodie joined the African Methodist Episcopal clergy in the mid-1850s. He was appointed secretary of the denomination's general conference in 1856 and spoke out at that meeting against the presence of black slaveholders in the denomination. He helped found the British Methodist Episcopal church that same year, but during the early 1860s, he joined with other BME dissidents in breaking away to establish the Independent Methodist Episcopal denomination. Brodie's most notable accomplishments came after the Civil War, when he returned to the AME ranks. In 1866 he was appointed one of six superintendents responsible for directing AME mission work among the southern freedmen. He was based in Raleigh, North Carolina, where he became a leader of the city's black community. The black clergyman served as secretary of the AME's missionary department from 1872 to 1876

and remained active in the denomination into the 1880s. He was the first cashier of the Raleigh Freedmen's Savings Bank after it opened in 1868, and he served as director of the North Carolina Insane Asylum during the following decade. Wayman, *Cyclopaedia of African Methodism*, 26; *PFW*, 22 August, 8, 22 December 1855, 1 March 1856, 10, 24 January, 14 March 1857 [9:0978, 0988, 10:0491, 0516]; *GSB*, 28 October 1858 [11:0393]; Delany, *The Niger Valley Exploring Party*, 12–13 [11:0336]; Payne, *History of the AME Church*, 328, 342, 361–92; Smith, *African Methodist Episcopal Church*, 38, 67, 90, 137, 343, 505–24; Osthaus, *Freedmen, Philanthropy, and Fraud*, 75, 107, 233; Howard N. Rabinowitz, *Race Relations in the Urban South, 1865–1890* (Urbana, Ill., 1980), 145.

57.
Editorial by H. Ford Douglas
17 May 1856

In the spring of 1856, black abolitionists H. Ford Douglas and Mary Ann Shadd Cary undertook an antislavery lecture tour through the small towns of Michigan, Illinois, and Wisconsin to garner support for the *Provincial Freeman*. When Douglas returned to Canada West, he composed a retrospective piece on the experience. "The Colored People and Slavery" demonstrated his weariness from the lengthy tour and his distress at the black attitudes he had encountered. The apparent lack of antislavery zeal he found among free black Americans concerned Douglas. He acknowledged the role that a slaveholding society played in molding black attitudes and shaping black behavior, yet he perceived little effort by free blacks to break out of the cycle of continual degradation that they faced. Douglas emphasized that the progress, elevation, and unity of free blacks directly affected the future of the American antislavery movement. *PFW*, 24 February, 8, 15, 29 March, 5, 12 April 1856 [10:0074, 0080, 0097, 0101, 0107].

The Colored People and Slavery

There is no one department of the anti-slavery enterprise, so well calculated to dispirit and dishearten the young, ardent, and impulsive genius in its first efforts to impress upon the world the practical necessity of anti-slavery principles, as that of public lecturing.

Nor is any one pursuit so well calculated to fill the mind with gloomy forebodings of the future, in view of the amount of labor required, and the absolute demand for that labor in order to ensure success, as that of attempting to awaken the blunted moral sense of the American people, to the injustice and sinfulness of Slavery. The insult and impudence of negro hating white men; the besotted ignorance and deplorable indifference of the colored people themselves in the free States, all combine in presenting a sad picture of that anti-slavery progress, so often vaunted by certain political leaders, who endeavor to make the colored people contented with their present wretched condition.

In our recent efforts to do good, among no class have we been so poorly received or treated with so much indifference as among them. No words of good cheer, or "God speed you" greeted our ear; but all *Delphi*[1] has been rife with rumor, croaking prophecies have been belched forth from malignant and perverted natures, in regard to our success.

We say this in no complaining spirit, for anything that has been done us as an individual; but regret it sadly for the sake of the cause, which we all as colored men and women profess to hold so dear. Although, we must confess we expected better things of our colored friends, with whom we are identified, and for whom we are laboring. We were foolish enough to think that when weary and well nigh broken down in our conflict, with the cruel spirit of prejudice and caste, that the approving smiles of the colored people would afford a solace for every wound thus received. Not so; and whoever are encouraged by ideas of this kind, will be doomed to disappointment. The anti-slavery reformer must be prepared to contend with foes without, and pretended friends within, colored as well as white; for it is not our purpose to flatter any, neither white nor colored; but endeavour in our humble way to expose the errors of both. We find the colored people in the States not only ungrateful and envious, but in addition to this, they have all the meanness of the whites, with scarcely any of their virtues. We have often wondered why it was, that the colored people of the United States were looked upon with such contempt by the colored people from other parts of the world.

We have sometimes condemned such treatment, as in bad taste as ungenerous in the extreme; but indeed, we must confess that although being "*American negroes*" ourselves, as the foreign gentry sometimes very sarcastically termed us, still we can discover palliating circumstances in their conduct. We think that the subjects of his imperial highness Faustin the first,[2] or even, if we should come nearer home, and take the sable and saddled colored subjects, in Her Britannic Majesty's Dominions,[3] that they have some very good reasons for declaring nonintercourse, socially with the colored people from the United States, for that government has stamped its peculiarities upon their individual character producing an anomaly impossible to describe. They are certainly ignorant, supremely selfish and mean, and present a combination of incongruities resulting from the local influences which surround them; for there is nothing more apparent among the colored people in the States, than want of an individuality, without which, it is morally impossible for them ever to rise politically and socially, in the scale of being. We have used some hard terms; but we feel justified in doing so, conscious as we are that every thing we have said is true.

One would naturally suppose from the condition of the colored people in the States, and the wrongs to which they are subject, that they were opposed to this condition of things, that is, that they are anti-slavery. Not so! our experience has been that they are pro-slavery in their actions, whatever may be their theories on the subject; continually playing into the hands of their oppressors. You will not find colored men patronizing one another as white men do; whenever they have money to spend, they always prefer to give to those that don't thank them for their custom. In the cities we find them walking a dozen squares to patronize a negro hating white man, when they can be accommodated just as well, by one of their own color on the next corner, they will not help each other; this is the reason why, almost every enterprise gotten up by colored men have failed. White men will not encourage them in any honorable occupation higher than that of boot-blacking or waiting, of course we don't pretend to say that these occupations are not honorable in themselves, for we believe that "*whatever is necessary to do, is honorable to do.*" But we object to them being set apart exclusively for colored men, as if they were not capable of any other calling.[4] We object especially, to colored men being made the instruments of their own degradation, by thus assisting in fostering and keeping alive these unjust distinctions. Let us learn brethren to help each other, instead of assisting those that don't thank us for our aid; encourage every manly effort put forth by colored men to do good, and above all, let us realize the truth. "That those who would be free themselves must strike the blow."

H. F. D.[5]

Provincial Freeman (Chatham, Canada West), 17 May 1856.

1. Delphi is the site of a venerated ancient shrine in Greece. According to legend, it was the source of a powerful oracle. In ancient Greek history and mythology, the Delphic oracle was frequently consulted in important personal and public matters.

2. Faustin Soulouque (1785–1867) was born a slave in Haiti and eventually became a general in the Haitian army. In March 1847, Soulouque became president of Haiti and, two years later, proclaimed himself Emperor Faustin I. In 1849 and again in 1855, he invaded Santo Domingo. Both incursions failed, and in 1859 Soulouque was overthrown and forced to flee to France. H. P. Davis, *Black Democracy: The Story of Haiti* (New York, N.Y., 1967), 119–25; Perusse, *Historical Dictionary of Haiti*, 97; *DUB*, 3:1021–22.

3. The author refers to blacks in the British North American Provinces.

4. An array of evidence gathered from the U.S. Census, state and local economic indices, city directories, and individual testimony demonstrates that black workers were systematically restricted to menial occupations in the free states. Black men were generally limited to jobs as servants, waiters, porters, barbers, mariners, coachmen, bootblacks, hod carriers, unskilled laborers, and second-hand clothing dealers. Black women frequently worked as servants, washerwomen, seamstresses, and cooks. A matrix of causes brought on the economic exploitation of northern blacks, but the central reason was the pervasive racial discrimination they experienced in white society. Blacks were barred from the education and apprenticeships necessary to improve their economic circumstances and excluded from trade unions, and they faced hostility from native white and immigrant labor. Litwack, *North of Slavery*, 153–87.

5. Hezekiah Ford Douglas (1831–1865) was born a slave in Virginia. He escaped from bondage in 1846, settled in Cleveland, and obtained employment as a barber. Although unlettered, he worked hard to educate himself, and his later speeches indicate that he acquired a remarkable mastery of the Bible, classical literature, history, drama, and poetry. Despite his youth, Douglas quickly made a name for himself in the Ohio black community. His handsome appearance and

exceptional oratorical talents, which he displayed at black state conventions during the early 1850s, also attracted attention among white abolitionists. Douglas's hatred of American slavery and racial prejudice and his perception that the Constitution was a proslavery document soon convinced him that blacks owed no allegiance to the United States. By 1852 he was a confirmed emigrationist. He played an influential role at the 1854 and 1856 meetings of the National Emigration Convention in Cleveland. At the latter gathering, he was appointed to the movement's National Board of Commissioners. Between the two sessions, Douglas moved to Chicago, where he helped revitalize Illinois's black state convention movement and led protests against the state's black laws. In early 1856, he became coproprietor of the *Provincial Freeman*. His earlier work as a Cleveland subscription agent for Henry Bibb's *Voice of the Fugitive* had convinced him that black success in Canada West would help uproot the institution of slavery. Douglas viewed this as a chance to contribute to that success. He assumed little editorial responsibility but contributed articles and toured Canada West and the northern United States to enlist new subscribers. He viewed the separate black institutions he found in Canada West as unnecessary and urged black Canadians to become full and loyal British citizens, a position that made him unpopular among some black Canadians. A disillusioned Douglas returned to Chicago in late 1858 and, within a few months, became an agent of Congressman Francis P. Blair's Central American Land Company, which promoted black settlement on the isthmus. After Blair's scheme failed, Douglas returned to antislavery lecturing. At the invitation of abolitionist Parker Pillsbury, he made an extensive antislavery lecture tour of New England in 1860, much of it as a lecturing agent of the Massachusetts Anti-Slavery Society. His speeches during this tour demonstrated a more militant tone and advocated violent overthrow of slavery. In January 1861, Douglas returned to Chicago as the midwestern agent for James Redpath's Haytian Emigration Bureau. The Civil War interrupted his Haitian efforts and, enthused by this prospect for a violent end to slavery, he enlisted in the Ninety-fifth Regiment of Illinois Infantry Volunteers in July 1862. The light-skinned Douglas was one of only a few blacks to serve in a white regiment during the war. In 1863 he was authorized to raise an independent black company. It was mustered in during early 1865, saw only limited fighting, and was mustered out within a few months. Douglas is believed to have been the only black officer to lead troops into combat during the war. After being mustered out, Douglas attempted to establish a restaurant in Atchison, Kansas, but weakened by bouts with malaria contracted during the war, he died in November 1865. Robert L. Harris, Jr., "H. Ford Douglas: Afro-American Antislavery Emigrationist," *JNH* 62:217–34 (July 1977).

58.
Editorial by Mary Ann Shadd Cary
5 July 1856

The emigrationist debate intensified during the 1850s. Just as Henry Bibb and James T. Holly dominated the discussion early in the decade, Martin R. Delany was the prominent figure after 1854. Delany directed the movement away from a concern for continental unity and the protection of the British crown to a search for black nationhood and emigration sites where blacks were dominant, particularly West Africa. He orchestrated the 1854 and 1856 National Emigration Conventions in Cleveland to generate support for his beliefs. Although initially skeptical about Delany's plans, Mary Ann Shadd Cary became a supporter in the period between the two conventions. Cary had considered Canada the only acceptable site, but by 1856 she appeared willing to tolerate other locations. Several factors prompted this shift, particularly attacks by the antiemigrationists, who argued that the United States could be salvaged as a black homeland through black institutions, black uplift, and united black action to eliminate slavery and racial prejudice. Her 5 July editorial in the *Provincial Freeman*, which was written in an uncharacteristically conciliatory tone, urged antiemigrationists not to reject emigration without considering its value for black Americans at the upcoming Cleveland convention. Miller, *Search for Black Nationality*, 105–69; *PFW*, 5 July 1856 [10:0199].

The Emigration Convention

For many, many years the colored men of the United States, have been assembling in Conventions, at stated periods, in order to devise ways and means by which to improve their condition. Calls are issued—in due time, delegates assemble, and after making very many speeches (and some of them very excellent ones too) and passing resolutions of similar tenor, from year to year, they return to their homes with but little hope of any very great amount of good to result from their deliberations; but painfully conscious of a reduction in the pocket. We respect a people who show a disposition to change an uncomfortable position, and we must respect the efforts made by any people, although convinced that the means they use to that end are inadequate to the object, but in so doing, we must not be silent upon the merits of their peculiar theory, much less, must we be expected to endorse their action. The anti-emigrationists of the States, require not only silence, but the most decided approval, by the people generally, of all they are pleased to advance; now in all kindness we think they require too much. Let them meet Emigrationists on the broad platform of free discussion and inquiry, without bickering, animosity or jealousy, and actuated only by the determination to do NOW for their advancement, what SHOULD NOT be imposed as a burthen upon coming generations, and our word for it, results will follow different, and of higher character for good, than any that we have yet seen. Now, personal interests and party manoeuvres absorb much of the time in meetings and out of them, and the great questions are made of secondary importance. Let men who clamor for free thought, speech and action, from their oppressors, tolerate their brethren in the exercise of these necessary rights, so that when those who do not accept for themselves the old policy of staying at *home* on sufferance, wish to be heard, they may not be made the victims of an opposition for opinion's sake, by a part of their own household, as verily, as the entire people are victims of the slave power.

The Convention to be held in Cleveland in August of the present year,[1] will be held by those who have long since out-grown the policy that has guided the colored people of the States for many years. Emigrationists hold that political elevation, the bone of contention, and which cannot be secured without unnecessary sacrifice of *time*, energy and means in the land of their birth, can be obtained by removal to foreign and more liberal governments. Their positions on this point, should be examined and not be cried down without investigation. They maintain that by emigration they would not only supercede the necessity of colonization to Africa, so strongly insisted upon, and strangely enough, by some white friends, and many colored anti-emigrationists, but that thereby they would be enabled to do Anti-Slavery work more effectually, instead of, as now, remaining where they must, to be popular with some of their leaders, oppose their best interests (to remove) and when in order to get their "bread and cheese," they must actually support their oppressors, and assist in maintaining the government that is in the hands of their enemies a tower of strength. Look calmly and without prejudice at your position anti-emigration brethren, and you too who are indifferent! Not only are your hands tied against your own redemption from political thraldom, but you encourage a people to remain, and you remain and accumulate wealth, the very taxes upon which are not only put into the United States Treasury, and used to maintain a government cemented with the blood of your brethren, but a portion of which, actually is appropriated by its legislators to send you to Africa;[2] thus you are forced to go, made to pay the expenses of your own expatriation in part, and made to contribute your quota to return the Burnses, the Simses and other brave fellows, who wish to escape from the tender mercies of its supporters, and, to pay the price demanded by the keepers of the blood hounds human and canine, who see the fleeing fugitives.[3] Verily brethren your responsibility is awful! but made more intense by the opposition you show, against those who would reverse this order of things.

Cease to uphold the United States government, if it will, and while it does uphold human slavery. Cease to grapple after the shadow while you disregard the substance. "Come out from" a government that begins its depredations upon the rights of colored men, and ends by destroying the liberties of white men: if they will not regard the members of the household, think you they will listen to you? No verily. Go to the Cleveland Convention, and determine to remove to a country or to countries, where you may have equal political rights, and thus be *elevated at once*. Where from the responsibilities of your position as freemen, you will have something else to do, and a higher tone of thought, than to *serve* a class of tyrants for reduced wages, and to speculate upon, and imitate the fashions and follies of a people who despise and deride you. Go up to Cleveland on the 26th of August.

M. A. S.

Provincial Freeman (Chatham, Canada West), 5 July 1856.

1. The second National Emigration Convention met at the African Methodist Episcopal church in Cleveland, Ohio, during 27–29 August 1856. Unlike the gathering two years earlier, this second convention was beset with problems that threatened the emigration movement's fragile momentum. Although many of the first meeting's leaders were present, the convention was sparsely attended. A struggle developed between supporters of Martin R. Delany and James T. Holly over the leadership and direction of the movement. Delany's supporters envisioned only secular aims for emigration; Holly's followers espoused Christian missionary objectives. Delegates also failed to agree on the most beneficial black emigration site. But the convention could claim some accomplishments: delegates enlarged the convention's organizational apparatus by adding boards of trade and publications, moved their official headquarters to Chatham, Canada West, designated Mary Ann Shadd Cary's *Provincial Freeman* as the official newspaper of the movement, and appointed H. Ford Douglas as an official lecturing agent. Future meetings were limited to members of the National Board of Commissioners (a majority of whom lived in the Chatham area) and of the boards of trade and publications. Miller, *Search for a Black Nationality*, 134–35, 160–66, 179.

2. Despite frequent requests, the federal government of the United States provided no financial support to the American Colonization Society or the broader African colonization movement prior to the Civil War. But some state legislatures did respond. In 1850 the Virginia legislature encumbered $30,000 annually for five years to support and encourage free black emigration. New Jersey, Pennsylvania, Missouri, and Maryland also appropriated significant but smaller amounts. Staudenraus, *The African Colonization Movement*, 244.

3. Cary refers to the fact that black Americans were required to indirectly support the enforcement of the Fugitive Slave Law of 1850 through the payment of taxes. She makes particular reference to the notorious extradition cases of Thomas Sims (April 1851) and Anthony Burns (June 1854), which were conducted at federal government expense. The Burns case was perhaps the most publicized of the fugitive slave extradition cases. Burns (1834–1862) was born to slave parents in Stafford County, Virginia. At age six, he became the property of

Colonel Charles F. Suttle, a local shopkeeper and deputy sheriff. Suttle hired the young slave out as a domestic servant and laborer. During this time, Burns joined the Baptist faith and secretly learned to read. In February 1854, he stowed away on a ship bound for Boston, and upon reaching the city, he obtained employment as a cook, then worked in a clothing store owned by Coffin Pitts, a local black. But Suttle traced Burns to Boston and obtained a federal warrant for his arrest. Burns was arrested on 24 March under provisions of the Fugitive Slave Law. Abolitionist lawyers, supported by the Boston Vigilance Committee, exhausted legal means to free Burns. When a federal commissioner ruled that the fugitive must be returned to slavery, an interracial mob led by white abolitionist Thomas Wentworth Higginson stormed the courthouse where he was held and attempted to free him. Their effort failed and Burns was returned to Norfolk, Virginia. After four months in the slave pen there, he was purchased by a North Carolina speculator, but in February 1855, members of the Twelfth Baptist Church, of which Burns had been a member, purchased his freedom. A Boston woman sponsored his study at Oberlin College, where he remained through 1857. He then briefly pastored a black congregation in Indianapolis, but he left because of his disgust for local prejudice against free blacks. Burns settled in St. Catharines, Canada West, in 1860 and served the Zion Baptist Church there until his death. Charles Emery Stevens, *Anthony Burns: A History* (Boston, Mass., 1856); Campbell, *Slave Catchers*, 124–32; Samuel Shapiro, "The Rendition of Anthony Burns," *JNH* 44:34–51 (January 1959); Fred Landon, "Anthony Burns in Canada," *OHSPR* 22:162–66 (1925).

59.
Editorial by Mary Ann Shadd Cary
26 July 1856

Black abolitionists attempted to refute the racial stereotypes that white Canadians held about blacks. Mary Ann Shadd Cary, who remained ever alert to racial insults, was particularly skilled at pointing up their absurdity. She chastised the Chatham *Western Planet*—a local journal that espoused moderate antislavery views—for its subtle racism. The *Planet*'s 16 July 1856 issue reported an incident of an inebriated black man who passed by the paper's office swearing and acting in a disorderly manner. From that example, the editor of the *Planet* drew a general conclusion that blacks were unable to use alcoholic beverages in a responsible fashion, and he called for a law prohibiting sale of liquor to blacks. Cary's 26 July editorial response in the *Provincial Freeman* addressed the bias inherent in the *Planet*'s reasoning. It was, Cary argued, unreasonable to hold the black race responsible for the behavior of one black drunkard without applying the same standard to whites. She also reminded the *Planet*'s editors that racial stereotyping did not mix well with the paper's professed antislavery sentiments. *CP*, 16 July 1856.

> INTEMPERANCE—A colored man passed under the windows of this office on Saturday, "full of strange oaths," and very indiscreet expressions, the promptings of the god to whom he had been pouring *in* his libations. We cannot tell whom he may have insulted or even hurt under this influence. There is a law against furnishing drink to Indians,[1] and we cannot but think that a similar restriction applied to the "son of Ham" would be a wholesome protection both to themselves and others. *Planet*[2]

The *Planet* gets worse, and worse! Something more than bare assertion of regard for colored people must take place to make the community believe it. We all heard, a few days ago, of the Editors of anti-slavery tendencies, and yet, whenever it can put a word in edge-wise, which will bear injustly upon colored men it does so. The colored people are not *wild* Indians, neither do they drink more whiskey than their white friends hereabouts. One colored man passed under your office window drunk, and if he had not "hurt" somebody he might have done so, bah! They must be out of a subject to write about down at that office! Every colored man must be prohibited from drinking because one drank freely. Who patronize the saloons, taverns &c., in this place? Indians and colored men only? No! We believe in passing a strictly prohibitory law that will not only prevent Indians and colored men from getting drunk, but will stop white men from drinking as well and not only the "inferior" classes about

Chatham, but a drunken Editor occasionally. But the Editor of the *Planet* must have too much good sense, must be too much of an abolitionist to propose a regulation of the sort in sober earnest, else he must have forgotten that while to see a drunken colored man is of so rare occurrence as to "call him out" on the subject. Drunken officers, "limbs of the law," a drunken M.P.P.,[3] or a drunken Editor of his class is quite common now adays.

M. A. S. CARY

Provincial Freeman (Chatham, Canada West), 26 July 1856.

1. The editors of the *Planet* refer to the Act for the Protection of Indians in Upper Canada from Imposition, which was approved by the Canadian Legislative Assembly in 1850. It outlawed the sale or other provision of alcoholic beverages to Indians in the province and established a fine for violators. Derek G. Smith, *Canadian Indians and the Law: Selected Documents, 1663–1972* (Toronto, Ontario, 1975), 40–47.

2. The Chatham *Western Planet* was established in 1853 by publisher Miles Miller. The weekly newspaper supported Reform party candidates and causes, moderate antislavery, and temperance. By 1856 it was published three times a week; in October of that year the paper was renamed the *Chatham Planet* (subtitled the *Tri-Weekly Planet*). It continued to publish under this and variant names until absorbed by the *Chatham Daily News* in 1922. J. J. Talman, "The Newspaper Press of Canada West, 1850–60," *TRSC* 33:166, 169 (1939); *CTWP*, 22 October 1856.

3. Cary refers to members of the provincial parliament.

60.
Robert Jones to William Still
9 August 1856

Black Canadians organized patriotic demonstrations, held Emancipation Day celebrations, and participated in Canadian politics to strengthen their Anglo-Canadian identity. They also affirmed that identity through military service. Canada's willingness to accept blacks for militia duty contrasted sharply with policy in the United States, where federal and state governments systematically excluded blacks. In a letter written to William Still shortly after arriving in Canada West, black abolitionist Robert Jones posited a clear connection between military obligation and black elevation. Jones recognized the personal pride and public esteem that an all-black militia unit could engender in the black community. He helped organize Queen Victoria's Rifle Guards, a volunteer black militia company. Three years later, blacks in Victoria, Vancouver Island, duplicated this effort by organizing the Victoria Pioneer Rifle Corps—British Columbia's first volunteer militia. Litwack, *North of Slavery*, 31–35; Winks, *Blacks in Canada*, 279–80.

HAMILTON, C[anada] W[est]
August 9th, 1856

MR. WM. STILL
Dear Friend:

I take this opportunity of writing you these few lines to inform you of my health, which is good at present, &c. * * * *[1]

I was talking to you about going to Liberia, when I saw you last, and did intend to start this fall, but I since looked at the condition of the colored people in Canada. I thought I would try to do something for their elevation as a nation, to place them in the proper position to stand where they ought to stand. In order to do this, I have undertaken to get up a military company amongst them. They laughed at me to undertake such a thing; but I did not relax my energies. I went and had an interview with Major J. T. Gilepon, told him what my object was, he encouraged me to go on, saying that he would do all he could for the accomplishment of my object. He referred to *Sir Allan McNab,*[2] *&c.* * * * * I took with me Mr. J. H. Hill[3] to see him—he told me that it should be done, and required us to write a petition to the *Governor General*,[4] which has been done. * * * * The company is already organized. Mr. Howard was elected Captain; J. H. Hill, 1st Lieutenant; Hezekiah Hill,[5] Ensign; Robert Jones,[6] 1st Sergeant. The company's name is, Queen Victoria's Rifle Guards. You may, by this, see what I have been doing since I have been in Canada.

6. Victoria Pioneer Rifle Corps during the 1860s
Courtesy of Provincial Archives of British Columbia/HP 19617

When we receive our appointments by the Government, I will send by express, my daguerreotype in uniform. My respects, &c. &c.,

ROBERT JONES

William Still, *The Underground Railroad* (Philadelphia, Pa., 1872), 272.

1. These and other asterisks in this document appear in the original.

2. Sir Allan Napier McNab (1798–1862) followed his father in a career built around military service. He was born in Newark, Upper Canada, and settled in Hamilton, where he became engaged in speculative business ventures and Conservative politics. As a militia commander during the Rebellion of 1837, McNab sparked an international incident by ordering the attack on the *Caroline*. His unscrupulous involvement in railroad development made him a wealthy, but controversial, public figure. *DCB* 9:519–27.

3. John Henry Hill (1835–?) was the slave of John Mitchell of Petersburg, Virginia, who hired him out to local artisans during the early 1850s. Mitchell arranged to sell Hill in January 1853, but the slave escaped from a Richmond slave auction and hid for nine months in the local free black community. Finally, in mid-September, Hill used a forged pass to travel to Norfolk, then stowed away aboard the *City of Richmond* until it reached Philadelphia. William Still and the Vigilance Committee of Philadelphia helped him flee to Toronto within a few weeks. In time Hill's relatives purchased his freedom. He settled in Toronto, found work in the local black community, attended antislavery meetings, and served as secretary to the Board of Directors of the *Provincial Freeman* Association. A frequent correspondent of Still's, he assisted other fugitive slaves forwarded to Toronto by the Philadelphia abolitionist, helping them to obtain food, clothing, shelter, and employment. Hill relocated in Hamilton in 1855. There he supported himself through his skills as a carpenter; he also served as an officer in Queen Victoria's Rifle Guards, a local black militia unit. By the early 1860s, he was a successful tobacco merchant. After the Civil War, Hill returned to Petersburg, where by 1872 he had become a justice of the peace. Blassingame, *Slave Testimony*, 427–29; William Still, *The Underground Railroad* (Philadelphia, Pa., 1872), 41, 43, 189–200, 203; Winks, *Blacks in Canada*, 246; *PFW*, 3 June, 1 July, 5 August 1854.

4. Sir Edmund Walker Head (1805–1868), an Oxford-educated nobleman, served as lieutenant governor of New Brunswick from 1848 to 1854. For his competent work toward "responsible government" on the provincial level, he was appointed governor-general of the British North American Provinces. During his seven-year tenure, he presided over the growth of party government and promoted the idea of a Canadian federation. *DCB*, 9:381–86.

5. Hezekiah Hill (ca. 1824–?), the uncle of John Henry Hill, spent the first three decades of his life as a Petersburg, Virginia, slave. He attempted to purchase his freedom several times, paid his master $1,900, but was not freed. When his master arranged to sell him to a slave trader in early December 1854, Hill fled to Richmond, where friends in the black community hid him for thirteen months. In early January 1856, Hill stowed away on the steamship *Pennsylvania* until it reached Philadelphia, where he obtained assistance from William Still and the local vigilance committee. By the end of the month, he arrived in Toronto, Canada

West. He soon settled in Hamilton. After the Civil War, Hill resettled in West Point, Virginia. Still, *Underground Railroad*, 200–203.

6. Robert Jones (1817–ca. 1890), a black Philadelphia barber, was born in Pennsylvania. He considered immigrating to Liberia during the mid-1850s but instead settled in Hamilton, Canada West, in 1856. There he assisted recently escaped fugitive slaves; he also organized and served as an officer in Queen Victoria's Rifle Guards, a black militia company. Jones returned to Philadelphia by 1863 and urged black men to join the Union war effort. He reestablished himself as a barber in Philadelphia and practiced his trade there from the 1860s until his death. United States Census, 1850; Still, *Underground Railroad*, 272; Board of Education, "Education and Employment Statistics of the Colored People of Philadelphia, 1856," 2 vols., Pennsylvania Abolition Society Papers, PHi, 1:31; "Men of Color, to Arms! Now or Never" (broadside), Leon Gardiner Collection, PHi [14:0945]; Philadelphia City Directory, 1866–90.

61.
Editorial by Mary Ann Shadd Cary
6 December 1856

During the 1850s, abolitionist optimism for a peaceful solution to the slavery question turned to despair. The early years of the decade brought passage of the Fugitive Slave Law of 1850 and the Kansas-Nebraska Act and witnessed the presidential administrations of Millard Fillmore and Franklin Pierce, both of whom catered to southern preferences. For black Canadian observers like Mary Ann Shadd Cary, the American presidential election of 1856 demonstrated that slavery had become the national policy. She saw the contest in terms of the "slave power conspiracy" (represented by Democratic candidate James Buchanan) aligned against the antislavery movement (represented by Republican candidate John C. Fremont). For Cary, Buchanan's victory ended hopes of peaceful emancipation. In an editorial written only a few weeks after the election, she asserted that the growing power of the proslavery forces made "a great and gory struggle" over slavery inevitable. Her words proved prophetic. The Dred Scott decision, "Bleeding Kansas," John Brown's Harpers Ferry raid, and finally the Civil War demonstrated the failure of political solutions to the sectional issue.

The Presidential Election in the United States

Since the great struggle of parties for the presidential candidacy, which recently agitated the American States,[1] a calm seems to have supervened, which the excited state of the contest would hardly justify if viewed from a surface point. But those acquainted with the minutia—with the great principles involved, discover in the apparent "hush" of the present, a suffocating and unnatural stillness, the precursor of a more terrific storm than has hitherto been witnessed. And, why should there not be a perfect hurricane of sentiment—a whirlwind of startling facts, of bloody deeds such as the contest of despotism against nominal freedom has never before realised? Before the result of Mr. Buchanan's election was announced, the pro and anti-slavery parties joined issue; the one for a dominance secured by a mistaken deference to weakness, at first, and held by unworthy advantage afterwards, the other, to maintain the integrity of free institutions for all men. Since the poll has been decided in favor of despotism, the adherents of that party, not only assume that they have beaten, but expect unyielding submission; unquestioned and unquestioning deference to their authority; but the genius and spirit of liberty is against them. Had the contest assumed the old form; had the abolitionists of the North, moved only by compassion for the slave, appealed to them to withhold their grasp, a result so decisive might be regarded as probably a quietus to further agitation for a time, only, the genuine abolitionist never giving up entirely; but it is no longer the "nigger in the wood pile." Compassion for the slave in his chains, is but secondary to the great necessity of a decided struggle for his own liberties, by the white man of the country. Instead of a handful of abolitionists, from motives of humanity, the world beholds millions of abolitionists from necessity, and depend upon it there will be hard and bloody work, before the struggle terminate[s]! We heartily deplore the prospect. There is no one so thoroughly depraved! as to love violence for its own sake, but the oppressor of the colored man has forced the necessity. Beginning upon the colored minority and aided in their work without dissent by the North, they went on, and on, until the increasing respect for self, and the opinion of the world, obliged northern men to hesitate—then came the rebound—from the black man to the white, and now we contemplate a great but gory struggle. Bleeding Kansas![2] Ostracism for opinion's sake. Ruffianism in the Halls of Legislation.[3] Impertinence on the high ways and by ways. Incarceration as in the case of the noble Passmore Williamson[4]—not for speaking, not for acting—but for silence; and lastly, the seal upon all these outrages by the election results. But into the future who can bear to look without a shudder at what must be, judging from the decided and demon-like attitude of the South, and her past history and present aggressions? When we remember that away down under all this mass of outraged humanity, the white men North and South, opposed to the institution from an instinct of self preservation and to slaveholders, because of their tyrannical and dictatorial policy towards them—away down under it all, buried nearly out of sight, lie the prostrate slave, and the mis-called free colored man, devoted to wrongs worse even than even were experienced in Kansas—not shot because they do not stay away from asserting their rights, but stripped of all rights—things without names, to "go on" bleeding and breeding in body and mind and spirit until the struggle over and around them should have terminated. A fearful thing is the result of that last Presidential election! The opinion expressed by that good woman [word illegible] Esther Moore of the Fugitive Bill, is true of this, "there is no name for it."[5]

M. A. S. C.

Provincial Freeman (Chatham, Canada West), 6 December 1856.

1. In the election of 1856, the Democratic party bypassed the incumbent president, Franklin Pierce, and chose James Buchanan (1791–1868) as its nominee. Buchanan had spent a lengthy career in national politics as a member of Congress, the expansionist secretary of state in the administration of James K. Polk, and minister to Russia and Britain. His candidacy was opposed by John C. Fremont of the newly organized Republican party and former president Millard Fillmore of the nativist American ("Know Nothing") party. The debate over the extension of slavery into the territories was the central issue of the campaign.

Republicans opposed slavery's extension and ran a lively campaign based on the slogan "free soil, free men, and Fremont." Democrats supported extension and the provisions of the Kansas-Nebraska Act. Buchanan won the election and became the fifteenth president of the United States. He carried the South, all of the border states except Maryland, and five northern states. The election demonstrated the growing division of American political parties along sectional lines. Once in office, Buchanan strictly enforced federal laws on slavery in opposition to abolitionist demands. During his last months in office, he witnessed the beginnings of Southern secession. *DAB*, 3:207–14.

2. Passage of the Kansas-Nebraska Act in May 1854 initiated the rapid development of Kansas by proslavery and free-state settlers. Each group sought to dominate the political process leading to statehood and thereby determine whether Kansas would be admitted to the Union as a slave or free state. By 1855 the struggle had erupted into civil war. The territory became a symbol of sectional controversy and earned the sobriquet "Bleeding Kansas."

3. Cary refers to the brutal caning of Massachusetts Senator Charles Sumner by South Carolina Congressman Preston Brooks on the floor of the Senate during May 1856 in response to Sumner's earlier antislavery speech, which vilified South Carolina Senator Andrew Pickens Butler.

4. Passmore Williamson (1822–1895), a Philadelphia conveyancer and liberal Quaker, joined the antislavery movement in the mid-1840s and became a lifelong member of the Pennsylvania Abolition Society in 1847. He served as PAS secretary (1848–51), then as secretary of the PAS Acting Committee. The latter position and his membership on the Vigilance Committee of Philadelphia brought him into regular contact with fugitive slaves during the 1850s. Williamson's role in a well-publicized slave escape brought him considerable notoriety. On 18 July 1855, he and several associates boarded a steamship in Philadelphia harbor and informed Jane Johnson, the slave of John H. Wheeler, U.S. minister to Nicaragua, that, because she had been transported into a free state, she was free. Johnson fled the ship with her two sons. Wheeler sought redress from the U.S. District Court; Judge John K. Kane summoned Williamson to produce the three slaves before the court. When Williamson answered that the slaves had never been in his custody, the judge imprisoned him for contempt of court. Despite legal petitions, Williamson was not freed until 3 November. Kane's ruling that Wheeler did not alter the legal status of his slaves by bringing them into Pennsylvania established a precedent clarified by the 1857 Dred Scott decision. Ralph Lowell Eckert, "Antislavery Martyrdom: The Ordeal of Passmore Williamson," *PMHB* 100:521–38 (October 1976); Samuel May, *The Fugitive Slave Law and Its Victims* (New York, N.Y., 1861), 46–47.

5. Esther Moore (1774–1854), a prominent Philadelphia Quaker, was active in the antislavery, women's rights, and spiritualist movements. A founding member of the American Anti-Slavery Society and a lifelong member of the circle of Philadelphia antislavery women that included Lucretia Mott, she was not a well-known public speaker, but she frequently introduced antislavery orators at reform gatherings. The context of Moore's comment about the Fugitive Slave Law remains unclear, but it was likely offered during the fall of 1851 in the wake of the Christiana slave riot. *NASS*, 25 November 1854; *Lib*, 8 December 1854; Merrill and Ruchames, *Letters of William Lloyd Garrison*, 2:127–28, 363–64, 3:60.

62.
Editorial by Mary Ann Shadd Cary
6 December 1856

Like most antebellum reformers, black abolitionists shared a belief in the perfectibility of society. This led them to support a diversity of reform interests and to join a variety of allied moral reform movements, including temperance, women's rights, and peace. Abolitionists—black and white—were probably more active in temperance than in any of the other crusades. Black leaders in Canada West were no exception. Samuel Ringgold Ward contended that "Rum" was one of the greatest evils degrading North American blacks. Both the *Voice of the Fugitive* and the *Provincial Freeman* advocated temperance and considered news of the movement noteworthy. The planned black settlements in the province either required or recommended temperance. In communities throughout Canada West, local blacks formed societies, like the African Temperance Society of St. Catharines, to promote abstinence from intoxicating beverages. As publication agent, editor, and lecturer for the *Freeman*, Mary Ann Shadd Cary frequently did her part for this effort. Her 6 December 1856 editorial, "A Good Boarding House Greatly Needed by the Colored Citizens," urged local blacks to organize a temperance boardinghouse in Chatham in order to combat the perceived proalcohol influence of other local boardinghouses. Such an establishment would, in Cary's view, eliminate the "temptation to beastly intoxication," while safeguarding the "physical health of the community." Ronald G. Walters, *American Reformers, 1815–1860* (New York, N.Y., 1978), 101; *VF*, 24 September, 5 November 1851, 12 February 1852; *PFW*, 24 March 1853, 25 March 1854; Hill, *Freedom-Seekers*, 179.

A Good Boarding House Greatly Needed by the Colored Citizens

It is very desirable that some one acquainted with managing properly a good Boarding House should open one in Chatham, at this time, both for the respectable entertainment of the public and the citizens of this place. A "house of all nations" wherein the essentials, good tables and lodging, excellent deportment from proprietors and visitors, could be insisted upon, and where the charges would be in keeping with the character of the place. A good *temperance house* of high tone,[1] and fitted up properly and managed by competent persons, would pay well! At the present time, we do not know of a public boarding house that is not also a drinking house. A most unworthy state of morals! and yet such houses, not 'gin palaces' either, are blazoned forth as desirable places of resort. We regard them as degrading in their tendency—as calculated to not only corrupt and demoralize the young, but as dangerous to the physical health of the community as the small-pox or cholera. For it is not only that they hold out the temptation to beastly intoxication—a fact that cannot be denied—the quality of their liquors is so inferior generally, as to facilitate disease and death with greater rapidity than ordinary. Some of our Chatham boarding houses *make* their own liquors and a "make" they may be supposed to be. While the character of houses here is indifferent so far as we have been informed, the rates for entertainment are enormous. The wants of the travelling community justify better provisions than have been made in this respect, and we sincerely hope some enterprising COLORED Canadian or American will take the matter in hand.

M. A. S. C.

Provincial Freeman (Chatham, Canada West), 6 December 1856.

1. During the 1830s, temperance associations in towns and cities throughout the United States established coffeehouses, restaurants, and hotels to service a temperance clientele and to combat alcohol consumption. Temperance hotels were generally quasi-religious establishments—some refused to serve on the Sabbath, many held daily worship services, and most provided guests with moral uplift literature. Ian R. Tyrrell, *Sobering Up: From Temperance to Prohibition in Antebellum America, 1800–1860* (Westport, Conn., 1979), 200, 232; W. J. Rorabaugh, *The Alcoholic Republic: An American Tradition* (New York, N.Y., 1979), 195.

63.
James T. Rapier to John H. Rapier, Jr.
27 January 1857

For many blacks Canada offered economic, educational, and other opportunities not readily available in the United States. Alabama free black James T. Rapier arrived in Canada West in 1856 and stayed eight years. His first years were spent at the Elgin settlement, where he received a classical education that prepared him for his future career as a black politician and U.S. congressman. Rapier's 27 January 1857 letter to his brother described everyday affairs at Elgin. As his letter suggests, the process of acquiring and developing the land was a difficult, uncertain enterprise, even at one of the more successful black Canadian settlements. Little progress could be made during the cold winter months; and the stringent property standards at Elgin placed an additional burden on the settlers. Rapier writes not as one who had discovered a permanent sanctuary in Canada West, but as an exile, anxious to return to his Alabama home. Ullman, *Look to the North Star*, 124–32, 289–94; Schweninger, *James T. Rapier and Reconstruction*, 30–33.

Buxton, C[anada] West
Jan[uar]y 27, 1857

Dear Brother[1]

Your welcome letter came to hand of the date [4]th instant with the cheque of Fifty dollars draune up in your favor and transferred to me[.] I have delayed no time in answering your letter for I considered it quite essential for you to know all about that piece of land belonging to you[.] I sold the cheque for forty eigth dollars and a half[.] I then went to the Rev. Wm. King and asked him what was behind and he told me that five installments were due yet[.] You know they are twelve dollars and half each with interest. The whole amount due 81 dollars and 25 cents[.] So i did not pay him any of the draught but I have it reserved for him if you say [p]ay it[.] The papers you spoke of i understood you to mean the deed which he tells me will probably be a year before you could get it after the money was all paid[.] I knew Fifty dollars were of no avail to wards getting the deed. That was the reason i did not pay him until I had farther orders from you[.] You can rest assured of that fact[.] The money is all safe enoug[h.] If you say pay him what you sent i will do so or wait until you send the balance. I suppose you & Father[2] have fixed that business up between your[selves.] You are doubtless aware that Father paid two installments when he was out here last summer and I suppose advanced Harris about forty dollars more on that land[.] There are only fourteen dollars more coming to Harris[.] I think you will have to pay the land out and give Father a mortgage on it[.][3] Rev. King told me that you would have to put you up a house to entitle you to the land[.] The house you have started is of the right dimension providing it was covered and a fence before it[.][4] This all has to be done by the first of June next or it is liable to be sold for he sold one about a week ago under the Same circumstances as I have wrote you all about [word illegible] i will comence my letter[.]

You asked me whether I was going back to alabama or not. Father told me when I started that I could go to school this winter & spring and then I could come there if I wanted. So I am going to take him at his word[.] You can look for me if life last and have good luck about the 15th of April[.] Uncle Henry wants to come there too a little later in the spring[,] so you must write to us & let us know which away to come[.] I was afraid i would have to run away when i had the row with Scott but it did not cost me any thing[.] Uncle wants to know whether you received that watch or not[.] I wrote you at [letter illegible]atab and also sent you a paper there[.] I hardly know how to thank you for these 10 dollars until i get able to pay you again[.] I am getting along at school very well but you will perceive this at once from my writing[,] grammar & spelling[.][5] John[,] this is sunday morning and every thing looks gloomy[.] The ground is covered with 12 inches of snow[.] The trees are covered with sleet and very smoky this morning and inclined to be a little rainy and being esconced in a neat little cottage by a log Fire and being all a lone i have a little chanc[e] to write[.] The church bells sound reechoes through the woods summoning the people to assemble together to hear the word of god proclaimed[.] All of these combined is enough to turn my thoughts back to the hom[e] of our boyhood where all four of us boys were together[,] where we all breathed as one but are we not scattered abroad on face of Earth[.] Do you expect ever to see us all together again[?] I do not[.] Just look where we are at[,] you in the west and myself in the north[,] Henry & Dick in california[6] & Father in Alabama[.] Did you ever think how small our Family is and Sarah the only female among them out of eleven[.] I think you and me might drive down stakes together and keep them down[.] What says you[,] John[?] I would write more but i have not room to express my feelings[.] I am going to get adams & co. to express [two or three words illegible] unusual for me to write so long a letter[.] [word illegible] all send their respects to you, sarah[7] in particular[.] John[,] i bid you fare well until we meet in April if both liv[es] [word illegible] Adieu I remain your Brother,

James T. Rapier[8]

P.S. Get me a situation and uncle Henry too if you can do it[.] Must i Bring a friend with me[?] Let me know[.] Answer [immediately] if not sooner[.] Look for me and give me som dirictins about that land what to do[.]

James T. Rapier

Rapier Family Papers, Moorland-Spingarn Research Center, Howard University, Washington, District of Columbia. Published by permission.

1. John H. Rapier, Jr. (1835–ca. 1865), was born to free black parents Susan and John H. Rapier, Sr., of Florence, Alabama. About the mid-1850s, he determined, upon his father's advice, to leave Alabama and settle in free territory. He briefly entertained the notion of immigrating to Liberia, but he abandoned the idea when he received no reply after making several inquiries to the American Colonization Society. In early 1856, he and his uncle, James P. Thomas, joined William Walker's filibustering campaign in Nicaragua. Rapier and Thomas were optimistic about the role of blacks in a new Nicaraguan government but returned to the United States when they learned that Walker planned to proclaim a dictatorship and reestablish black slavery. Settling in the Minnesota Territory, Rapier served as the personal secretary of Parker H. French, a coadventurer in Nicaragua, an association that ended in a dispute over wages. Rapier then worked as a free-lance journalist, and during the next four years, he contributed over one hundred articles to five Minnesota newspapers on such diverse topics as destruction of the environment, snuff and snuff dippers, the Republican party, Henry Ward Beecher, and his reminiscences of the Walker filibuster. The erudite Rapier also wrote poetry and penned several tracts chiding public officials for discrimination against blacks and advocating black emigration. In December 1860, Rapier left Minnesota for Port-au-Prince, Haiti, where he taught in a school for mulatto children. After observing Haitian poverty and corruption firsthand, he began to perceive slavery in a positive light and urged blacks to remain in slave societies. Yet he was soon disabused of this notion and advocated black immigration to the British West Indies. In February 1861, he left Haiti for Kingston, Jamaica, where he lived with a local government official and studied dentistry and anatomy with Canadian physician William Beckett. Upon returning to the United States in 1862, Rapier enrolled in the Department of Medicine and Surgery at the University of Michigan. He was the first black enrolled there, and the hostility of white students soon forced him to withdraw from the school. He enrolled at the medical school of the University of Iowa at Keokuk in autumn 1863 and received a doctor of medicine degree the following year. Rapier promptly sought and obtained a commission as an assistant surgeon in the Union army. He spent the remainder of his life on the staff of the Freedmen's Contraband Hospital in Washington, D.C. Schweninger, *James T. Rapier and Reconstruction*, 12, 15, 17, 24–29.

2. Rapier's father was John H. Rapier, Sr. (1808–1869), of Florence, Alabama. The elder Rapier was born in Virginia to a mulatto slave mother, Sally Thomas, and a white father. During John's childhood, his master moved the family to Nashville, Tennessee. There, the young slave was hired out as a waiter and pole boy for river barge captain Richard Rapier, who plied the Cumberland–Mississippi river trade between Nashville and New Orleans. In 1819 Captain Rapier sent young John and other slaves to Florence, Alabama, to clear land and build a retail store. John continued to work for Richard Rapier until he was manumitted in 1829. It is

not known when he adopted the Rapier name. Shortly after his emancipation, John Rapier settled in Florence, established a barbershop, and married Susan, a nineteen-year-old free black from Baltimore. They had four sons: Richard, John, Henry, and James Thomas. Susan died in 1841. In 1848 Rapier took a young slave woman, Lucretia, as his common-law wife; they had five children, all slaves, who were not emancipated until the Civil War. Rapier's success in the barbering trade provided the family with an annual income of $600 to $1,000. His success earned him the respect of local whites and allowed him to accumulate real estate. During the 1840s and 1850s, he purchased six lots in Florence, one hundred acres in Minnesota Territory, three lots in Toronto, and one hundred acres near Buxton, Canada West. He visited Canada West in 1856 and simultaneously helped a slave escape there from Florence. After the Civil War, Rapier became active in Republican politics. In 1867 he was selected voter registrar for the Forty-third District in Alabama, thus becoming the first black public official in the state's history. He died in Florence of stomach cancer in 1869. Schweninger, *James T. Rapier and Reconstruction*, 1–3, 15–18, 20–21, 45–46, 72.

3. When John H. Rapier, Sr., visited Buxton, Canada West, in the autumn of 1856, he made a $117 down payment to the Elgin Association on one hundred acres of wilderness land. He also paid black laborer Robert Harris an additional $70 to clear and fence the land. Harris, a longtime Buxton resident, was active in Elgin settlement affairs and later became a close friend of the Rapier brothers. Soon after hiring Harris, the elder Rapier returned to Florence, Alabama, and posted a second payment on the land. He eventually paid off the mortgage and received a deed to the property. Schweninger, *James T. Rapier and Reconstruction*, 21; *VF*, 8 April 1852; James T. Rapier to John H. Rapier, Jr., 9 March 1857, Rapier Family Papers, DHU [10:0574].

4. The Elgin settlement at Buxton had specific construction regulations. Each piece of property was to have a residence, and failure to comply with this condition of the contract could result in the loss of one's land. Each residence was to be no smaller than 18′ x 24′ x 12′. It had to stand 33′ back from the road, have land cleared around it 64′ from the center of the road, and have a garden in front enclosed by a picket fence. A drainage ditch, 4′ wide at the top, 18″ at the bottom, and 2′ deep, was to span the front of each property. Schweninger, *James T. Rapier and Reconstruction*, 21; Pease and Pease, *Black Utopia*, 97.

5. Rapier enrolled in the King School at Elgin in October 1856 and attended through the 1857–58 academic year. The interracial, free institution of 140 students first opened its doors in 1850. Although its initial objective was to provide students with a basic education in elementary English, arithmetic, and geography, by 1853 it also offered courses in Greek, Latin, and algebra. The school's reputation prompted many area whites to send their children to Elgin. During his tenure there, Rapier studied the basic subjects, plus the Bible, history, classical literature, the higher mathematics, and several ancient and modern languages. Schweninger, *James T. Rapier and Reconstruction*, 30–33; Pease and Pease, *Black Utopia*, 102.

6. Richard (Dick) Rapier (1831–ca. 1895) and Henry Rapier (1836–?) were two of the four sons born to free blacks Susan and John H. Rapier, Sr., in Florence, Alabama. When they were in their teens, their father sent them to Buffalo, New York, to live with their uncle Henry K. Thomas and to attend school. Both

later continued their schooling in Canada West. In 1855 the two brothers crossed the Rockies in search of gold, ending up along the Feather River in northern California (evidence also suggests that Richard had earlier gone overland to California around 1850). Finding that area played out, they turned to farming and purchased and planted three hundred acres near Auburn. Differences between the brothers prompted Henry to leave the farm; by 1861 he was an established barber in Sacramento. Richard continued to farm the land near Auburn for several years. In 1868 he married a local widow, Henrietta Stans. They abandoned the farm sometime before 1880 and settled in Auburn, where Richard also found work as a barber. Schweninger, *James T. Rapier and Reconstruction*, 15, 17, 19, 24; Abajian, *Blacks in Selected Newspapers*, 3 : 137; *Sacramento City Directory*, 1861; *ESF*, 21 August 1868.

7. Rapier refers to his cousin, Sarah Thomas (1845–?) of Buffalo, New York. In 1857 she was apparently the only female cousin in the Rapier-Thomas extended family. Sarah, the eldest daughter of Henry K. and Maria Thomas, taught in Canada West during the Civil War and later secured a position at a freedmen's school operated by the American Missionary Association in Mississippi. United States Census, 1850; Schweninger, *James T. Rapier and Reconstruction*, 15, 29, 113.

8. James T. Rapier (1837–1883) was born in Florence, Alabama, the fourth son of John H. Rapier, a moderately prosperous barber-realtor, and his free, Baltimore-born wife, Susan. In 1842 Rapier was sent to Nashville, Tennessee, to attend a private school for blacks and to live with his well-to-do uncle James P. Thomas. He completed his early schooling in 1854 and spent over a year working on Mississippi riverboats. In 1856 he moved to William King's Elgin settlement in Canada West, a community that had received support from his father. Rapier lived with his uncle Henry, formerly a successful Buffalo, New York, barber who had moved his family to a two-hundred-acre farm at Buxton after passage of the Fugitive Slave Law. Although Rapier enrolled in King's well-known settlement school (where he was preceded by brothers Richard and Henry), he initially devoted his energy to the search for a lucrative business venture. But early in 1857, he experienced a religious conversion, rededicated himself to his education, and began to study for the ministry. Rapier moved to Toronto in 1860 to attend a normal school and received his diploma three years later. He taught at Buxton for a year, then moved to Nashville, Tennessee, in 1864, hoping to employ his missionary zeal and teaching skills for the benefit of freedmen.

During the next twenty years, Rapier became one of the South's most dynamic and accomplished black leaders, distinguishing himself as a politician, labor leader, businessman, federal administrator, and editor. He was an outspoken and courageous critic of racism who steadfastly worked for racial reconciliation, black civil rights, and economic opportunity. Rapier immediately established himself as a successful planter and steamboat provisions merchant, first in Tennessee and, by 1866, near his Alabama home. His encounters with restrictive racial laws and policies simultaneously led him into politics. He attended the Nashville black suffrage convention (1865), led a voter registration drive in Alabama, and joined that state's Republican party. In 1868 he was driven from politics by Ku Klux Klan death threats, but he reentered public life in 1870 as an unsuccessful candidate for Alabama secretary of state. Between 1869 and 1872,

Rapier focused his attention on the National Negro Labor Union, attending national conventions and founding an Alabama chapter (1871).

In 1872 he was elected to the U.S. Congress from Alabama's Second District, one of only seventeen blacks sent to Congress during Reconstruction. As a congressman, he sponsored legislation to rehabilitate the southern economy and was an influential participant in debates over the Civil Rights Act of 1875. Rapier was also the first black federal administrator appointed in Alabama, serving as both assessor (1871) and collector (1878–83) of internal revenue in his home district. He represented Alabama at the Fifth World Exposition (1873) in Vienna, Austria, and edited a party newspaper, the *Republican State Sentinel* (1872, 1878). After 1879 he promoted emigration as the best answer to the South's reemerging racial caste system. He attended the Southern States Negro Convention (1879) and chaired its emigration committee, and he purchased land in Kansas for black settlers. Rapier remained active in politics until his death. Schweniger, *James T. Rapier and Reconstruction*; *DANB*, 514–15; Maurine Christopher, *Black Americans in Congress*, rev. ed. (New York, N.Y., 1976), 123–36.

64.
Editorial by Mary Ann Shadd Cary
31 January 1857

Mary Ann Shadd Cary envisioned that the black Canadian community would become an educated, self-reliant, British citizenry. Black Canadians' modest advance toward that ideal prompted her to write "Obstacles to the Progress of Colored Canadians." For Cary the primary obstacle was a lack of unity and common purpose, a condition she attributed to the lingering effects of slavery on many Canadian blacks. Their failure to achieve a consensus, she argued, had opened the way for three decades of incompetent leadership and demeaning begging operations. Cary's complaints were not new, but the critique she had presented in the early 1850s was just as appropriate in 1857. By restating her initial criticisms, she underscored the persistent, intractable character of the essential issues confronting black Canadians. *PFW*, 15 July 1854, 12 May 1855, 17 May, 19 July 1856 [9:0643; 10:0158, 0160, 0226].

Obstacles to the Progress of Colored Canadians

The colored people of these Provinces live in a land of equal laws—equal rights, and yet, no people that we know of are given to complaint more than they. In certain localities, parties can be found, who, taking advantage of the prevalent ignorance among the colored population, administer the law in a way clearly prejudicial to the interests of the latter; but, how far the former are censurable under the circumstances is with us a question, when viewed in the light of an ordinary transaction for the exact extent of the censure to be attached to the colored people themselves is not quite clear, we are convinced however, that the fault is not all on one side, but that to them belongs a fair share of blame. We make these remarks with no intention to shield white men from merited blame at all, but that the colored people may not take to themselves complete exemption from rebuke for their great indifference to their interests.

Courts of justice, corrupt judges nor any other grievance of which we may complain can injure them a tithe in comparison, with the treachery, want of confidence and down right wickedness one towards the other. In the United States, in slavery, the great aim of their oppressors was to destroy confidence the one in the other—to under-value one another in their person and pursuits; at the same time that they inculcate fear of the master, or the person of white complexion, to make him also the idol, the centre of homage, the one to be looked up to, to be clothed and fed by, although the very food to be furnished them, whether moral or other, should poison in the taking. Many in coming to Canada, have but fled from the sting, the bitterness of the dose, the direct result of the relation of master and slave, but not at all from these other evils which are as clearly concomitants of the relation.

A well organized insurrection for meeting out to the master his just deserts, must be nipped in the bud by the treachery of some "negro," who more in contempt of his own people than hatred to the actions of the man who trampled upon him, must reveal the plot.[1] He had no confidence in his fellows—there was no fellow feeling—he would save his oppressors at the expense of his suffering brethren.

The case of that slave, brutalized as he is, has many a counterpart in these Provinces, among colored men. Try any community—our own to begin with, and seek out if you can among its teeming hundreds, twenty men who see eye to eye upon the subject of their interests! They cannot be found! While upon one question some may unite, there will be the most rancorous and bitter division, upon others equally clear and conclusive; and rather than yield an opinion for the general good; their entire interests may go by the poor. The vulture now at the vitals of [word illegible] is the aim [one or two lines missing] other words, the desire of a few ignorant colored men to lead the people. To that love of power, and the "pickings and stealings" resulting from it may be traced [to] the greater part of the evils entailed upon us. We pause just here, to say by way of parenthesis (that no honest colored man or woman who knows the moral condition of the colored people of these Provinces can deny what we say), without telling a falsehood, and yet, for saying this much truth, we know as certainly that,

Tray Blanche and Sweet heart,[2]

and every contemptible cur in the pack will either be growling, snapping, barking, or secretly biting for it.

The time has come to "cry aloud and spare not." Instead of being like the Jews, who unite the more because of oppression, unlike every other people, the more the division the better; and unable to get along beautifully in the work of separation, a free invitation is indirectly given for inroads of the enemy, should he assume the garb of a friend, though not possessing one trait to merit the name. Take a retrospect of the colored people of Canada for the last thirty years. Their institutions—their divisions—the knots and "squads"—their white and colored beggars—begging in public for lands, clothes, schools, churches—the quarrels of these beggars, white and colored—the contentions about their lands—among their churches—the *immorality* among missionaries white and colored, teachers and preachers, male and female—the caucuses, conventions, resolutions, and after all, the return of the pretended leaders of the people,

"Like the dog to his vomit, or the sow to her wallowing in the mire," and that too, after years or weeks or months of sin, and after having before "God and the sun" foresworn for the twentieth time such vile deeds.

And now good reader, and friend to your race, look at the *condition* of the same churches, schools, institutions. Calculate if you can, the vast sums drawn from the benevolent of England and America, enough to have installed an empire; then, too, turn to the "mussy fussy" creatures who have been at this work—this business of degrading an entire people, back almost to their [first] estate, as fast as British law could make men of them, and what do we see? Who are these Atlases upon whose powerful shoulders rests this *colored* world?[3] Men generally among the whites, who could not be made available for any good work at home—men of fallen fortunes or of no fortunes, who have chosen this field to replenish empty purses, or to fill purses always empty; and among black men, knavish tools of these first named, or men of great ignorance, conceit and ambition, whose highest recommendation, whose certificate of reputation, is their ability to instal beggars and begging, and to squander the same. Think of it! The destiny of thousands of people to be confided to such keeping. Think of a people who when on the other side, was said by one of the greatest philanthropists of the county to be a "nation of servants," and when under British rule aspire to be a nation of beggars. Having spoken in general, we intend in future, to particularize. Instead of treachery, ignorance[,] servility, we want to see confidence, intelligence, independence and instead of a host of cold refugees formerly bond and free, aiming with might and maim to curse their people, with a pro-slavery–yankee training. We shall aim to persuade these "suffering" people, to cease hankering after the "flesh pots of Egypt," and as they have come under British rule from necessity, to become British at heart in reality.

M. A. S. C.

Provincial Freeman (Chatham, Canada West), 31 January 1857.

1. Few insurrection attempts by slaves in the American South ever proceeded beyond the planning stage. One reason was slave informers. Informers betrayed black rebels for a variety of reasons: objection to violence on religious grounds, fear for personal or family safety, distrust of rebel leadership, or loyalty to masters. Informers were frequently freed or otherwise rewarded. Except for the 1811 slave insurrection in St. Charles and St. John the Baptist parishes in Louisiana, the notable antebellum insurrection attempts—those organized by Gabriel Prosser (1800), Denmark Vesey (1822), and Nat Turner (1831)—were all betrayed by slave informers. Herbert Aptheker, *American Negro Slave Revolts*, 3rd ed. (New York, N.Y., 1969), 247, 249–50, 254; Eugene Genovese, *From Rebellion to Revolution: Afro-American Slave Revolts in the Making of the Modern World* (Baton Rouge, La., 1979).

2. Cary borrows a line from Act 3, Scene 6, of William Shakespeare's *King Lear*, in which three imaginary dogs turn against the insane king:

> The little dogs and all,
> Tray, Blanche, and Sweetheart, see
> They bark at me.

3. In Greek mythology, Atlas was condemned to support the sky on his shoulders. In the popular mind, the globe carried by Atlas in artistic renditions represented an overwhelming task or set of responsibilities.

65.
Resolutions by L. G. Spears
Delivered at the First Baptist Church, Amherstburg, Canada West 21 February 1857

Abolitionists used a variety of means to achieve antislavery goals. One common method was to break organizational ties with American churches and associations that supported slavery or remained silent on the issue. Black abolitionists in Canada viewed this as a way to influence American organizations. During the 1850s, Canadian black denominations, particularly the Amherstburg Baptist Association and the Canadian Anti-Slavery Baptist Association, employed a strict antislavery test, as did many local black churches. The black First Baptist Church of Amherstburg received regular financial assistance from the New York State Baptist Convention, unaware that many members of that body tacitly approved of slavery. When J. J. E. Linton, a white Canadian abolitionist and a leading opponent of "fellowshipping" with proslavery churches, informed them of this fact, the congregation immediately prepared to sever relations with the New York association. On 21 February 1857, church clerk L. G. Spears presented a series of resolutions to the congregation designed to accomplish that end. An "overwhelming majority" approved the resolutions and requested that they be published in the *Provincial Freeman*. Spears reported this action to the *Freeman*'s editors. Lewis, "Religious Nature of Negro Migration," 123–30; *PFW*, 7 March 1857 [9:0522].

Whereas, The Amherstburg Baptist Church did receive aid from the New York State Convention in 1853, and continued until 185[5].[1] And

Whereas, We do see with J. J. E. Linton and the American Baptist as relates to the different churches (North), being connected with or silent upon Slavery,[2] and

Whereas, The public do labor under a misunderstanding in thinking that we still remain in fellowship with them since our last reception of aid. Therefore

Resolved, That we will neither give nor receive aid nor hold fellowship with any church that does not look upon Slavery as a sin, or that holds its peace on the subject.

Resolved, We will not hold fellowship with any church or churches, that apologise for any such a scheme.

Resolved, That we will not *hold* fellowship with any minister who *will* not stand up and speak in loud tones and show the people their sins, and the churches their state of transgression in relation to Slavery. See minutes of the sixteenth Anniversary of the Amherstburg Baptist Association, held in Chatham, Sept. 18[5]6.[3]

Resolved, That we will not fraternize nor give credit to any so-called Christian Board, Press or Society, any longer than we find them to be pro-slavery.

Resolved, That any so-called Christian church, Press, Society or Minister, that remains silent or is afraid to speak the truth and the whole truth is not fit for the public use or service.

Moved that these resolutions be published in the *Provincial Freeman*.

Done by order, in behalf of the church.

L. G. SPEARS
Church Clerk

Provincial Freeman (Chatham, Canada West), 7 March 1857.

1. After J. J. E. Linton informed members of the black First Baptist Church of Amherstburg that the New York State Baptist Convention tacitly condoned slavery, the congregation prepared in January 1857 to sever all relations with the New York Baptists. Spears's resolutions represent the completion of this process. Murray, "Canada and Anglo-American Anti-Slavery Movement," 259.

2. Both John James Edmonstoune Linton (1804–1869) and the *American Baptist*, an American Baptist Free Mission Society organ, opposed fellowshipping with proslavery churches and those who avoided the slavery issue. Linton emigrated from Scotland to Upper Canada in 1833. He settled in Stratford, where he worked as a farmer, teacher, notary public, and clerk. His uncompromising convictions led him to assail North American churches for neglecting the slavery and temperance issues. Linton contributed articles to the *Provincial Freeman* and in 1856 started his own short-lived abolitionist paper, the *Voice of the Bondsman*. In later years, he carried on local charity work in Stratford. *DCB*, 9:469–70.

3. In 1855 the Amherstburg Baptist Association opposed fellowshipping with any religious denomination that attempted to apologize for slavery even while condemning it. Each local ABA congregation was asked to hold monthly antislavery rallies, a policy that was reiterated at the association's September 1856 meeting in Chatham. The ABA had been founded at Amherstburg in 1841 by three black Baptist congregations from Detroit, Amherstburg, and Sandwich. It grew quickly. The ABA operated as a religious denomination—ordaining clergy, disciplining members, interpreting doctrine, and establishing rules of behavior. During its early years, it was directed by some of Canada West's most prominent black clergymen—Anthony Binga, Horace Hawkins, Israel Campbell, William C. Monroe, and Madison J. Lightfoot. Throughout its existence, the ABA denounced begging and promoted black self-help and temperance. When the ABA joined the American Baptist Free Mission Society in 1849, a schism occurred. Objecting to "suspect" practices on the part of the society, particularly in the operation of the British-American Institute at Dawn, several churches withdrew from the ABA and formed the Canadian Anti-Slavery Association. But the ABA stepped up its antislavery activity in the early 1850s, and the disgruntled congregations rejoined the parent organization in 1857. Thereafter, the organization resumed its rapid

growth. By 1861 it claimed over a thousand supporters in twenty member churches. The ABA supported the Union during the Civil War. After the war, the association sent missionaries to work among the freedmen in the American South. The organization continued to operate under different names into the twentieth century. Hill, *Freedom-Seekers*, 54, 104, 143; Lewis, "Religious Nature of Negro Migration," 117–32; Simpson, "Negroes in Ontario to 1870," 112–14, 117–18; Winks, *Blacks in Canada*, 342–45.

66.
Circular by Mary Ann Shadd Cary, H. Ford Douglas, and Isaac D. Shadd
February 1857

Antislavery institutions had a precarious existence, and the black press was no exception. Of six attempts to establish black antislavery newspapers in Canada West, only two—the *Voice of the Fugitive* and the *Provincial Freeman*—survived long enough to influence the antislavery movement. In 1839 black abolitionists Peter Gallego and E. L. de St. Remy of Toronto announced their intention to publish *The British American Journal of Liberty*, but no evidence exists that the paper was ever published. *The British American*, published by fugitive slaves in Toronto in March 1845, survived less than a month. Nothing ever came of a resolution by the Drummondville Convention (1847) to create a black antislavery paper in Toronto. Augustus R. Green's *True Royalist and Weekly Intelligencer* (1860) was also short-lived. Lack of financial support was the usual cause of failure. *The Voice* and the *Freeman* worked to address that problem. Both had regular subscribers and advertising income. The *Voice* received a subsidy as the official organ of the Refugee Home Society. The *Freeman* created its own support organization, the Provincial Union Association. In addition, editors Mary Ann Shadd Cary, Isaac D. Shadd, and H. Ford Douglas made antislavery lecture tours in Canada West and in the northern United States to enlist subscribers to the paper. Even so, the *Freeman* engaged in a persistent financial struggle. By early 1857, after three years of continuous publication, the militant antislavery paper was on the verge of closing down. Ironically, Cary, Shadd, and Douglas—leading voices of black self-reliance in Canada West—responded with a plea for public assistance. "Slavery and Humanity," their February 1857 circular, was an unabashed appeal for funds. *CA*, 11 May, 22 June 1839 [3:0054, 0125]; Winks, *Blacks in Canada*, 395; *Convention of the Coloured Population*, 15; *PFW*, 22 July 1854, 5, 12 April 1856, 8 August 1857 [8:0935, 10:0101, 0107].

SLAVERY AND HUMANITY

You are respectfully entreated to consider the claims of the ***PROVINCIAL FREEMAN***, a Newspaper published among the Refugees in the Province of Canada, and now struggling to exist, that it may be an instrument in the hand of Providence, to improve their mental and moral condition, and to encourage habits of independence.

Ignorance and inexperience of individual responsibility, are bitter fruits of the Institution of Slavery; as an anti-slavery instrumentality, then, the

Freeman aims in an humble way to uproot the tree, by inculcating a healthy anti-slavery sentiment, in a country which, though under British rule, is particularly exposed, by intercommunication, to pro-slavery religious and secular influence; and to encourage the colored people to improve their minds, and to hold fast by their religious faith, and thus to dissipate the dark cloud hovering over their intellect, the direct result of their former condition.

In this work we believe good christians, men and women must sympathize, and therefore we feel emboldened to make this direct appeal to them for genuine and practical encouragement.

For nearly three years we have pursued our labors without aid, except the bare amount of our yearly subscription, $1.50 (except in a small amount, which altogether, would not make fifty-dollars), and we find that an effort commensurate with the work we have to do, and the liabilities we have incurred, must be made, else not only must our work cease, but we must remain in debt to a few good men, who encouraged us by their loans at first.

Shall we look for a patient consideration of our appeal, dear friends, and a response from your liberality to meet the exigencies of the cause in this particular? We have never appealed to you before, as we had hoped by severe self-denial, and untiring exertions, to succeed without aid except from the sale of the papers, but, after having labored long and being obliged to support ourselves by *other* means (for not one cent do we realize toward support from the papers as yet), the indifference of many indebted to us, and the little sympathy from friends of the slave arising from non-acquaintance with our enterprise, make our efforts to meet our liabilities impossible as yet.

We beg, therefore, that this simple Statement may not be unheeded by friends to the anti-slavery cause, but that by your generous consideration you will enable us to go on.

Any *Donations* in funds sent by friends to our address, will be duly and gratefully received, and acknowledged through the paper, and a copy sent to the friends so contributing. Here is an interesting though much neglected People to labor for—here is much work to do. The scars of oppression have to be healed, and the responsibilities belonging to men who live under the just and merciful rule of Her Majesty—and the British Government—the only shelter for this people—have to be inculcated. Shall we then be aided and encouraged in this work until abler heads and stronger hands can be induced to take hold, or until we secure the help of able and willing minds whose pens might be nobly employed, to carry our cause along safely and securely? Most respectfully and affectionately yours, in the cause of human freedom and elevation,

MARY A. S. CARY
H. F. DOUGLASS *Editors*

I. D. SHADD[1]
CHATHAM, C[anada] W[est]
Feb[ruary], 1857

Communications addressed to I. D. SHADD

Mary Ann Shadd Cary Papers, Public Archives of Canada, Ottawa, Ontario. Published by permission.

1. Isaac D. Shadd (1829–1896), the eldest son of free black parents Abraham D. and Harriet Shadd, was born in Wilmington, Delaware, but spent much of his youth near West Chester, Pennsylvania. He settled in Toronto, Canada West, during the early 1850s. Like his sister, Mary Ann Shadd Cary, he was a principal figure in the ongoing publication of the *Provincial Freeman*. Shadd became a Toronto subscription agent for the paper in the spring of 1855. When it relocated in Chatham the following summer, he assumed publishing responsibilities. Although he was the *Freeman*'s publishing agent and nominal editor, Cary retained editorial control. Shadd's occasional editorials were consistent with the general tone of the *Freeman*. He urged blacks to immigrate to Canada West and become full and loyal British citizens, and he despaired of the political apathy among free blacks, the persistence of begging practices, and the reluctance of black churches to speak out unequivocally for the antislavery cause. Shadd married Amelia Freeman, a black teacher, in 1856. During the years that followed, he became a respected figure in Chatham's black community. He also adopted an increasingly militant tone. Shadd was active in the Chatham Vigilance Committee during the late 1850s; he led the rescue of Sylvanus Demarest in September 1858 and was arrested and fined for his efforts. He hosted abolitionist John Brown when the latter visited Canada West in early 1858. Although Shadd participated in Brown's Chatham Convention, he remained ambivalent about the prospect of slave insurrection.

Shadd was attracted to Martin R. Delany's plans for a black settlement in the Niger Valley of West Africa during the late 1850s. He attended the National Emigration Conventions in Cleveland (1856) and Chatham (1858), served on the movement's National Board of Commissioners, and helped organize the ephemeral African Civilization Society of Canada. In 1861 he arranged to settle in the Niger Valley but abandoned those plans when West African chiefs abrogated their treaty with Delany. With the failure of Delany's African venture and the coming of the Civil War, Shadd considered returning to the United States. He visited the black communities on the Pacific coast in 1863 and then settled in Mississippi after the war, joining Isaiah T. Montgomery's Davis Bend colony during the early 1870s. He moved to Vicksburg in 1872 and became prominent in local Republican circles. Shadd was elected to the Mississippi House of Representatives later that year and served as speaker of that body from 1874 to 1876. Shadd Family Records, Mary Ann Shadd Cary Papers, CaOLU; Bearden and Butler, *Shadd*, 160–63, 188–200, 205, 219; *PFW*, 21 April, 30 June, 22 August 1855, 21 June, 25 November 1856, 4 April, 10 June, 8 August 1857 [9:0723, 10:0190, 0385, 0420, 0633]; Victor Lauriston, "Sampson in the Temple," *CM* (June 1932), 9, 40–41; *GSB*, 28 October 1858 [11:0393]; *NASS*, 30 October 1858; Simpson, "Negroes in Ontario to 1870," 237, 665, 710; Miller, *Search for Black National-*

ity, 160–66, 194, 252; Delany, *The Niger Valley Exploring Party*, 12–13 [11:0336]; *PA*, 28 March, 22 August 1863; *NNE*, 20 April 1871; Janet Sharp Hermann, *The Pursuit of a Dream* (New York, N.Y., 1981), 183–84, 197; William C. Harris, *The Day of the Carpetbagger: Republican Reconstruction in Mississippi* (Baton Rouge, La., 1979), 423.

67.
Editorial by Isaac D. Shadd
4 April 1857

In 1857 the Supreme Court's decision in the case of *Dred Scott* v. *Sanford* stripped blacks of any claims to American citizenship. Writing for the court, Chief Justice Roger Taney argued that blacks were "so inferior that they had no rights which the white man was bound to respect." The court's decision shocked black Americans into an awareness that, for them, the distinction between slavery and freedom was fading quickly. Some blacks staged militant protests, while many, convinced that the federal government had abandoned them to slaveholders and slave catchers, considered emigration. Canadian blacks urged others to join them. "Your national ship is rotten and sinking," counseled Mary Ann Shadd Cary from Chatham, "Why not leave it?" Her brother, Isaac Shadd, offered the same advice. His editorial on the Dred Scott decision, which appeared in the *Provincial Freeman*, was a brief for Canadian immigration. Shadd reminded black Americans that, after decades of struggle, they were further from equality than ever. He urged blacks to come to Canada, where they could enjoy the citizenship, political rights, and legal equality denied them in their homeland. Benjamin C. Howard, *Report of the Decision of the Supreme Court of the United States in the Case of Dred Scott* . . . (Washington, D.C., 1857), 13–14; Foner, *History of Black Americans*, 3:226.

Colored men of the States

After struggling for years for their political rights, holding convention after convention, spending much time and means to demonstrate their ability for self-government, what great good has resulted therefrom? Again in some of the States, the political Constitution serving brethren, have organized military companies, and occasionally march after the sound of the drum,[1] showing their determination to support the government that oppresses them; evidently wishing to exhibit their love of country, notwithstanding their conceded disabilities.

To what eminence in the scale of political equality have they attained? The recent decision of the United States Court has decided the controversy,[2] and prostrated all the past efforts of the colored man.

Who are American citizens among the masses of colored Northern State men? There are none according to the lately declared meaning of the Constitution. We are of opinion that people proscribed in their native land, denied the rights of citizenship, without claim to government protection, must feel to be but little superior in condition to the slave, and according to the "Fugitive Slave Law" they are all as liable to arrest, and may be subjected without the greatest difficulty on their part, to the same degradation; in reality a population of nonentities, without existence in the body politic.

We do not rejoice at their downfall, but regret that those whom we supposed had better judgment, should have remained in such utter darkness, in hope of surmounting the machinations of the pro-slavery people of the S. With all that has been said or done against them, we hear that now as formerly, the leaders are speaking out in commanding terms to the masses: "Do not leave the States; it is our home and we'll stay and contend for our rights." How determined! Now if they intend to repose under the shade of the tree that was planted at the Rochester convention,[3] we will not object, but according to the late decision the whole body are trespassers, and can be driven from under their tree at option. Again, should they *be permitted* to "repose under it," there will be but the glimmer of a shade, as the tree seems rootless and without proper nutriment. The contention for rights, then must end in talk, and the few great Orators, Journalists, &c., who have kept up the *hubbub*, like the eagle, after soaring above all, must come down to the earth to find a permanent resting place; while thousands that have been their adherents, will stand as living victims to the continual outpouring of superlative nonsense. The affinity between the Northern and Southern pro-slavists, is such, when considering the aid of Southern colored men—Slaves!—the unwitting promoters of the designs of their owners by the three-fifths representation[4]—together with the fact, that, the eloquent oratory and influence of the most popular colored men of the United States shields the blood stained pro-slavery political party from view as pro-slavery, thereby measuring arms with freedom, and adding strength to the South, that their whole efforts have been of a downward tendency, and leadership has proven abortive. We shall wait patiently, but look for a hurried emigration e'er long, of a large portion of the most intelligent nominally free men to these Provinces, in search of what they so long waited for but failed to get.

Here is a prosperous and free government, untrammeled in her laws and healthful in prospects; with lands and resources capable of sheltering and sustaining, the half million free colored people of the Northern States, and the same number of foreigners from Europe.

The Canadas have been reputed by the people of the States to be but a suitable refuge for the fugitive; but permit us to say, these fugitives are men! many of them acknowledged British subjects, and those that are not, in due time will be.

I. D. S.

Provincial Freeman (Chatham, Canada West), 4 April 1857.

1. Blacks were not allowed to join militia companies in the United States. Congressional legislation of 1792 prohibited blacks from enrolling in militias, and

many state constitutions included a similar prohibition. Shadd apparently refers to the uniformed, paramilitary black cadres that frequently marched in parades in northern towns and cities. These cadres represented various black benevolent, literary, and fraternal organizations, which devised formal dress for their members to wear at special public and private events. Leonard P. Curry, *The Free Black in Urban America, 1800–1850* (Chicago, Ill., 1981), 208–13; Litwack, *North of Slavery*, 31, 32, 33, 35, 60.

2. Shadd refers to the decision of the United States Supreme Court in the case of *Dred Scott* v. *Sanford* (1857). Chief Justice Roger B. Taney, writing for a majority of the justices, held that no black could be a citizen of the United States on the grounds of a constitutional presumption of black inferiority. Taney's decision responded to litigation begun in 1841 by Missouri slave Dred Scott. Scott sued his owner, John F. A. Sanford, for freedom, contending that he was free because a previous master had let him reside in free Illinois and the territory of Minnesota from 1834 to 1838. The court not only denied Scott's claim to freedom but rejected Congress's authority to legislate on the issue of slavery in the territories. Taney declared that slave property was protected by the due process clause of the Fifth Amendment to the Constitution. This overturned both the underlying premise of the Compromise of 1820 and the concept of "popular sovereignty" contained in the Kansas-Nebraska Act (1854). Abolitionists and free blacks reacted vigorously against the Dred Scott decision because it limited the authority of a free state to exclude slavery within its borders (if the slave was owned by a resident of another state), questioned black citizenship in free states, and allowed for the spread of slavery into the territories—thus upsetting the fragile congressional balance between slave and free states. Don Fehrenbacher, *The Dred Scott Case: Its Significance in Law and Politics* (New York, N.Y., 1978).

3. Shadd refers to the antiemigration position of many antebellum black leaders. Throughout the 1850s, antiemigrationist sentiment rose and fell in direct response to nationalist-emigrationist programs within the northern black community. Antiemigrationist leaders regarded the emigration movement as yet another expression of colonizationist thought, and they leveled many of the same charges against it that they had earlier against the colonization movement. They asserted that emigrationism was another attempt to "coerce" free blacks into abandoning the United States; that it postponed emancipation; that it capitulated to white racist determination to make the United States into a white man's country; and that it deterred blacks from taking the social, political, and institutional actions necessary to rectify their condition. This sentiment was best expressed by black leaders at the Colored National Convention held in Rochester, New York, during 6–8 July 1853. Approximately 170 delegates from ten states attended the gathering. The delegates—particularly Frederick Douglass, who drafted the meeting's Declaration of Sentiments—made it clear that most free northern blacks rejected what they saw as the resurgent efforts of the American Colonization Society and, by implication, the enthusiasm of some free blacks for emigration. Pease and Pease, *They Who Would Be Free*, 123, 139–40, 150, 253–55, 258–60; *Colored National Convention in Rochester*, 3–51; *FDP*, 15 July 1853.

4. Shadd refers to Article I, Section 2, of the Constitution, known as the three-fifths clause, which provided that three-fifths of the slave population should be counted in apportioning taxes and representation in the House of Representatives.

68.
William Fisher to Isaac D. Shadd
18 May 1857

Black intellectuals—Samuel R. Ward, Mary Ann Shadd Cary, and H. Ford Douglas among them—provided sophisticated critiques of the begging issue. Other black Canadians offered personal statements that, while not as refined, effectively delivered the message. Henry Johnson of the Elgin settlement insisted: "I wouldn't receive any of their help: I didn't want it: I felt't would do more injury than good." Thomas Johnson of Gosfield, Canada West, was more blunt: "I don't want anybody to beg for me in the United States." In a letter to the *Provincial Freeman*, Colchester farmer William Fisher presented his own antibegging protest, which emphasized that begging helped sustain the proslavery myth of black dependence. Drew, *North-Side View of Slavery*, 248, 306, 336, 381.

COLCHESTER, NEW LEBANON
May 18th, 1857

The slaveholders say that we are not created of God to be free, and if we were free we cannot get our living, but the white people in the States that call themselves our friends say we are created equal with themselves, and can get our living being free, but they deny it by their deeds. If we can get our living, what do they send their clothes here to us for? Why, to degrade us, that they may sell our names in the States and get money to make themselves rich. This shows that they are not our friends, but the friends of slaveholders. Their sending their old clothes here to prove what the slaveholders say of us to be the truth, for they witness what the slaveholders say of us. But we can get our living being free, and that without their old clothes. I have on hand now 1500 weight of as good pork as there is in Canada West for sale. This shows that the colored people can get their living here if they try. If the white people wish to be the friends of the colored people, they will be their friends by helping the slaves to Canada, and when they get here let them go to work and get their living or die. We have the same rights in law here that white men have and we can get our living without the old clothes, like they do. The agents, ministers, and the old clothes that are sent here to us by those in the States that call themselves our friends are a curse to us and to the free land of Canada.

Mr. Editor—Please give this place in your paper, and oblige your friend.

WILLIAM FISHER[1]

Provincial Freeman (Chatham, Canada West), 30 May 1857.

1. William Fisher (1814–?), a Colchester black, served as a vice-president of the Amherstburg Convention (1853). Assessment Roll, Colchester, 1860; *Minutes of Convention in Amherstburg*, 2–3 [8:0298].

69.
Editorial Correspondence by Isaac D. Shadd
12 June 1857

The antislavery lecture tour was unpredictable. Its success often depended upon luck, timing, persistence, and local support. H. Ford Douglas toured Canada West during the late spring of 1857 to recruit subscribers for the *Provincial Freeman*. He delivered well-attended, well-advertised addresses in London, Woodstock, Stratford, Paris, Brantford, Dundas, and Hamilton. In each case, Douglas allowed local abolitionists to arrange the details of meetings in advance. But once he reached Toronto, his tour faltered. Isaac Shadd, Douglas's advance agent in the city, obtained St. Lawrence Hall (Toronto's main meeting hall), placed a notice in George Brown's *Globe*, and hung posters "in all the main thoroughfares." But the *Globe* and local white abolitionists paid little attention. Douglas's first Toronto meeting attracted only sixteen people and was canceled. After a second unsuccessful attempt, Douglas began lecturing in local black churches and found that word of mouth could attract sizable audiences in the Toronto black community. Shadd's editorial correspondence recounts Douglas's successes and failures in Toronto. *PFW*, 16 May 1857 [10:0679].

EDITORIAL CORRESPONDENCE
NO. 1

Visit to Toronto—Anti-slavery Meeting in St. Lawrence Hall—Colored Regular Baptist Church, Corner Terauly and Edward Streets—Colored British Wesleyan Church, Richmond St.—Baptist Church, Corner of Victoria and Queen Streets

Our stay in this city has been a lengthy and discouraging one; shortly after our arrival here we procured the St. Lawrence Hall for the purpose of having an Anti-slavery Lecture to be delivered by Mr. Douglass: large posters were put in all the main thoroughfares to get out a good house. The *Globe*, generally characterized as the leading paper in the Province, the suckler for Reform, by being requested, found time and space for an editorial notice of *three or four lines*,[1] for which I suppose, we should feel very thankful, emanating as it did from such an influential source, and as colored men are expected to be forever thankful, and under obligations for these little condescensions or favors, I feel heartily glad there was no more of it. As the hour of meeting approached, the rain commenced falling, and continued until near meeting hour, though abating in sufficient time to have allowed persons from the various parts of the city to assemble, had there been the proper interest felt in the cause, but after the elapse of the appointed hour, on looking over the audience, and seeing but sixteen persons scattered over the seats of the splendid hall, Mr. Douglass thought best to abandon speaking. Now we were left to wonder, where the members of the Anti-slavery society were, of whom we have heard so much said at times, as being much interested in the welfare of suffering humanity, only one being present. No, we are inclined to think that the lengthy report of the Anti-slavery friends that appeared in the *Colonist* on the fourth of May was their main labor of the year,[2] rendering themselves popular by talking. After reading the lengthy report referred to and noticing some who took active part as speakers, and seemed to abhor the vile Institution so much, I thought I would call upon one Mr. Barras and solicit same information, and his name as a subscriber to our list, stating to him that the *Freeman* was actively Anti-slavery, and we were desirous of supporting it, as an organ of the kind was much wanted. He expressed his knowledge of the Paper, and its worthy cause, but was sorry to say that he could not do any thing just now, told that usual tale "*I have so many papers I have calculated to stop some*," [and] of all the friends he knew he could not refer to one who he thought would take interest enough to subscribe, but wished the Paper, great success, *which does considerable towards supporting it*. If I could see less profession and a little more practice I would look for a more happy demonstration in the end.

After such a complete failure in the St. Lawrence Hall we made application to the Trustees of the Coloured Regular Baptist Church, Corner of Terauly & Edward Sts.[3] and were granted the use of it for Sabbath evening, by Messrs. Adolphus Judah, & R. Richards,[4] but after having the Notices circulated in the different churches, one sister & church *mother in her own estimation*, backed up by some few ignorant brothers, all of whom ran as fast from Slavery on Sunday, and were as willing to receive the aid of Anti-slavery friends on Sunday as any other day, were first to object to the use of their sacred little house for the redemption of the yet oppressed bondsmen. A vote was taken upon the propriety of using the House on Sabbath for such purposes when unfortunately ignorance had two of a majority. When will ignorance cease to be the ruling influence in these Colored Churches? Mr. Judah, one of the pillars of the church and a thorough Anti-slavery man, who feels for the success of the freemen of Canada as he does for the Slaves in Chains, contended for the use of the Church for the fullest expression for the amelioration of the wrongs of the oppressed at all times, believing it to be truly Chistian to do so, and said he had left a white church for taking the pro-slavery position, and he would quit this. Since then, he and R. Richards have left the Trustee board. *Noble men!* and of course this was the second failure but our talented and indefatigable friend Dr. A. T. Augusta[5] having become so disgusted at the debased, ignorant and unchristian action of a portion of the Terauly St. Baptist church members, determined to have a meeting and applied to that noble little Spartan Band, on Richmond St. the colored British Wesleyans who recently came out from the white Wesleyans for their fellowship and union with the pro-slavery churches in the United States[6]—they were anxious and willing, to open their church and give the use of their altar, for the elevation and liberation of any portion of the human family, so on Wednesday Evening the 10th the House was opened at an early hour and soon filled with anxious hearers. On motion of A. Judah, second by I. N. Cary,[7] W. R. Abbott was appointed Chairman, and I. D. Shadd sec'y. The meeting was opened with prayer, and Mr. H. F. Douglass, addressed the audience at considerable length, showing up the Institution of slavery in its most horrid form, and descanting upon the fellowship existing between the northern and southern churches whose hands and garments are dripping with the blood of their fellow brethren and sisters in church: when these delicate portions of the subject were dwelt upon, quite an uneasiness was manifested among some of the Regular Baptist members, but after his conclusion, the whole of his remarks upon their pro-slavery fellowship was sustained by some honest members who were present, and the following Resolutions were adopted by an overwhelming majority.

> *Resolved*, That we as the subjects of Great Britain, feel it to be a christian duty to remember at all times the poor slave, whose liberty has been cloven down by an irresponsible Despotism, in the Republican Government of the United States: That we will use every effort, consistent with out duty as loyal British subjects, and the injunctions of our holy religion, to break his chains—and place him "Redeemed, and disenthralled, upon the worldwide platform, of a common humanity"—by H. F. Douglass.
>
> *Resolved*, That in the opinion of this meeting according to the teachings of the Holy Scriptures, christians of every denomination everywhere, are morally and religiously bound to plead the cause of the Slave and the oppressed, at all times, and in all places.
>
> By
> I. N. Cary

After the above resolutions were adopted the audience desiring a further statement in regard to church fellowship appointed a meeting to be held the next evening in the Queen St. Baptist Church;[8] when the appointed time arrived a large and respectable number were in attendance and addressed by Mr. Douglass, Wm. Harris[9] by appointment presiding as chairman, and I. D. Shadd as secretary. The hearers manifested great interest and satisfaction by their earnest attention and—frequent applause to say nothing of the liberal collection and some subscribers to our "paper." The only strange conduct we observed, in the audience was on the part of some half-dozen *pious looking beings*, with white neck cloths and the prefix Rev. to their names, who have been holding a conference at their church (white Wesleyan), but have not learned to pay that respect to the church that is done by almost every school boy, no these gentlemen came inside of the door placed themselves against the wall, and stared as if gasping for breath in a pit of nauseous gasses. Seats were frequently offered them by the friends but all in vain, and Mr. Douglass's assertions in respect to the Wesleyans being pro-slavery were sustained when subscribers were called for to sustain and carry on our paper devoted to Anti-slavery, by these Revs. slipping unceremoniously out into the street. Let colored Wesleyans, pray for them: they need it.

I. D. SHADD
Toronto, June 12th

Provincial Freeman (Chatham, Canada West), 20 June 1857.

1. The 3 June 1857 issue of the Toronto *Globe* printed a notice of H. Ford Douglas's antislavery lecture, which read: "Mr. Douglass, at present connected with the *Provincial Freeman*, Chatham, lectures to-night in the St. Lawrence Hall, on the subject of slavery. He is said to be a good speaker." *TG*, 3 June 1857.

2. Few issues of the Toronto *British Colonist* from this period, including that of 4 May 1857, are extant. But the article to which Shadd refers is probably the annual report of the Anti-Slavery Society of Canada, which was issued at the organization's 29 April annual meeting in Toronto. The *Colonist*, which was founded in 1838, was the organ of the Conservatives of the Church of Scotland. It appeared daily during the 1850s and frequently printed verbatim reports of legislative debates and other public meetings. The *Colonist* merged with the Toronto *Leader* in 1860. Anti-Slavery Society of Canada, *Sixth Annual Report* (Toronto, Canada West, 1857); Firth, *Early Toronto Newspapers*, 13, 16.

3. The Coloured Regular Baptist Church (or Teraulay Street Baptist Church) was located at the corner of Teraulay and Edwards streets in central Toronto. The congregation was formed when a schism developed within the city's black First Baptist Church in the early 1850s over an attempt by pastor William P. Newman and a majority of the members to limit the powers of the local church trustees. The trustees responded by closing the church to Newman and his followers, who were forced to form the Teraulay Street congregation, of which Adolphus H. Judah and Richard B. Richards were leading members. Newman and later William Mitchell pastored the new church. Mitchell went to England during 1859–61 to raise funds to construct a new church building for the congregation. The Coloured Regular Baptist Church was reunited with the First Baptist Church by 1864. Simpson, "Negroes in Ontario to 1870," 868–69.

4. Richard B. Richards was a respected member and trustee of the Coloured Regular Baptist Church of Toronto. A successful businessman, he owned the first ice business in the city in partnership with Thomas F. Cary; by 1854 he owned and operated four ice houses. *Toronto City Directory*, 1859; *PFW*, 3 November 1855 [9:0916]; Hill, *Freedom-Seekers*, 168.

5. Alexander Thomas Augusta (1825–1890) was born free in Norfolk, Virginia. He barbered in Baltimore while studying medicine before moving to Phila-

delphia to attend the University of Pennsylvania's medical school. When the university refused to admit him, he studied privately with one of the professors. Married in 1847, Augusta traveled to California to earn the funds necessary to pursue his goal of becoming a physician. He graduated from Trinity College of the University of Toronto with the bachelor of medicine degree in 1856. Augusta remained in Toronto, establishing a successful practice while supervising the city hospital and later an industrial school. He also participated in antislavery activities and founded the Provincial Association for the Education and Elevation of the Colored People of Canada, a literary society that sponsored lecture series. After 1860 Augusta spent some time in the West Indies, but by October 1862, he was back in the United States offering his services to the Union war effort. In April 1863, he accepted a major's commission as surgeon for black troops, becoming the army's first black physician and its highest ranking black officer at the time. Shortly afterwards, he was mobbed in Baltimore for wearing his uniform in public. In March 1865, his performance of his duties earned him the rank of lieutenant colonel. After the war, Augusta accepted an assignment with the Freedmen's Bureau in Georgia, where he took charge of the agency's Lincoln Hospital in Savannah. While there, he exhibited his belief in the self-help philosophy held by many white bureau officers and encouraged the freedmen to contribute to the support of their hospital. Augusta received his discharge in October 1866 and returned to private practice in Washington, D.C. Between 1868 and 1877, he served on the staff of the Freedmen's Hospital and taught at Howard University, becoming the first black to be appointed to any medical faculty in the United States. *DANB*, 19–20; *PFW*, 20 June 1857 [10:0733]; *Lib*, 7 August 1857 [10:0777]; *TG*, 3 March 1860 [12:0542]; *WAA*, 5 May 1860, 16 February, 30 November 1861 [12:0684, 13:0326, 0943]; *DM*, June 1863; Todd L. Savitt, "Politics in Medicine: The Georgia Freedmen's Bureau and the Organization of Health Care," *CWH* 28:49, 52, 58 (March 1982).

6. The Coloured Wesleyan Methodist Church of Toronto was formed when forty blacks, objecting to their treatment in local white Wesleyan churches and to the fellowship that these churches maintained with proslavery bodies in the American South, withdrew from those churches and established their own congregation. After worshiping briefly in a rented building on Richmond Street, members purchased the property in July 1838. Rev. Stephen Dutton served the congregation until 1843, when he and several other members left to found another church. An African Methodist Episcopal group then used the building until 1847–48, when the black Wesleyans again began to worship there under the direction of Rev. William Addison. In 1850 a schism divided that congregation, and a majority—over one hundred members—left and worshiped elsewhere. A small minority, led by Thomas Smallwood, continued to meet regularly in the Richmond Street church and eventually attempted to unite with a white Wesleyan congregation. In 1853 the former group, led by Wilson R. Abbott and Rev. Charles Hatfield, took possession of the building. A lawsuit between the two parties returned possession of the building to Smallwood's followers in 1855, but the two groups subsequently reconciled. The death of many members and the return of others to the United States after the Civil War led to the closing of the church in 1875. Remaining members joined local Anglican, Baptist, and British Methodist

Episcopal churches. The property was sold in 1891. Hill, *Freedom-Seekers*, 136; Anderson R. Abbott, Notes for a History of the Coloured Wesleyan Methodist Church, Abbott Family Papers, CaOTP; Winks, *Blacks in Canada*, 357.

7. Isaac N. Cary (?–1874), the second husband of Mary E. Miles Bibb, was an active Haitian emigrationist, who lived in Haiti for several years. Although he may have visited the island as early as 1821, it is certain that Cary visited Haiti in 1836, carrying a letter signed by President Andrew Jackson attesting to his good character. He resided for a time in Washington, D.C., where he operated a barbershop. In the mid-1850s, Cary settled in Toronto, Canada West, and participated in the reform activities of the city's black community. In May 1857, he became an agent for his sister-in-law Mary Ann Shadd Cary's *Provincial Freeman*—a working arrangement that apparently did not survive his marriage to Mary Bibb and his involvement with emigration. Later in the decade, Isaac Cary participated in local antislavery meetings and, in August 1858, chaired a meeting of Toronto's black voters that endorsed Reform politician George Brown. In 1859 he sat on the interracial board of directors of the Provincial Association for Education and Elevation of the Colored People of Canada, a black educational and moral improvement society. In September 1861, James Redpath's Haytian Emigration Bureau appointed Cary as a recruiting agent, first at Windsor (for the Canadas) and later, in 1862, in Washington, D.C. Cary was a selective recruiter who rejected blacks that would not strengthen the agricultural base of the immigrant community. In September 1862, with the movement a failure, he resigned from the bureau. During the latter years of the Civil War, he approached federal officials with an offer to assist in settling Washington's freed slaves in Central America, but apparently nothing came of it. In the early 1870s, Cary worked as a clerk and a tanner in Brooklyn, New York. *PFW*, 13 October 1855, 30 May, 20 June 1857 [10:0733]; *TG*, 17 August 1858; *PP*, 19 October, 9 November, 30 November, 14 December 1861, 20 March, 1 May, 14 August, 21 August, 4 September 1862 [13:0835, 0884, 0939, 0974]; Isaac N. Cary to [James Redpath], 3 September [1861], Redpath Letterbooks, Manuscripts Division, DLC [13:0735]; *Lib*, 28 February 1862 [14:0156]; Isaac N. Cary to A. J. H. White, 24 April 1863, RG48, M160, Records of the Secretary of the Interior Relating to the Suppression of the African Slave Trade and Negro Colonization, DNA [14:0818]; Winks, *Blacks in Canada*, 366–67; *New York City Directory*, 1872–74.

8. The First Baptist Church (or Queen Street Baptist Church) was located at the corner of Queen and Victoria streets in south central Toronto. The congregation originated in 1826, when a dozen fugitive slaves began meeting for prayer along the shore of Lake Ontario. Rev. Washington Christian soon organized the black worshipers into a congregation. Many white members joined at first, but they withdrew in 1829 to form the Jarvis Street Baptist Church. Under Christian's direction, the black members worshiped in rented halls until 1841, when the frame Queen Street church was erected. Christian visited Jamaica during 1843–45 and raised sufficient funds among the Baptists there to pay off the cost of construction. The church became the focal point of black antislavery activity in the city; it sheltered numerous fugitives, and dispersed missionaries inland to found other black Baptist churches in the province. During the 1850s, it was a "corresponding church" of the Canadian Anti-Slavery Baptist Association. William P. Newman followed Christian as pastor, and during his tenure, the congregation divided over

the issue of how much control should be retained by the church's trustees. Newman and the majority of the members were forced to leave and formed the Coloured Regular Baptist Church. The two groups were reunited by 1864. The congregation abandoned the Queen Street site in 1905 but has continued to exist to the present day. It remains Toronto's oldest black institution. Hill, *Freedom-Seekers*, 138–39; Lewis, "Pioneer Coloured Baptist Life," 265; Lewis, "Religious Nature of Negro Migration," 128.

9. William H. Harris.

70.
Resolutions by a Committee of Toronto Blacks
Presented by Alexander T. Augusta, Toronto, Canada West
June 1857

By the mid-1850s, blacks in Canada West had acquired sufficient political confidence to break from their traditional Conservative voting habits. They began to challenge racist Conservative candidates, as in the case of John Prince. Blacks in Kent and Essex counties had supported Prince's political career from the 1830s. Both the *Voice of the Fugitive* and the *Provincial Freeman* gave the Conservative politician strong endorsements. But relations between Prince and Essex County blacks deteriorated in the spring of 1857 when he called for the reinstatement of magistrates involved in a fugitive slave extradition case. Then, on 9 June, Prince attacked blacks in an address before the Legislative Council. In late June and early July, blacks in Toronto, Windsor, Sandwich, and Chatham held meetings to protest Prince's racist demagoguery and to petition for his resignation. The petition, with four hundred signatures, went to various government officials. Toronto blacks adopted a set of resolutions condemning Prince that were presented by Alexander T. Augusta at a meeting held for the purpose in late June. Although Prince endured this crisis of confidence in the black community, the loss of black support eventually cost him his parliamentary seat in 1861, when he was defeated by Archibald McKellar, a Reform party candidate and an executive of the Elgin Association. Winks, *Blacks in Canada*, 214–15; *VF*, 17 December 1851, 12 February 1852 [7:0233, 0415]; *PFW*, 8, 22 December 1855, 25 November 1856, 28 March, 4 April, 18, 25 July 1857 [9:0989, 10:0389, 0634]; *Lib*, 7 August 1857 [10:0797]; Thomas F. Cary to Mary Ann Shadd Cary, 11 June 1857, Mary Ann Shadd Cary Papers, CaOTAr [10:0722].

PREAMBLE

Whereas, it has pleased Colonel Prince, a member of the Legislative Council of this province,[1] in moving an address to the Governor-General (to restore to the commission of the peace, Messrs. Wilkinson and Woodbridge, who were dismissed from the same for conniving at the rendition of Archy Lanton,[2] a colored man, to the authorities of the United States) to use the following language relative to the colored citizens of the province:

That "they are extremely demoralized, repaying with ingratitude, with pilfering, theft, and other vices and crimes, the kindness they have received at our hands." In his opinion, they should be kept separate, and not allowed to taint the atmosphere and corrupt white society, and he advised that a colony of them should be founded in the Manitoulin Islands,[3] or some other place. Language which, for vituperation and prejudice against the colored man, can only be equalled by the most ignorant of mankind.

And whereas, the said Colonel Prince is the last man in this province, to speak so disparagingly of the colored people, inasmuch as, during the rebellion of 1837, when he was in command of the troops in the western part of this province, he walked arm in arm with colored men, and when his life was in danger for having as he very justly did executed without judge or jury the rebels or border-ruffians whom he fell in with or captured, it was colored men who guarded his person and household; not one of whom was ever a rebel, or traitor.

And whereas, this said Colonel Prince owes his election to the distinguished position which he now holds, to the votes of colored men; and much of his earthly gains, have been accumulated from a lucrative practice of the law, among his colored clients.

And, whereas, it has pleased Almighty God to enlighten the understanding of British statesmen to give that boon to the colored man, which few other countries have given—to be free as soon as his foot touches British soil, and ultimately enjoy all the rights and privileges of a citizen. Therefore, it ill becomes a petty counsellor, at this period of enlightenment to advise the government to colonize its citizens on a barren island of sand in Lake Huron. They who have fought, bled and died to keep this beautiful country from the grasp of the iniquitous slaveholding and despotic republic adjoining us, to starve them out, which is only in keeping with the black-hearted scheme of the American Colonization Society, which receives its impulse from the blood-stained gold of the South. And for aught we know, "Southern gold" is doing its work of corruption and bribery with the men of this province in high places, to carry out this new scheme of colonization, degradation and kidnapping, to deter colored men from emigrating to this province. Therefore,

1st. Resolved, That the charges made by Colonel Prince, the self-styled "model old English gentleman," against the character of the blacks (as reported in the *Daily Colonist* of the 10th inst.)[4] are treacherous and false in the extreme, and that the disgusting and despotic language used in making those charges, whether induced by bribes of Southern gold, or a base excited spirit did so "taint the atmosphere" of the Legislative Council, as to cause several ladies to withdraw from the Council Chamber.

2nd. Resolved, That we, the colored citizens of the city of Toronto, do cast back into the teeth of Col. Prince, the foul imputations contained in his speech, as a base slander of our character as citizens, calculated to foster prejudices against us and to degrade us.

3d. Resolved, That we will resist by every means in our power, any invasion of our rights as citizens; and will hold up to public scorn and contempt all such panderers to American prejudice against color.

4th. Resolved, That we recommend to the constituents of Colonel

Prince, that they request him to resign his seat in the Legislative Council immediately, as being morally unfit to represent them, and as exhibiting a pusillanimity toward the colored people, without a parallel in the legislative proceedings of this province, not excepting the resolutions of the notorious Larwill.[5]

5th. Resolved, That it is the opinion of this meeting that the colored people throughout the province should unite in the expression of a most decided detestation of both Prince and Larwill, who have shown themselves as mere despotic demagogues, and among the bitterest enemies of the colored man, and should set the seal of condemnation upon all disposed so to act.

6th. Resolved, That we return our heartfelt thanks to his Excellency the Governor-General, and his constitutional advisers, for the promptness with which they acted in defending our rights by dismissing Messrs. Wilkinson and Woodbridge, which will, no doubt, deter others from doing likewise. And they will ever hold a prominent place in our memory.

7th. Resolved, That we will ever hold dear the flag which gives us protection of life, liberty and property; and we pledge ourselves to Her Most Gracious Majesty Queen Victoria, to be ready at a moment's warning to defend the country of our adoption, at all hazards.

8th. Resolved, That we tender our sincere thanks to Mr. Garrat, for the prompt action he took in laying before His Excellency the Governor, the case of the man Lanton.

9th. Resolved, That a copy of this preamble and resolutions be forwarded to Her Majesty Queen Victoria, His Excellency the Governor-General, and the members of the Executive Council of this province.

Liberator (Boston, Mass.), 31 July 1857.

1. John Prince (1796–1870) was born in England but abandoned a successful legal practice and a promising political career to immigrate to Upper Canada in 1833. He settled in Sandwich and established himself in law and politics. During the Rebellion of 1837, Prince served with the Canadian militia along the Detroit frontier, rising to the rank of colonel. He represented Essex County in the Canadian parliament as an Independent (1836–54), sat on the legislative council (1857–60) for western Canada West, and later advocated Canadian independence and republicanism. *DCB*, 9:643–47.

2. Archy Lanton, a fugitive slave, stole two horses in Michigan during his escape to Sandwich, Canada West. In early 1856, two slave catchers arrived in Sandwich to obtain a warrant for Lanton's arrest and extradition to the United States. Magistrate Adolphus Woodbridge and Magistrate Wilkinson granted the warrant and entrusted it to Samuel Port, a local constable. Port arrested Lanton but left him in the custody of the two slave catchers while he went to inform the magistrates of the arrest. During Port's absence, the slave catchers returned Lanton to American soil. When Canadian blacks protested this obvious violation of extradition procedure, Sir George-Etienne Cartier, the attorney general for the Canadas,

removed the two magistrates from office. This action infuriated some white Canadians, who petitioned the governor-general to reinstate the magistrates. They were not reinstated. Murray, "Canada and Anglo-American Anti-Slavery Movement," 532–34; Hill, *Freedom-Seekers*, 95; *WH*, 2 May 1856.

3. Manitoulin Island, the world's largest freshwater island, is located in the northeastern part of Lake Huron near Georgian Bay and is part of Ontario, Canada.

4. On 9 June 1857, John Prince addressed the Legislative Council, requesting that Magistrates Woodbridge and Wilkinson—one a personal friend of Prince—be reinstated. In the course of his speech, Prince claimed that blacks were immoral, that their presence corrupted white society, and that black Canadians should be sent to "some sort of Liberia or Botany Bay to live in a colony by themselves." He suggested the Manitoulin Islands in Lake Huron. The Toronto *British Colonist* printed the text of Prince's remarks. Toronto blacks responded to Prince's remarks at a protest meeting, the proceedings of which were published in the 25 June *Colonist*. A series of angry letters between Prince and Alexander T. Augusta, the leader of the black protest, followed in the *Colonist*. *Lib*, 31 July, 7 August 1857; Winks, *Blacks in Canada*, 214.

5. Edwin Larwill.

71.
Elizabeth J. Williams to Mary Ann Shadd Cary
18 January 1858

After passage of the Fugitive Slave Law of 1850, blacks in Canada West organized to aid escaping slaves and to assist them after they arrived in the province. A few black abolitionists, such as John Mason and Harriet Tubman, went South to lead slaves out of bondage. Others created networks with American abolitionists that kept a steady flow of information, goods, and fugitives moving between the two countries. During the mid-1850s, John Henry Hill, a fugitive from Virginia slavery, corresponded with William Still of the Vigilance Committee of Philadelphia, who sent fugitives on to Toronto and placed them in Hill's care. Hill saw to it that they were settled in the local black community. Mary Ann Shadd Cary arranged through letters to Elizabeth J. Williams, her free black aunt in Wilmington, Delaware, to have fugitives forwarded northward to Chatham. Cary then eased their transition to freedom. Williams's 18 January 1858 letter to Cary was part of this exchange. Cary, Hill, and others like them—whose work made up the substance of the underground railroad—contributed to the influx of forty thousand refugees that reached Canada in the decades preceding the Civil War. Still, *The Underground Railroad*, 189–200; Elizabeth J. Williams to Mary Ann Shadd Cary, 2 November 1858, Mary Ann Shadd Cary Papers, CaOTAr [11:0395].

Wilmington, [Delaware]
Jan[uary] 18, 1858

Mary A. S. Cary
My Dear

Mary Ann[—]Some time a go I wrote to you concerning Mrs. [V]easy and r[equ]ested an answer but none has ever come. [I]f you remember I told you that she was a fugitive that her owners live in Baltimore and that there is a Coulred man living in fall river that knows her owners and She lives in continuel dread of him. She wants to come to Canada in the Spring. She is a good seamster and [what i] want to know is weather you [think] She can make a living by her neadle there and weather you would be willing to let her come to your house for a Short time and weather you would be willing to ade her in litting work when She first Comes out there. You will find her a real [n]ice woman and I know you will like her and all She wants is to have some one to go too when she firs arives [as is] a stranger their She does not want [to] come to live on you for She [words illegible] industress working woman and a very pleasant [agreeable lady?] [rest of letter—7 lines—virtually illegible]

E. J. Williams[1]

Mary Ann Shadd Cary Papers, Archives of Ontario, Toronto, Ontario. Published by permission.

1. Elizabeth Jackson Schad Williams (1797–?), a Wilmington, Delaware, free black, was the aunt of black abolitionist Mary Ann Shadd Cary. She taught at a local black school during the 1840s. After the death of her husband, Abraham J. Williams, in 1855, she assisted the underground railroad by aiding the escape of several fugitive slaves from Wilmington to Chatham, Canada West. Sometime after 1858, she moved to Chatham. Shadd Family Records, Shadd Family Papers, CaOLU; *PFW*, 3 November 1855; *Wilmington City Directory*, 1857; Elizabeth J. Williams to Mary Ann Shadd Cary, 18 January, 2 November 1858, Mary Ann Shadd Cary Papers, CaOTAr [11:0125, 0395].

72.
Sermon by Mary Ann Shadd Cary
[6 April 1858]

Antislavery women saw slavery as a metaphor for their own plight. "The investigation of the rights of the slave," wrote abolitionist Angelina Grimké, "has led me to a better understanding of my own." Prominent black antislavery women, including black abolitionists Sojourner Truth and Mary Ann Shadd Cary, moved freely between antislavery and feminism. Truth joined the nascent women's rights movement in 1850 and lectured for that cause for several decades. Beginning in the mid-1850s, Cary viewed her antislavery actions in feminist terms. She believed emancipation of the slave and equal treatment of women to be of identical importance. Generally acknowledged as the first black woman newspaper editor on the North American continent, she believed that her work for the *Provincial Freeman* had "broken the 'Editorial Ice'" for black women, and she urged others to "go to editing" or to take on other significant roles in the antislavery movement. Cary's growing antislavery feminism was typified by a Sunday evening sermon that she apparently delivered before a Chatham audience on 6 April 1858. Cary's feminism matured during the late 1850s and early 1860s, and after the Civil War, she frequently lectured for the women's suffrage movement. Walters, *American Reformers*, 101–6; *PFW*, 30 June 1855 [9:0724]; *DANB*, 553, 606.

Sunday Evening
Apr[il] 6, [1858]

1st business of life[,] to love the Lord our God with heart and soul, and our neighbor as our self.

We must then manifest love to God by obedience to his will—we must be cheerful workers in his cause at all times—on the Sabbath and other days. The more readieness we Evince the more we manifest our love, and as our field is directly among those of his creatures made in his own image in acting as themself who is no respecter of persons we must have failed in our duty until we become decided to waive all prejudices of Education birth nation or training and make the test of our obedience God's Equal command to love the neighbor as ourselves.

These two great commandments, and upon which rest all the Law and the prophets,[1] cannot be narrowed down to suit us but we must go up and conform to them. They proscribe neither nation nor sex—our neighbor may be Either the oriental heathen the degraded Europe and or the Eslaved colored American. Neither must we prefer sex the Slave mother as well as the Slave-father. The oppress, or nominally free woman of every nation or clime in whose Soul is as Evident by the image of God as in her more fortunate cotemporary of the male sex has a claim upon us by virtue of that irrevocable command Equally as urgent. We cannot successfully Evade duty because the Suffering fellow woman ~~be~~ is only a woman! She too is a neighbor. The good Samaritan of this generation must not take for their Exemplars the priest and the Levite when a fellow wom[an] is among thieves—neither will they find their Excuse in the custom as barbarous and anti-christian as any promulgated by pious Brahmin that [word crossed out] they may be only females.[2] The spirit of true philanthropy knows no sex. The true christian will not seek to Exhume from the grave of the past [word crossed out] its half developed customs and ~~offer~~ insist upon them as a substitute for the plain teachings of Jesus Christ, and the Evident deductions of a more Enlightened humanity.

There is too a fitness of time for any work for the benefit of God's human creatures. We are told to keep Holy the Sabbath day. In what manner? Not by following simply the injunctions of those who bind heavy burdens, to say nothing about the same but as a man is better than a sheep but combining with God's worship the most active vigilance for the resurector from degradation violence and sin his creatures. In thise cases particularly was the Sabbath made for man and woman if you please as there may be those who will not ~~exe~~ accept the term man in a generic sense. Christ has told us as it is lawful to lift a sheep out of the ditch on the Sabbath day, i[f] a man is much better than a sheep.

Those with whom I am identified, namely the colored people of this country—and the women of the land are in the pit figurat[ively] ~~speaking~~ are cast out. These were Gods requirements during the Prophecy of Isaiah[3] and they are in full force today. God is the same yesterday to day and forever. And upon this nation and to this people they come with all their significance within your grasp are three or four millions in chains in your southern territory and among and around about you are half a million allied to them by blood and to you by blood as were the Hebrew servants who realize the intensity of your hatred and oppression.[4] You are the government what it does to [th] you Enslaves the poor whites The free colored people The Example of slave holders to access all.

What we aim to do is to put away this Evil from among you and thereby pay a debt you now owe to humanity and to God and so turn from their chanel the bitter waters of a moral servitude that is about overwhelming yourselves.

I speak plainly because of a common origin and because were it not for the monster slavery we would have a common destiny here—in the land of our birth. And because the policy of the American government so singularly set aside alows to all free speech and free thought: As the law of God must be to us the higher law in spite of powers principalities selfish priests or selfish people to whom the minister it is important the we assert boldly that no where does God look upon this the chief crimes with the least degree of allowance nor are we justified in asserting that he will tolerate those who in any wise support or sustain it.

Slavery American slavery will not bear moral tests. It is ~~in~~ Exists by striking down all the moral safeguards to society by—it is not then a moral institution. Your are called upon as a man to deny and disobey the most noble impulses of manhood to aid a brother in distress—to refuse to strike from the limbs of those not bound for any crime the fetters by which his Escape is obstructed. The milk of human kindness must be transformed into the bitter waters of hatred—you must return to his master he that hath Escaped, no matter how Every principle of manly independence revolts at the same. This feeling Extends to Every one allied by blood to the slave. And while we have in the North those who stand as guards to the institution the must also volunteer as [s]hippers away of the nominally free. You must drive fr[om] his home by a hartless [os]tracism to the heathen shores when they fasted, bowed themselves, and spread sack cloth and ashes under them. Made long prayers [&c.] that they might be seen of men, but Isaiah told them God would not accept them. They must repent of their sins—put away iniquity from among them and then should their light shine forth.

But we are or may be told that slavery is only an Evil not a sin, and that too by those who say it was allowed among the Jews and therfore ought to be Endured. Isaiah sets that matter to rest he shows that it is a sin handling it less delicately than many prophets in this generation. These are the sins that we are to spare not the sin of Enslaving men—of keeping back the hire of the laborer. You are to loose the bands of wickedness, to undo the heavy burdens to break Every yoke and to let the oppressed go free.[5] To deal out bread to the hungry and to bring the poo[r] [word missing] speaking. Their cry has long been ascending to the Lord who then will assume the responsibility of prescribing times and seasons ~~and~~ [word crossed out] ~~for~~ for the pleading of their cause—of and righteous cause—and who shall overrule the voice of woman? Emphatically the greatest sufferer from chattel slavery or political proscription on this God's footstool? Nay we have Christs Example who heald the sexes indiscriminately thereby implying an Equal inheritance—who rebuf[f]ed the worldling Martha and approved innovator Mary.[6] [The Him] who respected not persons [two words crossed out] but who imposes Christian duties alike upon all sexes, and who in his wise providence metes out his retribution alike upon all.

No friends we suffer the oppressors of the age to lead us astray; instead of going to the source of truth for guidance we let the adversary guide us as to what is our duty and Gods word. The Jews thought to that they were doing [H]is requirements when they did only that which was but a small sacrifice.

Mary Ann Shadd Cary Papers, Archives of Ontario, Toronto, Ontario. Published by permission.

1. Cary's opening remarks are an exegetical treatment of Matthew 22 : 37–40, in which Jesus Christ informs Jewish leaders of his basic theology—that individuals should love God with their entire heart, soul, and mind, and should love others as much as themselves. Christ claimed that the Jewish scriptures (known as "the Law and the Prophets") were based on these two principles.

2. Cary alludes to the New Testament parable of the Good Samaritan to suggest that men should stop treating women as less than equals, a social custom she compares to the elitism of the Brahmin arbiters of New England culture. According to the parable, a Jew traveling from Jerusalem to Jericho was robbed, beaten, and left to die along the road. A Jewish priest and a Levite passed by him without offering assistance. Finally, a Samaritan, a foreigner not expected to show sympathy to a Jew, attended to his wounds, took him to an inn, and provided for his care until he recovered. Luke 10 : 29–37.

3. The Jewish prophet Isaiah proclaimed his message to Judah and Jerusalem between 742 and 687 B.C.

4. Cary compares the relationship between white Americans and black Americans (slave and free) with the relationship between "the Hebrew servants and their Egyptian masters."

5. Slavery existed in ancient Jewish culture and is occasionally mentioned in the Old Testament. The duties of masters to slaves are outlined in Exodus 21 : 1–11 and Deuteronomy 15 : 12–18. Slavery is mentioned several times in the book of Isaiah, but although Cary indicates that the book condemns slavery, Isaiah's position on slavery is not completely clear. The freeing of captives and the enslaving of captors is a major theme in the book. Cary generates antislavery meaning from the reference in Isaiah 58 : 6 that God sought

> to loose the bonds of wickedness,
> to undo the thongs of the yoke,
> to let the oppressed go free,
> and to break every yoke.

Job 31 : 13–15; Isaiah 14 : 1–2, 24 : 2, 45 : 13, 49 : 24–26, 61 : 1.

6. Cary alludes to the New Testament story of the sisters Martha and Mary. According to Luke 10 : 38–42, Jesus Christ approved Mary's preference for listening attentively to his teachings, while rebuking Martha for her excessive hospitality. Cary suggests that this demonstrates that Christ viewed women and men as intellectual equals.

73.
Circular by Mary Ann Shadd Cary
[October 1858]

Vigilance committees were a defensive apparatus that blacks created in the wake of the Fugitive Slave Law. Dedicated to aiding fugitives during their escape, then protecting them from slave catchers—with violence if need be—these loosely formed groups of blacks and antislavery whites were common in the northern states and in Canada West, particularly in communities with a sizable black population. The Chatham committee was among the most aggressive and saved several blacks from being returned to slavery during the 1850s. One of its most dramatic rescues occurred in September 1858, when 100 to 150 Chatham residents removed Sylvanus Demarest, a young free black, from a train. Demarest and W. R. Merwin, who claimed to be Demarest's owner, were spotted in London, Canada West, by the former mayor of the town. Word went down the line to the Chatham Vigilance Committee, and several armed members crowded into the train when it stopped to take on water. They rescued Demarest, but railroad officials brought charges against the committee, and five blacks and two whites were arrested. Demarest remained in the custody of Isaac D. Shadd, one of those arrested. Mary Ann Shadd Cary's circular pleaded for funds to aid in their defense, the cost of which nearly ruined the *Provincial Freeman*. The case was dismissed by the court when it was learned that Merwin had never owned Demarest and apparently was kidnapping him to sell him into slavery. Merwin returned to New York while Demarest briefly remained in Chatham with the Shadd family. The seven defendants were freed. Hill, *Freedom-Seekers*, 39–43; *PFW*, 24 March 1855; *GSB*, 28 October 1858 [11:0393]; *NYT*, 4 October 1858; *NASS*, 30 October 1858; Simpson, "Negroes in Ontario to 1870," 664–65.

As an agent appointed by our Vigilance Committee, established here to conduct the case growing out of the release of the slave boy spoken of by the *New York Tribune*,[1] and as Assistant Secretary of the same, I am authorized, and beg to enlist your pecuniary aid towards defending the suit brought against I. D. Shadd (editor of the *Provincial Freeman*), J. Sparks,[2] Edward Doston,[3] Shelby Smith,[4] Wm. Streets,[5] John Goodyear and John Hooper. One hundred and fifty others are also liable to arrest under a similar charge of riot and (indirectly) abduction. The parties, with the exception of Messrs. Goodyear and Hooper, are colored men and poor men. The editor of the *Freeman* (organ of the fugitives) holding the boy in his care, in spite of pro-slavery officials, is the most responsible party to the Court, yet he, the conductor of a struggling paper, must suspend it to meet the exigencies of the case. There is no other resort than to make a direct appeal to the friends of Freedom through those who stand on the watch tower of Freedom, in order that a part at least, of the heavy expense may be met by the 18th of the present month, at which time the trial will come on at the Assizes.[6] Please assure us of your sympathy by a word of encouragement, and whatever your generosity will prompt you to give or send.

Direct to I. D. Shadd, *Provincial Freeman* Office, Chatham, C.W.

Officers and Members of the Vigilance Committee: Wm. H. Day,[7] Chairman; I. D. Shadd, Vice-Chairman; J. M. Bell,[8] Secretary; M. A. S. Cary, Assistant Secretary; H. C. Jackson,[9] Treasurer; L. S. Day,[10] T. F. Cary,[11] M. R. Delany,[12] J. H. Harris,[13] G. W. Brodie, J. Pleasant, M. E. Pleasant,[14] Mrs. I. D. Shadd,[15] O. Anderson. Collecting Agents: I. D. Shadd, Wm. H. Day, Mary A. S. Cary, J. H. Harris, G. W. Brodie, Lucy S. Day.

Gerrit Smith Banner (New York, N.Y.), 28 October 1858.

1. The 26 September 1858 rescue of Sylvanus Demarest, a black youth, from white businessman W. R. Merwin at the Chatham railway station was discussed in two brief articles in the 4 October issue of the *New York Tribune*. The *Tribune*, the most influential newspaper in mid-nineteenth century America, was founded in 1841 by Horace Greeley. Under Greeley's guidance, it supported political anti-slavery and encouraged resistance to the Fugitive Slave Law of 1850. Greeley's support of westward expansion, as embodied in his famous exhortation, "Go West, young man," and the publication of numerous articles on agriculture attracted a wide readership in the Midwest, in addition to the concentrated readership in the Northeast. The paper continued to be published until 1924, when it merged with the *New York Herald*. *NYT*, 4 October 1858; Jeter Allen Isley, *Horace Greeley and the Republican Party* (New York, N.Y., 1965), 56–59; Frank Luther Mott, *American Journalism: A History, 1690–1960* (New York, N.Y., 1962), 267–78.

2. John Sparks (1817–?), an American-born mulatto, was a member of the Church of England who worked as a watchmaker in Chatham. Census of Canada, 1861.

3. Edward Doston (1828–?), an American-born mulatto, was a barber in Chatham. He belonged to the Wesleyan Methodist faith. Census of Canada, 1861.

4. Shelvey Smith (1811–?), a black laborer, was born in the United States but settled in Chatham in the late 1840s. He was a member of the Wesleyan Methodist church. Census of Canada, 1851.

5. William Street (1822–?) was trained and worked as a slave blacksmith in Tennessee. He escaped from slavery in 1850 and, after a year of eluding slave catchers in Tennessee, fled to Canada West. Street settled in Chatham and established a successful blacksmithing business. Drew, *North-Side View of Slavery*, 285–90; Census of Canada, 1861.

6. Assizes refer to periodic judicial sessions of the superior courts throughout much of the British Empire, including Canada West.

7. William H. Day (1825–1900) was born free in New York City, the son of Eliza and John Day, who were moderately prosperous and devoted members of the African Methodist Episcopal Zion church. Day's education in the city's public schools was supplemented by private lessons. He graduated from Rev. Rudolphus Hubbard's high school in Northampton, Massachusetts, and entered Oberlin College in 1843, the only black in a class of fifty. Already a veteran of local antislavery efforts when he received his degree four years later, Day continued his reform work, particularly in Ohio, at numerous black citizens' conventions. Day was a highly regarded speaker who displayed a rich knowledge of black history. A political abolitionist, he led the struggle to overturn Ohio's black laws, appeared before the state legislature on behalf of black suffrage, and represented blacks at the state's constitutional convention. During the early 1850s, he helped organize local and state black gatherings and called for national conventions to address black issues.

Day was an editor for the Cleveland *True Democrat*, but in April 1853, he founded his own newspaper, the *Aliened American*, a Cleveland weekly meant to serve the Ohio black community. In August 1854, Day split with the mainstream of black politics and with the leaders of the Rochester Colored National Convention (held a year earlier) by attending the National Emigration Convention convened in Cleveland by Martin R. Delany. Day was at first hostile to general emigration but decided that he "would not discourage individuals who are disposed to emigrate to Africa or the West Indies." The demise of the *Aliened American* and its successor (the *People's Record*), the continued assaults of northern racial prejudice, his own poor health, and his newfound tolerance for emigration prompted his settlement early in 1856 in Dresden, Canada West, a small town forty-five miles northeast of Detroit. Day farmed for a living, wrote occasionally for the *Provincial Freeman*, and challenged the discriminatory practices experienced by blacks on Great Lakes boats. He attended the National Emigration Convention of 1856 in Cleveland. While serving as president of the General Board of Commissioners for the 1858 National Emigration Convention in Chatham, Day retreated from his emigrationist position and led the commissioners to a tepid endorsement of Delany's Niger Valley Exploring Party.

In the summer of 1859, Day accompanied William King, founder of the successful Elgin community, on a fund-raising trip to England. He returned from England in the spring of 1862 and settled in New York City. In the mid-1860s, he edited the *Zion Standard and Weekly Review*, served as general secretary to the Freedmen's American and British Commission (1866), and was superintendent of schools for the Freedmen's Bureau in Maryland and Delaware (1867–68). Day continued his religious and educational activities into the 1880s, serving as general secretary of the AMEZ General Conference (1876–96), and as a district school director in Harrisburg, Pennsylvania (1878, 1881, 1886). Day received a doctor of divinity degree in 1887 from Livingston College in North Carolina. Oberlin College Alumni Records Office to [?], n.d., OClWHi; *Commemorative Biographical Encyclopedia of Dauphin County* (Chambersburg, Pa., 1896); *HT*, 3 December 1900; *HP*, 6 December 1900; *ASB*, 24 July 1846, 26 January 1849, 19 January, 29 June, 17, 24, 31 August, 14, 30 September 1850, 22 February, 3 April, 20 November 1851, 31 January, 25 December 1852, 14, 28 January, 4, 11 February 1854, 13 January, 27 October 1855, 25 October 1856; *FDP*, 1, 15

October 1852, 28 April, 5, 12, 19, 26 May, 6, 28 July 1854 [7:0756]; *DM*, February 1861; *VF*, 7 October 1852 [7:0776]; *AA*, 9 April 1853 [8:0208]; *PF*, 5, 19 June 1856 [10:0010, 0027]; *NASS*, 14 May 1864; *WAA*, 26 August, 4 November 1865; William H. Day to Gerrit Smith, 27 March 1856, Gerrit Smith Papers, NSyU [10:0093]; Miller, *Search for Black Nationality*, 180–225; *CP*, 26 August 1858 [11:0334]; *CTWP*, 3 September 1858 [11:0342].

8. James Madison Bell (1826–1902) was a free black born in Gallipolis, Ohio. From 1842 to 1854, he resided in Cincinnati, where he became a plasterer and a brickmason. At some point during his early years, he attended a private school connected with Oberlin College. In 1854 he left Ohio for Chatham, Canada West, and remained there until 1860. While at Chatham, he became involved in black community affairs and participated in antislavery meetings at which he contributed to the reform spirit by reading his original poetry. He also published some of his work in the *Provincial Freeman*. In 1858 Bell was secretary of the Chatham Vigilance Committee. That same year, he became acquainted with John Brown, and as late as September 1859, he corresponded with Brown's followers concerning the Harpers Ferry raid. In 1860 Bell moved to San Francisco, California, where he plied his trades and published poetry in the local press on topics as varied as the arming of former slaves and the death of Abraham Lincoln. He again became involved in community affairs, reading his poems on public occasions, assisting in the organization of local events, serving as president of a music association, and petitioning for better educational facilities for black public school students. As an advocate of black rights, he protested against stereotypical minstrel shows and color restrictions in San Francisco and served on the black executive committee, an organization dedicated to winning the franchise for California blacks. By early 1866, Bell had returned to Canada West, but shortly thereafter he made his home in Toledo, Ohio. In 1872 he was elected to the Ohio and national Republican conventions. Around 1901 a volume of his poetry was published in Lansing, Michigan. *DANB*, 38; *PFW*, 16 June 1855, 8 March, 19 April 1856, 24 January 1857 [9:0699, 10:0075, 0112, 0516]; *CP*, 26 August 1858 [11:0334]; *GSB*, 28 October 1858 [11:0393]; *Lib*, 24 December 1858; *PA*, 12 April, 24 May, 28 June, 5 July, 2 August, 27 September, 27 December 1862, 10 January, 16 May, 22 August, 3 October 1863 [14:0242, 0321, 0323, 0373, 0381, 0422, 0514, 0624, 0690, 1018, 1077]; *ESF*, 7, 21 April 1865 [15:0803, 0835, 0836]; Benjamin Quarles, *Allies for Freedom: Blacks and John Brown* (New York, N.Y., 1974), 43–45, 74–75, 131.

9. Harvey C. Jackson resided in Simcoe, Canada West, and drove a stage between Ingersoll and Port Burwell through the early 1850s. By 1855 he had moved to Chatham. As a member of the Provincial Union Association, he supported black self-help and opposed begging. Jackson organized and served as secretary of the Dawn Investigating Committee meeting at Chatham in August 1855. Apparently well-educated, he advocated education and professional training for blacks, worked with William Howard Day and Harriet Tubman to aid fugitive slaves arriving in the province, and probably collaborated with John Brown during 1858, when the abolitionist was in Chatham to organize the Harpers Ferry raid. Shortly after Brown's death, Jackson penned a "Response of the Colored People of Canada," in which he defended Brown's objectives and appealed for funds for the families of the "Harpers Ferry Martyrs." *PFW*, 6 May, 19 August 1854, 20 June,

22, 29 August 1855 [8:0776, 9:0723, 0788, 0807]; Benjamin Quarles, ed., *Blacks on John Brown* (Urbana, Ill., 1972), 32–33; Simpson, "Negroes in Ontario to 1870," 526, 796.

10. Lucie Stanton Day (ca. 1834–1910) was born in Cleveland, Ohio. She graduated from the Ladies' Course at Oberlin College in 1850, making her the first black woman college graduate in the United States. In 1852 she married black abolitionist-journalist William Howard Day, with whom she had a daughter, Florence (born ca. 1857). During the early 1850s, Lucie Day taught in the public schools of Columbus, Ohio. Later in the decade, she accompanied her husband to Canada West. When he visited Britain on an extended fund-raising tour in 1859, she returned to Cleveland and supported herself and her daughter by dressmaking. Distance strained the marriage, and the Days soon divorced. When she sought a teaching position at a freedmen's school in 1864, the stigma of divorce evidently led the American Missionary Association to reject her application. In 1871 she went south and obtained a public school teaching position in Mississippi; she continued to teach there and in other southern states until 1903. She also remarried, this time to Levi N. Sessions of Mississippi. An active black clubwoman and temperance worker, she died in Los Angeles in 1910. Dorothy Sterling, ed., *We are Your Sisters: Black Women in the Nineteenth Century* (New York, N.Y., 1984), 266–67; *DANB*, 163.

11. Thomas F. Cary (?–1860), a Toronto barber, became active in the antislavery movement and other black causes during the 1850s. Cary and Samuel Ringgold Ward became close friends after Ward arrived in Toronto during the winter of 1851, a friendship that encouraged Cary's growing antislavery activity. In 1853 Cary called for a black provincial convention at London, which became the Amherstburg Convention. The following year, he helped found the Provincial Union Association, a black self-help organization, and was elected one of its vice-presidents. When Ward declined the presidency of the association, Cary and Wilson R. Abbott directed its activities. During the mid-1850s, Cary became a partner of black Toronto businessman R. B. Richards in the ice business. He also raised funds for the *Provincial Freeman*. Cary and the *Freeman*'s editor, Mary Ann Shadd, married in January 1856. He brought three children from an earlier marriage to the union: Ann (b. 1842), Thomas, Jr. (b. 1845), and John (b. 1849); and he and Mary Ann had two others, Sarah Elizabeth (b. 1857) and Linton (b. 1861). The Carys were separated for long periods during their marriage; Thomas maintained his barber shop in Toronto, and Mary Ann and the children lived in Chatham. During the latter part of the 1850s, Thomas Cary worked with fugitive aid efforts and participated in numerous antislavery meetings in Toronto. In 1857 Cary and James C. Brown were chosen to act as legal representatives in the fugitives' attempt to regain legal title and control of the British-American Institute at Dawn and to demonstrate that institute agents did not act on behalf of the fugitives there. As economic conditions worsened in the province during the late 1850s, Cary broadened his business interests; he began selling lamps and lamp fuel. He participated in a July 1858 meeting to consider economic survival measures. When the *Provincial Freeman* resumed publication in 1858, Cary became copublisher of the paper with his brother-in-law, Isaac D. Shadd. That same year, Cary collaborated with abolitionist John Brown in the planning of Brown's unsuccessful Harpers Ferry raid. But because of worsening health, Cary

was unable to participate in the raid. He died on 29 November 1860. Bearden and Butler, *Shadd*, 185–86, 192–95, 201–3; S. L. Dannett, *Profiles of Negro Womanhood*, 2 vols. (Yonkers, N.Y., 1964–66), 1:150–57; Hill, *Freedom-Seekers*, 168, 179–80; *NAW*, 1:301; Thomas F. Cary to Mary Ann Shadd Cary, 21 May, 11 June 1857, 21 January 1858, Mary Ann Shadd Cary Papers, CaOTAr [10:0685, 0722, 11:0127]; *PFW*, 24 April 1853, 17 June, 19 August 1854, 19 May 1855, 24 January, 28 February 1857 [8:0175, 9:0017, 10:0516].

12. Martin R. Delany (1812–885) was born free in Charlestown, Virginia, the second son of a free seamstress named Pati and a plantation slave named Samuel. Delany's mother was caught educating her five children and was forced to resettle the family in Chambersburg, Pennsylvania. In 1823 she helped purchase her husband's freedom. At age nineteen, Delany moved to Pittsburgh, enrolled in Lewis Woodson's African Educational Society School (1832), and, a year later, began a three-year apprenticeship with a local doctor. Delany established himself as a significant figure within the Pittsburgh black community. He belonged to a number of black self-help organizations, was a member of the Philanthropic Society (a group formed to protect fugitives slaves), and led attempts to recover black suffrage in Pennsylvania. He also worked for the Liberty party.

In 1843 Delany founded and edited *Mystery*, a respected, weekly abolitionist newspaper that addressed social, economic, and political issues affecting black Americans. Delany discontinued the paper early in 1847 and, in December, joined Frederick Douglass as coeditor of the *North Star*, a position he held until 1849, when he resigned and returned to his Pittsburgh medical practice. After being rejected by a number of medical schools, Delany was accepted at Harvard in 1850, but student protests brought his dismissal from the program after a single term. Within a year, he had written *The Condition, Elevation, Emigration and Destiny of the Colored People of the United States*—a brief for emigration and black nationalism. In August 1854, Delany met with 106 delegates in Cleveland, Ohio, to consider immigration to Central America, South America, or the West Indies. Delany moved to Canada West early in 1856 and planned for a second convention, which met in Cleveland that August and marked a new direction in emigration thinking. Delany now focused on Africa.

From 1856 to 1858, Delany made plans to launch the Niger Valley Exploring Party, an executive agency for establishing a free-labor settlement in Africa. Delany and Philadelphia schoolteacher Robert Campbell sought the necessary funds. The American Colonization Society sponsored Delany's passage to Liberia in the late spring of 1859. In December 1859, the two men acquired land for a settlement through a treaty with the Alake (king) of Abeokuta. They journeyed to England in May 1860, and Delany conducted a successful seven-month speaking tour, describing his African plans and experiences.

When Delany returned to the United States, he became increasingly involved in the Union war effort as a recruiting agent for black soldiers and in 1865 became the first black officer commissioned to serve with a black regiment. Delany remained in the military for three and one-half years, working with the Freedmen's Bureau. In 1870 Delany briefly joined the staff of the *New National Era*—a Washington, D.C., newspaper—before resettling in Charleston, South Carolina. From 1870 to 1875, Delany was active in Republican party politics. He tried to develop a homestead plan for freedmen (1872) and briefly edited the Charleston

Independent (1875) before serving a three-year term as a minor court official during the tenure of Democratic Governor Wade Hampton. In 1878–9 Delany supported a short-lived emigration effort known as the Liberian Exodus Joint Stock Steamship Company. Delany wrote the novel *Blake; or The Huts of America*, which was serialized in the *Weekly Anglo-African* beginning in 1859. Victor Ullman, *Martin R. Delany: The Beginnings of Black Nationalism* (Boston, Mass., 1971), 1–507; Miller, *Search for Black Nationality*, 116–225, 265–67; Frank A. Rollin, *Life and Public Services of Martin R. Delany*, (Boston, Mass., 1868; reprint, New York, N.Y., 1969), 306; Dorothy Sterling, *The Making of An Afro-American: Martin Robinson Delany, 1812–1885* (Garden City, N.Y., 1971), 48–55.

13. James Henry Harris, a black upholsterer, settled in Chatham, Canada West, in the 1850s but apparently did not participate in antislavery and emigration activities there until late in the decade. Harris was appointed an agent of the National Emigration Convention (1858) at Chatham, was involved in anti-begging meetings in 1859, favored Martin R. Delany's Niger Valley Exploring Party, and opposed the Haitian immigration scheme of the early 1860s. *WAA*, 23 July 1859, 19 October 1861 [11:0876, 13:0837]; Simpson, "Negroes in Ontario to 1870," 710; Census of Canada, 1861; Delany, *The Niger Valley Exploring Party*, 12–13.

14. Mary Ellen "Mammy" Pleasant (ca. 1814–1904) claimed to have been born in Philadelphia, Pennsylvania, to a wealthy Sandwich Island merchant and a free black woman, but accounts of her birth and early life are contradictory. She eventually resided in Boston, where she made the acquaintance of several abolitionists and married a Cuban planter named Alexander Smith. She inherited a substantial sum when he died, then married John P. Pleasant, her first husband's former overseer. In 1849 Mary Ellen and John Pleasant moved to San Francisco, where Mary Ellen opened a successful boarding house. She also managed estates, loaned money, and operated brothels. Tradition credits her with rescuing newly arrived slaves held illegally by their masters. In 1858 she and John Pleasant left California for Canada West. During the fall of 1858, they stayed in Chatham, Canada West, where they purchased a house and probably met John Brown. Legend suggests that Mary Ellen donated funds to further Brown's slave insurrection, and she claimed to have traveled to Virginia to incite the slave population prior to Brown's raid on Harpers Ferry. The Pleasants later returned to California, where Mary Ellen renewed her business activities and became the housekeeper of San Francisco financier Thomas Bell. Her relationship with Bell was close, and she apparently had unlimited access to his funds. Her reputation was publicly sullied in 1881 when she was accused of having instigated a fraudulent divorce suit. She contributed to the cause of civil rights in California; in 1863 she helped blacks acquire the right to testify in the state's courts; and later in the decade, she filed a suit that opened San Francisco's streetcars to black passengers. After Thomas Bell's death, Mary Ellen Pleasant continued to live in his mansion until 1889, when she was evicted. She apparently died in poverty. *DANB*, 495–96; *NAW*, 3:75–77.

15. Amelia Freeman Shadd.

74.
Editorial by Isaac D. Shadd
29 January 1859

Black abolitionist support for emigration from the North American continent peaked in the years immedately preceding the Civil War. Between 1858 and 1862, increasing white Canadian racism prompted several black leaders in Canada West to advocate specific emigration programs. Black abolitionist Martin R. Delany of Chatham announced in early 1858 that he intended to locate a black settlement in the Niger Valley of West Africa. He spent the year organizing an expedition to explore the area. Delany hoped the third National Emigration Convention would endorse his venture, but when it met in Chatham in August 1858, it neither approved West African immigration nor offered assistance to his Niger Valley Exploring Party. Delany did persuade the convention's General Board of Commissioners to give him an "African Commission," which authorized him to explore the Niger Valley "for the purposes of science and general emigration." But Delany sought morc substantial support, particularly from Canadian blacks. On 23 November 1858, with the help of Isaac D. Shadd, he organized the African Civilization Society of Canada. Although the organization was composed entirely of Chatham blacks, Delany hoped that it would lend credibility to his claims of widespread black support. Shadd's 29 January 1859 editorial in the *Provincial Freeman* explained the objectives of the new society. But the organization proved to be short-lived. It attracted few members outside of the Chatham community and disbanded a few weeks after Shadd's editorial appeared. Hampered by a lack of black enthusiasm, Delany was unable to proceed with his Niger Valley expedition for several more months. Miller, *Search for Black Nationality*, 179–83, 193–95; Delany, *Niger Valley Exploring Party*, 12–13 [11:0336–37]; Isaac D. Shadd Diary, 23 November 1858, in Abraham D. Shadd Ledger, Shadd Family Records, CaOLU.

African Civilization Society of Canada

A number of our Citizens have formed an organization for the purpose of aiding in promoting the civilization of Africa, and thus destroying the slave trade—up-rooting slavery in the United States, and improving the condition of colored men here, and elsewhere.

Anti-Slavery men are now divided into two parties, the one opposed to any movement seeming to favor the emigration of intelligent colored men from the United States, to any country, the other in favor of the emigration of any class from the United States, to any country which invites to equal political privileges; on whose soil the fulcrum of a lever can be rested to move slavery. To the latter, Canada, Africa, Hayti, and the islands, conjointly, offer the soil and scope of territory for their aims, and earnest men who accept the theory are multiplying in numbers, marvelously, every day, and from among former advocates of the opposite doctrines. The improvement of the race of mankind without regard to clime or color, and especially the improvement of those to whom advantages have been long denied, is the constant concern of many amongst us. The hope of being able to help Africa, and of being instrumental in improving the condition of the colored man "wherever found," have been the reasons for founding our Canadian Society.

There are fears expressed that the new movement will supply the place of "something better." No such fears need be entertained. Old plans have been found to be impracticable, without giving a substitute more rational. This movement for Africa, however, supplies the desideratum. Working men and women take hold, and others will yet come to the work. There is a sad lack of information upon African affairs, and it is due to the rising generation to remedy deficiencies in this respect.

Africa is no inconsiderable portion of the Globe, and to become acquainted with her people, and the character of her institutions, should not, as many think, prevent us from acquiring information of Europe, Asia, and America. The young people of the present day should not be suffered to grope in the dark, as we have been doing; but the works of Livingston, Bowen, Anderson, Wilson, and other celebrated writers,[1] should be introduced into our schools, and families, and take their place upon the shelves, side by side with the works of authors who have written upon matters relating to other divisions of the Globe. The work properly promoted by aid of an efficient organization, such, as we trust, our Civilization Society may become, will effect a marvelous change among the colored people of Canada in a few years, and be an important instrument in up-rooting slavery, and advancing the welfare of Africa.

Provincial Freeman (Chatham, Canada West), 29 January 1859.

1. African missionaries and explorers produced a substantial body of literature during the mid-nineteenth century, which intensified interest in the "Dark Continent." The most celebrated explorer-missionary, David Livingstone (1813–1873), described his work in the widely read *Missionary Travels and Researches in South Africa* (1857). In *Central Africa: Adventures and Missionary Labors* (1857), Thomas J. Bowen (1814–1875) recalled his experiences as a Southern Baptist missionary in Yoruba. Karl Johan Andersson (1827–1867), a Swedish naturalist, recorded his observations in *Lake Ngami; or Explorations and Discoveries during Four Years' Wanderings in the Wilds of South-western Africa* (1856). John Leighton Wilson (1809–1886), a Presbyterian missionary, wrote *Western Africa: Its History, Conditions, and Prospects* (1856). *DAB*, 20:337–38; *DNB*, 11:1263–74; Miller, *Search for Black Nationality*, 183.

75.
John J. Moore to Amor de Cosmos
[February 1859]

The image of the Canadian haven persisted through the 1850s. Ohio blacks, seeking relief from the state's black laws, had established the Wilberforce colony in 1830; California blacks, reeling under a similar wave of racial prejudice and legal discrimination, looked to the Canadian Pacific coast for sanctuary three decades later. In the spring of 1858, representatives of the San Francisco black community visited Victoria, Vancouver Island, where Governor James Douglas extended them a hospitable invitation similar to that which Lieutenant Governor John Colborne had given Cincinnati blacks in 1830. As many as four hundred black families left California and settled in Victoria, where they confronted the same problems that blacks in Canada West had already encountered. In a letter to the *British Colonist*, Rev. John J. Moore described the motives and objectives of Victoria's black settlers. Winks, *Blacks in Canada*, 272–74; Crawford Kilian, *Go Do Some Great Thing: The Black Pioneers of British Columbia* (Vancouver, British Columbia, 1978), 15–25, 35–42.

COLORED EMIGRANTS

What do the colored people intend to do in this country? This interrogation has been frequently addressed to us. We would not have noticed it in public print were it not made by those whom we feel confident have an equal respect for, and interest in, colored men's welfare, in common with other races. Upon entering into the query we have found it simply this: Have the colored people come to this country to settle permanently for the future, or for pecuniary interest, intending only a transient stay? We would hesitate to array this portion of community before the public mind, were we not conscious that duty requires of us all public as well as private information that may set us in a true light before those who may speak, think, or act toward us with distinction. Colored men, like all other races of men, are induced to action in the same direction by various motives; and are subject to the same individual variety and social distinctions that other races are, therefore in judging their case, as a community, men must never expect them a unit; this would be as unnatural as unusual with men generally.

The writer having had the honor and pleasure of being one of the conductors of the educational, moral and religious, interests of the colored community of California, for the last 6 or 7 years, has some knowledge of the general character, condition, and intentions, of the colored people of this community, who hail from that region.[1] 1st. As to character—for sobriety, honesty, industry, intelligence, and enterprise, they will compare

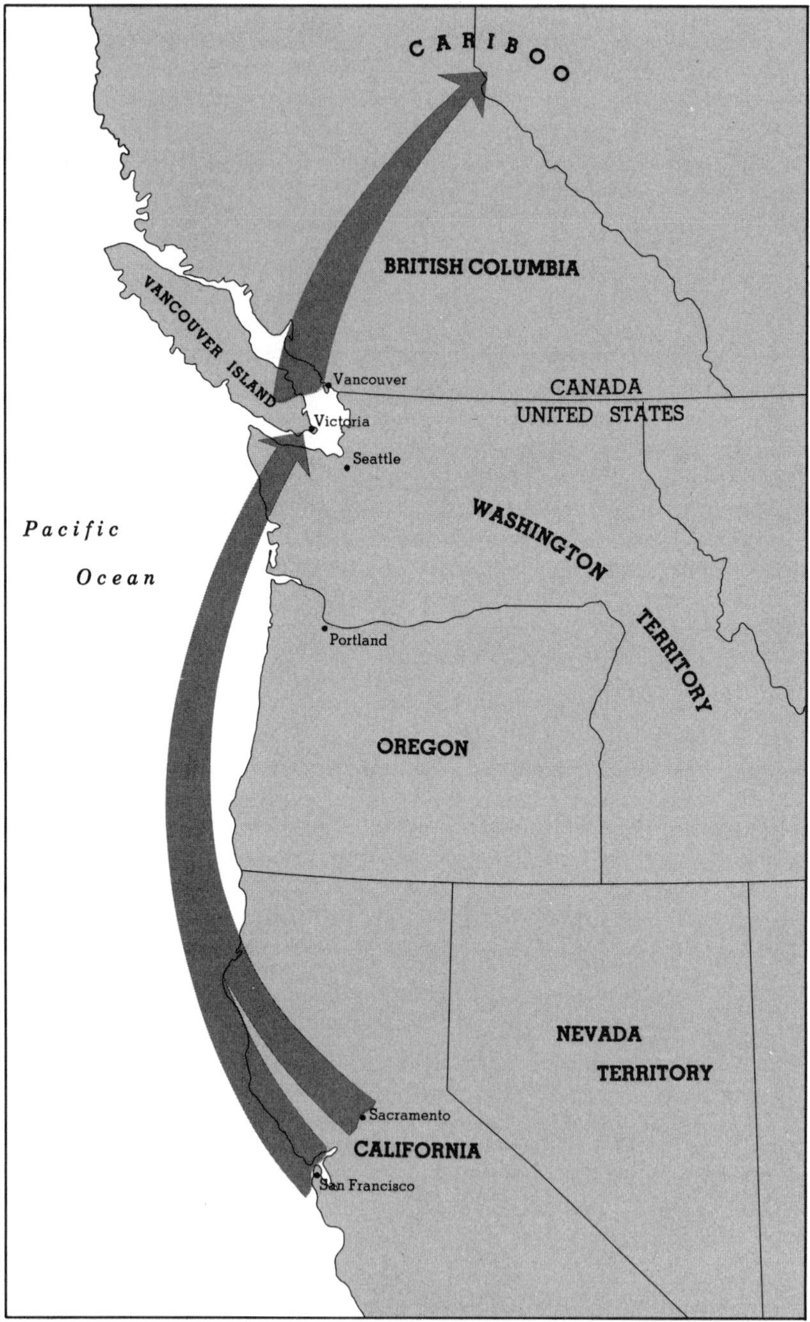

Fig. 3. Black migration and settlement on the Pacific coast, 1858–1866

with any. 2nd. As to condition—for respectability, domestic comfort, and wealth, take them per numerical ratio, they are on par with any. They have purchased thousands of dollars worth of real estate on this Island, and up the river.[2] 3rd. Respecting their intentions in migrating to this country—their object was three fold: 1—To better their political condition; in California they were disfranchised. Without the legal protection of life, liberty, and property; they were not admitted to testify in courts of justice, if against white persons; their veracity was only admissable when in no way against white parties. What mockery of justice—it would disgust antiquate barbarism. These outrages were not owing to our want of the true requisites of true and worthy citizens, for our oppressors have acknowledged those requisites in us, as intelligence, industry, honesty, and integrity. But we were victimized by a ruthless prejudice—(for the Moloch of American slavery, whose iron fingers are now dripping with human gore);[3] from this prejudice we have fled to a country governed by a nation far-famed for justice and humanity. Hasty fortunes we seek not; with some of us losses have been sustained, that the chief advantages of the country cannot briefly indemnify; but this is a secondary consideration with us: the full, free, and peaceable enjoyment of those highest inherent rights with which Heaven has gifted man, is the crowning thought with us, not dollars and cents. 2—We come here not to seek social favors, but to enjoy those common social rights that civilized, enlightened, and well regulated communities guarantee to all their members. We come not to seek any particular associations (those of us who understand ourselves); we only desire social rights in common with other men. Particular society is a creature of circumstances, and establishes and regulates its own government. Its admissions or restrictions no human legislation can interdict, except they come in contact with the general laws of community. Therefore we are not anxious about particular society, in view of caste. 3—We have come to this country to make it the land of our adoption for ourselves and our children. We have come to possess the soil; to till the earth; to reap its productions, extract its minerals; to mould its rocks and forests into firesides; and to fill the solitary places with joy and gladness; to gild the western verge of old ocean with white winged messengers to glide upon the bosom of every sea; and build up for ourselves and children, happy homes in the land of the free and home of the brave.

J. J. MOORE, V.D.M.[4]

British Colonist (Victoria, Vancouver Island), 8 February 1859.

1. Many blacks settled in California during the period of the gold rush. By the late 1850s, nearly five thousand blacks, or 1 percent of the total population, resided in the state, primarily in the San Francisco-Sacramento area. Blacks shared in the boom economy created by the gold rush, accumulating an estimated $4.5

million in property and business. A cohesive black community developed, and churches, schools, and newspapers—including the *Mirror of the Times* and the *Pacific Appeal*—were established. Despite these successes, California blacks were often the target of racial prejudice and legal discrimination. In order to challenge the discriminatory laws, blacks organized and held three state conventions (1855–57), launched petition drives, sought legal redress, and explored the possibility of resettlement on Vancouver Island. Rev. John J. Moore was an active participant in this process. Howard H. Bell, "Negroes in California, 1849–1859," *Phy* 28:151–61; Rudolph Lapp, *Blacks in Gold Rush California* (New Haven, Conn., 1977), 126–38; Kilian, *Go Do Some Great Thing*, 15–25.

2. When several hundred California blacks resettled on Vancouver Island in 1858, they brought with them substantial capital, which they reinvested in local real estate and business ventures. Many profited from the British Columbia gold rush of the late 1850s. Black businessmen like Mifflin W. Gibbs and Peter Lester accumulated large real estate holdings in and around Victoria, the island's major town. One source indicates that Victoria blacks owned $250,000 worth of real estate by 1861. Kilian, *Go Do Some Great Thing*, 34, 42–48, 124.

3. Moloch was an ancient Ammonite deity to whom children were sacrificed.

4. John Jamison Moore (1804–1893) was born to slave parents in Berkeley County, Virginia. He was originally named Benjamin Clawson but changed his name after his parents escaped with him to Pennsylvania during his youth. After embracing religion in 1833, Moore prepared for a preaching career, employing private tutors to instruct him in Latin, Greek, Hebrew, and theology. In 1839 he began itinerant preaching in Pennsylvania, Maryland, and Ohio and soon gained a reputation as a dynamic pulpit orator. He was later considered one of the outstanding black preachers of the antebellum period. Ordained into the African Methodist Episcopal Zion ministry in 1842, he spent the following decade serving AMEZ congregations in Philadelphia and Baltimore. Moore left Baltimore in 1852 for San Francisco, where he established the first AMEZ congregation west of the Mississippi River. His activism helped energize the nascent California black community. Moore opened and directed the city's first black school and agitated for appropriation of public funds for black education. He actively opposed the state's black laws. He penned numerous newspaper articles on local black politics and edited and published the *Lunar Visitor*, a black monthly. And he participated in the 1855, 1856, and 1865 California black state conventions and served on various black state committees. At the 1865 state convention, he urged California blacks to adopt a militant rhetoric in defense of their civil rights.

But Moore's concern extended beyond the local black community. He was a frequent antislavery speaker. He made several extended visits to investigate conditions in the black communities at Victoria, Vancouver Island (1859), and in the Cariboo mining region of British Columbia (1863–64). During the Civil War, he served as corresponding secretary of the California Contraband Relief Association and also did missionary work among the California Indians. He became one of the leading AMEZ clerics after the war. Elected to the bishopric in 1868, he returned East and led an effort to unite his denomination with the African Methodist Episcopal church. When that failed, he directed his energy to missionary work among the freedmen in the South, and during the latter years of Reconstruction, he organized numerous churches in North Carolina, Georgia, and the

Bahama Islands. In 1877 Moore was appointed to direct the AMEZ's publishing efforts; two years later, he traveled to England and successfully solicited funds for that purpose. He personally authored a number of AMEZ publications, including a catechism and a denominational history, and edited *The A.M.E. Zion Sunday School Banner* during the 1880s. Moore spent his last years in Salisbury, North Carolina. Walls, *African Methodist Episcopal Zion Church*, 129, 141, 149, 164–66, 199–200, 204, 212, 249, 268, 302, 337–38, 353, 360, 402, 437, 463, 478, 576–77, 632; Douglas Henry Daniels, *Pioneer Urbanites: A Social and Cultural History of Black San Francisco* (Philadelphia, Pa., 1980), 64, 113; G, 12 December 1885; Foner and Walker, *Proceedings of Black State Conventions*, 112–14, 126, 130, 133–35, 152, 169–71, 178, 192, 196, 201; *PA*, 16 August 1862, 17 January, 11 July, 25 September 1863, 20 February 1864 [14:0446, 0699, 0950, 1067, 15:0251]; *San Francisco City Directory*, 1863.

76.
Jackson Whitney to William Riley
18 March 1859

Narratives, interviews, and public lectures provided fugitive slaves with the opportunity to make a personal antislavery statement. The most personal, direct, and ironic statements came when former slaves wrote letters to their old masters. Jackson Whitney's letter addressed a specific grievance—his family's enslavement. In requesting freedom for his wife and children, Whitney appealed to the slaveholder's Christian conscience and the attendant prospect of perdition. The antislavery press welcomed the opportunity to publish such letters. Their literary quality and articulate expression were subtle indictments of slavery. Their high moral tone—civility, righteous indignation, and call to conscience, rather than the threat of violence—spoke to abolitionist sensibilities. Whitney's letter was reprinted in several antislavery papers, including the *Liberator* and *National Anti-Slavery Standard. Lib*, 2 September 1859; *NASS*, 3 September 1859.

"Fugitive's Home"
Sandwich, C[anada] W[est]
March 18, 1859

Mr. Wm. Riley
Springfield, K[entuck]y
Sir:

I take this opportunity to dictate a few lines to you, supposing you might be curious to know my whereabouts. I am happy to inform you that I am in Canada, in good health, and have been here several days. Perhaps by this time you have concluded that robbing a woman of her husband and children, of their father, does not pay, at least in your case; and I thought while lying in jail by your direction that if you had no remorse of conscience that would make you feel for a poor, broken hearted man, and his worse-than-murdered wife and children, and could not be made to feel for others as you would have others feel for you, and could not by any entreaty or persuasion be induced to do as you promised you would, which was to let me go with my family for $800—but contended for $1,000 when you had promised to take the same you gave for me (which was $660) at the time you bought me, and let me go with my dear wife and children! but instead would render me miserable, and lie to me, and to your neighbors (now if words mean anything, what I say is so), and when you was at Louisville trying to sell me! then I thought it was time to make my feet feel for Canada, and let your conscience feel in your pocket. Now you cannot say but that I did all that was honorable and right while I was with you, although I was a slave. I pretended all the time that I thought you, or some one else had a better right to me than I had to myself, which you know is rather hard thinking. You know, too, that you proved a traitor to me in the time of need, and when in the most bitter distress that the human soul is capable of experiencing; and could you have carried out your purposes there would have been no relief. But I rejoice to say that an unseen, kind spirit appeared for the oppressed, and bade me take up my bed and walk—the result of which is that I am victorious and you are defeated.

I am comfortably situated in Canada, working for Geo. Harris,[1] one of the persons that act a part in *Uncle Tom's Cabin.*[2] He was a slave a few years ago, in Kentucky; and now owns a farm so level that there not hills enough on it to hide a dog, yet so large that I got lost in it the other day. He says that I may be the means of helping poor fugitives and doing them as much good as he does, in time.

This country is not what it has been represented to me and others to be. In place of its being cold and barren, it has a beautiful, comfortable climate, and fertile soil. It is much more desirable in these respects than any part of Kentucky that I ever saw. There is only one thing to prevent me being entirely happy here, and that is the want of my dear wife and children, and *you* to see us enjoying ourselves together here. I wish you could realize the contrast between freedom and slavery; but it is not likely that we shall ever again meet on this earth. But if you want to go to the next world and meet a God of love, mercy, and justice, in peace; who says, "Inasmuch as you did it to the least of them my little ones, you did it unto me"—making the professions that you do, pretending to be a follower of Christ, and tormenting me and my little ones as you have done—had better repair the breaches you have made among us in this world, by sending my wife and children to me; thus preparing to meet your God in peace; for if God don't punish you for inflicting such distress on the poorest of His poor, then there is no use of *having* any God, or *talking* about one. But in this letter I have said enough to cause you to do all that is necessary for you to do, provided you are any part of the man you pretend to be. So I will close by saying that if you see proper to reply to my letter, either condemning or justifying the course you have taken with me I will again write you.

I hope you will consider candidly and see if the case does not justify every word I have said, and ten times as much. You must not consider that it is a slave talking to "massa" now, but one as free as yourself.

I subscribe myself one of the *abused* of America, but one of the *justified* and *honored* of Canada.

JACKSON WHITNEY

Evening Journal (Jamestown, N.Y.), 1 July 1859.

1. During his lifetime and afterward, Lewis Clarke, a black Sandwich farmer, was identified as the model for the character George Harris in Harriet Beecher Stowe's *Uncle Tom's Cabin* (1852). Although Stowe raised some questions about Clarke's claim in 1895, her *Key to Uncle Tom's Cabin* (1856) acknowledged that Clarke lived for a time in her sister-in-law's Ohio household and that she based Harris's character upon real slave experiences. Parallels in her book and in Clarke's own *Narrative* (1845) suggest that Stowe drew upon the Clarke family story. Both Lewis and his brother Milton Clarke reported that they provided Stowe with considerable information about slavery. *BT*, 7, [14?] December 1895; *NYSu*, 9 December 1900.

2. *Uncle Tom's Cabin* was Harriet Beecher Stowe's first novel. Initially published as forty installments in the *National Era* and republished as *Uncle Tom's Cabin; or, Life among the Lowly* (Boston, Mass., 1852), it sold over three hundred thousand copies the first year, and was made into a popular stage drama. A fictionalized indictment of slavery, the book helped crystallize northern sentiment against slavery. Southern reviewers vilified Stowe and challenged the accuracy of the book's depiction of the slaveholding system. Some thirty anti-Tom novels appeared in the South; in *The Key to Uncle Tom's Cabin* (Boston, Mass., 1853), Stowe provided evidence to rebut her attackers. David C. Roller and Robert Twyman, eds., *Encyclopedia of Southern History* (Baton Rouge, La., 1979), 1259; William R. Taylor, *Cavalier and Yankee: The Old South and American National Character* (New York, N.Y., 1961), 307.

77.
Daniel Webster to James Miller McKim
1 May 1859

Upon reaching their destination in Canada, blacks frequently wrote to friends and family to confirm their safe arrival. Daniel Webster reported back to Philadelphia abolitionist James Miller McKim. Webster, a free black from Pennsylvania, had been arrested and tried as a fugitive slave in April 1859. After his acquittal, he settled in Canada West to avoid additional legal problems and new threats of enslavement. Webster's experience, as outlined in his 1 May 1859 letter, typified the difficult period of adjustment that confronted many black settlers in the provinces. May, *Fugitive Slave Law*, 116–18.

Drummondville, Canada [West]
May 1st, 1859

Mr. McKim[1]
Dare Sir

I am well and safe in Canada[.] I have been here 2 weeks[.] Times is vary Hard in deed[.] There is no work to be had as yet[.] I have been trying to get work like all of the new comers and cannot get any till working times comes on that wont be till 25th of may. Sir I wish you would send me some money if you please for I am out of means[.] I am as ever thankful to you and all the Friends for all there Kindness to me in the Houre of distress[.] I will ever think of you all and beleive me to be a Friend[.] If you cannot send me any money please see or write to my Brothers and let them know where I am and have them to send me some money if you please for I am in want of some money[,,] at this time[.] My Love to Mr. Purvice[2] and all the Friends[,]

Danil Webster[3]

Anti-Slavery Collection, Olin Library, Cornell University, Ithaca, New York. Published by permission.

1. James Miller McKim (1810–1874) was born in Carlisle, Pennsylvania, and educated at Dickinson College. An early Garrisonian abolitionist and American Anti-Slavery Society member, McKim's liberal theology and antislavery immediatism forced his withdrawal from the Presbyterian ministry. McKim lectured on slavery, assisted fugitive slaves, and edited the antislavery newspaper *The Pennsylvania Freeman*. During the Civil War, McKim urged enlistment of black soldiers and supported freedmen's relief efforts through the Port Royal Relief Committee and the Pennsylvania Freedman's Relief Association. In 1865 he founded the *Nation* with his son-in-law Wendell Phillips Garrison. *DAB*, 12:103–4.

2. Webster refers to Robert Purvis (1810–1898). Purvis was born in Charleston,

South Carolina, the son of William Purvis, a cotton broker, and Harriet Judah, the mulatto daughter of a German Jewish merchant and his former slave wife. In 1819 the family moved to Philadelphia. When William Purvis died in 1826, he left a legacy of strong antislavery convictions that particularly influenced Robert, and he left an inheritance that provided for his family. Robert Purvis concluded his formal education with a year at Amherst College, then returned to Philadelphia, where he began his abolitionist career by contributing to William Lloyd Garrison's *Liberator* and by helping to organize the American Anti-Slavery Society in 1833. In 1834 Purvis married Harriet Forten, daughter of James Forten, the black abolitionist and wealthy Philadelphia sailmaker. He also traveled to England to blunt colonizationist appeals abroad and to fashion international antislavery cooperation.

Throughout the remainder of the 1830s, Purvis focused his attention on the problems of Pennsylvania blacks and on the creation of a Pennsylvania antislavery network. He joined the Young Men's Anti-Slavery Society of Philadelphia, led the formation of the Pennsylvania Anti-Slavery Society in 1837, and, in 1838, chaired the committee of black citizens that drafted the *Appeal of Forty Thousand*—a protest against the Pennsylvania Reform Convention's attempt to take away black suffrage. When the antislavery movement factionalized in 1840, Purvis remained with the American society. Although he supported the free produce movement, he vowed to "eschew all means [except] pure morality to end slavery." Passage of the Fugitive Slave Law and ferment among black abolitionists about their role in the movement redirected Purvis's antislavery activities after 1850. Purvis was always a supporter of fugitive slave rescue efforts, and in the 1850s, he became dedicated to that work. He built secret hiding places for fugitive slaves in his Philadelphia home and at his two Byberry farms, and in 1855 he advocated the impeachment of U.S. District Court Judge John K. Kane for his decisions in fugitive slave cases. By 1859 Purvis claimed to be ready "to kill every oppressor" that stood in his or any fugitive's way to freedom.

Purvis's antislavery commitment was reinforced by racial prejudice. The Purvis children were excluded from public schools, and Purvis was refused permission to participate in agricultural competitions and harassed by antiabolitionists. Purvis cautioned that some abolitionists, who were the "only true friends of the colored man, were not consistent in their conduct." During the Civil War, Purvis enlisted blacks in the Union army. After the war, he served as commissioner of the Freedman's Savings Bank, supported passage of the Fourteenth Amendment, and helped found the Pennsylvania Equal Rights Association, an organization dedicated to suffrage for women and blacks. In later life, Purvis continued his work for black equality as well as for municipal reform in Philadelphia. *DANB*, 508–10; William Wells Brown, *The Rising Son: or The Antecedents and Advancement of the Colored Race* (Boston, Mass., 1874; reprint New York, N.Y., 1970), 468–69; Still, *Underground Railroad*, 711; Janice Sumler Lewis, "The Fortens of Philadelphia: An Afro-American Family and Nineteenth Century Reform" (Ph.D. diss., Georgetown University, 1978), 44–46, 50–52, 65–76, 94–95, 106–8, 184–90, 205–7, 243; *PPr*, 3 August 1890, 16 April 1898; *PEB*, 16 December 1859; *NYH*, 12 May 1854; *PF*, 29 March 1838, 20 December 1848; *Lib*, 17 May, 14 June 1834, 10 August 1836, 10 January 1837, 10 May 1838, 19 August 1842, 1 September 1848, 9 September, 25 November, 6 December 1853,

5 May 1854; *NASS*, 25 October 1849, 20 May 1852, 12 November, 3 December 1853, 13 May 1854, 13 January, 8 September 1855, 7 February 1858, 6 March 1863, 8 April 1865, 22 December 1866, 14 January 1871.

3. Daniel Webster (ca. 1824–?), a Baltimore free black, settled in Philadelphia in the late 1840s. By 1853 he was resettled in Harrisburg, Pennsylvania, with his wife and children; there he found employment as the servant of W. W. Rutherford, a local physician and state senator active in the antislavery cause. Webster gained a measure of antislavery notoriety in April 1859, when he was arrested by a federal marshal as an escaped slave under the Fugitive Slave Law of 1850. French Simpson, a Virginia planter, claimed that Webster was his slave, Daniel Dangerfield, who had escaped in November 1854. Webster was tried before a federal tribunal in Philadelphia during 6–8 April. Although several white witnesses testified that he was Dangerfield, the contradictory testimony of black witnesses and factual discrepancies in the physical identity of the two men led to his release. Fearing further trouble, Webster immediately resettled in Drummondville, Canada West, where he became an active member of the local Missionary Society. May, *Fugitive Slave Law*, 116–18; Campbell, *Slave Catchers*, 205; *NASS*, 16 April 1859; John L. Johnson to the Anti-Slavery friends [in Philadelphia], 1 May 1859, Anti-Slavery Collection, NIC [11:0724].

78.
Fielding Smithea to Amor de Cosmos
10 June 1859

The black enclave established in Victoria, Vancouver Island, developed into a prosperous and influential community. Yet not all blacks were satisfied with conditions there. In a letter to the *British Colonist*, Fielding Smithea described the "mildew-like" racial prejudice that hounded blacks on the North American continent. Smithea recounted several instances of racial discrimination and insisted that British law alone could never insure equality for blacks; public sentiment determined social conditions. From his California and Victoria experiences, he concluded that persistent white prejudice meant that the two races could never coexist. Racial tensions in the British North American Provinces had undeniably increased with a substantial rise in black immigration in the 1850s. Those who found the Canadian promise unfulfilled agreed with Smithea and called for a black homeland in West Africa or the Caribbean. *BC*, 13 June 1859; Miller, *Search for Black Nationality*, 170–249.

VICTORIA, V[ancouver] I[sland]
June 10th, 1859

MR. EDITOR:[1]

Have the colored people realized their fond anticipations in coming to Vancouver's Island? I answer *no*. And if not, what is the position they occupy in this colony? I answer decidedly a degrading one, and certainly one not to be borne by men of spirit.

It is a fact generally known that in the United States of America, the colored people labor and live under many disadvantages, the result of prejudice. Yet while this is a truth, there are many States in which colored men vote and enjoy all the rights of citizens.[2] Hence we have in many of the northern States colored men practicing the law, medicine, and many other professions. We enter their colleges, and graduate in common with white students. In many of these colleges they have colored gentlemen professors and teachers. This state of things has been brought about by the untiring efforts of our friends, whose name is legion, and forming a connecting link with such men as Clarkson,[3] Burke,[4] and Wilberforce.[5]

Finally, we went to California in common with others, to make money, and very many were successful. In the early history of California, the very worst men, shoulder-striking, devil-daring fellows, fought their way into office, and when in, they tried to pass a law prohibiting any more colored persons and Chinamen from emigrating thither, and those already there must register their names in a Recorder's office,[6] and though they did not accomplish their diabolical purpose, yet we took the will for the deed and considered ourselves, not only outraged, but more degraded than ever. Hence we held mass meetings, and discussed the question of where we should go. Some said to Sonora in Lower California, others into Central America; but just at that time there was some talk about Vancouver's Island, where the majority concluded to go. A Roman general said "Veni, Vidi, Vici,"[7] and I can say, we came, we saw, and even conquered difficulties, but we have not conquered that mildew-like feeling that lurks in the hearts of our enemies, i.e., prejudice. Having from early boyhood cherished a friendly feeling for the British Government, which was the result of her liberal policy towards the colored people generally, we had hoped on coming here to occupy this virgin soil; that we would enjoy all the rights and privileges enjoyed by others, but how sadly have many of us been disappointed. All the hotels, inns, and whiskey shops, are closed against us, and a colored gentleman was ordered out of the cabin of the steamer *Gov. Douglas*, the other day—he had a cabin ticket. They shut us out from their concerts, and a member of the church says give him $500 and he will build a gallery in the English Church, in which to huddle us together.[8] I know nothing of English law, yet I believe the course these men pursue is contrary to all law, human or Divine. The Bible says 40 Jews banded themselves together not to eat or sleep until they had "slain Paul of Tarsus."[9] So I am informed that there is in town a secret association of wicked white men (I wonder if any are good singers), whose ostensible purpose is to keep colored men out of the jury box, and from serving on the Grand Jury. Now for myself, I care not if I never fill any office here, but in the language of one, "Fiat justitia, ruat coelum." In connection with the steamboat affair, I remember a case somewhat similar which took place some years ago in one of the northern States. A colored lady purchased a first class ticket, and on taking her seat in the cars she was ordered to go into the emigrant cars, which she declined. She afterwards sued and recovered damages from the company.[10] Some of our people whose susceptibilities are *not so keen* upon the subject of human rights, say having the law in our favor we ask no more. It is well said, "if ignorance is bliss." But when I consider how many ways there are to evade the law, I subscribe to no such doctrine, for there is a power behind the throne stronger than the throne itself, and that power is public opinion. Were it not so, men would have no regard for human society.

In view of these facts, I contend that the position we hold in this colony, is not only humiliating in the extreme, but degrading to us as a class. I will not now stop to enquire why it is that we are thus treated, hated and despised. Enough to know that it is so. I know some among us are inclined to whitewash these matters over, saying there will be a better state of things hereafter. But the obnoxious seeds of prejudice are so deeply rooted in the white man's heart, which he directs against us with such burning force, biting like an adder and stinging like an asp, that we naturally suffer from its deadly effects.

It is said that in war colored men make good and brave soldiers, but I think in the common walks of life they are viewed through different glasses. I believe it utterly impossible for the African and the Anglo-Saxon races ever to live together on terms of equality. *I am as firmly fixed in this opinion as I am that some day I shall go to judgement.* I am not alone in this feeling, for I reflect the views of very many of our people, even in Victoria, unless they say one thing and mean another.

When I contemplate the vast multitude of colored people scattered throughout the United States of America, the Canadas, and the West Indies, my heart yearns for the day when God, in his providence will gather us together in some favored country, where we cannot only be men, without any restraint, but grow and become a great nation like others; this inward desire does not only predominate over all others, but it does in very deed *consume me gradually away.* Yet homo sum atque nihil humanie a me alinum puto.[11]

F. S.[12]

British Colonist (Victoria, Vancouver Island), 13 June 1859.

1. Amor de Cosmos (1825–1897), a photographer, journalist, and politician, was born William Alexander Smith in Windsor, Nova Scotia. He joined the California gold rush, then resettled in Victoria, Vancouver Island, in 1858 and founded the *British Colonist.* De Cosmos edited the *Colonist* during its early years; it became a daily in 1860 and was renamed the *British Colonist and Victoria Chronicle* six years later, when it merged with another Victoria paper and absorbed the New Westminster *British Columbian.* De Cosmos became politically active during the early 1860s and led the fight in British Columbia for responsible government and union with the Dominion of Canada. He served in the provincial assembly (1863–67), represented Victoria in Ottawa (1871–72), and was briefly premier of British Columbia (1873). *MDCB*, 203.

2. By 1860 free blacks residing in Maine, Vermont, New Hampshire, Massachusetts, and Rhode Island enjoyed the unfettered right to vote. Only a small number of blacks met New York State's property and residence qualifications. Blacks in most other states were effectively denied the franchise. Litwack, *North of Slavery*, 74–93.

3. Thomas Clarkson (1760–1846) first became interested in slavery through a prize-winning dissertation he wrote on the subject at Cambridge in 1785. Thereafter, he collected information and statistics on the brutality of the Atlantic slave trade, wrote antislavery tracts, testified before parliamentary committees, held public meetings, and distributed pamphlets. Largely due to his indefatigable efforts, British public opinion turned against slavery. Clarkson helped found the Committee for the Suppression of the Slave Trade in 1779; in 1823 he became a vice-president of the new Society for the Mitigation and Gradual Abolition of Slavery throughout the British Dominion. Under the strain of constant work and

traveling, his health deteriorated. But he lived to witness the culmination of his efforts—the Emancipation Act of 1833. *DNB*, 4:454–57.

4. Edmund Burke (1729–1797) was an Irish-born, British politician and man of letters. In 1766 he was seated in Parliament, where he defended the right of the American colonies to self-government and spoke out against slave trade. Burke's classic moral indictment of revolutionary politics, *Reflections on the French Revolution*, made him the standard-bearer of English political conservatism. *DNB*, 3:344–65.

5. William Wilberforce (1759–1833) was born and raised in Yorkshire, England. After attending Cambridge, he sat in the House of Commons (1780–1825), where he led the parliamentary campaign against the slave trade. Wilberforce introduced the first bill for the abolition of West Indian slavery and helped organize the Society for the Mitigation and Gradual Abolition of Slavery throughout the British Dominion in 1823. His devotion to evangelical Christianity prompted him to champion a variety of reform causes, including penal reform, electoral reform, public education, and aiding the industrial poor. In his later years, Wilberforce was respected as the interpreter of the British national conscience. *DNB*, 21:208–17; John Pollock, *Wilberforce* (London, 1977).

6. In the spring of 1858, the California legislature attempted for the third time in nine years to pass a bill prohibiting black immigration into the state. During the debate over the bill, legislators discussed the possibility of also banning Chinese immigration. The bill would have required blacks already in the state to register and to carry free papers at all times. Like the two previous efforts, the bill passed overwhelmingly in the lower house but was defeated in the state senate. Lapp, *Blacks in Gold Rush California*, 128, 130, 148–54, 236, 239–40.

7. Smithea refers to a quote attributed to Gaius Julius Caesar (100–44 B.C.), a Roman general, dictator, and writer. According to Plutarch's *Lives*, Caesar characterized his brief but successful Pontic campaign (47 B.C.) in Asia Minor with the phrase "Veni, Vedi, Vici"—"I came, I saw, I conquered."

8. Although British law protected Victoria's blacks from political and legal discrimination, it did not shield them from social expressions of racial prejudice. The large number of American settlers in the community reflected "Yankee prejudice" and helped shape public attitudes toward blacks. During the Civil War, pro-Confederate sympathies further aggravated racial tensions. As a result, blacks sometimes found themselves unable to obtain service in American-owned businesses, excluded from the fire brigade, passed over for jury duty, snubbed at public celebrations, denied preferred seating at the local theater, and victimized by public ridicule and harassment. Despite these notable instances of discrimination, Victoria's multiracial character and frontier social dynamics mitigated the effect of white prejudice against blacks. The open political and economic life of the community permitted many blacks to prosper and a few to run for public office. Black residents also successfully resisted attempts to segregate local schools and churches. As the black population declined in the late 1860s, racial tensions abated. Winks, *Blacks in Canada*, 287; Kilian, *Go Do Some Great Thing*, 53–57, 75–76, 79–80, 116–38.

9. Smithea evidently extrapolates upon a reference in Acts 9:23–25 to a Jewish plan to assassinate St. Paul, the early Christian leader, while he was preaching in

Damascus. According to the book of Acts, Christians discovered the conspiracy and safely smuggled Paul out of the city.

10. Smithea refers to an incident that occurred in New York City in July 1854, when Elizabeth Jennings, a free black teacher and mental improvement lecturer, was refused the right to ride in a first-class streetcar operated by the Third Avenue Railroad Company. Jennings sued the company and was awarded $225 in damages. The decision also upheld the right of blacks to ride in the cars "if sober, well-behaved and free from disease." Sterling, *We are Your Sisters*, 80, 112, 223–24; *FDP*, 28 July 1854.

11. Smithea quotes from act 1, scene 1, line 23 of the comedy *Heauton Timorumenos* by the Roman author Terence (ca. 186–159 B.C.). "Homo sum: atque humani nihil a me alienum puto" translates as "I am human, so any human interest is my concern." Terence, *The Comedies*, ed. Betty Radice (Baltimore, Md., 1967), 86.

12. Fielding Smithea (1823–?) was born in Caroline County, Virginia, but later settled in Ohio. He attended Oberlin College during 1844–45, and there he was undoubtedly introduced to reform ideas. He continued to reside in the Oberlin area until going overland to California about 1850. Smithea initially settled in central California, where he located work as a steward, but he later moved to the Contra Costa-Alameda area. There he became active in the affairs of the San Francisco black community and was elected a delegate to and vice president of the First Convention of the Colored Citizens of California, which met in Sacramento in 1855. Disturbed by growing racial discrimination in California, he joined the blacks that left for Victoria, Vancouver Island, during the late 1850s. He worked as a messenger in the Victoria government offices and continued to actively protest discrimination. While in Victoria, Smithea entered the African Methodist Episcopal ministry, and in late 1862, he was appointed pastor of a local AME congregation by the denomination's California district. He returned to the United States by 1869, settling in San Francisco, where he worked as a whitewasher into the 1880s, except for brief periods serving AME congregations in Los Angeles (1873) and Petaluma (1878). He remained active in his quest for full black civil rights, worked to end racial discrimination in San Francisco's schools, lectured to local black societies, and frequently corresponded with the *Pacific Appeal* and the *Elevator*, two black San Francisco newspapers. Smithea was a delegate to the 1873 black national convention. *WAA*, 13 April 1861; California Census, 1852; United States Census, 1880; "Oberlin College Catalogue and Record of Coloured Students, 1835–1862," 9, Cowles Papers, OO [1:0541]; *ESF*, 20 August, 12 November 1869, 1 July 1870, 19 October 1872, 24 May, 8, 22 November 1873; Foner and Walker, *Proceedings of Black State Conventions*, 2:112–16, 122, 126, 128; Pilton, "Negro Settlement in British Columbia," 51; *PA*, 8 November 1862, 24 September 1870, 20 July, 17 August 1872, 14 February 1874, 10 August 1878; *San Francisco City Directory*, 1869, 1872, 1875.

79.
Mifflin W. Gibbs to Amor de Cosmos
[22 October 1859]

A sense of pan-African unity prompted black Canadians to follow black interests throughout the world. Even blacks in the frontier village of Victoria, Vancouver Island, viewed nineteenth-century slave emancipation in an international perspective. When the Victoria *British Colonist* published an antiemancipation article entitled "Effects of Emancipation on the African Race in the British West Indies" in its 21 October 1859 issue, local black merchant Mifflin W. Gibbs responded. The article, which first appeared in the London *Times*, characterized the former West Indian slaves as indolent, ungrateful, and arrogant. Bemoaning the fact that black farmers planted what they wished (foodstuffs), rather than what whites wanted (cotton, tobacco, sugar), it called emancipation an economic failure. The article was one in a litany of antiemancipation pieces by the *Times*; throughout the years between passage of the Emancipation Act of 1833 and the Civil War, the London newspaper repeatedly argued that former West Indian slaves were not ready for freedom. Gibbs's angry letter to Amor de Cosmos, the editor of the *Colonist*, refuted the *Times*'s characterization of West Indian emancipation as a failure. Rejecting the economic criteria used by the *Times*, he pointed to improvements in black education, family life, religion, politics, and behavior since freedom. The freedman could hardly be blamed, Gibbs argued, for refusing to work for their former masters for nominal wages when they could "admirably sustain themselves" by farming their own land. Gibbs believed that the *Times*'s tendency to measure emancipation "by the increase or diminution of a few pounds of sugar" dehumanized the former slaves. *BC*, 21 October 1859; Douglas A. Lorimer, *Colour, Class and the Victorians: English Attitudes to the Negro in the Mid-Nineteenth Century* (Leicester, England, 1978), 179, 182–83.

EDITOR *BRITISH COLONIST*:[1]

Noticing in your last issue a selection from the *London Times*,[2] entitled "The effect of Emancipation in the West Indies," I have taken the liberty to ask that you insert the following extracts. The charge of bad effects from emancipation, has been so frequently exploded, and its falsity made so apparent by facts and figures, that I never expected to see its dead carcass disinterred. The *Times*—though great in ability and powerful in influence—is neither the exponent of the religious element nor the moral worth of the people of England; but the mouthpiece of political conservatism and a soulless commerce. The idea of its measuring a

7. Mifflin Wistar Gibbs

From I. Garland Penn, *Afro-American Press and Its Editors* (Springfield, Mass., 1891)

great act of national righteousness, like the West India Emancipation, by the increase or diminution of a few pounds of sugar exhibits a depth of moral depravity, and a contempt for the essential principles of true national greatness, which is revolting to every friend of morality and justice. Point them to the schools once prohibited, but now in operation for the education of the masses—tell them that the marriage institution is now honored, where it was utterly repudiated—and that there is no longer separation of husband and wife, for the marriage relation is held sacred; tell them that every man is now owner of himself, a recognised and protected British freeman; tell them that he occupies high stations in the church and in the State, as minister, lawyer, doctor, judge, mayor and legislator; that complexional distinctions are fast fading out; that crime is diminishing, and improvement is everywhere visible—and what is their reply? "These things are nothing; what have you to say about the sugar crop?" What consummate folly and villany! Why, in the very nature of things, liberty and material prosperity must go hand in hand, while slavery is a withering curse, turning the most fertile soil into barrenness.

Now it is a fact that things differ in their appearance according to the standpoint from which they are viewed. Emancipation in the West Indies, viewed from the "easy chair" of the *London Times*, surrounded by the influence of disappointed planters, and proprietors, may not present a very pleasing aspect to the avaricious, and devotees of unrequited toil; for it is undoubtedly true that the laborers there, like mankind everywhere, refuse to work for mere nominal wages for others when they can admirably sustain themselves by the cultivation of their own soil. The fact of the negro laborer refusing to work for ninepence a day, does not prove that one shilling a day demanded by him is "ludicrously disproportionate"—or that he is unwilling to work for a fair compensation. Without trespassing further on your space, Mr. Editor, British Emancipation viewed from the stand-point of high moral duty, stern fact, and honest investigation, reveal it as a glorious success both in a moral and material light. Yours respectfully,

M. W. GIBBS[3]

British Colonist (Victoria, Vancouver Island), 24 October 1859.

1. Amor de Cosmos.

2. The London *Times*, which was founded in 1788 as the nonpartisan *Times and Universal Daily Register*, emerged as a leading metropolitan daily during the nineteenth century. It was noted for its extensive domestic and foreign news coverage and innovations in newspaper print technology. The politically powerful John Thadeus Delane edited the *Times* from 1841 to 1877. During his tenure, the paper openly expressed proslavery views, reflecting growing public disillusionment with the West Indian emancipation experiment. The *Times* believed slave emancipation to be a dismal failure and blamed the decline of the sugar-based

Caribbean economy on the indolence of black workers. H. R. Fox Bourne, *English Newspapers: Chapters in the History of Journalism*, 2 vols. (New York, N.Y., 1966), 1:254–68, 279–85, 354–62, 2:164–65, 333; Lorimer, *Colour, Class and the Victorians*, 122–23; *TL*, 19, 23 December 1857.

3. Mifflin Wistar Gibbs (1823–1915) was born into a Philadelphia, Pennsylvania, free black family, the son of a Methodist minister. He learned the building trade as a teenager, eventually becoming an independent contractor. By the time he was twenty-six years old, he had risen to prominence in the city's black community. Gibbs nurtured a lifelong belief in the importance of self-help; he was active in the Philomathean Institute (a literary society) and in the underground railroad. At several meetings during 1848–49, he denounced slaveholders, the American Colonization Society, and political and social discrimination. In early 1850, Gibbs broadened his antislavery activities by accompanying Charles Lenox Remond on a speaking tour of western New York State. While traveling, he learned of the California gold rush; he followed earlier fortune seekers west and in September settled in San Francisco, where he prospered as a partner in a clothing firm. At the same time, he continued his reform activities, joining other leading blacks in issuing a strong civil rights statement in 1851, participating in black state conventions in 1854, 1855, and 1857, and backing and editing an abolitionist journal, *Mirror of the Times*, in 1855. In 1857 he joined other disfranchised blacks in refusing to pay a poll tax.

By 1858 Gibbs had tired of struggling against American racism and left California for Victoria, Vancouver Island. There he established another successful store, sold real estate, organized a black militia, read law, and became the black community's chief spokesman. In 1866 he won election to the first of two terms on the city council and served as chairman of the city's finance committee. Despite his successes in Victoria, Gibbs became dissatisfied with the local political situation. In 1869 he returned to the States, where in 1871 he embarked on a new career as a lawyer in Little Rock, Arkansas. A loyal Republican until 1908, he held appointive offices, including that of U.S. consul at Tamatave, Madagascar (1898–1901). On his return to Little Rock, he wrote his autobiography (1902). Throughout his Arkansas years, Gibbs fought for black rights and supported Booker T. Washington's advocacy of black advancement through industrial training and the acquisition of property. *DANB*, 258–59; Simmons, *Men of Mark*, 597–602; Tom W. Dillard, "'Golden Prospects and Fraternal Amenities': Mifflin W. Gibbs's Arkansas Years," *AHQ* 35:307–33 (Winter 1976); *NSt*, 6 October 1848, 15 June 1849, 8 February 1850 [5:0802, 6:0014]; *PF*, 28 September 1848 [5:0797]; *IC*, 5 December 1849 [6:0233, 0234]; *Lib*, 3 July 1857 [10:0748]; *DM*, May 1859.

80.
Peter Lester to [William Still]
30 November 1859

The fresh perspective gained by living in a different culture led many black abolitionists to reexamine the black American experience and, occasionally, to offer advice to black friends in the United States. After enduring years of abusive treatment in Philadelphia, then in California, black merchant Peter Lester settled in Victoria, Vancouver Island, in 1859. The freedom and equality he found there contrasted with his earlier life. Lester's distance from the American scene brought him to a new understanding about the antislavery movement at home. In a 30 November 1859 letter to black Philadelphia acquaintance William Still, Lester offered four remedies to the failure of American abolitionism. First, black and white abolitionists should rejuvenate the free produce movement, which Lester believed would weaken slavery by making it unprofitable. Second, black Americans should emigrate rather than submit to a steady drumbeat of degradation in the United States; Lester suggested Africa but noted that the specific site was not as important as the act of securing a more favorable homeland. Third, white abolitionists should yield the leadership of the movement to blacks, who were more familiar with the feelings of slaves. Fourth, Lester encouraged black Americans to improve their economic conditions through self-help and hard work. By making themselves more valuable economically to whites, blacks could lessen racial prejudice. Lester's advice to American blacks reached a sizable audience when it was copied in the *Weekly Anglo-African*. Pilton, "Negro Settlement in British Columbia," 48; *WAA*, 12 May 1860 [12:0698].

VICTORIA, Vancouver Island
Nov[ember] 30, 1859

MUCH ESTEEMED FRIEND:

I have just been looking over a pamphlet which you had the kindness to send me; I would have acknowledged the receipt of it before, but it came just after I had left San Francisco for this my present home.

It has always been a source of wonderment to me why the friends of the slave did not refrain from the use of such articles as are cultivated by him. I fully agree with you that the great work of emancipation will be complete when we make slave labor unprofitable. I also believe that colored men must emigrate; whether it be to Africa or not, they must be the judges; but go we must, if we ever expect to be on a par with the more favored of mankind. It may appear very strange to hear me express myself thus, knowing as you do that ten years ago I advocated remaining here where we were. But why should I shut my eyes to the truth? It is no evidence to my mind that a man is right because he never changes; had I remained in Philadelphia until now, it is likely that my views would have undergone little or no alteration; but having got this far, I think I can judge of the good effects of emigration. Now, if Africa holds out good inducements to colored men, then I say go. I have no doubt the day will come when she will be one of the greatest countries on the globe; she is rich in all the minerals that are so valuable to the civilized world. You do not say much for America when you speak of the different countries that have acknowledged the independence of Africa (Liberia);[1] it is not more than reasonable to suppose that she would have been first on the list; but alas! to her shame be it spoken, I am afraid she never will. This whole matter of free labor I am sorry to say has not been rightly looked into by the colored people. They say, "Well, what little sugar, rice, tobacco, &c., I use, will never bind the fetters any tighter on the slave"—never thinking for a moment that their neighbors are doing the same thing, and are excusing themselves in the same way; and thus the slaveholder is enabled to sell at a high-figure his ill-gotten gain, otherwise there is no doubt the cause would have been advanced twenty-five percent at least. I know the friends of the colored man have been toiling for many years, and we feel grateful for what they have done, we will praise them for their good deeds, and at the same time thrash them for their short-comings.

The anti-slavery society has been too much like the political parties. The great question with them is, what can we make by this or that move? The money must be all kept in the family; we will give our agents liberal salaries to travel through certain counties where they are well known, or rather where there is no danger of being mobbed, and at the same time sure of getting a good collection. Now one word about this family. It is well known that there has been a few leading men and women who have had the control of the so-called Radical Abolition Society[2] from the beginning, and they are likely to hold their positions to the end of their natural lives. Do not understand me as finding fault with them for being radical, for I do not see how any one can be otherwise on the subject of slavery. But this is the ground upon which I arraign them: they have not given away for the colored man as he has become, or fitted himself for the work. I am one of the many who believe that colored men should be the agents in every anti-slavery office in the United States. In a word, I believe the white men (and women, too) should give the leadership of this reform into the hands of colored people, for the best reason, namely, it is our cause: therefore we claim to be the proper exponents of it. We know our wants, from the fact of having to wear the yoke. I look at the matter somewhat after this wise: The true friend of the colored man should not scruple to give way when he knows there are colored men qualified to lead; but I am sorry to say they appear of late years to think more of the loaves and fishes, than they do about the slaves' freedom. This may be a grave charge, but nevertheless I believe it to be true. It has become a question with me whether all this talking (by either colored or white) is of any benefit to the slave. The teaching we have received for the last thirty-five years has, I am afraid, caused a large majority of the colored people to think that if they learn to speak well on the subject of anti-slavery, it is all they need, especially when they have the privilege of traveling about the country on steamboats and railroad cars—now and then becoming martyrs, in the way of being dragged out and otherwise maltreated.

Now, the best and surest way to gain their rights in this particular, is, to seek to have the same interest in these different conveyances as the white man has. Do you tell me that if the colored men were conveying their wheat, corn, oats, barley, rye, potatoes, &c., together with their live stock and dry goods, as the more favored are doing to the different markets, they would not be treated better? The day that we are engaged in business matters, so as to bring about a commercial intercourse between the whites and ourselves, that very day our chains will commence to fall. I think as Horace Greeley[3] does with regard to our elevation—that one well cultivated farm will do more to remove the prejudice against us, than all the fine-spun speeches that we often hear. When we look closely into our history for the last twenty years, you will find we have done little but talk. This may be all well enough in its place, and I would not say one word if we did not talk to the exclusion of everything else.

Now, dear friend, I must bring this letter to a close. Hoping to hear from you soon, I remain, yours as ever,

(Signed)
PETER LESTER[4]

Weekly Anglo-African (New York, N.Y.), 12 May 1860.

1. Although Liberia declared its independence in 1847, the U.S. Congress refused to grant diplomatic recognition to the country long after many European nations had done so. No serious action was taken until 1862, when the exigencies of war forced Congress to extend formal recognition to the black nation. James A. Padgett, "Ministers to Liberia and their Diplomacy," *JNH* 22:50 (January 1937).

2. The Radical Abolition party and its kindred organization, the American Abolition Society, were organized in 1855 by Lewis Tappan, Gerrit Smith, William Goodell, and other former members of the defunct American and Foreign Anti-Slavery Society. Both the party and the society were envisioned as vehicles for political abolitionism. The party established a new antislavery organ, the *Radical Abolitionist*, held national conventions in Boston and Syracuse, and received encouraging endorsements from black abolitionists Frederick Douglass and James McCune Smith, but it failed to attract widespread abolitionist support. Although the New York-based party nominated Gerrit Smith for president and Samuel McFarland of Virginia for vice-president in 1856, it polled only 165 votes in the entire state. By 1858 both the party and the society were moribund. M. Leon

Perkal, "American Abolition Society: A Viable Alternative to the Republican Party," *JNH* 65:57–69 (Winter 1980); Wyatt-Brown, *Lewis Tappan and Evangelical War*, 332–34.

3. Horace Greeley (1811–1872) was born in New Hampshire and entered the publishing business at age fourteen. He settled in New York City and in 1841 founded the *New York Tribune*. The *Tribune*, which reflected Greeley's Whig politics and opposition to slavery, became the most influential American newspaper of the mid-nineteenth century. In 1872 Greeley ran unsuccessfully against Ulysses S. Grant for the presidency. *DAB*, 7:528–34.

4. Peter Lester (1814–?) was born in Philadelphia and studied at Clarkson's Hall, a local abolitionist school, during the late 1830s. He operated a successful bootmaking shop in the city during the following decade. Lester joined the antislavery movement in the late 1840s, served on the executive committee of the Pennsylvania Anti-Slavery Society (1849), and attended several black state conventions. He settled in San Francisco about 1851 and established a second bootmaking shop with Mifflin W. Gibbs, another Philadelphia black. Lester accumulated considerable wealth; he donated to charitable causes and helped finance the construction of the San Francisco Athenaeum, a local black library company. But the racism he encountered—he was the victim of racial violence, and his daughter Sarah was expelled from the city's public schools because of her race—prompted him to move to Victoria, Vancouver Island, in 1858. Together with Gibbs, he opened a large provisions house, which was rivaled only by the Hudson's Bay Company store. He again accumulated a small fortune. As one of the leaders of the local black community, he participated in local politics and battled racial prejudice. And he urged American blacks to emigrate. Lester helped raise funds for black contraband in Philadelphia during the Civil War. Although Lester and Gibbs ended their long partnership in 1864, the former continued to reside in Victoria after the Civil War. United States Census, 1850; *WAA*, 19 November 1859, 5 January 1861; *PF*, 28 January 1847, 16 February 1854; *NSt*, 10 November 1848, 2 February, 2 November 1849; *Philadelphia City Directory*, 1846–50; *San Francisco City Directory*, 1852–58; Pilton, "Negro Settlement in British Columbia," 43, 48, 55, 60, 94, 201, 209; Kilian, *Go Do Some Great Thing*, 15–16, 18, 135–36, 140.

81.
Speech by Osborne P. Anderson
Delivered at the Coloured Regular Baptist Church, Toronto, Canada West 9 April 1860

John Brown, the abolitionist martyr who led the ill-fated raid at Harpers Ferry in October 1859, played a part in building the Canadian antislavery mystique. Brown traveled to Canada in the spring of 1858, seeking support among fugitive slaves there. A "quiet" gathering of thirty-four blacks and twelve whites, known as the Chatham Convention, resulted. Information about what happened at Chatham is sketchy, but following Brown's raid and subsequent execution by the state of Virginia, the convention—and Canada's role in the raid—became legend. Canadians followed the story of the raid and Brown's execution with great interest. Although many deplored Brown's violent tactics, most considered him a true martyr; numerous memorial services and sympathy meetings were held in Canada West to eulogize Brown and to raise funds for his family. Osborne P. Anderson, a black Canadian who participated in the Harpers Ferry raid, recounted his experience at a memorial service held by blacks in Toronto. His address included an appeal for funds to publish a personal account of the raid. The following year, Anderson published *A Voice from Harpers Ferry*. Winks, *Blacks in Canada*, 267–70; Fred Landon, "Canadian Negroes and the John Brown Raid," *JNH* 6 : 174–82 (1921).

It has been my privilege to be present, under the command of Capt. John Brown, at the capture of Harper's Ferry.[1] I[2] had the honor of being one of the party that took prisoner Col. Washington, who, notwithstanding the illustrious name he inherits, submitted passively to a few volunteers; and I received from his hands the sword presented by Frederick the Great of Prussia to General George Washington, and with which Capt. Brown commanded his men at Harper's Ferry.[3] Gov. Wise[4] and his confederates of the slaveholding States were eager to have the world believe that the slaves of that section of the country refused to join in the insurrection—that they were pressed into service, and as soon as an opportunity offered itself they deserted their liberators. This false and wilful statement, which has been echoed and re-echoed by the pro-slavery press North and South, originated with Gov. Wise after he returned from Harper's Ferry, and was no doubt offered to the chivalrous inhabitants of Richmond to allay their panic. But Providence has been pleased to spare my life, to enable me to transmit to posterity a truthful history of that short but desperate struggle; and I thank God for this opportunity of

8. Osborne P. Anderson
Courtesy of Library of Congress

bearing testimony that the second Attucks[5] in the cause of freedom has forfeited his life. Yes, the first man whose blood was spilled to cleanse the soil of that country from the stain of slavery—the first martyr to liberty, I say (and may my words echo throughout this continent), *was a slave of that very neighborhood.* He fell at the beginning of the conflict, in the early part of the day.[6] I saw him offer up his life, and was by his side during his dying moments, until his spirit leaped from its earthly tenement to the world on high; and to-night he is seated on the right hand of God, in the full enjoyment of that great blessing for which he died—*liberty.* There were seven vacant places by his side, which were soon occupied by that noble little band which was captured by the banditti, *pre-judged and condemned, and then tried and executed.* You know too well how the apostle of liberty, Capt. John Brown, met his fate, and those who followed him have proven to the world that they were worthy to fight under the banner of such a chief. On the 16th of March terminated the bloody chapter; and, in the words of another, "It was the highest tribute Virginia could offer to true virtue, and the gallows on which the martyrs of liberty were wafted into heaven is now as sacred as the cross!"

Mr. Anderson related how that he was on his way to New York, Boston, and other cities in the United States, and having arrived at Rochester on the 3d inst., dame rumor too eagerly flew through the city with the intelligence that one of Captain Brown's men was in town; and the U.S. Deputy Marshal being apprised thereof, was cautiously endeavoring to arrest him, which compelled him to take passage on the underground railroad for this land of liberty. His mission to the States was for the purpose of publishing a history of the struggle at Harper's Ferry,[7] the facts of which he alone is in possession of. He said that it is known to all that colored men shared the perils of the Revolutionary War, as well as that of 1812, '14, and '15; and even here, in suppressing the Canadian rebellion, colored men took an active part. But is there anything in history to prove it? It was for this reason he urged the colored people to aid him in snatching from oblivion the heroism of the colored men who so nobly seconded the efforts of the immortal John Brown.[8] He hoped that the citizens of Toronto would liberally respond to his request, and with the assistance he expects to receive from other places he would ere long be able to issue a work so much needed by our race.

Weekly Anglo-African (New York, N.Y.), 28 April 1860.

1. John Brown (1800–1859) was a failed businessman and religious zealot who earned an antislavery reputation during the free-state proslavery struggle in the Kansas territory and, by 1859, considered himself God's providential instrument to end slavery. On 16 October 1859, Brown led a twenty-one-man cadre in an attack on the federal armory at Harpers Ferry, Virgina, hoping to incite a slave

insurrection. The effort failed after two days, and Brown was caught, tried, and hanged in Charleston, Virginia, on 2 December 1859. Before Brown went to the gallows, he delivered a stirring antislavery speech, which insured his martyrdom and pushed the North and South toward violent confrontation over slavery. Stephen B. Oates, *To Purge This Land with Blood: A Biography of John Brown* (New York, N.Y., 1970); Jeffery Rossbach, *Ambivalent Conspirators: John Brown, the Secret Six, and a Theory of Slave Violence* (Philadelphia, Pa., 1982).

2. Osborne Perry Anderson (ca. 1830–1872) was born to free black parents in West Fallowfield, Pennsylvania. As a young man, he attended Oberlin College and learned the printing trade. He immigrated to Chatham, Canada West, with the Shadd family in late 1850 and established himself in the printing business. Anderson slowly involved himself in the *Provincial Freeman*, serving as one of the paper's subscription agents in 1856 and becoming its printer and general assistant during 1857–58. On 29 July 1857, Anderson wrote a notable editorial for the *Freeman* that condemned the begging activities of some black settlements in the province. He charged begging agents with self-interest and argued that begging merely provided a rationale for slavery and colonization. During investigations of the Dawn settlement in 1857, Anderson served as secretary of several meetings and sat on the committee charged with regaining control of the Dawn lands for the fugitives. In 1858 he met abolitionist John Brown, attended the 8 May Chatham Convention at which Brown revealed his plans to provoke a slave uprising at Harpers Ferry, Virginia, and decided to join the raid. Prior to the assault, Anderson spent three weeks in secret military training in Virginia. Brown gave Anderson a prominent place in the raiding party. When it became apparent during the actual raid that Brown's party faced certain defeat, Anderson escaped and returned to Canada West. He wrote and published *A Voice from Harpers Ferry* (1861), a reminiscence of his experiences in John Brown's raid. Anderson served as a noncommissioned officer in the Union army during the Civil War. After the war, he settled in Washington, D.C., where he died on 13 December 1872. Osborne Perry Anderson, *A Voice from Harpers Ferry: A Narrative of Events at Harpers Ferry* (Boston, Mass., 1861; reprint, Freeport, N.Y., 1972), 28, 30–31; Bearden and Butler, *Shadd*, 195–97, 201–2, 206; Dannett, *Profiles of Negro Womanhood*, 1:157; Hill, *Freedom-Seekers*, 21, 23, 214; *PFW*, 7 June 1856, 24 January, 28 February, 8 August 1857 [10:0516, 0781]; *DANB*, 15.

3. Lewis Washington (ca. 1825–1871), a Virginia planter, was the great-grandnephew of President George Washington. An army colonel, he served as a staff aide to Governor Henry A. Wise of Virginia. Washington was held hostage by John Brown's meager force during the raid at Harpers Ferry but was eventually rescued. The sword referred to by Anderson was apparently given to George Washington by Frederick II, also called Frederick the Great, the Hohenzollern king of Prussia from 1740 to 1786. *ACAB*, 6:385; Oates, *Purge This Land with Blood*, 290–91.

4. Henry A. Wise (1806–1876), a Virginia lawyer and politician, served as a member of the House of Representatives (1833–44), where he was known for his dogged defense of southern interests, then as minister to Brazil (1844–47). As governor of Virginia (1856–60), he was responsible for repressing John Brown's raid at Harpers Ferry. Wise wielded considerable influence in the Democratic

party during the 1850s. Although initially ambivalent about secession, he served as a general in the Confederate army during the Civil War. *DAB*, 20:423–25.

5. Anderson refers to Crispus Attucks (ca. 1723–1770), a mulatto of black and Natick Indian ancestry, who was born in Framingham, Massachusetts. He apparently was the escaped slave of Deacon William Brown of Framingham. On 5 March 1770, Attucks led a protest against the presence of British soldiers in Boston. When the protesters taunted the British guards stationed at the Custom House, the soldiers fired into the crowd, killing Attucks and four others. Like the other victims of the Boston massacre, Attucks became a revolutionary symbol to American colonists. *DANB*, 18–19.

6. Anderson refers to Dangerfield Newby (ca. 1811–1859), one of five blacks who participated in John Brown's raid at Harpers Ferry, Virginia. Born in Virginia to a slave mother and a Scottish father, Newby was freed by his father at the time he died. Newby settled on a farm near Harpers Ferry, worked as a blacksmith, and married a slave from a nearby plantation; they had seven children. He joined Brown's raid because his family was threatened with sale to the South and because Brown needed Newby's familiarity with the area's geography. He entered Brown's base camp at the Kennedy farm outside of Harpers Ferry in late August 1859. When Brown and his raiders marched into the town during the evening of 16 October, Newby and two others were chosen to guard the Shenandoah Bridge, a railroad and wagon trestle spanning the Potomac River. An assault by a Maryland militia company forced Newby and the others from the bridge the following morning. Newby became the first of Brown's men to be killed; his body was savagely mutilated but was disinterred in 1899 and taken to North Elba, New York, where it was buried near Brown. *DANB*, 473; Quarles, *Allies for Freedom*, 86; Oates, *Purge This Land with Blood*, 276, 290, 296, 316.

7. In 1861 Anderson published *A Voice from Harpers Ferry: A Narrative of Events at Harpers Ferry*. Mary Ann Shadd Cary helped him prepare the manuscript for publication. The volume recounted the planning and course of John Brown's attempt to capture the federal arsenal at Harpers Ferry in western Virginia and provoke a slave uprising. He departed from accepted thinking about the raid by blaming Brown's compassion for prisoners taken during the raid as the primary reason for its failure and by denying the claim that blacks in the area of Harpers Ferry did not join the assault. Anderson, *A Voice from Harpers Ferry*; Bearden and Butler, *Shadd*, 195–97, 201–2, 206.

8. Five blacks joined John Brown's raid. They included Anderson; John A. Copeland, a freeborn, twenty-three-year-old Oberlin College student from North Carolina; Lewis Leary, Copeland's uncle, who left a wife and child living in Oberlin; Shields Green, a fugitive slave known as the "Emperor," who joined Brown after accompanying Frederick Douglass to a meeting with Brown in August 1859; and Dangerfield Newby, a former slave from the Harpers Ferry area, who hoped to liberate his family from a nearby plantation. Leary and Newby were killed during the fighting. Copeland and Green were hanged with Brown. Anderson escaped and wrote a memoir of the episode. Oates, *Purge This Land with Blood*, 224–350; Quarles, *Blacks on John Brown*, xii, 34, 40.

82.
The John Anderson Case

John Anderson to Edmund Walker Head
1 October 1860

William P. Paton to John Anderson
17 January 1861

The last slave extradition case to come before the Canadian courts severely tested the Canadian haven. It involved John Anderson, a fugitive slave from Missouri who murdered Seneca T. P. Diggs, a white neighbor of his master, during his flight to Canada West. In April 1860, seven years after the incident, Anderson was discovered and arrested near Brantford. He was released, then rearrested on a warrant sworn out in Detroit. Because Anderson had committed murder, there appeared to be a real chance that he might be surrendered to American authorities. On 1 October, Anderson petitioned Governor-General Edmund Walker Head with details of his escape and a request that he not be extradited. Late in November, Anderson was brought before the Court of Queen's Bench (Toronto) on the murder charge. In mid-December, the court recommended extradition. But Anderson's counsel, Samuel B. Freeman, appealed to the Court of Common Pleas. In the weeks that passed while they awaited a decision, the case became a cause célèbre in the transatlantic antislavery movement. Black Canadians and the Anti-Slavery Society of Canada sponsored mass rallies. The Toronto *Globe* called daily for Anderson's release. English and Scottish abolitionists petitioned key colonial officials and, on 15 January 1861, obtained a writ of habeas corpus on Anderson's behalf from the Court of Queen's Bench (London). Two days after the writ was granted, Scottish abolitionist William P. Paton wrote to Anderson for the Glasgow New Association for the Abolition of Slavery, praising the writ and expressing the society's belief that the fugitive would soon be freed. On 16 February, the Court of Common Pleas acquitted Anderson on a technicality arising from a defect in the warrant. Robert C. Reinders, "The John Anderson Case, 1860–1: A Study in Anglo-Canadian Imperial Relations," *CHR* 56:393–415 (1975); Winks, *Blacks in Canada*, 174–75.

Brantford, [Canada West]
1*st October*, 1860

To His Excellency the Governor-General of Canada, &c., &c.:

The petition of the undersigned, John Anderson,[1] confined in the jail of the county of Brantford, humbly showeth:

9. John Anderson

That your petitioner was born in the state of Missouri, one of the United States of America.

That to the best of his knowledge he is of the age of thirty years. That he was the slave of Burton and another, in the year one thousand eight hundred and fifty-one. That the plantation of Burton and the other, was within about thirty miles from the plantation of Samuel Brown. That in the last mentioned year your petitioner was married to one Maria Tomlin, who was the daughter of Tomlin, who had purchased his liberty from his master. That about six weeks before he formed the determination to come to Canada, for the purpose of obtaining his freedom, he was sold and transferred by said Burton, and his partner, to one MacDonnell, who lived about thirty miles distant from your petitioner's wife.

That your petitioner had always felt that he had a right to his freedom. That he had never done anything to forfeit his liberty, and was not subject to any restraint through crime.

That he might lawfully use any means within his power to obtain his liberty, and with that object ran away from MacDonnell. That he went to his wife, who was a slave of, and lived with Samuel Brown, and consulted with her as to his intentions, and she concurred with him in his views, with an ultimate hope as to herself, and a young child, then about eight months old, the issue of our marriage, obtaining their liberty.

That while he was then there he was pursued, but escaped. That in his course to Canada he had to pass the plantation of Seneca F. T. Diggs, and that while passing it he was accosted in nearly the manner mentioned in the evidence transmitted to your Excellency. That he made the excuse of wishing to go to Givens's so that he, Mr. Diggs, would allow him to pass.

That this will be manifest, or otherwise, your petitioner could have had no reason, under the evidence, for attempting to escape.

That when said Diggs refused to allow this excuse for not having a pass, your petitioner found it necessary to make his escape, and endeavoured to do so.

That your petitioner was run down, having been chased for nearly an hour in a circle, and at the moment he was looking for success, Mr. Diggs appeared before him.

That he could not turn, his pursuers being at his heels with clubs, and being borne on by the first impulse, he dashed against said Diggs with an open knife, with which he had threatened his pursuers, as will appear from the evidence of Phil, hereto annexed, which is nearly true; whether your petitioner struck with it more than once, he cannot recollect; but whatever sudden impulse bid, that he did to obtain his liberty. That your petitioner was imprisoned for about the space of three weeks last spring, on this charge; but as no one appeared against him, he was discharged. That another warrant was issued against him for his arrest for the same crime on the third day after his discharge, on an information quite insufficient, as he is advised.

That your petitioner was not aware of such second warrant having been issued until he was arrested in the town of Simcoe, about two weeks since. That he had gone from Caledonia, where he resided at the time of his arrest, in the hope of obtaining employment at his trade as a mason. That your petitioner therefore prays that your Excellency will be graciously pleased to withhold an order delivering your petitioner to the authorities of the state of Missouri, inasmuch as by the British law he is entitled to be free there, and the evidence shows that he only used such force as was necessary to maintain that freedom there; and your petitioner, as in duty bound, will ever pray.

(Signed)
his
JOHN X ANDERSON
mark

(Witness)
A. S. REACHIE, Deputy Jailor

John Anderson, *The Story of the Life of John Anderson, a Fugitive Slave*, ed. Harper Twelvetrees (London, 1863), 29–31.

Religious Institution Rooms
Glasgow, [Scotland]
Jan[uary] 17, 1861

Mr. John Anderson
Toronto, [Canada West]
DEAR SIR:

At a meeting of the Ladies' and Gentlemen's Committees of this Association,[2] held on the 14th instant, it was unanimously resolved that a letter should be sent to you, expressing their cordial sympathy with you in your present trying position, and their strong hope that you may not be allowed to be removed from British ground.

If the general voice of the people of Great Britain can prevent your rendition to those who seek your destruction, you may give thanks to the Almighty for a prospect of a speedy deliverance from a dreadful uncertainty.

While we greatly lament the existence of a system that placed you in the unhappy position which left no other alternative than to take away life to preserve your own, as well as to secure your God-given right of freedom, it is, at the same time, most repugnant to our feelings, as Christians and as men, to contemplate the inhuman vengeance of the slaveholder, if you should be delivered up to him.

In accordance with these feelings we are sending a memorial to the Right Honourable Lord Palmerston, Prime Minister of Great Britain,[3] on your behalf, and we think there is much ground of hope for you in the writ of habeas corpus which has just been granted by the Court of Queen's Bench in London.

We are satisfied that slaves are not contemplated in the Ashburton Treaty.[4] But supposing any law or treaty exists by which your rendition could be demanded, it is not in consonance with the feelings and sentiments of this country. Such a treaty should not be acted on nor complied with. Its provision would be alike at variance with humanity and religion, and it ought, therefore, to be immediately abrogated. When the people of this free country lift up their voice in a righteous cause, they will, by the Divine blessing, be found too strong for the advocates of injustice and oppression.

We believe that in this case you will find in the British public a bulwark that will successfully defend you from the assaults of your cruel and wicked enemies.

Commending you to the care and protection of the Almighty, the just and merciful God, whose ear is ever open to the cry of those that put their trust in His loving kindness and tender mercy, We remain, your faithful friends, Signed, on behalf of the Association,

WILLIAM P. PATON[5]
Chairman of the Meeting

Globe (Toronto, Canada West), 15 February 1851.

1. John Anderson (ca. 1831–?) was born in Howard County, Missouri, the son of slave parents. His mother was the property of Moses Burton, a tobacco farmer, and his father fled slavery for South America during Anderson's infancy. At age seven, Anderson was separated from his mother when she was sold by Burton. In 1850 Anderson married a slave named Maria Tomlin, who lived on an adjoining farm belonging to Samuel Brown, and within a year, they had a child. In mid-August 1853, Anderson was sold to another farmer named McDonald, who lived thirty miles away; the separation from his family so infuriated Anderson that he fled slavery. On the third day of his escape, when he was being pursued by Seneca T. P. Diggs, Anderson stabbed and killed Diggs during a struggle. Anderson fled to Chicago but soon moved to Windsor, Canada West, where he gained a rudimentary education during a brief enrollment in Henry Bibb's school for fugitive slaves. He also took the name John Anderson, having been known as Jack Burton in his slave days. Six months later, Anderson received a suspicious letter, which he believed was sent by a slave agent and which claimed his wife wanted to meet him in Detroit. It prompted his flight to Chatham, Canada West.

During 1859, while living in Caledonia, Canada West, he was betrayed by a friend, who informed a local justice of the peace about the Diggs killing. The magistrate ordered Anderson arrested and entertained American extradition requests. From the moment of his arrest in mid-April 1860, Anderson became a cause célèbre in British and American antislavery circles. His release that fall was regarded as a triumph for abolitionist forces because it reaffirmed long-standing British policy toward the extradition of fugitive slaves, which provided that no individual could be sent back to the United States for committing an act that was not against Canadian law. Because Canadian law prohibited slavery, his lawyer argued that Anderson killed Diggs in self-defense. The freed Anderson was feted at abolitionist meetings throughout the Canadas.

In mid-spring 1861, Anderson was invited to England by groups active in the English component of his legal defense. Anderson arrived there in June 1861 and found that a John Anderson Committee had been formed to raise funds for him. During the summer of 1861, Anderson attended numerous antislavery meetings and narrated the events of his life. In December he enrolled in the British Training Institution near Corby, where he spent the next year. The committee eventually decided that Anderson should move to Liberia, believing his settlement there would "furnish unequalled opportunities for . . . prosperity." Anderson was given five acres of land and sailed for Liberia on 24 December 1862, accompanied by black abolitionist Alexander Crummell. Anderson's narrative, *The Story of the Life of John Anderson, Fugitive Slave* (London, 1863), was published after he left for Liberia. John Anderson, *The Story of the Life of John Anderson, Fugitive Slave*, ed. Harper Twelvetrees (London, England, 1863); Thomas Henning to L. A. Chamerovzow, 20 December 1860, Thomas Henning to Joseph A. Horner, 5 July 18[61], Joseph A. Horner to L. A. Chamerovzow, 17, 20 July 1861, British Empire MSS, Rhodes House Library; British and Foreign Anti-Slavery Society Minutes, 4, 14 January, 8 February, 5 July, 6 December 1861, 1 May 1863, British Empire MSS, UkOxU-Rh; *ASRL*, 1 February, 1 May, 1 June 1861; R. C. Reinders, "Anglo-Canadian Abolitionism: The John Anderson Case, 1860–1861," *RMS* 19:72–97 (1975); Blassingame, *Slave Testimony*, 353–58.

2. Paton refers to the Glasgow New Association for the Abolition of Slavery and its women's auxiliary, the Glasgow New Ladies' Anti-Slavery Association. The GNAAS was organized in 1850 by a conservative, anti-Garrisonian group within the Glasgow Emancipation Society. About the same time, the new women's auxiliary emerged from the women's auxiliary of the parent organization. The GNAAS sponsored Harriet Beecher Stowe's 1853 visit to Scotland. Although the GNAAS lapsed into inactivity by 1857, the women's auxiliary remained the focus of female antislavery activity in Glasgow throughout the decade. C. Duncan Rice, *The Scots Abolitionists, 1833–1861* (Baton Rouge, La., 1981), 112, 148–49, 156–57, 188.

3. On 10 January 1851, the Executive Committee of the Glasgow Emancipation Society forwarded a memorial to the British Colonial Office urging that Anderson be freed. A few days later, the Glasgow New Association for the Abolition of Slavery sent a similar petition to Henry John Temple, Lord Palmerston (1784–1865), then prime minister of Britain. Palmerston made it clear that he believed Anderson to be innocent of murder and instructed Edmund W. Head, the governor-general of the Canadas, not to surrender the fugitive. A Conservative, Palmerston had served in Parliament and as foreign secretary during the 1830s and early 1840s. As prime minister (1855–58, 1859–65), he supported vigorous enforcement of international agreements outlawing the slave trade and pursued a

policy of strict neutrality during the American Civil War. Minutes of the Glasgow Emancipation Society, 10 January 1861, UkGM; *ASRL*, 1 March 1861; *DNB*, 19:496–513.

4. Paton rejects proslavery claims that extradition provisions in Article X of the Webster-Ashburton Treaty (1843) allowed slave catchers to return fugitive slaves from the British North American Provinces.

5. William P. Paton, a Glasgow commercial broker and city alderman, became a vice-president of the Glasgow Emancipation Society in 1839. During the early 1850s, he broke with the society's Garrisonian faction and helped found the more conservative Glasgow New Association for the Aboliton of Slavery. Paton hosted Calvin and Harriet Beecher Stowe during their 1853 visit to Glasgow. Rice, *Scots Abolitionists*, 45, 52, 178, 211.

83.
Martin R. Delany to James Theodore Holly
15 January 1861

On the eve of the Civil War, two emigration alternatives competed for the attention of North American blacks. Martin R. Delany urged blacks to resettle in West Africa; James Theodore Holly favored Haiti. Delany explored the Niger Valley region of West Africa in late 1859 and signed a treaty with local chiefs that provided land for a settlement of North American blacks. He spent the following year in Britain, seeking financial and moral support for his scheme. Delany returned to Chatham, Canada West, in late 1860 and began lecturing on "Africa and the African Race" and recruiting black Canadian emigrants. About that time, he began a correspondence with Holly that debated the relative advantages and disadvantages of West African and Haitian immigration. Delany's 15 January 1861 letter to Holly expressed his major reservation about Haitian immigration—it was controlled by James Redpath, a white man. To Delany, this demonstrated a sycophantic attitude toward the white race on the part of the Haitian government. He asked why black emigrationists like J. Dennis Harris, Henry Highland Garnet, or Holly himself had not been chosen to lead the movement. Holly responded on 29 January. He thought it foolish to question Haiti's black militancy, noted that Harris and Garnet were not appointed by Haiti because they had not visited the black nation, and confided that black clergyman William P. Newman had initially been chosen but had to forfeit the position because of legal troubles. According to Holly, the Haitian government then decided that the next best thing was to appoint Redpath, "a faithful and devoted *white* man." Holly's letter apparently ended the correspondence. Within a matter of months, the emigration impulse yielded to black enthusiasm for the Civil War and the prospects of emancipation. Miller, *Search for Black Nationality*, 198–228, 250–58; *WAA*, 9 February 1861 [13:0300].

King Street Hut
Chatham, C[anada] W[est]
Jan[uary] 15th, 1861

Rev. J. Theodore Holly
Rector St. Luke's Church
New Haven, Conn[ecticut]
Rector Holly, my Dear Sir and Friend:

Your kind favor without date in reply to mine written at Liverpool, England, the 11th ult., has just come to hand for which I thank you.

My duty and destiny are in Africa, the great and glorious (even with its defects) land of your and my ancestry. I cannot, I *will not* desert her for all things else in this world, save that of my "own household,"[1] and that does not require it, as it will thereby be enhanced.

I have nothing to say against Haytian emigration, except that I am surprised that in the face of the intelligent *black men* who favor it, two of whom have been to that country and one to Jamaica (yourself, Mr. Harris,[2] and Mr. Garnet),[3] the government would appoint *over them*, to encourage black emigration, a white man,[4] thereby acknowledging negro inferiority, and the charge recently made against them by Dr. J. McCune Smith, that according to their estimation, "next to God is the white man."[5]

You know that this is *not prejudice* in me, as my sentiments endorsed by yourself, and the whole Cleveland Convention are, that the black man should act and do for himself, just as the white man, under like circumstances, would be justifiable in doing—*self reliance*, on the principles of a Black Nationality. These sentiments conceived in my youth, many years ago, matured in manhood, promulgated in a public document in the great Emigration Convention at Cleveland, Ohio, U.S., in 1854,[6] have since been proclaimed in tones unmistakable upon the high seas, in the capitol of Liberia,[7] for twenty-five hundred miles along the coast of Africa, in the Metropolis of the world, and through the United Kingdom until they "career against the wind," reverberating from the top, and rippling the surface of Ben and Loch Lomond,[8] the home and haunt of the gallant highlander, where the slogan of the Campbell's and Cameron's, and of the McDonald's[9] have long since been heard, against the strife of battle and the groans of death. If thus uttered amidst my greatest friends and supporters of my scheme and adventure, I cannot I say be charged with prejudice when I object to a black government appointing over black men, a white, when black were competent to act and no policy requires the appointment of a white. I object to white men in such cases, getting all the positions of *honor* and *emoluments*, while the blacks receive only the *subordinate* with little or no pay! I maintain this position as necessary to self respect, and treat with contempt the idea, that it makes no difference in such cases whether the person be white or black, while black men are still occupying inferior positions in the midst of a people who deny their equality in all the relations of life.

My next exception is, that I fear that this movement is too precipitous—not sufficiently *matured*. There should be no *haste*, as such, at the commencement of such movements (and this is the commencement of yours), and all attempts at excitement should be avoided.

Neither do I regard or believe Mr. Redpath, the Haytian Government Agent, nor any other white man, competent to judge and decide upon the destiny of the colored people or the fitness of any place for the bettering of their condition, any more than I should be a Frenchman to direct the destiny of Englishmen. If they have not now, if we with our claim and boasted equality have not yet reached the point of competency to judge and decide for ourselves, what, when, and where is best for us to do or go, but must needs have white men to [act] for us, then indeed are we wholly unfit to fill the places they claim for us, and should be under white masters.

Do not misunderstand me as objecting to your movement, as conflicting with mine or ours. This is not the case, as we desire no promiscuous or general emigration to Africa (as the country needs no laborers, the[s]e everywhere abounding industriously employed in various occupations), but select and intelligent people to guide and direct the industry, and promote civilization by the establishment of higher social organizations and the legitimate development of our inexhaustible commerce, which promises not only certain wealth to us, but all the rest of the world, besides the certainty of thereby putting a stop to the infamous slave trade, with a reflex influence upon the [if] possible more infamous American slave trade. In this we desire not to shed their (the Southern monsters') blood, but make them shed their tears. I am, my dear Mr. Holly, very sincerely your friend and co-laborer in the cause of our race, for God and humanity,

M. R. DELANY

Planet (Chatham, Canada West), 21 January 1861.

1. In January 1861, Delany's Chatham, Canada West, "household" consisted of himself, his wife Catherine, and five children. Catherine Richards, a Pittsburgh mulatto of mixed black and Irish ancestry, married Delany in 1843. The marriage produced seven children between 1846 and 1864. Adhering to Delany's concept of race pride, they named their children after great black men or, in the case of a daughter, Ethiopia, after an ancient African nation. Children born by 1861 included Toussaint L'Ouverture (b. 1846), Charles Lenox Remond (1850–1879), Alexander Dumas (b. 1854), Saint Cyprian (b. 1856), and Faustin Soulouque (b. 1858). Later children were Placido Rameses (b. 1862) and Ethiopia Halle (b. 1864). Catherine and six children survived Martin Delany, who died in 1885. Ullman, *Martin R. Delany*, 45, 50–51, 292; *DANB*, 170, 172.

2. J. Dennis Harris, a black Cleveland plasterer, was active in the Ohio State Anti-Slavery Society during the 1850s. He endorsed black immigration to the Caribbean at the 1858 black state convention in Cincinnati and devoted the next few years to promoting various emigration plans. Harris initially supported proposals by Congressman Francis P. Blair and others to establish a black colony in Central or South America. In June 1859, he organized the short-lived Central American Land Company in Cleveland to encourage and assist black settlement in that region. Later that year, he promoted Jamaican immigration before black audiences in Chatham, Canada West. Harris visited the Caribbean in the summer of 1860 and published his observations in *A Summer on the Borders of the Caribbean Sea* (1860), a volume that drew attention to the emigration cause. After returning to the United States, Harris became a lecturer and recruiting agent for

James Redpath's Haytian Emigration Bureau. He toured Canada West for the HEB during the spring and summer of 1861. During the fall of that year, he settled in Haiti. Once there, he assumed responsibility for directing the "Flight Colony" near St. Marc, regularly corresponded with the *Pine and Palm*, and (with James Theodore Holly) attended to HEB affairs in the black nation. Frank P. Blair, Jr., *The Destiny of the Races of this Continent* (Washington, D.C., 1859), 34 [11:0433]; J. Dennis Harris to Frank P. Blair, Jr., 29 January, 22 February 1860, Blair-Lee Papers, NjP [12:0463, 0506]; *PP*, 8 June, 3, 17 August, 22 October 1861, 16 January, 29 May 1862 [13:0587, 0592, 0675, 0692, 0870]; Miller, *Search for Black Nationality*, 237–38, 240; Howard H. Bell, ed., *Black Separatism and the Caribbean, 1860* (Ann Arbor, Mich., 1970), 11–14, 67–184.

3. Henry Highland Garnet (1815–1882) was born in Maryland to slave parents. In 1824 Henry's father, George Garnet, led ten family members to freedom in the North, finally settling in New York City. Between 1826 and 1833, Garnet received an intermittent education in New York's African Free School, enrolled in the High School for Colored Youth, and met Rev. Theodore S. Wright, a leader of New York's black community, who became his mentor. In 1835 Garnet, Alexander Crummell, Thomas Sidney, and four other blacks were driven from Rev. William Scales's integrated Noyes Academy in Canaan, New Hampshire, by an antiintegration mob.

After graduating from Beriah Green's Oneida Institute in 1839, Garnet began an eight-year residence (1840–48) in Troy, New York, where he ministered to a black congregation (the Liberty Street Presbyterian Church), edited two short-lived reformist newspapers (the *Clarion* and the *National Watchman*), and founded a school for black children in nearby Geneva. Garnet also assisted the suffrage struggle of New York blacks and was active in Liberty party deliberations. His considerable reputation as an antislavery reformer was enhanced at the Buffalo National Convention of Colored Citizens (1843), when he gained notoriety as a strident black voice for freedom by delivering his "Address to the Slaves of the United States"—a speech generally perceived as a call to arm slaves. A supporting resolution was narrowly defeated.

In 1850 Garnet's support of the free produce movement brought an invitation from Henry and Anna Richardson, leaders of the British movement, to lecture on the subject. After a two-year stay in Great Britain, Garnet accepted an appointment by the United Presbyterian Church of Scotland to serve as a missionary in Jamaica. During his stay on the island (1853–55), Garnet established two elementary schools for black children and a female industrial school, which was directed by his wife, Julia. Illness forced Garnet to resign his post. He returned to New York City in 1856 to pastor the Shiloh Presbyterian Church. Although Garnet had spoken positively about limited black emigration as early as 1849, he institutionalized these beliefs in the late 1850s by helping found the African Civilization Society—an organization that did not repudiate a black presence in the United States but encouraged black missionary work and entrepreneurship in Africa. He traveled to England again in 1861 to promote the society. During the Civil War, Garnet recruited black troops for the Union army and afterwards became the first black man to preach a sermon in the House of Representatives (1865).

In 1868, after serving the Fifteenth Street Presbyterian Church in Washington, D.C., and directing African Civilization Society efforts to educate newly freed black children, he was appointed president of Avery College, a black college established by influential Pittsburgh cotton merchant Charles Avery. Garnet returned to his Shiloh pastorate in 1870. He was appointed United States minister to Liberia in 1881. Joel Schor, *Henry Highland Garnet: A Voice of Black Radicalism in the Nineteenth Century* (Westport, Conn., 1977), 3–217; Martin Burt Pasternak, "Rise Now and Fly to Arms: The Life of Henry Highland Garnet" (Ph.D. diss., University of Massachusetts, 1981), 1–269; *DANB*, 252–53.

4. Delany refers to James Redpath (1833–1891), who was appointed commissioner of emigration by the Haitian government in 1859. Redpath emigrated from Scotland to Michigan in 1850. A correspondent for Horace Greeley's *New York Tribune* during the 1850s, he covered the Kansas affray and published an account of his travels through the South, *The Roving Editor, or Talks with Slaves in the Southern States* (1859). Redpath's emerging abolitionism was strengthened through his acquaintance with John Brown, about whom he wrote several books. After accepting an appointment from Haiti, he worked tirelessly for black emigration, opening the Haytian Emigration Bureau in Boston, writing *A Guide to Hayti* (1860), and publishing the *Pine and Palm*. Immediately after the Civil War, he served as commissioner of education in Charleston. In 1868 Redpath founded the Boston Lyceum to encourage and manage public lectures and performances. He later became interested in the Irish question. *DAB*, 15:443–44.

5. Delany quotes from a 5 January 1861 letter written by black abolitionist James McCune Smith to Henry Highland Garnet. The letter, which was reprinted in the 12 January issue of the *Weekly Anglo-African*, was highly critical of African and Haitian immigration ventures and urged Garnet, a leading emigrationist, to abandon the movement. Smith claimed that the Haitian people believed themselves to be inferior to whites; to make his point, he repeated a supposed Haitian proverb: "Next to God is the white man." *WAA*, 12 January 1861 [13:0190].

6. In August 1853, Martin R. Delany, leader of the emerging black emigration movement, issued a call for a national convention that would consider ways to encourage development of a flourishing black nation outside of the United States. The first National Emigration Convention met at the Prospect Street Congregational Church in Cleveland, Ohio, on 24–26 August 1854. Although 101 delegates attended the gathering from eleven states (including four slave states) and Canada West, most participants were from the western states; only three delegates came from areas east of Pittsburgh. Unlike other antebellum black conventions, one-third of the delegates were women. The convention adopted a Declaration of Sentiments and heard Delany's seven-hour-long presentation of the "Report on the Political Destiny of the Race on this Continent"; both outlined Delany's philosophical position on emigration and black nationalism. The delegates also established a permanent administrative organization, known as the National Board of Commissioners, to oversee the movement and to assist the development of specific emigration plans. Three study committees were formed to acquire the information necessary to develop such plans. Miller, *Search for a Black Nationality*, 134, 137–57, 160–61, 166, 175, 194.

7. Delany refers to Monrovia, which was named after President James Monroe.

Founded by American free blacks in 1822 at Cape Mesurado on the West African coast, it became the capital of the newly established Republic of Liberia in 1848. J. B. Webster and A. A. Boahen, *A History of West Africa* (New York, N.Y., 1967), 147–50.

8. Ben and Loch Lomond refer to a mountain and lake located about twenty-five miles northwest of Glasgow, Scotland.

9. The Campbell, Cameron, and McDonald families were three of the largest and most widespread highland clans in central Scotland's early history.

84.
Speech by William J. Watkins
Delivered at the Hall of the Mechanics' Institute, Toronto, Canada West
25 June 1861

By the late 1850s, black voters in Canada West were turning to Reform party candidates. The Conservative government had disappointed blacks on specific issues, including integrated schools, railroad corruption, and the John Anderson extradition case. Blacks had also acquired the political understanding and confidence to move away from the tradition of voting for Conservative candidates simply to demonstrate their loyalty to the crown. They recognized in the Reform party a political philosophy more compatible with their reform interests. Reform party leaders understood the importance of the black vote and solicited black support for their candidates. William J. Watkins, John J. Cary, and other black abolitionists spoke at a Reform party rally held at the Mechanics' Institute in Toronto on 25 June 1861. The assembly condemned the Conservative government and endorsed the candidacies of Adam Wilson and Toronto *Globe* editor George Brown for the Canadian legislature. Winks, *Blacks in Canada*, 214–15, 282–86.

Whereas, we believe that a wise and virtuous government is necessary to the development of a country's greatness, and, whereas, agitation is the life-blood of all reform movements, therefore, *Resolved*—That all intelligent and honest men, all true conservators of the public weal, should stand shoulder to shoulder with the opponents of the present corrupt ministry; and we earnestly recommend our brethren throughout the Province to give the Reform party, in the present contest,[1] and in all future contests, which they believe to be right, their united votes and their active co-operation. We hate tyranny in all its forms, and whenever and wherever we can hurl against it an effective blow, in God's name, and in the name of humanity, shall that blow be given, for GOD WILL DEFEND THE RIGHT.

He[2] said he was well-known to the colored electors of this city and also to those throughout the country, and he was confident that they would be ready to acknowledge that he would not advise them to do anything that would not be for their good. (Cheers.) He then went on to refer to the many acts of corruption of the present Government in Canada, and said he was glad to learn that many of the colored electors of this city who had formerly voted for their supporters, were determined to vote for Mr. Brown and Mr. Wilson[3] at the coming election. (Cheers.) He was glad to learn it, and he trusted his brethren throughout the country would give their support to Opposition candidates, in order that the present corrupt Administration might be driven from power and honest men put in their places. (Great cheering and cries of "We will; we will.") He knew what they would do in Toronto. (Renewed cheering.) He then referred in most amusing terms, which created much amusement, to the attempt of Mr. Isaac Buchanan[4] to secure the support of the colored electors of Hamilton, by giving them a donation of $10 for their church. Speaking of the celebrated Anderson case, he said he did not think it was necessary to remind them of the noble stand which Mr. Brown had taken through the columns of the *Globe* in favour of Anderson's liberation.[5] (Cheers.) On the other hand, he did not think he needed to remind them of the action of the base and unrighteous Government in this case. (Cries of "It is not required.") He was aware they had known it, and he knew that the iniquitous action of the Government had brought Mr. Brown many friends. (Cheers.) After relating a number of most amusing anecdotes, he concluded a very eloquent speech by calling upon all present, whether Reformers or Conservatives, to record their votes early on the first day of the election, and resumed his seat, after reading the resolution, amid much cheering.

Globe (Toronto, Canada West), 27 June 1861.

1. Watkins refers to the Liberal-Conservative coalition government of Sir George-Etienne Cartier (1814–1873) and Sir John A. Macdonald (1815–1891), which administered the Canadas from 1857 to 1862. The Cartier-Macdonald ministry emerged victorious in the 1861 general elections that Watkins discusses; the Reform party suffered significant losses, including the defeat of George Brown and Adam Wilson in Toronto. J. M. S. Careless, *Brown of "The Globe,"* 2 vols. (Toronto, 1959–63), 2:43–48.

2. William J. Watkins (ca. 1826–?) was born to free black parents William and Henrietta Watkins in Baltimore. Although a machinist by trade, he occasionally taught at the Watkins Academy, his father's school, during his early years. Watkins moved to Boston in the late 1840s and became involved in the underground railroad and civil rights efforts. He petitioned for the formation of black militia companies, pushed for the integration of the city's public schools, and advocated immediate abolitionism. Watkins broke with the Garrisonians during the early 1850s over the issue of political antislavery; he was active in Free Soil and Republican politics throughout the remainder of the decade and labored diligently for the extension of black suffrage in New York State. After his break with the Garrisonians, he aligned himself with Frederick Douglass, moved to Rochester in 1853, and served as associate editor of *Frederick Douglass' Paper* for several years. About the same time, he began to actively participate in the women's rights and black convention movements. Watkins became known for his antislavery lecturing after he embarked on an extended tour of New York and Pennsylvania in the spring of 1854. Lecturing almost daily, he acquired a reputation as a tireless, articulate, and persuasive antislavery speaker. His antislavery critique was di-

rected primarily at the free black community, which he admonished for its petty factionalism bred by separate institutions. Watkins lamented the apathy among northern blacks and urged them to be more militant in defense of their civil rights. He even advocated slave violence in certain circumstances. Toward the end of the decade, Watkins abandoned his earlier antiemigrationism and joined the Haitian immigration movement. During 1861 he toured Canada West and Michigan as an agent for James Redpath's Haytian Emigration Bureau, recruiting prospective settlers. Watkins, who had earlier antagonized black Canadians with his persistent opposition to Canadian immigration, now attracted even sharper criticism. After the demise of the HEB in late 1862, he returned to Boston, studied law, and became one of the first blacks admitted to the legal profession in the United States. He died in the early 1870s. *FDP*, 24 March, 9, 16 December 1853, 24 March, 14, 28 April, 30 June, 14 July, 18, 25 August, 8 September 1854, 12 January, 2, 16, 23 February, 2 March, 4, 25 May, 24 August 1855 [9:0011]; Blassingame, *Frederick Douglass Papers*, 2:442n; Graham, *Baltimore*, 126–30; Gardner, "William Watkins," 623; *Proceedings of the Colored National Convention, Held in Philadelphia, 1855* (Salem, N.J., 1856), 6, 10; *Lib*, 7 September 1849, 20, 27 December 1850, 28 November, 5 December 1851, 9 January 1852, 13 May 1853, 23 August 1861 [13:0706]; *PP*, 13 July, 7, 21 September 1861, 4 September 1862 [13:0742, 0766]; *WAA*, 9, 30 November, 14 December 1861 [13:0844, 0886, 0943]; *TG*, 27 June 1861 [13:0603].

3. Sir Adam Wilson (1814–1891) emigrated from Scotland to Canada in 1830 and began the practice of law. In 1859 he became the first Toronto mayor elected by direct vote. After serving briefly in the legislative assembly during the early 1860s, Wilson entered upon a judicial career, sitting on the Court of Queen's Bench (1863) and serving as chief justice of the Court of Common Pleas (1878) and the Court of King's Bench (1884). *MDCB*, 895–96.

4. Isaac Buchanan (1810–1883), a Scottish merchant, immigrated to Canada in 1830. He became a prominent businessman in Toronto and was involved in matters ranging from politics to railroad development to the Free Church movement. An independent Conservative politician, he represented Toronto (1841–43) and Hamilton (1857–65) in the legislative assembly of the Canadas. Buchanan wrote several widely read pamphlets on economic and political issues. *DCB* 11:125–31.

5. From 28 November 1860 to 18 February 1861, George Brown of the Toronto *Globe* wrote sixteen editorials about the Anderson fugitive slave case. He denounced Anderson's arrest, rebutted arguments favoring the arrest, outlined the moral and legal principles that compelled Anderson's release, criticized court orders to return Anderson, and advocated Anderson's release on bond during the prolonged proceedings. Brown also favored British judicial intervention in the case in the event that Canadian authorities failed to rule in Anderson's behalf. When Anderson was freed by Canadian courts, Brown vigorously applauded the decision. *TG*, 28 November, 3, 5, 11, 17, 22, 24, 25 December 1860, 11, 28, 30 January, 2, 11, 12, 13, 18 February 1861.

85.
Speech by William J. Watkins
Delivered at the Sayer Street British Methodist Episcopal Church, Toronto, Canada West
12 August 1861

As support for Martin R. Delany's Niger Valley venture waned, the idea of Haitian immigration began to attract attention among black Canadians. Black agents for James Redpath's Haytian Emigration Bureau—Isaac N. Cary, William Wells Brown, William J. Watkins, John B. Smith, and others—crisscrossed Canada West and the Maritimes recruiting emigrants. Watkins's tepid endorsement of the Haitian scheme suggests the tenuous manner in which many blacks approached the issue. A prominent black abolitionist, he had earlier opposed black emigration; but by the early 1860s, he advocated limited black resettlement in Haiti, although he recognized that emigration was no panacea for blacks. On 12 August 1861, Watkins addressed the monthly meeting of the Provincial Association for the Education and Elevation of the Colored People, a Toronto black organization devoted to improving the educational opportunities available to the race. The session, which convened in the black Sayer Street BME Church, began with a prayer by local black clergyman Nelson H. Turpin. After members conducted some pending business, Watkins rose and spoke as part of the association's annual lecture series. Blacks, he noted, needed to emphasize mind over place. Emigration alone could not solve black problems; it must go hand-in-hand with self-help and moral uplift. After Watkins completed his address, the members of the association tendered him a vote of thanks. Miller, *Search for Black Nationality*, 243–46; *FDP*, 17 February 1860; *Lib*, 30 August 1861 [13:0713]; Simpson, "Negroes in Ontario to 1870," 236–38, 885–86; *WAA*, 5 May 1860.

Mr. W. J. WATKINS, who was present by invitation, proceeded to address them upon the duties and responsibilities of colored men. These he presented in a strong and forcible manner. He was not present, the lecturer remarked, to deal in intangible abstractions, but concrete realities. One reason why the colored people of the United States and of the Canadas occupied no higher position than at present is, said he, because they do not fully realize and appreciate the responsibilities which rest upon them, and which must be discharged by them, if at all. We have been more intent upon projecting new theories than in reducing old ones to practice. A theory may be as bright as the wing of an archangel, but it will be of but little advantage to the world unless it is made to sweep the circle of human activities. It must be crystalized into practical life. It does no good to form good societies, and there let the professed object of their formation evaporate into windy speeches and flaming resolutions and pic-nic excursions. Hannibal said to his army when the battle trembled to begin, "It is not words that are now wanted, but action." His men leaped into battle, and by united, determined action routed the enemy.[1] Let this be our motto, said Mr. Watkins, if we would rise superior to the crushing circumstances which affect us. The startling events which crimson the wing of the present hour bid us "awake, arise, or be forever fallen!" Our long-tried friends, the Abolitionists, can no more act for us and do our duty, than they can breathe and eat and die for us. We must act well our part by the assumption and performance, to the best of our ability, of all the duties and responsibilities of fully developed manhood. Too long already have we slumbered. What! sleep amid the thunder and smoke of battle, when the events of the next hour may seal our destiny! Are we so infatuated, when white men are sacrificing their earthly all? The man among us who can sleep now, would sleep, if possible, amid the thrilling clangor of the resurrection trumpet. Recently, all Europe shook beneath the majestic tread of Garibaldi.[2] He comes across the ocean to fling his ponderous weight against the Bastile of American despotism.[3] Let not our inertia, our indifference to the tragic realities of the hour fill his throbbing heart with sorrow, and chill his noble nature with the apathy of despair.

After presenting the claims of the Educational Association,[4] the lecturer alluded to the fact that many of the colored people of the United States, and some in the Canadas, are seriously contemplating emigration to Hayti. He had a word to say on this subject. It is useless to emigrate anywhere until we emigrate from the gross faults which have characterised us. Hayti needs men of the right stamp—those who feel the dignity of manhood, and act accordingly. Those who go thither should not be deceived. Hayti wants no one who will be an incubus upon her energies. Those who, in the States or in the Canadas, have been like driftwood washed down the stream, will be a valuable acquisition nowhere, and it is well for the struggling and noble people of Hayti if they remain where they are. Some are going there to be generals, judges, and legislators; some to marry their daughters to "Haytian noblemen." *Mirabile dictu*! But all such, if they go, will be, and ought to be, disappointed. Let solid men, who will help Hayti as well as themselves, go thither to develop the resources of the country, and thus conduce to its prosperity, and the government and the people will receive them with open arms. Remember that we go there to continue the warfare against that monstrous abomination, American Slavery—not to get rid of the conflict. The interests of Hayti, and of colored America, cannot be dissociated. We go to help to promote those interests, and therefore help the millions of our race who will continue in the United States until Gabriel shall sing the requiem of the world's departed spirit.[5] The speaker still held to the views he had always advocated concerning the expatriation of the race. It could not be effected. President Geffrard did not contemplate it.[6] We remain, then, on this continent in close proximity with our oppressed brethren, who may yet summon us from the land of the pine and palm, to help strike down the haughty Assyrian.[7] Onward, then, and upward! Never dream of peace until the last slave shall clank the last chain, and from among brutes and creeping things leap upon the broad and enduring platform of humanity, and swell the grand hallelujah of redeemed millions!

Liberator (Boston, Mass.), 30 August 1861.

1. Watkin's reference to Hannibal (247–183 B.C.) was taken from book three, part three of the *Histories* of the Greek historian Polybius, which recounted Hannibal's speech to the Carthaginian army on the eve of his victory over the Romans at Cannae in 216 B.C.

2. Giuseppe Garibaldi (1807–1882), a leader of the Italian unification movement, was exiled after the fall of the Roman Republic in 1849. He arrived in New York in the summer of 1850 but shunned publicity rather than supporting antislavery as Watkins hoped. In 1851 Garibaldi traveled on an American passport in the Pacific, returning to Europe from New York in 1853. Denis Mack Smith, *Garibaldi* (London, 1957), 48–56.

3. The Bastille, a fortified prison in Paris and a symbol of the tyranny of the French monarchy, was besieged during the popular uprising of 14 July 1789. Watkins equates the Bastille to the institution of slavery.

4. The Provincial Association for the Education and Elevation of the Colored People, a Toronto black organization dedicated to improving the educational opportunities available to the race in Canada West, was organized in May 1859 and continued to operate into the early 1860s. It was led by President Alexander T. Augusta, Isaac N. Cary, and Wilson R. Abbott. The association opposed separate schools, sponsored an annual lecture series, and attempted to organize a black convention in Toronto (1861). Simpson, "Negroes in Ontario to 1870," 236–38, 885–86; *WAA*, 5 May 1860.

5. Gabriel is one of four archangels named in Hebrew tradition. His name frequently appeared in nineteenth-century references to the end of the world.

6. Fabre Nicolas Geffrard (1806–1878), a popular Haitian general, overthrew Emperor Faustin Soulouque and became president of the Republic of Haiti on 23 December 1858. After taking office, he began an aggressive immigration policy by inviting black Americans to settle in Haiti and inducing his government to pay for their passage and to provide board and lodging during the initial period of settlement. But as Watkins suggests, Geffrard did not envision the expatriation of all black Americans to Haiti. Although Geffrard ruled more responsibly than his predecessor, lingering political corruption and economic misery caused chronic popular unrest and attempted coups. Threatened by a rebellion at Port-au-Prince, Geffrard resigned on 13 March 1867 and fled to Jamaica. Perusse, *Historical Dictionary of Haiti*, 41; Miller, *Search for Black Nationality*, 236–37.

7. The Assyrians, a warlike, ancient Semitic people, were known for their repression of captive nations. Watkins, who here uses the term to refer to southern slaveholders, likely draws this reference from a prophecy in Isaiah 10:5–12.

86.
George Cary to James Redpath
26 August 1861

Several hundred black Canadians settled in Haiti during the fall and winter of 1861–62. They came from throughout the province, recruited mostly by local emigration societies based in Toronto, Hamilton, St. Catharines, and Chatham. One of these, the Cotton Growing Association, was organized in Chatham during August 1861 by George Cary, Mary Ann Shadd Cary's brother-in-law. The association included twelve to fifteen local blacks who, distressed by growing white Canadian racial prejudice, planned to immigrate to Haiti and cultivate cotton on shares. Cary's letter to James Redpath, the chief figure in the Haitian movement, explained why the members chose to immigrate and what they expected to do in Haiti. Redpath replied in the 14 September issue of the *Pine and Palm*. He promised to arrange the best possible accommodations but cautioned that, with the coming of the Civil War, most available steamers had been pressed into military service. Cary and several other association members emigrated in December. Ironically, Cary died three weeks after his arrival in Haiti. Winks, *Blacks in Canada*, 164–65; *PP*, 14 September 1861 [13:0754], 13 February 1862.

DRESDEN, C[anada] W[est]
Aug[ust] 26, 1861

Mr. James Redpath
Sir:

I take the liberty to address you a few lines respecting the intentions of a few of us in this locality. I am forming a club of twelve or fifteen good, reliable men in this neighborhood, for the purpose of going to Hayti this ensuing fall, to cultivate cotton. Some of them have been engaged in that business down South, consequently have some knowledge of the *modus operandi*. The rest of us are farmers who have no practical knowledge of cotton-growing, but from theory and experience in other agricultural matters, flatter ourselves we can soon make a hand in the cotton field. At all events, we are willing and anxious to make a trial in the land of the palm.

Our intention at present is to go out in October (by which time we hope the number of applicants will justify your employment of a steamer), and take charge of some gentleman's estate somewhere in the neighborhood of St. Mark or Cape Haytian,[1] and go immediately into the cultivation of cotton on shares. While that is in progress, we can have an opportunity to make our selection of a permanent location.

Most of us have comfortable homes in this country, where the laws are equal; but we have a damning prejudice to contend against, which it, in our opinion, will take all coming time to eradicate. It is a preventative to a just and equal administration of the British Constitution.

As an instance of its violation, I will inform you how we are treated in school matters in this township, and the same state of things exists in many other places. The Government has established a system of common schools, in which the law says all children may be taught.[2] A-1-1 means those of the black man as well as those of the white, even in the United States, that land of rotten democracy, but especially everywhere under the British Constitution, which knows nothing of complexional distinctions. Well, I live in a township some fifteen miles in length, and some parts four or five miles in breadth. The municipal authorities have the power of forming all the school districts or divisions in the townships. There are some twelve or thirteen school divisions in my township, from all of which the children of colored people are excluded, save one. All our lands are taxed for school purposes, while all our children are actually excluded. Now, bear in mind, we are scattered all over the township, and have but one school-house erected for us; and that at one end of the township. You see the inconvenience labored under by those even four or five miles off, saying nothing about those from eight to twelve miles away. They will not permit a colored child to enter a school where white children are taught. The feeling seems to be gaining ground, for when I came into this section fifteen years ago, they all went to school together, and many of them to a colored master. Such a thing would not be tolerated now for a moment.

In view of this state of things, many are talking about leaving, and some of us think it will be no sacrifice to get half the value of our places, pull up stakes, and accept of President Geffrard's liberal offer.[3] War or no war, by Divine permission, if your emigration scheme continues until October, we expect to be on hand, for we are not among those who are willing to abide the "good time coming" on this continent.

Since I commenced this epistle, W. P. Newman has arrived here, and has held two meetings, one of which I attended. He endorsed everything said by you in the Guide,[4] relative to the country; but the people, from President Geffrard down to the humblest citizen, are a treacherous, debauched set, such as no person having any pretensions to decency or self-respect ought to carry his family among. Polygamy and nudity among men, women and children were to be met with at almost every turn. A people entirely incapable of self-government, &c. Well, in a word, he used every means to set the people against the Haytians; but I am happy to say that his temperament is too well known here to effect anything with any one in this neighborhood who entertained any serious notion of emigrating. From present prospects, I think there will be quite an emigration from this Western section of Canada this fall.

Within a few days a letter has been received here from Jordan Jones,[5] who left this place in May for Hayti; and one from David Cooper,[6] who left Windsor about the same time. Both of them are much pleased, and say "Come, one and all." Mr. Jones writes for his wife to come out with us without fail—that everything is right.

You will please answer this, and say what number would justify you in chartering a steamer. Respectfully yours,

GEORGE CARY

Pine and Palm (Boston, Mass.), 14 September 1861.

1. St. Marc is a small Haitian town located on the Gulf of Gonaïves. Cap-Haïtien, situated on the northern coast, is Haiti's second largest city. These two towns were frequently the destination of black immigrants to Haiti during the early 1860s.

2. Cary refers to the Common School Act of 1850.

3. Cary refers to the invitation of President Fabre Geffrard for black Americans to immigrate to Haiti.

4. *A Guide to Hayti* was published in 1861 by the Boston-based Haytian Emigration Bureau, an agency sponsored by the Haitian government. The *Guide*, a promotional device meant to encourage black emigration from the United States and Canada West to Haiti, was edited by the bureau's director, James Redpath. James Redpath, ed., *A Guide to Hayti* (Boston, Mass., 1861).

5. Jordan Jones, a resident of the Dawn settlement, sailed to Haiti from Boston on 31 May 1861. After visiting sites throughout the black nation, he eventually settled near St. Marc. *PP*, 15 June 1861, 7 August 1862.

6. David Cooper, a free black, was born in Virginia and reared in Pennsylvania. He and his wife, a former slave, later settled in Windsor, Canada West. During the early 1850s, he became involved with the Colored Industrial Society at Sandwich. The Cooper family left Canada West in the spring of 1861 and resettled in Haiti. Drew, *North-Side View of Slavery*, 334–35; Hill, *Freedom-Seekers*, 74; *PP*, 14 September 1861, 3 July 1862.

87.
Mary Ann Shadd Cary to Robert Hamilton
17 September 1861

Mary Ann Shadd Cary was never enthusiastic about emigration sites other than Canada. She found Haitian immigration especially offensive, particularly after the black republic hired white abolitionist James Redpath to organize its emigration effort. Redpath established a newspaper (the *Pine and Palm*), wrote a promotional pamphlet (*A Guide to Hayti*), and enlisted several agents—including black abolitionists Isaac N. Cary, William J. Watkins, and William Wells Brown—to canvass Canada West for potential emigrants. Cary was their chief critic. She charged that Haiti was unhealthy and unchristian, that it did not compare with the Canadas, and that Redpath and his agents were more concerned about their wages than black advancement. She likened Redpath to white colonizationists and slave traders. Her 17 September 1861 letter to Robert Hamilton is one of a series she wrote opposing Haitian immigration. Hamilton published these in his *Weekly Anglo-African*, a New York City-based black newspaper and a leading antiemigration journal. Cary's advocacy of permanent resettlement in Canada, support for Delany (but not his plan for West African repatriation), and objection to Haitian immigration suggests the complexity of the emigration issue for black abolitionists. *WAA*, 17, 28 September, 19, 26 October, 9 November, 14 December 1861 [13:0777, 0836, 0886, 0976].

CHATHAM, C[anada] W[est]
Sept[ember] 17, 1861

EDITOR OF THE *ANGLO-AFRICAN*
Sir:

It is extremely gratifying to know that the *Anglo-African* is in circulation once more.[1] When your paper "went out," the hopes of many who had only heard of it, seemed to die out with it; some feared, they felt by intuition, that mischief was brewing, and very soon the evil was upon them in its full extent.

In the interim between the transfer of the *Anglo-African* to other parties, and its republication, a doubtful scheme, said to be for the benefit of our much injured people, was securely matured and established, (?) and it has been pushed forward since with a vigor, a tact, and an unscrupulousness worthy of the early days of African Colonization.

For the first time, since colored men dared to canvass questions relating to their own interests, have they been summarily silenced—forbidden to examine both sides; for the first time have they been ruthlessly thrust out of doors by those loud in their protestations of friendship. Not only is this a part of our sad history, but in the prosecution of the Haytian Colonization scheme we have, singularly enough, all of the old, and worn out, and repudiated arguments, about the extinction of our race—extinction from 20 persons in 1620, to 4,000,000 in 1861[2]—the invincibility of American prejudice, common schools, churches, railroads in 1832, and 1861 in States and Canada, the incongeniality of climate—do we not live as long, and are we not as exempt from disease as the pure Anglo-Saxon? We have, with these, the exhumed relics of the past; the fact that instead of unrelenting Democrats and heartless slaveholders, to push forward this new crusade against the best interests of the free colored man of the North, we have Republican abolitionists, and fugitive-slaves, who "once upon a time" fought bravely against the dogma, and when its now cherished arguments were the pet theme of the fierce negro-hater and the great conservators of slave property.

To be consistent, would it not be well for the new colonizationists to dig up their buried foes, and make haste and repair the damage to this generation by singing in praise of their wise foresight, and their genuine friendship for our poor people?

But not only has another doubtful scheme been "set a going," now said to be in the name of the black man, and for black men, but for the first time in thirty years have our Pennington's, our Delany's, our Smith's and Downing's, been cuffed into silence. Our so-called enemies, the African Colonizationists, never dared to stigmatize as drunkards, "renegade negroes" and snobs, those of our men known to be among the leaders in defence of our rights.[3]

Once upon a time brave men and women, with bugle-blast of indignation, spoke out against wrong when it was perpetrated against black men, at the risk of the halter. I have a dim recollection of one noble man called William Lloyd Garrison in such peril. Why cannot there be a strong and manly voice now? There has been a slight murmur down about Boston; why does not somebody speak OUT? Are not you recording the dead and buried? Do not you tell of the disappointments? Are not Mother Holly and John Anthony, and numbers, gone? and have not Mrs. Monroe, Sarah Underwood, Mason, and others spoken?[4]

We are told that only the lazy complain, or tell tales; what must we say of the dead? they tell no tales.

I have spoken of the sins of commission, in the interim of your silence—now for the sins of omission during the same period: The American Union is one scene of distraction; must we for the same cause be at our wits ends? There never was a time when the colored man could afford to be more calm and collected than now. There are thousands of "contrabands"[5] peering cautiously from your forests, and skulking behind corners in your cities, not knowing in their extremity what way to go, and finally starved into asking the first "massa," though it may be an enemy, "am this Canada?" Has the North Star, the old beacon light, gone out, that these men cannot be encouraged to follow the ONLY safe and long tried road to freedom? It seems to me that the devil is let loose to hound the poor fugitives for a season. From the faith of our people being in God, and the North Star, a James Redpath and a star never before heard of, a South Star, now dazzle with a sort of "foxfire" light,[6] to the neglect of our duty to God, our true interests, and our obligations to humanity.

Who, may I ask, is this James Redpath, in the hollow of whose hand lies trembling the destiny of our people? This man, who by a species of moral jugglery, beyond my stupid comprehension, has succeeded in throwing glamour over the optics of all our friends, and who has made the bitter pill of colonization sophistry long since discarded by them, a sweet morsel to hundreds of devotees of the god *Palm*?[7] In all sincerity I ask this question. In a letter to the *Planet* of our town, Mr. Redpath complains that the Rev. W. P. Newman, whom he calls a "renegade negro," is trying "to destroy whatever influence my anti-slavery service may have given me with Americans of African descent."[8]

What have been and what are the anti-slavery services of Mr. Redpath, upon which he claims to be entitled to influence with—colored Americans of African descent.[9] In the name of common sense and common fairness what are they? When Wm. Lloyd Garrison, Lewis Tappan, Wendell Phillips,[10] Gerrit Smith, and a host of such speak of services rendered, we know what they mean—they have looked in the opposite direction from Mr. Redpath for thirty years—they toiled in our cause when it cost something, and their noble sacrifices, crop out into a harvest of gratitude from the entire colored people. But what has Mr. Redpath done?

Is it this leading men and women by reason of their ignorance and credulity, to untimely graves in the island of Hayti?

A child, say our wise educators should be at least five years old before he should be instructed in the rudiments; it may be that moral precosity entitles Mr. Redpath to some consideration, but keeping in view the fact that John Brown has not been dead three years, and that Redpath for all practical anti-slavery purposes, must have been borne since then—I cannot forbear again asking what special labor since he came into being entitles him to teach, to dictate a destiny? and to make of no effect—the work of friendly laborer's who toiled hard heretofore? Who can tell!

Brother Newman tells you we have some excitement here in Canada, so we have, the most of it, is caused by the advocacy of this Haytian scheme about which I write. It is not that the thousands about which you have heard so much, are going to leave and throw off their British allegiance, but that a few agents, using the name of Brown[11] and talking Redpath have, by working upon an imaginative and hitherto overworked people, set afloat stories of genial skies, plenty to eat, and little to do, and have, at the same time, plied vigorously the old story about their attaining to the "greatest height" among the whites; these rigmaroles, which they have been scattering broadcast for a few months, have caused excitement. Before then, our people in Canada, thanked God for this Asylum; they went on adding to their statement, and were surely removing the local obstacles to unbounded progress.

A few have gone to Hayti, a few more will go; a few will go to Jamaica; already some have written back from Hayti who are not too well pleased; some more await further advice. Another record of deaths and they will fall back into their former industrious persevering ways; that is what this new scheme will come to here, and in the meantime, in answer to the question of a good woman in Wisconsin, who writes to know "what to do with the contrabands," we say over here, send them to Canada! Send them over here as you have done thousands before, who now sit in the shade of their own noble forests, with none to disturb them. Canada is just as large as ever, and though they may suffer a little for a time, the people will rally to help them; our government will give them one hundred acres of land, in a region where now she gives the same to Norwegians, Irish, English and Scotch, and where colored men can get it if they will, or they can settle down readily, and do well in this western section, with friends and relatives to help them. Do not let the question be asked what shall we do with them? send them along.

M. A. S. CARY

Weekly Anglo-African (New York, N.Y.), 28 September 1861.

1. The *Weekly Anglo-African* began publication in New York on 23 July 1859. Edited by Thomas Hamilton, who simultaneously published the monthly *Anglo-African Magazine*, it reflected a growing self-identification by blacks as both African and American. One of the most militant of black papers, it emphasized the necessity of resisting oppression. The paper functioned as an advocate for slaves and free blacks and as a liaison among northern black communities; a host of unofficial correspondents regularly reported black news from their locale. By late 1860 it also displayed increased interest in Haitian and African immigration. In mid-March 1861, Hamilton was replaced by George Lawrence, Jr., New York agent for James Redpath's Haytian Emigration Bureau. Under his guidance, the paper was rechristened the *Pine and Palm* and became the official organ of Redpath's bureau. It continued to be published through 1862. By early August 1861, another *Weekly Anglo-African*, financed in part by James McCune Smith, began publishing as an antiemigrationist weekly. It was edited by Robert Hamilton, Thomas's brother, and a third Hamilton, William G., served as business agent. Despite the threat of financial insolvency in early 1862, the paper continued through December 1865, although in 1863 the title was shortened to the *Anglo-African*. In July 1865, Henry Highland Garnet became editor of the *Anglo-African's* southern department, and supplied news from that region. The weekly then functioned primarily as a general black newspaper. Martin E. Dann, ed., *The Black Press, 1827–1890: The Quest for National Identity* (New York, N.Y.,

1971), 26, 55, 57, 78, 83–84, 261, 265; *WAA*, 23 July, 29 October 1859, 17 March, 29 December 1860, 16 March, 17, 24 August, 21 December 1861, 6 April 1862; *AAN*, 12 August, 3 September 1865; *PP*, 25 March 1861; Miller, *Search for Black Nationality*, 170, 242–43, 279; Schor, *Henry Highland Garnet*, 221.

2. Cary refers to the growth of the black population in America from the first twenty Africans who were landed at Jamestown, Virginia, in 1619, to the estimated four million by 1861.

3. James McCune Smith, J. W. C. Pennington, and George T. Downing were the most effective black American critics of the Haitian immigration movement during the early 1860s. Known collectively as the Smith clique, they argued that emigration was a poor solution to American racial problems and charged that James Redpath and his Haytian Emigration Bureau agents were deluding prospective colonists. Through Smith's influence, the *Weekly Anglo-African* shifted from modest support for emigration to strong opposition and published considerable criticism of Redpath and his cohorts. To silence the Smith clique, Redpath used funds from the government of Haiti to purchase the *Anglo-African* in April 1861. Renamed the *Pine and Palm*, it served as the official organ of the Haitian immigration movement. This quieted the Smith clique for a time, but in August, Smith financed publication of a new, antiemigrationist *Anglo-African*. Dean, *Defender of the Race*, 35–36, 117–18n.

4. Reports of intolerable living conditions, sickness, and death filtered back from the blacks that immigrated to Haiti. Mary O. Monroe, the widow of African missionary William C. Monroe, returned from Haiti in the fall of 1861 and reported several deaths. Other returning immigrants told of unsanitary water, inadequate shelter, poor farming conditions, and widespread disease and death. The high death rate at James T. Holly's New Haven Colony received particular attention. Three months after reaching Haiti, Holly's mother and infant daughter were dead, as were John P. Anthony (a member of Holly's New Haven congregation), Anthony's parents, and nine other members of the colony. Such reports from Haitian settlers returning to the United States slowly destroyed the Haitian immigration movement. Miller, *Search for Black Nationality*, 245–47.

5. Slaves who sought sanctuary behind Union lines during the Civil War were defined as *contrabands*. The contraband policy was devised in May 1861 by Brigadier General Benjamin F. Butler, when three slaves who had been working at a nearby Confederate battery took refuge in Fortress Monroe, a Union position located in southeastern Virginia. Because the slaves had contributed to the Confederate war effort, Butler considered them "contrabands of war" and refused to return them. Congress essentially approved Butler's policy on 6 August by passing the First Confiscation Act, which provided that owners of slaves engaged in hostile military service forfeited claims to their slaves' labor. The term contraband was broadly used to describe Southern blacks displaced by the war. *CWD*, 172.

6. Foxfire light is a term given to a phosphorescent light given off by certain fungi found on decaying wood.

7. Cary sarcastically refers to the *Pine and Palm*, the official organ of the Haitian immigration movement, which was edited by James Redpath, George Lawrence, and Richard Hinton. It was created when Redpath used funds from the Haitian government to purchase the *Weekly Anglo-African* in April 1861 and re-

named it the *Pine and Palm*. The paper was published weekly in New York City and Boston and provided readers with news of the Haitian immigration movement, correspondence from Haytian Emigration Bureau agents, lists of emigrants, letters from settlers in Haiti, and informational articles on the history, government, culture, geography, and climate of the black nation. It paid increasing attention to the conduct of the Civil War. William Wells Brown, John B. Smith, James T. Holly, and M. Saint Amand contributed frequent articles. The *Pine and Palm* ceased publication in September 1862, when the Haitian government withdrew its support. Dean, *Defender of the Race*, 35–36, 117–18n; *PP*, 18 May 1861, 4 September 1862.

8. In 1861 Canadian whites hired an agent, black abolitionist William P. Newman, to discourage interest in Haitian immigration among black Canadians. Newman informed blacks in Canada West that Redpath meant to sell them into slavery and force them to become Roman Catholics once they arrived in Haiti. Newman hoped to divert settlers to Protestant Jamaica, from which he received a fee. Winks, *Blacks in Canada*, 164.

9. Cary suggests that James Redpath was a recent convert to the antislavery movement and that his abolitionist reputation rested solely on *Echoes of Harpers Ferry* and *The Public Life of Captain John Brown*—his posthumous accounts of John Brown. Redpath actually embraced abolitionism in his early twenties when, as a New York newspaper correspondent in the mid-1850s, he witnessed the political turmoil in Kansas. Between 1854 and 1859, Redpath also traveled through the South and published his observations in *The Roving Editor, or Talks with Slaves in Southern States*. *DAB*, 15:443–44.

10. Wendell Phillips (1811–1884) was the son of a patrician Massachusetts family and was educated at Harvard College and Harvard Law School. Early in 1837, Phillips declared his commitment to the antislavery cause and to the moral suasionist principles of his friend William Lloyd Garrison. For the next twenty-four years, he made vigorous antislavery efforts; he regularly spoke out against the institution, attended local, national, and international abolitionist gatherings, and denounced the usurpations of the slave power. Phillips was a member of the Boston Vigilance Committee. In the mid-1850s, he supported aid to Kansas free-state settlers and advocated the disunion of the North and South as a way of ending slavery. After the Civil War, he opposed Garrison's effort to disband the American Anti-Slavery Society and used the organization to support passage of the Fourteenth and Fifteenth amendments. In the 1870s, Phillips devoted himself to temperance, penal, and labor reform. *DAB*, 14:546–47.

11. Cary probably refers to black abolitionist William Wells Brown and to John Brown, Jr. (1821–1895), who were agents for James Redpath's Haitian Emigration Bureau in Canada West. John Brown, Jr., was born in Ohio, the eldest son of the abolitionist martyr John Brown. He settled in Kansas, where he became active in the free-state movement. Although not directly involved in the planned raid on Harpers Ferry, he toured the Northeast and Canada as an agent for his father, soliciting funds, weapons, and recruits for the cause. Brown served as a company commander for the Union army during the Civil War. After the war, he settled on Put-In-Bay Island, Ohio. Oates, *Purge This Land with Blood*; *NYT*, 23 September 1872; Winks, *Blacks in Canada*, 164.

88.
William Wells Brown to James Redpath
[October 1861]

Emigrationist lecturers engaged in the most sustained black speaking tours of the British North American Provinces. During 1861–62 John Brown, Jr., Alexander Tate, Simon T. J. Spencer, and black abolitionists Isaac N. Cary, William J. Watkins, John B. Smith, and William Wells Brown toured Canada West and the Maritimes to gather converts for the Haitian immigration movement. William Wells Brown, an agent for James Redpath's Haytian Emigration Bureau, arrived in Canada West in mid-August 1861. During the next two months, he lectured to large audiences and held emigration meetings in every major black community between Toronto and Windsor. In late October, he submitted a report to Redpath on his recent "labors" in the province. Like his colleagues, Brown wrote in glowing terms of the inroads he believed the Haitian cause was making in Canadian black communities. But circumstances soon proved him wrong. By the time Brown completed his tour, he discovered a great deal of opposition to the Haitian movement among blacks in the province. William Edward Farrison, *William Wells Brown: Author and Reformer* (Chicago, Ill., 1969), 342–51.

REPORT OF WM. WELLS BROWN
UP TO FRIDAY, OCT. 18, 1861

James Redpath, Esq.
Sir:

I beg to submit to you the following report of my labors:

On Sunday, Sept. 29, I visited the "Refugee House,"[1] eight miles from Windsor, in Canada, where I found a large school-house, filled with persons, every one of whom were farmers, anxious to hear something about Hayti. At the conclusion of my lecture many questions were asked, and I warned all who were not intending to cultivate the soil, or to make themselves useful to the country and to themselves, to remain in Canada. In fact, this has been my advice to intending emigrants at every place where I have spoken.

I had a large audience at the Baptist church at Amherstburg, on Monday, September 30, who appeared much interested in the past history and the present condition of the Republic of Hayti.

By earnest invitation of several highly-influential farmers in Colchester, I went there on Tuesday, October 1, and spoke in the Town Hall to a full house. This is the most beautiful of all the agricultural towns through which I passed; and although the people seem to be in good circumstances, many of them are anxious to make their homes in Hayti, for the benefit of their children. On Wednesday, October 2, I had another meeting in the same town, but at a different place.

Thursday and Friday, the 3d and 4th, I held meetings again at Amherstburg, and, seemingly, with renewed interest amongst the people. On my return to Windsor, Mr. Cary[2] felt anxious for me to visit London, Hamilton, and Toronto, to facilitate the departure of the emigrants from those places. At London, I found a fiddler, ready with his wife and children, to start in the first train; also, a carpenter. Both of these, however, I refused. The first-named, because he could do nothing but *fiddle*, and I felt that his services would not be needed in Hayti; the second, because a red nose showed that he was more accustomed to drink bad rum than to work for a living.

In Toronto, I found the second colony of emigrants ready, and their leader called them together,[3] seventy-five in number, and I must confess that a nobler looking set of men and women I never beheld—all going out to Hayti with the determination to commence the culture of cotton. Most of these people take out their own farming implements, and many of them have considerable means. This colony was to leave Toronto on Tuesday morning, October 14.

At Hamilton, were eight more emigrants waiting for an opportunity to reach New York, and I arranged for these to join the Toronto colony, and all go on together. The last named were sober, industrious persons. Respectfully,

W. WELLS BROWN[4]

Pine and Palm (Boston, Mass.), Supplement, 2 January 1862.

1. Brown refers to the Refugee Home Society.

2. Brown refers to Isaac N. Cary.

3. The Haitian immigration movement made some inroads in the Toronto black community during the early 1860s. An emigration society was formed in mid-1861 under the direction of John W. Stokes, a local black leader. By September it claimed ninety members. Late that month, Stokes and fifty-three other members left to establish a black colony at St. Marc, Haiti. Several, including Stokes, died shortly after their arrival. A second group of Toronto colonists was organized in early October but apparently never sailed. *PP*, 21 September, 2 November, 21 December 1861, 13 February, 17 April 1862 [13:0761, 0987].

4. William Wells Brown (ca. 1814–1884) was born in Lexington, Kentucky, the son of Elizabeth, a slave woman, and a white relative of her owner. After twenty years as a slave, Brown escaped to freedom in January 1834. He spent the next two years working on a Lake Erie steamboat and running fugitive slaves into Canada. In the summer of 1834, he met and married Elizabeth Spooner, a free black woman; they had three daughters, one of whom died shortly after birth. Two years after his marriage, Brown moved to Buffalo, where he began his career in the abolitionist movement by regularly attending meetings of the Western New

York Anti-Slavery Society, boarding antislavery lecturers at his home, speaking at local abolitionist gatherings, and traveling to Cuba and Haiti to investigate emigration possibilities.

Brown's abolitionist career reached a turning point in the summer of 1843, when Buffalo hosted a national antislavery convention and the National Convention of Colored Citizens. Brown attended both meetings, sat on several committees, and became friends with a number of black abolitionists, including Frederick Douglass and Charles Lenox Remond. Brown joined these two in their appeal to the power of moral suasion, their rejection of black antislavery violence (particularly the course espoused by Henry Highland Garnet in his "Address to the Slaves"), and their boycott of political abolitionism. Brown's expanded service to the antislavery movement, his increasing sophistication as a speaker, and his growing reputation in the antislavery community brought an invitation to lecture before the American Anti-Slavery Society at its annual meeting in New York City; in May 1847 he was hired as a Massachusetts Anti-Slavery Society lecture agent. Brown moved to Boston and, by the end of the year, had published the successful *Narrative* of his life.

In October 1849, he began a lecture tour of Great Britain. Brown remained abroad until 1854. The length of his stay was conditioned by personal and political motives. He was exhilarated by the tour, had time to write, and enjoyed the benefits of reform circle society. He was also trying to recover from the dissolution of his marriage. Quite as important, once the Fugitive Slave Law was passed in 1850, it was dangerous for the escaped slave to return to America. Concern for Brown's safety prompted British abolitionists to purchase his freedom in 1854.

When Brown did return, he had written *Clotel*, the first novel published by an Afro-American, and was finishing *St. Domingo*, a work that suggests Brown's growing antislavery militancy. The publication of those works, as well as a travelogue, a play, and a compilation of antislavery songs, established his reputation as the most prolific black literary figure of the mid-nineteenth century. During 1861–62 he was a lecturing agent in Canada West and the Northeast for James Redpath's Haytian Emigration Bureau. For the remainder of his life, Brown lived in the Boston area, producing three major volumes of black history and continuing to travel, lecture, and write. He completed his last book, *My Southern Home: Or, the South and Its People*, in 1880. Farrison, *William Wells Brown*.

89.
"The Colored People of Canada" by William Wells Brown

In the fall of 1861, William Wells Brown toured Canada West to promote Haitian immigration on behalf of James Redpath's Haytian Emigration Bureau. He reported on his travels and activities in a series of articles written for the *Pine and Palm*, the bureau's official journal. These reports provided a detailed portrait of black communities in Canada West at their most developed stage, on the eve of the return migration to the United States. Brown understood the antislavery message inherent in discussing black success in Canada. A temperate, pious, and industrious black community made an eloquent statement against slavery and racial prejudice. Brown's positive description of black Canadian life seemed to contradict his efforts for Haitian immigration: If life was good in Canada, why would blacks decide to emigrate? His personal ambiguity reflected the debate between those who wished to build a model black community in Canada West and those who wanted to create a black nation in the Caribbean. Whatever their purpose, Brown's writings offer a rich look at black life in Canada.

THE COLORED PEOPLE OF CANADA

BY WM. WELLS BROWN

[I]

No section of the American Continent has been watched with so much interest, both by the oppressor, the oppressed, and the friends of freedom and civilization, as the Canadas. The only spot in America, where every child of God could stand and enjoy freedom, and the only place of refuge for the poor whip-scarred slave of the Southern plantation, it has excited the malignant hate of all slaveholding Americans, while it shared the sympathy and approving interest of the friends of the African race everywhere. The colored population of the Canadas have been largely overrated. There are probably not more than 25,000 in both Provinces, and by far the greater number of these are in Canada West, and in a section of country lying west of Toronto, and near Chatham.

TORONTO. The number of colored people in Toronto is about 1,400. Every Southern state of the American Union is here represented, and every shade of color from purest white to midnight darkness, is among these sons and daughters of oppression. The dialects of the rice fields of Carolina, the cotton plantations of Georgia, the sugar estates of Mississippi, the tobacco plains of Virginia, the corn fields of Kentucky, and the hemp lands of Missouri, are all here amalgamated into one conglomerated mass; and these are scattered in every part of the city.

CHURCHES. There are three churches: one Baptist, situated on Queen Street, and under the pastoral charge of the Rev. Mr. Mitchell,[1] now in England collecting money for his society. This church has about one hundred members, but is not in a very flourishing state, owing to internal division, which has caused a *secession* of a portion of the congregation. The Methodist church, in Sayer Street, under the ministerial charge of the Rev. Mr. Turpin,[2] has seventy-five members, and appears to be in a good condition. Mr. Turpin is himself a man of much energy, of a progressive nature, and deeply interested in the moral, social, and religious elevation of his race. He is a forcible preacher, and is doing great good in the community, and claiming the respect of all. The Wesleyan church, in Richmond Street,[3] numbers about sixty members, but has no regular pastor. The edifices in which these societies worship are all good substantial buildings, but not *gaudy*.

SABBATH SCHOOLS. The Sayer Street church has a large Sabbath school, recently organized by Rev. Mr. Turpin, and the people, both members and attendants, seem deeply interested in it, and it appears to be doing a good work in bringing the children in from the streets. There is also a school in each of the other churches.

EDUCATIONAL FACILITIES. Toronto has the finest educational institutions of any city I have yet visited in America. The common schools, high schools, college, and university—to all of these the colored student can enter, upon terms of perfect equality with the whites. Nevertheless, many are unable, through want of books, charts, and other necessaries to take their position in these schools, and therefore an Educational Institute,[4] for the purpose of aiding such persons, has been established, and incorporated by Parliament. Dr. A. T. Augusta, the worthy president of this association, was one of its founders. The Educational Institute has during the past two years got up a course of Lyceum lectures, which were open to all who wished to avail themselves of the opportunity. This institution has about one hundred members.

SOCIETIES. Of the beneficial societies, the most prominent are St. John's Benevolent Association, which has a large amount of funds on hand, and allows its sick $2 per week, and $15 for the burial of its dead. This society has fifty members. The Victoria is composed of females, has forty members, provides for its poor and sick, and buries its own dead.[5] The Daughters of Prince Albert is a society similar to the last. The Rising Star consists of young ladies who have resolved to get up early in the morning, walk a mile before breakfast, and marry no man that either chews tobacco, smokes, or drinks intoxicating beverages. Their numbers are small, but their heads are strong.

PROFESSIONS. Dr. A. T. Augusta is a physician of decided merit, and has been in practice in this city some four or five years, and seems to have the entire confidence of his patrons. Dr. S. C. Watson is a young man, a graduate of Oberlin, and at the head of his profession.[6] He has lately come to Toronto from Chatham, where he was considered very skilful. Professor S. Goutier,[7] one of the finest music teachers in Canada, has his share of public patronage. Few persons can handle the Spanish guitar equal to the professor. As a French teacher he has no superior. There are two students in the university, one at law, and the other at medicine.

BUSINESS. There is one drug store, one book store, two cabinet shops, six tailors, two umbrella makers, ten plasterers, one splendid livery stable, four masons, three shoe dealers, eight shoemakers, three carriages, one carter, forty-five artists in water colors, sometimes vulgarly called "whitewashers." There are also a large number in small saloons, dealing in fruits, ice cream, and nuts, and one man is employed in the custom house at a salary of $500 per annum. There are a large number of hair dressers, seven carpenters, and four blacksmiths.

MORALS. Considering the early training, or I would say, the want of early training, of the colored people of Canada, the morals of Toronto are far above what they are among the same number in many places in the States. While crime seems to be on the increase among the whites, it is pleasing to find that it is on the decrease among the colored population. This is, no doubt, in part owing to the exertion and influence of such men as Wilson Abbott, Esq., John J. Cary, Dr. Augusta, Geo. W. Cary,[8] Dr. Watson, Prof. Goutier, the Watkins,[9] and some others, whose names I have forgotten. In these gentlemen I found a strong, intelligent, reformatory sentiment, and they appear to be devoted to the education and social elevation of their race.

WEALTH. There is a fair proportion of wealth among the colored people, especially when we take into consideration the indigent circumstances under which so many came to Canada. I found one man in Toronto, said to be worth $120,000, and upon inquiry I am satisfied that I have set the sum too low.[10] Others, whose wealth was estimated at from $5,000 to $40,000 were also given to me. In Toronto, there are probably five hundred persons, men and women, who are deeply tinged with the African hue, but who pass for white. Twenty or thirty of these were pointed out to me in a single day's walk, and several of them were much deeper dyed than myself. Many of these pass for foreigners, and under that guise, almost any mulatto may push himself through the crowd,[11] if he can rattle off a little French, German, or Spanish. With some of our class, this is an inducement to study the languages.

HAMILTON. I found about 500 colored persons in this city, and apparently doing well. They have two churches, a Baptist and a Methodist. Rev. Mr. Stuart is the Methodist minister,[12] and the Rev. Mr. Broadwater presides over the Baptist.[13] Like Toronto, the colored children here go to the schools in common with the whites.

BUSINESS. The American Hotel is kept by William Richardson, a *col-*

ored white man. Thomas Morton, who is not ashamed of his identity with the race, has two public carriages, one of which he drives himself.[14] There are four shoemakers, one tailor, three plasterers, one cooper, two carpenters, one blacksmith, and thirteen artists in *water colors*. They have several benevolent societies, similar to those already mentioned in the notice of Toronto. The morals of the people here will compare very favorably with the whites. There is considerable wealth here: one man is set down at $20,000. This must close my letter. In my next I write of the people in St. Catharines and London.

[II]

St. Catharines. Only ten miles from the American side of the Niagara river, and the principal depot for fugitive slaves who escape by way of New York, Philadelphia, Harrisburg, and Buffalo, St. Catharines has long been an important place for the oppressed, and consequently has become the home of many of these people. In the village and its environs, there are not far from eight hundred colored people, representing every Southern State in the late American Union. Scattered around, and within five miles, are a large number of farmers, many of whom have become wealthy since escaping into Canada. Going into the market on Saturday morning, I counted 37 colored persons selling their commodities, consisting of ducks, chickens, eggs, butter, cheese, hams, bacon, vegetables, and fruits of all kind. This reminded me more of the vegetable markets of the Slave States, than anything that I have yet witnessed. The venders are men and women, old and young. The broad-brimmed straw hat of the women of the South has been transferred to the market-women of this place.

Hearing the hearty laugh of one of these daughters of Africa, and looking upon her smiling face, I ventured to approach her, and the following conversation took place. "Good morning, Aunty!" "How de do, honey?" "How much do you ask for pears?" "Well, sonny, dese big ones is quarter dollar fer haf a peck." "Is not that rather high?" "Well, yer see, honey, I is bin out here sefenteen years, an when de ole man an I fust come out, we plant de trees dat dese pars growed on. Now, yer see dat dese is pars dat is pars; dey is as rich as cream. Jess try one, it'll melt in yer mouf like butter." I took a pear, paid for it, and commenced eating, and found it even better than had been represented. I continued, "You speak as if you came from the eastern shore of Maryland." "God love yer heart, honey, I jess is—is you from dar, too?" "No," I replied, "I am from old Kentucky." "Yer don't say so—well, den, gib me yer han; dar is plenty here from ole Kentuck," and she gave me a hearty shake of the hand, that made my fingers ache. "Is yer jess come to de promis' lan'?" "Yes, madam, I came here last night," I replied. "You was house servant, down dar, I spose." "Yes." "Well, you see, honey, you is got yer freedom now, you must make good use ob it. Did you leave any wife and chillen back dar?" "No, madam, I had no wife when I came off." "Now I tell yer, honey, yer must be on yer *p's* and *q's* here—many dese women ain't no count, and you musn't go and get a wife de fust week yer is here, like some ob um. Wait a little while, honey, till yer knows who's who." The throng of customers around the old lady cut short our conversation, and I passed on.

THE COLORED SETTLEMENT. The colored settlement is a hamlet, situated on the outskirts of the village, and contains about 100 houses, 40 of which lie on North Street, the Broadway of the place. The houses are chiefly cottages, with from 3 to 6 rooms, and on lots of land of nearly a quarter of an acre each. Most of the dwellings are wood-colored, only a few of them having been painted or whitewashed. Each family has a good garden, well-filled with vegetables, ducks, chickens, and a pig-pen, with at least one fat grunter getting ready for Christmas. The houses, with the lots upon which they stand, are worth upon an average about $500 each. Some of them have devoted a small part of the garden to the growth of the tobacco plant, which seems to do well. Entering North Street at the lower end, I was struck with surprise at the great number of children in the street. On passing a gate, I inquired for Mr.——; and a good-looking woman coming out of her door, informed me, and in return said, "Stranger here, I spose." "Yes, madam," I replied. "Come from behind the sun?" continued she. I replied that I had. "Den as you is light and well dressed, I speck you is yer marster's son, ain't yer?" "No, I am my uncle's son," [15] I said. "Well," she continued, "dat is strange—I never heard of any one being dar uncle's son before, but heaps of 'em who comes out here is dar marster's sons. De war makes good times now for our people, while de white folks is fightin', de colored people can run away. Heaps of 'em comes along now."

The houses in the settlement are all owned by their occupants, and from inquiry I learned that the people generally were free from debt. Out of the eight hundred in St. Catharines, about seven hundred of them are fugitive slaves. I met one old lady who escaped at the advanced age of eighty-five years—she is now *one hundred and four*.

Among them I found seventeen carpenters, four blacksmiths, six coopers, and five shoemakers. Two omnibuses and two hacks are driven by colored men. Not long since, a slave run away from Virginia, came here, and settled down; a few months after, his master "broke down," cheated his creditors, escaped to Canada, came and settled by the side of his former chattel. Their families borrow and lend now, upon terms of perfect equality.

SUNDAY AT THE SETTLEMENT. They have two churches, both on North Street, and in the centre of the settlement. In the morning I listened to a good discourse from Anthony Burns, formerly the chattel of Col. Suttle [16] of Virginia, and made somewhat noted by being returned under the Fugitive Slave Law from Boston, in 1854. His congregation is not large.[17] The Methodists have a very commodious church,[18] finely finished, and have about 250 members. In the afternoon I listened to one of the "locals," the pastor being absent; in the evening I was invited to occupy the pulpit, and did so. Perfect order was observed all day on Sunday. Indeed, the settlement made a very neat and clean appearance. Taking an early walk, I found that during the previous night the street had been swept, and every door-yard looked as clean as a pin. Even the pigs that had been a little noisy on Saturday, seemed to understand that it was Sunday, and behaved themselves accordingly. The people appeared at church well dressed, many of them coming ten miles from the country.

The different styles of dress and the Southern look of some of the bonnets, contrasted strangely with the turban, the scuttle, the scoop, the glengarrie, and the jaunty Scotch cap,[19] that I had seen upon the heads of the ladies of Toronto, the previous Sunday. Nevertheless, no matter how much out of fashion, these coverings were always clean and neat. The Methodists have a large Sabbath School, and there are several benevolent societies among the women; the only name of them that I learned, was the "Harrywines of Jericho." This village is the home of Hiram Wilson, long known as the fugitive's friend. I called at his residence, but he was from home—probably on some errand of mercy.

III

LONDON. All the way from St. Catharines to London, a distance of more than a hundred miles, I saw, on either side of the railway, unmistakable evidence that the U.G.R.R.[20] had been doing good service to the oppressed people of the Southern States. As I came West I found a larger proportion of colored inhabitants. There are from 500 to 700 in this place, where they have two churches, two Sabbath schools, and one benevolent society.[21] I met here Rev. L. C. Chambers,[22] an old acquaintance, who invited me to speak to his people in the Methodist church twice during the Sabbath, which I did, to a crowded house on both occasions.

PREJUDICE AGAINST COLOR. Canada has so long been eulogized as the only spot in North America where the Southern bondsman could stand a freeman, and the poetical connection of its soil with the fugitive, the "North Star," and liberty, had created such an enthusiastic love in my heart for the people here, that I was not prepared to meet the prejudice against colored persons which manifests itself wherever a member of that injured race makes his appearance.

That old, negro hating cry of "Crow, crow," which used to greet the well dressed colored person on the other side of the line twenty years ago, and which I had not heard for a long time, sounded harshly upon my sensitive ears as I passed through the streets of this city. Indeed, in none of the States, not even in Pennsylvania, is the partition wall between the blacks so high as in Canada. Amongst the colored men here, are some first class mechanics, yet none of these can get employment in shops where white men are at work. I have been informed by the best authority, in every place through which I have passed, that the introduction of a colored mechanic in any establishment here, would be taken as an insult by the white men, who would instantly leave their work. A splendid carpenter has just gone by with his whitewash bucket and brush; unable to get employment at his trade, he resorts to the latter for a livelihood. The equality meted out to colored persons in the hotels of New England, are unknown in Canada. No where here, are our people treated with any kind of respect in the hotels; they are usually put off into inferior rooms by themselves, fed at separate tables from the whites, and not permitted to enter the common sitting rooms of the inn. Most of the towns have excluded the colored children from the common schools. In this place the proscriptive measure has just commenced, and I here give a portion of a recent editorial from the *Free Press*,[23] the *liberal* paper of this section of Canada. In urging the exclusion of colored children from the public schools, the editor says:

> We are confident, however much our fellow-citizens, as a people, may sympathize in the sufferings and mortal degradation of the unfortunate African in the neighboring Republic, and throughout the world, that were each to express the genuine sentiments of his own heart, he would boldly declare his unwillingness that his daughter, verging upon womanhood, should be constrained to associate, for six hours in the day, with negroes of either sex. Nor can we esteem this feeling erroneous or unnatural in itself. Who will boldly advocate an amalgamation or intermarriage between the races? Will any one pronounce such a fusion desirable? Will any one deny, that unrestrained intercourse may lead, and has led, to such results? Cases of such *mesalliance* have frequently occurred, in which the feelings of friends have been outraged, and the happiness and prospects of families blighted by permitting the society of negroes on a footing of equality. So long, then, as the colored children are admitted as students into our public schools, they must be received as the associates and equals of the most respectable children of the city, enjoy the same advantages, and receive the same care, kindness, and consideration at the hand of the teachers. This is all right while they are there, but is it right they should be there?
>
> This, then, is the question at issue. Will the people of London sustain the Board, or that portion of the Board that proposes to take initiatory steps for securing this desirable object? If we may credit the report, emanating from the Board at the close of the last year, their schools are in a most flourishing condition, doing almost the entire work of education among us, and embracing within their

> Ward and Central schools nearly the whole juvenile population, of the city. Would it be wise, then, to risk the popularity and usefulness of the schools, by forcing into the senior classes, contrary to the feelings and wishes of the white population, a great number of well-grown boys and girls of the negro race?
>
> Some of the lads educated in these schools will, in the course of a few years, assume a high position in the community, but a union of the races can only produce a deterioration of the one, without any compensating advantage to the other, and ought to be carefully guarded against. The trustees need not, therefore, be surprised, if the wealthier classes, who are able to afford their daughters an education in a private school, refuse to have them seated at the same desk with the children of the colored inhabitants. We have it from the best authority, that the annual examination for transfer now proceeding, will result in removing from the Ward schools to the Central, a large number of negroes of both sexes—rude in speech, uncouth in manners and address, and untidy in attire. It can hardly be hoped—it can hardly be desired, that the parents of the pupils, whose appearance impresses every visitor so favorably, should feel gratified by the step. It remains then for the people to make their wishes known to the Board by petition or otherwise. If they approve of keeping the races united for purposes of education—well; if not, the law has wisely provided the remedy—let the Board adopt it.

It will be observed that the objections here urged, and the reason assigned for turning the colored children out of the schools, are the same that were put forth by the mob who broke up the school of Prudence Crandall, in Canterbury, Conn., twenty-five years ago, because she admitted children of the proscribed class.[24] I think that the prejudice against the colored people in Canada, arises mainly from the following causes: First, the colored inhabitants withdrawing themselves from the whites, forming separate churches, taking back seats in public meetings, and performing the menial offices of labor, and thereby giving the whites an opportunity to regard them with a degree of inferiority.

Second, the main body of the population of Canada appears to be made up of the lower class of the people of England, Scotland, and Ireland. As I walk the streets here, I look in vain for that intelligent portion of the middle classes that I used to meet in London, Edinburgh, and Dublin. This lower stratum, coming from the old world, and feeling keenly their inferiority in education and refinement, and being vulgar and rude themselves, try, like the editor of the London *Free Press*, to draw attention from their own uncouthness, by directing the public eye to the other degraded class. It would, however, be doing injustice to the cause of

Reform, to say that the entire population of Canada is of the class above mentioned, or that the editor of the *Free Press* represents the highest idea of liberalism in the Western Province. Mr. Brown, the gentlemanly proprietor and editor of the *Toronto Globe*, is an exception to this.

Notwithstanding there is so much prejudice, and the colored people are shut out from the more profitable employments, they are nevertheless thrifty, and doing well. Although bad beer and poor whiskey appear to be in good demand in this city, and I have met several persons who seemed to have an over stock on hand, I have not yet seen a colored inhabitant intoxicated. In the vicinity of London there are many of our race who own good farms and carry them on in the best manner. A man I once knew at the South as a slave, now resides upon a beautiful place of sixty acres in a high state of cultivation, fine grafted fruit on it, a well finished house, and large, comfortable barns, all of which he owns himself, without a single debt. Although there seems to be such hatred of the negro here, if one is known to be wealthy, the whites vie with each other to see which shall do him the most honor. In confirmation of this I will relate an incident told me by a respectable gentleman since I came here. A colored man arrived in this city, a few years ago, from New Orleans, intending to purchase a family residence, and to invest several thousand dollars in real estate. Before making any inquiries about situations, or selecting a locality, he deposited $80,000 in one of the banks. From that moment he was a marked man, by those in and about the bank. Some days after, our Southern planter called on an extensive real estate dealer, and proposed purchasing a very valuable lot of land on one of the principal streets. The broker looked for a moment at the black man, curled his lip, turned up his nose, wheeled around, and started in an opposite direction. He had not, however, gone but a few rods when he met the cashier of the bank in which the black planter had made his deposit. The cashier whispered to the broker, "put a flea in his ear," and the latter started off in full chase after the "wealthy nigger." Catching up with the planter, the broker seized his hand and exclaimed: "I am sure, my dear sir, that you will pardon me for not answering your question about the lot of land. I am subject to fits of dizziness; they are hereditary in our family, and they come on us at times very suddenly, but I am now recovering from it. Will you walk in and be seated?" The next day the black man dined with the real estate broker in company with the mayor and the president of the bank.

In point of size, strength, physical development, and fleetness, I think that the bedbugs of Canada surpass anything of the kind I have ever before met. And the hotel-keepers appear to have paid the strictest attention and care to their cultivation and training, for they are found in large numbers. They are much larger and have teeth far sharper than any raised under the stars and stripes; and strange to say that a hotel life has not created in these creatures the slightest prejudice against colored persons, unless they made a mistake when waiting upon me. Indeed, I am almost of the opinion that they have a particular liking for the colored man.

[IV]

CHATHAM. At every place on the line of the railway, coming west, where I had an opportunity of conversing with the people, they all pointed to Chatham as the most important spot in Canada for the colored man. "Wait till you get to Chatham, and you'll see heaps of our people," fell from many lips on the route. The appearance of the village to the right, as the train neared the depot, with its straggling low, unpainted houses contrasted strangely with the beautiful villas, and finely cultivated grounds of the wealthier classes of Toronto, Hamilton, and London, through which I had so recently passed. In my walk from the railroad station to the hotel, I was at once impressed with the fact that I was at Chatham, for every other person whom I met was colored. The population here is made up entirely from the Slave States, with but few exceptions. Every shade of the Southern sons and daughters of oppression, from the polite house-servant down to the coarsest field-hand, is seen upon the unpaved and dusty streets of this little town. Those who have ever passed down the valley of the Mississippi, or walked on the banks washed by the Potomac, will have his liveliest recollections of the appearance of the slaves revived by spending an hour in Chatham.

CHURCHES. The British M. E. Church is a brick building just finished, and capable of seating 1,500 persons. The edifice was planned by Wm. H. Jones, the minister now in charge;[25] every brick in the vast building laid by one man, and every hod of mortar carried up by a single individual. From the laying of the first stone to the putting on of the last brush of paint, the workers were men of color, and nearly all of them fugitives from slavery. Not as large as the Bethel in Philadelphia, or as finely finished as St. Phillips in New York,[26] the Chatham church is more beautiful than either. This edifice cost $5,000, all of which was collected by Mr. Jones, its architect, its builder, and its pastor. The church has 200 communicants, and a Sabbath school numbering about the same. The Baptist church is a neat frame building, capable of seating 600 persons, has 150 members, a flourishing Sabbath school, and appears in good condition.[27] The Secessionists, a society that "split off" from the B. M. E. Church, worships in the City Hall, under the pastoral care of the Rev. Mr. Pearce.[28] It has 100 communicants, a Sabbath school of 120 members, and claims to have in it the most educated of the followers of Wesley.[29]

EDUCATIONAL FACILITIES. I am informed that this was the first town in Canada to exclude children of colored parents from the common schools. There is one Government School for children, the principal of which is Mr. St. Clair, assisted by Mrs. Armstrong.[30] A Grammar School, established by, and under the charge of Mrs. Shadd[31] and Mrs. Cary, and sustained entirely by individual benevolence, has been in operation four or five years. This school seems to have a worthy claim upon the friends of education everywhere, from the fact that the prejudice here keeps the colored children out of the other Grammar Schools.

One grand feature in the career of the fugitives and colored people generally in Canada is, that they seldom if ever become a charge upon the towns or counties. Aside from their own industry, they have benevolent societies in sufficient numbers to take care of their own poor and sick. "Love and Charity," is an association of females, numbering about 90. They allow their sick $2 per week, and $20 to bury their dead. "The United Daughters of Zion" has 80 members, gives their sick $1 per week, and allows $15 to bury their dead. Both of these societies are in good condition, in a pecuniary point of view.

PROFESSIONS. Dr. T. Joiner White, a graduate of the oldest University in the State of Maine, and for some time a student at Paris, is here.[32] In point of education, medical skill, and patronage, I should judge that the doctor stands first on the list of his profession in Chatham. Dr. A. Array is what may be termed a reformer in medical practice, being an allopathist, hydropathist, homeopathist, and an eclectic.[33] I think the doctor wise, for he can suit the million in practice, whether he cures or not, yet there are those here who are willing to stake their earthly existence on Dr. Array's skill.

Dr. M. R. Delany, though regarded as a man high in his profession, is better and more widely known as a traveller, discoverer, and lecturer. His association with Professor Campbell in the "Niger Valley Exploring Expedition" has brought the doctor very prominently before the world, and especially that portion which takes an interest in the civilization of Africa. The doctor, however, seems destined not to reap the many honors which he had evidently set his heart upon, in that beautiful land that flows with milk and honey, for he had scarcely left Lagos ere some evil disposed persons urged Alake and his chiefs to repudiate the treaty which they had made with Messrs. Delany and Campbell. Lord Russell hearing this, made inquiry of Lord Woodhouse, under-secretary for the colonies, and this brought about a correspondence between Lord Alfred Churchill, chairman of the "African Aid Society," and Mr. McCoskry, acting consul at Lagos. Mr. McCoskry informed Lord Russell through Lord Churchill that Alake and his chiefs did sign a treaty with Messrs. Delany and Campbell, granting a tract of land and certain privileges to them for a colony of colored Americans; but that, after the departure of the commissioners, Alake and his chiefs were advised not to permit American emigrants to settle in their section, for fear that the new-comers would wage war against the natives, and thereby take possession of the country. They pointed to Liberia as an example, and said that the Americans being more intelligent and enterprising would not be satisfied without governing. Upon receiving this information Lord Russell advised the officers of the "African Aid Society" not to encourage the emigration to Lagos for fear of arousing the evil spirit of the rulers there.[34] Dr. David Livingston also gives it as his opinion that the natives would not quietly permit settlers in other parts of Africa.[35] The wars between the Liberians and king Joe Harris appear to have given warning to the natives far and near; and the apprehensions of Alake and his chiefs seem not to have been without some foundation, for I am informed that Dr. Delany, in a speech at London, C.W., some weeks since, announced that the first act which he would commit after reaching Lagos would be to "take off the head of the old king."[36] Had the doctor been a Yankee he would have held his tongue till he was fairly settled in his new dominion. As it is, the king's head will be allowed to remain on his shoulders a little while longer, and the doctor permitted to return to the practice of his profession; for the "African Aid Society" holds the *motive power*, and those in Chatham who for a year or two past, have been troubled with dreams and nightmares on account of the "sixty million pounds sterling" that was to *come over* may now sleep sweetly.[37] But there are some honors which the doctor gained while abroad, that no African chiefs can rob him of. Some men obtain renown by unremitting study, toil, research, and energy, while others reach the utmost top of the ladder by a single bound. It was a lucky day for Martin R. Delany, when Lord Brougham called the attention of Minister Dallas to the fact that a negro was a member of the "International Statistical Congress," and I am glad that the doctor appreciates so highly the laurels gained in other lands, for I see by one of the doctor's handbills announcing himself to lecture, that he says—"Dr. M. R. Delany, chief of the Niger Valley Exploring Expedition, Member of the International Statistical Congress (H. R. H. Prince Albert, president), London, Member of the National Society for the Promotion of Social Science of Great Britain, and Member of the Social Science Congress (Right Honorable Henry Lord Brougham and Vaux, president), Glasgow, Scotland; who read a paper before the Royal Geographical Society (Lord Ashburton, president), London, and recently travelled extensively in Africa; whose lectures have been presided over by Lord Alfred Churchill, M.P., &c., the Right Honorable Lord Calthrope, Member of Her Majesty's Privy Council, London, the ex-Lord Provost of Glasgow, &c., will give a lecture on Africa, &c." I have copied the above *verbatim et literatim*, so that those who prize the ribbon of honor and the highfalutin, may see that the colored man is rising.[38]

Considered in respect to hatred to the Anglo-Saxon, a stentorian voice, a violence of gestures, and a display of physical energies when speaking, Dr. Delany may be regarded as the ablest man in Chatham, if not in America. Like the Quaker, who when going to fight pulled off his coat, and laying it down, said, "Thee lie there, Quaker, till I whip this fellow," so the Doctor, when going to address an audience, lays aside every classic idea of elocution and rhetoric, and says, "Remain there till I frighten these people."

Dr. S. Russell is a Thomsonian.[39] I called at his gate, read his sign, my mouth beginning to feel peppery, I passed on.

Taking a seat in a front pew last Sunday, I listened to a well conceived and eloquently delivered sermon from the Rev. H. L. Simpson, at the Baptist Church.[40] Born in Columbia County, N.Y., a faithful student, and finely educated, Mr. Simpson is an honor to his profession, as well as to his race. His well turned periods, faultless dramatic gestures, short, but forcible sentences, and his overpowering earnestness, reminded me of the best efforts of Henry Melville, the master of the English pulpit.[41] In his younger days I should judge that the Rev. gentleman often looked upon the *boards*, and took delight in the sock and buskin, for certain am I that no man ever became such a master of the art of the tremble of the uplifted hand, without gazing upon Macready's Hamlet, or Forrest's *Gladiator*.[42] I think him the most polished preacher, colored or white, that I have heard for years.

Nearly every Methodist whom I met on my way to Chatham spoke of the Rev. William H. Jones as the most distinguished preacher of their denomination in or out of Canada, and invoked me by all means to see and hear him. Fortunately I found the Rev. gentleman in the midst of a religious revival in his own beautiful church, which gave me an opportunity of seeing him to advantage. 500 or 600 had already taken their seats when I entered the building. Inside the altar and near the table, sat the centre of attraction, with a smile upon his countenance. Mr. Jones is a man of medium size, of pure African descent, and with a head which Fowler[43] would pronounce to belong to a financier. He opened the services with prayer, commenced singing a hymn, and calling upon sinners to come forward to the anxious seat. Five or six women, mostly young girls of from 14 to 20 years of age, went forward, kneeled upon the floor, leaning their heads on the mourners' bench. The minister now called on the sisters to press forward and form a ring around the mourners. It was at this point that I began to discover the power of the preacher. A magnetizer of great influence, he needed only his subjects to work upon. The altar, inside and out, and the aisles near by were soon crowded, when Mr. Jones began singing in a musical voice:

The devil and me can't agree, can't agree, can't agree,
I don't like him, and he don't like me.
We are washed in the blood of the Lamb;
I intend to run, and never stop, never stop, never stop,
Until I reach the mountain top, mountain top,
We are washed in the blood of the Lamb.

The women had now fallen flat on the floor, and Jones ordered the bench to be removed so as to "give the sisters a fair chance." He is a poet as well as a preacher, and like Dr. Watts,[44] made up the verses for the occasion. As the women began to roll, he changed the tune, and sang:

See how we roll upon the ground, I am washed in the blood of the Lamb;
I wish my Lord would come down, I am washed in the blood of the Lamb;
Fit me for to wear the crown, I am washed in the blood of the Lamb.

With three or four men inside the altar, clapping their hands and stamping their feet, and nine or ten women in different parts of the house shouting at the top of their voices, I could now fairly see through the secret of Jones' power. Fatigued, he would retire to the back of the pulpit, and leave the working oar in the hands of his assistants. When the interest would begin to flag, the master spirit would step forward, throw his head back, and with uplifted hand would begin to sing:

The devil and me can't agree, can't agree, can't agree, I don't like him, and he don't like me—we are the people of God.

Never did I see a congregation so completely under the control of the preacher, as these people trained up by, and led by Wm. H. Jones. I had witnessed the performances of J. N. Maffitt,[45] the celebrated Methodist revivalist in his palmiest days, but this son of Africa threw the former entirely into the shade. He is the preacher of feeling instead of reason, and is the highest representative of the lowest religious idea, that I have ever beheld. I am informed that at a late camp-meeting he held the large audience, colored and white, in breathless silence, for two hours and a half, and that whites came twenty miles to hear him.

The Rev. Mr. Pearce is the minister in charge of the Secessionists. I did not hear him, but understand that he ranks high as a preacher. I. D. Shadd, Esq., ex-editor of the extinguished *Provincial Freeman*, is a man of talent and of humor. If Charles Dickens[46] could spend an evening with Mr. Shadd, his next novel would be "The Colored Preacher," and "I. D." would be its hero. Mrs. Cary (and as Widow Bedott[47] would say, "she that was Mary Ann Shadd") is the most intelligent woman I have met in Canada. She is widely and favorably known on our side of the line, as an able public speaker, and a devoted friend to the oppressed.

BUSINESS. Amongst the colored citizens are many engaged in the different mechanical branches. There are six boot and shoe stores, four blacksmith shops, one cabinet shop, one carpenter shop, one large jewelry store, besides many journeyman mechanics. In the neighborhood of Chatham are several splendid farms, owned and paid for by men once held in slavery. A very extensive merchant here told me that his best customers were colored persons.

MORALS. An officer in the Police Court informed me that out of 27 cases before the last term, only two were persons of color; and yet these people make up nearly half of the population. Not one of them has been seen drunk in the streets for a long time, so I am told. Their credit is good with the merchants generally, and most of the accounts in bank are in favor of the colored farmers, mechanics, merchants, butchers, and provision dealers.

[V]

BUXTON. With a one-horse conveyance, Mr. J. D. Harris and I started for the Elgin settlement, lying in the town of Buxton, and about fifteen miles from Chatham. Taking the turnpike from the latter place, we soon found ourselves passing the "Bee-Hive." This is a rather noted country inn, with a bee-hive painted on the sign, with the following poetical invocation to the weary and dusty traveller:

Within this hive we are all alive,
Good whiskey makes us funny;
If you are dry, just stop and try,
The flavor of our honey.

We did not, however, accept the call, but went on to fulfil our engagement. Two hours' ride over a bad road, brought us to the Elgin settlement, a district comprising 9,000 acres of land, six miles in length, and three miles in breadth, and is situated between the Great Western Railway and Lake Erie, being a mile and a quarter from the latter. The Rev. Wm. King, formerly a slaveholder in Louisiana, emancipated his people, brought them out here, and settled them with others, upon land purchased from the Government. There are now nearly 600 persons in this settlement, all of whom have comfortable homes, and are characterized by a manly, independent air and manner. Most of these people were slaves at the South, and came into Canada without a single dollar. The land here, though good in itself, nevertheless lies too low, and is covered with water during the spring when they should be planting; yet, with eight months' winter, land cold and undrained, these fugitives have demonstrated the fact that the colored man, though once a slave, can and will take care of himself, and even lay up treasures for the future, if he gets the opportunity. Some of the settlers have their land under a good state of cultivation. My old and intellectual friend, Henry K. Thomas, a man deeply interested in the welfare of his race, has a beautiful farm in the settlement, where he is raising up his children as tillers of the soil, instead of leaving them to the chance of filling menial positions in the city. Mr.

King is a kind-hearted and benevolent man, and deserves the respect and esteem of friends of freedom and justice everywhere.

OLD ACQUAINTANCES. One of the most pleasing features in a tour through Canada, is the meeting with friends whom we knew in our boyhood. While at London I renewed my acquaintance with Mrs. Rose Breckenridge and Mrs. Julia Clamorgan,[48] two ladies from St. Louis, and whom I had not seen for more than 25 years. How strange to look upon the faces that have been dead to us for so long a period! Not far from Chatham I met another, with whom I had played in the meadows and around the slave-quarters on the old farm from earliest remembrance till the "sum of all villanies" separated us at the age of twelve years. More than 30 years had passed since we last met, and each had thought the other dead. This was the object of my first love, in my boyish days, when we were both running about the plantation, our only garb being that unmentionable garment that buttons around the neck. How strange the scene now! A son 20 years old, a daughter of 18, and another of 16 gazed at us while I sat with the youngest child upon my knee, and talked with the mother about old times! With what fleetness one's recollection runs back, when the conversation has once begun. The names of all the slaves on the plantation even to Uncle Sam, Uncle Jim, Aunt Dolly, and Uncle Ned, long since dead, were called over. The little family quarrels between the old master and mistress were freely canvassed. I could almost see the old lady as I had in days gone by, sitting in her rocking-chair, with me fanning her, and could almost hear her say to the old man, as she used to when angry: "Never mind, I won't be here always, for you to hector and aggravate, for one of these days the Lord will make up his jewels and take me home to glory, and then I'll be out of your way, and I'll be devilish glad of it, too!"

How we laughed, and caused the household around to join in, when we brought up the conversations between the old mistress and the Rev. Mr. Pincher, the slaveholding preacher, who used to *pinch* our ears, occasionally. Near by I met another lady, considered the handsomest quadroon in St. Louis, 30 years ago. I scarcely knew her bowed form, wrinkled features, and almost snow white hair. Such meetings and such greetings make us sad.

CHURCHES. They have two churches at the Elgin settlement. Rev. Mr. King preaches in the Congregational, to which most of the colored people are attached. The other is a Baptist church—the name of its pastor I did not learn. Of course there is no distinction made in these denominations at Buxton. A fine Sabbath School is in connection with Mr. King's church. The colored population are so strong in this town, that they have succeeded in electing two members to the Council,[49] and a colored teacher for the district school.[50] This last move so enraged the Pro-Slavery whites, that they took their children out, and not a white pupil has entered the house since. The morals of the people of Buxton are good, and their habits of the most industrious character.

DRESDEN. At the head of the Big Bear Creek, in the gore of Camden, lies the little village of Dresden, with a population of about 300, one third of whom are colored. The land here, is in the highest state of cultivation, and the farmers, the most thrifty that I have yet seen in Canada.

Within one mile of the village, and on the banks of the Sydenham, is the Dawn Institute. No place in the Western Province has excited more interest, or received a greater share of substantial aid, than this Association, and no place has proved itself less deserving. Every town in the Northern States, and every city, village, and hamlet in England and Scotland has been travelled over by the agents of the Dawn, begging money to "pay for the land, and to build school houses for the poor fugitives," and yet to-day there is not a foot of land upon which the runaway slave can rest the soles of his feet, or a school house in which to put his head. It would be charitable to the legion of agents of Dawn, to say that, within the last twenty years, they have collected not more than $50,000, for the sole benefit of the Institution.[51] There is about 300 acres of land belonging to the Institute, which is now in the hands of Mr. John Scoble, the superannuated secretary of the British and Foreign Anti-Slavery Society, London, England.[52] Although there are some 500 colored persons in the neighborhood of Dawn, no one of that sable race has anything to do with the Institute, it having passed entirely out of their hands, and is no longer used for their benefit. I was informed that a son of Mr. Scoble holds possession of the place, and farms the lands for the sole use of his father. The mill, for the erection of which one Boston philanthropist gave a thousand dollars, has been bereft of its machinery, engine, boilers, and all, and is now fast rotting down. A half finished school house has been torn away, and the materials carried off, and nothing but the beautiful and well cultivated land remains.[53] There is a Baptist church in the village, under the pastoral charge of my old friend, Rev. Samuel H. Davis,[54] formerly of Buffalo, N.Y., Mr. and Mrs. George Cary, who extended to me their generous hospitality, resides near Dawn. "Father Henson,"[55] also has a fine farm, and "a big bag of flour," in his house, near to the Institution. Many others here have farms that would do honor to any race.

WINDSOR. Directly opposite to Detroit, and at the terminus of the Great Western Rail Road, lies the village of Windsor, a place of 2,500 inhabitants, 600 of whom are colored, and most of the latter class are fugitives from slavery. Henry Offet, a colored man, is the most extensive provision dealer in the place.[56] His store is frequented by farmers, white and colored, from within ten miles of Windsor. The morals of the people are good. Rev. Wm. Troy, just returned from England, is an educated and enterprising man, and is building a fine church, for his congregation, which is of the Baptist order.[57] Bishop Green, of the split wing of the Methodist church, resides here, and preaches to a small congregation,[58] in a little hall; Rev. Mr. Disney, presides over the old wing, of the Methodist denomination.[59]

The colored children here, are separated from the whites, as they are in Chatham, St. Catharines, London, and Amherstburg. Mr. and Mrs. Isaac N. Cary, reside here, Mr. Cary was formerly from Washington City, where he enjoyed the respect and entire confidence of the people, both colored and white. In 1836, he visited Hayti, and carried with him an autograph endorsement of "Old Hickory," as the following will show:

> Washington
> July 10, 1836
>
> Isaac N. Cary, a free colored citizen of the United States, and about making his residences in St. Domingo, is represented to me, by respectable citizens a bearing and fair character for integrity, industry, and general propriety of deportment.
>
> ANDREW JACKSON
> *President of the United States*

Mr. Cary is one of the most enterprising and intellectual men in Canada, and is deeply interested in the moral, social, and political elevation of all classes. Mrs. Cary, is better known as the beautiful and accomplished Mary E. Miles, afterward, Mrs. Henry Bibb. Her labors during the lifetime of Mr. Bibb, in connection with him, for the fugitives, and her exertions since, are too well known for me to make mention of them here, Mrs. Cary has a private school, with about 40 pupils, mostly children of the better class of the citizens of Windsor.

VI

The past history and present condition of the colored population of Canada, differ widely from that of any other race in the world. Brought up under the strong arm of oppression, bought, sold, made to toil without compensation, from early dawn till late at night; the tenderest ties of nature torn asunder, deprived of all the rights of humanity, by both law and public opinion, at the South, they escape to Canada with all the hope and enthusiasm that such a long-dreamed of change can bring. On arriving here they are met by two classes; the mongrel whites, half French, Indian and Spanish on the one side, and Irish, Scotch, German and English, on the other. These *natives*, employ the fugitive, work him late and early, and pay him off in old clothes and provisions, at an exorbitant price, or cheat him entirely out of his wages. If he is so fortunate as to slip through the fingers of these, he then falls into the hands of another class, a set of land speculators, under the guise of philanthropy, owning large tracts of wild, heavy timbered, and low, wet land, which has been purchased for a shilling an acre, or thereabouts, and is importuned to "come and buy yourself a home; you can have ten years to pay for it in. Come now, get you a farm and be independent." The land is bought, the contract duly signed, and the poor man with his family settles in a log hut, surrounded by water a foot deep, in the spring of the year. By hard work, and almost starvation, they succeed in making their annual payments, together with the interest. The "Benevolent Land Association" has its Constitution and By-Laws,[60] with any number of loop-holes for itself to get out at, but none for the purchaser. The fugitive is soon informed that he must fulfil certain obligations, or he will forfeit his claim. Unable to read, he takes his paper, goes to a lawyer, pays a fee, and is told that it is all right, he is bound by the contract. This unexpected stipulation is scarcely settled, ere he is again informed that if he does not comply with another oppressive act, he will forfeit his claim. Away he starts to the lawyer; another fee, and he returns with a flea in his ear. The last requirement is fulfilled with a sigh and a heavy heart. After years of toil, he has paid all that he agreed to, and demands his deed, when he is met with the reply that the "Association" has passed an act that every settler shall erect a frame house, twenty-four by thirty feet, must put a post and paling fence in front, and must ditch his land, or he cannot get his deed. Once more he goes to the lawyer, pays a fee, and then begins to think that "all that glitters is not gold," and gets upon his knees and prays to the Lord to give him patience to bear up under his multitude of misfortunes, or damns the "Benevolent Land Society," and swears that philanthropy in Canada is a humbug. Should he have health, strength, religion, and physical courage enough to pass safely through the meshes of the "Land Society," he then falls into the hands of the political jugglers. In Canada, one must possess a certain amount of property, or pay rent in a given sum, to entitle him to a vote for a member of Parliament. On the "Refugee Home" lands the colored residents voted for the candidates, at the election preceding the last, when it was found that they held the balance of power in their district, and at once it was resolved to disfranchise them. Consequently, at the last election, these people were assessed so low, that they fell under the required sum, and lost the right to vote. Still their taxes are just the same as they were when exercising the franchise. Thus, the names of more than fifty persons in one town were struck from the voters' list, on account of color.

The more I see of Canada, the more I am convinced of the deep-rooted hatred to the negro, here. In no hotel, can a colored person receive the respect given to the same class in New England. In every place except Toronto and Hamilton, they are excluded from the public schools, and in one district, where there were not enough colored children to entitle them to a separate school, the district school was abolished entirely rather than permit the colored children to attend it. One of the wealthiest and most influential colored farmers, and almost white, too, was lately refused a membership to a county agricultural society. Whenever a colored man is employed by a white man, the former is invariably put to a side table to take his meal; in the farming districts it is the same; and even when a white man works for a colored person, he demands a side-table, for he feels himself above eating with his master. The Rev. William King, of Buxton, is the only white person who has yet invited me to partake of his hospitality.

VII

COLCHESTER. Ten miles from Amherstburg, and on the shores of Lake Erie, lies the agricultural town of Colchester. This is the warmest section of Canada, and the land here, is the best that I have yet seen. Sweet potatoes of good size, pumpkins three feet high, and watermelons two feet long, are all brought to perfection in this climate. Two hundred farms in Colchester are owned by colored men. Mr. Joseph Mason, once a slave, and son of ex-Gov. Mason of Virginia, has a splendid farm, and conducts a saw-mill, owned by himself and neighbors.[61] Mr. Wm. McCurdy, is an able farmer and an enterprising citizen, having the elevation of his race deeply at heart.[62] Cursey & Harris, own and carry on a large brickmaking establishment. Mr. John White and Mr. James Harris,[63] each have a brickyard, also. As farmers, I consider the colored people of Colchester, far in advance of the same class in other sections through which I have passed. There is a Wesleyan Methodist Church here, presided over by the Rev. Wm. Ruth, a veteran preacher, farmer and mechanic.[64] Mr. Ruth combines the useful with the ornamental.

AMHERSTBURG. At the entrance to the Detroit river, and 18 miles below Windsor, lies the village of Amherstburg, with a population of 2,200, of whom 400 are colored. This is one of the oldest towns in this section of Canada, and the small, low, unpainted houses, the muddy streets, with pigs, dogs, and cattle running at large, the almost smothering smell of the hog-pens, as one passes through the thoroughfares, and the dark French and Indian look of its white inhabitants, distinguishes this, from every other place in Canada West. Lying so near to Detroit, Amherstburg has long been one of the principal receiving depots of fugitives escaping by the Underground Railroad from the South. The colored population here, seem to be in comfortable circumstances, most of them occupying their own dwellings, and appear to get ready employment. The Baptist Church is a neat building, capable of seating 400 persons, and has 150 members; Rev. Anthony Binga, is the pastor.[65] The Methodists have a small church and are erecting a new one, which they expect to occupy during the next year. Rev. Mr. Christine has the pastoral charge of the last named.[66] Another branch of the Methodists have a small society, with the Rev. Mr. Broady, as their minister.[67] There is a

Union Sabbath School,[68] which meets and holds its sessions at the Son's Hall, and in which all denominations are represented.

BUSINESS. There are seven grocery stores, all owned and conducted by colored persons. The most finished carpenter and joiner in the place is Mr. William Lyons, a colored man.[69] To see him bossing half a dozen whites, contrasts strangely with the mean prejudice which shows itself wherever a dark skin is seen. There are four plasterers, seven carpenters, five blacksmiths, two stone masons, and two bricklayers. Levi Foster, Esq., owns and carries on a fine livery establishment, and his horses are the best in the town. At a recent county fair Mr. Foster took four prizes. His corn, cows, and horses were the best on the grounds. His beautiful horse, "Whitelock," is the most splendid looking animal I have ever seen, and is said to be worth $1000. Mr. Foster is an enterprising man, and during the winter runs a line of stages between Amherstburg and Windsor. No man in the place is more respected than he. Mrs. Foster is an accomplished lady from New England, and I am deeply indebted for a congenial home at their residence while at Amherstburg. Should I meet any young men in search of wives, and worthy of good ones, I would direct them to the home of Levi Foster, Esq., for his amiable daughters, will, I think, make the best of wives.[70]

There are many finely cultivated and valuable farms in the vicinity of Amherstburg, owned and paid for by colored men. Mr. Thomas Buckner is one of the most scientific farmers in Canada,[71] and has his place stocked with the best breed of horses, cattle, and sheep, his orchard is the most splendid I saw in the Province. A squash weighing 100 pounds was raised in his garden this year. He, like Mr. Foster, has taken several first class prizes at the county fairs. Three of his beautiful daughters were engaged at spinning, weaving, and sewing, when I arrived, getting ready for the severe Canada winter. These young ladies will no doubt be snatched up like hot cakes. The British M. E. Church,[72] has no presiding minister, now, I believe. The Baptists, also, have a small church here. The separate school system is felt in this town, as well as in other places, and under such circumstances the education of the children will always be poor, for the educated portion of the whites feel no interest in them, and both teacher and building generally appear sadly deficient. This does not apply to Colchester, more than to other places.

The farmers throughout Canada suffer severely from the long winters, and the last week give indications that cold weather is at hand. Already the farmers are expressing fears that the frost will spoil the corn, which is still in the fields, with many other products.

One of the greatest pests, in Canada, is the rat; farmers are very much annoyed with them. They infest the barns, corn cribs, hay lofts, stables, and the dwellings, to an extent unknown in the States, or in Europe. The specimens that I have seen appear to be an enlarged edition of the Norway rat, finely improved. Many of them are as large as a woodchuck, and almost as tame as a kitten. Few cats will have the courage to tackle to one of these animals. While I write, two are playing on the floor, and puss lays under the table, not daring to disturb them. Last night I awoke, found five or six on my bed, and kicked them off. This morning I discovered that a hole had been cut through my coat pocket, and a stick of cough candy taken out during the night, by these scamps. Nothing but my religion kept me from swearing.

MORALS. Everywhere, the whites testify to the high moral standing of the colored people; and this is the more commendable from the fact that so many of them are from slavery, where there is no inducement for them to be chaste and virtuous. I have not seen any ardent spirits in a private house, since coming into the Province, and I am told that it is never bought and taken home, by the colored farmers or mechanics. The people here have one bad habit, and that is, the use of tobacco. Men, women, and children, not only smoke, but it is common to see a woman with her chew of tobacco in her mouth. I cannot blame the women for using the weed, where the men are given to the filthy practice; for, like the woman who takes a bite of onion to keep up with her husband's breath, after he has eaten half-a-dozen, so the wife must chew tobacco, that she may not be repulsed by the unbearable breath of her husband, whose teeth and gums have been steeped and soaked in the nasty juice.

The practice of taking children to meetings of every kind is well understood and carried out in Canada. I have counted as many as twenty-five babies in a single audience. Being in a country district a few evenings since, and being very much annoyed by the cries of the little ones, and hearing that a larger grist of them was to be expected the following evening, I went to the nearest village, got a bottle of paregoric, and prepared for the interesting occasion. My host enquired what I was going to do with the medicine, when I informed him that I intended to give each baby a teaspoonful, at the beginning of the lecture. News soon spread from house to house, and from neighborhood to neighborhood, until the whole community of mothers understood upon what condition their children were to make up a part of the audience that night. Evening came, and with it came the people, but no babies. The laughing, the crying, and the snoring of the babies, as experienced the previous evening, vanished before my little bottle of paregoric. I now take a farewell of the people of Canada, and in making my bow, I must acknowledge my gratefulness to Isaac N. Cary, Esq., and lady, of Windsor, Rev. Wm. King of Buxton, Mr. and Mrs. Joshua Howard of London, and Mr. and Mrs. Thomas Morton of Hamilton.

Pine and Palm (Boston, Mass.), 7, 14, 21, 28 September, 19 October, 30 November, 7 December 1861.

1. William N. Mitchell (?–ca. 1879) was born free in Guilford County, North Carolina, to an Indian woman. Mitchell's parents died when he was young, and he was raised in the custody of local authorities, who indentured him as an apprentice for twelve years. His study of Christianity convinced him to end his association with slavery and to prepare for the ministry. He moved to Ross County, Ohio, with his wife (they had at least one daughter after settling there) and assisted runaway slaves on the underground railroad. In 1855 Mitchell became a missionary for the American Baptist Free Mission Society and moved to Toronto, Canada West, where, as pastor of the Coloured Regular Baptist Church, he ministered to many of the city's estimated one thousand fugitive slaves. In the late 1850s, Mitchell joined the Provincial Association for the Education and Elevation of the Colored People of Canada. In that capacity, he toured Canada West, accumulated information and statistics about black life in the country (especially on the needs of newly arrived fugitives), and contributed to the *Report of the Fugitive Mission*, which assessed those needs.

In early 1859, Mitchell traveled to Britain seeking funds to build a chapel and school for his congregation. He often shared the rostrum with Rev. William Troy of Windsor, Canada West, who was in Scotland and England on a similar mission. During his stay, Mitchell published *The Under-Ground Railroad* (London, 1860), which detailed underground railroad activity in the United States and addressed what Mitchell believed were misrepresentations being made about the true condition of fugitive slaves in Canada West. During a return trip to England in 1863, Mitchell became embroiled in controversy; he was arrested for failing to pay his room rent, censured for using references from his earlier tour, and accused of not maintaining collection accounts. Mitchell insisted that all of the four hundred pounds he had collected was sent to Canada, less expenses and salary. Mitchell is listed as a deceased member of the Consolidated American Baptist Missionary Convention in the minutes of the annual meeting for 1879. William N. Mitchell, *The Under-Ground Railroad* (London, 1860), 1–172; Winks, *Blacks in Canada*, 227, 238; Gara, *Liberty Line*, 161–63; Wilbur H. Siebert, *The Underground Railroad: From Slavery to Freedom* (New York, N.Y., 1898), 2, 3, 45, 46, 183, 184, 222, 233, 239, 462; *PtL*, 25 June 1863; Michael Willis to L. A. Chamerovzow, n.d., British Empire MSS., UkOxU-Rh; *ASRL*, 2 May 1864; *Minutes of the Thirty-Ninth Annual Meeting of the Consolidated American Baptist Missionary Convention* (Lexington, Ky., 1881), 32.

2. Nelson Harmon Turpin was born in Delaware. As a young man, he entered the African Methodist Episcopal Zion ministry, but he left the AMEZ and in 1854 was received into the Ohio conference of the African Methodist Episcopal church. Turpin remained in the Ohio conference through 1860, serving a congregation in Columbus, Ohio, then the Wylie Street Church in Pittsburgh. He was pastor of the Sayer Street British Methodist Episcopal Church in Toronto during the Civil War. That congregation, which had been formed by the AME in 1833, worshiped in several locations during its first two decades. Between 1842 and the mid-1850s, Rev. Jeremiah Taylor built it into the third largest AME congregation in Canada West. By the time of Turpin's pastorate, the church was well established on Sayer Street. After the war, Turpin was transferred to the New York conference. He served AME congregations in South Carolina during the 1880s. Wayman, *Cyclopaedia of African Methodism*, 169; Smith, *African Methodist Episco-*

pal Church, 88, 97; *Columbus City Directory*, 1856; *WAA*, 17 December 1859, 19 May 1860; Hill, *Freedom-Seekers*, 134–35; Simpson, "Negroes in Ontario to 1870," 342, 870–71.

3. Brown refers to the Coloured Wesleyan Methodist Church on Richmond Street.

4. Brown refers to the Provincial Association for the Education and the Elevation of the Colored People of Canada.

5. The Queen Victoria Benevolent Society, a self-help organization, was established by Toronto black women in 1840 and functioned into the 1860s. Ellen Abbott, the wife of black abolitionist Wilson R. Abbott, led the society throughout most of those years. In addition to providing its members with poor relief, aid for the sick, and burial insurance, the organization assisted newly arriving fugitive slaves. Hill, "Negroes in Toronto," 21; Hill, *Freedom-Seekers*, 179.

6. Samuel C. Watson (1832–?) was born to free black parents in South Carolina. Orphaned at the age of nine, he lived for a time with a Presbyterian clergyman in Washington, D.C. Watson received an excellent education; he was tutored by the wife of Leonard A. Grimes (a noted black clergyman), attended Union Seminary, and at the age of sixteen enrolled in Phillips Academy. In 1853 Watson followed his brother to Oberlin College, but he left within the year to study medicine at the University of Michigan. Four years later, with his studies at the Western Homeopathic College in Cleveland completed, he established a medical practice in Chatham, Canada West. Although lured to British Columbia in 1858 by the discovery of gold, he returned to Chatham one year later to manage the *T. Whitney*, a boat owned by William Whipper that ran between Sandusky, Ohio, and Detroit. He married the daughter of black abolitionist Joseph Cassey of Philadelphia during the winter of 1861. They initially settled in Toronto, where Watson again worked as a physician. In 1863 he and his wife moved to Detroit, where he abandoned medical practice and opened a successful pharmacy. He quickly became a prominent member of the city's black elite and a powerful force in local Republican politics. He gained a seat on the city's board of estimates (1875), twice ran unsuccessfully for the state legislature, and was eventually elected to the city council (1883). In 1884 Watson became the first northern black elected as a delegate to the Republican National Convention and represented Michigan as an honorary commissioner at the World's Exposition in New Orleans. But Watson's political moderation—he warned blacks against "overzealous action" in testing the 1875 Civil Rights Act—and his preference for white social circles alienated many blacks and limited his political effectiveness among blacks. His political ambitions frustrated, he joined the Democratic party during the late 1880s, but this action brought further condemnation from blacks—including Frederick Douglass—for abandoning his race. Simmons, *Men of Mark*, 860–65; Katzman, *Before the Ghetto*, 127–28, 136, 149–52, 163, 167, 179–84.

7. S. Goutier, a Toronto black, tutored French, accounting, and music and was a frequent correspondent of black newspapers. He was involved with the John Anderson extradition case and reported on the legal proceedings of that case, Haitian immigration, and other black concerns in letters to the *Weekly Anglo-African*. Goutier resettled in Haiti in 1862. *PP*, 14 August 1862; *PFW*, 13 September 1857; *WAA*, 17 March, 28 April, 5 May, 15, 29 December 1860, 12, 19

January, 16 February, 2, 9 March 1861 [12:0571, 0660, 0684, 13:0039, 0073, 0191, 0207, 0326, 0382, 0396].

8. George W. Cary, a hairdresser, was a leading member of the Toronto black community during the 1860s. He served as secretary of the Mental and Moral Improvement Society (a local black literary and self-help association), chaired numerous black meetings, and served on several committees appointed to investigate the concerns of Toronto blacks. Cary condemned race prejudice in Canada West and urged blacks to vote for Reform candidates who dealt favorably with black issues. *Toronto City Directory*, 1859; *TG*, 3 March 1860; 27 June 1861 [12:0542, 13:0603]; *WAA*, 7 April 1860 [12:0622].

9. Brown refers to William Watkins, who died in 1858, and his son, William J. Watkins.

10. Brown refers to Wilson R. Abbott, the wealthiest black in Toronto, who by 1858 had assets valued at over $100,000. He continued to extend his real estate holdings and by 1871 owned forty-two houses, five vacant lots, and a warehouse in Toronto, Hamilton, and Owen Sound. *ASR*, 1 April 1858; *DCB*, 10:3.

11. In the racial context, "passing" refers specifically to the experience of those blacks who were unwittingly accepted as white by white society because of their light complexions, cultivated mannerisms, and refined speech. Wentworth and Flexner, *Dictionary of American Slang*, 377.

12. Benjamin Stewart was a prominent member of the Trenton, New Jersey, black community through the early 1850s. He held a high position in the state's black Masonic order and served as pastor of a local African Methodist Episcopal congregation. After publicly endorsing Canadian immigration for several years, Stewart resettled in Canada West in 1854. Although he initially labored as an itinerant AME preacher, he gained notoriety when he submitted a resolution to the 1855 annual meeting of the Canada conference calling for its separation from the AME church. Stewart was active in the resulting British Methodist Episcopal denomination and eventually accepted the pastorate of the Hamilton BME Church. Under his guidance, the congregation reached a membership of 178 by the early 1860s. Stewart remained active in the affairs of the BME church after the Civil War. During the late 1860s, he served as a trustee of the Nazrey Institute, a BME seminary in Chatham. He pastored a BME congregation in Windsor during the following decade. Stewart also continued to be an active Mason, eventually becoming Grand Master of Ontario's black lodges. Simpson, "Negroes in Ontario to 1870," 100, 241, 416, 683–685n, 847; *PFW*, 10 April 1851 [6:0896]; Payne, *History of the AME Church*, 321–22; *CR*, 16 December 1875.

13. M. Broadwater was pastor of St. Paul's African Methodist Episcopal Church in Hamilton. He assumed ministerial responsibilities in Hamilton in the late 1840s. Brown incorrectly identifies Broadwater as a Baptist. Hill, *Freedom-Seekers*, 135.

14. Thomas Morton (1818–?), a Hamilton black, was born in Canada West. He signed the call for the 1851 North American Convention at Toronto. His wife, Mary (1823–?), was originally from New York. The Mortons and their five children resettled in Sacramento, California, after the Civil War. Abajian, *Blacks in Selected Newspapers*, 2:683–84; *VF*, 13 August 1851.

15. Brown claimed that his father, a white Kentuckian named George Higgins,

was a half brother of Dr. John Young, his first master. On occasion Brown referred to Young as his uncle. Farrison, *William Wells Brown*, 5.

16. Charles F. Suttle.

17. Anthony Burns was pastor of the Zion Baptist Church in St. Catharines, Canada West. Hill, *Freedom-Seekers*, 140.

18. Brown refers to the North Street Methodist Chapel.

19. Scuttle, scoop, and glengarry all refer to types of head apparel. The scuttle is a cowl; the scoop bonnet is so-named for its elongated, curved brim; and the glengarry, of Scottish origins, is an oval-shaped woolen cap.

20. Brown refers to the underground railroad.

21. During the early 1860s, there were two black churches in London, Canada West—the Second Baptist Church, which had been founded by Rev. Daniel A. Turner in the 1840s, and Rev. Lewis C. Chambers's British Methodist Episcopal congregation. Each operated their own Sabbath school program. The "benevolent society" to which Brown refers was probably the Ladies Association in Aid of Colored Refugees, a black fugitive relief organization. Hill, *Freedom-Seekers*, 143–45; Simpson, "Negroes in Ontario to 1870," 212, 759.

22. Lewis C. Chambers was born a slave in Cecil County, Maryland. He acquired a rudimentary education as a slave and, for eight years, managed the farm of his third owner, William Little of Nottingham, Maryland, before purchasing his freedom for $1,250 in 1844. Chambers settled in Philadelphia, joined the African Methodist Episcopal church, worked in a "chemical establishment," and earned enough to buy a farm in New Jersey. In the mid-1850s, he financed the resettlement of himself and fourteen other blacks in Canada West. Chambers rented a fifty-acre plot in London and divided his time between farming and missionary activity. Ordained by the British Methodist Episcopal church in 1858, Chambers pastored several black congregations in Kent and Middlesex counties. About that same time, the American Missionary Association followed Henry Highland Garnet's recommendation and appointed Chambers to serve in the Dresden area. From the late 1850s through 1863, Chambers worked for the AMA's Canada Mission. His correspondence contains frequent comments on white prejudice against blacks in Canada. Chambers was harassed by hostile whites in Wallaceburg and had his newly built home destroyed by arsonists in 1860. In 1863 Chambers relocated in St. Catharines, where he and his wife opened a school. But Chambers's congregations dwindled with the decline of the black population in Canada West, precipitated by the American Civil War. He made several unsuccessful appeals to the AMA for support to do missionary work in the American South or in Africa. Chambers returned to the United States in the fall of 1868, settled in New Brunswick, New Jersey, and served a small AME congregation there. Blassingame, *Slave Testimony*, 412–14n; Wayman, *Cyclopaedia of African Methodism*, 34; *AM*, January 1859; Simpson, "Negroes in Ontario to 1870," 647, 794; Johnson, "American Missionary Association," 353–54; Clara M. De Boer, "The Role of Afro-Americans in the Origin and Work of the American Missionary Association, 1839–1877" (Ph.D. diss., Rutgers University, 1973), 99–132.

23. Brown reprints an excerpt from an editorial entitled "Shall We have a Separate School for the Coloured Children," which appeared in the 22 July 1861 issue of the *London Free Press*. It attracted angry letters of rebuttal from black cler-

gyman Lewis C. Chambers and others. Initially named the *Canadian Free Press*, the paper was founded as a weekly by William Sutherland in 1849. Under the direction of Sutherland and Josiah Blackburn, who edited the paper throughout much of the 1850s and 1860s, it functioned as a Liberal organ. Publication of a daily edition began in 1857 and continues today. *LFP*, 22, 27 July, 6 August 1861; H. Orlo Miller, "The History of the Newspaper Press in London, 1830–1875," *OHSPR* 32:132–33 (1937).

24. Prudence Crandall (1803–1889) was born in Hopkinton, Rhode Island, received a Quaker education, and in 1831 opened a school for girls in Canterbury, Connecticut. A year later, when Crandall admitted a black girl to the school, parents withdrew their daughters. Crandall then established a boarding school for black girls. The school opened in April 1833 and occasioned a furious public debate and passage of a law banning schools for nonresident blacks (the Connecticut Black Law). Crandall had abolitionist support, especially from William Lloyd Garrison and Arthur Tappan. She was eventually arrested (June 1834), tried, and found guilty for violating the Black Law but appealed and won the case on a technicality. The school continued to operate until September 1834, when violence by townspeople closed it. Crandall's heroic posture during the affair made her one of the decade's most celebrated antislavery figures and an early catalyst of antislavery feminism. Crandall married Calvin Philleo, a Baptist minister, shortly before the closing of the school and moved with him to Illinois. After her husband's death, she moved to Kansas, where she died in 1889. *DAB*, 4:503–4; Edmund Fuller, *Prudence Crandall* (Middletown, Conn., 1971); Helen Catterall, *Judicial Cases Concerning American Slavery and the Negro*, 5 vols. (Washington, D.C., 1936), 414–16.

25. William H. Jones (?–1915), an African Methodist Episcopal clergyman of "pure African descent," spent his early years in the free black community of Baltimore. He was named traveling agent for the AME church press in 1852 and published new editions of early black works like *The Life of Richard Allen* and William C. Nell's *Colored Patriots of the Revolution*. During the next three years, he frequently visited Canada West and served as secretary to the AME's Canada conference. When conflict arose within the AME publishing committee over his financial reporting methods, he resigned and moved to Chatham, Canada West. Jones participated in the founding of the British Methodist Episcopal church in 1856 and pastored a Chatham BME congregation during the late 1850s and early 1860s. His successful fund-raising tour of the northern United States in 1859 enabled his congregation to build a spacious new brick structure. Under his direction, the church's membership increased to over three hundred people, making it the largest black congregation in the province. But the charismatic and flamboyant Jones offended some of the more staid black clergy, who made his questionable religious and moral conduct part of a broader struggle for control of the BME. Jones authored several works during the early 1860s, including a history of the BME and an antislavery songster. A vigorous supporter of Union conduct during the Civil War, he revisited the northern United States in 1863–64 with a panorama of slave and war scenes to raise funds for American sanitary aid associations. After the war, Jones turned his attention to the plight of the southern freedmen. From 1865 to 1868, he made a successful lecture tour of Britain to raise funds for the freedmen's aid cause. After returning from Britain, he did mis-

sionary work among the freedmen in Tennessee. Jones died in Arkansas in 1915. Smith, *African Methodist Episcopal Church*, 25, 27, 49, 305; Payne, *History of AME Church*, 278, 318, 334; *CR*, 13 July, 17 August, 16 September 1854; *VF*, 12 August 1852; *WAA*, 7 October 1859, 8 March 1862 [12:0115, 14:0177]; A. R. Green and Samuel Venable, *A Brief Account of the Re-Organization of the BME Church* . . . (Detroit, Mich., 1872), 8–36, 45–46, 74–82, 88–102, 114–30; *AAN*, 8 August, 24 October 1863, 9 April 1864; Christine Bolt, *The Anti-Slavery Movement and Reconstruction: A Study in Anglo-American Co-operation, 1863–77* (London, 1969), 66; *FML*, July, November, December 1866, March, April, July, November 1867, June, August 1868; William H. Jones to John J. Cary, 27 May 1870, AMA-ARC.

26. The Bethel African Methodist Episcopal Church of Philadelphia and St. Philips Episcopal Church of New York City were two notable black churches of the nineteenth century. The former, considered the mother church of the AME denomination, had its origin in 1792, when discriminatory seating practices prompted Rev. Richard Allen to lead black parishioners out of St. George's Methodist Episcopal Church. Brown refers to the congregation's third meeting hall, a large, brick and stone structure erected in 1841 and used until 1889. St. Philips Episcopal Church, the first black Episcopal congregation formed from another Episcopal body, was established in 1818 when black members, led by Rev. Peter Williams, withdrew from New York's Trinity Episcopal Church. The building to which Brown refers was constructed in 1822. Ruby C. Boyd, comp., *On this Rock: The Mother Church of African Methodism* (Philadelphia, Pa., 1976); George F. Bragg, *History of the Afro-American Group of the Episcopal Church* (Baltimore, Md., 1922; reprint, New York, N.Y., 1968), 81–89.

27. Chatham's First Baptist church was established in 1843 by Rev. Stephen White and nine other blacks. It joined the Amherstburg Baptist Association the same year. In 1846 the congregation suffered a schism, which resulted in the founding of the Second Baptist Church in Chatham under the direction of Rev. Eli Highwarden and, later, Stephen White. Rather than join the ABA, the Second Baptist Church affiliated with the Canadian Anti-Slavery Baptist Association. Both congregations erected church buildings in 1848. A third congregation, the Union Baptist Church, was founded in 1848 when several blacks attempted to reunite the First Baptist Church and the Second Baptist Church. Rev. Israel Campbell served this congregation of thirty members. In September 1856, the three churches reunited into a single congregation called the First Baptist Congregation of Chatham. The new church served as a meeting place for the town's black community, and it became the local headquarters for the antislavery campaign. Hill, *Freedom-Seekers*, 142–43; Lewis, "Religious Nature of Negro Migration," 122, 126–29; Lewis, "Pioneer Coloured Baptist Life," 270–71; Simpson, "Negroes in Ontario to 1870," 678–80; Walton, "Blacks in Buxton and Chatham," 26, 74.

28. Charles H. Pearce (1817–1887) was born into slavery in Queen Annes County, Maryland. After purchasing his freedom, he settled in New Haven, Connecticut, and preached to black Methodist congregations. He was ordained into the African Methodist Episcopal ministry in the early 1850s. Pearce soon resettled in Chatham, Canada West, and participated in the founding of the British Methodist Episcopal church in 1856. He became embroiled in a bitter personal

rivalry with the charismatic and controversial William H. Jones, another local BME pastor, in the early 1860s. This feud, which was part of a broader challenge to the leadership and organization of the BME, prompted the new denomination to expel Pearce. He then joined other BME "secessionists" in establishing the new Independent Methodist Episcopal church. Pearce returned to the United States in 1865, gained readmission to the AME church, and was appointed to supervise denominational missionary work among the freedmen in Florida. His forceful leadership and tireless organizing in the northern section of the state earned him considerable respect in the black community—the freedmen referred to him as "Bishop" Pearce. He recognized that the black ministry served both religious and political functions. When in Chatham, he used his pulpit to condemn Haitian immigration. During Reconstruction he became a powerful figure in the state Republican party and was elected to the state senate in 1868. As chairman of the senate education committee, he blocked efforts to segregate public schools. He also served briefly as superintendent of education in Leon County, Florida. Pearce was removed from the senate in 1872 on questionable bribery charges, but he was quickly reelected and continued to serve black interests. Census of Canada, 1861; *CR*, 17 November 1887; Payne, *History of AME Church*, 306, 369; Smith, *African Methodist Episcopal Church*, 66–67, 505–23; Green and Venable, *Re-Organization of the BME Church*, 8–37, 56–58, 67–82, 109–37; *WAA*, 26 May 1860, 9 November 1861, 5 April 1862 [12:0733, 13:0886, 14:0222]; Walker, *Rock in a Weary Land*, 120–21; Joe M. Richardson, *The Negro in the Reconstruction of Florida, 1865–1877* (Tallahassee, Fla., 1965), 84–85, 113, 120–22, 154, 190–92; Dorothy Dodd, "'Bishop' Pearce and the Reconstruction of Leon County," *Apal* (1946), 5–12.

29. Brown refers to adherents to Methodist doctrine.

30. Chatham's black public school opened in about 1848, making the village the first in Canada West with a segregated common school system. Forty-nine students were instructed by James E. Grant, a local black. The number of students had doubled by 1851, but attendance became erratic during the following decade. A black, Alfred Whipper, was hired as instructor in 1856, and he continued to serve periodically through 1860. A second black public school was opened in Chatham in 1858 but closed the following year. The original school was enlarged in 1861, and a Mr. Sinclair, a white opponent of racially integrated education, was hired as principal. Sarah Armstrong taught at the school and served as Sinclair's assistant. After the Civil War, Armstrong returned to the United States to teach at a black school in Newport, Rhode Island, and was replaced by James Ward. Although Chatham blacks protested against segregated education for decades, the local black public school remained active until 1891. Simpson, "Negroes in Ontario to 1870," 332, 570, 667–72, 674, 675, 686–89, 719; Walton, "Blacks in Buxton and Chatham," 76; *PP*, 28 September 1861; *PF*, 10 April 1851 [6:0896]; *PFW*, 31 May 1856; *WAA*, 12 August 1865.

31. Amelia Freeman Shadd (1833–?), a black teacher and underground railroad activist, was hired in 1856 to establish and operate a school for black students at Chatham, Canada West. Born and reared in Ohio, Amelia Freeman was educated at Oberlin College and under the tutelage of Rev. Charles Avery of Pittsburgh. After completing her education, she taught art and music in Pittsburgh during the early 1850s, first at Avery College, then at the Allegheny Institute. Her

work so impressed Martin R. Delany, William King, and William Still that they recommended her for a position in Chatham. Her April 1856 arrival there was greeted with much acclaim. Within a few months of her arrival, she married black abolitionist Isaac D. Shadd and opened her school. The school grew rapidly during the late 1850s and early 1860s, enrolling 259 day and evening students by 1864. Sarah M. Shadd, Mary Ann Shadd Cary, and the latter's stepdaughter, Ann Cary, periodically assisted Amelia Freeman Shadd in operating the institution. Its broad curriculum included philosophy, music, American history, algebra, and botany; Amelia Freeman Shadd also privately instructed students in embroidery, art, music, and written composition. The school suffered continuing financial difficulties despite subsidies received from the American Missionary Association and the Refugee Home Society during the early 1860s and from fund-raising tours conducted by Mary Ann Shadd Cary; in 1864 Amelia Freeman Shadd was forced to teach in the local public schools in order to keep her own school open. She played an important part in the cultural life of the Chatham black community, organizing lecture series, literary circles, nondenominational religious services, and various fund-raising projects. Her contributions to the *Provincial Freeman* included service as a subscription agent, a contributor, and in early 1857 as temporary editor. Isaac and Amelia Freeman Shadd moved to Mississippi in the early 1870s; she taught school at Davis Bend and in Vicksburg during the following decade. United States Census, 1850; Abajian, *Blacks in Selected Newspapers*, 1:296, 3:729; Bearden and Butler, *Shadd*, 190–203; Hermann, *The Pursuit of a Dream*, 183; *FDP*, 27 January 1854; *PFW*, 19 April, 31 May 1856, 3 January, 13 June, 15, 22 August 1857, 28 January 1859 [10:0786–87, 0789, 11:0553]; *PP*, 28 September 1861; *WAA*, 7 January 1860, 28 December 1861, 5 April 1862; Mary Ann Shadd Cary to George Whipple, 21 June 1859, 7 May 1864, AMA-ARC [11:0794, 15:0266]; *DANB*, 552–53; Winks, *Blacks in Canada*, 204–8, 225–26.

32. Thomas Joiner White (1831–1863) was born a free black in Petersburg, Virginia. In 1840 his family resettled in New York City, where White studied medicine under Dr. W. C. Roberts. He graduated from Bowdoin Medical College in 1852 and became a respected physician and activist in New York City's black community. White served as secretary of both the Committee of Thirteen—a black anticolonizationist and vigilance organization—and the Legal Rights Association. He married Emma Glouchester, the daughter of black abolitionist James N. Glouchester, in 1856. Shortly thereafter, he moved to Canada West, settling first in Hamilton, then in Chatham in 1859. During the summer of 1863, while preparing to return to the United States to join a black Union regiment, he was fatally stricken with cholera. *FDP*, 15 January 1852, 7 September 1855; *WAA*, 12 September 1863.

33. Amos Aray (1831–?) was the son of black farmers James and Ann Aray (also spelled Array) of Pittsfield, Michigan. Details of his life are vague before early 1856, when he settled in Chatham and opened a general medical practice. William Wells Brown described Aray as "a reformer in medical practice, being an allopathist, hydropathist, homeopathist, and an eclectic." Aray was an eloquent speaker; he frequently delivered local lectures on various nineteenth-century medical panaceas and gained prominence in the Chatham black community. An emigrationist, he was selected in 1858 to be surgeon for Martin R. Delany's Niger

Valley Exploring Party but failed to accompany the 1859 expedition to Yoruba. His interest in West African immigration continued, and in 1861 he planned to settle in Yoruba with a group of Chatham blacks sponsored by the African Aid Society; once again, he remained instead in Chatham. During the Civil War, he returned to the United States and was hired by Delany to examine black Union recruits. By the early 1870s, Aray was in Nashville, Tennessee, where he served as a subscription agent for Frederick Douglass's *New National Era*. United States Census, 1850; *PFW*, 8, 29 March 1856; *PP*, 28 September 1861; Miller, *Search for Black Nationality*, 182, 252; Ullman, *Martin R. Delany*, 284–85; *NNE*, 2 March 1871.

34. Martin R. Delany attracted considerable interest in the North American black community when he undertook an expedition to explore the Niger Valley in West Africa during 1859–60. His Niger Valley Exploring Party, the formal name given to the effort, consisted of himself and Robert Campbell, a black teacher from Philadelphia. The black explorers arrived at Lagos, the principal nineteenth-century port for the slave trade and commerce in the Niger Valley, then proceeded inland. On 27 December 1859, they signed a treaty with the Alake and chiefs of Abeokuta. Despite confused negotiations and ambiguous language in the treaty, Delany and Campbell believed that the agreement provided a separate grant of tribal land for an Afro-American colony. They were mistaken. According to Yoruba land law, tribal land was owned by kinship groups and could not be transferred. Anglican missionary pressure led the Alake and chiefs of Abeokuta to repudiate the treaty in February 1861. William McCoskry, the British consul at Lagos, supported the repudiation. Upon hearing of the chiefs' action, Lord John Russell, foreign secretary, and Lord John Wodehouse, colonial secretary, initiated a correspondence on the matter with Lord Alfred S. Churchill of the African Aid Society, a year-old British organization that supported Delany's West African settlement scheme. Acting upon word from McCoskry, Lord Russell advised Churchill to abandon the emigration project. Miller, *Search for Black Nationality*, 213–15, 220–30, 251–60; *DNB*, suppl. (1901–11), 3:695–99.

35. David Livingstone (1813–1873), a Scottish missionary and explorer, studied medicine in Glasgow before being sent to South Africa in 1840 by the London Missionary Society. He made several daring exploratory excursions into the interior of Africa that generated European interest in the African continent. *DNB*, 11:1263–75.

36. Joe Harris, the king of Grand Bassa, raided and destroyed a Liberian colonial settlement at Bassa Cove on 10 June 1835. He was later defeated by a militia from Monrovia and forced to rebuild the settlement at his own expense. Brown points to this incident as one example of the suspicion and animosity that existed between black settlers and indigenous peoples in nineteenth-century West Africa. He compares it to the repudiation of the 1859 treaty with Martin R. Delany's Niger Valley Exploring Party by the Alake and chiefs of Abeokuta. Brown implies that Delany was politically naive and lacking in diplomatic skills. Cassell, *Liberia*, 85, 107.

37. Using the 1860 gold price as a standard, £60 million sterling was equivalent to $320 million. Brown clearly offers an exaggerated estimate of the funds that Chatham blacks expected Martin R. Delany and the African Aid Society to generate in Britain for their Niger Valley settlement scheme. He suggests that

since the treaty had been repudiated and the settlement scheme was moribund, Chatham blacks no longer needed to concern themselves with those funds.

38. Martin R. Delany arrived in Britain in mid-May 1860 and spent the following seven months generating support for his Niger Valley Exploring Party's West African settlement scheme. He argued that free land, abundant labor, and black American expertise could turn the Niger Valley into a major cotton-producing region. The public initially failed to distinguish Delany's project from a similar proposal being espoused by the New York-based African Civilization Society and its agent, Theodore Bourne. But members of the aristocracy—particularly Lord Alfred S. Churchill, founder and chairman of the African Aid Society; Lord William Ashburton, president of the Royal Geographical Society; and Lord Frederick Gough-Calthrope, a member of Parliament—gained him a fair hearing. Delany's British tour came to international attention when he attended the International Statistical Congress in London in July 1860. Prince Albert chaired the prestigious scientific gathering. Lord Henry Peter Brougham, a Scottish abolitionist, introduced Delany to the congress's cheering delegates. Brougham's introduction and Delany's reply were thinly veiled condemnations of American slavery and focused attention on George M. Dallas, the American minister to Britain, who was in attendance. A delegate from South Carolina responded by walking out in anger; Dallas suffered in silence. The incident was widely publicized, evoked an official American diplomatic protest, and brought Delany to public attention. He addressed several other distinguished assemblies, including the Royal Geographical Society (London) and the Social Science Congress (Glasgow), during the remainder of his tour. He left Britain in December 1860, having achieved a measure of success in his efforts to interest British textile manufacturers, abolitionists, and government officials in his project. But a tepid response by black Americans and the repudiation of his land treaty by West African chiefs eventually stymied Delany's efforts. Miller, *Search for Black Nationality*, 217–28; Richard Blackett, "In Search of International Support for African Colonization: Martin R. Delany's Visit to England, 1860," *CJH* 10:307–24 (December 1975); *MEB*, 4:582–83.

39. Samuel Russell, a black physician and herbalist, kept a medical office next to the *Provincial Freeman* in the Charity building in Chatham, Canada West. He adhered to medical theories popularized by Samuel Thomson (1769–1843), a New England herbalist and traveling physician. In his medical journals and compendiums, Thomson emphasized the salutary effects of steam treatments and emetic herbs. *PFW*, 26 January 1855; *DAB*, 18:488–89.

40. Henry L. Simpson, pastor of the First Baptist Church of Chatham, settled in the town during the mid-1850s. He promoted black education and moral improvement and was interested in West African exploration and settlement. Census of Canada, 1861; *WAA*, 15 February, 5 April 1862 [14:0129, 0222]; *CP*, 29 March 1861 [13:0433].

41. Henry Melvill (1798–1871), an Anglican minister, was the most popular London preacher of his day. Many of his sermons were published in collected editions. Melvill served as a chaplain to Queen Victoria and became a canon residentiary of St. Paul's in 1856. *MEB*, 2:838.

42. Edwin Forrest (1806–1872), the first American-born actor of international renown, was best known for his portrayal of Spartacus in *The Gladiator*, a trag-

edy by Robert M. Bird. Forrest's roughhewn and passionate presentations contrasted markedly with the refined and studied form of his personal rival, William Charles Macready (1793–1873). A British Shakespearean, Macready won acclaim, especially from upper-class audiences, for his rendition of Hamlet and Macbeth. *DAB*, 6:529–31; *DNB*, 12:721–27.

43. Brown refers to Orson Fowler (1809–1887), a phrenologist, well known for his theories on health and for his writings on phrenology and sex. His lectures attracted large audiences in the United States and Canada. *DAB*, 6:565–66.

44. Isaac Watts (1674–1748), a Calvinist clergyman and author, was the most famous English hymnist of his time. Watts composed over six hundred hymns, whose poetic verses added an emotional dimension to the traditional Calvinist liturgy. *DNB*, 20:978–81.

45. John Newland Maffitt (1795–1850), an itinerant Irish-American, Wesleyan evangelist, was known for his preaching style, which made him popular with southern audiences. With Lewis Garrett, he founded the *Western Methodist*, which later became the *Christian Advocate*, the organ of the Methodist Episcopal church in the South. Maffitt also published an autobiography and collections of his sermons, poems, and other religious literature. *ACAB*, 4:172.

46. Charles Dickens (1812–1870) was the leading popular novelist in mid-nineteenth-century Britain. His best-known novels include *Pickwick Papers*, *A Christmas Carol*, *Oliver Twist*, *David Copperfield*, *Great Expectations*, and *A Tale of Two Cities*. He also edited two successful popular journals, *Household Words* (1850–59) and *All the Year Round* (1859–70). Dickens, who toured the United States twice, criticized American ways and particularly the peculiar institution. *DNB*, 5:925–37.

47. "Widow Bedott" is a female comic figure in the writings of Frances M. Whitcher (1814–1852), a New York Down East humorist who wrote her popular satirical pieces in local dialect. Her stories first appeared as magazine sketches, but many were later collected in *The Widow Bedott Papers* (1856). *DAB*, 20:82.

48. Brown refers to a member of the Clamorgan family, a St. Louis free-black elite. He evidently made Julia Clamorgan's acquaintance while he was a slave in St. Louis during the late 1820s and early 1830s. Cyprian Clamorgan, *The Colored Aristocracy of St. Louis* (St. Louis, Mo., 1858), reprinted in *Missouri Historical Society Bulletin* 1:8–31 (1974).

49. One of the blacks to whom Brown refers was Abraham Shadd, the father of black abolitionists Isaac Shadd and Mary Ann Shadd Cary. The elder Shadd was elected to the Raleigh Town Council in 1859. He later served as the census enumerator for Raleigh Township in 1861. Walton, "Blacks in Buxton and Chatham," 109; Winks, *Blacks in Canada*, 215.

50. Brown refers to Alfred S. Shadd, a son of Abraham D. and Harriet Shadd, who taught at the public North Buxton School during the early 1860s. He had studied at the Toronto Normal School and held a second-class teaching certificate. Hill, *Freedom-Seekers*, 89, 205.

51. Brown refers to Josiah Henson, James Canning Fuller, Hiram Wilson, and other representatives of Dawn, who raised funds in Britain and the United States during the 1840s and 1850s for the British-American Institute at the Dawn settlement.

52. John Scoble was secretary of the British and Foreign Anti-Slavery Society

from 1841 to 1851. The society, which was founded in 1839, united disparate elements of the British antislavery movement into a general crusade for worldwide emancipation and, for its first thirty years, was the only antislavery organization of national stature in Britain. It published the *Anti-Slavery Reporter*, sponsored numerous black and white antislavery speakers from the United States, and hosted four international antislavery conventions (1840, 1843, 1854, 1867). The BFASS functioned throughout the nineteenth century. In 1909 it merged with a similar organization to form the Anti-Slavery and Aborigines Protection Society. Temperley, *British Antislavery*, 62–70, 73, 75–90, 147–52, 209–17, 267–69.

53. When John Scoble moved away from the Dawn settlement in 1861, he left his son in charge of the property of the British-American Institute. The institute was moribund by this time, although Josiah Henson and the elder Scoble were seeking to resolve their dispute over control of the institute's property in the Canadian courts. The settlement's sawmill, which Boston Unitarian Amos Lawrence had partially funded, was destroyed by disgruntled mill workers in the late 1850s, when their employer absconded with three shiploads of lumber. Henson, *Autobiography*, 119–27; Pease and Pease, *Black Utopia*, 67–68, 75.

54. Samuel H. Davis, a black Baptist clergyman, was originally from Buffalo, New York, and later served black Baptist congregations in Detroit. Active in the black convention movement, Davis chaired the National Convention of Colored Citizens at Buffalo (1843) and attended the Colored National Convention at Rochester (1853). When the American Baptist Free Mission Society assumed responsibility for the black settlement and school at Dawn in 1850, Davis was appointed to manage the settlement. He revived the British-American Institute but only briefly. After control of the Dawn settlement passed to John Scoble in 1852, Davis returned to Detroit to pastor the Union Baptist Church. During the mid-1850s, he settled in Dresden and founded a Baptist church. Initially an agent for the Amherstburg Baptist Association, Davis broke with the organization to join the Canadian Anti-Slavery Baptist Association and was its leading figure during the 1850s. In the mid-1860s, he served a Baptist congregation at Puce River. After the Civil War, Davis did missionary work among the freedmen in the American South and later returned to Canada West, where he completed his ministerial career. *SL*, 16 January 1843 [4:0525]; *CTWP*, 19–21 July 1859 [11:0863]; *VF*, 12 March 1851, 21 October 1852; Simpson, "Negroes in Ontario to 1870," 733–34; *FDP*, 10 June 1853, 27 October 1854; *PFW*, 29 September, 1 December 1855; Lewis, "Religious Nature of Negro Migration," 125–26, 128; Carlesimo, "Refugee Home Society," 141.

55. Josiah Henson.

56. Henry Offitt (1824–?), a mulatto Windsor grocer, was born in the United States. Financially comfortable, by 1861 he had $4,000 invested in other local businesses. Census of Canada, 1861.

57. William Troy (1827–?) was born free in Essex County, Virginia. Troy's mother was the free mulatto daughter of an Englishwoman. His father was a slave who contracted his labor, became a modestly successful shoemaker, and eventually purchased his freedom. Both of Troy's parents insisted on an education for their son, although Troy indicates that antiblack education statutes in Virginia meant that his early training sometimes took place in secret. Troy was raised an Episcopalian but became a Baptist in 1843 at age fifteen. In the late spring of

1848, Troy and his wife moved to Cincinnati, where he continued his education under the tutelage of Rev. William Henry Brisbane, M.D., and Rev. Wallace Shelton, pastor of the Zion Baptist congregation to which Troy belonged. By 1851 Troy was a licensed minister and antislavery reformer. The same year, he moved to Canada West and briefly served as pastor of the Amherstburg Baptist Church before moving in 1856 to Windsor, where he ministered to a congregation chiefly composed of fugitive slaves. During the late 1850s, Troy lectured in the United States, hoping to raise money to assist Canadian fugitives. From 1859 to 1862, Troy—who was often accompanied by fellow black abolitionist William Mitchell, also a minister to a Canadian fugitive slave congregation—toured Scotland and England, trying to raise funds for a chapel and school for his congregation. During the summer of 1861, Troy raised £600 and, at one meeting, displayed the photograph of a chapel built in Canada with funds he had sent home. Troy also published *Hair-Breadth Escapes from Slavery to Freedom* (Manchester, 1861), which contained a short narrative of his life and the escape stories of over a dozen fugitives who had found haven in Canada West. After leaving Britain, Troy sailed to Kingston, Jamaica. He endorsed black immigration to the island and to the West Indies in general. In 1869 Troy returned to Virginia as a missionary and pastor of the Second Colored Baptist Church in Richmond. He continued his affiliation with the American Baptist Missionary Convention throughout the 1870s, serving in a variety of administrative positions and traveling throughout the state as a preacher. William Troy, *Hair-Breadth Escapes from Slavery to Freedom* (Manchester, England, 1861), 1–10, 110, 114; *FDP*, 1 January 1852; *LI*, 3 August 1861; *DM*, October 1861; *WAA*, 29 March 1862; *Report of the Nineteenth Annual Meeting of the American Baptist Convention* (New Bedford, Mass., 1859), 8; *Report of the Third Annual Meeting of the Consolidated American Baptist Convention* (New York, N.Y., 1869), 12, 23; *Report of the Thirty-First Annual Meeting of the Consolidated American Baptist Convention* (New York, N.Y., 1872), 2; *Report of the Thirty-Second Annual Meeting of the Consolidated American Baptist Convention* (New York, N.Y., 1872), 10; *Report of the Triennial Meeting and Thirty-Seventh Annual Meeting of the Consolidated American Baptist Convention* (Brooklyn, N.Y., 1877), 6, 30, 34; *Minutes of the Consolidated American Baptist Convention* (Lexington, Ky., 1861), 2, 33; Rabinowitz, *Race Relations in Urban South*, 203; Drew, *North-Side View of Slavery*, 249–52.

58. Augustus R. Green (?–1878) was born to free black parents in Virginia. His family later resettled in Pennsylvania, where he acquired a basic education and apprenticed as a blacksmith before redirecting his efforts to religious pursuits. In 1841 he joined the Ohio conference of the African Methodist Episcopal church. After an unsuccessful attempt to establish an AME manual labor school near Columbus, Ohio, he returned to Pennsylvania. In 1848 he became editor of the *Christian Herald*, an AME organ, and he later supervised the denomination's book concern in Pittsburgh. Green turned his attention to the black emigration cause during the early 1850s. He particularly endorsed the *Provincial Freeman*'s editorial preference for Canadian immigration, was a prominent delegate to the 1854 and 1856 National Emigration Conventions held in Cleveland, and demonstrated considerable interest in black Canadian affairs. Although he opposed the British Methodist Episcopal church's separation from the AME, he attended the BME's founding convention in Chatham (1856). Green moved to Windsor in

1860 and joined the BME church. With encouragement from BME Bishop Willis Nazrey, he attempted to revive the black Canadian press by publishing the *True Royalist and Weekly Intelligencer* in Windsor, but it was a short-lived effort. Green was expelled from the BME in 1861 after formulating a challenge to the leadership of the denomination. He subsequently served as bishop of the Independent Methodist Episcopal church—a black Canadian body organized by BME dissidents. Green returned to the United States during the late 1860s, rejoined the AME, and settled in Washington, D.C. In 1876 he was assigned to a pastorate in Vicksburg, Mississippi, where he died while providing medical assistance during a yellow-fever epidemic. *CR*, 10 October 1878; Wayman, *Cyclopaedia of African Methodism*, 68–69; Winks, *Blacks in Canada*, 261, 397–98n; Miller, *Search for Black Nationality*, 136, 146–49, 156–66; *PL*, 16 October 1844; Green and Venable, *Re-Organization of the B.M.E. Church*; Payne, *History of the AME Church*, 324, 341, 344, 361–92; Smith, *African Methodist Episcopal Church*, 27–41, 97, 115–16, 340.

59. Richard Randolph Disney (1835–1891) was born to free black parents in Cecil County, Maryland. As a youth, he moved to Baltimore and found work in the barbershop of Solomon McCabe, a local free black. Disney also converted to Christianity while attending Rev. Daniel Payne's Bethel African Methodist Episcopal Church. In 1851 Disney enrolled in Osgood Seminary, a Congregationalist theological school in Springfield, Massachusetts; after graduating in 1855, he entered the African Methodist Episcopal ministry. He took charge of a British Methodist Episcopal congregation in Chatham, Canada West, in 1857. In succeeding years, he served BME churches at Buxton (1859–61), Windsor (1861–64), St. Catharines (1864–69), and Toronto (1869–72). Disney returned to Chatham in 1872. While serving his congregation there, he became an assistant to BME bishop Willis Nazrey. Upon Nazrey's death in 1875, Disney succeeded him. As bishop, he worked to reunite the AME and BME denominations; this reunion took place in 1884. In that year, Disney was named AME bishop for Ontario, Nova Scotia, Demerara, the West Indies, South America, and Bermuda. He made an extended evangelical visit to the West Indies during 1887–88. He died on 18 April 1891. *AMECR*, July 1885, July 1891; Smith, *African Methodist Episcopal Church*, 72, 111, 133, 338; Simpson, "Negroes in Ontario to 1870," 666; Winks, *Blacks in Canada*, 357.

60. Brown refers to the Refugee Home Society.

61. Joseph Mason (1809–?) escaped from slavery in Virginia in the 1830s. He settled at Painesville, Ohio, where he lectured on slavery and served as a subscription agent for the *Colored American*. Mason later acquired a ninety-acre farm near Colchester, Canada West, where he participated in antislavery and fugitive slave relief activities. His former master cannot be identified. No one named Mason has ever been governor of Virginia. Brown may refer to one of the politically prominent slaveholding members of antebellum Virginia's Mason family, particularly John Young Mason (1799–1859)—a member of the U.S. Congress, secretary of the Navy, federal judge, and minister to France—or James Murray Mason (1798–1871)—a member of the U.S. Senate and a leading Confederate diplomat. *ASB*, 23 October 1846, 4 January 1851 [6:0725]; *VF*, 13 August 1851 [7:0050]; *CA*, 11 November, 23 December 1837; Census of Canada, 1861; *DAB*, 12: 364–65, 369–70.

62. William McCurdy (1820–?), a Pennsylvania-born mulatto, owned and farmed a seventy-eight-acre plot in Colchester Township. He was born in the United States but settled in Colchester in 1857. Census of Canada, 1861; Simpson, "Negroes in Ontario to 1870," 584.

63. Brown probably refers to black laborers John S. White (1832–?) and James Harris (1849–?) of Colchester, Canada West. White settled in Colchester in the mid-1850s. He was married and had two sons, both born in Canada West. Harris, who was born in the province, was the son of local mulatto farmer Jeremiah Harris. Census of Canada, 1861.

64. William Ruth (1796–?) was born a slave in Bourbon County, Kentucky. At age twenty-seven, he escaped from slavery, settled in Colchester, Canada West, in 1825, and acquired 150 acres of farmland. Ruth was active in the affairs of the black community. He served on an Amherstburg vigilance committee that assisted newly arrived refugee slaves and was appointed to a Colchester committee that monitored black fund-raising activities in the area. Ruth also participated in the black convention movement; he attended the Colored National Convention at Cleveland (1848) and represented Colchester blacks at the North American Convention (1851) at Toronto and the Amherstburg Convention (1853). A respected preacher, he served as pastor of a black Wesleyan congregation at Colchester during the 1850s and 1860s. *NSt*, 29 September 1848; *VF*, 1 January, 17 August, 24 September 1851; Drew, *North-Side View of Slavery*, 375–77; *Minutes of Convention in Amherstburg*, 2.

65. Anthony Binga organized the Amherstburg First Baptist Church in the late 1830s. He was a leading member of the Amherstburg Baptist Association, a black organization established in 1841 to promote the Baptist denomination and its educational programs in Canada West. A founder and vice-president of the Provincial Union Association in 1854, he encouraged black self-help and opposed begging, although he had earlier been accused of mishandling funds collected for fugitive slave relief. In the late 1850s, Binga undertook church-related work in Hamilton. *PFW*, 19 August 1854 [9:0017]; Hill, *Freedom-Seekers*, 140; Simpson, "Negroes in Ontario to 1870," 112–13, 121–22, 312, 850; *VF*, 24 September 1851; David Hotchkiss to George Whipple, 6 August 1851, AMA-ARC; "Report of the Canada Amherstburg Mission Office (1853)," 2, 9, MWA.

66. Isaac Christine, a former slave, worked as a watchmaker and served as pastor of the Amherstburg British Methodist Episcopal Church during the early 1860s. He joined the Amherstburg circuit in 1861 but was later removed from his position because of alleged misconduct. Assessment Roll, Amherstburg, 1861; Green and Venable, *Re-Organization of the B.M.E. Church*, 26, 37–39.

67. Brown refers to George W. Brodie.

68. The Union Sabbath School, a Sunday school for fugitive slaves and their children, was opened by the Refugee Home Society in January 1851. By the following month, thirty-six students of various ages were reported in attendance. In response to a plea by Henry Bibb, Dr. J. W. King of Michigan contributed the bibles, New Testaments, and other printed religious materials necessary to operate the school. Laura Smith Haviland, a white abolitionist, became the school's instructor in 1852. The Union Sabbath School continued to teach black fugitives into the 1860s. Pease and Pease, *Black Utopia*, 114; *VF*, 12 February, 18 June 1851.

69. William Lyons, a carpenter and joiner, was born to free black parents in Virginia. He later settled in Columbus, Ohio, where he continued to ply his trade. But the racial discrimination he encountered there led him to resettle in Amherstburg, Canada West, in 1853. Drew, *North-Side View of Slavery*, 358; *PFW*, 26 January 1856.

70. In 1861 Levi Foster's family included himself, his wife, and six children—George (23), James (19), Louisa (17), Elizabeth (15), Sarah (9), and Anne (3). Census of Canada, 1861.

71. Thomas Buckner, a successful black farmer, lived in Amherstburg, Canada West, during the 1850s. He signed the call for the North American Convention (1851) and was appointed to a vigilance committee by the Amherstburg Convention (1853). There is inconclusive evidence that Buckner was a Wesleyan clergyman. In correspondence with Egerton Ryerson, Canada's superintendent of education, he expressed concern for black education in Canada West. Buckner resettled in Detroit about 1862. A white mob besieged his residence and threatened his life during the Detroit riots of March 1863. *VF*, 13 August 1851; Abajian, *Blacks in Selected Newspapers*, 1:296; *Minutes of Convention in Amherstburg*; Simpson, "Negroes in Ontario to 1870," 578; "Report of Amherstburg Mission Office (1853)," 9, MWA; S. G. Howe, *Report to the Freedmen's Inquiry Commission, 1864* (New York, N.Y., 1969), 67; *The Late Detroit Riot* (Detroit, Mich., 1863), n.p. [14:0641].

72. The Amherstburg British Methodist Episcopal Church emerged from a black Methodist congregation founded in the village in 1826 by Rev. George Ferguson. It became affiliated with the African Methodist Episcopal church under Rev. Noah C. W. Cannon in 1828. The church continued to meet under AME auspices until 1856, when it joined the nascent British Methodist Episcopal church. The congregation prospered under the ministry of Willis Nazrey in the late 1850s but declined during the early 1860s. When Rev. Walter Hawkins was assigned to the congregation in 1866, he complained that the church was in both physical disrepair and spiritual trouble. Hill, *Freedom-Seekers*, 132, 136–37; Simpson, "Negroes in Ontario to 1870," 116, 570–71.

90.
Wellington D. Moses, Jacob Francis, Fortune Richard, William Brown, and Richard H. Johnson to James Douglas
[November 1861]

Black Canadians struggled to achieve a social equality commensurate with the political and legal rights they enjoyed. In Victoria blacks converted segregated theaters into symbols of social injustice. From 1860 to 1865, they employed a variety of tactics to challenge the theaters' discriminatory practices. Blacks openly defied seating policy, wrote letters of protest to newspapers, sought legal redress, and petitioned government officials. In November 1861, following a disturbance at a benefit concert in which ruffians dumped flour on two prominent blacks seated in the theater's dress circle, the management served notice that blacks would only be allowed in the gallery. Victoria's blacks responded with a petition to Governor James Douglas. The letter reminded the governor of his assurances to blacks when they first arrived from California in 1858. Douglas met with the black committee but apparently did little to ease the situation. Blacks petitioned the governor a second time in 1864. Racial tensions finally eased as the black population declined in the mid-1860s. By 1865 the theaters' segregation policy was quietly abandoned. Kilian, *Go Do Some Great Thing*, 116–24.

To His Excellency James Douglas C.B. &c. &c.[1]
Sir,

We the undersigned committee appointed by the colored people of this Colony, desire to memorialize your Excellency with reference to the gross insult and shameful proscription of places of public amusements by inserting upon hand-bills and posters, "Colored people not admitted to any part of the House except the Gallery."

Proscription solely on the ground of color, we believe to be an insufferable wrong, but the outrage is still more apparent, when it is known that the gallery is the only sole resort of the lowest order.

Coming to this colony to found our homes, and rear our families, we did so advisedly, assured by those in authority that we should meet with no disabilities political or conventional on the ground of color.

Your memorialists would submit that in point of sobriety, intelligence, and industry, as well as other requisites for good citizenship, they compare favorably with any other class; they are in possession of real estate to the amount of £50,000, which awaits taxation for the support of Government. We are here investing our means, and zealously laboring for the well being of the colony, and are influencing large numbers of our class to do likewise, and desire to have our families untrammeled by the perpetuation of a mean and senseless prejudice against color—a prejudice having no foundation that is honorable, and alone supported by the ignorance and brutality of the lowest order of society.

Earnestly deprecating all resorts to violence, desiring to be law-abiding, and feeling that the proscription practices to which we call the attention of your Excellency to be slanderous, and injurious to a large and respectable body of Her Majesty's subjects, that they are inimical to the genius of British Law and world-renowned British sentiments. We therefore petition your Excellency to make such recommendations that will guarantee the rights of your petitioners in common with all other men.

And we your humble petitioners as [in] duty bound will ever pray. Signed on behalf of Two Hundred and Sixty colored residents,

Committee
Wellington D. Moses[2]
Jacob Francis[3]
F. Richard[4]
Wm. Brown[5]
Richard H. Johnson[6]

Provincial Archives of British Columbia, Victoria, British Columbia. Published by permission.

1. Sir James Douglas (1803–1877) emigrated from Scotland to the British North American Provinces as a commercial apprentice in 1819. Successful business ventures at Fort Vancouver led to his appointment as governor of Vancouver Island (1851–64) and British Columbia (1858–64). In those positions, Douglas was primarily responsible for the establishment of British authority on the Pacific coast, despite border disputes, disruptive gold rushes, and chaotic growth. *DCB* 10:238–48.

2. Wellington D. Moses (1814–1890) was born in the British West Indies but spent his early adult life in New York City. While there, he made the acquaintance of Arctic explorer Sir John Franklin and nearly accompanied him on his ill-fated 1845–48 expedition. Moses settled in California by the early 1850s and became an active and articulate participant in black community affairs. He represented Santa Clara County blacks at the 1855 and 1856 black state conventions and was a vocal supporter of the *Mirror of the Times*, a San Francisco black paper. By 1857 Moses moved to San Francisco and became coproprietor of the Western Hotel. Local blacks named him to the Pioneer Committee that investigated the possibility of black migration to Victoria, Vancouver Island, in 1858. He visited the island, and his positive report on conditions there helped motivate the resettlement. Soon after arriving in Victoria, Moses opened a barber shop and bathhouse. He led several protests against the discriminatory treatment that blacks encountered in the city. Moses remained in Victoria until 1862. After working in the mining camps along the Fraser River, he eventually settled in Barkerville in the Cariboo mining region of British Columbia and opened another

barber shop, a general store, and a moneylending business. Moses became well-known for his own "Hair Invigorator," which he marketed through the Cariboo and Victoria papers. He served as a local subscription agent for the *Pacific Appeal* during the early 1870s, and he remained in Barkerville until his death. San Francisco County Census, 1852; Winks, *Blacks in Canada*, 276; Pilton, "Negro Settlement in British Columbia," 33–34, 50–51, 97–98, 161, 163–68, 197; Kilian, *Go Do Some Great Thing*, 37–38, 46, 79, 90–95, 100, 124; Foner and Walker, *Proceedings of Black State Conventions*, 2:112, 133, 154–55; *MT*, 12 September 1857; *PA*, 3 September 1870, 3 January 1874.

3. Jacob Francis was born in England but moved to New York City and participated in local civil rights and temperance efforts during the 1830s and 1840s. Francis settled in California about 1849 and soon became prominent in the San Francisco black community. He served as president of the Young Men's Association—a local civil rights organization—and helped found and direct the San Francisco Athenaeum, a black library company and debate society, which was the first black literary society formed in California (1853). He represented local blacks at the 1855 and 1856 black state conventions and chaired the former session. Francis moved to Victoria in 1858 and opened a saloon. He became an outspoken opponent of local prejudice, battled to keep the city's schools and churches free of caste distinctions, and twice sued local bar owners who refused to serve him. Francis entered local politics, ran for the Victoria legislative assembly in 1861; he won, but was refused his seat on a technicality. He served as Victoria subscription agent for the *Pacific Appeal* during the early 1860s. Francis returned to New York City at the end of the Civil War. Pilton, "Negro Settlement in British Columbia," 98–100, 185–86, 197, 199; *E*, 6 October 1836, 21 December 1837 [1:0706, 2:0308]; *NASS*, 16 July 1846 [5:0249]; *FDP*, 22 September 1854, 6 April 1855; *MT*, 12 December 1857; *WAA*, 19 November 1859; Foner and Walker, *Proceedings of Black State Conventions*, 2:112, 132–33, 155; *San Francisco City Directory*, 1858; Kilian, *Go Do Some Great Thing*, 66–67, 75–76, 136; *PA*, 19, 26 April 1862, 20 June 1863, 30 July 1864; *ESF*, 30 June 1865; *AAN*, 8 July 1865.

4. Fortune Richard (ca. 1805–?) was one of three delegates sent by the Pioneer Committee of San Francisco blacks to consult Victoria's Governor James Douglas and to investigate the British colony as a potential site for black settlement. Richard, his wife, and their fourteen-year-old daughter soon settled in Victoria. There, Richard supported his family by farming and working as a ship's carpenter. He vigorously protested the antiblack discrimination he encountered there. In 1863, when he and two black friends were denied entrance to a Victoria theater for racial reasons, he unsuccessfully pursued damages in court. Richard served as an officer in the black Victoria Pioneer Rifle Corps from 1861 until it disbanded in 1864. Thereafter, he took little part in Victoria's public life, although in 1882 he published a protest against the actions of a clique within Victoria's Baptist Church that attempted to exclude blacks from membership in the congregation. Pilton, "Negro Settlement in British Columbia," 197–98, 210, 216, 230–31; Kilian, *Go Do Some Great Thing*, 77, 124–25, 153–54.

5. William Brown, a black merchant, was a leading figure in the San Francisco black community in the mid-1850s. He owned a clothing emporium in partnership with Thomas W. Pierre until 1858, when he moved northward to Victoria,

Vancouver Island. Brown operated a store in Victoria and served as a captain in the Victoria Pioneer Rifle Corps during the early 1860s. On several occasions, he helped lead public protests against racial discrimination in the city's public facilities. Abajian, *Blacks in Selected Newspapers*, 1:283; *San Francisco City Directory*, 1858; Pilton, "Negro Settlement in British Columbia," 199, 207, 230–31.

6. Richard Henry Johnson, a Victoria black, actively protested racial discrimination in the city on several occasions. A captain in the Victoria Pioneer Rifle Corps, he presented a written address to Governor A. E. Kennedy in 1864 that protested the unit's exclusion on racial grounds from the gubernatorial inauguration and parade. After the corps disbanded later that year, Johnson briefly opened a temperance house and mission in Victoria. A small gold rush prompted him to go to the Leech River area north of Victoria during the winter of 1864–65. He opened the Mount Ararat Hotel there, and the hotel gained a reputation throughout the province for its fine food and comfortable rooms. Johnson operated the hotel until his death in the late 1860s. Pilton, "Negro Settlement in British Columbia," 117, 120, 174–75, 197, 209; Kilian, *Go Do Some Great Thing*, 99–100, 124, 135; Winks, *Blacks in Canada*, 279.

91.
James T. Rapier to John H. Rapier, Jr.
17 March 1862

With the coming of the Civil War, black Canadians turned away from the emigration issue. Despite the personal and everyday concerns of their busy lives, blacks read newspapers and letters from American friends to keep abreast of the progress of the war, especially in those American locales they still considered home. James T. Rapier's 17 March 1862 letter to his older brother and frequent correspondent, John H. Rapier, Jr., is typical. James, who was then struggling with the economic hardships and academic demands of student life at a Toronto normal school, found time to follow military events in the American South, rejoicing as Union forces occupied his hometown of Florence, Alabama. Like many other black Canadians, Rapier's concern with American affairs prompted him to return southward in late 1864. Schweninger, *James T. Rapier and Reconstruction*, 35–36.

Chatham, [Canada West]
March 17th, 1862

John H. Rapier, Esq. [word illegible]
Dear Brother

With both sorrow and pleasure I recd. your last and had answered to com by last steamer but owing something or other the letter was carried to New York and returned again to Buxton and as I have not been there for some time not since December of course I did not get it[.] As that letter explains my [course] betters than I will have time to write in this[,] you may look for it by next steamer. [It explains] reasons why I did not comply with [promis] viz. I was thrown out of my situation and as a consequence I had no money to let you have I do not mean spare for [I] have one dollar[.] I can spare you 75 cents of it[.] Being thrown out I was left without 4.00 to commence the winter on[.] I had to get credit for my board until spring[.] I was hoping to hear from my other application[s] befor I wrote but I can not expect to hear before two or three days and if I should wait longer than to day this will not meet the steamer and I do hate above all things to look for a letter and be disappointed[.]

I say it gave me sorrow because I always [hate] to hear [o]f a Brother's hard circumstances and unable to help him[.] It was pleasure as it always is to hear from my dearest Brother[.] I tell you again if the situation terminates favorably to me you m[a]y expect me to mail you some money by the first steamer in may[.] If I do not John I have n[o]ne and as a consequence I will not be able to send you any[.] I have worked hard and I have not made the sure progress in the world that some have, but there are those who have made less progress than I have[.] They may have more money than I have for I have not two Dollars to save my life but I am now very nearly out of debt a good [name] and a tolerable fair Education and should I miss my situations I will try and work hard hire out or something to raise money enough to enter the normal school next session which opens in august and six months more[.][1] I can produc[t] then I think[.] I must close[.] I wish to start this Evenings mail. The Federal[s] are making good heading down south[.] They have been to Florence and every body unionists there[.][2] If you are desirous of writing to Father you had better address me as I believe the mails will soon be open up to that point and I can forward it better than you[.] The other letter will explain all that this fails [word illegible]. Your Brother,

James T. Rapier

Rapier Family Papers, Moorland-Spingarn Research Center, Howard University, Washington, District of Columbia. Published by permission.

1. Rapier enrolled in a Toronto school, probably the Toronto Normal School, in 1860 and, despite financial problems, enrolled again for the 1861–62 academic year. His studies there included Latin, Greek, geometry, and ancient history. Although evidence is sketchy, he apparently graduated from the school in October 1862. Schweninger, *James T. Rapier and Reconstruction*, 35, 196n.

2. On 8 February 1862, three Union gunboats navigated up the Tennessee River behind Confederate lines as far as Florence, Alabama. Union forces occupied Florence and the immediate area throughout the remainder of the year. Except in the black community, Unionist sentiment in Florence was limited. Despite Rapier's contention, most Florentines remained sympathetic to the Confederacy. Rapier evidently based his assumption of widespread Unionist sentiment in Florence upon an erroneous report that local citizens had offered to organize a grand ball for the officers of the Union gunboats. Kenneth R. Johnson, "Slavery and Racism in Florence, Alabama, 1841–1862," *CWH* 27:166–71 (June 1981).

92.
"One of the Sons of Ham" to George Brown
2 October 1862

Black abolitionists in Canada carefully monitored what the Canadian press published about emancipation. They praised proemancipation newspapers and criticized those that questioned black readiness for freedom, and they attempted to educate white Canadians about American race relations. A 2 October 1862 letter from an anonymous black to George Brown, the abolitionist editor of the Toronto *Globe*, summarized the divergent responses of the Toronto press to President Abraham Lincoln's announcement of his Emancipation Proclamation. The author applauded recent editorials in the *Globe* that favored emancipation but chided the Conservative Toronto *Leader* for its hesitant and unenthusiastic response to the prospects of black liberation. The letter was reprinted in the American antislavery press. *TG*, 23, 30 September 1862; *Lib*, 31 October 1862.

Toronto, [Canada West]
Oct[ober] 2, 1862

SIR:

I have read with much satisfaction your recent articles on the emancipation of slaves in the United States;[1] they were in direct contrast and a just rebuke to that *pro-slavery* sheet, the *Leader*.[2] It out-herods Herod[3] in its love and praise for the manstealer, and his hellish institution. The colored man, as well as every member of the human family, has much cause to rejoice that we have here such an advocate of the rights of man, without distinction of color; one that is not dependent upon the *blood-stained money* of a few slaveholders and their sympathizers to keep up his circulation, but rises above low prejudice and pecuniary consideration to take up the cause of the oppressed. And, sir, when the history of this rebellion is written, the *Globe* will hold a prominent place in that galaxy of stars which shall be noted for their advocacy of freedom to all men. The *Leader* has all his sympathy laid up in store for the Slaveocrat, who has grown fat, rich and arrogant upon the bones, blood and muscles of human beings, and deals it out with a profusion that knows no bounds; but he has none for the poor defenceless slave, who has been cut, slashed, burnt, and outraged in all manner of ways, his flesh been torn by bloodhounds, his daughters prostituted, his wife and children sold away thousands of miles from him, and the sleeping babe of his wife stolen from the cradle while its mother is absent on her daily duties.

The *Leader* pretended some time since that, if the North was fighting for the freedom of the slave, he and the people of Canada could sympathize with her; but as soon as Congress passed the Confiscation Act, to liberate the slaves of the rebels,[4] he labored with all his might to prove it to be barbarous and unconstitutional! And when President Lincoln performs the crowning act of his administration, and issues his proclamation of emancipation[5]—for which millions of hearts all over the world will beat in thanksgiving to God—the *Leader*, true to his instincts, commences to hurl his epithets against him and his proclamation!

It seems the *Leader* fears that emancipation will cause an influx of free colored people into Canada. Nothing can be more erroneous. On the contrary, it will be the best thing that could be done to prevent an influx either into the North or Canada. And I think any one who asserts that the slaves will, when free, desert the places of their nativity in the Sunny South, and come to this cold and inhospitable climate, where they will be subject to the diseases incidental to it, and from which they enjoy perfect immunity there, to say nothing of the cold-hearted and cruel prejudice exhibited towards them here by certain evil-disposed persons, must either be a fool or a knave. But suppose, Mr. Editor, for argument's sake, a few thousands of those stout fellows, with whom John Mitchell,[6] the convict, wished to have a plantation down South well stocked, and who have made the South what it has been by the sweat of their brow, who have kept the Lancashire looms going so long, the stoppage of whose productions is now dealing such a heavy blow to Britian, and reducing her operatives to famine and beggary,[7] were to settle upon some of our rich lands not now under cultivation, and make them to yield their natural productions so as to increase their value, what objection could there be to it? For the country is certainly in want of laborers, and it cannot be said that we have not good farmers amongst us; for it is proverbial that some of the best farms in Western Canada are owned by colored men, and some, too, that they have bought from white men who had failed to succeed, and were obliged to sell out themselves, to prevent the sheriff from doing it for them.

It cannot be disguised, Mr. Editor, that both the North and South are getting well scourged for their oppression of the colored man; and Canada may now learn a lesson from which she should profit, rather than take a retrograde movement to oppress the poor and helpless. And let her not forget the words of Thomas Jefferson who said, "When I remember that God is just, I tremble for my country."[8] But, says the *Leader*, you are better off as slaves than if you were free. Well, if slavery is such a benign institution, let him and his coadjutors make a trial of it; and as old uncle Abe is going to deprive the black race of its great blessings and benefits, they will have a good chance of monopolizing it. Nor need they fear any competition, or that they will not succeed for want of capital. It only wants willing hearts, with union and perseverance; and although at first it will come a little awkward to them, they have only to keep trying, when I am sure they will be able to transmit to their posterity some of the imprints of its beauties—namely, flat noses, retreating foreheads, projecting teeth, thick lips, large feet, and long heels; and, should they get down in some of the rice swamps of South Carolina, perhaps they may even succeed in handing down a black skin and a woolly head of hair. For Hugh Miller tells us, in his *Testimony of the Rocks*, page 272, that "There are cases in which not more than from two to three centuries have been found sufficient thoroughly to alter the physiognomy of men." And further, "On the plantation of Ulster in 1611, and afterwards on the success of the British against the rebels in 1641 and 1689," says a shrewd writer of the present day, himself an Irishman, "great multitudes of the native Irish were driven from Armagh and the south of Down, into the mountainous tract extending from the Barony of Fleurs eastward to the sea; on the other side of the kingdom the same race were exposed to the worst effects of hunger and ignorance, the two great brutalisers of the human race. The descendants of these exiles are now distinguished physically by great degradation. They are remarkable for open, projecting mouths, with prominent teeth and exposed gums; and their advancing cheek bones and depressed noses bear barbarism on their very front."[9]

In conclusion, Mr. Editor, I have to express to you, what I am satisfied every intelligent colored person feels, gratitude for your noble and manly advocacy of our cause, with a wish that God may speed you in the work of imbuing in the minds of the people pure principles of liberty and equality to all men. I remain, dear sir, Your humble servant,

ONE OF THE SONS OF HAM

Globe (Toronto, Canada West), 8 October 1862.

1. Between 23 September and 4 October 1862, four items in the Toronto *Globe* responded to President Abraham Lincoln's announcement of the forthcoming Emancipation Proclamation. A 23 September notice briefly described the terms of the proclamation and characterized it as "a war measure," but one likely to produce "an army of blacks ready to fight for freedom." A 30 September editorial called the proclamation "one of the most important events of modern times," again criticizing it as a "war measure," not an executive order designed to provide "justice" for blacks. On 3 October, another editorial stated that black freedom would ultimately become the "grand issue" of the war and suggested that the proclamation would compel all Canadians to support the Union cause. A third editorial, published on 4 October, chided Southerners for "threatening a war of extermination" and characterized as "absurd" their anxious talk of black "servile insurrection" while the region was engaged in the "greatest rebellion of the century." *TG*, 23, 30 September, 3, 4 October 1862.

2. The Toronto *Leader* was founded as a weekly in 1852 and it became a daily one year later. Under the direction of publisher James Beatty and editor Charles Lindsey, it functioned as a Conservative organ throughout most of its existence. In the 1860s, it claimed the largest circulation of any paper in the province. A

leading Canadian critic of Union policy during the Civil War, it regularly chided President Abraham Lincoln's conduct of the conflict, particularly the recruitment of black soldiers, passage of the Second Confiscation Act (1862), and issuance of the Emancipation Proclamation. The *Leader* defended slavery and argued that blacks were contented with bondage and incapable of coping with freedom. The paper generally favored the Confederacy and called for recognition of the Southern nation as early as July 1862. The *Leader* ceased publication in 1878. Middleton and Landon, *Province of Ontario*, 2:791; Firth, *Early Toronto Newspapers*, 24; *Toronto City Directory*, 1867; *TL*, 1, 14 July, 1, 2, 12, 25, 28 August, 13, 29, 30 September 1862.

3. The popular expression "to out-herod Herod" comes from act three, scene two of William Shakespeare's *Hamlet*. It refers to Herod Antipas (4 B.C.–40 A.D.), a tetrarch of ancient Galilee and Perea, who is described in the New Testament as excessively violent and indulgent. Matt. 14:1–11; Mark 6:14–28.

4. The U.S. Congress approved two confiscation acts during 1861–62. The First Confiscation Act provided for the seizure of all property, including slaves, used for "insurrectionary purposes." The Second Confiscation Act established penalties for those convicted of treason against the United States and subjected individuals in "rebellion or insurrection" to fine, imprisonment, and the liberation of their slaves. J. G. Randall and David Donald, *The Civil War and Reconstruction*, 2d ed. (Lexington, Mass., 1969), 283–84.

5. Abraham Lincoln (1809–1865), an Illinois Republican, achieved national prominence during the late 1850s, particularly for his opposition to the extension of slavery. Elected president of the United States in 1860, he is best remembered for preserving the Union and for issuing the Emancipation Proclamation. Early in the war, Lincoln was reluctant to consider slave emancipation for political reasons, but by the spring of 1862, he was moved to do so by military and political necessity, by abolitionist pressure, and by his own sense of justice. He drafted and issued a Preliminary Emancipation Proclamation on 22 September 1862. On 1 January 1863, Lincoln signed the Emancipation Proclamation, which declared slaves in rebel-held areas to be free. The proclamation did not free slaves in Union-occupied areas of Louisiana, the border states of Maryland, Delaware, Kentucky, and Tennessee, or in the forty-eight counties of Virginia (later West Virginia) that had refused to join the Confederacy. But it was a significant step toward dismantling the institution, and it tacitly recognized that the Civil War was being fought both to free slaves and to save the Union. *DAB*, 6(1):242–59; John Hope Franklin, *The Emancipation Proclamation* (New York, N.Y., 1965), 13–134.

6. John Mitchel (1815–1875), an Irish journalist and nationalist, graduated from Trinity College in 1834 and entered upon a legal career. He was soon attracted to the Young Ireland movement and founded and edited the Dublin *Nation* and the *United Irishman* to further Irish nationalism. His radical politics led to his deportation to a Tasmanian penal colony in 1850. Mitchel escaped and surfaced in New York City in 1854 as the publisher of the *Citizen*. An unabashed defender of slavery, he soon gained national notoriety and lectured throughout the South. Mitchel published the Knoxville *Southern Citizen* (1857–59) and edited the *Richmond Enquirer* and the *Richmond Examiner* in Virginia during the Civil War. After the war, he continued to work as a journalist in New York

City before returning to Ireland in 1874. Blassingame, *Frederick Douglass Papers*, 1:139–40n; *Lib*, 27 January, 3 February, 17 March 1854.

7. In the decades preceding the Civil War, the economy of the English county of Lancashire (which included Liverpool) became increasingly dependent upon cotton produced in the American South. Nearly one-sixth of the area's population was employed in processing raw cotton into cloth. The Union blockade of Southern ports during the war sharply reduced the supply of Southern cotton available in Britain, and this had a devastating economic impact in Lancashire. Cotton imports dropped from nearly a million pounds in 1859 to less than seventeen thousand pounds three years later; the number of unemployed rose to more than 247,000, and nearly twice that number of people were dependent on public welfare. Mary Ellison, *Support for Secession: Lancashire and the American Civil War* (Chicago, Ill., 1972).

8. Thomas Jefferson (1743–1826), a Virginia politician, scientist, philosopher, and author of the Declaration of Independence, served as governor of Virginia (1779–81), minister to France (1784–89), vice-president under John Adams, and third president of the United States (1801–9). Although a slaveholder, Jefferson conceded the immorality of slavery in his *Notes on the State of Virginia* (1785), Query 18: "Indeed I tremble for my country when I reflect that God is just, that his justice cannot sleep forever. Commerce between master and slave is despotism. Nothing is more certainly written in the book of fate than that these people are to be free." *DAB*, 10:17–35.

9. Hugh Miller (1802–1856), an Edinburgh stone mason, banker, newspaper editor, and author, became nineteenth-century Scotland's foremost geologist. He wrote several books on the subject including *The Testimony of the Rocks* (1857), which offered an incomplete and contradictory racial theory. Miller accepted Caucasian superiority but did not believe that the alleged inferiority of other races was either innate or predestined. Rather, he suggested, it resulted from the cumulative effect of decadent, but freely chosen, acts by members of a race. He illustrated this point by demonstrating that even whites (though not the white race) declined under unfavorable conditions. He cited the work of a "present-day Irish author" on the inferior status of the nineteenth-century descendants of those seventeenth-century Irish rebels driven into a desperate rural existence by the British; Miller indicated that the interplay of environment and group choice led to their precipitous decay. Hugh Miller, *An Autobiography. My Schools and Schoolmasters; or, the Story of My Education*, 2d ed. (Boston, Mass., 1862); Hugh Miller, *The Testimony of the Rocks; or, Geology and its Bearing on the Two Theologies, Natural and Revealed* (Edinburgh, 1857), 252–56, 270–72.

93.
Emily Allen to Hannibal Hamlin
13 April 1863

After emancipation, some reformers began collecting funds and supplies for recently freed blacks in the American South. Despite strenuous solicitation, freedmen's aid societies generated little interest and few contributions among white Canadians. But black Canadians, whose own experiences made them acutely aware of the difficulties involved in starting a new life, embraced the freedmen's aid cause in hopes of easing the slave's transition from bondage to freedom. Black associations in Canada West and on Vancouver Island collected sizable amounts. The Committee of Colored Ladies of the British Colony of Victoria sponsored bazaars, Sabbath-school exhibitions, and other events during 1862–64 on behalf of black contrabands. Committee members—some of them former slaves—collected nearly $800 during 1863. In a 13 April 1863 letter to Vice-President Hannibal Hamlin, Emily Allen, president of the committee, forwarded a donation designated for contrabands in the Beaufort, South Carolina, area. Hamlin requested that General Rufus Saxton, military commander of the Union occupational forces along the south Atlantic coast, disperse the funds. Saxton used the donation to support a freedmen's school at Fernandina, Florida. Allen's letter was published in the *New York Tribune*. Winks, *Blacks in Canada*, 289; *NASS*, 4 July 1863; Rufus Saxton to Hannibal Hamlin, 9 July 1863, Hannibal Hamlin to Rufus Saxton, 22 July 1863, Hannibal Hamlin Papers, MeU; Pilton, "Negro Settlement in British Columbia," 54; *PA*, 6 February 1864 [15:0236].

VICTORIA, [Vancouver Island]
April 13, 1863

HON. HANNIBAL HAMLIN[1]
SIR:

By order of the Committee of Colored Ladies of the British Colony of Victoria, V.I.,[2] please find inclosed a draft for £86 14 9 sterling on London, made payable to your order.[3]

Please send it to Beaufort, S.C., for the benefit of the contrabands. One of the reasons for sending this money to Beaufort is, its being the first place a colored regiment was formed, according to law.[4] This money has been raised by and through the colored people of this place, and who are originally from the United States.

We have also sent $170 to the City of Philadelphia for the same purpose, to be used there.[5] You will please accept our thanks as a people for the great interest you have taken in the cause of humanity; and though many miles divide us from those who have the burden to bear in this great struggle for human liberty, our hearts are with you even unto death. Please acknowledge the receipt of this money through the THE N.Y. *TRIBUNE.* Respectfully,

EMILY ALLEN, President[6]

New York Daily Tribune (N.Y.), 2 June 1863.

1. Hannibal Hamlin (1809–1891), a Maine lawyer, served in the state legislature during the 1830s before embarking on a national political career. Hamlin was a member of Congress (1843–47) and later served in the U.S. Senate (1848–57). Dissatisfied with his party's proslavery position, he bolted from the Democratic ranks in 1856 and joined the Republicans. As Abraham Lincoln's vice-president during the Civil War, he staunchly supported emancipation and other Radical Republican policies. He lost his renomination bid in 1864 but was returned to the U.S. Senate (1869–81), where he continued to support the Radicals on Reconstruction issues. *DAB*, 8 : 196–98.

2. The Committee of Colored Ladies of the British Colony of Victoria, a benevolent society that raised funds to assist contrabands and Afro-American institutions, was active throughout the Civil War. The organization also solicited subscribers for the *Anglo-African* (a black newspaper published in New York City), collected donations to the paper, and contributed to a fund that supplied issues of the *Anglo-African* to black soldiers in the Union army. Leading members of the committee included President Emily Allen, Elizabeth Leonard, Lucinda Hamilton, Susan Brown, Emma Ringo, Emily Coons, and Louisa E. Wilcox. *AA*, 9 April, 24 December 1864; *PA*, 6 February 1864; Pilton, "Negro Settlement in British Columbia," 54.

3. This amount was equivalent to $604.20. Hannibal Hamlin to [Rufus] Saxton, 22 July 1863, Hannibal Hamlin Papers, MeU.

4. The Union War Department authorized General Rufus Saxton of the Department of the South to organize a black regiment in late 1862. When he mustered in the First South Carolina Volunteers at Beaufort, South Carolina, on 7 November, it became the first official Union regiment consisting of former slaves. Thomas W. Higginson, a Massachusetts abolitionist, commanded the unit, which saw action in Georgia, Florida, and South Carolina. In 1864 it was renamed the Thirty-third United States Colored Troops. Stationed in Charleston after the Civil War, the black regiment was mustered out on 9 February 1866. Benjamin Quarles, *The Negro in the Civil War* (Boston, Mass., 1969), 118–19; Thomas Wentworth Higginson, *Army Life in a Black Regiment* (Boston, Mass., 1870; reprint, Williamstown, Mass., 1971).

5. In early 1863, the Committee of Colored Ladies of the British Colony of Victoria forwarded $150 to the central committee in Philadelphia to be used for contraband relief. They had raised the money at a 31 December 1862 New Year's Eve "donation party" held to celebrate the Emancipation Proclamation. In May 1863, Peter Lester and several other black Victoria residents sent an additional $152 donation to the Social, Civil, and Statistical Association of Colored People of Pennsylvania. Pilton, "Negro Settlement in British Columbia," 54–55.

6. Emily Allen (1816–?), a Virginia-born black, resided for a time in Pennsylvania before settling by 1852 in Sacramento, California. While in Sacramento, she worked as a laundress and a hotelkeeper. During the late 1850s, Emily Allen and her husband, William, immigrated to Victoria, Vancouver Island, where she played an active role in the public life of the Victoria black community during the 1860s, particularly as president of the Committee of Colored Ladies of the British Colony of Victoria. California Census, 1852; *MT*, 12 December 1857; Pilton, "Negro Settlement in British Columbia," 55, 207.

94.
Address by a Committee of Toronto Blacks
21 April 1863

Most black abolitionists in the British North American Provinces viewed the Civil War as a crusade for emancipation and equality. They used a variety of means to rally black Canadians behind the Union war effort—convening mass meetings, drafting addresses, and writing letters to local, religious, and reform newspapers. Black leaders in Toronto called a 6 April 1863 meeting of city blacks to endorse efforts by the United States government to emancipate and "elevate" blacks. The session was held at the Coloured Wesleyan Methodist Church and chaired by R. Phillips. The audience resolved to appoint a committee of seven prominent blacks—Thomas Smallwood, Thomas W. F. Smallwood, John J. Cary, George W. Cary, Rev. James Harper, R. P. Thomas, and C. F. Francis—to draft a pro-Union address to black Canadians. The committee submitted the resulting "Address to the Colored Citizens of Canada" at a 21 April meeting. *AA*, 9 May 1863.

ADDRESS

To the Colored Citizens of Canada

Having been silent observers of events as they have recently occurred in different parts of the world; and being interested in and closely identified with some of the most important of them, we think it becoming and proper that we should at this time give a few expressions and thoughts in relation to them. We have heard with sorrow and joy of the unhappy and desolating war which has been and is at present being carried on in the neighboring republic. Our hearts have been moved with tender emotions of sorrow, because so many of our fellow beings have been mangled, and pained, and hurled unprepared into eternity, and families and firesides rendered sad and unhappy. Our hearts have thrilled with the pleasanter emotions of joy because in that fratricidal war we recognize freedom and slavery marshalled against each other; because we believed that the impartial and Supreme Maker of all, would overrule this sanguinary event for good; that slavery in that land was doomed never to fetter its victims again; and that our brethren, beings stamped in their Creator's own image, will enjoy liberty, full and perfect, both soul and body.

Our hearts hail with pleasure and delight, President Lincoln's proclamation of emancipation of January last, and although that edict does not at present break the clamps of every fetter in that land, still we ardently hope that ere the conflict is ended, its effects will give liberty to every slave, and every hut become a solemn witness that it dwells therein. We extend our sympathy to President Lincoln in the prosecution of the great work for freedom. We trust that the Union armies will be strengthened and sustained, and that they will go on "conquering and to conquer."[1]

We recommend our brethren in Canada to do all in their power, consistently with the laws under which they live, to assist the President and the Union. Our brethren in the United States, we trust, will quickly rally to the defence of freedom, that they will enter without hesitation the Union armies; send terror and dismay by their undaunted valor into the hearts and ranks of the enemy, and be ever encouraged to go on and endure hardships by cherishing that noble and earnest sentiment, that "those who would be free themselves must strike the blow."

We rejoice that we are subjects of Her Most Gracious Majesty the Queen, and that we live under a flag that has "braved a thousand years the battle and the breeze."[2] As loyal subjects we cannot but regret that there are subjects of Her Most Gracious Majesty living in Canada and England, who by their expressions and acts, countenance and aid the fierce onslaught on human freedom and the effort to establish a Confederacy whose chief corner stone is slavery.[3] As members of one common family, we sympathize with the cotton operatives in England, in their deep distress, and we feel that the Great Disposer of all events will gradually remove those severe trials and touching bereavements, and institute where utter destitution reigned, full and plenty. Finally we tender our heartfelt thanks to the Hon. George Brown of the *Globe*, and those connected therewith, for their urbanity and readiness at all times to advocate human rights—irrespective of color or clime.

Anglo-African (New York, N.Y.), 9 May 1863.

1. The committee quotes from Revelation 6:2.
2. The committee quotes from the poem "Ye Mariners of England" by Scottish poet Thomas Campbell (1777–1844).
3. The Confederacy found support both in Britain and in the British North American Provinces during the Civil War. By 1862 the lack of cotton, created by the Union blockade of Confederate ports, encouraged pro-Confederate feeling among the British working class as unemployment increased in the textile industry. Some dominant British and Canadian political figures and many members of the London aristocracy were sympathetic to the Confederate cause. The Confederacy also earned the support of British and Canadian newspapers, particularly the Toronto *Leader* and the Montreal *Gazette*, which publicly announced their pro-Southern sympathies. Anglo-Canadian support for the Confederacy developed for a variety of reasons, including economic ties, disgust for American tariff policies, a belief in the inherent right of self-determination, recognition that the Union's main purpose in fighting the war was not the abolition of slavery, and a suspicion that the North might invade Canada once the South was defeated. Despite the efforts of Confederate diplomats, propaganda agents, and sympathizers, the British government maintained a policy of neutrality. Ellison, *Support for Secession*, 5–14, 24–25, 162; Brian Jenkins, *Britain and the War for the Union*, 2 vols. (Montreal, 1974), 2:41–43, 317–19, 343; Winks, *Canada and the United States*, 15, 18, 63, 117, 129, 229–31, 244–63.

95.
Sarah A. Lester to William Still
21 April 1863

The Civil War demonstrated the extent to which most black Canadians thought of themselves as Americans-in-exile. Writing from Victoria, Sarah A. Lester described the United States as "the fatherland" and American events as "our national affairs." Lester confided to William Still that she spent much of her time thinking about the war and its meaning for North American blacks. Although recognizing that emancipation and the organization of black regiments were acts of expediency, not conviction, by the federal government, she urged blacks to participate in the war on the Union side. She realized that racism and discrimination existed in the North and would remain after the war ended, but she believed that the conflict provided blacks with an opportunity to exhibit their manhood and prove their readiness for freedom, thus tempering the nature and extent of that racism. After Appomattox, Lester returned to San Francisco and took an active role in the affairs of the city's black community. *ESF*, 25 October 1867.

Victoria, [Vancouver Island]
April 21st, 1863

DEAR FRIEND STILL:

Perhaps you can spare a few moments to chat with me about our national affairs. I have been thinking very much lately of the war and its consequences, particularly since the organization of colored regiments.[1] I am so anxious that they shall prove themselves worthy to shoulder arms in the contest. There is great diversity of opinion as to what should be their course. Some persons say it is foolishness for them to fight at all; that they have suffered long enough. True they have suffered, but the cloud of ignorance that has so long obscured the black man's horizon is passing away; it appears he is awakening to feel his power as a man, and his future suffering will no longer be the result of *meek submission* to tyrants. Others say, since neither the North nor the South is the true friend of right, it matters not which side is assisted, and again others wish, that they could be removed until the scene of bloodshed is past. Now here I am on this far off side of the Rocky Mountains and the great valley of the Mississippi, and yet I believe no heart more truly sympathises with or is more deeply interested in the progress of events in the fatherland than mine. In the *Standard*[2] I saw that Mr. Robert Purvis had offered to assist in mustering a regiment.[3] I hope his efforts, if put forth, will be crow[n]ed with success. From an extract of a Tennessee paper, I learned how the spirit of prejudice still fires the people: this time roused by the attack of black rebels upon the Federals. They think it very galling indeed to have their sons slain and the bodies stripped upon the battlefield by negroes of the Confederate army. But the ball is only beginning to move, and I am inclined to think that the galling times have not fairly arrived. I *hate* the spirit which desires us to stand still and in no way identify ourselves with present circumstances: be mere spectators, and where we cannot avoid it, fall before the bayonet, without even lifting a hand to ward off the blow. I say out upon such doctrine! 'Tis thus that cowards die, but men,

> High minded, honorable men,
> Men who their *duties know*,
> But *know* their *rights* and knowing *dare maintain*,

are found by death facing the foe till the last moment. I hope that we will prove our claims to "life, liberty, and the pursuit of happiness" by manly conduct, and let the enemy see that while as Christian soldiers, we can pray for those who despitefully use us, we can also, like David, beat them as small as the dust when they oppose the cause of God and human progress in the path of right.[4] To say it matters little which side is helped shows lack of consideration. In the North, surely, our position is in part owing to the fact that a progressive people cannot have any element of humanity among them, and all the while compel that element to remain uninfluenced by the same causes that procure their own advancement: and so in spite of opposition it is beneath northern skies that the eloquence of Fred. Douglass and others are poured forth. And where institutions of learning dispense knowledge to the despised negro. Where earnest antislavery men and women have employed their time and talents in endeavors to overthrow not only the cursed system of slavery, but also to destroy in the minds of men the principle that recognises property in man, and rear instead that fabric of a faith that recognises the fatherhood of God and the brotherhood of man. The name of William Lloyd Garrison, the noble champion of freedom, I am sure should ever be honored. We must consider which section owns the purest and most abundant stock of the seeds not of the black man's promotion alone, but the ingredients of the intellectual, moral, and physical exaltation of humanity in general. We must stand upon a platform broad enough to afford a place for every soul on God's earth, and allow no craven set of villains to drive us off. On the other hand the faults of the North are glaring. She has lent her military forces to quell mob violence, and ensure the safe return of the trembling fugitive to a cruel, remorseless man-stealer.[5] Her churches, by silence on the subject, have assented to all the gross violations of the moral law which slavery's disgusting rites involve.[6] She has enacted laws whose sentiments disgrace Christendom; and for all this is she punished, and will, I trust, after this scourge rise to the dignity of a Christian nation, in a thorough practical sense. Notwithstanding the monstrous evils, there are germs of good whose development our course can greatly retard or promote. Viewing the President's Emancipation Proclamation in the true light, it is clear, that motives of policy rather than conviction of duty in the matter prompted him, but I think we can turn even presidential policy to a good account if we will. I hope we, in the language of a dying soldier at Vienna, will "stand by the flag." Take up arms for the North and sustain the President. On such ground we have an opportunity of identifying ourselves in the interests of the country, and I certainly think we will be fools if we do not use every means to secure a more auspicious future. We have no right to stand upon our native soil as neutral as the cows and horses roaming o'er the western prairies. If like God-fearing men we fight, like God-fearing men we must prevail. If when in sacking town or village we meet women disloyal, her brains we'll scatter to the winds; but we will not abuse ourselves and mankind by making defenceless woman the victim of our lust; here is a point wherein we can show *loyalty to manhood's honor*. Mentally we must become the equals of our foes, and morally as far superior as a more faithful adherence to the divine precept of our holy religion can make us. If the bloody spirit of the South holds out, that body will be quite reduced before it is subdued. I trust that spirit will fail not, as thereby the valor of northern souls may be fully tested. It is not unlikely when the victory is won that the North, though she cannot reduce things to their former state, will seek, as far as possible to prevent the intellectual and consequently social and political advancement of the colored race. Then it is that we must prove whether we be men or not. Then our swords will be required to meet the insolence of the "degenerate dastards" who may strive to revive the dying notion that we have no right to be respected, and while we lay not by the sword we must bring sublime, spiritual, mental and moral agencies to bear, for not until the human mind is redeemed from error will it be possible to refrain from warfare. We must not throw away God's truth because we see it abused by those who know better. We must remember that God exalts those who honor Him, and believing this we must help to raise the shattered structure of our republic to a lofty rank among nations upon the foundations of a truth and justice that God will approve and bless. We live in an enlightened age, and let us resolve that the mark we make in the world shall glorify our God and dignify humanity. Then will our page in history glow with the *just deeds* of *just men*. I have looked on the bright side. Suppose, however, all our best exertions perish. Should we retreat? No! Never!!

> Still, still forever,
> Better tho' each man's life blood was a river,
> That it should flow and overflow, than creep
> Thro' thousand lazy channels in our veins
> Damned like the dull canal, with locks and chains,
> And moving, as a sick man in his sleep

Three paces and then faltering: better be
Where the extinguished colored men still are free
In their proud channels of the United States
Than stagnate in the marsh

of *stupidity and indifference.*

The hour for decisive blows is coming, therefore we must nerve ourselves in Heaven's panoply, that like men we may greet the music of

The bursting shell
The rattling musketry, the clashing blade,
And ever and anon in tones of thunder,
The diapason of the cannonade.

Well I have written only of the war, and really I think most of it just now, so it seems easier to write about, besides there is nothing very stirring here, and perhaps you will patiently read my ideas, if indeed they are worth the name. I am anxious to hear of my bundle of stray thoughts. We are all very well. Kind regards to Mrs. S. and the little ones.[7] Hoping to hear from you all shortly, I remain, yours truly,

SARAH A. LESTER[8]

Christian Recorder (Philadelphia, Pa.), 13 June 1863.

1. The decision to recruit and arm black regiments was an important step in radicalizing Union objectives during the Civil War. During the opening months of conflict, the federal government refused the services of black volunteer regiments. But political and military needs forced it to reconsider this policy in 1862. A few Union commanders, faced with the twin problems of contrabands and recruitment, organized black military units on their own authority in the early part of that year. The First South Carolina Colored Regiment, for example, was formed on the Sea Islands in the spring of 1862 but never mustered. Passage of the Second Confiscation Act and the Militia Act of 17 July 1862 by Congress opened the way for recruitment of black soldiers. Three militia regiments of Louisiana Native Guards, organized by General Benjamin Butler, were the first black units to be officially mustered. The War Department issued its initial call for a black regiment, the First South Carolina Colored Volunteers, in August 1862. After President Abraham Lincoln issued the Emancipation Proclamation, organizing of black regiments began in earnest. By the end of the war, 139 black regiments had been formed; 123,000 of the nearly 180,000 black Union soldiers saw action in black regiments. Dudley Taylor Cornish, *The Sable Arm: Negro Troops in the Union Army, 1861–1865* (New York, N.Y., 1966), 29–93, 288.

2. Lester refers to the *National Anti-Slavery Standard*, which began publishing on 11 June 1840 in New York as the organ of the American Anti-Slavery Society. Plagued by continuing financial problems, the *Standard* nevertheless established itself as a leading Garrisonian paper with a fairly wide circulation. The *Standard* was published weekly and covered abolitionist news and events as well as a broader range of subjects, including foreign affairs. Originally edited by James C.

Jackson, the paper eventually had a number of editors—a fact best explained by William Lloyd Garrison's constant influence; these editors included Nathaniel P. Rogers (1840–41), Lydia Maria Child (1841–43), David Lee Child (1843–44), Sydney Howard Gay (1844–58), and Oliver Johnson (1858–65). The *Standard* ceased publication in 1871. Joseph Anthony Del Porto, "A Study of American Anti-Slavery Journals" (Ph.D. diss., Michigan State College, 1953), 184–88; Merrill and Ruchames, *Letters of William Lloyd Garrison*, 2:xxvi, xxviii, 553, 577, 660, 662, 681, 694, 704, 708, 719, 725, 729, 730, 3:2, 27, 161, 163, 175–76, 305–6, 309–14, 340–42.

3. The 14 February 1863 issue of the *National Anti-Slavery Standard* carried a notice that black abolitionist Robert Purvis had agreed to help recruit black troops for the Union army. He apparently represented the Philadelphia Supervisory Committee for Recruiting Colored Regiments, an interracial group of seventy-five local leaders organized for the purpose. *NASS*, 14 February 1863; Fred Binder, "Pennsylvania Negro Regiments in the Civil War," *JNH* 37:389 (October 1952).

4. David was a military leader and the king of ancient Israel during the tenth century B.C. Many of the psalms attributed to him speak to the theme of smiting one's adversaries when they oppose divine law and justice.

5. Lester refers to federal enforcement of the Fugitive Slave Law of 1850.

6. No major denomination denounced slavery before the Civil War. The reasons for this silence varied by denomination but included a fear of offending slaveholding members and fiercely independent local churches. Powerful denominational hierarchies easily suppressed antislavery debate in general councils and purged the antislavery message from religious publications. Yet the relationship between northern churches and the antislavery movement defies comfortable generalization. Many of the movement's most prominent leaders were clerics, and concerted efforts by immediatist abolitionists heightened the sensitivity of northern churches to the issue of slavery by the late 1850s. Certain evangelical sects, particularly the Society of Friends and the American Baptist Free Mission Society, were active in the movement. John R. McKivigan, *The War Against Proslavery Religion: Abolitionism and the Northern Churches, 1830–1865* (Ithaca, N.Y., 1984).

7. William Still married Letitia George in 1847. They produced four children. *DANB*, 573.

8. Sarah Lester was the mulatto daughter of prominent black merchant Peter Lester of Victoria, Vancouver Island. Reared in San Francisco, she attended the city's public schools until they were racially segregated in January 1858. At that point, she was expelled from the school she had been attending, although a minority on the San Francisco school board argued that an exception should be made in her case because of her light complexion. During the summer of 1858, Lester and her parents moved to Victoria, where she supported herself by teaching piano lessons in the Lester home. Lester returned to San Francisco at the end of the Civil War. She taught religious education there at Trinity Episcopal Church until dismissed from her position in October 1867. Pilton, "Negro Settlement in British Columbia," 60; Kilian, *Go Do Some Great Thing*, 18; *ESF*, 25 October 1867.

96.
Martin R. Delany to Mary Ann Shadd Cary
7 December 1863

As the Civil War dragged on, black abolitionists in Canada were presented with increasing opportunities to participate directly in the Union war effort. A few—most notably Martin R. Delany, Osborne P. Anderson, and Mary Ann Shadd Cary—became aggressive and successful recruiting agents. Delany spent much of 1863–65 enlisting volunteers for black Massachusetts, Rhode Island, Connecticut, and Ohio regiments. He encouraged several former friends in Chatham, Canada West, to assist in this effort. Soon after Delany's 7 December 1863 letter to Cary, she returned to the United States and recruited volunteers for black Connecticut and Indiana regiments. Like many black Canadians, both Delany and Cary remained in the United States after the war. Ullman, *Martin R. Delany*, 283–313; *DANB*, 553; Benjamin S. Pardee to Mary Ann Shadd Cary, 3 March 1864, Mary Ann Shadd Cary Papers, DHU [15:0266].

Box 764 P. O.
172, Clark, St[reet]
Chicago, Ill[inois]
Dec[ember] 7th, 1863

Mrs. Cary
Madam:

I have just returned from the East, where I have completed a contract with the State authorities, of Connecticut, with the sole right of raising Black Troops in the west and South-west. She wants 5,000, men to make up her quot[a], and as many of them as can be obtained may be Black.[1]

The first black regiment to be raised is the "29th Regiment Connecticut Volunteers."[2]

To all "slaves" obtained, a state Bounty of $120, cash will be paid immediately on being sworn in, with the same pay per month, clothing, and political status as white men. Free colored men get $200, Bounty cash.

This difference in the Bounty has to be made, in consequence of all the contingencies attending the obtaining of our "slave" brethren.

I will pay you $15, (fifteen dollars) cash for all slave men (or freedmen as the case may be) on delivery and examination by me here in Chicago, I bearing the expense of transportation.

This is one of the best measures yet entered into, and presents a good opportunity to do good to the oppressed, and justice to those who help them.

I should have said, that I will pay $5, (five dollars) on delivery for evry

10. Martin R. Delany in his Civil War uniform
From W. J. Simmons, *Men of Mark* (Cleveland, 1887)

free born man, but do not desire to get many from so great a distance, as the cost is hardly justifiable.

Please write me by return of mail, as I am anxious to hear from you, and to get all the men I possibly can in the shortest posible time.

I am still an Agent for Rhode Island, and if any prefer Heavy Artillery, you may take them for that, always designating the one of service intended for, whether Infantry or Artillery. Very Respectfully dear sir,

M. R. Delany

[Marcellina] M. Wagoner[3]
Secry.

Mary Ann Shadd Cary Papers, Moorland-Spingarn Research Center, Howard University, Washington, District of Columbia. Published by permission.

1. In late 1863, Martin R. Delany accepted the task of recruiting Connecticut's quota of five thousand troops for the Union army. He opened recruiting offices in Cleveland and Chicago and hired his old friend and medical colleague Amos Aray of Chatham, Canada West, to examine black recruits. He also employed Mary Ann Shadd Cary to help recruit troops for black Connecticut regiments. Delany's arrangement with the state of Connecticut was part of a broader recruiting effort; he was, however, the first black to be awarded a recruiting contract by any state. Ullman, *Martin R. Delany*, 283–87.

2. The Twenty-ninth (Colored) Regiment Connecticut Volunteer Infantry was organized at Fair Haven, Connecticut, between August 1863 and January 1864 and mustered into Union service on 8 March 1864. The regiment performed distinguished duty in South Carolina and Texas and was actively engaged in the 1864–65 Virginia campaigns against Petersburg and Richmond. Two companies of the Twenty-ninth were the first Union infantry to enter the fallen Confederate capital in April 1865. The regiment was discharged on 25 November 1865 after suffering 198 deaths due to battle casualties and disease. Isaac J. Hill, *A Sketch of the 29th Regiment of Connecticut Colored Troops . . .* (Baltimore, Md., 1867); *Record of Services of Connecticut Men in the United States, During the War of the Rebellion* (Hartford, Conn., 1899), 859–91.

3. Marcellina M. Wagoner, the daughter of black Chicago barber and abolitionist Henry O. Wagoner, served as secretary to Martin R. Delany in his efforts to recruit black troops for the Union army during 1863–64. By 1870 she had moved to Denver, Colorado, and married black painter Robert L. Moss. Together they produced at least one child, Robert, Jr. After the death of her husband (ca. 1877), Marcellina Moss continued to reside in Denver well into the 1880s, apparently supporting herself as a seamstress. Martin R. Delany to Mary Ann Shadd Cary, 7 December 1863, Mary Ann Shadd Cary Papers, DHU [15:0108]; Martin R. Delany to Edwin M. Stanton, 15 December 1863, Record Group 94, Adjutant Generals Office, 104th United States Colored Infantry, Colored Division Letters Received, DNA [15:0119]; United States Census, 1870; *Denver City Directory*, 1871, 1873–76, 1878, 1880–81.

Index

Page numbers in boldface indicate the main discussion of the subject.